The Black
Church in
the African
American
Experience

The Black Church in the African American Experience

C. Eric Lincoln and Lawrence H. Mamiya

Duke University Press

Durham and London   1990

© 1990, Duke University Press
All rights reserved.
Printed in the United States of America
on acid-free paper ∞
Second impression, 1991.

Library of Congress Cataloging-in-Publication Data
Lincoln, C. Eric (Charles Eric) 1924–
The Black church in the African American experience
C. Eric Lincoln & Lawrence H. Mamiya.
Includes bibliographical references, index.
ISBN 0-8223-1057-0
ISBN 0-8223-1073-2 (pbk.)
1. Afro-American churches. 2. Afro-Americans—Religion.
3. United States—Church history. I. Mamiya, Lawrence H.
II. Title.
BR563.N4L55 1990
277.3'08'08996073—dc20 90-34050 CIP

To Robert Wood Lynn and
Lawrence Neale Jones

To May, Mae, Ralph, and Rachel

Contents

List of Tables

Preface

A good way to understand a people is to study their religion, for religion is addressed to that most sacred schedule of values around which the expression and the meaning of life tends to coalesce. The study of a people's religion is not guaranteed to provide *all* of the answers to what gives a culture its characteristic definitions, of course, for religion is essentially a subjective experience, and an external study or investigation will inevitably miss some of the critical nuances experienced (and valued) only by those on the interior of belief. Nevertheless, a critical observer with an open mind can gain invaluable insight into the structural and motivational cosmos out of which particular behaviors emerge as distinctive earmarks particularizing a given population. Religion, seriously considered, is perhaps the best prism to cultural understanding, not as a comparative index, but as a refractive element through which one social cosmos may look meaningfully at another and adjust its presuppositions accordingly. This study has the advantage of both interior and exterior perspectives both methodologically and experientially.

The prevailing American sentiment has traditionally held that the mainline white churches constitute the only relevant spiritual pulse in the nation, and that whatever is outside this narrow ambit is of little if any significance to the American religious profile. This conventional wisdom is widely reflected in seminary curricula and denominational policies to the end that misperception is compounded, and the religious experience of some 30 to 35 million African Americans is clouded in consequence.

The burden of the conventional views regarding the Black Church and black religion has to do with the uncritical assumption that the black experience in religion is but the replication of the white experience, shadowed by an African patina predisposing it to an inordinate exoticism and emotionalism which distorts to a significant degree the proper expression of the faith. This study is not concerned with the confirmation or the refutation of that point of view. Rather our primary concern is to present as authentic and as objective a profile of the Black Church and black religion as we found to be possible consistent with contemporary sociological theory and methodology, with the hope that clearer insights might make for a less simplistic understanding. To do this we have examined carefully the history of the Black Church and the findings of other social scientists as a backdrop for our own field study covering the major black communities in the United States.

Our basic premise has been that black religion, whatever its distinctive expressions, is significantly part and parcel of the American experience in religion and that to exclude it arbitrarily from the normative study of religion in America runs the risk of a seriously distorted picture of what American religion is like. After all, seven major black denominations account for more than 80 percent of black religious affiliation in the United States, and that is a sizable segment of the total church population at a time when most white denominations are in decline. Moreover, the remaining 15 to 20 percent of black Christians are scattered among numerous small black sects, the Roman Catholic Church, and the mainline white Protestant denominations. The overwhelming majority of the latter are in predominantly black congregations, despite denominational affiliation with white communions.

But mere numbers aside, the impact of the Black Church on the spiritual, social, economic, educational, and political interests that structure life in America—including the mainline white churches themselves—can scarcely be overlooked in any realistic appraisal of our common religious experience. It is our hope that this study will be a useful instrument of clarification and illumination in church and academe alike for all those Americans of whatever creed or color, who are in search of a more authentic understanding of our religious environment.

However, because there has been such a dearth of serious research on black churches up to very recent times, the Black Church has often experienced difficulty in conceptualizing or knowing itself except as an amorphus, lusterless detail on some larger canvas devoted to other interests. In consequence the Black Church has often found itself repeating history it had already experienced, and relearning lessons it had long since forgotten. Perhaps this offering will help the Black Church establish with finality its true identity, whatever that may be, so that it can get on with the business of history with appropriate self-confidence and direction. That is certainly a principal motivation for this undertaking.

There are probably few studies of such limited scope which have embraced the contributions, direct and vicarious of so many scholars, researchers, and clerical professionals. We can list but some of them here, but our gratitude to all those who helped in this endeavor, whether or not their names appear here, is real, heartfelt, and complete. Our very first vote of thanks must be reserved for the hundreds of black pastors who received us in their churches, opened their hearts and their records to us, and gave generously of their time, their wisdom, and their experiences to lend viability and authenticity to our efforts to profile the Black Church—their church. Without their help, this book could never have come into existence, and could scarcely have been justified in conception.

We next pay tribute to the teams of seminarians, graduate students, clerical trainees, and others who blanketed the field from New York City to Los Angeles, and from Detroit to the rural counties of Florida and Mississippi to interview church personnel, and to carefully record the data of their response. For this our warmest thanks and appreciation is extended to the regional and local coordinators of the survey: Charles A. Brown, coordinator, Birmingham, Alabama; Dr. Lillian Ashcraft Easton (Clark Atlanta University), regional coordinator for St. Louis, Kansas City, Missouri, and the Midwest and national researcher; Rev. Dr. David Hurst (pastor, Los Angeles), coordinator, southern California; Rev. Samuel A. Lockhart, national researcher, southern urban areas; Rev. Dr. Larry Murphy (Garrett-Evangelical Theological Seminary), coordinator, Chicago area; Rev. Dr. James Shopshire (Interdenominational Theological Center), regional coordinator, Atlanta area and southern rural black churches; and Rev. Dr. Archie Smith (Pacific School of Religion), regional coordinator, San Francisco-Oakland Bay area.

Field-workers under the direction of the coordinators included Marlene Bailey, M. Kathy Brown, Rose Brown, John A. Cade, David E. Cann, Vernon Carroway, Dr. J. King Chandler III, Tim Cyrus, Warren L. Dennis, Kofi Dumfour, Earl Dunstan, Arnette Edelmann, Cynthia Faison, D. A. Gaines, Arlene Hambrick, Wilma Joyce Irvin-Grooms, Richard Johnson, Jr., Evans Kote-Nikoi, Michelle Lanchester, Bernard Mayhew, Jr., Sabrina Miles, Ralph J. Miller, Nathaniel Milton, Otis I. Mitchell, Vincent F. Mitchell, Cynthia Moore, Mae C. Morrow, Tracy Poole, Frank Portee III, Ronald E. Ramsey, Fred Smith, Sherman Tribble, Erwin D. Ward, Jerry Welch, and Jeanne Wilkerson. Inevitably, the names of many more field-workers are no longer available after so many years since their involvement. Nevertheless, for those named and those anonymous, we are grateful for their contributions, and we hope that the summers they sacrificed in this effort will find some reward in seeing the results of their work in print.

Simultaneous with the collection of field data, our research was strengthened immeasurably by the consultation and advice of a distinguished cadre of men and women from church and academe whose expertise in a wide spectrum of religious interests helped to gauge, direct, and confirm our investigation. We take this occasion to record our thanks to the following consultants for their understanding, cooperation, and advice: Bishop John H. Adams (A.M.E. Church); Bishop Moses Anderson (Roman Catholic Church); Dr. Lewis V. Baldwin (Vanderbilt University); Dr. Delores Carpenter (Howard University School of Divinity); Bishop James L. Cummings (C.M.E. Church); Rev. F. Benjamin Davis (NBC America); Bishop J. H. Dell (COGIC); Mr. Richard Dozier (Black Church architect); Bishop Alfred G. Dunstan (A.M.E. Zion Church); Bishop John Exum (C.M.E. Church); Bishop J. Clinton Hoggard (A.M.E. Zion Church); Dr. Lawrence Neale Jones (dean, Howard University School of Divinity); Rev. William A. Jones (PNBC); Rev. Thomas Kilgore, Jr. (PNBC); Rev. George W. Lucas (NBC); Dr. William B. McClain (Wesley Theological Seminary); Bishop S. S. Morris, Jr. (A.M.E. Church); Dr. Mance Jackson (C.M.E. Church in Georgia and the Interdenominational Theological Center); Dr. Larry Murphy (Garrett-Evangelical Theological Seminary); Dr. Douglas Nelson (Black Church historian); Dr. Clarence G. Newsome (assistant dean, Howard University School of Divinity); Mr. Richard Poilucci (computer consultant, Vassar College); Dr. Alton Pollard (Wake Forest University); Dr. Harry Richardson (president emeritus, Interdenominational Theological Center); Dr. Grant Schockley (former president of the Interdenominational Theological Center); Bishop German Ross (COGIC); Dr. John Satterwhite (editor, A.M.E. Zion Review); Rev. Manuel L. Scott (NBC, U.S.A., Inc.); Dr. James Costens and Dr. David Shannon (president and vice president of the Interdenominational Theological Center, respectively); Dr. James Shopshire (Wesley Theological Seminary); Dr. Jon Spencer (Duke University); Dr. James B. Stewart (Pennsylvania State University); Dr. Sonja Stone (University of North Carolina, Chapel Hill); Dr. Harold Dean Trulear (Eastern Baptist Theological Seminary); Dr. James Washington (Union Theological Seminary); Professor Leon Watts (Yale University Divinity School); and Dr. Kenny Williams (Duke University). All of the consultants mentioned provided indispensable help in the form of position papers, consultative advice, professional commentary, and necessary contacts with key church leaders.

After the survey data were collected, we turned to Dr. David Roozen, at the Hartford Seminary Foundation for help in determining what they meant and how that meaning might best be expressed statistically. His computer projections and statistical analysis were not only illuminating, they greatly reduced the time between the collection of data and their presentation in this book. Others whose contributions deserved a special measure of thanks and appreciation include Professor Doris L. Saunders of the Department of Journalism of Jackson State University and a lay member of the Episcopal Church, who served as senior research associate for the project and a consultant on women in the Black Church. We also thank Dr. Mary R. Sawyer of the State University of Iowa who was intimately involved with various aspects of the project during several years of graduate study at Duke University, in addition to her subsequent contributions as consultant and editor after joining the faculty in the Department of Religion at Iowa State University. We are also indebted to the members of the working group on Afro-American religion and politics of the W. E. B. Du Bois Institute at Harvard University who read and critiqued two key chapters of the manuscript.

For manuscript preparation and for critical management of field assignments, research assistance, retrieval of data, payroll preparation, and a hundred other details vital to the progress of the study, we owe an incalculable debt to Dolores J. Morehead and Wanda Camp at Duke University, and to Marlene Bailey and Lenore Cypress-Ferrill at Vassar College. Mrs. Faye Stickles of Vassar provided expert keypunching for computer cards as a back-up system.

The primary funding for this study came from the Eli Lilly Endowment. For their generous support and encouragement on behalf of the Endowment, and for their warm, personal involvement over the entire life of the project, it is impossible to adequately express our appreciation to Dr. Robert Wood Lynn, retiring vice president for religion and program officer, Jacqui Burton. Despite the inevitable delays and inadvertencies which sometimes plagued the best intentions of our carefully planned research, they stayed the course that finally saw this project through to publication, and for this we are most grateful.

Supplementary funding was graciously provided by the Ford Foundation at a time when additional help from our primary sponsor was simply beyond our willingness to request. We are very grateful to Ford and to the program officer Lynn Jones-Walker for their understanding and their rescue.

We also thank the librarians at the following institutions for their kind assistance in the historical and cultural phases of our research: Duke University; Vassar College; the Schomberg branch of the New York Public Library; Union Theological Seminary; Howard University School of Divinity; Interdenominational Theological Center; and Hartford Seminary Foundation.

Finally, the support from our wives—Lucy Cook Lincoln and May Lawson Mamiya—was of a kind no other sources could match. They and our children made the truest sacrifices and gave the most enabling support of all as one year succeeded another in a project that always seemed to be turning the final corner. These dear ones have our deepest appreciation for their love, their sacrifice, and their encouragement.

If this work has any merit, all those whose contributions we have cited have a share in it. Its deficiencies are our own and ours alone.

1 The Religious Dimension: Toward a Sociology of Black Churches

In this book we have attempted to provide a wide-ranging study of the churches and clergy that comprise the seven major historic black denominations: the African Methodist Episcopal (A.M.E.) Church; the African Methodist Episcopal Zion (A.M.E.Z.) Church; the Christian Methodist Episcopal (C.M.E.) Church; the National Baptist Convention, U.S.A., Incorporated (NBC); the National Baptist Convention of America, Unincorporated (NBCA); the Progressive National Baptist Convention (PNBC); and the Church of God in Christ (COGIC). We use the term "the Black Church" as do other scholars and much of the general public as a kind of sociological and theological shorthand reference to the pluralism of black Christian churches in the United States. Since the late 1960s "the Black Church" has replaced the older reference, "the Negro Church," which was used by scholars of a previous generation.[1] In general usage any black Christian person is included in "the Black Church" if he or she is a member of a black congregation. In this study, however, while we recognized that there are predominantly black local churches in white denominations such as the United Methodist Church, the Episcopal Church, and the Roman Catholic Church, among others, we chose to limit our operational definition of "the Black Church" to those independent, historic, and totally black controlled denominations, which were founded after the Free African Society of 1787 and which constituted the core of black Christians.[2] Today the seven major black denominations with a scattering of smaller communions make up the body of the Black Church and it is estimated that more than 80 percent of all black Christians are in these seven denominations, with the smaller communions accounting for an additional 6 percent.[3] Historical overviews of these seven major black denominations are provided in the chapters on the Baptist, Methodist, and Pentecostal communions.

Although the main intent of this study is one of social description, providing historical overviews as well as statistical data and analyses, we want to make clear in this chapter what our underlying assumptions are in regard to the study of black churches. Thus far, a general theory for the social analysis of black religious phenomena and a sociology of black churches has not yet appeared,[4] but we want to contribute the following theoretical assumptions to the scholarly dialogue: (1), the religious dimension: the black sacred cosmos; (2), the Black Church as the central institutional sector and partial differentiation; and (3), the dialectical model of the Black Church.

1   The Religious Dimension: The Black Sacred Cosmos

In any attempt to gather statistics and other data about black religious phenomena, it is easy to forget about the experiential dimension which gave rise to the set of social institutions called "churches." Religion, or the religious dimension consists of the encounter of human beings with the "sacred" or "divine." Rudolf Otto has given a classical description of this encounter with the sacred as eliciting feelings of "*mysterium, tremendum, et fascinans*" (the mysterious, terrifying, and fascinating).[5] While Otto's phenomenological description of the awesomeness and attractiveness of the sacred is useful as a generalized and universal description of the religious dimension, attention must also be given to the particular cultural and historical configuration in which that experience takes place. This investigation is addressed to the religious worldview of African Americans, which we have called the "black sacred cosmos."[6] Above all, religion is, as Durkheim has made clear, a social phenomenon, a shared group experience that has shaped and influenced the cultural screens of human communication and interpretation.[7]

The black sacred cosmos or the religious worldview of African Americans is related both to their African heritage, which envisaged the whole universe as sacred, and to their conversion to Christianity during slavery and its aftermath. It has been only in the past twenty years that scholars of African American history, culture, and religion have begun to recognize that black people created their own unique and distinctive forms of culture and worldviews as parallels rather than replications of the culture in which they were involuntary guests.[8] As slaves on the farms and plantations, then as domestic servants in white households, black people were privy to some of the most intimate aspects of white life and culture, from worship to sexual behavior; but very few whites knew anything about black people or their culture, or cared to. In fact, some scholars have viewed aspects of black cultural creations as aberrational attempts to mimic mainstream white culture.[9] Other scholars have claimed that, "The Negro is only an American and nothing else. He has no values and culture to guard and protect."[10] Such arguments seem unwilling to grant to African Americans the minimum presuppositions all other hyphenated Americans are permitted to take for granted, which is to say that their origins were elsewhere, and that coming from elsewhere, if they have a viable history, they must also have an effective culture. That a large gulf separated the black world from the expectations of the white is undeniable, but hardly inexplicable. Culture is the sum of the options for creative survival. Two hundred and fifty years of slavery were followed by one hundred years of official and unofficial segregation in the South and the North. Even today the gulf still persists, bolstered in large measure by racial segregation in the place of residence, education, religion, and social life.[11] However, the more limited the options for approved participation in the cultural mainstream, the more refined and satisfying become the alternatives to those excluded from the approved norms.

Depending upon the culture and history of a particular African-related religious tradition, different sacred object(s) or figure(s) will be at the center of the black sacred cosmos. For the more African-based syncretic religions of the Caribbean and Latin America like the Voudou of Haiti, the Obeia of Jamaica, the Santeria of Cuba, and the Candomble and Umbanda of Brazil, African deities and spiritual forces played a more prominent role in the rituals and worship of the people.[12] For African American Christianity, the Christian God ultimately revealed in Jesus of Nazareth dominated the black sacred cosmos. While the structure of beliefs for black Christians were the same orthodox beliefs as that of white Christians, there were also different degrees of emphasis and valences given to certain particular theological views. For example, the Old Testament notion of God as an avenging, conquering, liberating paladin remains a formidable anchor of the faith in most black churches. The older the church or the more elderly its congregation, the more likely the demand for the exciting imagery and the personal involvement of God in history is likely to be. The direct relationship between the holocaust of slavery and the notion of divine rescue colored the theological perceptions of black laity and the themes of black preaching in a very decisive manner, particularly in those churches closest to the experience.

Nonetheless, as Henry Mitchell, James Cone, and Gayraud Wilmore have all agreed, throughout black religious history the reality of Jesus as the Son of God made flesh finds a deep response in black faith and worship. The experience of oppression is more likely to find immediate resonance with the incarnational view of the suffering, humiliation, death, and eventual triumph of Jesus in the resurrection than with an abstract concept of an impersonal God.[13] Another example of this difference in emphasis concerned the greater weight given to the biblical views of the importance of human personality and human equality implicit in "children of God."[14] The trauma of being officially defined by the U.S. Constitution as "three-fifths" human, and treated in terms of that understanding, the struggle of the African American people to affirm and establish their humanity and their worth as persons has a long history. The black Christians who formed the historic black churches also knew implicitly that their understanding of Christianity, which was premised on the rock of antiracial discrimination, was more authentic than the Christianity practiced in white churches.

A major aspect of black Christian belief is found in the symbolic importance given to the word "freedom." Throughout black history the term "freedom" has found a deep religious resonance in the lives and hopes of African Americans. Depending upon the time and the context, the implications of freedom were derived from the nature of the exigency. During slavery it meant release from bondage; after emancipation it meant the right to be educated, to be employed, and to move about freely from place to place. In the twentieth century freedom means social, political, and economic justice. From the very beginning of the black experience in America, one critical denotation of freedom has remained constant: freedom has always meant the absence of any restraint which might compromise one's responsibility to God. The notion has persisted that if God calls you to discipleship, God calls you to freedom. And that God wants you free because God made you for Himself and in His image. Although generations of white preachers and exhorters developed an amazing complex of arguments aimed at avoiding so obvious a conclusion, it was a dictum securely anchored in the black man's faith and indelibly engraved on his psyche. A well-known black spiritual affirms that:

> Before I'll be a slave
> I'll be buried in my grave
> And go home to my Father
> and be free. . . .

Implicit is the notion that unfreedom puts at risk the promise of salvation. No person can serve two masters, and freedom as a condition of spiritual readiness was no less critical to the religious strategies of Martin Luther King, Jr., than to those of Richard Allen, Nat Turner, Sojourner Truth, and Fannie Lou Hamer. Each person developed a modus vivendi consistent with their times and the resources at hand. Their objectives were the same: freedom to be as God had intended all men and women to be. Free to belong to God.

For whites freedom has bolstered the value of American individualism: to be free to pursue one's destiny without political or bureaucratic interference or restraint. But for African Americans freedom has always been communal in nature. In Africa the destiny of the individual was linked to that of the tribe or the community in an intensely interconnected security system. In America, black people have seldom been perceived or treated as individuals; they have usually been dealt with as "representatives" of their "race," an external projection. Hence, the communal sense of freedom has an internal African rootage curiously reinforced by hostile social convention imposed from outside on all African Americans as a caste. But Dr. Martin Luther King's jubilant cry of, "Free at last, free at last, thank God Almighty, we are free at last," echoed the understanding black folk always had with the Almighty God whose impatience with unfreedom matched their own.[15] In song, word, and deed, freedom has always been the superlative value of the black sacred cosmos. The message of the Invisible Church was, however articulated, *God wants you free!*

In describing the key religious elements of the black churches he visited in the South, W. E. B. Du Bois was particularly impressed with "the preacher, the music, and the frenzy."[16] In later chapters we will examine more closely the situation of the black preacher and the development of music in black churches. For this examination of the black sacred cosmos, a deciphering of the frenzy is particularly important. Like most observers and visitors to black worship services, Du Bois was referring to the intense enthusiasm and the open display of emotions and feelings exhibited by the worshipers. Some worshipers "got the Spirit" and were propelled into a paroxysm of shouting. While others "fell out" and rolled on the floor in a shaking, trance-like state, possessed by the Holy Ghost. Some people stood up in the pews and waved their hands over their heads, while others clapped their hands in time with the music. Even in the midst of preaching, the worshipers carried on a dialogue with the preacher by shouting approval and agreement with ejaculations like "Amen!" or "Preach it!" or "Tell it like it is!" At other times they encouraged the preacher to work harder to reach that precipitating point of cathartic climax by calling out, "Well?" . . . "Well?" The highlight of the service was to worship and glorify God by achieving the experience of mass catharsis; a purifying explosion of emotions that eclipses the harshness of reality for a season and leaves both the preacher and the congregation drained in a moment of spiritual ecstasy. Failure to achieve this experience often resulted in polite compliments of "good talk" or "good lecture," and not the ultimate, "You *preached* today!" being offered the preacher. The Black Church was the first theater in the black community. Like the Greek theater its functional goal was catharsis, but beyond the Greeks, the Black Church was in search of transcendence, not a mere emptying of the emotions, but an enduring fellowship with God in which the formal worship service provided the occasion for particular periods of intimacy.

Above all, the core experience of the black sacred cosmos was the personal conversion of the individual believer. The Christianity that was spread among slaves during the First and Second Awakenings was an evangelical Christianity that stressed personal conversion through a deep regenerating experience, being "born again." The spiritual journey began with an acknowledgment of personal sinfulness and unworthiness and ended in an emotional experience of salvation by God through the Holy Spirit. The rebirth meant a change, a fundamental reorientation in the approach to life. While white Christians also stressed personal conversion, the historical and narrative evidence indicate that the black conversion and visionary experience was of a qualitatively different level. As Mechal Sobel has argued in her analysis of the black Baptist's cosmos, "black religious experiences began to be singled out as particularly ecstatic by white Baptists, signifying consciousness of a difference."[17] As time passed the black-white difference intensified. "Analysis of the black visionary experiences indicate," wrote Sobel, "that they were very different from the outset, and that their uniqueness was highlighted as the whites grew less concerned with spiritual journeys."[18]

We can also extend Sobel's argument about the forging of a new cosmos from the seventeenth to the early nineteenth centuries that "united African and Baptist elements in a new whole."[19] What was really created was a black sacred cosmos that cut across denominational lines—largely Baptist and Methodist at first, but also Roman

Catholic, Pentecostal, and others in later years. Wherever black people were gathered in significant enough numbers, the distinct quality of a shared Afro-Christian religious worldview and faith was felt. Even in predominantly white denominations with a million or more black members like the United Methodist Church and the Roman Catholic Church, the surges and eruptions of the black sacred cosmos were constant and influential.[20] A qualitatively different cultural form of expressing Christianity is found in most black churches, regardless of denomination, to this day.

Culture is the form of religion and religion is the heart of culture. Paul Tillich's insight about the relationship between religion and culture is important in a discussion of the black sacred cosmos.[21] Religion is expressed in cultural forms like music and song, styles and content of preaching, and modes of worship, to give a few examples. But religion is also the heart of culture because it raises the core values of that culture to ultimate levels and legitimates them.[22] The relationship between the black sacred cosmos and black culture in general is similar. The core values of black culture like freedom, justice, equality, an African heritage, and racial parity at all levels of human intercourse, are raised to ultimate levels and legitimated by the black sacred cosmos. Although this cosmos is largely Afro-Christian in nature due to its religious history, it has also erupted in other black militant, nationalistic, and non-Christian movements.[23] The close relationship between the black sacred cosmos and black culture has often been missed by social analysts who impose sacred/secular distinctions too easily upon the phenomena of black culture.[24] What is often overlooked is the fact that many aspects of black cultural practices and some major social institutions had religious origins; they were given birth and nurtured in the womb of the Black Church.

2   The Black Church as the Central Institutional Sector and Partial Differentiation

The assumption that black churches constituted the central institutional sector in black communities is common in the American understanding of the black subculture. Reliable investigators have consistently underscored the fact that black churches were one of the few stable and coherent institutions to emerge from slavery.[25] Slaves not only worshiped with their masters or under the conditions of their masters' control, they also held their own secret, independent worship services in the backwoods and bayous of plantations, and sometimes in their own slave quarters: a phenomenon which Frazier called the "invisible institution."[26] Among quasi-free blacks, mutual aid societies and churches were among the first institutions created by black people. For example, the Free African Society, a mutual aid society founded by Richard Allen and Absalom Jones in 1787, gave birth to Mother Bethel A.M.E. Church in 1794. During the antebellum period of Reconstruction the pattern for their central and dominant institutional role was set when churches became the centers of the numerous black communities in the South that were formed as former slaves were separated from the plantation base to which they previously belonged. Du Bois has called the building of these black churches the "first form of economic cooperation" among black people.[27] Even in northern urban black communities the early historic black churches like Mother Bethel in Philadelphia, Mother Zion and Abyssinian Baptist in New York City, and First African in Boston also became the central institutions of those communities.[28]

The Black Church has no challenger as the cultural womb of the black community. Not only did it give birth to new institutions such as schools, banks, insurance companies, and low income housing, it also provided an academy and an arena for political activities, and it nurtured young talent for musical, dramatic, and artistic development. E. Franklin Frazier's apt descriptive phrase, "nation within a nation," pointed to these multifarious levels of community involvement found in the Black Church, in addition to the traditional concerns of worship, moral nurture, education, and social control. Much of black culture is heavily indebted to the black religious tradition, including most forms of black music, drama, literature, storytelling, and even humor. The first black publisher was the A.M.E. Church which, with the A.M.E. Zion Church, pushed the black experience into its first national organizations.

Among blacks the process of differentiation began in the late nineteenth century and it was accelerated by the urban migrations of the twentieth century after World War I through the 1960s. Differentiation took several forms: class differentiation, the development of secular institutions, and the rise of competing black religious groups. Although there were class distinctions forming during the period of slavery between freed men and slaves, and gradations among slaves according to the type of labor they performed and skin color, the process of class formation was largely a twentieth-century phenomenon, developing a black middle class from a largely rural proletariat. In 1890 about 90 percent of the black population resided in the South, and more than 80 percent of them lived in the rural "black belt" counties. The vast majority of this rural population were either farmers, sharecroppers or tenants, and unskilled workers. One hundred years later, close to one-third of the black population has achieved middle-class status and more than 80 percent of the black population live in urban areas. African Americans now constitute one of the most highly urbanized populations. A more detailed description of the development of class stratification and the rise of competing black religious groups is given in chapters 6 and 9.

The twentieth century also saw the development of black secular organizations like the black college fraternities and sororities starting in 1907, the National Association for the Advancement of Colored People in 1909, and the National Urban League in 1911. Independent black newspapers, which began in the early nineteenth century, also multiplied in urban areas during the twentieth century. The important fact about the development of these secular institutions such as the NAACP or National Urban League is that they were often founded with the help and support of Black Church leaders; their memberships also often overlapped with Black Church membership. Some of the more astute and visionary church leaders saw the need to develop secular vehicles in order to cope with more complex and pluralistic urban environments. In other words, a partial differentiation of these institutions, spheres, and functions occurred, which did not require a complete separation from the Black Church. These black secular organizations also allowed clergy and church members to influence the institutions and political processes of the larger society without raising questions about the constitutional separation between church and state. There is often an interplay, an interaction between black churches and these secular institutions, particularly in the spheres of education, politics, and economics. In fact, there is often more cooperation than conflict between black churches and secular organizations as we will show in later chapters. Most social scientific views of religion in modern society assume a posture of complete differentiation, where the spheres of the polity and the economy are completely separated from religion, do not intersect, and have very little interaction. Religion in modern society becomes privatized.[29] Our contention is that such a view of complete differentiation when applied to the Black Church confuses the historical uniqueness of that institution, and leads to a misinterpretation of the data and to a misunderstanding of black churches and black culture.

The view of partial differentiation also emphasizes the fact that the black religious tradition forms a central part of the black cultural heritage and continues a dynamic interaction with the secular forms of black culture. The interplay is seen most clearly in the area of black music, where so many black musicians and singers received their initial training and first chance for a public performance in their churches. While some of them went off to play and sing the "devil's music" like the blues and jazz in nightclubs, these secular cultural traditions gradually affected Black Church music. For example, the rhythm and blues genre was transformed into urban Negro gospel music by Thomas A. Dorsey, son of a country preacher, and a bluesman.[30] Jazz musicians such as Duke Ellington and Mary Lou Williams composed sacred music and masses for use in worship settings. Another example of partial differentiation and interaction is found in the area of education. As we will show later, some of the nation's best black colleges, like Morehouse and Spelman, were started in the basements of black churches. Like their famous counterparts, Fisk and Howard universities, they were also the training grounds for the religious professions, such as the ministry in the case of Morehouse and for missionaries and teachers at Spelman. Their early curricula were steeped in the maxims of moral education. Although the schools became secularized in the twentieth century, Morehouse College still produced outstanding religious leaders such as Rev. Dr. Martin Luther King, Jr., who profoundly affected the directions of Black Church history. Where the black cultural heritage was vibrant and alive, so was the black religious tradition. Much of black culture was forged in the heart of black religion and the Black Church. A demise of the black religious tradition would have profound implications for the preservation of black culture.

3   The Dialectical Model of the Black Church

In their important work, *Black Church in the Sixties,* Hart Nelsen and Anne Kusener Nelsen have identified three different types of interpretive schemes or social scientific models found in the work of past researchers of the Black Church, which we have summarized as follows:[31]

1. The Assimilation Model—The essence of this view is the belief in the necessity of the demise of the Black Church for the public good of blacks. The Black Church is seen as a stumbling block to assimilation in the American mainstream. The assimilation model also views the Black Church as anti-intellectual and authoritarian. This model is found in the views and studies of E. Franklin Frazier.[32]

2. The Isolation Model—The Black Church is characterized by "involuntary isolation" which is due to predominantly lower-class statuses in the black community. Isolation from civic affairs and mass apathy are the results of racial segregation in ghettos. Thus, black religion is viewed as being primarily lower class and otherworldly. The isolation model is found in the work of Anthony Orum and Charles Silberman.[33]

3. The Compensatory Model—The Black Church's main attraction is to give large masses of people the opportunity for power, control, applause, and acclaim within the group which they do not receive in the larger society, as St. Clair Drake and Horace Cayton asserted in *Black Metropolis*. This view is also related to Gunnar Myrdal's perspective in *An American Dilemma* that the black community is essentially pathological and black culture is a "distorted development" of general American culture, so black people compensate for this lack of acclaim and for lack of access to mainstream society in their own institutions.[34]

4. The Nelsens' fourth alternative (developed by themselves) is the "ethnic community-prophetic" model which gives a more positive interpretation of the Black Church. This model emphasizes the significance of the Black Church "as a base for building a sense of ethnic identity and a community of interest among its members." It also accentuates the potential of the Black Church or its minister as "prophet to a corrupt white Christian nation."[35]

Our own view of the Black Church, which is closer to the Nelsens' model, may be called the "dialectical model" of the Black Church. Black churches are institutions that are involved in a constant series of dialectical tensions. The dialectic holds polar opposites in tension, constantly shifting between the polarities in historical time. There is no Hegelian synthesis or ultimate resolution of the dialectic. Although this dialectical model is not completely new, we feel that it is time to reassert the dialectical tensions in order to obtain a holistic picture of black churches. The task of the social analyst is to examine the social conditions of any particular black church, including the situation of its leadership and membership, in order to determine what its major orientation is in relation to any pair of dialectical polarities. There are six main pairs of dialectically related polar opposites, which are discussed below.[36]

The dialectic between priestly and prophetic functions. Every black church is involved with both functions. Priestly functions involve only those activities concerned with worship and maintaining the spiritual life of members; church maintenance activities are the major thrust. Prophetic functions refer to involvement in political concerns and activities in the wider community; classically, prophetic activity has meant pronouncing a radical word of God's judgment. Some churches are closer to one end than to the other. Priestly churches are bastions of survival and prophetic churches are networks of liberation. But both types of churches also illustrate both functions, which means that liberation churches also perform the priestly functions and priestly churches contain liberation potential. Much of the discussion of black liberation theology has tended to neglect the priestly element within black churches.

The dialectic between other-worldly versus this-worldly. While the previous dialectic referred to functions, other-worldly versus this-worldly project the orientation that believers have toward the world. "Other-worldly" means being concerned only with heaven and eternal life or the world beyond, a pie-in-the-sky attitude that neglects political and social concerns. "This-worldly" refers to involvement in the affairs of this world, especially politics and social life, in the here and now. Past studies have overemphasized the other-worldly views of black churches. The other-worldly aspect, the transcendence of social and political conditions, can have a this-worldly political correlate which returns to this world by providing an ethical and prophetic critique of the present social order. In some instances eschatological transcendence can help to critique the present. One example of this is found in the mysticism of Nat Turner, whose eschatological visions directed him to attempt a strategy of violence to overturn the system of slavery.[37]

The dialectic between universalism and particularism. As ethnic institutions the historic black churches reflected the dialectical tension between the universalism of the Christian message and the particularism of their past racial history as institutions emerging out of the racism of white Christianity and the larger society. While all of the historic black churches have maintained a universal openness to all races and proudly asserted a strong antiracial discrimination position, they have differed and varied in their views and support of particularistic racial views, especially in regard to black consciousness. After the watershed period of the civil rights movement and the rise of black consciousness, it is important to understand the dialectical tensions which exist in every black religious group in matters regarding the racial factor. Race has played a very important role in the lives of black people and in the history of black institutions. Assessments of the racial factor, both positive and negative, ought not be avoided. For example, when confronted by the radical and particularistic demands of a phenomenon like black liberation theology, many white Christians, including theologians, have quickly hoisted the flag of a universal Christendom, as "brothers and sisters in Christ," while trying to escape responsibility for the contemporary pain and suffering inflicted upon black people. Similarly, some black Christians, including pastors, have felt uncomfortable in dealing with their racial past and present, and would prefer to assert the universalism of the gospel as an alternative to confronting the nettlesome problems of Christian racialism.

The dialectic between the communal and the privatistic. The communal orientation refers to the historic tradition of black churches being involved in all aspects of the lives of their members, including political, economic, educational, and social concerns. The privatistic pole of this dialectic means a withdrawal from the concerns of the larger community to a focus on meeting only the religious needs of its adherents. This dialectic is useful in assessing the degree to which the process of secularization has affected black churches. In sociological theory the effects of secularization are to push toward privatism, a more personal and individualistic sense of religiousness. Secularization also results in a psychologizing of religion, a focus on personal counseling and producing a sense of individual well-being.

The dialectic between charismatic versus bureaucratic. Max Weber's typology of organizational forms is useful in analyzing the organizational style of any black church or denomination. As an overall generalization, the majority of black churches and denominations tend to lean toward the charismatic pole of the continuum, especially when compared to white mainstream denominations and churches which tend to have more bureaucratic forms. This charismatic tendency is seen in the great difficulty which most of the historic black denominations have encountered in trying to establish a centralized national headquarters for their denominations. Among the seven black denominations, only the Christian Methodist Episcopal Church and the Church of God in Christ have been able to establish national headquarters, both in Memphis. The National Baptist Convention, U.S.A., Inc., established a national headquarters in Nashville in 1989. The charismatic tendency is also seen in the lower priority given by black churches and clergy to bureaucratic organizational forms like keeping accurate membership and financial records. From their beginnings in the "invisible institution" of slave religion, African Americans have invested far more authority in the charismatic personality of the preacher than in any organizational forms of bureaucratic hierarchy. The origins of this charismatic emphasis stemmed from the oral traditions of African cultures and religions, where people with the best speaking abilities were viewed as divinely gifted, and in the United States from the prohibition against teaching slaves to read and write, which resulted in a greater stress upon the development of an oral tradition in African American culture.[38] The charisma of church leaders was demonstrated both in the appeal of their personalities and especially in their ability to preach and elicit a strong cathartic response. Rising educational levels and upward mobility among black people have not diminished the appeal of charisma in black churches. While middleclass black churches have been more careful in keeping better records and in adopting more efficient organizational forms, their pastors must not only possess the proper educational credentials but also a charismatic preaching ability. The nickname of a famous black preacher, Rev. Dr. Charles Adams of the Hartford Avenue Baptist Church in Detroit who is called the "Harvard whooper," is an illustration of this ideal. Dr. Adams is widely celebrated as an educated preacher who can still preach in the traditional black style. The "organization man and woman," those who embody the bureaucratic style, are seldom found among the pastors of the leading black churches in the United States.

   The dialectic between resistance versus accommodation. The crucial axis of black history, according to Manning Marable, has consisted of two decisive political options, that of resistance versus accommodation.[39] Every black person and every black institution has participated in making compromises between these two poles.

The pole of accommodation means to be influenced by the larger society and to take part in aspects of it, however marginal that participation may be. In their accommodative role, black churches have been one of the major cultural brokers of the norms, values, and expectations of white society. Black churches are viewed as "mediating institutions."[40] For example, after the Civil War the church was the main mediating and socializing vehicle for millions of former slaves, teaching them economic rationality, urging them to get an education, helping them to keep their families together, and providing the leadership for early black communities. Sometimes accommodation also meant that black preachers were manipulated and used by whites. But the pole of resistance meant that it was possible to resist the accommodative forces and pressures of the American mainstream. Resistance meant affirming one's own cultural heritage, in this case an African American or black heritage. As one of the few totally black controlled and independent institutions, black churches played a major role in resistance. Politically, resistance has included both self-determination and self-affirmation. Since the civil rights movement and the attempts to desegregate American society, the accommodative pressures on black people and black institutions have grown considerably. One of the major roles of black churches in the future will be as historic reservoirs of black culture and as examples of resistance and independence.[41]

These six pairs of dialectical polarities give a more comprehensive view of the complexity of black churches as social institutions, including their roles and functions in black communities.[42] The strength of the dialectical model of the Black Church is that it leads to a more dynamic view of black churches along a continuum of dialectical tensions, struggle, and change. The problem of single, nondialectical typological views of black churches is that they tend to categorize and stereotype black churches into rigid pigeonhole categories like "other-worldly"; they miss the historical dynamism of institutions moving back and forth in response to certain issues or social conditions. Besides allowing for institutional change, the dialectical model of the Black Church offers methodological flexibility. For example, six major polar dimensions have been mentioned above, but other polarities could be added to the model such as the dialectical polarities involved in sexual politics (male-female), or those of liberation theology (oppressor-oppressed). Whatever polarities are used, the most important aspect of the model is to stress the dialectical tensions and constant interactions.

The dialectical model of the Black Church is helpful in explaining the pluralism and the plurality of views that exist in black churches and black communities. For example, in regard to politics the dialectical model of the Black Church is helpful in understanding Gayraud Wilmore's statement that black churches have been "the most conservative" and "the most radical" institutions at the same time.[43] It also helps to clarify Manning Marable's political assessment of what he has called the "ambiguous Black Church."[44] Unless one understands that black churches are involved in a dynamic series of dialectical tensions, a serious misunderstanding of these institutions can occur because the usual tendency is to collapse the dialectic and assert one side of the polarity, which often results in a simplistic view. The models of black churches that were summarized earlier share the danger of oversimplification when certain insights about black churches are made the major defining categories.

The dialectical model allows for a more objective analysis of black churches as social institutions because it takes a broader, more comprehensive perspective. It moves beyond the simplistic positive or negative assessments of personal observation and places black churches along a dynamic continuum allowing for change in response to changing social conditions.

The dialectical model of the Black Church is reflective of W. E. B. Du Bois's phenomenology of consciousness, his poetic articulation of "double-consciousness" as summarizing both the plight and potential of the African and Euro-American heritage of black people; "two struggling souls within one dark body."[45] Du Bois did not provide any final resolution of this double-consciousness, but he did recognize the need for complete freedom for African Americans in order that their human potentials could be fully realized. The Black Church institutionalizes the dialectical tensions and constant struggles that Du Bois wrote about. The black churches are not reified social institutions, but they represent the collective double-consciousness of the African American subculture expressing itself as a religious community in the uncertain shadow of an established tradition.[46]

Conclusion

The purpose of this brief introductory chapter has been to make clear the main theoretical assumptions that underlie our interpretation and analysis of black churches. Although the major intent of our study was to provide descriptive historical overviews and contemporary statistical data and information about black churches and clergy in the seven historic black denominations, we felt that an elaboration of these theoretical assumptions would contribute to the ongoing scholarly dialogue about ways of interpreting black religious phenomena, especially the Black Church.

The religious dimension of black churches is found in the black sacred cosmos, a unique Afro-Christian worldview that was forged among black people from both the African and Euro-American traditions during the eighteenth and nineteenth centuries. The black sacred cosmos permeated all of the social institutions and cultural traditions of black people. While the general structure of beliefs, rituals, and organization of black churches remained the same as white churches, black Christians often gave different nuances and emphases to their theological views. For example, the paladin God of deliverance is given a much more prominent role in black worship practices. Black worship and religious experiences are also much more ecstatic, emotionally expressive, and enthusiastic compared to whites. The black sacred cosmos also reflects the deepest values of African Americans, giving primal consideration to the necessity of freedom as an expression of complete belonging and allegiance to God.

As the only stable and coherent institutional area to emerge from slavery, black churches were not only dominant in their communities but they also became the womb of black culture and a number of major social institutions. While the social processes of migration, urbanization, and differentiation have diminished aspects of this centrality and dominance, black churches have continued their interactions within the spheres of politics, economics, education, and culture so that only a partial differentiation has occurred and not a complete separation. Examples of this partial differentiation will be given in later chapters.

The "dialectical model of the Black Church," which conceives of black churches along a continuum of six major dialectical polarities held in dynamic tension, has been our way of obtaining a more comprehensive view of this significant institutional sector. Many past studies of black churches have been flawed by using a single rigid typological label like "other-worldly" or "compensatory" to characterize all black churches. While these typologies may contain aspects of truth, they fail to present the whole picture. Furthermore, they also tend to become ahistorical with the passage of time.

The complexities of black churches as social institutions require a more dynamic and interactional theoretical perspective because they have played more complex roles and assumed more comprehensive burdens in their communities than is true of most white and ethnic churches. Hence, the theoretical assumptions cited above are only the first steps in the quest for a more comprehensive theory of black religious phenomena and a sociology of black churches.

In chapters 2, 3, and 4 we present overviews of the seven historic black denominations, denoting their organizational forms, and the main aspects of their history. Unfortunately, a listing of all of the people who contributed to the historical development of a particular denomination is impossible in a brief overview, and readers are referred to the in-house histories published by the denominations themselves.

In chapters 5 and 6 we present summary profiles of black rural and urban churches and clergy for our field survey of black churches nationwide. We have attempted to place our results in historical perspective, using comparisons with past studies wherever possible.

Chapter 7 consists of an examination of the impact of the black consciousness period of black power and black pride upon black churches and clergy. These findings represent the first attempt to examine this phenomenon by any survey study. A black consciousness scale was constructed from the survey questions and used to examine the degree of black consciousness expressed by black clergy, and the relationship between black consciousness and the sponsorship of community outreach programs by black churches.

In chapters 8 and 9 we present both historical summaries and contemporary data regarding the relationship of black churches to the areas of politics and economics. The arguments of partial differentiation and the dialectical model of the Black Church are reiterated, giving concrete examples of how black churches still continue to interact with and play important roles in the politics, economics, and education of African Americans.

Chapter 10 focuses on one of the difficult problems which confronts black churches, the situation of black women clergy. Again, our survey findings on black women clergy are presented in the context of historical overviews of the struggle of black women to become preachers and pastors in black churches.

In chapter 11 we examine the problems which black churches have experienced in regard to black youth and young adults. Some data on a growing sector of unchurched urban teenagers and young adults are presented, as well as a summary of the kinds of programs which black churches have sponsored for black youth. The chapter concludes with a listing of some of the creative programs being attempted by some black churches.

Chapter 12 offers a broad overview of the development and types of music from spirituals to civil rights hymnody in black churches. Although most sociologists have tended to ignore music in their studies of black churches, we felt that it could not be excluded. All black churches have been sustained and revitalized by their rich musical heritage.

In the concluding chapter 13, some major trends among black churches and religious groups are noted. The study ends with a brief statement on policy recommendations for the historic black denominations. We felt that a study of the scope and magnitude such as ours should not only describe what is happening but also provide some reflections on policy alternatives for the future. In this sense, our study has been "proactive," scholarship with some practical application. We turn next to an overview of the seven historic black denominations, the black Baptists, Methodists, and Pentecostals.

2 The Black Baptists:
The First Black Churches in America

The cultural origins of the black Baptists are to be found in the South rather than the North as was the case with the founding of the mother congregations of the African Methodist Church and the African Methodist Zion Churches in the mid-1790s. This basic difference still holds true for the black Baptists—even though they now dominate the urban scene. Regardless of this preponderance, these churches are still characterized by a distinct Southern religious milieu which stresses enthusiastic and demonstrative worship.*

Overview

The first independent black Baptist congregations were organized in the last half of the eighteenth century, at a time when the American colonies and black Methodists alike were issuing their respective declarations of independence. The black Baptists were pursuing no overt political revolts but rather were struggling to carve out a religious space in the midst of the southern plantations that defined their lives as slaves. During the antebellum period, however, fugitive slaves and free Blacks in the North did form abolitionist missionary associations and societies, the leaders of which then organized the first regional black Baptist conventions. Many of the participants in these associations and conventions were for a long time simultaneously involved in white Baptist organizations. Miles Mark Fisher reports that:

> After Nat Turner's insurrection in 1831 one must define anew a Negro Baptist church. That movement sent hot hate back and

*James M. Washington, *The Origins and Emergence of Black Baptist Separatism, 1863–1897*, p. 257 (Ann Arbor, Mich.: University Microfilms, 1983).

20

wide consternation all over the Southland. Generally, what independence Negro churches had enjoyed was taken away. A
revised black code was enacted . . . silencing . . . colored preachers. A [white] church . . . [and] association . . . would take a Negro church as a branch; and thus the independence of the Negro
church was further postponed. . . .[1]

Early in the Reconstruction era, however, an emergent ideology of
separatism gave impetus to the organizing of a national black convention.[2] While this first national organization lasted but a dozen
years, it established a critical precedent for subsequent efforts.

Today there are eight identifiable black Baptist communions in
the United States, the largest ones being the National Baptist Convention, U.S.A., Inc.; the National Baptist Convention of America;
and the Progressive National Baptist Convention, Inc. These three
conventions, along with the Lott Carey Baptist Foreign Mission Convention share a common ancestry and are the principal focus of
Baptist development. Of the remaining four, the largest is the National Primitive Baptist Convention, U.S.A., which originally withdrew from the white Primitive Baptists in 1865 and organized formally in 1907. The National Primitive Baptists have an estimated
250,000 members. The United Free Will Baptist Church began in
1870, but did not formally organize as a denomination until 1901. It
has an estimated membership of 100,000.

The National Baptist Evangelical Life and Soul Saving Assembly
of the U.S.A., a group originally formed in 1920 as part of the National Baptist Convention of America and becoming independent in
1937, has some 50,000 members. The Free For All Missionary Baptist
Church, Inc., formed in 1955, has perhaps 10,000 members. In addition to the predominantly black groups, at least 75,000 blacks belong
to the Southern Baptist Convention, and at least 150,000 to the
American Baptist Churches in the U.S.A.[3] The American Baptist
Churches of the South, an initially integrated but now predominantly black regional unit of the ABC, organized in the early 1970s.

Emergence of Black Baptists

The formal Baptist movement, like the Methodist, has its origins in
England, although the Baptists antedate the Methodists by a century.
The first Baptists evolved from a group of Puritans compelled to take

refuge in Holland as a result of persecution in their homeland. While in Holland, these Separatist Puritans became persuaded that only baptism of adult believers and baptism by immersion were doctrinally correct. They also came in contact with Anabaptists, the radical wing of the Protestant Reformation who, among other convictions, gave primacy to the separation of church and state. In this milieu the exiles established the first English Baptist church in 1609. Upon their return to England, members of this group organized a Baptist church in London around 1612. This was followed by a second church in 1616, which split over doctrinal differences in 1638. The resultant new church in turn split in 1641, giving rise to a third variation of the proliferating Baptist movement.

The American Baptist movement emerged in the colonies during the same period as the movement in England, and is generally dated from the arrival in America of Puritan Roger Williams in 1631. Exiled from the Massachusetts Bay Colony because of his fierce opposition to the intermingling of church and state interests, Williams obtained a charter from the British monarch to establish the Rhode Island colony, and the first Baptist Church in America was established by Williams in Providence in 1639. A second church was organized by John Clarke in Newport, Rhode Island, in 1641. A few congregations were subsequently established in Massachusetts, but the inhospitable reception there caused Rhode Island to develop as the Baptist stronghold. Throughout the seventeenth century the Rhode Island churches were typically known as "General" Baptists, a reference to their Arminian inclinations.[4] In 1670 these congregations organized the first Baptist association, but thereafter gradually declined.

In the eighteenth century the orientation of the Baptist churches in Rhode Island and throughout the Middle Colonies became more rigorously Calvinistic in contrast to the earlier General churches. These new churches were known as "Particular" Baptists, and by 1707 five such churches in New Jersey, Pennsylvania, and Delaware united in the formation of the Philadelphia Baptist Association. By 1767 associations had also been organized in New England, Virginia, and the Carolinas. This growth in the Baptist movement was attributable in part to the mission work of the Philadelphia Association, but even more to the impact of the Great Awakening which made large numbers of people receptive to the Baptist appeal. At the same time, however, the Awakening led to a division of Baptists into two distinct groups. The "New Light" or Separate Baptists, initially concentrated in New England, became even more extreme in their Calvinistic emphases and the intensely emotional tactics of revivalism. The "Old Light" or Regular Baptists, consisting largely of the Philadelphia Association, were more moderate in their doctrinal requirements and more traditional and decorous in their rituals of worship.

Before the end of the century Old Lights and New Lights had set aside their differences in the interests of cooperative mission efforts, and by 1800 some twelve hundred churches were organized in nearly fifty local associations. The first step toward denominational structure was taken in 1814 with the formation of the General Missionary Convention of the Baptist Denomination in the United States of America for Foreign Missions. This fellowship subsequently was known as the American Baptist Missionary Union, and was joined by two complementary organizations, the American Baptist Home Mission Society, and the American Baptist Publication Society. But long before this degree of unity and organization was achieved, both the New Light and the Old Light Baptists had extended their missionary efforts to southern states where slaves attending revival services were introduced to evangelical Christianity.

The first known black Baptist, identified only as Quassey, was listed as one of fifty-one members of the Newton, Rhode Island, church in 1743. The Providence, Rhode Island, Baptist Church had nineteen black members in 1762, and blacks were first received into membership in the First Baptist Church of Boston in 1772. But by far the preponderance of black Baptists were in the South.

The National Baptists

The ancestry of the National Baptist Convention reaches back to the first known black churches in America, generally acknowledged to have been the African Baptist or "Bluestone" Church on the William Byrd plantation near the Bluestone River in Mecklenberg, Virginia, in 1758, and the Silver Bluff Baptist Church, located on the South Carolina bank of the Savannah River not far from Augusta, Georgia.[5] Although historical records indicate that the Silver Bluff Church was established by a slave named George Liele sometime between 1773 and 1775, the cornerstone of the present church building claims a founding date of 1750.[6] Like many other slaves, Liele embraced Christianity during the evangelistic revivals that followed the Great

Awakening. He was subsequently licensed as an exhorter to perform
mission work among other slaves on neighboring plantations, which
included the Galphin plantation and trading post at Silver Bluff. The
church was shortlived, as a consequence of conflicts associated with
the Revolutionary War. After being freed by his master, however,
Liele went to Savannah where he preached for some time. He emigrated to Jamaica in 1782 or 1783, leaving behind him a baptized
group of slaves, among whom was Andrew Bryan who organized the
First African Church of Savannah around 1788. Bryan was assisted by
another slave, Jesse Peters (also called Jesse Galphin), who was previously a member of the Silver Bluff Church and had become a
preacher as a result of Liele's work. Peters became the pastor of the
Springfield Baptist Church of Augusta, Georgia, which was organized
around 1787.[7]

As these early churches grew and multiplied in the Savannah area,
other independent black churches were established in cities such
as Williamsburg, Richmond, and Petersburg, where there were greater numbers of blacks and proportionately more free blacks. Two
black ministers, Josiah Bishop at Portsmouth and William Lemon at
Gloucester are known to have pastored white Baptist churches in
Virginia. Nor was it uncommon for black churches to have white
pastors. Robert Ryland was the white pastor of the First African
Church of Richmond for twenty-five years.[8] Baptist churches were
also established early in North Carolina and South Carolina. At the
turn of the century the number of black Baptists was estimated to be
in excess of 25,000.

The degree of independence diminished, however, as the number
of slave members increased despite the strict regulations requiring
that they have written permission to leave the plantations for worship. Many of the slaves were permitted to attend only the white
churches of their masters or black churches pastored by white clergymen. Very often the slave members of nominally white churches
outnumbered the white membership. In 1846 a church in Georgetown, South Carolina, had thirty-three white members compared to
798 black, while a church in Natchez, Mississippi, had sixty-two
white members and 380 black.

Many slaves were obliged to worship clandestinely in hidden enclaves on the plantations as units of what came to be called the
"invisible institution." But even when secrecy was not mandated,
under no circumstances were the scattered independent churches

allowed to develop formal black associations, though some of them did seek to join with existing white Baptist organizations. Miles Mark Fisher has summarized the situation with sensitivity when he observes that:

> A Negro Baptist church was somewhat independent in the North, although associations like those in Philadelphia and New York could appoint preachers for Negro churches. In the South a large congregation of colored people could lay no claim to sovereignty apart from the white people. This point is illustrated in the First African Baptist Church, Savannah, whose membership of seven hundred was divided into three churches by the Savannah Association in 1802. . . . Only after emancipation can complete autonomy be called a distinguishing mark of a Negro Baptist Church.[9]

As the spirit of the Revolutionary era waned and tensions were aggravated by incidents such as the planned slave uprising by Gabriel Prosser in 1800, the Denmark Vesey revolt of 1822, and the Nat Turner rebellion of 1831, increasingly severe restrictions were imposed on religious activities until "independent" became a misnomer where southern black congregations were concerned. The status of blacks grew even more tenuous when the Baptists split in 1845 over the issue of slavery. Nevertheless, the number of black Baptists continued to grow, reaching 150,000 by 1850, and nearly 500,000 by 1870 as independent churches proliferated with the demise of slavery.

In the early nineteenth century organized black Baptist activity became a distinguishing feature of the northern churches. In northern states, as in the South, the move toward racially separate churches was not a matter of doctrinal disagreement, but a protest against unequal and restrictive treatment. Out of this interest emerged such historic institutions as the Joy Street Church in Boston, originally organized as the African Baptist Church by Thomas Paul in 1805; the Abyssinian Baptist Church, also founded by Thomas Paul, in 1808; and the First African Baptist Church in Philadelphia, organized by Henry Cunningham in 1809.

The separation of northern black Baptists from white churches was made easier by the nature of Baptist polity. In contrast to the elaborate connectional structure of the Methodists, the hallmark of Baptist polity is the absolute independence of each local church. A group of churches may join together in an "association," that is, a cluster of congregations within a given geographical area which may encompass several towns or counties, or only a portion of one city. Similarly, states with a substantial Baptist population invariably have one or more "state conventions." But the affiliation of a given local church with larger organizations is strictly voluntary and may be terminated at any time on the vote of the local congregation. Similarly, it is the prerogative of a state convention to affiliate or not with one of the national conventions. Furthermore, a local church may vote to affiliate directly with one or more of the national conventions, completely bypassing the state structure. So jealous are local churches of their independent status that many Baptists take exception to the very use of the word denomination in describing their loose-knit structures. This sensitivity has historically been in tension, however, with the struggles of black Baptists to create and maintain regional and national organizations.

While the departure of black Baptists from white churches in the late eighteenth and early nineteenth century was easier than for the black Methodists, the formation of a national denomination was more difficult. Indeed, that effort preoccupied the better part of a century. From 1815 to 1880, many black Baptists worked through existing national white Baptist organizations via the African Baptist Missionary Society. The ABMS was first under the auspices of the American Baptist Union. After the 1845 division of the white Baptists over slavery, the Society became associated with the Southern Baptist Convention. The primary objective of the African Baptist Missionary Society was mission work in Africa, and the best known of its representatives was Lott Carey, one of its founders who established the First Baptist Church in Monrovia, Liberia, in 1821.

The earliest all-black Baptist associations were organized not in the South, but in the "West": Providence Association in Ohio in 1834; Union Association, also in Ohio, 1836; Wood River Association in Illinois in 1839; and Amherstburg Association in Canada and Michigan in 1841. In contrast to the white associations, the black groups generally assumed a strong abolitionist posture, and many of their members were active in the Underground Railroad in Ohio and Canada. In 1844 the Wood River Association organized the Colored Baptist Home Missionary Society, whose efforts resulted in the formation of the Western Colored Baptist Convention. The WCBC was an expanded association with representatives from seven states, and it endured from 1853 to 1859. In 1864 this effort was revitalized by the Wood River Association with leadership assistance from the other three associations. Out of this relationship emerged a regional grouping known as the Northwestern and Southern Baptist Convention, with representatives from eight states.

The Northwestern and Southern Baptist Convention was actually the second regional convention to be formed. The first, the American Baptist Missionary Convention, had been organized fully two decades before emancipation at the Abyssinian Baptist Church in New York City in 1840, for purposes of evangelization, education, and general racial uplift. This convention was restricted in its activities to the New England and Middle Atlantic areas until after the Civil War, when it sent black ministers to the South as missionaries.

In 1866 in a meeting of the Plan of Union Committees held in Richmond, these two regional conventions merged in what was the first attempt to create a national convention. The Consolidated American Baptist Missionary Convention, as it was called, held its first official meeting in August 1867 in Nashville, and in 1868 reported a constituency of 100,000 black Baptists, with 200 ministers. The Consolidated Convention, consisting of six subdivisions called district conventions, lasted for twelve years. It held its final meeting in 1879, by which time it was already fragmenting into separate regional conventions.

Partly as a result of heightened race consciousness, partly in reaction to the discrimination of southern white Baptists and the paternalism of northern white Baptists, the independent church movement initiated among black Baptists in the antebellum period intensified during the Reconstruction and its aftermath. Though in tension with a competing school of thought which favored working on a cooperative basis with whites within the existing northern Baptist organizations, the separatist ideology prevailed and ultimately culminated in the establishment of an independent Baptist denomination. The first national effort at consolidation, the Consolidated American Baptist Missionary Convention, foundered on the shoals of inadequate financial support and internal class conflicts between the educated northern blacks and the southern ex-slaves on such issues as emotional fervor and political activism. Upon the demise of this convention, however, three new organizations came into existence.

The Baptist Foreign Mission Convention of the United States of

America was formed at a meeting of 151 delegates from 11 states convened by Rev. W. W. Colley in Montgomery, Alabama, on November 24, 1880. It was originally headquartered in Richmond, with Rev. Mr. Colley serving as corresponding secretary. The convention not only sent missionaries to Africa, but concerned itself with such domestic social issues as the use of alcohol and tobacco.

The American National Baptist Convention was organized August 25, 1886, at a meeting of 600 delegates from churches in 17 states convened in St. Louis, under the leadership of Rev. William J. Simmons, who became its first president. This convention, which claimed over one million constituents in some 9,000 churches with 4,500 ministers, represented the most ambitious effort to date to create a black Baptist denomination, an initiative pursued in spite of resistance from northern white Baptists.

The third convention, the National Baptist Educational Convention of the U.S.A., was formed in Washington, D.C., in 1893 under the leadership of Rev. W. Bishop Johnson for the primary purpose of educating and training clergy and missionaries.

At the 1894 annual meeting of these various bodies in Montgomery, a motion was made proposing their merger into one convention, whereupon a joint committee was appointed to report on the proposal the following year. The merger was accomplished at a meeting convened in Atlanta on September 28, 1895, and attended by over 500 delegates and observers. The resulting organization was the National Baptist Convention, U.S.A., with subsidiary Foreign Mission, Home Mission, and Education boards, to which a publishing concern was added in 1897. Rev. E. C. Morris was elected the first president of the new convention.

The display of unity was timely because African Americans had entered into an era of intensified repression. From 1890 to 1910 legislation was passed by all southern states which effectively disenfranchised African Americans, and gave license to lynchings and other forms of racial suppression. The Supreme Court also ratified the Jim Crow segregation by approving "separate but equal" railroad cars and, by extension, in all other public facilities in *Plessy v. Ferguson* in 1896. In the process, the ranks of the black churches, which constituted the sole place of sanctuary, expanded accordingly. Between 1890 and 1906 the number of black Baptist ministers increased from 5,500 to over 17,000.

Baptist unity was short lived, however. When a new corresponding secretary was appointed to the Foreign Mission Board and its head-quarters moved from Richmond to Louisville, some of the original members of the board declined to cooperate and withdrew in 1897 to form the Lott Carey Foreign Missionary Convention. The issues involved loyalties to the old Foreign Mission Convention which had been based in Richmond (as had the original African Baptist Mission-ary Society) and resentment of the publishing activities of the new convention, which jeopardized the relations of the Richmond group with the white Baptist organizations.

Withdrawal of the Lott Carey contingent, made up of better-educated members from Virginia, North Carolina, and the District of Columbia, was an expression once again of the class and ideological differences that had long plagued the movement for denominational independence.

In 1905 the Lott Carey Convention and the National Baptist Con-vention were ostensibly reconciled. Today they continue to function as independent bodies, although most of their members and officers have a dual affiliation. The National Baptist Convention, U.S.A., meanwhile, became a distinctly black denomination but internal conflicts persisted. The convention was to experience schism twice more in the next century, once in 1915 with the formation of the National Baptist Convention of America, and again in 1961, with the organizing of the Progressive National Baptist Convention.

To some degree, these divisions are transcended, if not obscured, in efforts supported cooperatively by the different conventions. A number of black institutions of higher learning have Baptist origins and maintain Baptist affiliations. They are not, however, generally under the direct jurisdiction of one particular convention. They may receive support from the various black conventions, as well as from one or both of the major white conventions, or they may be spon-sored principally by a state convention. Many of these institutions were founded in the years immediately following emancipation (of-ten as secondary schools) by the white American Baptist Home Mis-sion Society. Others were established by black Baptists around the turn of the century. A dozen of these schools survive today as junior colleges, and another dozen as four-year colleges. Among them are Benedict College, in Columbia, South Carolina; Virginia Union Uni-versity, Richmond; Shaw University, Raleigh, North Carolina; and Morehouse College and Spelman College in Atlanta. Some schools like Tuskegee Institute were closely aligned with the Baptists due to the influence of leaders like Dr. Booker T. Washington. The American Baptist Theological Seminary in Nashville is jointly operated by the Southern Baptist Convention and the National Baptist Convention, Inc.

National Baptist Convention, U.S.A., Inc.

After the schism in 1915 which produced the National Baptist Convention of America, the NBC, U.S.A., incorporated and its other boards became subordinate to the convention.[10] Rev. E. C. Morris, who had first been elected president when the NBC was created in 1895, continued in that capacity with the incorporated body until 1922. Following the loss of the publishing concern in 1915, a new board was created, the Sunday School Publishing Board of the National Baptist Convention. The Foreign Mission Board, however, replaced the publishing concern as the center of the convention's operations.

The convention also involved itself in domestic interests. Even before the turn of the century the NBC was active in education, supporting nearly 100 elementary and secondary schools and colleges, as well as providing for the education of African missionaries. In the first decade of the new century the NBC spoke out against racial violence and waged campaigns against segregation in public accommodations and discrimination in the armed service, education, and employment. These and other activities were generally carried out within the prevailing ideological framework of self-help. While both Booker T. Washington and W. E. B. Du Bois were frequent speakers at the annual conventions, it was Washington's program which the convention formally endorsed in 1909. The NBC, Inc., strongly supported the NAACP, however, and was vocal on such matters as the right to vote and to serve on juries.

At the time of the split in 1915 the National Baptist Convention represented nearly 3 million black people in over 20,000 local Baptist churches. Spurred by the northern migration of African Americans over the next several decades, both conventions experienced a shift from rural to urban churches, and a rapid growth in membership.

E. C. Morris was succeeded as convention president by W. G. Parks, who served only one year before L. K. Williams took office in 1924. D. V. Jemison was elected president in 1941 and served until 1952. In 1953 J. H. Jackson became president and held that office for a record twenty-nine years.

At the time of Rev. Dr. Joseph H. Jackson's election, the NBC, Inc., had nine boards and commissions. To these the new president added an additional thirteen. The program expansion was not reflective of social concerns, however, as the convention took a decidedly conservative turn. Jackson represented a strong vocal opposition to Martin Luther King and King's strategy of civil disobedience and nonviolent protest. Under his slogan of "from protest to production!" he located himself in the patriotic, law and order, anticommunist, procapitalist, school of gradualism. Although his was a position out of favor with most younger African Americans, Jackson succeeded in blocking the participation of the convention as an institution in the civil rights movement. King, for his part, left the NBC, Inc., as one of the leaders of the Progressive National Baptist Convention, a splinter group founded in 1961.

In contrast, Jackson's successor, Rev. Dr. Theodore J. Jemison, was a veteran of the civil rights movement, having organized a bus boycott in Baton Rouge, Louisiana, in 1953, and having served as the first general secretary of the Southern Christian Leadership Conference. Upon his election in 1982 Jemison pledged his support for social action in pursuit of civil rights, and initiated a nationwide voter registration drive.

The National Baptist Convention, U.S.A., Inc., is by far the largest of all the black denominations, and is considered the largest organization of African Americans in existence. The NBC, Inc., reports about 7.5 million members, of whom all but 100,000 are in the United States. The membership thus encompasses nearly one-fourth of the entire black population of the United States, and at least one-third of the estimated number of black members of Christian churches. Over 29,000 clergy and 30,000 local churches are affiliated with the convention, as are 4,700 associations and 59 state conventions. The annual budget of the National Convention in 1989 was about $4.5 million.[11]

NBC, Inc., convenes once a year, at the same time in September as the National Baptist Convention of America. Local churches, associations, and state conventions are required to pay a fee of from $10 to $50 for representative delegates, depending on the size and type of the sponsoring group, except that state conventions pay $200 for the first two messengers. Individuals may join the convention by paying an annual membership fee of $10, but they are not entitled to vote. Life membership is awarded upon payment of $200.

The officers of the convention are elected annually. Offices specified in the constitution include president, vice president-at-large, four vice presidents, vice presidents from each of the states represented, general secretary, four assistant secretaries, treasurer, statistician, historiographer, executive editor, and attorney. The convention is governed by a board of directors, which consists of fifteen members-at-large elected by the convention in addition to the named officers. The board of directors and its nine-member executive committee are responsible for conducting the business of the convention when it is not in session.

Traditionally, the purpose of the National Convention has been to carry on work in areas such as education, mission, and publishing which could not be done effectively by individual churches and would be done less efficiently by multiple regional bodies. More recently the national body has also assumed responsibility for matters such as ministerial pension plans. Current information on the organization of the convention is restricted inasmuch as no literature setting forth the president's program has been published since the change in administration in 1982. (The convention is empowered to create each year whatever boards are deemed necessary to carry out its work.) The scope of its activity is suggested by the auxiliary conventions and boards officially reporting at the 1980 session of the convention. These included Foreign Mission, Home Mission, Sunday School Publishing, Baptist Training Union (B.T.U.), Education, Evangelistic, and Benefit boards, and Usher's and Moderator's Auxiliaries. The Laymen's Movement Auxiliary, Women's Convention Auxiliary, and Congress of Christian Education (formerly Sunday School and B.T.U. Congress) are specifically provided for in the constitution. A Young People's Department, operated as a subsidiary of the Women's Convention, is subdivided into several units based on age and marital status of the girls and young women. The Laymen's Auxiliary has a department for boys. Various commissions appointed from time to time address such matters as social service, rural life, theological education, theology, church-supported schools, ecumenical Christianity, the United Nations, civil rights, and intercultural relations.

According to the constitution, each board is to be made up of one member from each state and territory represented at the convention, plus an additional eight members from the state in which the board is located. Each board determines its own laws and regulations, nominates its own officers, and selects its own employees, who are then subject to ratification by the convention or its board of directors. Several of the boards have counterpart departments to implement the various programs. The auxiliary conventions generally meet in session at the same time as the National Convention. They have their own officers and committee structures, and in some instances a separate constitution and their own publications.

The convention presently has no permanent national headquarters, although it has plans to complete a new $12 million National Baptist World Center in Nashville in 1990, adjacent to the American Baptist Theological Seminary (jointly supported by National Baptists and Southern Baptists). Its current president, T. J. Jemison, pastors the Mount Zion First Baptist Church in Baton Rouge, Louisiana, while the general secretary resides in Mount Vernon, New York, and its publishing house, the Sunday School Publishing Board, is located in Nashville.

National Baptist Convention of America

The National Baptist Convention of America (NBCA), originally called the National Baptist Convention, Unincorporated, is a product of the 1915 split in the National Baptist Convention, U.S.A., which was founded in 1895. The central issue in this conflict was the publishing concern, which had also been a factor in the 1897 schism resulting in the Lott Carey Convention. This time the dispute involved the "Boyd faction" led by R. H. Boyd, secretary of the Publishing Board, and the "Morris faction," led by E. C. Morris, president of the convention. Ultimately, the Boyd faction took the name "National Baptist Convention of America" and remained unincorporated. The Morris faction retains the original name of the convention, but incorporated to become the National Baptist Convention, U.S.A., Inc.

Both groups claim to be the original parent body. Both claim the founding date of 1880. In fact, no unified National Baptist Convention existed in 1880, which was the founding date of the oldest of the three entities that merged in 1895. In short, while three Baptist bodies went into the funnel in 1895, two emerged from the other end in 1915.[12]

The conflict was set in motion shortly after the NBC, U.S.A., Inc., was created, when the American Baptist Publication Society, upon complaints from Southern Baptists, withdrew its invitation for black leaders to write articles for one of its publications. As a result of this impasse, the National Baptist Convention determined to establish its own publishing capabilities. The new Publishing Board was initially placed under the Home Mission Board of which R. H. Boyd (who introduced the resolution proposing the printing committee) served as corresponding secretary.

Under Boyd's leadership and on the basis of his personal credit the Publishing Board quickly became a successful business venture. New facilities were built on land owned by Boyd in Nashville, who had the agency incorporated in the state of Tennessee, and materials produced by the publishing house were copyrighted in his name. When in 1905 the Rev. Mr. Morris acted to separate the publishing house from the Home Mission Board, Boyd and the other members of the board resisted, and a decade-long controversy ensued centered around the question of ownership and control of the publishing interest. Ultimately the conflict was resolved in Boyd's favor by the courts of Tennessee. The convention itself was unincorporated and so unable to own property in its own name and although it had created the Publishing Board, it had neglected to make proper provisions for legal claim to it.

The National Baptist Publishing Board became the nucleus of a separate National Baptist body, which was organized in Chicago on September 9, 1915. As this convention moved to establish additional boards, an agreement was struck whereby all foreign mission work of the new group would be conducted through the Lott Carey Convention. The latter thereby strengthened its hand in missions, while the NBCA gained an enlarged audience for its literature. Over the years, however, this working relationship declined and NBCA ultimately organized an independent Foreign Mission Board. In addition to the issues of prohibition, evangelism, and education, the NBCA gave early support to civil rights organizations, urban social service programs, and the antilynching campaign.

The Boyd family continues to be prominent in the NBCA publishing concern. Henry Allen Boyd succeeded his father, R. H. Boyd, in 1922, and he in turn was succeeded by his nephew, T. B. Boyd, Jr., who led the publishing house from 1959 to 1979. Since 1979 the Publishing Board has been headed by T. B. Boyd III, in his capacity as executive director.

Rev. E. P. Jones was elected president of the convention at the time of its organizing. His successors were J. E. Woods, 1923; J. W. Hurse, 1930; G. L. Prince, 1933; C. D. Pettaway, 1957; J. C. Sams, 1967; and E. E. Jones, 1985.[13]

The National Baptist Convention of America is the second largest of the three black Baptist conventions having a national constituency, and the third largest of all the black denominations. In 1989 its estimated membership of 2.4 million in 7,800 local churches indicates an average congregation of about 280, which is somewhat larger than the average congregation of the National Baptist Convention, Inc. (235), but far smaller than that of the Progressive National Baptist Convention (a thousand). These churches are served by from 2,500 to 3,000 clergy, suggesting a substantial number of small rural churches. Some four hundred associations, ranging from five to a hundred local churches, and thirty-five state conventions in twenty-seven states, are affiliated with the convention.[14]

The NBCA convenes every year on the Wednesday following the first Sunday in September. Convention delegates called "messengers" include lay and ministerial representatives from local churches, associations, and state conventions. Each church is assessed a minimum of $50, or $1 per member for the first messenger, and $10 for each additional messenger. Each district association pays $50 for the first two messengers, and $10 for each additional messenger; each general association and state convention pays $100 for the first five messengers, and $10 for each additional messenger.

The officers of the convention are elected annually and include a president; first, second, and third vice presidents; recording secretary; first, second, third, and fourth assistant recording secretaries; corresponding secretary; statistical secretary; treasurer; auditor; director of public relations; historian; and secretary of youth activities. The presidents of the state conventions and moderators of the general associations are associate vice presidents. The Executive Board, which conducts the business of the convention when it is not in session, consists of the elected convention officers and presidents of the state conventions. The constitution provides for five administrative committees: Registration, Budget, Finance, Bills and Accounts, and Credentials.

The NBCA has seven program boards: Home Mission, Foreign Mission, Baptist Training Union, National Baptist Publishing, Evangelical, Benevolent, and Educational. The membership of each board consists of one member from each state convention and general association. The auxiliaries of the convention include two Women's Missionary auxiliaries, Junior Women's Auxiliary, Brotherhood Union, Ushers, Nurses' Corps, and Youth Convention. Each board and auxiliary elects its own officers, although the officers of the latter are subject to ratification by the convention. The constitution also specifies four commissions: Transportation, Christian Education, Social Justice, and Army and Navy Chaplains.

The NBCA does not have centralized national headquarters. The publishing house is in Nashville. The principal officers do not ordinarily relinquish their offices as local pastors.

In 1988 a new schism occurred in the NBCA over the question of the Boyd family's control of the Publishing House. With an estimated 25 percent of the membership, the Boyd faction styled itself the National Missionary Baptist Convention of America (NMBCA). It remains to be seen whether this group will emerge as the fourth major black Baptist denomination.

Progressive National Baptist Convention, Inc.

The Progressive National Baptist Convention, U.S.A., Inc., (PNBC) came into existence in 1961 as a result of conflict within the National Baptist Convention, U.S.A., Inc. The dissension began in 1957 when ten pastors were expelled from the NBC, Inc., for challenging the president, J. H. Jackson, in court on his ruling that an amendment setting a four-year limit on tenure was invalid, inasmuch as it had been adopted in 1952 in a manner that was procedurally unconstitutional. Jackson's position was upheld by a federal court.[15]

His opponents, reacting to the larger issue of what was perceived as autocratic rule, subsequently organized around the candidacy of Rev. Dr. Gardner C. Taylor.[16] The "Taylor team," as it was called, included Martin Luther King, Sr., Martin Luther King, Jr., Ralph David Abernathy, Benjamin Mays, and a number of other clergy committed to King's social change strategies which Jackson condemned as inadvisable and injurious to the cause of racial advance and harmony.

At the 1960 convention in Philadelphia, the nominating committee unanimously presented Jackson's name for another term, whereupon he was declared reelected. When the Taylor team protested, demanding a roll call vote by states, the convention was declared adjourned. The delegates remained, however, and conducted an election in which Taylor won. When the Jackson faction refused to acknowledge the vote results, the Taylor team proceeded to conduct a sit-in at the convention. The Taylor faction claimed throughout the following year to be the rightful officers of the convention, but the courts again ruled in Jackson's favor.

The next year, in Kansas City, Missouri, the Taylor delegates, who had been meeting in separate session, were initially denied admission to the larger assembly. When they were admitted, physical confrontations erupted as they moved to take control of the platform. Ultimately, a court-supervised election was held, and Jackson emerged victorious. Taylor acknowledged the results, and he and King both called for unity. Before the convention was ended, however, Martin Luther King, Sr., Martin Luther King, Jr., D. E. King, Marshall L. Shepard, C. C. Adams and others were removed from any offices they held, including membership on the board of directors.

Rev. L. Venhael Booth assumed leadership of the opposition and, as the chairman of the "Volunteer Committee for the Formation of a New National Baptist Convention," called for a meeting in November 1961 at his church, Zion Baptist Church, in Cincinnati. The thirty-three people who attended from fourteen states voted to start a separate convention. The first annual meeting was held in Philadelphia the following year. Rev. T. M. Chambers was elected the first president; he was succeeded in 1967 by Gardner Taylor.

The new convention adopted as its motto: "Unity, Service, Fellowship, Peace." PNBC was actively involved in the civil rights movement, was supportive of the black power movement, and was one of the earliest groups to publicly oppose the war in Vietnam.[17] In more recent years it has given emphasis to black political development, economic development, education and job training, and strengthening of the black family. Around 1970 several white churches established dual affiliations with PNBC. Conversely, many PNBC churches today maintain dual affiliations with one of the white conventions.[18]

The Progressive National Baptist Convention, Inc., is the smallest of the three National Baptist conventions. In 1989 the denomination claimed 1,000 clergy with 1.2 million members in 1,000 churches, giving it an average congregation of 1,000. Its estimated budget was $1.2 million for that year. The unusually large size of the congregations is attributable to the fact that the convention's membership consists primarily of churches in major metropolitan areas, many of which have memberships of from two to three thousand, while including relatively few rural churches.[19] Unlike the other two conventions, PNBC is divided into regions. Within the four regions, a total of thirty-five state conventions are affiliated with the convention; the number of associations is not known.

The departments of PNBC include Women, Laymen, Youth, Ushers and Nurses, Moderators, and the Congress of Christian Education. Other agencies include the Board of Christian Education and Publication, Home Mission Board, Foreign Mission Bureau, Progressive Pension Plan Board, and Chaplaincy Endorsing Agency. Committees and commissions are Program, Convention Arrangements, Internal Affairs, Cooperative Christianity, Civil Rights, and Community Economic Development.

For several years PNBC met in September at the same time as NBCA and NBC, Inc. In the mid-1970s the convention began convening during the week following the first Sunday in August to accommodate school schedules and encourage the participation of families. The constitution calls for affiliated churches to pay membership fees equivalent to 1 percent of their previous year's operating budget, with the number of official messengers or delegates from each church determined by the size of the church. Each state convention, upon payment of $200, is entitled to two messengers. Fellowships must pay $150 for two messengers, and associations $50 for one messenger. Any member of an affiliated church may attend the convention; however, only representative members so designated by the churches, associations, or state conventions may vote. Individuals may secure life memberships, with voting privileges, upon payment of $500.[20]

In a departure from the other conventions, PNBC presidents since 1967 have been limited to two consecutive one-year terms. Thus, in its twenty-five-year history the convention has already had a dozen different presidents. Most of the other officers including first and second vice presidents, regional vice presidents, general secretary, recording secretary, assistant recording secretaries, treasurer, historian, and editor are subject to the same tenure rule.

The sixty-member Executive Board, which is responsible for oversight of the convention when not in session, consists of the elected officers, the heads of the departments, chairpersons of all boards and commissions, past presidents, the general secretary, and one representative chosen by each state convention. An executive committee, consisting of the president, vice presidents, general secretary, recording secretary, treasurer, and five additional members, may be empowered to act on behalf of the Executive Board. Standing committees of the Executive Board are Personnel, Planning and Evaluation, and Finance and Property.

National headquarters with a permanent staff are located in Washington, D.C. In another departure from the other conventions the general secretary of PNBC is a full-time employee responsible for the day-to-day administration of the convention's program. Consequently, the role of the president aside from presiding at official sessions, is largely that of ambassador to the larger world. PNBC has no publishing house of its own.

Baptist Polity and Ministry

As noted previously, in addition to the national conventions, many Baptists are also organized into state conventions and associations. Like the national conventions, most state conventions convene once a year, with delegates participating from all associations and local churches within the jurisdiction who have elected to affiliate. The North Carolina General Baptist State Convention, for example, involves 1,666 churches, with a membership of nearly 400,000 individuals. The state conventions may be legal corporations in their own right, and thus commonly maintain permanent offices with paid staffs. The business conducted at the annual session includes electing messengers to national conventions, if any, with which it may choose to affiliate, whether formally or informally; raising funds for national mission efforts; and receiving reports from its various auxiliaries. These may include such units as Laymen's League, Sunday School Congress, Training Union, Usher's Convention, Young Adult and Youth departments, and Woman's Convention.

State conventions may support various institutions such as colleges or orphanages, provide training for local ministers and lay officers, assist college and seminary students, contribute to retirement plans, administer community social service projects, and issue publications. The governmental structure of the conventions varies from state to state, but generally consists of a president, Executive Committee, and Administrative Board, which includes the heads of the various auxiliaries. The conventions frequently contain the word

"General" in their title, which distinguishes them from white state conventions.

Associations, consisting of churches within a smaller geographical area are independent entities which may be legally incorporated.[21] Many associations, particularly in the South, date back more than a century, and have a long tradition of service to the community and to its member churches. The more elaborate associations may have a number of subsidiary units, such as a Parent Body (Pastors) or Ministers, Deacons, and Deaconesses Union; Woman's Federation, Department, or Auxiliary; Youth or Young People's Department; Church Training Department or Baptist Training Union; Sunday School Convention or Christian Education Department or Congress; Nurses' Department; and Laymen's League. Many of these auxiliaries have their own constitutions, officers, departments or committees, and budgets, and meet independently of the annual or semiannual meetings of the association itself.

Officers of the association, who may be either ministers or lay persons and are elected annually, include a moderator, vice moderator, recording secretary, treasurer, financial secretary, members of the Executive Board, and presidents of the auxiliaries. All pastors and members of the churches belonging to the association are members of the association; however, each church and auxiliary is allotted a given number of delegates, and only the delegates may vote for officers.

In addition to the auxiliaries, an association may have a number of committees, such as Finance, Budget, Time and Place, Nominations, Resolutions, Recommendations, Admission of New Churches and Members, and others as needed. Of particular import is the Ordaining Council, which in some associations is the standing subunit of the Ministers and Deacons Union responsible for establishing qualifications for ordination, and for examining candidates for the ministry within the association. Other associations convene an ordination committee or council as needed. Local churches, however, are not bound by association guidelines.

As might be expected given the autonomy of the associations, the theological and ideological orientations vary from one to another. In some parts of the country, for example, ministers who ordain women or admit them to association membership are subject to reprisal and retribution. In contrast is this resolution adopted in 1984 by a North Carolina association:

Whereas, ours has been a history of oppression from all institutions including the white religious institutions; therefore:
Be it resolved that the East Cedar Grove Association publicly disassociate itself from the decision of (the) Southern Baptist Convention in their rejection of support for the ordination of women,
Be it further resolved that we inform the General Baptist State Convention that our position is one of ordaining and supporting called and qualified women in their attempts to pastor.

At the same session, this association passed a second resolution which to a substantial degree typifies black Baptist churches—their diversity notwithstanding—and, indeed, is characteristic of the Black Church as a whole: "Whereas, all of our lives are affected by the political process, be it hereby resolved, That the Association urges our churches to impress upon their members the sacred duty of registering to vote and to vote in the upcoming election."[22]

The motive for coming together in these associations and conventions is fellowship and mutual support; no "book of discipline" or any other denominational authority makes participation obligatory. Because Baptists do have a congregational polity, local members often are less concerned or informed about the national organization than is the case in connectional denominations. In many areas the state convention, rather than the national, serves as the principal arena of activity. Involvement is primarily by the ministers, with only marginal lay participation. Characteristically, the preferences of the local pastor determine largely whether there will be any external affiliation or activities and how they will be expressed.

Most ministers participate in an additional Baptist form of organization called ministerial conferences or fellowships. These conferences, made up of the pastors in a given city or metropolitan area, generally meet once a week and serve as forums for teaching, preaching, in-service training, evaluation and endorsement of candidates for political offices, addressing current community and civic issues, and general mutual support.

In the Baptist churches there are but two categories of official ministry, the one being preliminary to the other. Candidates are first licensed by the local church, usually in consultation with an association, upon the satisfactory preaching of a trial sermon. The "licensed preacher," to become a minister, must satisfy the study requirements of the local association, if any; be examined by a group or council of ministers and lay persons convened by the local church; and experience the ritual of ordination which is performed by the laying on of hands by ministers who usually are members of the local association. Great emphasis is placed on being "called" to the ministry, while less significance is attached to formal education and training, although this varies from one locale to another. Those ministers who are responsible for a local church are called pastors, (that is, all pastors are ministers; but not all ministers are pastors). In contrast to other denominations, Baptist pastors are not appointed to a church by a higher ecclesiastical authority, but are elected by majority vote of the local congregation. Unlike the Methodist churches, deacons in the Baptist churches are lay persons. Traditionally, deacons were to be ordained, and that practice continues in most black churches, but they remain lay persons, and are not considered to be in preparation for a higher ministry.

Once ordained and called to pastor a particular church, ministers generally are granted considerable autonomy in conducting the affairs of the church. As one observer put it over sixty years ago, "These separate (black Baptist) churches are a law unto themselves. They vary widely in doctrine and method. In government they may be absolute monarchs ruled by a strong pastor who, in fact, is responsible to nobody. Usually, however, some power is in the hands of the trustees and in many cases they acquire dominating power, making the church a little oligarchy." Still, the power ultimately redounds to the membership, for "always there exists the power of secession to curb the tyranny of the pastor or trustees or as a method of expelling them. In nearly every city or town, one will have pointed out 'the First Baptist' and then one or two splits or withdrawals, making a 'Second Baptist' or a 'Siloam' or 'Shiloh.' "[23]

However much or little this characterization may apply today, Baptists do in fact share a common doctrinal foundation, and local churches manifest much the same pattern of organization, which often is set forth in a church constitution and bylaws. The Board of Trustees is responsible for financial matters and maintenance of church property. There may be a finance committee as well. The duties of the deacons vary from church to church. In some instances deacons and trustees are combined in one board, but in general they are to assist the pastor in maintaining the quality of the spiritual life of the church. They assist with communion, visit the sick, care for the needy, conduct devotional services, and administer the affairs of the church in the absence of a pastor. In some churches these duties are shared with deaconesses. Other church auxiliaries commonly include Missionary societies or circles; Sunday School, and a board or committee of Christian education; Youth Department, Pastor's Aid, several choirs, Benevolence Committee, Usher boards, and various men's and women's clubs. There may also be committees on stewardship, evangelism, nominations, music, flowers, and social concerns, depending on the size of the congregation.

In addition to the heads of these units, church officers may also include a clerk, treasurer, financial secretary, moderator (who may be the pastor or a lay person), historian, and Sunday School superintendent. In some churches, these officers collectively constitute an advisory council or board; alternatively, the Board of Deacons serves this function. However, the church itself, that is, the congregation, is the supreme governing body. In some churches certain responsibilities may be delegated to various boards and committees. And as suggested, considerable power is wielded by the pastor and by the chairman of the Deacon Board. But traditionally, all matters of substance, whether concerning finances, program activities, spiritual affairs, or social concerns are to be considered in regularly convened church meetings of the entire membership.

Baptist Autonomy in Modern Urban Society

Because Baptist "denominations" are so loosely knit and local churches largely autonomous, an examination of the denominations alone is misleading insofar as a survey of Baptist activity is concerned. It is true that the president of the convention can exercise a certain degree of control over individual pastors through the patronage system of prestigious appointments to various boards and committees. But at the same time, individual pastors have the option of not participating in that arena. The pastors of very large churches, in particular, are able to build substantial power bases in their own right and thereby effect significant change in their local communities, as well as nationally. Because Baptist ministers are essentially free of accountability to a denominational hierarchy, they have often been less vulnerable to civil and economic suppression, a factor of significance in their traditional involvement in political activity and community advocacy. For example, no event of recent times highlighted this circumstance more than the civil rights movement. Although Martin Luther King, Jr., was himself in disfavor with the head of the convention to which he belonged, for example, the mass movement he led was populated disproportionately by pastors and members of local Baptist churches.

As we will point out in our chapters on black churches in politics and economics, the principle of autonomy has made black Baptist churches quite successful in adapting to the conditions of modern urban society in the twentieth century. Although this autonomy has been reflected largely among black Baptist preachers in political careers or in carrying out large-scale economic projects, it is by no means limited to them alone. Lay black Baptist women like Nannie Burroughs played important political roles prior to the civil rights movement, while Fannie Lou Hamer, Ella Baker, Diane Nash, Marianne Wright Edelman, and Bernice Reagon Johnson, among many others, were key leaders during the struggles of the 1960s. The whole area of the relationship between religious principles and values among black congregations and the kind of socialization that is produced has been inadequately studied, so no firm conclusions can be drawn at this time. However, field observations and some of the data collected on politics and economics tend to support the view that black Baptist churches have been more successful in adapting to modern urban society.

Status of Women

Ostensibly in defense of the authority and autonomy of local churches, none of the national conventions has taken a formal stand either for or against ordination of women. Neither NBCA nor NBC, Inc., has officially reported any known instances of women pastoring churches affiliated with their conventions. However, the three known cases of black Baptist women pastors have usually occurred when wives replaced their pastor husbands who died unexpectedly.[24] PNBC has a few women clergy; how many of these were ordained in other denominations before coming to PNBC is not known. Attitudes toward ordination of women vary from church to church and association to association. The Baptist Ministers Conference of Baltimore, for example, has admitted a number of women pastors to its membership since 1979. The neighboring conference of Washington, D.C., on the other hand, severed its relationship with the Baltimore Conference in protest of this action. Thus, while the principle of congregational autonomy has helped black Baptist churches successfully adapt to the urban scene, it also has had a negative side in the failure to produce resolute collective action to improve the situation for women clergy. The issue of black women clergy is explored in more detail in chapter 10.

Women may presumably serve in any lay office in the local church; in practice, only a very few are trustees, and fewer still serve as deacons. In NBCA women generally hold no offices, either locally or nationally, in any but the traditional women's organizations. Women officers at the national level of NBC, Inc., are restricted to the usher's auxiliary and the women's convention movement, except that a woman serves as executive director of the Sunday School Publishing Board. In PNBC a woman heads the Congress of Christian Education, and the constitution specifically states that women, clergy or lay, may hold any office of the convention.

The International Dimension of Foreign Missions

As early as 1815 the African Baptist Missionary Society of Richmond was organized by two black ministers, Collin Teague and Lott Carey, with the aid of a white deacon, William Crane.[25] In 1821 Lott Carey became the first black Baptist missionary to Africa. Like the black Methodist Daniel Coker, he was sent to Liberia under the auspices of the American Colonization Society on the second ACS expedition to West Africa. However, Carey also voiced the sentiments of some free African Americans regarding the lack of justice and equality in the United States, and their desire to emigrate. He said, "I am an African and in this country, however meritorious my conduct and respectable my character, I cannot receive the credit due either. I wish to go to a country where I shall be estimated by my merits not by my complexion."[26] Carey also laid the foundation for a theology of missions in Africa for the Baptists. However, much of the black Baptist missionary endeavors were limited to Liberia and the West Coast of Africa during the nineteenth century. In 1889 the Baptist Foreign Mission Convention published a magazine called *The African Missions*.[27] During the twentieth century missionary efforts were extended to Central and South African countries.

The missionary ventures of the African American Baptists in the Caribbean basin were carried out by one of the organizers of the earliest black Baptist churches in the Savannah River region, Rev. George Liele. As early as 1784 Liele had established the First Baptist Church of Kingston, Jamaica.[28] Since then the missionary efforts of the black Baptists have spread extensively throughout the Caribbean island nations.

While the black Baptists founded the earliest churches and still have the largest numbers of black Christians, the Methodist movement among African Americans organized the first black denominations, which were their first national organizations. We turn now to a consideration of the black Methodists and their organizing efforts in the late eighteenth and early nineteenth centuries.

3   The Black Methodists: The Institutionalization of Black Religious Independence

"African" and "Christian" in the names of our denominations denote that we are always concerned for the well-being of economically and politically exploited persons, for gaining or regaining a sense of our own worth, and for determining our own future. We must never invest with institutions that perpetuate racism. Our churches work for the change of all processes which prevent our members who are victims of racism from participating fully in civic and governmental structures.*

Overview

The first separate denominations to be formed by African Americans in the United States were Methodist. The early black Methodist churches, conferences, and denominations were organized by free black people in the North in response to stultifying and demeaning conditions attending membership in the white-controlled Methodist Episcopal churches. This independent church movement of black Christians was the first effective stride toward freedom by African Americans. Unlike most sectarian movements, the initial impetus for black spiritual and ecclesiastical independence was not grounded in religious doctrine or polity, but in the offensiveness of racial segregation in the churches and the alarming inconsistencies between the teachings and the expressions of the faith. It was readily apparent that the white church had become a principal instrument of the political and social policies undergirding slavery and the attendant degradation of the human spirit. Against this the black Christians quietly rebelled, and the Black Church emerged as the symbol and the substance of their rebellion. In 1863 a group of African Ameri-

*John H. Satterwhite, "The Black Methodist Churches," unpublished background paper prepared for "The Black Church in the African American Experience" research project, p. 29.

47

cans in Nashville asked to be admitted to the A.M.E. Church, citing as their reasons the fact that:

> A vast majority of the ministers and members of the Methodist Church, South, have proven themselves disloyal to the Constitution and Government of the United States by identifying themselves with those who are now in open rebellion against it. . . . We believe it to be our duty as Christians and citizens to bear our testimony against such unjustifiable conduct, as also to testify to our own loyalty to the country which gave us birth and the constitutional government which controls us as well by deeds as by words.[1]

During the Civil War black defections from white churches were massive as the Union armies opened up new territories for the crusading "African" evangelists from the North. The challenge to join an "African Church" was interpreted as a challenge to assume the full responsibility of freedom, both physical and spiritual, and African affiliation became a concrete symbol of the will and capacity to be independent. In 1860 the Methodist Episcopal Church, South, had a black membership of around 207,766. By 1866 that membership was less than 78,742 souls.[2] Yet, despite these implications, the severance from the white Methodist Church was not universal, North or South. In consequence of that historic contradiction, the contemporary United Methodist Church has the largest black constituency of any mainline denomination, and one with a history so distinctive as to raise the popular allegation of it being "a church-within-a-church." We shall have an opportunity to look more closely at the black United Methodists after these main denominations of independent black Methodists have been considered.

Black Methodism ordinarily refers to the African Methodist Episcopal Church (A.M.E.), the African Methodist Episcopal Zion Church (A.M.E.Z.), and the Christian Methodist Episcopal Church (C.M.E.). Five smaller black Methodist communions merit mention. One of these, the Union American Methodist Episcopal Church (U.A.M.E.), is actually the oldest of all the black Methodist denominations. Originally called the Union Church of Africans, it was founded by Peter Spencer in Wilmington, Delaware, in 1813.[3] Today it has approximately 28,000 members. Other groups are the product of schisms within the A.M.E. or A.M.E.Z. churches. These include the Reformed Methodist Union Episcopal Church (1885), with some 16,000 members; the Reformed Zion Union Apostolic Church (1881), also claiming 16,000 members; and the Independent African

Methodist Episcopal Church (1907), with perhaps a thousand members. There is also the African Union First Colored Methodist Protestant Church (known as A.U.M.P.), with approximately 8,000 members. This church was organized in 1866 in a merger of the African Union Church, which had split from the original Union Church of Africans, and the First Colored Methodist Protestant Church.[4]

Emergence of the Black Methodists

The original Methodist movement, so named for its distinctive "methods" of organizations and its spiritual disciplines, began as a "Holy Club" of students at Christ Church College in Oxford University in the mid-1720s. Led by Charles Wesley, who was later joined by his brother, John, this small group of Anglicans, some of whom were ordained priests, developed an evangelical style of worship and service which focused upon ministering to the social needs of the impoverished classes of London. So great was the response to their efforts that Wesley was compelled to organize new converts into "classes" and "societies" under "class leaders" and "lay preachers" serviced by an "itinerant ministry," all of which became institutionalized in the emergent Methodist Church. Although Wesley had no intentions of founding a separate denomination at the outset, the uniqueness of his ministry and organization, conjoined with rejection by the Anglican Church, eventuated in the establishment of an historically distinctive Protestant movement.

The Wesleyan movement crossed the Atlantic as early as the mid-1730s. Under the leadership of Thomas Coke, Francis Asbury, and George Whitefield, it was enthusiastically received among the lower classes in the colonies who welcomed the emphasis on religious experience, that is, a "warm heart," in contrast to the cold intellectualism of the austere Puritan churches, and the neo-catholicism of the Episcopalians. By 1773, when the first annual conference (a Methodist innovation) was held, itinerant preachers had spread the evangelical vision of Christianity along the eastern seaboard and westward to the Appalachians. At the General Conference held in 1784, known historically as the Christmas Conference, the various societies scattered among the newly independent colonies were formally organized into the Methodist Episcopal Church. In little more than a decade the church grew in membership from 18,000 in 1785 to nearly 57,000 by 1796.

Large numbers of slaves were among those who responded to the Methodist preachers, exhorting the revivals and camp meetings of the First Great Awakening in the 1740s. John Wesley recorded in his *Journal* that he baptized his first two black converts, one of whom was a woman, on November 29, 1758. Historical records indicate that African Americans were among the charter members of the very first Methodist society which was organized in Frederick County, Maryland, in 1764. Listed on the roll of the first class was a woman called Aunt Annie, the slave of a family named Sweitzer.[5] Similarly, among the 1776 charter members of the John Street Society in New York City was a black servant named Betty.[6] In 1789, seventy of the 360 members of John Street Church were African Americans.[7] At St. George's Church in Philadelphia the membership included 270 white members and seventeen African Americans. In 1786 the Methodist Episcopal Church as a whole acknowledged 1,890 African American members, representing approximately 10 percent of its total membership.[8]

The opposition of Methodists to slavery was expressed officially in the original *General Rules* set forth by Wesley in 1743 and in the rules adopted at the 1784 Christmas Conference. This antislavery sentiment was reaffirmed repeatedly on many intervening occasions and it enhanced significantly Methodism's attractiveness to African Americans, both slaves and free. Although after 1785 the church retreated from its original opposition to slavery, the number of black members continued to increase in the lingering aura of Methodist benignity, and as the African Americans experienced the evangelical fervor of the Second Great Awakening at the turn of the century. So powerful was the attraction of Methodism to the slaves of the period that even in rebellion against the slave system in 1800 Gabriel Prosser was constrained to admonish his followers to "spare the Methodists and the Quakers." This poignant footnote to history is all the more remarkable in that it occurred in Virginia more than a decade after Richard Allen had felt compelled to withdraw from fellowship with the white Methodists of Philadelphia.

The African Methodist Episcopal Church

The A.M.E. Church dates from 1787 when Richard Allen, Absalom Jones, and other black worshipers withdrew from St. George's Methodist Episcopal Church in Philadelphia after being pulled from their knees during worship in a gallery they did not know was closed to black Christians. In protest, "All went out of the church in a body," according to Allen, "and they were no more plagued with [us] in that church."[9]

Richard Allen was a former slave who had joined a Methodist society in Delaware around 1780, and since 1783, he had been preaching as a licensed exhorter in New Jersey and Pennsylvania. Upon arriving in Philadelphia in 1786 he "established prayer meetings" and "raised a society . . . for forty-two members."[10] That same year he proposed a separate place of worship for blacks, but desisted in the face of opposition from white Methodist officials. In April 1787, however, a mutual aid society called the Free African Society[11] was organized by Allen and Absalom Jones for benevolent purposes and "without regard to religious tenets."[12]

Whether the Free African Society was organized prior to the departure of blacks from St. George's is a matter of some conjecture, but November 1787 is commonly believed to have been the approximate date of the separation, placing it seven months after the incorporation of the society.[13] The Free African Society assumed religious as well as secular functions, meeting initially in a rented storeroom. From 1788 to 1791 the society met at the Friends Free African School House, and there they began holding regular worship services in 1790. In the interim Allen and Jones began soliciting subscriptions to build a meeting house but with the intention of remaining under the jurisdiction of the Methodist Church. However, upon completing this "African Church," as Allen termed it, he was rebuffed first by the Methodist Church which refused to supply a minister, and then by the members of the society, the majority of whom voted to affiliate with the Church of England. Allen then proceeded to move an old blacksmith shop onto a lot he owned, where the structure was renovated to serve as a place of worship.

On July 17, 1794, the original building the Free African Society had erected was dedicated as St. Thomas' African Episcopal Church and Absalom Jones, after being ordained the first black Protestant Episcopal priest, became the pastor. Richard Allen had first been asked to pastor St. Thomas's, but insisting that he could "not be anything else but a Methodist" he had declined that honor. He was confident, he explained, that "no religious sect or denomination would suit the capacity of the colored people as well as the Methodist." Later, Allen succeeded in having Methodist Bishop Francis Asbury dedicate the building he had purchased, and Bethel Church of Philadelphia, as it was named, became the mother church of what was to be a new denomination, the African Methodist Episcopal Church.

The Free African Society in Philadelphia which spawned Episcopal and Bethel A.M.E. churches was replicated by several other such organizations in the surrounding areas of Pennsylvania, Maryland, Delaware, and New Jersey. These, too, evolved into black Methodist churches. After corresponding with one another for several years, sharing their frustrations and conflicts with white Methodists over ownership of property and assignment of ministers, representatives of five such congregations came together at Bethel Church in 1816 to officially organize the African Methodist Episcopal Church. Richard Allen, who had been ordained a deacon by Bishop Asbury in 1799 was now ordained an elder. At the same meeting he was elected bishop of the fledgling denomination after Daniel Coker, who was first elected, declined the office.

It should be noted that two principal interests of the Free African Societies were racial solidarity and abolitionist activity, a tradition that persisted with the institutionalization of a formal church. Bethel Church, among others, served as a station of the Underground Railroad. Many of the four thousand members of the first A.M.E. church in Charleston, South Carolina, were deeply involved in the 1822 slave insurrection led by Denmark Vesey. The church was burned to the ground by the outraged whites who had never felt comfortable with its presence, but Rev. Morris Brown who pastored the church managed to escape with his life by secreting himself aboard a ship bound for Philadelphia.[14] In 1830 Richard Allen organized the first of several "Negro Conventions" for the purpose of bringing the common efforts of the Black Church leadership and other potential sources to focus on the galling issues of slavery.[15]

From the beginning, the A.M.E. Church was concerned with providing social service relief to those in need. Today the church maintains seven housing projects in as many cities across America to help house the needy in settings conducive to Christian social development. An equally strong interest of the emergent A.M.E. Church was education. The church leaders were not educated people, but they had a clear perception of what education would mean to the interests of the church and to the advancement of the African people then held in abject slavery. Bishop Daniel Payne, who had been a schoolmaster in Baltimore, set the educational goals for the fledgling institution by insisting upon a trained ministry, and by encouraging A.M.E. pastors to organize schools in their communities as an aspect of their ministry.

An excerpt from the Quadrennial Address of the Bishop of the A.M.E. Church to the General Conference of 1864 underscores the high premium the church placed on education: "We assure you, dear brothers, this is no time to encourage ignorance and mental sloth; to enter the ranks of the ministry, for the education and elevation of millions now issuing out of the house of bondage, require men, not only talented, but well educated; not only well educated, but thoroughly sanctified unto God."[16]

Payne himself was instrumental in founding Wilberforce University in 1856. Wilberforce was the first institution of higher learning founded by African Americans in the United States. Bishop Payne also developed a course of studies required of all A.M.E. preachers as an acceptable alternative to the seminary education which he hoped would become the norm for A.M.E. ordinations. Altogether the A.M.E. Church established more than a score of academic institutions. Some eventually merged with each other to avoid duplication of effort; some have been closed. Today, the best-known A.M.E. colleges include Wilberforce (Wilberforce, Ohio, 1856); Morris Brown (Atlanta, Georgia, 1881); Allen (Columbia, South Carolina, 1870); Paul Quinn (Waco, Texas, 1881); Shorter Junior College (North Little Rock, Arkansas, 1886); and Edward Waters (Jacksonville, Florida, 1901). The A.M.E. Review founded in 1881 is the oldest journal in the world owned and published by black people.

Missions were another early emphasis of the A.M.E. Church as is evident by its rapid growth. Within two years of its founding the denomination's membership increased from 1,000 to nearly 7,000. Four years later in 1822 the original five charges (or church units) had grown to forty-three, encompassing a territory from Washington, D.C., in the South, to Pittsburgh in the West, and New York City in the North. Much of this early growth was attributable to the efforts of William Paul Quinn and Morris Brown whose missionary zeal was legendary, and whose fame lives on to this day in two A.M.E. colleges which bear their names. Even before slavery was abolished the A.M.E. Church sent hundreds of missionaries into the South on the heels of the Union armies. Thousands of new members from what had been the "invisible institution" of slave religion, as well as from the large black constituency of the Methodist Episcopal Church, South, flocked into the new African Church where they found an unaccustomed dignity and sense of self-worth. From a modest 20,000 members at the beginning of the Civil War, the church had grown to nearly 400,000 by 1884, and to over 450,000 by 1896. The path of growth and expansion returned to the North and West as African Americans emigrated from the South in the early decades of the twentieth century. Missionary efforts at home were augmented by a strong desire to plant the flag of African Methodism wherever that flag would fly. In consequence, the A.M.E. Church has been the most effective of all the black denominations in its overseas missionary efforts, claiming 1 million members and over 22,000 churches in Africa and the Caribbean.[17]

The African Methodist Episcopal Church is the largest of the black Methodist communions, with a 1989 membership in the United States of 2.2 million. Its congregations average about 285 members. The clergy-to-local church ratio (5,000 and 6,000, respectively) suggests about one in five ministers serves more than one church. The annual budget of the denomination is approximately $6.8 million.[18]

The A.M.E. Church functions under the motto, "God Our Father, Christ Our Redeemer, Man Our Brother." The doctrine and polity of the church, set forth in *The Book of Discipline*, were modeled after the original Methodist Episcopal Church, as was the case with each of the major black Methodist bodies. Their original dispute was not with matters of belief or structure, but with the failure of the white church to honor its own commitments to love and brotherhood and respect for all of God's children. Some relatively minor differences in organization have since developed, the most significant being the greater power vested in the bishops of the black churches, but the principal difference remains a matter of ethnic identity and the determination of the black Methodists to stand before God and man as fully committed and fully responsible Christians without any conditions imposed upon them by their fellow believers.

The "Mission and Purpose of the Church," presented in the *Discipline* as a preface to the Wesleyan "Articles of Religion," declares that:

> Each local church of the African Methodist Episcopal Church shall be engaged in carrying out the spirit of the original Free

African Society out of which the A.M.E. Church evolved, that is, to seek out and save the lost and serve the needy through a continuing program of: (1) preaching the gospel, (2) feeding the hungry, (3) clothing the naked, (4) housing the homeless, (5) cheering the fallen, (6) providing jobs for the jobless, (7) administering to the needs of those in prisons, hospitals, nursing homes, asylums and mental institutions, senior citizens' homes, caring for the sick, the shut-in, the mentally and socially disturbed, and (8) encouraging thrift and economic advancement.

To accommodate these objectives, a local church typically has a range of auxiliaries that includes the Board of Stewards (responsible for finances), Board of Trustees (responsible for property), one or more boards of Stewardesses (who prepare for the rituals of Holy Communion and baptism), and Deaconesses (who attend to the social welfare of church members and community residents). There are also class leaders, Usher boards, Missionary societies, one or more choirs, a Sunday School, Young People's Department, and other lay organizations, and various supportive clubs. Local churches may also have commissions on Membership and Evangelism, Christian Education, Missions and Welfare, Stewardship and Finance, Public Relations, and Christian Social Relations. The administrative body of the local church is the official board, comprised of the ministers and principal officers (trustees, and deaconesses) of the church.

The supreme legislative body of the A.M.E. Church at the national level is the General Conference, which meets once every four years. Participants include the bishops, general officers, heads of colleges and seminaries, armed forces' chaplains, and ministerial and lay delegates from all the annual conferences. The General Conference conducts its business through some 30 committees and is responsible for electing general officers (for example, editors, publishers, secretaries of departments, treasurer, historiographer), establishing the budget, receiving reports from the various agencies, determining organizational structure and regulations, assessing the work of the bishops, and electing new bishops.

Below the General Conference are four other major denominational divisions. The Council of Bishops constitutes the executive branch of the church, assuming oversight of superintendence of the entire church between quadrennial sessions of the General Conference. A judicial council functions as an appellate court to hear appeals from any decision affecting any member or minister within the church. The Board of Trustees is responsible for church property. The budget and programs of the church are administered by the General Board whose eleven vice presidents each chair one of the standing commissions: Finance and Statistics, Pensions, Publications, Minimum Salary, Church Extension and Evangelism, Missions, Higher Education, Research and Development, Christian Education, Social Action, and the Lay Commission. Each commission in turn is responsible for one or more departments that actually implement the programs.

The A.M.E. Church has no centralized national headquarters, and no one chief administrative officer. It does have a general secretary whose responsibilities do not require relocation on election. The publishing house is located in Nashville. The church supports five colleges, one junior college, two Job Corps centers and two seminaries—Payne Theological Seminary at Wilberforce, and Turner Theological Seminary which is affiliated with the Interdenominational Theological Center in Atlanta, Georgia.

The African Methodist Episcopal Zion Church

Like the A.M.E. Church, the A.M.E. Zion Church has its origins in the late eighteenth century when a delegation of black members broke from the white-controlled John Street Methodist Episcopal Church in New York City. As previously indicated, the English-based Methodist societies had taken an early stance against slavery and welcomed African Americans into their membership. By 1793, however, the proportion of black members had risen to over 40 percent, and the resulting tension and discriminatory treatment in conjunction with the refusal to fully ordain black preachers and allow them to join the conference as itinerants sparked the move toward separation.[19]

In 1796, at the urging of Peter Williams, a former slave employed at John Street Church, some members of one of the black classes of that church organized an African chapel in a cabinetmaker's shop owned by another of the members, William Miller.[20] Services were conducted there by black local preachers of the John Street Church until the building of a new house of worship was completed in September 1800. In 1801 the chapel was incorporated as the "African Methodist Episcopal Church [called Zion] of the City of New York," with Peter Williams and Francis Jacobs as signatories.[21] Provisions at that time required that church property be owned by the Board of Trustees and that only trustees of African descent could act for the corporation. Further, only Africans or their descendants could be members and only male members could vote on church matters. Pastoral supervision, however, continued to be provided by elders appointed by the New York Methodist Episcopal Conference, and usually through John Street Church.

Not until 1816 did the conference establish a separate "circuit charge" consisting of Zion Church and Asbury African Methodist Episcopal Church in New York City.[22] In 1820 William Stillwell, the white pastor appointed to Zion Church by the Methodist Episcopal Conference withdrew from the conference along with several hundred other ministers over the issue of control of church property. Subsequently, the two black churches also left the New York Conference after deciding at a meeting held August 11, 1820, to start their own separate African Conference, still under the jurisdiction of the Methodist Episcopal Church. However, this African Conference was ultimately developed into a separate denomination largely through the continued recalcitrance of the parent church over racial issues.

In October 1820 the two black churches adopted their own *Discipline*, "with a little alteration from that of our Mother-Church," as the Founder's Address puts it.[23] Though they adopted the name African Methodist Episcopal, the new entity declined to come under the supervision of Bishop Richard Allen. Allen had incurred the Zionist's resentment for using a former member of Zion Church to do mission work in New York City for Allen's own denomination. This action was regarded by the New York African Methodists as an encroachment on their territorial prerogatives. In consequence, they convened their first annual conference on June 21, 1821, in New York City, with representatives from four other congregations in Pennsylvania, Connecticut, and New York, with the determination to establish a distinctive identity from the A.M.E.S or "Allenites" based in Philadelphia.

This 1820 conference is commonly accepted as the official organizing meeting of what was to become the African Methodist Episcopal Zion denomination, although a total break with the Methodist Episcopal Church did not occur until after the 1824 General Conference of the M.E. Church. In 1822 James Varick, then pastor of Zion Church, was elected the first bishop or superintendent. Varick, who is traditionally regarded as the founder of the denomination, served in this capacity until the 1828 annual meeting of the affiliated churches, a meeting which is generally considered to have been the first General Conference of the A.M.E. Zion Church. In 1848 the word Zion was officially added to African Methodist Episcopal to make clear the distinction of this denomination from the A.M.E. Church originating in Philadelphia.

Because of internal dissension and of competition from the Allenites, the A.M.E. Zion Church experienced only modest growth prior to the Civil War. Starting with 1,400 members and 22 preachers in 1821, the church in 1860 numbered 4,600 with 105 preachers. What growth did occur generally is attributed to the talents of Christopher Rush, who succeeded Varick as the general superintendent (bishop) in 1828. Expansion was limited in these years to the Northeast but gained momentum in the South following Emancipation. By 1884 the church had grown to 300,000, and in 1896 membership stood at 350,000. In the second half of the nineteenth century foreign mission programs were established in South America, Africa, and the West Indies. The twentieth century brought a third major period of expansion with the growth of cities and the migration of African Americans to the North and West following the two world wars.

Currently, the African Methodist Episcopal Zion Church is the second largest of the black Methodist denominations, numbering in 1989 1.2 million members in the United States and an additional 100,000 in Africa and the Caribbean. It has fewer churches than the A.M.E.s, but proportionately larger congregations, which average four hundred members. The church claims three thousand clergy who serve 2,900 churches, two hundred of which are overseas. The budget of the denomination in 1989 was $4 million.[24]

Long known as "The Freedom Church," A.M.E. Zion claims such abolitionist luminaries as Sojourner Truth, Harriet Tubman, Rev. Jermain Louguen, Catherine Harris, Rev. Thomas James, and Frederick Douglass who was licensed as a local A.M.E. Zion preacher. Like the A.M.E.s, many members, pastors, and church officials were abolitionists and were intensely involved with the Underground Railroad. That commitment to social justice has persisted to the present time. The A.M.E. Zion Church was the first among all of the Methodist denominations, including the Methodist Episcopal Church, to extend the vote and clerical ordination to women. In all of the black Methodist denominations, whites have long been admitted to membership and may hold any office in the church. Their numbers, however, have remained small.

The General Conference, which convenes every four years, is the supreme lawmaking body of the A.M.E. Zion denomination. Made up of ministerial and lay delegates elected from the annual conferences, the General Conference establishes the rules and regulations of the church; defines Episcopal Districts; elects, assigns, and receives reports from the bishops; and elects and receives reports from the general officers. The General Conference, which is presided over by one of the bishops, also acts as a court of appeals.

The administrative arm of the church is the Connectional Council, which meets once a year and is composed of the bishops, general officers, and administrative board members. It is responsible for making budget recommendations and assuring effective operation of the various connectional boards (except for the Board of Bishops). These boards, in turn, have oversight of corresponding national departments, which include Publication, Christian Education, Church Extension, Home Missions, Overseas Missions, Woman's Home and Overseas Missionary Society, Bureau of Evangelism, Historical Society, Public Relations and Social Service Department, and Council of Laity. There is also a Board of Connectional Trustees (responsible for church property), Connectional Budget, Relief Department, and Brotherhood Pension and Benefit Plan.

The Board of Bishops has responsibility for supervision of the church in between the quadrennial sessions of the General Conference. This board meets twice a year, once at the same time as the Connectional Council, and a second time to review the work of each bishop and the status of conditions in respective jurisdictions.

Members are guided by the *Doctrines and Disciplines,* but like other denominations actual practice may depend upon official interpretation of what the *Discipline* intends, and the authority of the bishops is such that they enjoy substantial interpretive discretion. Bishops in all the black Methodist denominations exercise considerably more power than in the United Methodist Church. This circumstance is probably more pronounced in the A.M.E. Zion Church by virtue of the fact that, unlike the A.M.E. and C.M.E. churches, there is no judicial council or court independent of the bishops to which decisions may be appealed. The traditions of the particular local church may also override or supplement aspects of the *Discipline.* Many churches, for example, do not conduct "Love Feasts" as the *Discipline* requires, and while most recognize the desirability of classes and class leaders, the extent to which these historically sanctioned units actually function fluctuates from congregation to congregation.

But while there is diversity among local churches, there is also a high degree of consistency. The majority of churches observe most of the organizational units required or recommended by the *Discipline*, including a Board of Stewards, Board of Trustees, Deaconesses, Christian Education Board, Sunday School, Varick Christian Endeavor societies, Committee on Music, one or more choirs, Home Mission Society, Committee on Overseas Mission, Woman's Home and Overseas Missionary Society (including Parent Body, Young Adult, Young Woman's, and Juvenile or Buds of Promise Missionary societies), Bureau of Evangelism, Committee on Church Extension, Board of Lay Activities, and Lay Council. Local churches may organize additional auxiliaries to accommodate various interests and age groups.

The church supports two junior colleges, and Livingstone College and Hood Theological Seminary, both in Salisbury, North Carolina. The denomination has no central headquarters and no chief administrative officer. The offices of the general secretary and the A.M.E. Zion Publishing House are located in Charlotte, North Carolina.

The Christian Methodist Episcopal Church

The C.M.E. Church is distinguished by the historical circumstances of its origins. Born in the post-slavery South the church began with a different consciousness than its northern predecessors as is evidenced in the name by which it chose to be known. Originally called the Colored Methodist Episcopal Church in America, the name was changed in 1954 to Christian Methodist Episcopal Church. While the A.M.E. Church in 1876 rejected a proposal to change its name from African to American, the C.M.E.s, voting in an era when an ideology of integration was beginning to emerge, opted to eliminate the racial designation to avoid any exclusionary suggestion. "Christian" was selected both to retain the traditional initials and to affirm the understanding of the church as being universal.

Unlike the African Americans of the A.M.E. and A.M.E. Zion churches in the North, which generally had affiliated with the northern Methodist Episcopal Church, those black Christians destined to become the C.M.E. Church were affiliated with the Methodist Episcopal Church, South, that branch of white Methodism that came into being with the split in Methodism in 1844 over the issue of slavery. Their departure from the M.E. Church, South, was not only a protest of the segregated and demeaning treatment to which northern and southern blacks alike were subjected, but an explicit declaration of self-determination by a new citizenry, almost all of whom were without experience beyond the conditions of slavery. The separation was accomplished amicably, a circumstance no doubt attributable to vested interests on both sides as much as to the reported spirit of altruism infusing the transition.

The religious taboos and practices of white Christians in the South were substantially unchanged by the outcome of the Civil War. African Americans were still considered less than human, whether in or out of the church. Some whites saw the breakup of slavery as sufficient reason to be done with the inconvenience of a black constituency. While the more general sentiment was for a retention of the black membership, there was no room for the expectation that they would be accorded anything other than the conventional status of subservience and segregation in all significant aspects of church life. The Methodist Episcopal Church, South, was clearly a case in point, for it was declared to be "unprepared to revise radically its conception of the proper place of blacks in the Connection. Though the Negro was invited to remain in the church, it was expected he would continue in an inferior and subordinate relation."[25]

Following Emancipation, intensive mission work initiated in the South by the A.M.E., A.M.E. Zion, and northern M.E. churches reduced the black membership of the M.E. Church, South, to 40,000 by 1870. The large numbers of blacks who left the M.E. Church, South, for these other Methodist denominations was testimony not to any doctrinal disputes as such, but to the restrictiveness of the southern church and to the desire on the part of blacks to exercise their own cultural forms of religious expression and to participate fully in all dimensions of church life, including leadership and decisionmaking. However, all of those wishing to leave did not view the northern churches as attractive options. This was partly because of the more radical politics of the "Republican" northerners and the hostility these engendered among white southerners, thus placing local black/white relations in jeopardy. It was also partly because the intense rivalry between the A.M.E.s and the A.M.E.Z.s was at times bewildering, and the practice of the northern churches of summarily taking over church properties along with their congregations were often considered offensive and illegal. In 1866 the General Conference of the M.E. Church, South—in response to the twin pressures of blacks who wanted autonomy and whites who wanted to dispense with the black membership—made arrangements for the eventual withdrawal of its black constituents at their petition. The strategy appeared to be to formulate an arrangement that would create a separate church for the former slaves which would retain unofficial ties with the parent church rather than become a part of the existing African movement.

Between 1867 and 1870 a concerted effort was made to ordain black ministers to assume responsibility for pastoring black congregations. Eight black annual conferences were organized in Tennessee, Kentucky, Georgia, Mississippi, South Carolina, Alabama, Arkansas, and Texas. The first General Conference was held at Liberty Church, the mother church of the denomination in Jackson, Tennessee, in December 1870. A *Discipline* modeled on that of the M.E. Church, South, was adopted at this founding meeting. Two bishops were elected—William H. Miles, who had been ordained a deacon in 1859 and had been briefly affiliated with the A.M.E. Zion Church, and Richard H. Vanderhorst, who had been a member of the A.M.E. Church. Both men were former slaves, as indeed were all of the first seven bishops of the denomination.

The separation from the M.E. Church, South, agreeable as it may have been to both parties, was not accomplished without certain restrictions. As a condition of transferring ownership of church property to the new denomination, political activity of any sort in the recipient churches was strictly prohibited. Criticisms by northern blacks notwithstanding, the condition was accepted by many southern blacks who had but recently escaped the bonds of slavery and were maneuvering their way to independence and self-sufficiency. A strategy of discretion became even more functional as Ku Klux Klan terrorism intensified and the M.E. Church, South, itself was increasingly fashioned into a harshly discriminatory institution during the Reconstruction period. Because the C.M.E. Church began under such strictures and because it lacked the tradition of the African societies and abolitionist involvement, its early development bore the stigma of ultraconservatism and political inconsequence. But despite the delicate circumstances of its origins and the peculiar history of its development the contemporary C.M.E. Church shares with other black Methodist bodies a firm commitment to the quest for social justice. The positions of the church on many current social issues are set forth in "The Social Creed" of the C.M.E. Church, the *Discipline*, and the denomination's "Episcopal Greetings" define the mandate of the church as "the salvation of sinners and the liberation of the oppressed from all forms of human bondage."

The new church defined itself as national in scope and aspiration, its southern origins and its association with the M.E. Church, South, notwithstanding. As early as 1866 black leadership in the M.E. Church, South, had rejected overtures from the A.M.E.s and had communicated that rejection to the white bishops who "readily agreed with them." Isaac Lane who was to become a bishop in the new church recalled that ". . . we made it known that we preferred a separate organization of our own, regularly established and organized after our own ideas and notions. The Bishops and the General Conference of the Southern Church readily agreed with us."[26]

The separate organization desired by the blacks came into being with the blessings of the southern Methodists when on December 15, 1870, at a general conference called for that purpose the Colored Methodist Episcopal Church in America was formally organized. Senior bishop Robert Paine of the M.E. Church, South, presided and he was assisted by three ministers from that church. This first resolution established the name of the church and declared its membership to be a part of the original Methodist Episcopal Church. A secondary resolution declared: "We most sincerely pray, earnestly desire, and confidently believe that there will ever be the kindliest feelings cherished toward the Methodist Episcopal Church, South, and that we may ever receive their warmest sympathy and support." While a third requested the M.E. bishop and his aides to "organize our General Conferences on the basis of the Discipline of the Methodist Episcopal Church South, in its entire doctrine, discipline and economy."

On the sixth day of the conference William H. Miles and Richard H. Vanderhorst were elected bishops and duly consecrated by Bishop Paine in the First Methodist Church in Jackson, Tennessee.[27]

Although it grew more slowly than the African churches, by 1890 the C.M.E. Church had a membership exceeding 103,000, 75 percent of whom were to be found in Alabama, Georgia, Mississippi, and Tennessee.[28] By 1945 it had expanded to eighteen states in the North and West, a process intensified by the emigration of blacks out of the South during the two world wars and the Depression era. The Christian Methodist Episcopal Church remains the smallest of the three black Methodist denominations, having a national constituency with a membership in 1989 of 900,000 in the United States, and

75,000 overseas. Like the A.M.E. Church, the C.M.E.s have more churches (3,000) than clergy (2,400). They also have church congregations of similar size, averaging 285 members. Their 1989 national budget was $3 million.[29]

Both the local and national organization of the C.M.E. Church follow closely the established model of Methodism. A typical local church has boards of Trustees, Stewards, Stewardesses, and Ushers; several choirs; Christian Education Department, Sunday School, Membership and Evangelism Committee, and Christian Youth Fellowship; Missionary Society (with subunits having names such as Adult Christian Council, Fragment Gatherers, and Helping Hand) and Laymen Council. Many also have a Department of Social Concern, Pastor's Aid Society, and various other clubs and boards. They may have class leaders, although classes commonly do not meet. The administrative body of the local church is the official board, consisting of the preacher in charge (pastor), local preachers, and church officers.

The General Conference, which meets every four years, is the national legislative body of the church. Its delegates, who by law must be half lay members and half ministers, consist of representatives from all the annual conferences. It is presided over by the bishops on a rotating basis. The College of Bishops, then, meets twice a year to carry out the actions of the General Conference and gives oversight to the church as a whole.

The Judicial Council interprets the laws, *Discipline*, and constitution of the church, acting as a court of appeals. It consists of nine members (four ministers and five laypersons) who are nominated by the College of Bishops and elected by the General Conference. The council convenes once a year.

The program of the national church is implemented by general departments, these being Finance, Publication Services, Personnel Services, Missions, Christian Education, Evangelism, Social Concerns, Legal Affairs, Connectional Laymen's Council, and Women's Missionary Council. Each departmental board is composed of a bishop designated by the College of Bishops to function as the chairman, and one representative from each of the episcopal districts. The departments are administered by general secretaries, who are general officers of the church elected by the General Conference. The members of the departmental boards, along with other representatives from each episcopal district who are apportioned on the basis of population, comprise the General Connectional Board. This board, which meets once a year to coordinate and supervise the departments and generally carry on the work of the church, has a number of committees and commissions, each chaired by a bishop whose areas of responsibility include such matters as Budget, Long-Range Planning, Hymnal and Ritual, Ecumenical Affairs, Archives, Chaplains, and Legislative Review.

The church supports five colleges (Lane, Paine, Texas, Miles, and Mississippi Industrial). It also maintains Phillips School of Theology, a seminary which is affiliated with the Interdenominational Theological Center in Atlanta. The national headquarters of the denomination was established in Memphis in 1970. Memphis is also the location of the c.m.e. Publishing House and the William H. Miles Bookstore. The c.m.e.s do not have a general secretary for the whole church; instead, each national department has its own general secretary.

Black United Methodists

In 1790 the 12,000 black members of the Methodist Episcopal Church represented about one-fifth of its total membership. By 1816 the m.e. Church had some 42,300 black members. Of these 1,066 withdrew to become part of the a.m.e. Church led by Richard Allen. Four years later, in 1820, 1,406 withdrew to join the a.m.e. Zion Church. By 1840 the black membership of the m.e. Church exceeded 87,000, but in 1844 the church split over the issues of slavery into northern and southern factions. The black constituency of the resultant Methodist Episcopal Church, South, withdrew following the Civil War into the separate Christian Methodist Episcopal Church, and because of the competition from the African Methodists, black membership in the northern wing of the Methodist Episcopal Church languished at barely more than 26,000. With the termination of the Civil War, however, the northern m.e. Church instituted an aggressive mission program in the South. By 1896 black Methodists numbered nearly 250,000, compared with the 130,000 c.m.e.s, 350,000 a.m.e.z.s, and 450,000 a.m.e.s.

From the beginning, part of the attraction of the Methodist Church (as well as the Baptist tradition) was the opportunity to preach. Blacks early established reputations as preachers, or "exhorters," and missionaries. Among the better known were "Black Harry" Hosier, who traveled with Bishop Francis Asbury; Henry Evans, a free-born African American of Virginia credited with establishing Methodism among both the black and white residents in Fayetteville, North Carolina; and John Stewart, who served in Ohio among the Wyandotte Indians and gave birth to the home missions' enterprise in the Methodist Church. Inspired and nurtured by these early black leaders, small black congregations began to spring up wherever they were allowed. And where they were not, the slaves congregated in secret as part of the "invisible institution."

In 1852 the northern M.E. Church elected Francis Burns as its first black bishop. Burns in turn was succeeded in 1866 by John W. Roberts. Both were elected as missionary bishops to serve in Africa, and so had no supervisory authority over whites. Indeed, not until 1864 were black preachers even permitted to be fully ordained as traveling elders. That same year the first two separate black conferences, the Delaware and the Washington, were organized, representing the culmination of forty years of petitioning on the part of black members. In 1868 there were eight black conferences, and their status was changed from mission conferences to annual conferences, thereby according them elected representation in the General Conference of the church. These black annual conferences existed as segregated units in the Methodist Church for more than a century, the last one—the South Carolina Conference—merging with the white annual conference in 1972. Since the election of Francis Burns there have been thirty-one black bishops in the United Methodist Church, including four missionary bishops. Eleven black bishops were active in 1987. Five others were retired.

During the same period in which the first black conferences were organized, the northern M.E. Church organized dozens of elementary and normal schools for southern blacks through its Freedmen's Aid Society. Ultimately twelve colleges were founded, including Bennett College, Bethune-Cookman College, Clark University, Dillard University, Meharry Medical School, and Gammon Theological Seminary which is now associated with the Interdenominational Theological Center in Atlanta.

In 1939, after nearly a century of division and years of negotiation, a plan for union was adopted which brought together the major white Methodist bodies—the Methodist Episcopal Church, the Methodist Episcopal Church, South, and the Methodist Protestant Church. The price of union, however, was the creation of a separate black unit within the new church. In addition to the five geographical regions or jurisdictions into which the Methodist Church was organized, a sixth entity called the Central Jurisdiction was created which consisted of all the black conferences and missions in the United States and encompassed 315,000 black Methodists. While this jurisdiction participated equally with the others at the national level of the church, at every other level African Americans were officially segregated. They could elect their own bishops, but black bishops could function only as bishops of black Methodists.

The effect of this action was to institutionalize a black Methodist church, literally a church within a church. Not until 1966 when a merger with the Evangelical United Brethren Church was effected was the Central Jurisdiction officially abolished. True integration in the church, however, as in society at large, failed to follow local desegregation. In practice if not in policy, black Methodists remained separate from white Methodists. The ambiguity of being neither members in an independent church nor full participants in a truly inclusive church was a factor in the organizing of Black Methodists for Church Renewal in 1968. To the extent that it continues to express and celebrate the historic religious traditions and understandings of black people in America, this black caucus within the United Methodist Church is a vital counterpart of the independent black denominations as an authentic segment of the "Black Church."

Presently, of the forty-six United Methodist bishops within the United States, eleven are black—a percentage greatly disproportionate to the number of black members and churches. Out of 9.4 million Methodists, 360,000 are black; and 2,600 of the 38,000 churches are predominantly black. The United Methodist Church has the distinction of having the first woman bishop among Methodist denominations, Leontine T. C. Kelly, who is one of the eleven black bishops. It is clear that despite a high degree of racial sensitivity and separation at the congregational level, African Americans in the United Methodist Church are uniquely positioned for a high level of participation in the national and international affairs of the church.

The General Conference is the legislative body of the church, while the Council of Bishops provides ongoing oversight and the Judicial Council serves as the court of appeals. The Council on Finance and Administration, located in Evanston, Illinois, is responsible for the overall budget of the church. The General Council on

Ministries, located in Dayton, Ohio, coordinates the program agencies of the church, which consist of numerous boards and commissions: Church and Society, Discipleship, Global Ministries, Higher Education and Ministry, Religion and Race, Status and Role of Women, and Christian Unity and Interreligious Concerns. Each one of the several support service agencies—Publication, Pensions, Communications, Archives and History—is located in a different city. The United Methodist Church, in short, has no national headquarters and no single top administrative officer.

The local churches generally mirror the program emphases of the national body having chairpersons and committees on religion and race, social concerns, education, evangelism, and missions. In addition to the traditional Methodist boards of trustees and stewards, *The Book of Discipline* mandates committees on Nominations and Personnel, Pastor-Parish Relations, and Finance. The churches invariably have organizations of United Methodist Women and United Methodist Men, as well as church schools, choirs, and youth groups. A local Council of Ministries works closely and sometimes is combined with the Administrative Board which is the governing body of the local church.

Methodist Polity

Each of the Methodist denominations combines an episcopal structure with the unique Methodist form of polity known as "connectionalism." As a connectional body, each local church maintains its own identity, yet is subject to a centralized governmental authority. No local Methodist church is an entity unto itself, but rather is "connected" at various levels to other units and offices of the national body. The structure may be conceptualized as a ladder of conferences, the top rung of which is the General Conference, that is, the national legislative body composed of ministerial and lay delegates.

In the black Methodist denominations, bishops are elected by the General Conference. Each bishop has oversight of an episcopal district, which is made up of two or more annual conferences. The bishop presides over the yearly meetings of the annual conferences, determines presiding elder districts (also called district conferences or districts), appoints the presiding elders, assigns pastors to the local churches within his or her jurisdiction, and ordains candidates for the ministry who have been approved by the annual conference.

As of 1985, the A.M.E. Church had thirteen episcopal districts within the United States, with fourteen active bishops and four retired bishops. An additional six bishops were supervising episcopal districts in Africa and the Caribbean. The A.M.E. Zion Church had twelve active bishops, one of whom was assigned overseas, and two retired bishops. The C.M.E. Church had nine episcopal districts in the United States, and one in Africa. Correspondingly, the church had ten active bishops—nine in the United States and one in Africa, and two retired bishops.

In contrast to the black denominations, bishops of the United Methodist Church (U.M.C.) are elected by the five jurisdictional conferences, rather than the General Conference, and are assigned responsibility for an episcopal area (for example, the New York area), rather than an episcopal district. Each area includes one or more annual conferences. Outside the United States the church has central conferences, which are the counterparts of the jurisdictional conferences. These also meet quadrennially and elect their own bishops. Presently, in addition to the forty-six bishops in the United States, the U.M.C. has fifteen bishops in other parts of the world.

Annual conferences may encompass all or a portion of a state. The delegates to the annual conferences, which convene once a year, include elected lay representatives from the local churches and all traveling ministers within the conference, that is, all ministers in full connection with the conference. Functions of the annual conferences include establishing the conference budget; electing delegates to the General Conference; examining candidates for ordination; appointing pastors to local charges; addressing various ministerial needs such as retirement benefits and salary supplements; receiving membership and financial reports from pastors and presiding elders; and hearing reports from the various conference-wide boards and committees. These may vary from denomination to denomination but generally reflect the national church interests and may include such entities as Women's Missionary Society, Christian Education, Lay Activity Council, and Young People's Department.

In 1985 the A.M.E. Church had eighty annual conferences; the A.M.E. Zion Church, forty; the C.M.E., thirty-six; and the U.M.C., seventy-four.

Each annual conference is in turn made up of two or more presiding elder districts. (In the u.m.c. the presiding elder is referred to as the district superintendent.) Convening of district conferences is more common in the black denominations than in the u.m.c. In the former a meeting of all ministers and lay representatives from all local churches or circuits within the designated geographical boundaries of the district is convened once a year by the presiding elder. The business of the meeting may include reviewing the status and work of the ministers, churches, schools, and benevolent societies in the district; granting or renewing licenses to preach and recommending candidates for ordination to the annual conference; evaluating benevolent and connectional financial collections; planning cooperative mission and training activities; and receiving reports from district committees and/or interchurch committees on such matters as social services, mission programs, voter registration, political action, and the establishment of credit unions or other financial entities.

In addition to this meeting, a separate meeting may be held of church school and youth organizations—called a "District Convention" by the A.M.E.Z.S, and "District Sunday School and Christian Youth Fellowship Convention" or "District Youth Conference" by the C.M.E.S.

The presiding elder (district superintendent) also chairs the quarterly conferences of each church within the district. Quarterly conferences are meetings held every three months of the ministers and officers of the local church to review the work of the various auxiliaries, certify delegates to the district and annual conference, recommend candidates for licenses or for orders (ordination), and appoint church officers and committees following their nomination by the pastor. In the United Methodist Church this level of meeting is referred to as the charge conference, rather than quarterly conference, and commonly is convened only once a year.

The base step on the connectional ladder, usually called the church conference, consists of all the members of a particular local church. In the u.m.c. these are optional and must be approved by the district superintendent. In the C.M.E. Church, on the other hand, church conferences are an integral part of its organization, and are convened once every month, with the pastor presiding, to plan and evaluate church activities. The A.M.E. Church also provides for the convening of church conferences to transact local business and prepare reports or recommendations to the quarterly conference. The *Discipline* of the A.M.E. Zion Church provides for "members' meetings" on an as-needed basis to transact business of the church that is outside the purview of the board of trustees, leaders' meeting, or quarterly conference. A "leaders' meeting" of the pastor, class leaders, and stewards is to be held monthly to review the spiritual condition of class members, and to report monies collected and paid out.

Ministry

The ministerial categories in Methodism are scarcely less complicated than its polity. Although there is much consistency, some minor deviations are found from denomination to denomination. In the three historic black Methodist denominations the first category of formal ministry is the "licensed preacher," also referred to as the "local preacher," since they generally function only in the local church, under the supervision of the pastor. If accepted by the annual conference as an "itinerant," a term denoting eligibility for appointment by the bishop to a charge within the conference, then the licensed preacher is referred to as a "traveling preacher" and may be appointed to pastor a local church. The United Methodist Church has a similar category termed "local pastor," denoting laypersons licensed and approved to pastor a local church.

Candidates for the itinerant ministry in the A.M.E. Church, whether deacon or elder, are required to be college graduates. A candidate for ordination as a local or itinerant deacon must have been a licensed preacher (local or traveling) for two years, and either be attending seminary (if itinerant) or have completed a two-year course of study set forth in the *Discipline*. A candidate for ordination as elder (local or itinerant) must have been a deacon (local or traveling) for two years, and either be a graduate of a seminary (if itinerant), or have completed a four-year course of study. Candidates for both itinerant and local deacon and elder must be recommended to the annual conference at the request of their quarterly conference. They must pass an examination administered by the Annual Conference Board of Examiners and be elected for "orders" by the annual conference, following which they are ordained by the supervising bishop.

In the A.M.E. Zion Church candidates for the office of deacon must first be licensed to preach and then serve for two years either as a local preacher or as a "traveling preacher on trial," during which they complete a two-year course of study prescribed by the *Discipline*.

Following examination by the annual conference they may be admitted to "full connection," whereupon they are eligible to become deacons, assuming the approval of the District Committee on Admission and election by the annual conference. Candidates for "elder's orders" must be local deacons for four years or traveling deacons in full connection for two years, complete the four-year course of study prescribed by the *Discipline*, be approved by the Conference Committee on Holy Orders, and be elected by the annual conference. Neither deacons nor elders are required to have college degrees, although this is encouraged. Both can be ordained only by a bishop.

In the c.m.e. Church aspiring deacons must be recommended by the quarterly conference, pass a committee examination on the course of study set forth in the *Discipline*, and have a high school diploma or equivalent. They may then be admitted to the annual conference on trial as a traveling preacher and must serve one year in itinerant work—that is, pastoring a charge (one or more local churches). A traveling deacon may perform all the duties of an elder except administering the Lord's Supper.

In addition to these requirements, candidates for traveling elder must serve as a traveling deacon for two years. Candidates for both offices must be recommended by the Examining Committee of the Annual Conference, and upon election to orders by the annual conference are ordained by the bishop. To be admitted to full connection with the annual conference, that is, full membership including entitlement to an appointment by the bishop, eligibility for transfer to another conference, and eligibility for insurance and retirement benefits, elders must be employed pastoring a church for two years and must complete two years of college.

In the United Methodist Church persons seeking to become candidates for the ministry must be high school graduates, be recommended by the charge conference of their local church and the district Committee on Ordained Ministry, and secure a license as local pastor. Deacons may perform all ministerial functions, except they may only assist an elder in administering the sacraments unless themselves appointed to a pastoral charge, in which case their rights to do so are local only. Candidates for elder must have completed four years of college, three years of seminary, and two years of field practice under the supervision of a district superintendent.

An elder may serve in one of three capacities: a pastor has been appointed to a local church (or circuit); a presiding elder is an elder appointed by the bishop of the annual conference to preside over one of the districts within the conference; or a bishop is also an elder, but one who has been consecrated by the laying on of hands of one or more bishops.

Other categories of "ministry" (the term "clergy" generally is reserved for elders only) are evangelists and exhorters. Exhorters, more common in the A.M.E. and A.M.E. Zion than in the C.M.E. churches, are laypersons elected by the quarterly conference and licensed by the presiding elder to teach the Scriptures. Such persons cannot preach and can work only in their local church with the permission and under the supervision of the pastor. In contrast, evangelists, who are common to all three denominations, are licensed precisely to travel and preach at various churches and revivals on invitation. They may also be ordained, but more commonly as a deacon than as an elder.

The A.M.E. Church also has deaconesses, who are designated by the pastor and consecrated by the bishop, but are not regarded as ministers in a formal sense of the term. Nor are "licensed missionary workers" so regarded, these being laymen and women who are licensed by the presiding elder, on the authorization of the bishop, to perform missionary work in the local community.

Status of Women

Technically, women are eligible in all four Methodist denominations to hold any office at the local church, district, annual conference, and national levels. In recent years they have increasingly moved beyond the traditional women's organizations to become trustees and stewards, offices traditionally held by males.

The A.M.E. Church began ordaining women as elders in 1948. Today there are an estimated five hundred to six hundred women elders in that denomination. A woman is currently the editor of the A.M.E. *Review.*

The C.M.E. Church voted to ordain women in 1954 and they were extended full clergy rights in 1966. The number of women clergy is not known. The first female presiding elder was appointed in 1985. At least one member of the Judicial Council is required by law to be a woman.

Women have been ordained deacons in the A.M.E. Zion Church

since 1894, and elders since 1898. The number of ordained women in the church is not known, but in 1986 there were at least three women in the office of presiding elder, and the Financial Department was headed by a woman. The quadrennial assembly (General Conference) is required to have equal lay and ministerial representation, and women outnumber men in the lay component, reflecting the make-up of the local membership.

Women are regularly ordained in the United Methodist Church and, as noted, have achieved the office of bishop.

The International Dimension of Foreign Missions

In 1820 Rev. Daniel Coker, the former pastor of the Bethel A.M.E. Church in Baltimore, became the first black Methodist missionary to Africa. Under the auspices of the American Colonization Society, Coker formed the first A.M.E. church aboard ship, ready to operate in Sierra Leone.[30] While the motives of the American Colonization Society were highly suspect due to the desire of some white slave-owners who wanted to send a growing free black population back to Africa, the black participants like Coker were far more interested in missionary work and spreading the gospel among Africans.[31] Beginning with its work in Liberia and Sierra Leone on the West African coast, the A.M.E. Church broadened the jurisdiction of its mission field to South Africa in the late nineteenth century when Bishop Henry McNeill Turner visited and began missionary efforts there.

While the A.M.E. Church has had the longest experience and the most extensive mission operations in West, Central, and South Africa, the other black Methodist denominations—the A.M.E. Zion and C.M.E. Churches—have also been active in Africa.[32] Through the work of Rev. Andrew Cartwright in 1878 in Liberia, the foreign missionary efforts of the A.M.E. Zion Church were started on the African continent. At the present time A.M.E. Zion mission churches and schools have been established in African countries such as Liberia, Ghana, and Nigeria, and in Georgetown, Guyana. Due to its prominence in the Underground Railroad to Canada, a number of Zion churches were established among the former slaves in that country. Apart from their role in educating native Africans in church colleges in the United States, the C.M.E.s began their formal work in Africa in 1911 in a joint venture with the M.E. Church, South, in

Zaire (Belgian Congo). Since then, the c.m.e. Church has sponsored missionary efforts in South Africa, Ghana, and Nigeria.[33] All of the black Methodist denominations have also carried on missionary efforts in the Caribbean.

Although the black Methodists were the first to organize themselves into independent denominational structures in the nineteenth century, especially the a.m.e. and a.m.e. Zion churches, it was the black Pentecostals who have shown the most rapid growth in the twentieth century. We turn now to a consideration of the black Pentecostals, especially the Church of God in Christ, the largest black Pentecostal denomination.

4   The Black Pentecostals: The Spiritual Legacy with a Black Beginning

It may be concluded that the Church of God in Christ is justified in likening itself to the scriptural day of Pentecost insofar as both fellowships began with the disappearance of racial and other barriers between believers amid exuberant joy and glossolalic utterance. . . . White Pentecostals and charismatics invariably understand the distinction to be primarily speaking in unknown tongues, quite overlooking the black perspective which understands tongues to be a mark or sign of that divine power and presence which brings all peoples together in reconciliation. . . . Throughout church history there have been numerous instances of glossolalia recorded but none within the context of creating a new community of Christian brotherhood beyond the usual human barriers preventing full fellowship; that is to say, none prior to the arrival of free black American Christian leaders upon the scene, with their previous insight forged during 400 years of slavery and oppression.*

Overview

Among the seven historic black denominations, the black Pentecostals have a unique historical origin. Unlike black Methodists and Baptists, they trace their origins not to white denominations, but to a movement initiated and led by a black minister. Also unlike black Methodists and Baptists, these black Pentecostals began not as a separatist movement, but as part of a distinctly interracial movement from which whites subsequently withdrew.

The modern Pentecostal movement in the United States, inclusive of both black and white people, dates from the Azusa Street

*Douglas J. Nelson, "A Brief History of the Church of God in Christ, Inc." Background paper prepared for the Black Church in the African American Experience research project, pp. 21–22.

Revival held in Los Angeles from 1906 to 1909 under the leadership of William J. Seymour, a black Holiness preacher. Pentecostalism, in turn, as suggested by Seymour's background, had roots in the Holiness movement of the latter part of the nineteenth century.

A confusion as to the distinction between Holiness and Pentecostal groups persists to the present time, and is exacerbated by the fact that in actual practice the lines distinguishing the two groups have been substantially blurred. So far as some believers are concerned there is no distinction, for these groups embrace both the requirements of conversion and of holiness or sanctification as prerequisite for salvation as well as the "third work of grace" called the "baptism in the Holy Ghost," which is manifested in glossolalia or "speaking in tongues."

Some of the black Pentecostal groups existing today actually began as Holiness groups, subsequently adopting the characteristics of Pentecostalism. Some Pentecostal groups have the word "Holiness" incorporated in their name; a few others reject the Holiness doctrine of sanctification and are strictly Pentecostal. The conventional practice of using the terms Holiness and Pentecostal interchangeably is more disconcerting, however, for those groups which are decidedly Holiness, but which reject the tongue-speaking practices of the Pentecostals.

Accurate statistics for either Holiness or Pentecostal groups are problematical, although the Pentecostals are widely acknowledged to be the fastest-growing segment of the black religious family. There are fewer Holiness bodies than Pentecostal; estimates of a total black Holiness membership of 100,000 have been put forth in recent years. Most of these are accounted for by four Holiness groups, the largest of which is the Church of the Living God (or Christian Workers for Fellowship, known locally as C.W.F.F.), organized in 1889. The Free Christian Zion Church of Christ began in 1905, the Church of Christ (Holiness), U.S.A., in 1907, and the National Convention of the Churches of God, Holiness in 1914. Some 10,000 blacks are estimated to be members of the white Holiness denomination, the Church of the Nazarene.

The Church of God in Christ with an estimated membership of 3.5 million members is by far the largest of the black Pentecostal groups.[1] The next eight largest Pentecostal bodies have a combined estimated membership of 300,000. These include the Apostolic (originally, Ethiopian) Overcoming Holy Church of God (75,000); Triumph the Church and Kingdom of God in Christ (55,000); Pentecostal Assemblies of the World (45,000); Bible Way Churches of Our Lord Jesus Christ, World Wide (30,000); and the United House of Prayer for All People (15,000). All of these were founded in the twentieth century, although the United Holy Church of America had its beginnings in 1886. An additional 50,000 blacks are estimated to belong to some fifty smaller black Pentecostal bodies, while perhaps 40,000 may belong to predominantly white Pentecostal groups, most notably the International Church of the Foursquare Gospel. In contrast, very few blacks are affiliated with the Assemblies of God.[2]

Emergence of Pentecostalism

Just as Methodism was originally a part of the Puritan movement within the Anglican Church, so did Holiness originate as a reform movement within Methodism. The Wesleyan tenet of sanctification or Christian perfection distinguished the Methodist movement from its earliest days. During the 1840s and 1850s the idea of "perfectionism" became widespread among other denominations as well, in large part because of the revivals and camp meetings of the Second Great Awakening. However, in the South the emphasis on spiritual perfection was eclipsed by the Civil War, and the revitalized enthusiasm for the doctrine that emerged in reaction to this conflict ultimately proved to be schismatic.

The Holiness movement dates from 1867 when a group of Methodists organized the "National Camp Meeting Association for the Promotion of Holiness." This National Holiness Association, as it came to be called, held nearly seventy interdenominational camp meetings in the two decades from 1867 to 1887. Simultaneously, local Holiness associations were formed, many of them within Methodist districts and annual conferences, but others were nondenominational. Baptists especially were among those drawn to the new emphasis on sanctification.[3] During the 1880s dissension arose within the movement between the reformers and the "come-outers," or those who believed it essential to work within the Methodist structure, and those who left Methodism and other churches to organize independent congregations and new denominations. The conflict came to a head in the 1890s as the Holiness churches, like all schismatics, sought to purify and preserve the faith believed to have been corrupted by the increasingly middle-class churches from which the dissenters withdrew.

The Holiness movement involved African Americans and Caucasians alike. Accordingly, both black and white people were drawn to the Azusa Street Revival in Los Angeles, which became the principal source of the more radical manifestations of the concerns embodied in the initial Holiness movement. As the Holiness associations organized into the more formal structures of sects and denominations, some of them embraced the additional features of Pentecostalism advanced by William Seymour. Seymour, who had studied briefly at a school in Houston run by Charles F. Parham, the head of the Apostolic Faith movement, is generally acknowledged as the founder of the Pentecostal movement. Although some continue to recognize Parham as a co-founder and even as the principal founder, Seymour was unquestionably the person responsible for the extraordinary spread of the Pentecostal movement in the twentieth century through his activities at the Azusa Street Revival.[4]

Both Holiness and Pentecostalism gained momentum in reaction to liberal tendencies at the turn of the century expressed in Darwinism, the ecumenical emphasis, and the Social Gospel movement. The antiliberal orientation of the Pentecostal movement led also to the termination of its interracial character as separatist white denominations were organized. As this racial divergence occurred, certain practices evolved in different directions as well. White Pentecostal churches do not have bishops, for example, while black churches do; and white Pentecostals ordain women and black Pentecostals do not. Ministers itinerate in the white churches, while they commonly serve for life in black churches. Black churches tend to be less rigorous and legalistic in doctrinal requirements, while giving more attention to education and social concerns.[5]

In an ironic development black Pentecostals, who founded the movement, have historically been excluded from ecumenical Pentecostal bodies such as the Pentecostal Fellowship of North America, as well as the National Association of Evangelicals. Internationally, however, Pentecostalism is very much a Third World movement, having spread rapidly in Africa, Asia, and Latin America. By 1970 there were estimated to be from 25 to 35 million Pentecostals worldwide, while the original Holiness movement could be credited with having given impetus to the founding of well over a hundred new denominations.

The Church of God in Christ

The Church of God in Christ, Inc., (COGIC) was among the numerous denominations formed at the turn of the century in the wake of the Holiness movement. Since much of the history of COGIC for over fifty years was closely tied to the life and actions of its founder, a brief biographical sketch is in order. The founder of COGIC, Charles Harrison Mason, was born on September 8, 1866, to former slaves, Jerry and Eliza Mason, who had been converted to Christianity during the Second Awakening on the Prior farm outside Memphis. They became staunch members of a Missionary Baptist church. In 1878 the Mason family moved to Plumersville, Arkansas, where Charles was converted in 1880. He became a Baptist minister who received his local license from the Mount Gale Missionary Baptist Church. Mason received his experience of "sanctification" in Preston, Arkansas, in 1893, and he also studied at the Arkansas Bible College. Dismissed from his Baptist church in Arkansas in 1895 because of his beliefs in sanctification, he continued preaching as an evangelist.[6] Joining with Rev. Charles P. Jones and others, Mason held revivals in Jackson and Lexington, Mississippi, in 1896 which resulted in both Jones and Mason being excluded from the state Baptist Association because they continued to preach the doctrine of sanctification. In 1897 when he returned to Lexington he found the doors of all the churches closed to him, so he preached from the south entrance of the county courthouse. After the space for worship services in the home of Brother John Lee proved inadequate because of growing numbers, the owner of an abandoned cotton-gin house, Dane Watson, allowed it to be used for services. Elder Mason was assisted in the cotton-gin house meetings by the Elders C. P. Jones and W. S. Pleasant. The revival meetings were highly successful and sixty converts became charter members of a Holiness church that Mason organized in Lexington. The meetings at the cotton-gin house were also interrupted by a pistol and shotgun attack where some members were wounded. This attack, presumably by other hostile black people in the Mississippi town has served as an example of the kind of persecution that early members faced. In succeeding years, as the membership steadily grew, a new building was erected in 1906 and named the St. Paul Church of God in Christ, the first church of the fledgling denomination.[7] Originally called the Church of God, the denomination was incorporated as the "Church of God in Christ" in Memphis in 1897.

Mason claimed that the name was revealed to him while he was walking down the street in Little Rock.[8]

While in attendance at the Azusa Street Revival in 1907 for five weeks, Elders Mason, D. J. Young, and W. J. Jegter were baptized "with the Holy Ghost and fire," the practice of glossolalia, and later urged their church to embrace the doctrine and practice. Describing his experience at Azusa Street, Mason said: "The Spirit came upon the saints and upon me. . . . So there came a wave of glory into me, and all of my being was filled with the glory of the Lord. . . . When I opened my mouth to say Glory, a flame touched my tongue which ran down to me. My language changed and no word could I speak in my own tongue. Oh! I was filled with the Glory of the Lord. My soul was then satisfied."[9] The General Assembly of COGIC was divided in its views of the legitimacy of the doctrine of the baptism of the Holy Ghost, however, with the majority rejecting it. Elder C. P. Jones assumed leadership of the non-Pentecostal faction, which subsequently became the Church of Christ (Holiness), U.S.A. Those accepting the practice of tongue-speaking continued to follow Mason, retaining the name, corporate status, and most of the property of the original body.[10]

The first Pentecostal General Assembly of COGIC, attended by representatives of twelve churches, was convened by Elder Mason in Memphis in November 1907. Accordingly, this has come to be regarded by the denomination as the official founding date of the church. Mason was at that time designated "General Overseer and Chief Apostle" (later, senior bishop) of the church, with absolute authority in matters of doctrine and church organization, as well as in the appointment of state overseers. Elder D. J. Young was elected editor of the *Whole Truth* paper.[11] Already established in Tennessee, Mississippi, Arkansas, and Oklahoma, the church quickly expanded into the states of Texas, Missouri, and California.

Because COGIC was the sole incorporated Pentecostal body in existence from 1907 to 1914, it was also the only ecclesiastical authority to which independent white Pentecostal churches could appeal. Consequently, many white ministers were ordained by Mason and were officially designated as Church of God in Christ ministers. When the Pentecostal movement began to succumb to secular social sanctions mandating segregation, it was the men ordained by Mason who organized what has become the largest white Pentecostal denomination, the Assemblies of God, in 1914.[12] The brief interracial period among black and white Pentecostals ended by 1924.[13]

The expansion of COGIC was itself phenomenal, particularly in the industrial areas of the North. Unlike many denominations, COGIC was created not so much by existing congregations coming together from the grass roots to form a national denomination as by the efforts of one charismatic and visionary leader, C. H. Mason, working from the top down. Among Bishop Mason's strengths was his ability to cultivate leadership and delegate responsibility. His strategy of sending evangelists to accompany the northerly migration of African Americans and of charging bishops with the establishment of new jurisdictions in such metropolitan areas as New York, Philadelphia, Detroit, and Chicago resulted in COGIC becoming a predominantly urban church. Although COGIC started as a rural church in Mississippi, it has far fewer rural churches than the Baptists and Methodists. Between the mid-1920s and the early 1960s membership increased eightfold, from some 50,000 to over 400,000.

In one of the rare extant works available on the spread of COGIC mission churches during the urban migrations, Mother Mary Mangum Johnson reflected on the experiences that she and her husband, Elder William G. Johnson, encountered in migrating from Memphis to Detroit to begin the work of COGIC in the state of Michigan in 1914. In a letter, Elder Johnson wrote:

> We left Memphis, Tennessee, March 16, 1914 for Detroit Michigan. We began work among the Colored people. God gave me to rent a mission for Him. I paid my last eighteen dollars for it. I did not have the money to pay the man for moving, so I helped him to load the things, and I left trusting in the Lord to give me the money to pay him. So on my way to the mission, the people in the streets gave me enough money to pay him. Then we had nothing to eat. I borrowed twenty-five cents to buy supper and gave it to my wife. She asked me, "What are you going to do?" I replied, "I will do without." My wife then said, "I know it is the Lord, who makes you willing to suffer, praise His Name." She had one dollar, which I did not know she had, so she gave it to me. I bought food for us both, and we were glad and happy that the Lord had counted us worthy to suffer for His Name, that other souls might be saved.[14]

Mother Johnson also recounted how Bishop Mason constantly traveled to visit them and to oversee the spread of the church in Michigan.

Mason's activities did not go unnoted. During the World War I era Mason was jailed a number of times for his pacifist views, despite his explicit support of the law and of the war bond drive. The FBI placed him under official but secret surveillance nationwide, working closely with the War Department, the Justice Department, and the local police in many cities. Not least among the FBI's concerns was the fact of Mason's interracial following. The growth of the denomination was scarcely impeded by this mark of notoriety, however, and in fact was probably enhanced by the repressive character of the times.

Mason's work is especially notable because it took place amid the rising tide of racism that swept through the country from the end of the Civil War through Reconstruction, past the turn of the century, and on into World War I with its crest in the orgy of racial hatred and violence that gripped the nation in the "Red Summer of 1919." The decorated black American soldiers returned from their overseas' service with the French forces only to discover that, far from proving their worth in the eyes of white Americans, they had instead proven the depth of white racism. The stories of urban warfare, suppression, lynchings, and burnings alive—even of veterans still in uniform—portray the urgent background against which the labors of Mason were consummated in the early years. One of his biggest dreams was fulfilled in 1945 when he dedicated the C. H. Mason Temple in Memphis at a cost of $400,000. This auditorium was the largest convention hall owned by any black religious group in the United States.[15] C. H. Mason Temple also became the headquarters of the sanitation strike when Martin Luther King was assassinated in 1968.

Following the death of its charismatic leader Bishop Mason on November 17, 1961, the church entered into a period of considerable turmoil and litigation, which it has called its "Wilderness Wanderings." Until his death COGIC had been deeply influenced by Mason's charismatic personality, so that the questions of his successor and lines of authority were inadequately provided for. The questions of who was to succeed Bishop Mason and how that was to be decided were the major issues between the contending parties: the power and authority of the senior bishop, Ozro T. Jones, Sr., versus the power and authority of the Executive Board. The period of the legal struggle from 1964 to 1968 culminated in a court-ordered constitutional convention on January 30, 1968. The drafting of a formal constitution defined the offices to be created and their vested authority.[16] Later that same year the first general elections in the history of the church were held, at which time Bishop James Oglethorpe Patterson, Sr., Mason's son-in-law and overseer of the state of Tennessee, was elected presiding bishop, a position which replaced the office of senior bishop. As a result of the conflict of this period, a splinter group broke away in 1969 and was organized as the Church of God in Christ, International. Many dissenting churches have since returned to the parent body.

Prior to becoming presiding bishop, Patterson was appointed to the Executive Committee (later called Executive Board) by Bishop Mason and he has also served as general secretary of the denomination. Bishop Patterson's background reveals the following complex ingredients of a successful career path in a major Black Church denomination: being the son of a COGIC elder, William Patterson of Derma, Mississippi; serving several large COGIC churches successfully; developing a shrewd business acumen in independent business enterprises like a laundry business, a coal business, and the large J. O. Patterson Funeral Home; marrying Deborah Mason, Bishop Mason's daughter; and quietly maintaining good relationships with his fellow bishops and elders. The Patterson family has also been active in local politics in Memphis. Bishop Patterson's son, J. O. Patterson, Jr., a lawyer, became the first successful black candidate from Shelby County to be elected to the state senate since Reconstruction.[17] Until his death in December 1989 Bishop Patterson had led COGIC in developing the bureaucratic structures necessary to accommodate the expansion of the most rapidly growing black denomination.

Church growth has been as phenomenal in the past twenty years as in the preceding forty. COGIC is currently the second largest of all the black Christian bodies, outranked by only the National Baptist Convention, Inc. The church has more than 10,000 clergy (pastors) and about 10,000 local churches, indicating an average congregation of 400 members. COGIC is well represented overseas, particularly in Africa and the Caribbean. Accurate current statistics on these churches are not available but in 1989 their total membership was estimated to be more than 3.7 million. The budget for that year was about $3.5 million.[18] Even statistics on U.S. churches are not precise, a circumstance reflective of the loosely organized character of the church, the polity of which is a paradoxical Episcopal, Presbyterian, and Congregational mixture.

COGIC Polity

The organizational structure and doctrines of COGIC were set forth in the 1973 edition of the *Official Manual with the Doctrines and*

Disciplines of the Church of God in Christ, which represented the
first revision of the manual since 1952. Reflecting the social climate
of the times, the revised manual includes a section on "The Church
and Welfare Concern," which addresses issues ranging from drug and
alcohol abuse to capital punishment to war and military service.
Bishop Mason's pacifist views are reflected in COGIC's official stance
in regard to military service in time of war; induction into the army
as conscientious objectors is supported and COGIC members can only
serve in noncombatant roles.[19] A section on human rights declares
that "the concern for involvement in and dedication to the principles
of equality of rights, justice and opportunity in all segments of our
society should be considered as a basic and integral part of the everyday Christian ministry of all members of the Church. This is so, not
because of the governmental proclamation that 'all men are created
equal and endowed with inalienable rights,' but because of the more
fundamental Christian philosophy of the brotherhood of man."[20]

According to the constitution as revised in 1972, the General
Assembly is the legislative and doctrinal authority of the church.
The delegates of the General Assembly include the members of the
General Board, all jurisdictional bishops, all pastors and elders, jurisdictional supervisors of women's work, two district missionaries and
one lay delegate from each jurisdictional assembly, and designated
foreign delegates. The General Assembly meets twice a year, once
during the National Convocation in April, and again during the
International Convocation in November. The Women's Department,
which functions with substantial autonomy, holds a separate convention each year in May.[21]

The General Council of Elders, consisting of all ordained elders in
the church, serves as an ecclesiastical council to hear any matters
referred to it. The General Assembly, however, functions as the supreme judicial body of the church.

The Board of Bishops is composed of all the bishops of the church.
The General Board, composed of twelve bishops elected by the General Assembly from the Board of Bishops for four-year terms, acts as
the executive arm of the church, providing oversight when the General Assembly is adjourned. The presiding bishop is elected from the
General Board (known as the "Board of Twelve") by the General
Assembly, also for a four-year term, but with no limitation on the
number of successive terms that may be served. The presiding bishop
acts as the chief executive officer of COGIC, administering the affairs
of the church on a day-to-day basis in between meetings of the Gen-

eral Board. The presiding bishop, acting in concert with the General Board, appoints all bishops, department heads, and national officers, except that the general secretary, financial secretary, and treasurer are elected by the General Assembly. Bishops are selected by the presiding bishop from among the ordained elders of the church, although the pastors of the particular jurisdiction to which the appointment is to be made may recommend persons for the position. Candidates for the office of bishop are consecrated by the laying on of hands by the presiding bishop and the members of the General Board.[22]

The church has six major departments: Women, Sunday School, Young People, Evangelism, Missions, and Music. The administrative offices include general secretary, financial secretary, Board of Trustees, Clergy Bureau, superintendent of properties, and counsel general. It also has a Board of Education and a Board of Publications.[23] COGIC maintains a bookstore as well as the Charles Harrison Mason Foundation, which supports educational scholarships. All of these organizational units as well as the mother church known as the Pentecostal Temple Church of God in Christ are located in Memphis, which is both the national and world headquarters of the denomination. COGIC refurbished a downtown hotel for its headquarters building.

COGIC has more bishops proportionately than the Methodist bodies and, correspondingly, each bishop has oversight of a smaller geographical area. In 1984 COGIC had 126 active bishops in 116 "Ecclesiastical Jurisdictions." Of the total number of bishops, 116 are jurisdictional, and ten are auxiliary, serving either as assistants to jurisdictional bishops or in an administrative capacity with a national agency. The church has another eight bishops overseas.

A given state may have from one to eight jurisdictional bishops (formerly called overseers or state bishops, and sometimes called prelates). Thus, as a structural unit, the jurisdiction (also sometimes referred to as a diocese) more closely resembles the annual conference of the Methodist Church than the Episcopal district. Or put another way, whereas a Methodist bishop might be responsible for several annual conferences, in COGIC a bishop is responsible for the equivalent of one annual conference.

Jurisdictional assemblies meet semi-annually, or at the discretion of the bishop. The assembly, which is presided over by the bishop, consists of all pastors, elders, and district missionaries within the jurisdiction; the supervisor of the Women's Department and other jurisdictional department heads; and one lay delegate from each district within the jurisdiction. The departments of the jurisdictions generally correspond to the national departments—that is, Women, Youth, Missions, Evangelism, and Sunday School. Officers of the departments are appointed by the bishop. Delegates to the General Assembly are selected during the jurisdictional assembly meetings, and reports are heard on the financial and programmatic status of the jurisdiction.

The jurisdictions, then, are subdivided into units called districts (in 1984 there were an estimated 600 to 800), which correspond more or less to the presiding elder districts of the Methodist churches. A given jurisdiction may have from two to forty-five districts. Each district, which generally consists of ten to fifteen churches, is headed by a district superintendent who is appointed by the jurisdictional bishop. Responsibilities of the district superintendent include presiding at the Annual District Meeting, serving as an intermediary between the local pastors and the bishop on programmatic and financial matters, and supervising the work of the local churches.

COGIC is not strictly connectional, however, although local churches are obliged to pay assessments to the jurisdiction, which in turn pays assessments to the national office. Local pastors and congregations enjoy a greater degree of autonomy than in Methodist denominations. While COGIC churches are not totally freestanding as in the Baptist tradition, local pastors exercise considerable independence from their superiors. For example, rather than being appointed to churches, COGIC has encouraged their clergy to start their own churches, a practice which has been partly responsible for the rapid growth of COGIC churches from a dozen congregations in 1907 to over 10,000 churches in 1989. In fact, the degree of authority of the clergy and the correspondingly lesser degree of participation by laity more aptly characterizes COGIC polity as presbyterian than congregational.

In part, these features reflect the fact that the church is still relatively young, still growing and developing bureaucratic structures and lines of authority. Traditionally, COGIC pastors have served for life. Until very recently most COGIC churches were still being pastored by their respective founders, or by the person designated by the founder as his successor. Only as this older generation of pastors has begun to experience significant mortality has succession become a major issue. Many COGIC churches tended to be "family" churches, not only bearing the name of the founder like Washington Temple or Mason Temple, but the pastorate of the church is usually handed on to family members, usually to a son, nephew, or son-in-law, and in unusual circumstances to the surviving widow of the pastor. The close involvement of family members in COGIC churches has made the succession issue extremely complicated and it has raised the question of whether bishops will ever have the opportunity to exercise their responsibility to appoint pastors to local churches.

Local churches, to become part of the denomination, must be registered by the jurisdictional bishop with the national general secretary, whereupon the local church receives a certificate of membership and is entitled to elect delegates to the Jurisdictional Assembly. Local churches may adopt their own constitutions, but must conform to the national constitution as well. The organizations of the local churches stipulated in the national constitution generally correspond to the national and jurisdictional departments. Under the Women's Department, each church may have subsidiary auxiliaries such as the Prayer and Bible Band, Young Women's Christian Council (YWCC), Purity Class, and Sunshine Band. Other organizations include the Sunday School, Young People's Willing Workers (YPWW), Home and Foreign Mission Department, and various choirs. They usually have boards of Deacons and Trustees, and sometimes a Deaconess Board, Usher Board, Men's Council, and/or various clubs as well. The Mothers' Board, made up of "retired" missionaries, is indicative of the respect and deference paid by the church as a whole to older women. Black Pentecostal churches and many Baptist ones as well usually have an organization for church nurses or nurses aides, women who are trained to keep members from injuring themselves in the enthusiastic and ecstatic phases of worship services.[24] The organized presence of church nurses during worship is one area where black churches tend to differ significantly from white ones. But aside from these common units, the programs and orientations of the local churches are highly individualized. For example, one church may prohibit participation in sports, while another may sponsor athletic activities. The bounds of propriety generally are specified by the pastor, who, as the chief executive officer, also has the authority to appoint and remove all officers of the church.

Ministry

The categories of ministry in COGIC include licensed minister (also called local preacher), elder, pastor, and bishop. Lay members of local churches intending to be ordained may be licensed to preach by their pastor. These licensed ministers continue to have lay status, but may temporarily pastor a church should the need arise. Their licenses must be renewed annually until they are ordained. To enter the ordained ministry, such persons must be recommended by their pastor to the Ordination Committee of the jurisdiction. Candidates must be active in their local church, be tithers and complete the course of study approved by their respective jurisdictions, usually involving one to two years attendance at one of the seventy bible colleges sponsored by COGIC. Upon the approval of the Ordination Committee, candidates are ordained as elders by the jurisdictional bishop. Except as noted, only elders may pastor churches, and only ordained elders in good standing can be appointed bishops.

In a departure from the pattern of other denominations, any given local church may have from five to fifteen ordained elders who rotate preaching responsibilities. The designation "pastor" thus has a distinctive meaning; the majority of persons who are ordained elders are not in charge of a church. The title of "Reverend" has only recently begun to come into usage in COGIC; the more accepted forms of address are "Elder" or "Pastor."

Evangelists, who may be men or women, as well as district missionaries and missionaries who are women only, are also considered categories of ministry and must be licensed. Missionaries are appointed by their pastors and licensed at the jurisdictional level by the bishop through the Women's Department to work in the local community. Missionaries may found new churches, although that is not customary, and in any such instances the church must be turned over to elders to be pastored.

Status of Women

In addition to the bible colleges, COGIC maintains a junior college, Saints Academy, in Lexington, Mississippi, while the All Saints University in Memphis remains in the planning stages. Arenia C. Mallory served as the president of Saints College for many years, and in many respects her accomplishments have been the equivalent of her more famous counterpart, Mary McLeod Bethune.[25] The Charles H. Mason Theological Seminary in Atlanta is the official seminary of the denomination and a participating member of the Interdenominational Theological Seminary. Significantly, over half the graduates of

Mason Seminary are women, which poses a problem for COGIC since the church does not permit women to be ordained. Provisions are made for women to have charge of a local church in exceptional circumstances, but without use of the title of pastor or elder. Occasionally, the wife of a deceased pastor does assume such responsibilities in an ex officio capacity. Recently a few women seminary graduates have been specially ordained to serve as chaplains. Women licensed as missionaries who also become evangelists officially are permitted to "speak," but not to "preach," although a few local churches now permit women access to the pulpit.

Women may hold any office in the local church except that of pastor. They commonly serve as trustees, and may function as deacons, though without that title. The only women officers at the jurisdictional level are the supervisors of the women's departments. The supervisor is responsible for the district missionaries, who in turn are responsible for the missionaries in the local churches. The majority of lay delegates to the general and jurisdictional assemblies are missionaries; consequently, most of the lay delegates are women.

The International Dimension of Foreign Missions

Since the Church of God in Christ was the most recently established of the seven historic black denominations, its involvement in foreign missionary endeavors has been largely a post-World War II phenomenon. Throughout much of the twentieth century COGIC's resources have been directed to domestic missionary work, especially in urban areas, building congregations from house churches and storefront churches to regular church edifices. Since the end of the civil rights period, COGIC has emphasized foreign missions in Africa and the Caribbean. According to recent studies, the fastest-growing sector of Christianity in African countries has consisted of African independent church movements, which are usually Pentecostal in form.[26] If COGIC succeeds in establishing relationships with this sector of African independent churches, it has the potential of becoming the largest of the historic black denominations. COGIC missionaries have also been active in establishing churches in the Caribbean region. At present the overseas membership of the Church of God in Christ, International, is estimated to be more than a half million members.

This historical overview of the Church of God in Christ completes our institutional summaries of the seven major historic black denominations. We turn next to our empirical findings regarding the general descriptive demography of black rural and urban churches in chapters 5 and 6, and then to more specific aspects of African American religious life throughout the remainder of the book.

5 In the Receding Shadow of the Plantation: A Profile of Rural Clergy and Churches in the Black Belt

It is generally agreed that the Negro church is the greatest institution developed by Negroes on American soil. It has held in common unity more Negroes than any other organization, and it has had more influence in molding the thought and life of the Negro people than any other single agency. The fact is often overlooked, however, that in its major development and until comparatively recent years, the Negro church was predominantly a rural church.*

A former Mississippian, an A.M.E. pastor in Denver, told me, "When I graduated from seminary, I went back to Mississippi, and they gave me a plantation church out near Leland. The second day I was there, the boss-man called me in. He handed me a ten-dollar bill and said, 'Your job is to keep my niggers happy. Do that, and I'll keep you happy.'"

"I packed up," he said, "and left Mississippi the next day."**

Historically, black churches have been the most important and dominant institutional phenomenon in African American communities.[1] The proscriptions of 250 years of slavery, followed by another hundred years of Jim Crow segregation, permitted only the religious enterprise among black people to become a stable, cohesive, and independent social institution. As a consequence, black churches have carried burdens and performed roles and functions

---

*Harry V. Richardson, *Dark Glory: A Picture of the Church Among Negroes in the Rural South,* p. xi. An earlier draft of this chapter, with the same title, by C. Eric Lincoln and Lawrence H. Mamiya was published in *Review of Religious Research* 29 (June 1988), no. 4.

**Bruce Hilton, *The Delta Ministry,* pp. 183–84.

beyond their boundaries of spiritual nurture in politics, economics, education, music, and culture. Elsewhere we have written:

> The black pilgrimage in America was made less onerous because of their religion. Their religion was the organizing principle around which their life was structured. Their church was their school, their forum, their political arena, their social club, their art gallery, their conservatory of music. It was lyceum and gymnasium as well as sanctum sanctorum. Their religion was the peculiar sustaining force that gave them the strength to endure when endurance gave no promise, and the courage to be creative in the face of their own dehumanization.[2]

In spite of this compelling historical and cultural significance, the sociology of black churches remains an underdeveloped area of scholarship and investigation.

Current scholarship on black churches is plagued by a lack of reliable statistical data. For example, since surveys are lacking, no one knows the accurate membership figures for most black denominations. There is also a paucity of other kinds of data on the finances of the black churches; the education, income, and occupational status of black clergy; and the kinds of groups and programs which support the churches' internal life and community outreach. The last major field study of both urban and rural black churches covering these kinds of information was done by Benjamin Mays and Joseph Nicholson in 1933, almost sixty years ago. Their study covered 609 urban churches and 185 rural churches.[3]

In 1978, with funding from the Eli Lilly Endowment, the authors of this article conducted a national survey of black churches in the United States, focusing on the seven historic mainline denominations comprising the Black Church.[4] We estimated that the membership of these seven denominations, considered to be the core of the Black Church, include more than 80 percent of all black church members. The major goals of our study were to gather descriptive statistical data about black churches nationwide and to establish a large base of survey data on black churches on which future studies can build. The field survey took five years to complete and involved personal interviews with 1,895 black clergy representing 2,150 urban and rural churches. Since rural clergy tended to have more than one church, the rural phase consisted of interviews with 363 clergy who were pastors of 619 churches.[5] The clergy were selected as the key informants concerning black churches due to their central leadership position within individual churches. After reviewing the methodology, and the impact of black migrations and the civil rights movement on rural churches, a descriptive demographic overview of rural churches and clergy is presented, based on our rural sample.

Methodology

The absence of national membership lists of black churches and clergy constitutes the major obstacle for undertaking survey research on the mainline black denominations. Without such lists rational random samples cannot be drawn. The representativeness of any sample of black churches, especially for the black Baptist groups, is currently questionable and will remain so until record keeping for membership and clergy has improved. In the face of these problems and limitations regional surveys were conducted, using personal interviews with clergy who were randomly selected from lists provided by local clergy associations in cities and towns in each region (Northeast, Midwest, South, Southwest, and West). Thus, our national sample was drawn from regional subsets.

Depending upon the demographic size of a town or city, black local clergy associations can cross or remain within denominational lines. Almost all of the black clergy in the mainline denominations belong to their local denominational association. The Baptists, however, tend to have more fluid, and often multiple affiliations with several Baptist associations. In small cities, towns, and rural areas there usually is one black ministerial alliance that includes all black clergy, regardless of denomination. In large cities the associations follow denominational lines. For example, most of the black Baptist clergy in the five boroughs of New York City belong to the Empire State Baptist Association. From these lists of local clergy associations a random sample was drawn. In view of the problems of an unknown universe and a lack of national lists, our basic research strategy was to aim at a large sample size of interviews from different regions throughout the country, which would help to correct the biases of past studies of black churches that tend to focus on one or a few elite black churches and clergy as being representative of the total picture.[6]

The rural part of the study was done totally in southern black belt counties which met one of two criteria. First, a county was included if previous data on rural black churches were found in past studies.[7] Second, a county with a black population of 30 percent or more was included to economize on the logistical factors of time and distances traveled by interview teams in rural areas. Demographic maps of the black belt counties published by the Southern Regional Council in 1974 were used to identify the counties, and the council's definition of "rural" as consisting of a standard metropolitan statistical area of under 50,000 population was adopted for this study.

All of the interviewers were black and displayed some knowledge of and sensitivity toward black churches. Rural churches had a sufficient number of characteristics that differed from urban churches to warrant preparation of a separate questionnaire which was pretested in the Mississippi Delta. The headquarters of the rural study was the Interdenominational Theological Center (ITC) in Atlanta, a consortium of black theological seminaries. The interview teams were supervised by a sociologist of religion from the ITC faculty.[8]

Black Migrations and Rural Churches

Migration has become a central social experience for African Americans. The 1890 census, the first to give an urban-rural breakdown of the black population, indicates that nine out of ten black people lived in the South and more than 80 percent of them in rural areas designated as the black belt.[9] By 1980, 85 percent of the black population resided in urban areas and only about 53 percent of them lived in the South.[10] The vast migrations from the rural South to the urban North and the West were clustered around the periods of the two world wars and the Korean War, transforming the demographic landscape as millions of African Americans relocated in search of jobs and a better life. Among the major causes for black migration were the mechanization of southern agriculture, the boll weevil attacks on the cotton crops, the lynchings and violence of a rigid system of Jim Crow segregation, the long-term decline of sharecropping and individual farm ownership, and the need for cheap labor in northern factories and industries.[11] Ironically, the exigencies of war opened up more avenues for labor mobility and improved standards of living for African Americans than all of the less sanguine efforts at economic parity combined.

From their beginnings in the mid-eighteenth century and throughout most of their history the majority of black churches in the South have been rural institutions, and the major effect of the migrations was to produce a largely "absentee pastorate" among these churches. Despite the conventions of a certain degree of itinerancy for the black clergy, due to the manner in which Christianity was spread on the plantations by traveling evangelists and circuit riders during the period of frontier revivalism, the migrations accentuated the situation of the absentee pastor. The studies by Richardson and Felton reflected the growing concern over the absentee pastor during the World War II period. As Richardson has pointed out, "there is a serious shortage of ministers in rural areas. Almost any pastor today can find a church of some kind. This is partly accountable for the fact that some ministers have three, four, and in a few cases even more churches. If a church is too greatly hampered by loss of members, the pastor can usually find another church without great difficulty."[12]

Since World War II the ubiquitous use of the automobile, the paving of roads, and the building of parkways and interstates have led to the increased mobility of absentee rural pastors and they typically travel several hundred miles to preach in different churches. In fact, close to two-thirds of the rural clergy in our study live in urban areas, away from their congregations. Our data indicate that the distances traveled by rural clergy to reach their churches range from one to 400 miles, with an average of 36.4 miles. When asked by an interviewer how he was able to pastor five different rural churches, a minister replied that he preached at services on Sunday morning, afternoon, and evening, and all he needed was "a fast mouth and a fast car." Although the case cited is not typical, the example does illustrate the logistical problems rural clergy face in serving their churches. In spite of the hardships involved, the majority of rural clergy are among the most dedicated of religious professionals.[13]

Despite his dedication, the phenomenon of the absentee pastor inevitably means that most black rural churches are inordinately dependent upon a network of loyal and devoted laypersons for their continued survival. Even if the congregation meets for worship only once a month, other church activities like weekly Sunday School, prayer meetings, choir rehearsal, and Usher Board meetings are frequently carried on by the laity in the interim. Rural church members seldom receive the kind of pastoral attention normally expected in other churches such as counseling, pastoral visits, and community leadership; but in spite of the dearth of conventional pastoral services and the impact of out-migrations, studies show that very few rural churches close their doors without a protracted struggle.[14] Consequently, in proportion to the total number of black churches in existence, a very large number of them are rural churches. Estimates are that 20 to 25 percent of all black churches are rural, close to double the percentage of the black rural population.[15]

The Civil Rights Watershed and Rural Churches

Besides black migrations, the period of the civil rights movement from 1954 to 1968 stands as a watershed in the annals of Black Church history and the sociology of black churches.[16] The past two decades have dimmed the memories of the conflict and turmoil of the period, the complex picture of successes and failures, violence and nonviolence, of courage and cowardice. The dust has settled and Martin Luther King, Jr., has become the symbolic, mythic figure of that era. The movement has produced a lasting positive effect among black churches because many of them, especially rural ones, participated in the struggle.

Confounding the sociological prophecies of the decline of religion or black religion as the opiate of the masses, at the height of the conflict many black rural and urban folk stood up in their churches to be counted.[17] Although their exact numbers may never be known, from 1962 to 1965 in the South ninety-three churches, most of them rural, were burned or bombed.[18] The rural congregations fed and housed the voter registration volunteers and were the centers for political agitation and protests in their communities. Not all pastors and churches participated in the movement, but enough did so that they can point to that period of sacrifice and service with pride.[19]

The most important result was the desegregation of public accommodations and other aspects of southern life such as education and voting. Although housing and religious worship remain persistent bastions of segregation, any study of rural churches must take into account the impact of the civil rights movement. This movement, which had both visible and invisible repercussions, was largely southern, and it changed forever the social and political profile of life in the South. Rural churches were an agent and a catalyst in that change.

A Profile of Black Rural Clergy

In our sample of 363 clergy, 346 were males and seventeen were females. On marital status, 93 percent were married, while 2 percent were divorced, 3 percent were widowed, and only 1.7 percent were single. In the South, although there is the phenomenon of child preachers who began at age eleven or twelve, the tendency has been toward having older preachers in rural churches. For Felton's sample of 424 pastors, the average age was 51.1 years.[20] The results of our study showed that the median age was fifty-two. Despite the practice among several black denominations of placing beginning ministers or seminarians in rural churches to test their commitment and develop their skills in a less demanding environment, the clergy who continue in the rural ministry tend to be older.

The educational level of rural clergy in the current sample show an increase in the years of schooling completed in comparison with earlier studies by Richardson (1947) and Felton (1950). This change probably reflects the effects of the civil rights movement and the desegregation of education. In 1947 Richardson's survey of eighty rural ministers showed that 46.2 percent had eighth-grade schooling or less, and only 10 percent were professionally prepared with some seminary education.[21] Felton's 1950 study yielded similar results, with 43.3 percent of the ministers who had less than an eighth-grade education and 58.2 percent who had never gone beyond high school.[22] In this study the average educational attainment was "high school graduate," with the median education at one year of college. A significant finding is that the majority of rural clergy, 194 (58.3 percent), achieved at least some level of college education (if the categories found in table 1 of "some college," "college graduate," and "college graduate plus" are combined). Since desegregation, the expansion and proliferation of community colleges and junior colleges have enhanced the opportunities for black clergy to acquire some level of college education. Of the sample, 28.8 percent had some seminary training. The tendency of all the black denominations to place seminarians in rural churches probably skewed the higher educational achievement results to some degree. Table 1 shows the distribution of the years of education completed by rural clergy in relation to their denominational affiliation.

The major denominational categories of Baptists, Methodists, and Pentecostals (Church of God in Christ) were used in analyzing the

Table 1: Years of Education Completed and the Denomination of
Rural Clergy

| | DENOMINATION | | | |
Education	Baptist	Methodist	Pentecostal	Total
Less than high school	45 (25.1%)	40 (28.4%)	2 (17.4%)	87 (26.2%)
High school graduate	37 (21.0%)	13 (9.5%)	2 (17.4%)	52 (15.5%)
Some college	24 (13.3%)	21 (14.8%)	3 (26.1%)	48 (14.5%)
(1 to 3 years)				
College graduate	24 (13.3%)	25 (17.2%)	1 (8.7%)	50 (15.0%)
College graduate plus	49 (27.3%)	43 (30.1%)	4 (30.4%)	96 (28.8%)
Totals	179 (53.8%)	142 (42.6%)	12 (3.6%)	333 (100%)
No response=30 (12.1)				
$N = 363$				

date of table 1. Although the chi-square results were significant at
the .01 level, showing some degree of relationship between education
and denomination, chi-square is also a test which can be affected by
the size of large samples. As a measure of the strength of association
between the two variables, Cramer's V was .11683, which indicates a
relatively weak relationship. Furthermore, the sample of only twelve
responses from COGIC pastors was also too small to make reliable
generalizations. However, it should be noted that the Church of God
in Christ is a predominantly urban denomination, although it began
as a rural church in Lexington, Mississippi.

Data on the personal income of rural clergy ("last year's gross
income") were extremely difficult to obtain. There was a high "no
response" rate, 142 (39.1 percent), in our sample, which indicates
the need for caution in interpreting the results. The responses of
221 rural clergy show that their median income is in the range of
$8,000 to $10,000. However, the authors feel that the real range for
median income may be somewhat higher, probably nearer $10,000 to
$15,000. Although the question asked for gross income during the
last year, most clergy tended to underreport their income or only gave
their church support figures, especially if the minister worked at a
secular job, which is often the case.[23] Given the part-time nature of
their ministry, many rural pastors are satisfactorily supported by
their churches economically.[24] A persistent factor is that, in spite of

Table 2: Occupations of Rural Clergy

Occupational Category	Number	Percent
Full-time clergy (No other occupation)	153	(42.9)
Other church (denominational administrative positions)	3	(0.8)
Other religious (e.g., chaplain of military, prison, police, etc.)	0	(0.0)
Professional/manager	12	(3.4)
Teacher/Professor	31	(8.8)
Social worker/service	24	(6.6)
Other white-collar (sales, insurance, business)	36	(10.2)
Other service (military, fire, police)	1	(0.1)
Other blue-collar (maintenance, including farm)	92	(25.8)
Unemployed	0	(0.0)
No response	5	(1.3)

$N=357*$

*Missing=6 (1.6%)

their poverty, most black rural church members exhibit a deep and abiding loyalty to both pastor and church and often strain their resources to take care of the pastor through offerings, monetary gifts on "anniversary" days, or if money is scarce, gifts of food and produce (called "pounding the preacher"). There is also an important sense of vicarious identity and gratification in having the pastor dress well and drive an attractive automobile.

Table 2 presents the occupational categories of the rural clergy. The income of pastors and their need for secular jobs reflect the general economic conditions of black people in rural areas. Over the past fifty years black family median income in rural areas has ranged from one-third to one-half of white family median income.[25] In response to a question on whether they have had "any other nonchurch occupation," 55.7 percent of our sample answered affirmatively. The rate for nonchurch occupations is probably higher—if seminary students who pastor rural churches were controlled for—since closer to two-thirds of all rural pastors had another job.

The level of full-time clergy in rural areas (42.9 percent) is less than the urban level (57.9 percent) in our study. The rural clergy are

Table 3: Number of Rural and Urban Churches
Pastored by Rural Clergy

Number	Rural	Urban
One	174 (47.5)	26 (7.2)
Two	121 (33.2)	3 (0.8)
Three	35 (9.6)	3 (0.7)
Four	20 (5.4)	3 (0.8)
Five	1 (0.3)	0 (0.0)
No response	32 (4.0)	328 (90.5)
N=363		

also employed as blue-collar workers at almost twice the rate of the urban clergy, 25.8 percent versus 13.6 percent, respectively. Most of the rural clergy in the blue-collar category do farm work.

The high percentage rate of rural clergy holding nonchurch occupations is related to the *lack of benefits* provided by their churches. Most black rural clergy cannot expect to receive the kinds of economic fringe benefits which most white clergy take for granted. In responding to questions on "benefits provided by the church," 289 (79.5 percent) of the pastors replied that their church did not provide a "residence for the pastor," and 70 (19.2 percent) responded affirmatively. Asked if "car allowances" were provided by the church, 276 (76.0 percent) answered no and 83 (22.9 percent) said yes. Asked about "any other benefits" provided by the church, 40 pastors (11.0 percent) said they received "health insurance"; 60 (16.4 percent) had a "pension plan"; 18 (5 percent) said a form of "housing allowance"; and 31 (8.6 percent) were recipients of other benefits like "life insurance, books, or travel."

Often the lack of any pension benefits or health insurance plans provided by the churches or by the denominations forces many black clergy to continue working long beyond their retirement age and effectiveness.

Table 3 shows the distribution of the number of rural and urban churches pastored by the clergy.

In table 3 the reason for both rural and urban categories is due to the fact that some clergy serve both rural and urban churches at the same time. The large "no response" (90.5 percent) under the heading of urban churches indicates that the majority of rural clergy tend to pastor only rural churches. Close to 81 percent of them have one or two churches at most. However, there were a few instances (9.5 percent) where the clergy have a combination of rural and urban churches. This is usually the case when the urban church has a regular Sunday morning service and the rural church meets once or twice a month during the afternoon. It is interesting to notice the fact that some urban churches are beginning to fall into the rural pattern where a pastor can have several urban churches which meet on an occasional basis each month and services rotate for the membership. Whether this pattern becomes widespread for urban churches remains to be seen. If it does, there may be economic repercussions since close to half of the clergy already hold full-time secular jobs apart from their pastorate. This pattern may lead to a greater weakening of the myriad support services ranging from daily counseling to informal group leadership and community involvement which the pastor can provide. The rural clergy with several churches on a rotating basis can only be relied on to preach and to officiate at certain ceremonial occasions. Their current involvement in the community is greatly diminished since the majority of them do not live in rural areas.

A Profile of Black Rural Churches

Rural churches were from one to more than two hundred years old. The oldest church in the study was the Silver Bluff Baptist Church of Beech Island, South Carolina, which on its cornerstone claimed a founding date of 1750. It is generally regarded as the first known black church. The average age for a rural church is eighty-four years, with the median age at eighty years. Our data parallel Felton's claim that the majority of black rural churches were organized in the late nineteenth and early twentieth centuries.[26] In response to the question whether the church was founded by blacks or by whites, 574 (95.7 percent) claimed that their church was organized by blacks and only 18 (3 percent) said by whites; missing data were recorded for 19 (3.1 percent) churches. Regarding churches that were organized on plantations, 158 (28.3 percent) of the churches stated that they were, and 400 (71.7 percent) that they were not.

A major change has occurred in the type of building which rural churches use for worship. In 1950 Felton observed that 87 percent of the 570 churches were "wooden frame" buildings.[27] In this study only 19.9 percent, or 123 out of 619, churches were frame buildings; and 76.6 percent or 473 were brick buildings. Four congregations (0.6 percent) were meeting in private homes. Brick buildings in rural areas carry prestige. Over the past thirty years church members have probably attempted to improve the physical conditions of the rural churches that have survived. A total of 232 (39.6 percent) of the rural churches claimed that they were not incorporated as nonprofit organizations in their state. The lack of incorporation prevented many black rural churches from acquiring federal historical designation, although a number of them could qualify under the criteria of age and historical significance to their communities. Community fundraising efforts are also hampered by this failure to incorporate.

The total membership of 619 rural churches was 105,011 members, with an average church membership size of 171. The study focused on aggregate membership or "membership on the rolls." A lack of adequate resources prevented a close monitoring of church attendance patterns over a period of time.[28] However, in light of our experience in rural churches, we estimate that slightly more than half of the members on the rolls attend church regularly, which makes the average rural church attendance size between eighty to one hundred members. Female members outnumber males by three-to-one.

Financial Information on Black Rural Churches

The survey questionnaire attempted to examine a range of financial information on black rural churches, such as yearly income, other financial holdings, church debt, and ownership. Table 4 shows the distribution of responses to the question "what is the average yearly income of this church?"

According to table 4, average rural church income of 619 churches is in the $10,000 to $15,000 range. Median income also falls within that range. However, given the tendency to underestimate income and the large size (21.2 percent) of the "no response" or "missing" category, a more realistic revised median income figure would be from $15,000 to $25,000.[29]

The financial disbursements of local church income vary with the church polity of the denomination. Denominations with a centralized connectional polity—the Methodists and the Church of God in

Table 4: Annual Income of Rural Churches

Income	Number	Percent
$1–4,999	122	(19.8)
$5,000–9,999	108	(17.4)
$10,000–14,999	76	(12.3)
$15,000–24,999	80	(12.9)
$25,000–49,999	72	(11.6)
$50,000 and over	30	(4.8)
No response	131	(21.2)
N=619		

Christ—pay "general claims" or yearly apportionments to the general church. The average general claims paid by 213 churches was $2,190. For the Baptists with their independent congregational polity, each local church decides its own disbursements. For the 406 Baptist churches in our study, the range of corrected income expenditures was found to be missions and benevolence, 5 to 10 percent; program of the local church, 80 to 90 percent; national programs or causes, 3 to 5 percent; and secular institutions, 1 to 3 percent. Much of the total income of black rural churches is spent on the pastor's salary, building upkeep, and local church maintenance programs. If rural churches contribute to national causes or programs, these usually are civil rights programs. The secular institutions that receive the most church support are educational institutions.

A large majority (88.2 percent) of rural churches indicated that they supported church-related black colleges either through special offerings or annual contributions. When asked "how much is given to educational institutions," only 349 (74.5 percent) of those churches gave dollar amounts, with 108 (23.6 percent) not responding. The average annual contribution reported was $508.00, which seems to be a realistic amount for rural churches.

In examining the sources of income for rural churches, all of the churches reported traditional strategies like offertory collections, pledge system or tithes, and special fund-raising drives (church dinners and special musical events). Only thirteen (2 percent) of the churches have any endowment income. When asked whether "any members included this church in their wills," twenty (3.6 percent) churches answered yes and 540 (96.4 percent) said no. The data reflect the economic condition of most black rural people, and their general lack of financial sophistication. Black denominational leaders have not generally provided programs that teach their clergy and lay people about financial vehicles like endowment income and wills. A developed tradition of willing money to institutions has not evolved.

In regard to other sources of income, sixty-six (11.3 percent) churches reported that they had investments, usually held in high interest bank accounts or certificates of deposit; while twenty-nine (4.8 percent) churches said that they derived additional revenues from income producing property and commercial businesses, farm cooperatives, and day-care centers. Most of the additional income comes from rental houses or leased land. One rural church outside Jackson, Mississippi, earned money from a natural gas well on its property.

Historically, black churches have been the most independent and stable institutions in black communities. Our survey of rural churches confirms this fact. Of the 619 churches, 566 (92.3 percent) reported that they owned their church building, 16 (2.3 percent) rented, and 31 (5.1 percent) had "other" arrangements. Of those churches that owned their property, 452 (76.9 percent) had paid up their mortgages and only 136 (23.1 percent) still owed on their mortgages. There are very few institutions in black communities that can match this record of ownership.

The average value of rural church property according to this study is $100,486.33. This figure seems to be somewhat inflated, although the real estate market over the past decade has been highly inflated even in the rural black belt. Rural church buildings range from dilapidated shacks to elaborate modern structures. One rural A.M.E. church outside of Hillsborough, North Carolina, had just completed an $800,000 building project. The average church debt for 197 rural churches is $19,100. Out of the 619 churches, 422 (68.2 percent) reported no debt and 197 (31.8 percent) claimed some level of debt. Most rural church debt is due to the construction of new church buildings or the renovation of older structures.

Internal Maintenance: Rural Church Programs

Mays and Nicholson once observed that all black rural churches have Sunday schools because "they are second in importance only to preaching."[30] Our study confirms this observation with 598 (97.4

percent) churches claiming Sunday schools. Roughly four-fifths, 442 (82.6 percent) said that their Sunday school met "every week," 59 (9.9 percent) churches said "twice a month," and 40 (6.7 percent) churches "once a month." The church schools are usually run by the laity; ministers seldom supervise or attend.

Besides worship services and Sunday schools, the internal life of rural churches is also sustained by midweek services, such as prayer meetings and Bible study. Seven out of ten churches claimed that they had midweek services, and 187 (30.2 percent) said they did not. Of those who have these services 349 (79.1 percent) also reported that they met "once a week," 45 (10.2 percent) met "once every two weeks," and 34 (7.7 percent) met once a month. When asked "who leads the midweek services," 250 (56.9 percent) churches said the pastor led, while 189 (43.1 percent) replied that the laity did so.

The absentee nature of rural pastoral leadership means that church members are more independent and must develop their own networks of spiritual care and nurture. Lay leaders take active roles in midweek services with roughly half of the services unattended by the pastor. The fabled stories of strong and authoritarian deacons and deaconesses have their roots in the absentee and itinerant nature of the rural ministry. The lay leaders have developed a strong sense of ownership of their churches and the pastor is often regarded as a necessary but an occasional visitor. Conflicts between deacon or trustee boards and the pastor are found in many local communities; church splits are often the results of such conflicts.[31] As one of the few institutions that is completely owned and controlled by black people, the sense of possessiveness, pride, and power are unparalleled in other phases of African American life. Charles Hamilton noted that there is a complete identification with "my pastor, my church," not found elsewhere.[32] Black people very seldom speak of "my NAACP" or "my Democratic party," but they often speak of "my church."

The late summer months, and sometimes the early fall, comprise the "revival season" in black belt counties. This is the slack period when the crops have been "laid by," but are not yet ready for harvesting. The revival season is also the time when many lynchings have occurred in rural areas since white farmhands were also free to do their deadly deeds. The revival is the major form of religious renewal used by Protestant churches. Although urban churches and television evangelists also rely on revivals, the classic form of revival is still found in southern rural churches, both black and white. As a form and technique of religious renewal the revival can be traced back to the Great Awakenings, especially the Second Awakening during the early nineteenth century. Beginning in the frontier states of Kentucky and Tennessee, the camp meeting revivals swept up white masters and black slaves alike in a religious frenzy. It was, as Strout described it, "a jamboree and an awesome rite, a family picnic and a religious crisis" all rolled into one.[33] Our study shows that revivals were held in 542 (87.7 percent) churches; two-thirds (67.2 percent) of the churches had one revival, the rest had two or more. Revivals can last from one day to two weeks or more. Churches that had revivals which lasted from "four to six days" numbered 394 (68.5 percent), while 154 (26.8 percent) claimed revivals of "seven days or more." Mays and Nicholson predicted that the "day of the professional evangelist" is rapidly passing.[34] While the professional evangelist who earned a living primarily by conducting revivals in churches may have suffered a demise, our data indicate that "guest evangelists" are still popular in black belt counties. The churches which had guest evangelists to conduct their revivals numbered 490 (85.8 percent), and only 73 (12.8 percent) churches relied on their regular pastor. Guest evangelists are often pastors of other churches who are known for their preaching or ability to elicit the emotional fervor necessary for religious conversion or reaffirmation of the spiritual life.

In revival evangelism all Black Church denominations make concessions to women preachers. Denominations, like the Church of God in Christ and some Baptist groups that have strict rules controlling or forbidding women pastors, will permit women to be evangelists. They can preach in revivals or special meetings, but they cannot pastor a church. One rural clergyman reiterated this view in his opinion of women as pastors: "Women have been preaching for years but [they were] not identified as preachers. That role [as] pastor has not been distinguished for her. As one within, I could not accept a woman pastor—a masculine role."

In this survey of groups and organizations in the church, 79.3 percent of the rural churches said that they had youth groups and 64.9 percent had women's groups. About half of the sample (49.4 percent) had organizations for men. Senior citizen groups (38.2 percent) seem to be the most neglected area. Rural churches have more active programs for young adults (49.5 percent) than the urban churches

(22.8 percent) surveyed. Close to two-thirds (63 percent) claimed that they had a lay group to help plan and conduct the worship service. The usual stereotype of rural churches as inactive, occasional meeting places is not sustained. They may lack continuous pastoral leadership, but many of them conduct a greater range of activities in the church and community than previously thought.

Rural Churches and Community Outreach

To assess the extent of participation of black rural churches within their communities, the survey examined interdenominational and interracial cooperation; cooperation with social agencies or nonchurch organizations; participation in any government funded programs (city or county, state, and federal); and the church as a meeting place for nonchurch organizations.

Past studies of black rural churches have shown an extreme paucity of community activities initiated by the churches or held in church-owned buildings. For example, in Felton's study only 16.1 percent of the churches in his sample sponsored 4-H clubs, 13.9 percent had home demonstration clubs, and 12.8 percent were affiliated with the NAACP. These had the highest rates of participation in a list of eighteen community activities. Felton concluded that "these churches are lacking in community work. This type of work is doubly important because it is so greatly needed by these Negro families and because the Church is about the only organization to promote it."[35]

In this survey community outreach programs show mixed results. In some areas there are marked improvements in community participation over the past thirty years and in others black rural churches still lag in vitally needed community activities. On interdenominational cooperation with churches of other denominations on various projects, 357 (61 percent) claimed that they cooperated. The average number of projects in which churches participated was 4.34. The types of interdenominational projects that churches took part in were as follows: 152 (26.4 percent) churches had "fellowship with other churches and pulpit exchanges"; 139 (24.2 percent) conducted "evangelism programs with other churches (revivals, crusades, etc.)"; 17 (3 percent) were involved in "community-oriented service programs"; 9 (1.6 percent) sponsored "education programs with other

Table 5: Cooperation with Social Agencies or Nonchurch
Organizations by Rural Churches

Types of Agencies and Programs	Number	Percent
Civil rights organizations and activities	310	(50.1)
Employment agencies and problems	2	(0.3)
Day-care centers and nurseries	2	(0.3)
Drug and alcohol abuse agencies and problems	4	(0.6)
Senior citizen or elderly groups	13	(2.1)
Welfare rights and housing	2	(0.3)
Police community relations	5	(0.8)
Food programs and clothing banks	4	(0.6)
Tutoring and educational programs	5	(0.8)
Health-related agencies and problems	5	(0.8)
Local community crisis events and problems	4	(0.7)
Emergency land fund	2	(0.3)
Youth agencies (YM/YWCA, 4-H Club, Scouts, etc.)	4	(0.8)
Other agencies and programs	21	(3.4)
No—no cooperation	201	(32.5)
No response	35	(5.6)

N=619

churches"; 2 (0.3 percent) had "social problem-oriented programs"; and 21 (3.7 percent) claimed involvement in other projects. More than one-third of the churches, 221 (38.4 percent), said that they did not participate.

Most of the interdenominational cooperation occurred between black church denominations. Only 10 (1.7 percent) black rural churches said that they took part in "interracial cooperation with white churches." This finding confirms Felton's, for only 2 black rural churches in his study took part in "interracial relationships between churches."[36] These results continue to underscore the highly segregated nature of religion in American society.

Roughly 65 percent indicated that they cooperated with social agencies or other nonchurch organizations in dealing with community problems. There were 201 (32.5 percent) that did not cooperate. Table 5 shows the variety of social agencies and types of nonchurch programs that black rural churches participated in.

About half of the rural churches (50.1 percent) are involved with civil rights organizations and activities, such as the NAACP, in sharp contrast to Felton's earlier finding of only about 12.8 percent of the churches. The most obvious explanation for the difference is the tremendous impact that the civil rights movement had on all black churches. Mass based organizations like the Southern Christian Leadership Conference with a largely all black church leadership, and the use of churches by civil rights groups for mass meetings and as bases of operation contributed to a degree of involvement and activism which had not been seen before in rural areas. But much of the church's involvement in the community has remained with civil rights issues and organizations. Although there are many other pressing concerns, the results of table 5 show a scattered and sparse degree of involvement. A little more than one-third of the churches (35–38 percent) are consistently uninvolved in either interdenominational activities or community problems and agencies.

Our research shows that the vast majority of rural churches, 589 (95.2 percent), did not participate in any government funded program, while only 17 (2.7 percent) claimed involvement in such programs. Of these participants 8 churches (1.3 percent) received government funds as centers for Headstart programs; 11 (1.8 percent) sponsored day-care centers or nursery schools; 2 (0.3 percent) participated in other programs. The survey found no participation in government funded programs like food services (breakfast or Meals on Wheels), CETA programs housing for the elderly and the indigent, and other tutorial and remedial education programs. In comparison, the black urban churches in our sample, 121 (7.9 percent) participated in government funded programs at a higher rate. Probably the lack of knowledge and technique of applying to such programs and the absentee pastorate contribute to the lower rates for rural churches.

Historically, black churches have usually played a major role in providing a meeting place for community events. During the slavery period and after, church buildings were often the only large halls available for such events in black communities. As both Frazier and Lincoln have observed in their respective studies, black churches were multifunctional and multipurpose institutions.[37] The survey examined whether black churches continue to play such a role. The results show that 171 (28.9 percent) churches responded affirmatively, while 420 (71.1 percent) said no. For the churches that provided their buildings as meeting places, the following nonchurch organizations ranked in the top three: 122 (19.7 percent) churches permitted civil rights organizations; 52 (8.4 percent) allowed fraternity and sorority groups and lodges (Masons, Elks, and Eastern Star); and 71 (11.5 percent) allowed civic associations.

One of the unintended consequences of the civil rights movement and the desegregation of public accommodations is the decreased use of black churches as meeting places for community groups and events. If at one time they were the only meeting places available, desegregation has since opened up a wide range of choices like public schools, town halls, civic auditoriums, hotel conference rooms, and other facilities for large meetings. Secular nonchurch black organizations no longer depend on black churches for meeting places. A similar, unintended consequence has exacerbated the financial plight of black colleges because now a wider range of choices is available to black students. Yet, as ethnic institutions which have been the major carriers of African American culture, the churches and colleges will continue to play important but different roles in the future.

Conclusion: Present Trends and the Future of Black Rural Churches

Although there are a number of competent anthropological analyses of black church life in individual churches in recent years, a descriptive statistical social profile of black rural churches and clergy is missing.[38] Since 1950 the sociology of black rural churches has been largely neglected. Most contemporary scholarship has examined urban black churches where the majority of black people are now located.[39] However, rural churches have been and will remain as the historical and cultural reservoir of the "black folk" religious experience. Many of the distinctive features of black worship like styles of preaching, shouting and falling out, spirituals and gospel music, and enthusiastic antiphonal audience responses were developed in the womb of the rural church. Black rural churches also played important historical roles in helping black people survive the dehumanization of slavery,[40] in providing economic and educational uplift after the Civil War,[41] and in acting as major centers for political activities like slave rebellions, civil rights protests, and, more recently, mobilizing the black vote.[42] Our study attempts to help fill the information gap which presently exists about black rural churches. Thus far, we have presented a profile of the present status of this institutional sector, but what of its future?

There are several present trends which will affect the future of black rural churches. First, the major financial crisis among farmers will affect the occupations of many black church members. There has been a continued rapid decline of small individual farms, tenant farming, and sharecropping, and an increase of large agribusinesses and farm factories like Frank Perdue's chicken industry. For example, census data on farm ownership show that there were 924,000 full- or part-time black owners of farms in 1910; by 1969 their numbers had declined to 104,000.[43] In 1989 black-owned farms have declined even more sharply, and they are quietly slipping away so that by the year 2000 there will be few black independent farmers left.[44] Farm foreclosures, rising taxes, and the difficulty of obtaining bank loans created a major depression in farming and farm-related industries. Many blacks who remain in rural areas will work as managers, skilled workers, and common laborers in large farm industries and agribusinesses. Rural areas will not disappear but agriculture is changing, and the tenant farmers, sharecroppers, and small individual farmers who appeared in past studies of black rural churches will experience a change in occupations.

Another trend is the gradual but noticeable reverse migration among black people to the South and the sunshine states of the Southwest. Studies indicate that during the 1970s the South gained more than 259,000 black reverse migrants.[45] The causes for reverse migration are complex. Like their white counterparts who also are moving, the primary reasons are the search for jobs and the continued industrialization of the South. More heavy industries are moving away from northern states to escape high taxes and strong labor unions. For example, American and Japanese auto manufacturers have chosen rural southern areas to locate new plants. Besides jobs, there is also the growing disillusionment with the northern dream. In the black psyche, the North has always been historically associated with freedom, less violence, and greater opportunities. But drugs, crime, street gangs, depressing living conditions in urban ghettoes, cold weather, and rising fuel costs have taken their toll of the northern dream. Changes wrought by the civil rights movement have also made the South more tolerable. Finally, extended family ties provide another motivation to move. The majority of black people in the North have relatives in southern states, and many of them still regard the South as home. Although the reverse migration will probably not match the previous out-migrations, it is a trend that will increase the black population base of the South and provide a potential constituency for some rural churches.

These trends mean a mixed picture for the future of black rural churches. Those near southern cities and growing black suburban areas will probably experience a rise in membership. In the field we have seen scattered examples of rural churches that have constructed large, expensive new buildings. But there will also be a decline of some plantation churches and others in deep rural areas as young people seek their fortunes elsewhere.

A final trend that will affect rural churches is the growing class split in the black community. Studies are showing an increase in the black middle and working classes who have been the major beneficiaries of affirmative action and civil rights policies. But there is also a corresponding increase among poor black families and female-headed households.[46] Lower-class and uneducated black people have provided the major constituency for many rural churches. These churches will continue to have a needed ministry and services to provide. Since the pastor usually reflects to some degree the economic conditions of his members, the pattern of a part-time, absentee pastorate in black rural churches will continue.

One of the great strengths of black rural churches, which has continued into the 1980s, is the loyalty of their members. In his reanalysis of the Gallup data on the "unchurched American," Nelsen has shown that black people residing in the nonmetropolitan South, or the traditional rural black belt, have the highest rates of being churched among all African Americans. Rural church members also tend to be among the poorest sector of the black population, having the lowest socioeconomic status.[47] In spite of the severe effects of urban migration upon rural churches, they have continued to hold the loyalty of a faithful remnant.

The high degree of racial segregation in religion and housing in the United States reflects the persistent difficulties that American society has had in adjusting to the realities of our racial and economic insensitivities. A total of 30 million African Americans are still trying to find a more comfortable place in their native land, a place they feel to be consistent with the expectations other Americans take for granted. The enduring search for respect and respectability, for acceptance and acceptability takes many forms, and the fallout of the effort is not always predictable. Black rural churches became the first institutions to carry the hopes and dreams of an outcast people.

If they were not always heroic institutions, they at least contributed to the survival of their people in the most extreme and violent circumstances. This study reflects the continuing saga and history of a neglected but remarkable institutional sector in the black community.

6   In the Streets of the Black Metropolis:
A Profile of Black Urban Clergy and Churches

It is a matter of continuous surprise that churches in America's large urban communities are able to compete with secular interests and to emerge even stronger than the church in rural areas.*

Although the rural churches and clergy described in the previous chapter were among the earliest institutions founded by African Americans, there have always been black people in the urban centers of the United States either as slaves or as quasi-free people. As John Hope Franklin has pointed out, even free Negroes had to carry passes because they were always in danger of being captured and turned into slaves.[1] In 1790 there were about 60,000 urban free blacks, who were almost divided equally between the North and the South, and by 1860 their number had risen to half a million. Prior to the Civil War the major areas of black urban concentration were tidewater Virginia and Maryland; the Virginia and North Carolina piedmont; the southern coastal cities of Baltimore, Washington, Charleston, Mobile, and New Orleans; and the northern cities of Boston, Cincinnati, New York, and Philadelphia.[2] It was among this sector of free blacks that the independent black church movement received its greatest organizational impetus. Independent black urban churches were founded only a few years after their rural counterparts and the first formation of the independent black denominations—the African Methodist Episcopal Church in 1816 and the African Methodist Episcopal Zion Church in 1822—were primarily urban phenomena which occurred in the cities of Philadelphia, Baltimore, and New York. These black Methodist denominations along

*St. Clair Drake and Horace Cayton, *Black Metropolis: A Study of Negro Life in the North*, vol. 2, p. 387.

with their black Baptist counterparts in the late nineteenth century became the first national organizations of African Americans.

Apart from the black extended family network, the earliest social institutions created by black people were the church and the mutual aid society. As Meier and Rudwick pointed out, "Historically the two were closely interrelated. The distinction between sacred and secular was not closely drawn. In a period when there were hardly any ordained ministers it was natural for the mutual aid society to perform both religious and secular functions. Moreover, leaders were few in the relatively small urban black communities, and where there were ministers it was natural that they would play an important role in all Negro affairs."[3]

The two earliest mutual aid societies recorded were the African Union Society of Newport, Rhode Island, in 1780 and the Free African Society of Philadelphia in 1787, which formed under the leadership of Richard Allen and Absalom Jones. Both of these societies gave rise to black urban churches: Mother Bethel A.M.E. Church under Allen's leadership was founded in 1794; the predominantly black St. Thomas Episcopal Church was led by Jones when he became the first ordained black priest in 1804; and in 1824 a black nonsectarian church, the Colored Union Church was established in Newport.[4] The symbiotic relationship between churches and mutual aid societies yielded two organizational patterns: sometimes black churches grew out of such societies and at other times churches helped to establish mutual aid groups for their members.[5] There is not much extant evidence of the organization of mutual aid societies on the plantations. However, it is presumed that each slave quarter on the plantations and large farms functioned as a quasi-mutual aid organization in the effort to survive the brutalities inflicted upon them by whites who did not consider them as human beings. Slaves buried their dead in anonymous graves, marked only by the innocuous symbols associated with the meagerness of life. They helped and comforted each other in times of serious illness, injury, or childbirth, and often shared their meager portions of food or material possessions. As we will point out in chapter 9, churches and mutual aid efforts formed the core of the black self-help tradition.

In this chapter we will present a historical overview of the development of black urban churches and point to some of the consequences which the process of urbanization had for African Americans and their institutions, particularly during the period of the great migrations to urban centers from the rural South. We will also present a demographic profile of black churches and clergy in our survey.

North to the Promised Land: The Impact of Migration and Urbanization on the Black Church

The northern and western cities offered employment possibilities, more freedom, greater choices, and more diversity than the rural areas, but they also led to a greater class stratification and a gradual erosion of the close kinship and communal bonds among some families. The social control and enforcement of moral codes of behavior by the clergy and leading lay members which occurred in small rural communities were also weakened. However, during the migrations there was no evidence of a great decline in church membership in urban areas. In fact, the majority of black migrants did not abandon their churches, but continued to seek refuge, help, fellowship, and collective community efforts in the confines of the only institution they had known. If they did not feel comfortable in the large established black churches, they helped to create smaller ones by first meeting in homes, then renting storefronts, and later purchasing their own church edifices. Black preachers attracted people by their personal charisma and ability to preach and lead, and sometimes by their moral charisma of earnestness and hard work. In less than a century a largely rural population had been transformed into an urban one.

In his study, *A Century of Negro Migration*, Carter G. Woodson dispelled the notion that black migration was only a twentieth-century rural to urban phenomenon. It is an old movement because black people have always been seeking to change their unhappy condition ever since they were brought in chains on a forced migration from Africa.[6] Many fugitive slaves and underground railroad conductors like Harriet Tubman—a staunch member of the A.M.E. Zion Church—learned to follow the North Star in their harrowing journey to freedom. The estimates are that about 90,000 African Americans went North on the Underground Railroad.[7] They became the first of millions of black migrants who chose "to get out of this land of sufring" so they could begin life anew in the promised land.[8] After the Civil War close to 60,000 migrants left for Kansas and Indiana in 1879. The depression of 1870, the failure of Reconstruction, and the institutionalization of a system of Jim Crow violence and segregation in southern states were some of the reasons for leaving.[9] But economic reasons, the search for jobs, and the ability to support a family were the primary motivators. At the turn of the twentieth century W. E. B. Du Bois observed that "the most significant economic change among Negroes in the last ten or twenty years has been their influx into northern cities."[10] During the years of the first Great Migration from 1910 to 1930, 1.2 million black people left the South. The steady trickle of 10,000 yearly migrants had become a flood. Between 1930 and 1970 more than 5 million people joined them. Over the course of a century from 1870 to 1970 more than 7 million black people had become part of the largest internal migration America has experienced.[11]

As mentioned in the last chapter, the major effects of the massive migrations on black rural churches were to leave a depleted population behind and to establish a pattern of irregular worship services and an absentee ministry. Some astute labor agents promised free passage on trains to Negro ministers if they could convince their people to leave.[12] Excerpts from a letter written by a Methodist pastor from Newbern, Alabama, during the Great Migration in 1917 give some insight into the reasons for leaving:

> Doubtless you have learned of the great exodus of our people to the north and west from this and other southern states. I wish to say that we are forced to go when one thinks of a grown man's wages is only fifty to seventy five cents per day for all grades of work. He is compelled to go where there is better wages and sociable conditions, believe me. When I say that many places here in this state the only thing that the black man gets is a peck of meal and from three to four lbs. of bacon per week, and he is treated as a slave. As leaders we are powerless for we dare not resent such or to show even the slightest disapproval. Only a few days ago more than 1,000 people left here for the north and west. They cannot stay here. The white man is saying that you must not go but they are not doing anything by way of assisting the black man to stay. As a minister of the Methodist Episcopal Church (north) I am on the verge of starvation simply because of the above conditions.[13]

It is misleading to view urbanization as only a northern phenomenon since black people also moved from rural areas to southern cities. In the first decade of the twentieth century large percentage increases in the black population occurred in cities such as Birmingham (215 percent) and Atlanta (45 percent). But the 1910 census showed that of the five cities with the largest black populations, of over 80,000, only one (New Orleans) was in the Deep South; the others were New York, Washington, D.C., Baltimore, and Philadelphia.[14] Later the focus of migration shifted to the industrial cities of the north-central region like Chicago, Detroit, and Cleveland. Much of the black migration to urban centers in the Deep South occurred as a post-World War II phenomenon when the cotton tenant-farm system collapsed throughout most of the Southeast and the process of industrializing the South began in earnest.[15]

Black Churches and the Urban Environment: Church Growth, Residential Segregation, and Economic Stratification

Studies done on black urban churches during the period of the great migrations from 1915 to 1950 indicate that they underwent a period of phenomenal growth, not only in the membership rolls of the older, established urban churches, but also in the founding of numerous new churches, often started in rented storefronts in the poorer sections of the city. In their study Mays and Nicholson reported that a comparison of the figures given in the *Federal Census of Religious Bodies* of five northern cities (Chicago, Detroit, Cincinnati, Philadelphia, and Baltimore) showed a 151 percent increase in the number of black Baptist churches, and a 200 percent increase in Baptist membership between 1916 and 1926; the A.M.E. churches in these cities showed an increase of 124 percent for churches and 85 percent for members.[16] The waves of black migrants swamped the resources of many churches.

The first reaction of many pastors and church leaders was to build—new additions to old structures or to erect completely new buildings that added a tremendous debt pressure to their already precarious financial situation. Other pastors bought older church buildings and synagogues from whites at inflated prices.[17] In retrospect, this prevalent "edifice complex" was the wrong reaction to the social crisis engendered by the migrations. In their fine study of churches in the late 1920s, Mays and Nicholson constantly raised the problem of overchurching in the urban environment. They also realized that the Great Depression of 1929 had nearly turned the folly of church expansion into a devastating catastrophe since the vast majority of black churches were stretched to their financial limits and strapped with large debts. They estimated that about 71.3 percent of urban churches in their sample were indebted.[18] St. Clair Drake Horace and Cayton reported that Negro churches in Chicago in 1933 were carrying the second highest per capita indebtedness among all urban Negro churches.[19] However, in a strange place it was natural for many of the black migrants to seek help from the dominant social institution they knew back home in the rural South, and it was also reasonable for a pastor to think that his ministry was prospering because of the many new faces he saw each week. Moreover, a new church building was a symbol of success. Excerpts from a letter of May 21, 1917, by a female migrant to Akron, Ohio, give us some insights:

> ... Their is no place like home. How is the church getting along ... the people are coming from the south every week the colored people are making good they are the best workers. I have made a great many white friends. The Baptist Church is over crowded with Baptist from Ala & Ga. 10 and 12 join every sunday. He [the pastor] is planning to build a fine brick church. He takes up 50 and 60 dollars each sunday he is a wel to do preacher.[20]

This phenomenal growth in church membership and the rise of new urban churches and storefronts, however, did not represent a major spiritual revival bringing in new converts. On the whole, the growth represented a transfer of memberships from rural to urban ones. The letters from migrants to their former pastors are often replete with reminders to send them a letter of "dismission" or transfer.[21] Sometimes a majority of members from a single church migrated together and it was not unusual to find migrants from the same rural county or town living in proximity to each other in new urban areas. The pattern of "chain migration" involved the verbal and written pleas of migrants to close friends and relatives to come North and most of the time they painted an optimistic picture of the promised land as a place of unrestricted freedom, friendly whites, and upward mobility.[22] Some migrants took advantage of the move to the city to break free of confining church traditions in rural areas; thus a small but steadily growing population of unchurched blacks, mainly composed of black men, began.

Not all of the black mainline churches joined this church expansion strategy. In each city there were a few leading churches and preachers who took a prophetic stance in attempting to meet the great needs of the migrants by using their church's resources to provide help with food, shelter, clothing, and employment. In the 1920s Rev. Adam Clayton Powell, Sr., opened one of the first soup kitchens for the hungry migrants just after his church, Abyssinian Baptist, had moved uptown to Harlem. In 1939 his son, Rev. Adam Clayton Powell, Jr., involved the church in welfare work, seeking employment, and supported black workers in their strikes and attempts to unionize. Powell himself was the publisher of a Negro newspaper and a member of the New York City Council before he became the first elected black congressman from New York State. In his famous 1944 study of *An American Dilemma*, the Swedish sociologist Gunnar Myrdal pointed to some examples of what he called "social work" among the black churches. In Chicago the Good Shepherd Church sponsored a community center which was directed by a Negro sociologist and coauthor of *Black Metropolis*, Horace Cayton.[23] During the period of the migrations, Bishop Reverdy C. Ransom of the Institutional A.M.E. Church in Chicago became one of the more outspoken political activists.

The social outreach of these larger churches, however, appeared to be the exception rather than the rule. The majority of the black churches were small in size and numerous in quantity. The main function of these churches from World War I until the mid-1950s was to act as a "cultural broker," a mediating institution, to help acculturate rural migrants to the urban environment. To some outside observers it appeared that most of the black urban churches during this period had withdrawn into a revivalistic Christianity and a defensive accommodationism. It is still a matter of scholarly debate whether the black churches during this period had been completely "deradicalized" as Gayraud Wilmore has contended, or whether the sudden expansion brought on by the migrations followed by a catastrophic worldwide economic depression simply overwhelmed black preachers and their churches.[24] In either case the consequences appeared to be the same, a relative quietism and an apparent vacuum of church leadership which was filled by flamboyant messiahs and cultists like Father Divine and Daddy Grace, whose promise of utopias and provision of social services to the abject poor caught the attention of the press and the imagination of the people.

While the northern urban environment did provide some economic mobility which gradually led to a differentiated social class
structure in black communities, the common thread which linked
the North and the South for many black migrants was the experience
of racial caste and segregation. From the beginnings of urbanization
in America, small residential pockets in most cities were usually set
aside for Negroes, slave or free; sometimes they were visible; at other
times they were hidden away in alleys and behind the tracks. But as
the migrations reached their peak, the small segregated areas like San
Juan Hill and the Tenderloin in Manhattan expanded to include
whole districts like the northern part of the island called Harlem, or
areas like the Southside of Chicago.[25] Although there were no signs
designating separate entrances for whites and colored, there was a
tacit understanding in northern cities developed from custom and
practice that certain hotels, restaurants, theaters, social clubs, parks,
residential areas, and even churches were off-limits to black people.
Violations of that understanding usually resulted in a forcible evic-
tion or severe beating, and sometimes they erupted in riots like those
in Chicago, New York, Omaha, and elsewhere during the bloody
"Red Summer" of 1919.[26] But the heart of de facto desegregation in
the North was found in the place of residence, and that fact has
continued to have major implications for the high rates of segregation in public education in northern cities, even after the removal of
racial restrictions in public accommodations which occurred with
the civil rights movement.[27]

As one of the few independent mass institutions created by the
people themselves, it was inevitable that the established black
churches would begin to reflect the differentiation, stratification,
and pluralism which the urban environment encouraged. During
slavery and the post-Civil War era, black churches performed multifarious roles in moral nurture, politics, education, economics, and
black culture in general, as described in our statement on theoretical
assumptions. A gradual process of separating these spheres from the
influence of the church occurred in the late nineteenth and early
twentieth centuries, which the process of urbanization accelerated.
Since black people were by and large excluded from most white
groups, they created parallel institutions such as lodges, fraternities
and sororities, and civil rights organizations such as the NAACP and
the National Urban League. Although these groups can be viewed as
competitors to black churches, it is a mistake to overemphasize the

competition or the sacred/secular tensions.[28] Throughout most of their history in local black communities, many of these groups depended upon black churches and pastors for meeting places, leadership, financial resources, publicity, and members. Furthermore, as we will point out in later chapters, particularly in the areas of politics and economics, some astute church leaders saw the need to create secular organizations to meet the more complex demands of an urban environment. In other words, a partial differentiation of these spheres of activity occurred rather than a complete separation from black churches. The notion of partial differentiation emphasizes the continuous interaction and interrelationships between churches and areas like politics, economics, education, and culture. The view of the complete differentiation of religion, a withdrawal into a private religious sphere which is prevalent in the social sciences, leads to a misunderstanding of the role of black churches in urban society.

The development of a class hierarchy among African Americans began in slavery with the major division between the elite few who were free and the masses who were enslaved. Class distinctions throughout much of black history have been intersected with color caste preferences; those with a lighter skin color or mulatto status received more privileges. Although there were status distinctions among the slaves like house slaves, artisans and craftsmen, and field slaves, much of the socioeconomic class divisions began with urbanization. For example, between 1890 and 1920 the beginnings of a petit bourgeoisie had formed among professional and businessmen who were completely dependent upon servicing the black community for their livelihood. They were largely self-made men, of lower-class origin, ambitious, and had somewhat darker skin color, but they were still mulattoes.[29] Black insurance agents, morticians, barbers, owners of small business enterprises like restaurants and stores, and some black clergy of newly founded black urban churches were part of this strata.

During the six decades from 1920 to 1980 this petit bourgeoisie developed into a viable black middle class, comprising about one-third of the black population, which internalized the major American middle-class values of individualism, privatism, pragmatism, conspicuous consumption, and upward mobility. The major effect of urbanization was to introduce a greater differentiation of social class and pluralism into the African American community. According to Andrew Billingsley, social class criteria must be modified when they are applied to the black community because the community has its own definitions of class, which differ somewhat from the white standards of income, occupation, and education. For example, what is considered middle class in the white community may be upper class in the black community like the vocations of high school principal, college president, or bishop of a black denomination. Class lines in the black community are also more fluid and subject to greater fluctuations, precariousness, and changes. Often two incomes are required for a black family to be considered middle income.[30]

Several studies have focused on the economic stratification of black churches in cities like Chicago. Between 1937 and 1939 Vattel Daniel studied forty Southside churches and developed a typology that he felt reflected the class structure in the black community. Contending that ritual, ceremony, and emotional content perform different functions for different classes among urban blacks, Daniel proposed a scheme of four "ritual types": (1) "ecstatic sects or cults," (2) "semidemonstrative groups," (3) "deliberative" or sermon-centered services, (4) "liturgical denominations." He felt that the urban liturgical and deliberative services had already evolved their types of services for a largely middle- and upper-class clientele, and the newly arrived migrants were thereby forced to develop their own worship styles, which either became semidemonstrative or ecstatic in character.[31]

In their 1945 study St. Clair Drake and Horace Cayton also observed the class stratification which developed among black religious groups in Chicago. About 10 percent, mainly the upper class in Bronzeville, were attracted to the predominantly white denominations such as the Episcopal, Congregational, and Presbyterian churches. The middle class were usually Baptist or Methodist and occasionally Roman Catholic, who expected their ministers to be "advancing the Race" and wanted their churches to "save the youth." They also tended to belong to large, mixed type churches which had a segment of lower-class members. The genius of the mixed type church is the use of many subgroups that provide close association and comfort to people of similar backgrounds. Like Daniel's typology, Drake and Cayton used overt emotionalism as being distinctive of lower-class religion. "When a person in Bronzeville says that he is 'sanctified,'" they commented, "or that he attends a Spiritualist church or one of the 'cults' he is immediately marked down as 'low status.' "[32] The masses of the black lower class were also pushed and pulled by a plethora of religious groups that competed for their souls and allegiance. The Holiness-Pentecostal movement expanded rapidly after the Azusa Street Revival in 1906 and became a largely urban phenomenon. Numerous black gods and prophets of the metropolis appeared during the Depression years, movements such as Father Divine's Peace Mission, Daddy Grace's United House of Prayer for All People, Elder Solomon Lightfoot Michaux's Church of God, Rabbi Cherry's Black Hebrews, and Mother Artemius Horne. The seeds for a number of black militant and separatist groups were also planted during the urban migrations by Noble Drew Ali, Marcus Garvey, Master Fard, and Elijah Muhammad.[33]

The period of the massive black migrations from the rural South to the urban North and West came to an end during the late 1950s, the beginning years of the civil rights struggle. It was somewhat of an irony that E. Franklin Frazier, the leading black sociologist, wrote his definitive study on religion, *The Negro Church in America*, during this period, and made the negative judgments that Negro churches were a hindrance to the assimilation of Negroes into the mainstream of American life, and that they were also responsible for the "so-called backwardness of American Negroes."[34] Frazier's untimely death in 1959 prevented him from seeing the activism of black rural and urban churches in the struggle to desegregate the South, and from hearing eloquent black clergy leaders like Martin Luther King, Jr. It also prevented him from feeling the resurgence of black ethnicity and pride in the black power and black consciousness movement of the 1960s, whose ideological foundations were articulated by another brilliant religious leader, Minister Malcolm X of the Nation of Islam. Instead, Frazier's negative judgments and pessimism were consonant with his training and the prevailing scholarly opinion that Negro Americans had no culture or heritage to call their own and that any manifestations of an independent cultural style were aberrant expressions of mainstream Euro-American behavior.[35] Like other social scientists of that era, Frazier was also influenced by the myth and metaphor of the "melting pot" of American society, where all ethnic differences would be melted to produce the new homogeneous American which curiously resembled the old WASP model. However, African Americans did not and could not melt. As Herbert Gutman has astutely pointed out, Frazier's "monocultural" model of the Negro family and religion did not allow the development of an indigenous, bicultural African American heritage, a unique ethnic culture fused from the strands of Africa, America, and Europe.[36] The metaphor for cultural pluralism in the United States is not the "melting pot" but the "rainbow," as the Jesse Jackson 1984 and 1988 presidential campaigns suggested. Studies of black churches and black religion beyond Frazier must come to terms with the new awareness of the black cultural heritage and to some extent a renewed activism by clergy and churches. In their study, *Black Church in the Sixties,* Nelsen and Nelsen examined the question of whether black religion acted as an opiate to civil rights militancy; an issue which we will reexamine in chapter 8.[37] Unfortunately, Ida Rousseau Mukenge's political economy approach to the study of black churches, *The Black Church in Urban America,* tends to dismiss the influence of the black consciousness movement upon black clergy and black churches. In succeeding chapters we will examine in greater detail aspects of this new awareness and activism in the impact of the black consciousness movement in politics, in economics and education, and in the growing feminist movement among black clergywomen. For the remainder of this chapter we present the results of our field study of black urban clergy and churches.

A Profile of Black Urban Clergy

A total of 1,531 urban clergy from the seven major black denominations were interviewed in fifteen major urban areas in the Northeast, Southeast, Southwest, Midwest, and West.[38] The denominational distribution is given in the appendix. The regional sampling strategy using local clergy associations, which was described in chapter 5, was also followed in the urban phase. In terms of denominational affiliation, about 90 percent of all of the clergy respondents said that they identified with one primary black denomination. Only the Baptist groups (NBC, U.S.A., Inc.; NBC, America, Uninc.; and PNBC) had multiple denominational affiliations, either with another black Baptist denomination, usually between the NBC, U.S.A., Inc., and the PNBC, or with the white Southern Baptists and American Baptists. The black Methodists' groups (A.M.E.; A.M.E. Zion; and C.M.E.) remained within their primary denominational affiliation and so did the black Pentecostals (COGIC).

The sex distribution of our sample included 1,462 (98.8 percent) male and 149 (3.2 percent) female. Although our interviewers were instructed to oversample and to interview any woman pastor in the mainline black denominations they could find, even if they were not included in the original list for random sampling, only 3.2 percent of the urban clergy were found to be female. Our best estimate is that fewer than 5 percent of all black clergy in the seven historic denominations are female. The implications of this fact will be considered in more detail in chapter 10. The rural sample showed a similar result with 94.6 percent of the clergy who were male and only 4.6 percent female. In regard to marital status, 1,329 (88.7 percent) were married while 54 (3.6 percent) were divorced. Only seventy-five (5 percent) of the clergy were single, and forty (2.7 percent) were widowed. There are great social pressures and preferences within black churches for the pastor to be married or to get married. Because of the predominance of female members in black churches, unattached single clergy, especially males, tend to be viewed as a threat to the stability of congregational life.

Clergy Income

Table 6 shows a comparative distribution of the gross income of both urban and rural clergy. As expected, the income of urban clergy tends to be higher than that of their rural counterparts. The median income for rural clergy was in the $10,000 to $15,000 range, while urban clergy reported a median income in the category of $15,000 to $25,000. It is interesting to note that about 151 (9.8 percent) of the urban clergy said that they earned more than $25,000 while only 11 (2.9 percent) of the rural clergy claimed that income level. The rural-urban difference reflects both a greater level of affluence in urban areas and the larger size of urban congregations. As was indicated in chapter 5, questions regarding accurate income figures in black churches remain problematic. The large number of clergy (27.7 percent) who did not respond to the question on personal income indicates the need for caution in interpreting the results. The clergy income results of our study are comparable to the findings of Brown and Walters's study of twenty-one black churches in Washington, D.C. They reported a pastor's family median income of $13,000.[39] The slight difference between the surveys on clergy income is due to the fact that our study focused on clergy in the seven mainline black denominations, while theirs included all black churches in a census tract, without regard to denominational lines. The mainline black denominations probably include more middle-income church mem-

Table 6: Clergy Income

Income Categories	Total	Urban	Rural
Zero earnings	27 (1.4%)	27 (1.8%)	0 (0.0%)
$1–2,999	100 (5.3%)	78 (5.1%)	22 (5.9%)
$3,000–$5,999	191 (10.1%)	142 (9.3%)	49 (13.5%)
$6,000–$7,999	141 (7.5%)	106 (6.9%)	35 (9.8%)
$8,000–$9,999	135 (7.1%)	110 (7.2%)	24 (6.9%)
$10,000–$14,999	262 (13.8%)	228 (14.8%)	34 (9.4%)
$15,000–$24,999	350 (18.5%)	305 (20.0%)	45 (12.4%)
$25,000 and over	162 (8.5%)	151 (9.8%)	11 (2.9%)
No response	526 (27.7%)	383 (25.1%)	143 (39.2%)

Total N=1,894
Urban N=1,531
Rural N=363

bers than the small, independent Apostolic and Pentecostal churches and storefronts. A cross-tabulation of reported clergy income from the seven denominations showed no significant variations. Cramer's V was 0.12507 for 1,368 respondents. However, it is interesting to note that clergy from the three Baptist denominations (14 percent average) and from the Church of God in Christ (15.7 percent) tend to have slightly larger percentages of their clergy earning more than $25,000 per year than the three black Methodist denominations (8.37 percent average). This is probably due to the influence of the connectional polity among Methodists that tends to standardize salary scales for pastors in their churches. In the churches with an independent or congregational polity such as the Baptists, each church determines such matters. As mentioned earlier, the Church of God in Christ has a mixed polity. Although it is a connectional church with bishops, COGIC clergy are also encouraged to be independent spiritual entrepreneurs and establish their own churches rather than waiting for appointment by the bishop.

Education of the Clergy

In their 1934 study Mays and Nicholson lamented the educational level of the Negro ministry. They reported that 80 percent of the urban pastors are not college trained and that 86.6 percent do not have the bachelor of divinity degree.[40] As we mentioned in our chapter on the rural church, the educational level of both rural and urban clergy has risen considerably over the past fifty years, reflecting in part the desegregation of public education and the other social changes which have occurred in the black community since the Depression. Table 7 shows that the median level of education of our urban sample is close to four years of college. Moreover, 70.2 percent of the urban clergy have some level of college training. It is estimated that about one third (35.9 percent) of all black clergy, in both urban and rural situations, have had some seminary or Bible school training beyond the college level. Although the survey did not ask about completion of a master of divinity program or graduation from a theological seminary, it is estimated that only about 10–20 percent of the clergy nationwide have completed their professional training at an accredited divinity school or seminary.[41] Unfortunately, this rate of professional training for the ministry, as measured by a seminary degree, has not improved very much since the time of Mays and Nicholson's study. On the other hand, the requirements of modern technological society have made professional education for the ministry a prerequisite for pastors of the mainline black churches. As more and more African Americans are entering professions that were once closed to them, the pastors of black churches must have both the educational credentials and the ability to preach if they are to be acceptable to an increasingly well-educated clientele. While the black clergy overall have kept pace with the general rise in educational levels in the black community, they still lag behind in professional training when compared to other black professionals. It is difficult to imagine a profession, whether it is medicine, law, engineering, teaching, or social work, where two-thirds of the professionals have not had any advanced training, and more than 80 percent have not completed professional degrees. However, that is the case with the majority of the black clergy in the 1980s. Most black clergy have learned about pastoring a church through an informal system of apprenticeship which exists in all black denominations. But the days when pastors could brag about being "untrained" and still build a large church are rapidly passing. Similarly, the time when the minister was looked upon for leadership because he was the best-educated, or among the best-educated people in the black community are also gone. To win the respect of the new black professionals and college-educated black people, the clergy must also, at a minimum, achieve professional parity.

If the Black Church is to have a viable future the need for professional seminary education appears to be critical. As the results of our survey will show, educational level has been a key variable in determining a pastor's awareness of social problems in the surrounding community, cooperation with social agencies, attitude toward politics, and awareness of internal problems in church structures. In our field interviews with black clergy the churches that sponsor the most creative and innovative programs in the community and in the church usually have well-educated, well-trained pastors. The educational issue is problematic for most black churches because the historical evangelical background of the Baptists, Methodists, and Pentecostals did not have stringent educational demands but only required evidence of a personal call from God to the ministry. The anti-intellectual and fundamentalist strains of that tradition have made it difficult for innovative church leaders and bishops to make professional seminary education a requirement for the ministry. The response of nineteen clergy in the Brown and Walters's study of Washington, D.C., were similar to our results. Their median educational level was four years of college with 42 percent having had some level of college or postsecondary education, and 21.1 percent having attended graduate school.[42]

Table 8 presents the cross-tabulation data on educational levels among the urban and rural clergy in the seven denominations. Overall, there were no significant differences among the denominations in terms of the educational levels of the clergy in the total sample of 1,894 respondents. Median educational levels ranged from College (one to three years) to College graduate (four years) for all seven denominations. The clergy of the A.M.E. Church and the C.M.E. Church had the highest median levels of college graduates. Cramer's V was 0.12412. However, the cross-tabulation does reveal that in the category of college plus 5, or graduate study, clergy in the Church of God in Christ denomination tended to have the smallest percentage. Only 56 (18.7 percent) out of 298 COGIC respondents said that they had done graduate study. The C.M.E. (51 percent) and the A.M.E. (48.2 percent) clergy had the highest reported rate of graduate study among the seven denominations. Among the Baptists, the Progressive denomination (43.7 percent) claimed a slightly higher rate than the NBC, U.S.A., Inc. (39 percent). The COGIC results reflected its transi-

Table 7: Clergy Education

Years of Schooling	Total	Urban	Rural
Grammar (1–3)	9 (0.5%)	4 (0.3%)	5 (1.4%)
Grammar (4–6)	30 (1.6%)	19 (1.2%)	11 (3.0%)
Grammar (7–8)	92 (4.9%)	63 (4.2%)	30 (8.1%)
High school (1–3)	166 (8.8%)	117 (7.7%)	49 (13.5%)
High school (4)	260 (13.7%)	206 (13.5%)	54 (15.0%)
College (1–3)	347 (18.3%)	295 (19.2%)	52 (14.4%)
College (4)	251 (13.2%)	201 (13.1%)	50 (13.8%)
College 5 plus	680 (35.9%)	581 (37.9%)	99 (27.3%)
No response	59 (3.1%)	45 (2.9%)	13 (3.5%)

Total N=1,894
Urban N=1,531
Rural N=363

tion to a more middle-income, denominational status from a largely lower-class, sectarian background. From field observations and reports from theological seminaries, it appears that the Church of God in Christ is moving rapidly to catch up with the other black denominations in the area of educational achievement for its clergy.

The age range of clergy in the urban sample was 18 to 92 years old with a median age of 51.5 years. There were no significant differences with the rural sample where the median age of clergy was 51.3 years and the age range was 17 to 89 years old. As mentioned in the previous chapter, the majority of black clergy tend to be older, which probably reflects an economic situation where many pastors cannot afford to retire because of low or nonexistent retirement benefits and pension plans. In a profession where the median age is close to 52 years old, critical questions must be raised about the future of the ministry in the black denominations and the source of new recruits. This issue will be examined in more detail in chapter 11.

Nonchurch Occupations of Black Clergy

Long before the idea of tent-making ministries or the notion of the worker-priests holding full-time, secular jobs became a feature in white theological seminaries, that tradition was well established

Table 8: Black Urban and Rural Clergy Education by
Denomination

Denomination	NBC, U.S.A.	NBC, America
Educational Level		
Grade school (1–8 years)	44 (8.7%)	15 (8.8%)
High school (1–4 years)	93 (18.5%)	59 (33.4%)
College (1–3 years)	90 (17.5%)	29 (16.2%)
College graduate (4 years)	81 (16.0%)	23 (13.1%)
College plus 5 (graduate school)	197 (39.0%)	50 (28.4%)
Totals	505 (27.5%)	176 (9.6%)
Median education	College (1–3)	College (1–3)
No response=130 (6.9%)		
N=1,894		

among black churches.[43] For example, most of the slave preachers
labored in the fields or worked as artisans and blacksmiths, besides
carrying out their duties as preacher. Rev. Richard Allen, for example,
founded Mother Bethel A.M.E. Church while he worked successfully
in a variety of business enterprises. He continued to pursue his civic,
economic, and pastoral tasks even after he became bishop of his denomination. Tradition aside, most contemporary black clergy work
at other occupations out of financial need. Although many may
prefer to be full-time pastors, their churches often cannot pay them
an adequate salary or provide adequate medical and pension benefits.
Inevitably the frustrations, difficulties, and conflict of loyalties and
commitments exacts their toll on productivity.[44] Black churches
with pastors who have other full-time jobs are usually open only on
designated weekends, and members of such churches often do not
receive the kind of pastoral care and attention that full-time clerical
oversight can offer.

In response to the question of having a nonchurch occupation, 845
(55.2 percent) of 1,439 urban clergy respondents claimed that they
were full-time pastors and had no other occupations. About 586
(38.2 percent) reported that they had other jobs than church employment; the no response rate was 71 (4.6 percent). The category "other
church" referred to clergy who took denominational administrative
positions, while "other religion" meant jobs as chaplains in prisons,

PNBC	A.M.E.	A.M.E.Z.	C.M.E.	COGIC
8 (5.5%)	9 (3.6%)	15 (7.0%)	2 (1.2%)	31 (10.4%)
39 (27.4%)	35 (13.4%)	48 (23.0%)	33 (19.9%)	106 (35.7%)
21 (14.2%)	49 (18.7%)	49 (23.3%)	26 (15.4%)	71 (23.8%)
13 (9.2%)	43 (16.1%)	23 (10.9%)	21 (12.5%)	34 (11.4%)
63 (43.7%)	126 (48.2%)	75 (35.8%)	86 (51.0%)	56 (18.7%)
144 (7.8%)	262 (14.3%)	211 (11.5%)	168 (9.2%)	298 (16.2%)
College (1–3)	College (4)	College (1–3)	College (4)	College (1–3)

or with the military and police services. As table 9 on nonchurch occupations shows, close to 54.8 percent of the rural clergy held other jobs. This rural-urban difference probably reflected the more depressed economic conditions in rural areas. The table also shows that after the blue-collar category (15.4 percent), which included maintenance and farm work, most black clergy were employed in either the teaching profession (8.0 percent) or in white-collar occupations (8.3 percent) like sales, insurance, or business.

Clergy Benefits

In regard to benefits provided to clergy by their churches and denominations, 579 (38.6 percent) of the urban clergy replied that a residence was provided for the pastor, while the majority, 922 (60.2 percent) said that no residence was provided. Table 10 shows a similar situation with other benefits such as car allowance, health insurance, or pension plans. The majority of urban clergy, 927 (60.5 percent) claimed that no car allowance was provided, while 546 (35.7 percent) replied affirmatively. As table 10 on benefits for the clergy indicates, the major black denominations lacked adequate health insurance and pension plans for their clergy. Less than one-quarter of the urban churches (24.8 percent) provided health insurance and only 15.7 percent had provisions for pension and retirement. These results

Table 9: Nonchurch Occupations of Clergy

Occupations	Total	Urban	Rural
No other occupation	998 (52.7%)	845 (55.2%)	153 (42.2%)
Other church	22 (1.2%)	19 (1.2%)	3 (0.8%)
Other religions	6 (0.3%)	6 (0.4%)	0 (0.0%)
Professional/manager	57 (3.0%)	45 (2.9%)	12 (3.4%)
Teacher/professor	152 (8.0%)	121 (7.9%)	31 (8.7%)
Social worker/service	82 (4.3%)	58 (3.8%)	24 (6.5%)
Other white-collar (sales; insurance, etc.)	156 (8.3%)	120 (7.8%)	36 (10.0%)
Other service (fire; police; military)	19 (1.0%)	18 (1.2%)	1 (0.1%)
Other blue-collar (maintenance; farm)	291 (15.4%)	199 (13.0%)	92 (25.3%)
Unemployed	8 (0.4%)	8 (0.5%)	0 (0.0%)
No response	103 (5.4%)	71 (4.6%)	11 (3.0%)

Total N=1,894
Urban N=1,531
Rural N=363

indicate that the lack of basic benefits like adequate health and retirement plans has become a crisis area that requires the attention of black denominational leaders. The continued lack of such benefits in the black denominations is certain to make the ministry less attractive in the future. It also compounds the age and generational problems of succession in these denominations when black clergy must continue to work long past retirement age in order to survive economically. Better-trained apprentice clergy experience exaggerated frustration as their succession to desirable pulpits or other positions of challenge seem inordinately delayed. As will be shown, age is a significant variable in determining the attitudes of clergy toward areas of social change.

The data on the income and benefits of the black clergy sharply contradict the pervasive stereotype of the expensively dressed black preacher in an expensive automobile. While there are a few wealthy preachers, the reality is that the vast majority of black clergy do not have even the minimal incomes and benefits that most American

Table 10: Clergy Benefits

	Total	Urban	Rural
A. Residence for Pastor (Parsonage)			
Yes	649 (34.3%)	579 (37.8%)	70 (19.2%)
No	1,211 (63.9%)	922 (60.2%)	289 (79.5%)
No response	34 (1.8%)	30 (2.0%)	5 (1.3%)
B. Car Allowance			
Yes	629 (33.2%)	546 (35.7%)	83 (22.9%)
No	1,203 (63.5%)	927 (60.5%)	276 (76.0%)
No response	61 (3.3%)	58 (3.8%)	4 (1.2%)
C. Other Benefits			
No other benefits	1,040 (54.9%)	826 (54.0%)	214 (58.9%)
Health insurance (medical plan)	419 (22.1%)	379 (24.8%)	40 (11.0%)
Pension plan (retirement plan)	300 (15.8%)	240 (15.7%)	60 (16.4%)
Housing allowance	29 (1.4%)	11 (0.7%)	18 (5.0%)
Other (travel, books, etc.)	106 (5.6%)	75 (4.8%)	31 (8.7%)

Total *N*=1,894
Urban *N*=1,531
Rural *N*=363

workers expect and that most white clergy routinely enjoy. At the same time the majority of black pastors are not poor but generally fall within the middle-income range.

In regard to the number of clergy employed by black churches, our survey showed that 1,476 (77.9 percent) have only one paid pastor, 203 (10.7 percent) churches have two paid clergy, and 64 (3.4 percent) claimed three. Only 45 (2.3 percent) had four or more clergy on their staff. In other words, paid multiple staffed ministries were very rare among the black denominations, but many black churches had a number of unpaid assistants or trainees, especially in Pentecostal and Baptist churches.

Pastoral Responsibilities

To assess which of their pastoral responsibilities the black clergy considered most important to them, we asked the ministers to give a rank order of common pastoral duties which were listed on a separate

Table 11: Pastoral Responsibilities (Urban Clergy Only)

Q. Please list the following pastoral responsibilities in order of their importance to you: Civic leadership, teaching, preaching, leading worship, visitation and counseling, fund-raising, administration of the church, leadership
of groups within the church.

Pastoral Responsibility	Urban	Rank Order
1. Civic leadership	14 (0.9%)	Sixth (tie)
2. Teaching	358 (23.4%)	Second
3. Preaching	919 (60.0%)	First
4. Leading worship	22 (1.4%)	Fifth
5. Visitation and counseling	14 (0.9%)	Sixth (tie)
6. Fund-raising	3 (0.2%)	Seventh
7. Church administration	62 (4.0%)	Third
8. Leadership of groups within the church	38 (2.5%)	Fourth
9. No response	101 (6.7%)	

$N=1,531$

card handed to them. Only the clergy of black urban churches were
given this task to perform since it became clear from our rural survey
that the prevailing absentee pastorate in most black rural churches
would obviate a listing of common pastoral responsibilities. The
results in table 11 show that for the black urban clergy, the task
of preaching far outranks any other, 919 (60.0 percent). Second and
third places, respectively, included teaching, 358 (23.4 percent), and
church administration, 62 (4.0) percent. The least desired task among
pastoral duties was fund-raising, 3 (0.2 percent). This survey of pastoral responsibilities lends factual weight to the perceived importance of preaching in the ministry of black churches. As we pointed
out in the introduction, black churches have been far more charismatic than bureaucratic institutions in their general value orientation. A large amount of emphasis is placed upon the black minister's
personal charisma as reflected in his or her ability to preach. This
stress upon the central role of preaching in the Black Church underscores the continued importance of the oral tradition in black culture.[45]

It is remarkable that the institutional sector of the black churches
has been able to attract some of the most talented people to its ranks

over more than two hundred years, in spite of the often meager benefits and the precarious economic security that the call to ministry often entails. To recite the litany of famous black preachers and church members is to recall the African American journey toward freedom in black history.[46] It is also a testimony to the deep religious commitment that was always a corollary of that pilgrimage. In spite of its venerable tradition, whether the Black Church will continue to attract the most talented men and women and whether it will continue to flourish in an increasingly complex urban society are serious questions for the future. These questions are addressed in more detail in chapters 11 and 13. Here we have presented a demographic profile of the urban black clergy with some comparisons with rural clergy data and among the denominations themselves. We now turn to a demographic profile of urban black churches.

A Demographic Profile of Urban Black Churches

It is a common convention in the black community that the church is the oldest and most stable institution. Our survey of 2,150 black rural and urban churches once again confirms that wisdom. The churches in our survey range from one to two hundred years old. The oldest church is the rural Silver Bluff Baptist Church in Beech Island, South Carolina, which claimed a much disputed founding date of 1750 on its cornerstone.[47] Among the oldest urban black churches were Bethel A.M.E. Church in Baltimore (1785); First African Baptist Church in Savannah (1787); Springfield Baptist Church in Augusta, Georgia (1788); Mother Bethel A.M.E. Church in Philadelphia (1794); Mother Zion in New York City (1796). The median age for all black churches in the study is one hundred years. Close to half of the urban churches, six hundred (47.6 percent), have moved only once, and another three hundred (23.9 percent) have changed locations twice. In other words, about 71.5 percent of the black urban churches surveyed have moved fewer than two times and have remained remarkably stable. The average number of years in the present location is 46.5. Black urban churches that change locations frequently tend to be storefront churches usually found in the poorest sections of black communities where the rents are lowest and the population transient. Here, their tenure may range from a few months to several years, while their unstable nature makes them difficult to study.[48]

But like their more stable counterparts, the goal of many storefront churches and congregations is to move up to a regular church edifice in due time or to build one of their own.

The characteristic progression of building black churches is often from small meetings in private homes (usually the preacher's), to a rented hall or storefront, and finally to a regular church edifice. Table 12 shows the type of building used for worship by the black urban churches in our study. The distribution indicates that the vast majority of urban churches in the mainline black denominations, 1,326 (86.6 percent), worship in regular church edifices, 107 (7.0 percent) churches were storefronts, while 48 (3.1 percent) rented halls for their worship services from YMCAs or from other public or private institutions. Only 30 (2 percent) of the church groups were meeting in homes.

The type of building used for worship can also be used as an indicator of the class stratification among black churches. While the seven denominations include the broad range from abject poverty to upper middle class, much of their membership is composed of a coping middle-income strata, made up mostly of middle- and working-class people. Close to 88 percent of the churches surveyed worship in regular church buildings and about 12 percent use storefronts, rented halls, and individual homes. However, caution must be taken in regard to social class generalizations. From our field visits and observations, we know that even the most elite black churches tend to have some poor members on welfare in their congregations. Most of the large black churches tend to be the mixed type that Drake and Cayton described earlier, composed of the middle class, working class, and poor. Depending on the church and the denomination, underclass members may range from 5 to 33 percent of the congregation. The black Methodist denominations, A.M.E., A.M.E. Zion, and C.M.E., tend to be more solidly middle class and have the fewest storefront churches.[49] Most of the storefront churches in the study were either Baptist or Pentecostal (COGIC).

A question on the incorporation status of both rural and urban black churches was included in the survey because incorporation as a nonprofit institution in a state is required for participation in federal programs such as the national historic landmark preservation program. As historic institutions in local communities, many urban and rural black churches would probably be eligible for federal funds to preserve their buildings. Incorporation requires a constitution and

Table 12: Type of Building Used for Worship

Type of Building	Urban Sample
Home (private residence of a member)	30 (2.0%)
Hall (the basement or a social hall of a church or voluntary association)	48 (3.1%)
Storefront (any building that would traditionally house a commercial enterprise)	107 (7.0%)
Edifice (any type of building traditionally used to house a Christian church or synagogue)	1,326 (86.6%)
No response	20 (1.3%)
N=1,531	

Type of Building	Rural Sample
Home (private residence of a member)	4 (0.6%)
Wooden frame building	123 (19.9%)
Brick building	473 (76.6%)
No response	19 (2.9%)
N=619	

by-laws. Our survey found that 1,233 (80.5 percent) of the urban churches have incorporated and a little more than half, 354 (57.2 percent), of the rural churches have done so. It is probable that the lack of knowledge among church leadership about the benefits of incorporation accounts for the failure to utilize incorporation more widely. But the independent strain among some black churches contributes to the notion that the church is not the business of the state and that it should avoid the state's intrusion wherever possible.

In examining the incorporation status of black churches, our fieldwork discovered that relatively few institutional histories of local black churches have been written or preserved, but a number of these churches, urban ones in particular, have created their own archives and museums. For example, the First African Baptist Church of Savannah; the Springfield Baptist Church of Augusta; the Sixteenth Avenue Baptist Church in Birmingham, Alabama; the Abyssinian Baptist Church in New York; Mother Bethel A.M.E. Church in Philadelphia; and Bethel A.M.E. Church in Baltimore have extensive historical holdings in their archives. Some other smaller black churches have also attempted to collect fragments of their past history which they often publish in church bulletins or other literature to commemorate the anniversary of the founding of their church. A survey and catalog of these local historical materials and other yet undiscovered church archives is critical for the preservation of black institutional history. Unfortunately, among the major black denominations, only the Church of God in Christ has made some substantial progress toward creating a central archives and museum in its headquarters building in Memphis. To date, only COGIC and the C.M.E.s have established central headquarters, both in Memphis. The three Baptist denominations and the A.M.E. and A.M.E. Zion churches have not established denominational headquarters, although the National Baptist Convention, U.S.A., Inc., is in the process of establishing a world headquarters in Nashville. Perhaps as the major black denominations centralize and consolidate their denominational identities, the centralization of historical records and archives will follow in due course.

Membership Estimates of Black Urban Churches

An accurate assessment of total black church membership in the seven mainline black denominations is still a task for the future. Until all of the denominations are willing to participate in field membership surveys, any membership figures must be taken as tentative estimates. At the present time only some of the black Methodist denominations have taken part in partial surveys. In table A.1 in the appendix we have presented our best estimates of the total membership figures in each of the seven historic black denominations. The estimates are based on interviews with denominational leaders, deans and presidents of black theological seminaries, our survey results, and field experience in a large number of black churches. Just as the federal census has had continuous difficulty in their decennial undercount of the black population (a phenomenon that still continues), it will take time, experience, and the training of clergy and lay leaders in keeping records before an accurate assessment of black church membership can occur.

As was indicated in chapter 5 on rural churches, the survey asked for total church membership on the rolls. All of the respondents were

Table 13: Church and Sunday School Membership

	CHURCH MEMBERSHIP ON THE ROLLS		
	Total	Urban	Rural
Average total	390	479	171
Average adult men	70	90	30
Average adult women	199	240	88
Average total youth	101	120	54
Average male youth	29	35	16
Average female youth	77	91	38

	SUNDAY SCHOOL MEMBERSHIP ON THE ROLLS		
	Total	Urban	Rural
Average S.S. adult men	10	12	7
Average S.S. adult women	25	30	19
Average S.S. male youth	15	18	12
Average S.S. female youth	33	38	24

$N=2,150$
Urban $N=1,531$
Rural $N=619$

clergy of black churches and not laity. Although we were aware of the problem that many churches had not updated their membership lists, our major concern was to obtain a baseline figure of overall membership data that was presently available to the pastors, which would be a start in the more involved task of deriving more accurate figures. Monitoring the church attendance patterns of lay members in the black community is a far more complicated task than our research project could afford. Table 13 shows the results of church membership data in terms of the total sample and its urban and rural totals. The average total church membership was about 390 members on the rolls, while the average for urban church membership was 479 and 171 for rural churches. In our interviews with pastors and denominational leaders they estimated that about half or close to half of the members on their rolls were active church members, that is, participating more than occasionally. By dividing the membership on the rolls total in half, the average active black urban church membership is estimated to be 240, with an average of about eighty-five for rural churches. This estimate of 240 members in the average black urban church in our survey was found to be in agreement with the results of the study of twenty-one black churches in Washington, D.C., which reported a mean membership of 260.[50] The male-female ratio was between 2.5 to 3 adult women to 1 adult male. For youth membership, females held close to a 2-to-1 ratio.

The vast majority of black urban churches have Sunday school programs. Sunday school classes traditionally have been held for both adults and for youth. In our field visits and interviews it was found that black urban churches in the South as a region tend to have more active Sunday school classes for adult members. For example, the late Rev. Ralph Abernathy in Atlanta expressed strong feelings about Christian education for adults and hired seminary students from the Interdenominational Theological Center to teach a variety of classes in his Baptist church. At the Bethel A.M.E. Church in Baltimore, Rev. John Bryant has even established a Bible school for adults. However, these examples tend to be exceptional. The survey results of Sunday school membership on the rolls like the situation with church membership tended to be highly inflated. Most Sunday school programs in black urban churches tend to be smaller, attracting between ten to twenty adults and about twenty-five to fifty children, depending on the size of the church. Many of the urban church Sunday school programs also do not receive the kind of pastoral attention and leadership that they deserve. Quite a few Sunday school classes that we observed tended to be more babysitting situations for youth rather than challenging and stimulating sessions, a phenomenon that will be elaborated on in chapter 11. As Mays and Nicholson indicated in their study, black urban churches have had considerable difficulty in setting up viable Sunday school programs, many of which tended to put youth of all ages into one department.[51]

Table 14 presents the data on the size of churches in our total sample. The range included storefront and rural churches with a membership under fifty, to what is believed to be the largest black church in the United States, the Concord Baptist Church of Brooklyn, pastored by Rev. Dr. Gardner Taylor, with an estimated membership of 12,000 to 15,000. The Abyssinian Baptist Church in Harlem, which claimed to be the largest black church during the days of the

Table 14: Size of Black Churches

Size of Membership	Number of Churches (Total Sample)
1 to 99	564 (26.2%)
100 to 199	381 (17.7%)
200 to 599	576 (26.8%)
600 plus	349 (16.3%)
No response	280 (13.0%)
$N=2,150$	

clergyman-politician Representative Adam Clayton Powell, Jr., had an estimated membership of eight thousand. This shift in the location of the largest black church from Harlem to Brooklyn in the 1980s also reflects the demographic fact that the borough of Brooklyn presently has the largest black population in the nation. More than 80 percent of the churches sampled were under six hundred members, with the median size between two hundred to two hundred fifty members. The fact that close to one-fifth of black churches have more than six hundred members is a significant one. As we will show, the size of a black church is an important variable in the number and kinds of programs that churches carry on in their communities. The vast majority of creative and innovative programs are usually established by these larger black churches, partly because they have the resources and the staff required but also because they can attract more capable and talented clergy leadership.

Since black churches are also financial and economic institutions, receiving and disbursing money, we have placed most of our findings on the finances of black urban churches in chapter 9. But we have included table 15 on church income here as part of the profile of black urban churches. The income of these urban churches shows a range from under $5,000 for the year, 110 (7.2 percent), to those that have a budget of $50,000 and over, 513 (33.5 percent). The rural-urban comparisons were quite startling with 122 (19.7 percent) of the rural churches in the lowest income category and only 30 (4.8 percent) rural churches reporting annual incomes over $50,000, which illustrate again the depressed conditions of the rural economy and the diminishing demographic base. The median income for black urban

Table 15: Annual Church Income

Income Categories	Total	Urban	Rural
$1 to 4,999	232 (10.8%)	110 (7.2%)	122 (19.7%)
$5,000 to 9,999	224 (10.4%)	116 (7.6%)	108 (17.4%)
$10,000 to 14,999	212 (9.9%)	136 (8.9%)	76 (12.3%)
$15,000 to 24,999	242 (11.3%)	162 (10.6%)	80 (12.9%)
$25,000 to 49,999	342 (15.8%)	270 (17.6%)	72 (11.7%)
$50,000 and over	543 (25.3%)	513 (33.5%)	30 (4.8%)
No response	355 (16.5%)	224 (14.6%)	131 (21.2%)

Total N=2,150
Urban N=1,531
Rural N=619

churches in 1983 fell in the $15,000 to $25,000 category, while the median income for rural churches was between $9,000 to $15,000. The rural-urban church income data also underscore the importance of the urban environment for black upward mobility: that it is in the cities that the major economic changes would occur.

Black Urban Church Internal Maintenance Profile: Church Staff, Internal Organizations, and Facilities

The daily functioning and internal life of black churches is carried on by a variety of people connected to the church besides the pastor. In examining how black churches are able to maintain themselves, we asked about their staffing needs and what kinds of groups and organizations are found within black churches. Table 16 presents a summary of the type of people and jobs that comprise the usual staff of a church. About two-thirds of black urban churches, 1,025 (66.9 percent), reported that they had a church secretary, and 480 (31.4 percent) said no. The rural church figures were slightly higher, with 467 (75.4 percent) saying yes, and 145 (23.4 percent), no. About 547 (35.7 percent) of the urban churches had at least one secretary and 294 (19.2 percent) had two. Between 50.7 percent (rural) to 49.8 percent (urban) of the churches said that they paid their secretary a regular

Table 16: Church Staff Members

	Total	Urban	Rural
A. Secretary?			
Yes	1,492 (69.4%)	1,025 (66.9%)	467 (75.4%)
No	625 (29.1%)	480 (31.4%)	145 (23.4%)
No response	33 (1.5%)	26 (1.7%)	7 (1.1%)
1. How Many?			
One	792 (36.8%)	547 (35.7%)	245 (39.6%)
Two	438 (20.4%)	294 (19.2%)	144 (23.3%)
Three plus	223 (10.4%)	139 (9.1%)	83 (13.5%)
No response	697 (32.4%)	551 (36.0%)	146 (23.6%)
2. How Paid?			
Regular salary	1,076 (50.0%)	762 (49.8%)	314 (50.7%)
Some other way	347 (16.1%)	218 (14.2%)	129 (20.8%)
No response	727 (33.8%)	551 (36.0%)	176 (28.4%)
B. Custodian?			
Yes	1,550 (72.1%)	1,078 (70.4%)	472 (76.3%)
No	566 (26.3%)	425 (27.8%)	141 (22.7%)
No response	34 (1.6%)	28 (1.8%)	6 (1.0%)
1. How Many?			
One	1,086 (50.5%)	745 (48.7%)	341 (55.1%)
Two	281 (13.1%)	218 (14.2%)	63 (10.2%)
Three plus	156 (7.2%)	86 (5.6%)	70 (11.3%)
No response	627 (29.2%)	482 (31.5%)	145 (23.4%)
2. How Paid?			
Regular salary	1,202 (55.9%)	853 (55.7%)	349 (56.3%)
Some other way	274 (12.7%)	169 (11.0%)	105 (17.0%)
No response	673 (31.4%)	509 (33.3%)	165 (26.7%)
C. Musician?			
Yes	1,685 (78.4%)	1,211 (79.1%)	474 (76.6%)
No	441 (20.5%)	300 (19.6%)	141 (22.8%)
No response	22 (1.1%)	20 (1.3%)	4 (0.6%)
1. How Many?			
One	558 (26.0%)	367 (24.0%)	191 (30.9%)
Two	522 (24.3%)	377 (24.6%)	145 (23.4%)
Three plus	587 (27.2%)	449 (29.3%)	138 (22.3%)
No response	483 (22.5%)	338 (22.1%)	145 (23.4%)
2. How Paid?			
Regular salary	1,297 (60.4%)	930 (60.7%)	367 (59.3%)
Some other way	298 (13.9%)	212 (13.8%)	86 (13.9%)
No response	553 (25.7%)	389 (25.5%)	166 (26.8%)

Total $N=2,150$
Urban $N=1,531$
Rural $N=619$

salary. But 218 (14.2 percent) of the urban churches and 129 (20.8 percent) of the rural churches paid their church secretaries in some other way. The most usual way of paying staff who work in black churches that cannot afford to pay a regular salary is the use of "love offerings," a special offertory collection taken up in regular worship services for the church staff on periodic occasions. Some churches also paid their staff by giving them gifts. The percentages for custodians were similar to those of church secretaries. About 70 percent of both urban and rural churches have at least one custodian. However, it is interesting to note that in the vast majority of black churches, urban and rural, a paid musician on the church staff seems to have the highest priority. The percentages for musician tend to be slightly higher than either secretary or custodian: 1,211 (79.1 percent) of urban churches and 474 (76.6 percent) of rural churches claimed to have musicians and about 60 percent of both rural and urban churches said that they paid their musicians a regular salary. The paid musician is usually a pianist and/or organist, probably with the added responsibilities of directing at least one church choir. The higher priority given to having at least one paid musician on the staff is indicative of the very important role that music in general has in black churches, which we elaborate on in chapter 12.

In *Black Metropolis*, Drake and Cayton observed that the large, mixed type of black urban churches, and sometimes even smaller ones, generated a variety of subgroups in which lay members of similar social status, needs, and interests could interact with each other.[52] The internal life of most black churches is defined by small groups and auxiliaries who perform much of the work of organizing, planning, and executing the events and activities which distinguish each local congregation. Table 17 shows a list of the most common types of organizations and activities. Bible study groups, 1,413 (92.3 percent), and prayer meetings, 1,394 (91.0 percent), led the list of weekly activities for the majority of urban churches. Next came youth groups, 1,297 (84.7 percent), women's clubs, 1,039 (67.9 percent), lay groups to help plan and conduct regular worship services, 971 (63.4 percent), and men's clubs, 810 (52.9 percent). Finally, 593 (38.7 percent) churches had senior citizen's groups, and only 329 (21.5 percent) had young singles clubs. Almost all black churches have auxiliary organizations like Usher boards that routinize such details as seating the worshipers and collecting the offering. This rank order of groups gives a schematic view of where black urban churches have placed their priorities. After groups dealing specifically with the spiritual life—Bible study and prayer—youth groups rank high in importance, an indication of urban church priorities. However, the fact that young singles clubs were ranked much lower is indicative of the unique problems the contemporary black churches experience with this age group as we will elaborate in chapter 11.

Young adults (ages eighteen to thirty-five) seem to be the most problematic group for black churches. Our field observations confirmed that representatives of the young adult age groups tend to be conspicuously missing from many urban churches. There is a significant difference with rural churches that claim to have more than double the percentage of young singles clubs, three hundred (48.5 percent) of the rural sample. The rural-urban difference is explained by the fact that young adults in urban areas tend to have more distractions and greater competition for available time than those who live in rural areas. Besides a much narrower range of social opportunities, young adults in rural areas are also more subject to the mores and social controls of their families and communities. Going to church in rural areas is much more of a social habit and recreational outlet for the whole family than it is for urban families.

Depending upon size and denomination, black churches may also have other internal groups than those mentioned above. Usher boards provide trained ushers for the church services, and most churches have such offices as deacons, stewards, and trustees. Some Baptist and many Church of God in Christ congregations may also maintain a nurse corps, that is, women who are trained in basic first aid, and who stand by to provide assistance to worshipers who faint, or who may be overcome with religious ecstasy.

The proliferation of such internal service groups in black churches helps to spread the available quantums of status, dignity, and recognition among lay members. Black people who are largely invisible or who have only marginal identities in their workday roles in the larger society receive confirmation of their humanity and dignity through such church activities. As Drake and Cayton recognized, small organized groups of otherwise anonymous people within large black urban churches tend to ease the problems of class differentiation and anomie.

As part of the examination of the maintenance of the internal life of the urban churches, we asked about availability of facilities for social and recreational activities. According to table 18, slightly

Table 17: Internal Organizations and Activities

	Total	Urban	Rural
A. Men's Group?			
Yes	1,105 (51.4%)	810 (52.9%)	295 (47.7%)
No	990 (46.0%)	688 (44.9%)	302 (48.8%)
No response	55 (2.6%)	33 (2.2%)	22 (3.6%)
B. Women's Group?			
Yes	1,435 (66.7%)	1,039 (67.9%)	396 (64.0%)
No	676 (31.4%)	462 (30.2%)	214 (34.6%)
No response	39 (1.8%)	30 (2.0%)	9 (1.5%)
C. Senior Citizens Group?			
Yes	820 (38.1%)	593 (38.7%)	227 (36.7%)
No	1,266 (58.9%)	892 (58.3%)	374 (60.4%)
No response	64 (3.0%)	46 (3.0%)	18 (2.9%)
D. Youth Group?			
Yes	1,776 (82.6%)	1,297 (84.7%)	479 (77.4%)
No	344 (16.0%)	219 (14.3%)	125 (20.2%)
No response	30 (1.4%)	15 (1.0%)	15 (2.4%)
E. Lay Group to Help Plan and Conduct Regular Worship Services?			
Yes	1,342 (64.0%)	971 (63.4%)	371 (59.9%)
No	755 (35.1%)	537 (35.1%)	218 (35.2%)
No response	53 (2.5%)	23 (1.5%)	30 (4.8%)
F. Young Singles Group?			
Yes	629 (29.3%)	329 (21.5%)	300 (48.5%)
No	1,469 (68.3%)	1,162 (75.9%)	307 (49.6%)
No response	52 (2.4%)	40 (2.6%)	12 (1.9%)
G. Bible Study Group? (Urban only)			
Yes		1,413 (92.3%)	
No		108 (7.0%)	
No response		10 (0.7%)	
H. Prayer Meeting? (Urban only)			
Yes		1,394 (91.0%)	
No		122 (8.0%)	
No response		15 (1.0%)	
I. Midweek Services for Prayer and Bible Study (Rural only)			
Yes			421 (68.0%)
No			187 (30.2%)
No response			11 (1.8%)

Total *N*=2,150
Urban *N*=1,531
Rural *N*=619

Table 18: Church Facilities for Social and Recreational Activities

	Total	Urban	Rural
A. Fellowship Hall?			
Yes	1,110 (51.6%)	822 (53.7%)	288 (46.5%)
No	993 (46.2%)	677 (44.2%)	316 (51.1%)
No response	47 (2.2%)	32 (2.1%)	15 (2.4%)
B. Gymnasium?			
Yes	149 (6.9%)	140 (9.1%)	9 (1.5%)
No	1,954 (90.9%)	1,362 (89.0%)	592 (95.6%)
No response	47 (2.2%)	29 (1.9%)	18 (2.9%)
C. Outdoor Basketball Courts?			
Yes	249 (11.6%)	219 (14.3%)	30 (4.9%)
No	1,866 (86.8%)	1,281 (83.7%)	585 (94.5%)
No response	35 (1.6%)	31 (2.0%)	4 (0.6%)
D. Athletic Program?			
Yes	613 (28.5%)	548 (35.8%)	65 (10.5%)
No	1,493 (69.4%)	947 (61.9%)	546 (88.2%)
No response	44 (2.0%)	36 (2.4%)	8 (1.3%)

Total N=2,150
Urban N=1,531
Rural N=619

more than half of the urban churches, 822 (53.7 percent), had a fellowship or social hall; only 288 (46.5 percent) of the rural churches had such facilities. Although more than 80 percent of both urban and rural churches claimed to have youth groups in their churches, our survey discovered that very few of these churches have built recreational facilities for their young people. Only 140 (9.1 percent) urban churches had a gymnasium available, as did nine (1.5 percent) rural churches. The situation with outdoor basketball courts was only slightly better since about 219 (14.3 percent) urban churches and thirty (4.9 percent) rural churches had them. In spite of the lack of facilities of their own, 548 (35.8 percent) urban churches and sixty-five (10.5 percent) rural churches sponsored athletic programs.

Beyond the concern for maintaining their own internal spiritual nurture and fellowship, black churches have an extensive history of involvement in their local communities. What is the extent of out-reach to the community and in what kinds of programs do today's black urban churches involve themselves? We turn next to the matter of community outreach.

Black Urban Churches and Community Outreach Programs

In this section we will briefly present some of our data on the com-munity outreach programs that black churches have sponsored. The topic of outreach and activism in the community involves political and economic questions and dimensions we will examine in more detail in chapters 8 and 9. In both of these chapters we will relate our findings to the contemporary participation of black churches in the political and economic spheres.

In examining community outreach programs we asked, "Has your church cooperated with social agencies or other nonchurch programs in dealing with community problems?" The results of table 19 shows that 1,459 (67.9 percent) of the total sample of black churches re-sponded affirmatively, while 596 (27.7 percent) said no. For urban churches 1,086 (70.9 percent) answered yes and 392 (25.6 percent) responded negatively, while the results for rural churches were 373 (60.3 percent) positive and 204 (33.0 percent) negative. Black churches and clergy, on the whole, were much more supportive of community outreach programs, thus undermining once more the stereotype of the Black Church as a withdrawn, insular, and privat-ized institution. As table 19 indicates, both urban and rural black churches cooperated with a wide variety of social agencies and pro-grams that focused on problems within the African American com-munity and in the larger society. As an overall generalization, the data show that black urban churches are far more active than rural ones in cooperating with social agencies and in dealing with commu-nity problems. The most popular nonchurch agencies were the civil rights organizations with which 625 (40.8 percent) of the urban churches and 310 (50.1 percent) of the rural churches indicated coop-eration. The slightly higher rural rate of cooperation with civil rights groups is due to the fact that there is a paucity of social agencies in rural areas, and as we mentioned previously, many southern rural churches were heavily involved in the civil rights movement. This high rate of cooperation between black churches and the major civil

Table 19: Community Outreach: Cooperation with Social Agencies and Nonchurch Programs

A. Has your church cooperated with social agencies and other nonchurch programs in dealing with community problems?

	Total	Urban	Rural
Yes	1,459 (67.9%)	1,086 (70.9%)	373 (60.3%)
No	596 (27.7%)	392 (25.6%)	204 (33.0%)
No response	95 (4.4%)	53 (3.5%)	42 (6.8%)

B. If yes, which agencies and programs? Possible to list more than one.

	Total	Urban	Rural
1. Civil rights organizations (NAACP, SCLC, etc.)	935 (43.5%)	625 (40.8%)	310 (50.1%)
2. Employment agencies and problems	114 (5.3%)	107 (7.0%)	7 (1.1%)
3. Day-care centers and nurseries	46 (2.1%)	41 (2.7%)	5 (0.8%)
4. Drug and alcohol abuse agencies and programs	95 (4.4%)	89 (5.8%)	6 (1.0%)
5. Senior citizen or elderly agencies and programs	163 (7.6%)	141 (9.2%)	22 (3.6%)
6. Welfare rights and housing problems	157 (7.3%)	153 (10.0%)	4 (0.6%)
7. Police/community relations (crime, delinquency, minority recruitment, etc.)	162 (7.5%)	158 (10.3%)	4 (0.6%)
8. Food programs and clothing banks (breakfast programs, clothing for the poor, etc.)	146 (6.8%)	128 (8.4%)	18 (2.9%)
9. Tutoring and educational programs (reading, unwed mothers, legal rights, etc.)	111 (5.2%)	101 (6.6%)	10 (1.6%)
10. Health related agencies and problems (hospitals, Red Cross, sickle cell, etc.)	177 (8.2%)	148 (9.7%)	29 (4.7%)
11. Local community crisis events (school desegregation, local demonstrations, etc.)	258 (12.0%)	249 (16.3%)	35 (5.7%)
12. Emergency land fund	2 (0.1%)	0 (0.0%)	2 (0.3%)
13. Youth agencies (YM/YWCA, Scouts, etc.)	404 (18.8%)	367 (23.4%)	37 (6.0%)
14. Other	159 (8.0%)	138 (9.8%)	21 (3.6%)
15. No—No cooperation	588 (29.5%)	387 (27.5%)	201 (34.4%)
No response	159 (7.4%)	124 (8.1%)	35 (6.7%)

Total N=2,150
Urban N=1,531
Rural N=619

rights organizations underscores the fact that black churches have been a key support system for these groups. Besides civil rights, black urban churches were also active in participating with youth agencies like the Scouts and YM/YWCA groups, 367 (23.4 percent); local community crisis events like school desegregation, local demonstrations, and closing of hospitals, 249 (16.3 percent); welfare rights and housing, 153 (10 percent); and police/community relations issues like crime and delinquency, recruitment of minorities, and police brutality, 158 (10.3 percent). Overall, the results of our survey were similar to the findings of Brown and Walters in Washington, D.C., where they found that 88.2 percent of the clergy replied that their churches had provided outreach services or worked in the local community. However, only 52.4 percent of the churches in their sample had cooperated with secular social agencies or organizations, compared to our rate of 70.9 percent for black urban churches.[53] The difference is explained by our focus on the seven mainline black denominations.

As part of our examination of community outreach, we inquired whether black urban churches continued the traditional historic practice of permitting nonchurch community groups to use the church building as a place for meetings and/or special programs. The data in table 20 indicate that the practice still continues to some extent, particularly in black urban churches, 673 (44.0 percent), and to a lesser degree in rural churches, 171 (27.6 percent). At one time black churches were the only places where black nonchurch groups could hold a meeting or special event. That is no longer true since more options are available even in the rural South since the civil rights period. There is, however, a rural-urban difference in the types of groups allowed to use the church building. For black urban churches, civic associations like block associations, neighborhood improvement groups, citizens' patrols, and community organizations, 471 (30.7 percent) led the way, while for rural churches, civil rights groups, 122 (19.7 percent), were first. Civil rights groups came in second for black urban churches, 289 (18.8 percent), while the fraternal orders and lodges placed second for rural churches, 52 (8.4 percent). These fraternal orders and lodges, the Masons and Elks, and their female counterpart, the Order of the Eastern Star, seem to represent a declining phenomenon in black communities. At one time most of the members of the black elite in a town or city belonged to the lodges and they played a very important economic and

Table 20: Use of Church Building by Nonchurch Groups

Q. Is the church building used by nonchurch organizations as a meeting place for special programs?

	Total	Urban	Rural
Yes	844 (39.3%)	673 (44.0%)	171 (27.6%)
No	1,221 (56.7%)	801 (52.3%)	420 (67.9%)
No Response	85 (4.0%)	57 (3.7%)	28 (4.5%)

Q. If yes, please list the organizations (more than one allowed, up to 3).

Organizations	Total	Urban	Rural
1. Civil rights organizations (NAACP, SCLC, etc.)	411 (19.1%)	289 (18.8%)	122 (19.7%)
2. Civic associations (block associations, neighborhood groups, citizens patrol, etc.)	542 (25.2%)	471 (30.7%)	71 (11.5%)
3. Political organizations (political meetings and rallies)	138 (6.4%)	114 (7.4%)	24 (3.9%)
4. Fraternal orders, lodges, fraternity and sorority groups	161 (7.5%)	109 (7.1%)	52 (8.4%)
5. Boy and Girl Scout troops, 4-H clubs, etc.	59 (2.7%)	57 (3.7%)	2 (0.3%)
6. Schools and educational groups	92 (4.3%)	74 (4.8%)	18 (2.9%)
7. Professional group meetings (teachers, social workers, etc.)	49 (2.3%)	45 (2.5%)	4 (0.6%)
8. Labor group meetings (labor unions, etc.)	41 (1.9%)	33 (2.2%)	8 (1.3%)
9. Other	190 (8.8%)	153 (7.1%)	37 (6.0%)

Total $N=2,150$
Urban $N=1,531$
Rural $N=619$

---

service role. But many members of the contemporary college educated, black middle class have preferred to join the national black fraternity and sorority groups, thus leaving an aging and declining sector of secret societies behind; a parallel phenomenon has also occurred among whites. The urban churches which reported that the orders, lodges, and fraternity and sorority groups which used the church building for their meetings numbered 109 (7.1 percent). In regard to political meetings, urban churches, 114 (7.4 percent), were more active than rural churches, 24 (3.9 percent).

Our survey gathered the only known data about the participation of black churches in government-funded programs (federal, state, and city). Although the numbers were not large, the information is important because some politicians and government bureaucrats, as well as a growing number of black urban clergy, have begun to see black churches as important bases for the delivery of some government-related social services, educational, food, and housing programs. More concrete examples of this tendency will be given in chapters 8 and 9. According to table 21, 138 (6.4 percent) of all black churches have participated in government funded programs, including 121 (7.9 percent) urban churches and 17 (2.7 percent) rural churches. For the black urban churches the top four government funded programs were Day-care centers, 60 (3.9 percent); food programs like the federal breakfast/lunch programs, 47 (3.1 percent); Headstart programs, 30 (2.0 percent); and Federal Housing, 32 (2.1 percent). Rural churches participated only in the Headstart, 8 (1.4 percent), and Day-care center programs, 11 (1.8 percent). It is important to note that all of our survey data were collected before the twin crises of hunger and homelessness in the United States became major issues during the waning years of the Reagan administration. The data now would probably show a larger increase in participation by black churches in government programs. Many black churches, especially those in poor neighborhoods, became distribution points for the surplus cheese program, and a number of others have provided shelters for the homeless or set up soup kitchens. The participation of black churches in government funded programs is fraught with both opportunities and problems. On the one hand, black churches are a natural way of channeling federal, state, and city government resources and services into black communities because they remain one of the few stable social institutions with a broad base of support from the community. As we will show, some black church groups have brought about important changes in their surrounding neighborhoods through the use of government funds and programs. On the other hand, black clergy and churches that participate in government programs also face the dilemma of losing their prophetic voice; the proverbial problem of "biting the hand that feeds you" becomes a real one.

Table 21: Church Participation in Government-Funded Programs

Q. Does your church participate in any governmental program for which it receives funding?

	Total	Urban	Rural
Yes	138 (6.4%)	121 (7.9%)	17 (2.7%)
No	1,975 (93.5%)	1,386 (90.5%)	589 (95.2%)
No response	37 (1.7%)	24 (1.6%)	13 (2.1%)

Q. If yes, list the programs (can list more than one, up to four).

Government-funded Programs	Total	Urban	Rural
1. Headstart programs	38 (1.8%)	30 (2.0%)	8 (1.3%)
2. Food programs (breakfast, lunch, etc.)	47 (2.2%)	47 (3.1%)	0 (0.0%)
3. CETA (job training)	12 (0.6%)	10 (0.7%)	2 (0.3%)
4. Federal housing	40 (1.9%)	32 (2.1%)	8 (1.4%)
5. Day-care center	71 (3.3%)	60 (3.9%)	11 (1.8%)
6. Other educational programs	12 (0.6%)	12 (0.8%)	0 (0.0%)
7. Other government-funded programs	24 (1.1%)	20 (1.3%)	4 (0.6%)

Total N=2,150
Urban N=1,531
Rural N=619

As a final item of community outreach, we also examined the attempts of black churches to reach out beyond themselves by participating in projects that required cooperation with churches of other denominations. Table 22 on interdenominational cooperation shows that 1,280 (59.5 percent) of all black churches participated in interdenominational projects, with 923 (60.3 percent) of the urban churches and 357 (57.7 percent) of rural churches taking part. Slightly more than one-third of the churches, 776 (36.1 percent), responded negatively. The data indicated that two of the top three programs were the traditional types of interdenominational cooperation among black urban and rural churches such as fellowship with other churches and pulpit exchanges, 572 (26.8 percent), and evangelism programs (such as crusades and revivals) with other churches,

Table 22: Interdenominational Cooperation by Black Churches

Q. Has your church participated in any ongoing projects that required cooperation with churches of other denominations in the past year?

	Total	Urban	Rural
Yes	1,280 (59.5%)	923 (60.3%)	357 (57.7%)
No	776 (36.1%)	540 (35.3%)	236 (38.1%)
No response	94 (4.4%)	68 (4.4%)	26 (4.2%)

Q. If yes, briefly describe the programs.

Type of Program	Total	Urban	Rural
1. Fellowship with other churches, pulpit exchanges, etc.	572 (26.8%)	420 (27.2%)	152 (24.6%)
2. Evangelism	303 (14.2%)	164 (10.7%)	139 (22.5%)
3. Educational programs (Bible classes, vacation Bible school, etc.)	29 (1.3%)	20 (1.3%)	9 (1.4%)
4. Community service oriented programs (tutoring, day care, elderly, youth, etc.)	123 (5.7%)	106 (6.9%)	17 (2.7%)
5. Social problem oriented programs (drug and alcohol abuse, crime, welfare, housing, etc.)	32 (1.5%)	30 (2.0%)	2 (0.3%)
6. Interracial cooperation with white churches	120 (5.6%)	110 (7.2%)	10 (1.7%)
7. Other	70 (3.4%)	49 (3.2%)	21 (3.4%)
8. No—no cooperation	741 (34.9%)	520 (34.0%)	221 (35.7%)
No response	160 (6.6%)	112 (7.5%)	48 (7.7%)

Total N=2,150
Urban N=1,531
Rural N=619

303 (14.2 percent). Interdenominationally sponsored community
service-oriented programs (such as tutoring, day care, senior citizens,
youth, counseling, and voter registration drives) ranked third with
123 (5.7 percent) churches.

As mentioned in the previous chapter, the de facto segregation of American society has resulted in very little interracial cooperation with white churches, and table 22 shows that only 120 (5.6 percent) of the total 2,150 black churches took part, with 110 (7.2 percent) black urban churches and 10 (1.7 percent) rural churches. The urban-rural difference is partly explained by the fact that black urban clergy have more opportunities to participate in interracial church councils or ministerial alliances in their areas. But rural areas in the South have also exhibited high degrees of racial segregation as evidenced by a long history of lynchings and racial violence, especially during the civil rights era.[54] Lower-class whites have generally felt threatened by the gains of lower-class blacks. It is significant to note that less than 10 percent of all black churches have taken part in any kind of interracial cooperation with white churches. Racial segregation in American society is most clearly seen in religion.

Conclusion: Present Trends and the Future of Black Urban Churches

The major focus of this chapter has been twofold: to provide a summary overview of the impact of urbanization on black churches and a largely rural black migrant population, and to present a descriptive profile of black urban clergy and their churches from the data gathered through our national survey. As we mentioned in the previous chapter, the studies of black urban churches since the 1950s have consisted largely of detailed ethnographic and sociological studies of one or a few congregations, or focused on one issue such as civil rights militancy.[55] Only Brown and Walters's study of 21 black urban churches in Washington, D.C., paralleled our concerns, but even their study was limited to one city.[56] A much broader portrait of black clergy and churches of the mainline black denominations nation-wide, especially a baseline statistical profile, was missing. We have attempted to fill that gap by a five-year survey consisting of face-to-face interviews with the pastors of 2,150 black urban and rural churches. Other aspects of our survey data that are relevant to the topics of black consciousness, politics, economics, women, youth, and music will be presented in the following chapters. For the remainder of this chapter we will discuss some present trends which may have an impact upon the future of black urban churches.

Black urban churches and the mainline black denominations have maintained themselves fairly well since the 1950s. None of the mainline black denominations have experienced the kind of severe decline in membership that has affected some mainline white denominations like the Disciples of Christ and the United Presbyterian Church, U.S.A., which have lost about 40 and 30 percent of their members, respectively.[57] Some black denominations have grown in membership, with the Church of God in Christ showing the most rapid growth from about 800 churches to over 10,000 churches since 1950.[58] The African Methodist Episcopal Church has also experienced some spurts of church growth in some Episcopal districts and in some individual churches with most of this growth stemming from the influence of a neo-Pentecostal or charismatic movement among some A.M.E. churches, which is described more fully in chapter 13. Other black denominations like the Christian Methodist Episcopal Church and the African Methodist Episcopal Zion Church have neither grown nor declined but they have reached a static state and are concerned about impending decline, which may be one of the motivating forces for their serious talks and plans in the mid-1980s about merger.[59] Whether these two denominations will merge remains to be seen since there have been other attempts at union in black religious history which have not succeeded.[60] There have also been overtures for union between the National Baptist Convention, U.S.A., Inc., and the Progressive National Baptist Convention following a change in the leadership of the incorporated convention and this may have removed some of the obstacles that precipitated the splinter movement that became the Progressive Baptists.[61] The individualism of the black Baptist churches, partly due to the principal of congregational autonomy, has made it very difficult to make any assessment of church growth or decline for Baptist denominations.

For many black urban churches, residential segregation has meant that their locations have been relatively constant, almost to the point of permanence.[62] While white churches and synagogues have moved to follow their members to the suburbs, the vast majority of black urban churches have remained in the central cities. The creation of new black suburban housing areas, especially around cities like Atlanta, Nashville, Philadelphia, and Washington, D.C., will have some implications for the relocation of some of these black churches and the development of new churches.[63] For example, demographic studies have recently shown that about 48 percent of the 570,000 black residents of Atlanta and the seven contiguous counties now live outside the city limits, mostly in DeKalb and the southern part of Fulton counties.[64] Some of the new black suburban churches in areas like Fort Washington, just outside of Washington, D.C., have shown rapid growth.[65] However, the creation of predominantly black suburbs for the black middle class will also mean that residential segregation will continue to be a major part of the fabric of American life. In spite of the fair housing laws, most African Americans still cannot live where they want to, even when they can afford it. Instead, the assigned "place" is still a prominent feature of black life in the United States.[66]

In the mid-1950s E. Franklin Frazier, along with other scholars, noted a tendency of upwardly mobile African Americans to become members of churches in white denominations like the Episcopal Church, partly out of the effort to confirm their new status.[67] While such inclinations were never of massive proportions, since the resurgence of black consciousness and black pride in the late 1960s the need to change religious identity by switching to white churches by the black middle class has dwindled to insignificance. As a matter of fact, the search for roots and for a black historical heritage has often led to a renewed appreciation of the multiple and significant roles that black churches have played in the security of black identity, and there is no evidence that any of the major white denominations, except the Roman Catholic Church, have experienced an appreciable surge in black membership.[68] Since 1985 black Roman Catholics have grown from 990,000 to close to 2 million members, with the gains coming largely from Caribbean immigrants and upwardly mobile African Americans seeking parochial educational alternatives to urban public school systems.[69] But even the Roman Catholic Church has felt the effects of the resurgence of black consciousness among its black bishops, priests, nuns, and laity.[70] Members of the black middle class tend to join the elite congregations of the historic black denominations. Many of these elite churches tend to be very large with several thousand members, thus providing a spectrum of class and social options for the new affiliates. They also sponsor a wide range of social service projects in the community and are politically active. Furthermore, these black elite churches have often developed a sizable commuter population of middle-class people who usually drive in from the suburbs or from metropolitan areas away from the central city; they no longer live in the neighborhood of the church.

The majority of black urban churches are still strong, vibrant institutions and they have continued to attract and to hold the loyalty of a significant sector of the national black community. Gallup Poll data indicate that about 78 percent of the black population in 1987 were "churched," that is, claiming church membership and attending church within the last six months.[71] In their 1987 study of *American Mainline Religion,* Roof and McKinney have pointed to the "relatively strong socioreligious group ties" in the black community: "Black Protestants attend worship services more than any other group except white conservative Protestants: 56 percent are regular attenders and 25 percent are occasional attenders. . . . Generally blacks have a high level of denominational commitment, much higher in fact than most other groups."[72]

While black churches are still the central institutions in their communities, some cracks have begun to appear at the edges of the religious stronghold. Despite the universal claims of the Black Church for the whole black community, there has always been a small sector of unchurched black people. Mostly they were younger black males or other maverick types determined to resist the powerful social control of black churches in the small rural towns and in urban areas. They were given various names by past studies of black communities: Du Bois called them "criminal and vicious classes" in *The Philadelphia Negro;* Drake and Cayton referred to them as "the Shadies" and the "Non-Church Centered Respectables" in *Black Metropolis.* Liebow described them as "the street corner men" in *Talley's Corner.* In black folk terminology, they were simply known as "the low life," those who frequented the bars and clubs and listened to the "Devil's music."[73] Recent studies have begun to show a significant growth among young, unchurched blacks, especially males in northern urban areas.[74] From his reanalysis of the April 1978 Gallup study of "The Unchurched American" and the data of other studies, Hart Nelsen has found that "race," "residence," and "region" were among the most significant variables in determining the degree to which African Americans were churched or unchurched. Using the definition of "churched" mentioned earlier, Nelsen's study found that black people residing in rural areas of the South, or "nonmetropolitan South," had both the highest rates of being churched (85.2 percent) compared to whites (48.8 percent) and the strongest degree of religious socialization. While African Americans in the northern and western urban areas—the "non-South metropolitan"—had the lowest rates of being churched, especially in

central cities (28.4 percent). Black residents in the urban areas of
the South, or "metropolitan South" had rates between 45.5 to 50
percent of being churched. Nelsen found no significant differences
for education, occupation, or income. Because of the small size of the
sample of black respondents ($N=182$) in the Gallup survey, questions
can be raised with regard to how representative the sample is, and the
method of sampling.[75] We will return to a discussion of this trend
of unchurched black Americans and consider the implications of
this phenomenon in relation to the future of black churches in chapter 11.

In spite of this trend of a small but growing population of unchurched blacks, it is a bit premature to conclude as Frazier, Mukenge, and Nelsen have that black churches in the urban environment have lost their major communal functions in politics,
economics, education, and culture.[76] In other words, their argument
is that differentiation has gone so far that religion has become a privatized matter and the Black Church has withdrawn into a sphere of
religiosity. As Nelsen has written, "With the migration of blacks to
the metropolitan area, the black church is subject to differentiation,
to increasingly being coupled with religious motivation rather than
being identified with meeting the whole panoply of black needs. Increasingly, religion becomes a private matter, with the black church
not tied to meeting the many functions it once served."[77] In contrast
to this privatization scenario and view of complete differentiation,
we will point out in later chapters that there are far more interactions
and interrelationships between black churches and the spheres of
secular life such as politics and economics so that only a partial
differentiation has taken place. Many black churches have not yet
given up their communal functions and withdrawn from the "whole
panoply of black needs." In fact, a holistic view of the ministry of the
Black Church, of being involved with all aspects of life, has been one
of the continuing major attractions for many black clergy throughout
history; the holistic view represents a major historical strand among
black churches that calls for continuous prophetic involvement in all
phases of black communal life.[78] With the growing specialization of
professions, ministry in black churches, both urban and rural, is one
of the few vocations that has legitimated care and concern for all the
needs in the black community.

Besides missing this theological self-understanding of the task of
ministry in black churches, one of the major problems of the privati-

zation scenario is that it tends to ignore the continuous and insidious role that racism in American society has played and the communal bonding effects that racism has stimulated in black communities. As one of the major bulwarks and voices against racism, black churches and clergy have played and will continue to play a far more communal role than they have been given credit for. The privatization scenario tends to project onto blacks the results of social processes from white ethnic groups, some of which may be relevant, but almost all have to be reinterpreted because of the racial factor. For example, while many white churches have tended to withdraw from an active role in the political and economic scene because there are strong, competing institutions that can fulfill those functions, in most urban and rural black communities there is a paucity of strong institutional alternatives. In many cases black churches have had to help create and nurture these institutions like banks, insurance companies, low-income housing projects, employment training centers, or political vehicles like the major civil rights organizations. They still do so, as we will show in later chapters. Most black people do not feel a sense of ownership or of partnership with the major American political parties, even with the Democratic party, as the Jackson candidacy in 1988 has shown; nor do they have a sense of ownership of a significant sector of American business enterprises, or the American economy. There may come a time when racial discrimination is completely eradicated in American society and African Americans are treated fairly and justly like any other American. When that happens black churches and clergy may no longer feel compelled to involve themselves in all aspects of black life. But that point has not yet been reached in the late twentieth century. As Roof and McKinney have correctly argued,

> With respect to membership in a church group—perhaps the best measure of communal bonds—they (Black Protestants) exceed all the other families. They are the only family for which more than one-half claim involvement in a church group. Strong bonds to church and community have served to buffer the trends toward greater religious individualism dominant in the society.[79]

Just as social class factors cannot be adequately applied to black people without taking into account their "definition of the situation," as Billingsley cogently argued, a realistic assessment of the black religious situation must also take into account what black churches and black clergy have been doing and are doing.[80] To dismiss this side of the ledger is to miss more than half of the picture. We contend that the relationships between black churches and clergy and other aspects of black institutional life are far more interrelated and finely woven together—and more dynamic—than most social scientists have been willing to concede. The present picture of black urban churches is a complicated, mixed picture of some effects of privatization among unchurched sectors of the black population, and the withdrawal of some black churches into a sphere of personal piety and religiosity; but there are also numerous signs of a continuing tradition of activism and involvement in the political, economic, educational, and cultural aspects of black life among the majority of black clergy and churches. Much of the recent upsurge in activism by black churches can be traced to the legacy of the civil rights movement and the period of black pride and black power that followed it. We turn now to an examination of the impact that the black consciousness movement of the late 1960s and early 1970s has had upon black clergy and churches.

7 The New Black Revolution: The Black Consciousness Movement and the Black Church

You know yourselves that we have been a people who hated our African characteristics. We hated our head, we hated the shape of our nose—we wanted one of those long, dog-like noses, you know. Yeah. We hated the color of our skin. We hated the blood of Africa that was in our veins. And in hating our features and our skin and our blood, why, we had to end up hating ourselves. . . . Our color became to us a chain. We felt that it was holding us back. Our color became to us like a prison which we felt was keeping us confined . . . and it became hateful to us. It made us feel inferior, it made us feel inadequate. It made us feel helpless. And when we fell victims to this feeling of inadequacy or inferiority or helplessness, we turned to somebody else to show us the way.[*]

Probably the most powerful force, however, in breaking down the barriers of segregation is the determination of the Negro himself. . . . Once plagued with a tragic sense of inferiority, resulting from the crippling effects of slavery and segregation, the Negro has now been driven to reevaluate himself. . . . He has come to feel that he is somebody. And with this new sense of "somebodiness" and self-respect, a new Negro has emerged with a new determination to achieve freedom and human dignity whatever the cost might be.[**]

---

[*]Malcolm X, "Africa and Self-Hate," excerpt of speech delivered in the Audubon Ballroom, December 1964, in *Malcolm X on Afro-American History*, edited by George Breitman, p. 74; also in *Malcolm X Speaks*, edited by George Breitman, pp. 184–85.

[**]Martin Luther King, Jr., "The Case Against Tokenism," *New York Times Magazine* (August 5, 1962), p. 11ff.; reprinted in James M. Washington, editor, *A Testament of Hope: The Essential Writings of Martin Luther King, Jr.*, p. 108.

The 1934 national study of "The Negro's Church," as Mays and Nicholson's work was entitled, was noteworthy for its conservative characterization of Negro pastors and churches. In the half century since that study was conducted, the African American community has undergone a veritable revolution—a revolution in consciousness that encompasses all black institutions, including the Black Church.

The antecedents of the black consciousness movement were several. The first of these was the very process of urbanization, and its by-products. With the concentration of large numbers of black people in the cities came a greater awareness of African Americans as a distinct social group. Through the labor movement, urban black workers were exposed to the protest tactics and possibilities of organizing for social change. Black churches grew in size, establishing relationships with one another through citywide and later statewide ministerial alliances. In addition to this vital communication network, new modes of communication—radio, telephones, movies, and later television—presented themselves. Each of these factors contributed to group identity.[1] The sense of solidarity was then further reinforced by the experiences African Americans had abroad during the World Wars, by the political independence movements in Africa, and by the 1954 Supreme Court decision outlawing school segregation.

The most potent catalyst for the black consciousness movement, however, was the civil rights movement led by Martin Luther King, Jr., beginning with the Montgomery bus boycott in 1955. From the beginning, the civil rights movement was anchored in the Black Church, organized by both activist black ministers and laity, and supported financially by black church members. Even secular civil rights groups such as CORE (Congress of Racial Equality) and SNCC (Student Nonviolent Coordinating Committee) were influenced by black church culture; James Farmer of CORE was the son of a clergyman, and John Lewis of SNCC was a seminary student. Thus, as Aldon Morris has written, it was the Black Church which provided an "ideological framework through which passive attitudes were transformed into a collective consciousness supportive of collective action."[2] The Black Church was not unanimous in its affirmation of solidarity and social activism, however, and in dialectical fashion it became a beneficiary of the black consciousness movement it had helped to spawn.

The term revolution is usually reserved for political eruptions which involve the taking over of power by a new group of people and the institutionalization of a new set of principles to reorient a society.[3] Revolutions also signal a sharp break with the status quo ante, with old ways of thinking and doing. C. Vann Woodward dismisses as a revolution any movement "that derives overt support from the established government, that strives to realize rather than destroy traditional values, that seeks to join rather than overthrow the social order."[4] Nevertheless, although the civil rights movement and the period of black consciousness referred to as the "new black revolution" did not involve a transfer of political and economic power, the radical change in consciousness among black people which yielded new perceptions of self and society warrants use of that term. Fundamental social changes in society require a reorientation in human consciousness without which the needed structural changes cannot occur. In the long perspective of black history in the United States, the ferment of the black cultural revolution fueled by the activism of the civil rights movement marked an entirely new stage. Even the nationalist social movement led by Marcus Garvey and the advent of the "New Negro" during the Harlem Renaissance did not match the impact of the new black revolution.[5] Minister Malcolm X and the Nation of Islam paved the way for the most recent resurgence of black nationalism. They were joined by other militants and cultural nationalists such as Stokely Carmichael, Ron Karenga, Huey Newton, Bobby Seale, and Angela Davis. The quest for black power also invoked personal self-affirmation and a radical change in black consciousness that fully complimented the sense of "somebodiness" that Martin Luther King was striving to articulate. The assault on epithets such as "Negro" and "colored" was furious as those traditional slave terms were dropped in favor of "black." Even the beckoning vision of integration in Dr. King's dream had its counterpart in a hard-nosed separatism in the caucuses and consciousness-raising groups which made the strains of "black and white together" seem somewhat perfunctory at times. The birth of a new consciousness was difficult and painful, but it was authentically liberating as African Americans gained in self-respect and self-confidence in this strange new confrontation of a world they had never had the opportunity to plumb before.

Since the civil rights period, the black revolution in consciousness has had a profound impact on the black community and on the larger society. Rev. Jesse Jackson's presidential campaigns in 1984 and 1988 and the election of thousands of black officials in large urban areas and small towns are among the visible signs of this revolution manifested in the political sphere, which we shall examine in more detail in the next chapter. Other signs included a large increase in the numbers of black students in colleges and graduate schools, an enlarged black middle class, and a period of creative ferment of black literary and intellectual talent reminiscent of the achievements of the Harlem Renaissance. Tragically, gains made in these areas were partially reversed in the 1980s during the Reagan era.

Although there have been calls by black leaders like Jesse Jackson in 1989 to shift from the usage of "black" to "African American," the major battle of a shift in consciousness and an affirmation of ethnic identity, physical features, culture, and history had been fought and won during the black consciousness movement.[6] That movement made it possible for African Americans to affirm their links with Africa and the African diaspora. Indeed, the future will probably see a mixed usage of terminology including black, African American, and Afro-American.

In the area of religion the transition from "Negro Church" to "Black Church" was first noted in *The Black Church Since Frazier*, published in 1974 as a companion volume to E. Franklin Frazier's *The Negro Church in America*.[7] Just how complete that transition is, how pervasive black consciousness is in the church, is difficult to measure. Clearly the Black Church is not monolithic, but rather encompasses a continuum of sociopolitical and theological views and postures. Nevertheless, that the Black Church as an institution has been influenced by the new black revolution is beyond question. There have been numerous theological positions, statements, and pronouncements about the importance of this phenomenon of black consciousness by individuals, groups, and even denominations but there has been a paucity of social science studies documenting the change among black churches.[8] Our study is one of the first systematic, empirical attempts to begin charting the influence of the black consciousness movement upon the black clergy since the civil rights period. Given their strong leadership role in African American congregations, we assumed that this clerical elite will have an influence upon lay members through their sermons, personal theology, and educational methods. Our study was limited to the views of the clergy, and a further examination of the views of congregational members needs to be done in the future.

The Black Consciousness Profile

In our personal interviews with black clergy representing 2,150 churches or 1,531 urban churches and 619 rural churches, we included a series of seven questions that were designed to elicit the views of the clergy on the impact of the black consciousness movement upon them and their churches. Chart 1 presents a summary of the data on black consciousness, including questions asked, response percentages, and chi-square and eta coefficient test results. Both chi-square and eta scores help to distinguish between statistical and substantive significance in a relationship of two variables, since large sample sizes like ours can usually achieve statistical significance at the .01 level with chi-square results. Substantive significance, which is usually indicated by an eta coefficient score of 0.2 and above, means that there is a real relationship between the variables rather than merely a statistical one due to a large sample size. The independent variables included the following: age, sex, education, region of the country (Northeast, South, Midwest, and West), location (urban/rural), and denomination. Of these independent variables, the age and education of the black clergy were found to have the strongest relationships with the black consciousness items tested. In some cases, denomination was also a major factor. On the whole, sex differences between the clergy were not significant. The high mobility of black clergy tended to negate regional and urban-rural differences. As we mentioned in chapter 5, it was found that two-thirds of the pastors of these churches resided in urban areas.

Black Consciousness: Ministry and Mission of the Black Church

Questions 1 and 2 of the Profile examined the views of black clergy on whether the ministry and mission of the Black Church differs from the white church, that is, whether there is anything distinctive about ministry in a black denomination. The data indicate that 54.8 percent of the clergy responded positively and 45.2 percent negatively on question 1 regarding ministry. The responses on the variable of ministry are strongly related to the age and education of the clergy; younger and more highly educated clergy tend to respond positively, while older clergy and those with less education have more negative responses. The eta coefficient on age is .20907 and on education .26720, indicating a strong substantive relationship.

Chart 1: Summary of the Black Consciousness Profile

Questions	Percentages		Eta Coefficient	
1. Ministry				
Q. Do you think your ministry is essentially different because you are in a black denomination?	Yes	54.8	Age	*0.20907
	No	45.2	Education	*0.26720
			Denomination	*0.13807
2. Mission				
Q. Does the black church have a different mission from the white church?	Yes	36.6	Age	*0.16714
	No	63.4	Education	*0.16074
			Denomination	*0.15293
3. Church-related black colleges				
Q. Does your church support church-related black colleges?	Yes	86.1	Age	*0.09409
	No	13.9	Education	*0.18489
			Denomination	*0.37562
4. Children				
Q. Are the children in your church taught about the distinctiveness of the black church?	Yes	71.6	Age	*0.10719
	No	28.4	Education	*0.13531
			Denomination	*0.23048
5. Sunday school literature				
Q. Is it important to have black figures in your Sunday school literature?	Yes	68.0	Age	*0.06411
	No	32.0	Education	*0.20603
			Denomination	*0.20179
6. Sermons				
Q. Do your sermons reflect any of the changes in black consciousness (black pride, black is beautiful, black power, etc.) since the civil rights movement?	Yes	64.3	Age	*0.19868
	No	35.7	Education	*0.24684
			Denomination	*0.20535
7. Black liberation theology (1,531 urban clergy only)				
Q. Have you been influenced by any of the authors and thinkers of black liberation theology (e.g., James Cone, Gayraud Wilmore, De Otis Roberts, Major Jones, William Jones, etc.)?	Yes	34.9	Age	*0.24320
	No	65.1	Education	*0.23976
			Denomination	*0.29419

*Asterisk indicates in all these data a chi square that is significant at the .01 level.
Unless otherwise indicated, $N=2,150$.

In interviews with the clergy, the negative answers of "no difference" generally appealed to the universalism of the Christian ministry and its primary task as the saving of souls. As one Baptist minister said in his interview, "The ministry of both black and white preachers is the same: the saving of souls. . . . Skin color is of no great significance in relating the message of Jesus."

On the other hand, the clergy who affirmed the distinctiveness of the black ministry stressed the problems of racism in American society and the different social, economic, and cultural conditions of African Americans, which the black clergy have to deal with. One cleric said, "Black people have different needs; different concepts of what the church ought to do. Since we are oppressed (we) have to deal more with what religion really means. Have to deal with practical (needs)." Another pastor replied, "Black folks have a different religious orientation from white folks. There is little emphasis put upon Home and Foreign Mission and Christian Education. White folks work from the building of their educational department, but black folks operate from the pulpit as great preaching stations. Great emphasis is put on preaching in black churches." Other pastors stressed the independence of the Black Church and its central role in the community. Ministry in a black denomination was different, said a Methodist preacher, "because of what the church means to the community as a center for black caring and social-political nurture. . . . It is the one 'free' institution in the black community and lends the pastor the freedom to respond to problems and issues without fear."

In responding to question 2 on whether the mission of the Black Church differed from that of the white church, 36.6 percent replied yes and 63.4 percent answered no. Although the chi-square scores indicated a .01 level of significance, this was due largely to a large sample size because the eta test also showed that there was a lack of substantive relationship with the variables of age and education. There was also a decline in the number of affirmative responses from 54.8 percent on question 1 to 36.6 percent on the question of mission. The decline may be due to both the lack of clarity in the question and the semantic confusion which the term mission may have for the clergy. Although we meant "purpose" by the word mission, the term also has other meanings in a religious context, for example, mission field or foreign mission. Another explanation is that the majority of black clergy tend to follow the orthodox understanding that the main purpose of Christian churches is to spread the Word and to save souls.

To the extent that this is the case, certainly black clergy would see their mission as no different from white clergy.

The qualitative responses tended to reflect the ambiguity in the question. Pastor number 1810 said, "Main Christian mission is the same but the Black Church has to be related to social issues of black people, pointing to hope." In a similar vein, interviewee number 1950 declared, "Theologically, no, but practically yes. And that difference is to get people liberated on racial grounds and to get their personhood together. The difference is to get the whites to loosen up from bigotry and prejudice—subtle differences. Not to blame the white man for everything. [But] the white man does not just deal with entities in the community." Finally, the pastor of a rural church said, "Primarily, the Black Church has a responsibility to be involved in the total liberation of black personhood and to help empower the black community."

Black Consciousness: Education and the Black Church

Questions 3, 4, and 5 of the black consciousness profile can be broadly grouped under the rubric of education or, more specifically, the support of church-related, black educational institutions and the educational content relating to opportunities to learn about the distinctiveness of the Black Church and to the provision of black role models in Sunday school materials.

On question 3 regarding the support of church-related black colleges, the response was on the whole overwhelmingly positive with 86 percent responding yes and only 14 percent saying no. The variable of age was not very strongly related to the direction of the responses. There was not much difference between the older and younger categories (85 percent for those under age thirty and 89.7 percent for those over age sixty-five). The educational level achieved by the clergy has some relationship to the support of black colleges, although the relationship was not strong enough to raise it to a level of substantive significance (eta score=.18489). Clergy in the categories of college graduate or college 5 plus show a somewhat higher positive response rate than those who are below high school or high school graduates (91 percent average versus 78.4 percent average).

The denomination variable shows a strong relationship (eta score = 0.37562) to the question of supporting black colleges. The results show some slight differences between Baptists and Methodists in their level of support for education, with the Methodists indicating higher support (96.7 percent average for Methodists versus 88.3 percent average for Baptists). In contrast, the Pentecostals, the Church of God in Christ, showed a significantly lower rate of support for church-related black colleges with a 58.5 percent average. Several factors may explain this lower rate of support. First, as a former urban lower-class sectarian movement, cogic has only recently achieved denominational status. Second, cogic has only one denominational school at the high school and junior college level, Saints College in Lexington, Mississippi. It also has only one official theological seminary, C. H. Mason at the Interdenominational Theological Center in Atlanta. As our earlier historical chapters on the different denominations have shown, the Baptists and Methodists have had a much longer history of developing their own colleges and theological institutions than the Pentecostals. Although the support for more education is currently growing among Pentecostals, especially among young people, most of the existing cogic clergy are older and have not yet been influenced by that trend.

The differences among the historically black denominations in regard to the support of educational institutions are related to their past historical, social class differences and their differing requirements for ordination to the ministry. Traditionally, many black Methodists have been either from middle-income groups or were middle-class oriented; they have also stressed education and an educated clergy through their connectional polity. During the post-Civil War era, for example, a.m.e. Bishop Daniel Payne not only advocated an educated ministry and membership but he also derisively criticized some aspects of the black folk worship tradition.[9] The independent polity of the Baptists has only required evidence of a divine calling with no educational requirements. However, there are exceptions reflecting the diversity of social classes among black Baptists. Pastors of the elite black Baptist churches, those having the largest and wealthiest congregations, often have extensive graduate education. The clergy of poorer Baptist churches generally have a high school or community college education. However, of the seven historic black denominations examined in this study, the Pentecostals still reflect their lower social class origins to a greater degree. Although their socioeconomic situation is changing rapidly, the majority of cogic members were still located in either the working class or the working poor.[10]

In response to question 4, "Are the children in your church taught about the distinctiveness of the Black Church?" the results showed that the age of the clergy had no relationship to the direction of the response. The level of education has a slight relationship with those clergy who are college graduates or higher responding more positively (76.7 percent average), versus those whose educational levels are below college (64.5 percent average). The eta test score of .13531 for educational level does not indicate the presence of a strong substantive relationship.

Denominational differences were also evident surrounding the issue of teaching children about the distinctiveness of the Black Church. From two-thirds to three-fourths of all black churches do emphasize this distinctiveness in youth classes, but Methodists do so much more systematically than Baptists, and Baptists in turn more than COGIC. The variable of denomination showed a very strong relationship to the direction of response on question 4. The eta score of .23048 indicated that a strong substantive relationship was present. The variation ranged from a high positive response of 89.1 percent among the clergy of the A.M.E. denomination to a low of 58.3 percent among COGIC pastors. The black Methodist denominations also showed a higher positive average rate (83.4 percent) than the Baptists (67 percent). The Methodist-Baptist difference may be due simply to the fact that the Methodists have a longer history as organized denominations than do the Baptists. Although individual black Baptist churches were founded somewhat earlier than Methodist ones, their organization into a national denomination did not occur until the late nineteenth century. Furthermore, as organizations with a centralized connectional polity, it has been easier for Methodists to write their institutional histories than for Baptists. The Methodists also take unusual pride in passing on their denominational history to their young people. The much lower rate for the Pentecostals of stressing the "blackness" of the church is also possibly related to its interracial past, its recent establishment as a denomination, as well as to some of the factors mentioned previously such as the lower socioeconomic background and lower levels of educational achievement among COGIC clergy.

The results on question 5, "Is it important to have black figures in your Sunday School literature?" indicate that the majority of clergy are in favor of including black figures in Sunday School literature (68.0 percent yes versus 32.0 percent no). The variable of age has no relationship to the direction of response (eta=.06411). However, both education and denomination show significant levels of relationship. The educational level of black clergy is strongly correlated with positive attitudes on the presence of black figures in Sunday School literature (eta=.20603). There is an ascending symmetrical relationship with clergy of lower educational levels having fewer positive responses and those with higher levels of education having more positive views. For example, the data show that there is a very significant difference in positive responses between the highest educational category, college 5 plus (78.9 percent), and the lowest, less than high school graduate (52.4 percent).

The eta score of .20179 indicated a strong substantive relationship on the variable of denomination. There was almost no difference between Baptists (72.8 percent average) and Methodists (70.4 percent average) regarding their views of including black figures in their Sunday School materials. However, there was a substantial variation in the views of COGIC pastors who are almost evenly divided on this question (51.7 percent). The somewhat lower level of educational achievement, on the whole, among COGIC clergy may account for the variation.

Our qualitative interview data on questions 4 and 5 indicated that those who answered negatively in regard to the distinctiveness of the Black Church or to the importance of having black figures in Sunday School literature usually felt like the pastor who said, "Skin Color is of no great difference in relating the messages of Jesus. There is no black church but God's church." A few pastors felt that there was a need to deemphasize the racial aspect. Pastor number 1094 said, "Children are taught that race as such has no place in the Christian religion—that whatever it may mean as a physical distinction, it must never be a real barrier to fellowship or aspirations."

On the other hand, the majority of pastors who responded positively pointed to the importance of teaching the African American historical heritage and providing role models to black youth. Pastor number 1188 argued, "Our culture is different. If you send a black child to a white church, he would not know he has been to church. . . . The [Black] Church has an obligation to teach about the contributions of our race. If we don't do this, where are our kids gonna get it?" Another minister replied, "Because it gives them a self-awareness and self-esteem so they don't feel inferior. If they see white images, they think you have to be white to succeed."

Black Consciousness: Sermon Content and the Black Revolution

Sermon content may well be one of the indicators most revealing of black consciousness. Black churches place a premium on the charisma of the pastor, a most important expression of which is preaching ability. The sermon assumes a degree of importance in the black worship service which cannot be matched by its institutional counterparts in other religious communities.[11] Throughout the historical development of the Black Church over the past two hundred years, the sermon has served a wide variety of functions and purposes: its primary purpose has been to glorify God but it has also served as theological education and Sunday School; ritual drama and show time; singing and humming; encouragement and political advice; and moralizing and therapy—all rolled into one. Everything in the sermon is directed toward the point of emotional climax and catharsis. Shouts of "Amen" and "preach it" fill the air to show agreement, while the ubiquitous calls of "well?" tend to urge the preacher on. The congregational members do not sit passively but are intimately engaged. Sermons that stir the whole being mark the difference between a fine lecture and the heights of good preaching.

Responses to question 6, "Do your sermons reflect any of the changes in black consciousness (black pride, black is beautiful, black power, etc.) since the civil rights movement?" indicated that age and education were strongly related variables. Again, younger clergy and/ or those with more education tended to reflect more positive attitudes toward emphasizing aspects of black consciousness in their sermons. Older and less educated pastors tended to respond negatively. The eta score on age is .19868 which is on the border of indicating a substantive relationship. On the variable of age, clergy under forty years old have a 79.4 percent positive response average versus a 53 percent average for those older than sixty years. The eta score on education is .24684, indicating a strong relationship. For the clergy with the highest levels of education, 71.1 percent of them responded favorably compared to 49.2 percent of those with the lowest levels of education.

The variable of denomination is also strongly related to sermon content reflecting black consciousness. The eta score is .20535. As chart 1 indicates, there are some variations between the Methodists and Baptists, with the Methodists showing a somewhat higher degree of positive attitude (72.5 percent versus 64.2 percent average). The greatest difference is again noted with the Pentecostals (46.2 percent). This difference in attitude and practice is related not only to the fact of the lower-class and educational background of the majority of Pentecostals, but also to the strong emphasis of the denomination upon religious experience, a deep evangelical piety reinforced by charismatic phenomena like glossolalia.

Clergy who decline to include black consciousness-type content in their sermons expressed the conviction that their job is only to "preach the Christian Gospel" or that there is "too much emphasis on race." In contrast is the view of Dr. Gardner C. Taylor, pastor of the largest black church in the United States, the Concord Baptist Church in Brooklyn. Taylor, who is often referred to as the "dean" of black preachers, is among those black clergy who acknowledged that their preaching changed with the commencement of the civil rights movement. Prior to the mid-1950s, he preached more of an evangelical gospel, leaving racial matters out. Since that time he has included racial concerns, although Taylor also voiced some caution: "We need to reflect [on] the aberrations and also some of the futile aspects of the Civil Rights [movement]." COGIC Bishop Dr. Ozro T. Jones, Jr., of Philadelphia said in his interview regarding the impact of the civil rights and black consciousness period on his preaching, "I always attempt to identify, to be relevant to the consciousness of my hearers."

It is obvious from the data that the civil rights movement and the black ideologies that followed it have had a very significant impact on the consciousness of black preachers, two-thirds of whom have acknowledged changes in their sermons since that era. However, this should not obscure the fact that an evangelical gospel largely unconcerned with racial matters still has a strong following among at least another one-third (36 percent) of the pastors of the historic black denominations. Rev. William Holmes Borders, pastor of the Wheat Street Baptist Church in Atlanta, summarized the black consciousness issue by saying in his interview, "Black people must relate semantically to their own conditions through the power of words and symbols."

Black Consciousness: The Influence of Black Liberation Theology

One of the most important expressions of the consciousness movement was the emergence of black liberation theology. The seminal ideas of black theology were far from new, however, as a brief historical review will establish. The idea that God is black, for example, was set forth in David Walker's antislavery *Appeal* of 1829 where he used the phrase "God of the Ethiopians"; and in A.M.E. bishop Henry McNeil Turner's pointed reply in *Voice of Missions*:

> We have as much right biblically and otherwise to believe that God is a Negro, as you buckra or white people have to believe that God is a fine looking, symmetrical and ornamented white man. . . . Every race of people since time began who have attempted to describe their God by words, or by paintings, or by carvings, or by any other form or figure, have conveyed the idea that the God who made them and shaped their destinies was symbolized in themselves, and why should not the Negro believe that he resembles God as much as other people?[12]

The idea that God or Jesus or the ultimate values of a religion should be viewed and interpreted from a people's own experience and social location was further radicalized by the black religious and social movements during the first half of the twentieth century. Marcus Garvey's pronouncement that "a Black God was coming" was quickly confirmed by Father Divine's claim that he, a short (five foot two), charismatic black man, indeed, was everybody's God. The Black Muslims also claimed that Master Fard was "Allah" and the Honorable Elijah Muhammad was his "Prophet."[13] Examples of this reinterpretation of the major symbols of Christianity occurred on the African continent itself. In Central Africa as early as 1703 a young woman named Kimpa Vita called herself "Beatrice the Madonna" and led an independent religious movement, which was replete with an African Christ and Saint Anthony, in reaction to the teachings of Portuguese Capuchin missionaries.[14]

Liberation motifs even older than this view concerning a "Black God" may be identified within the historical tradition of black churches. The motif of "independence" can be found in the movement prior to the American Revolution in the desire for founding independent black Baptist churches and then later Methodist ones, and their subsequent development into independent denominations. Aside from private family life, black churches became the first independent economic and sociopolitical sphere among African Americans. The theme of freedom that emerged among an enslaved people has developed a deep religious symbolic significance among all sectors of the black population. Freedom meant freedom from all forms of racial oppression. "Freedom now!" became the chant of the civil rights movement, and numerous songs, sermons, and speeches dwelt on the theme of freedom in both reformist and militant movements. In addition, the motif of "self-help" was also disseminated through the pulpits by the practical moral advice given by preachers to their congregations to "get an education," "save for a rainy day," "work hard," or "buy some land." However, this older liberation tradition within the Black Church remained relatively unsystematized until recently.

The significance of the present new movement of black liberation theology is that for the first time in American religious history, a group of Christian theologians in major divinity schools and theological seminaries have attempted to construct systematic theologies from a black perspective. Influenced by the period of black consciousness and black power in the late 1960s, the first seminal ideas were elaborated by James Cone's *Black Theology and Black Power*, which appeared in 1969.[15] Since then, a host of other theologians and scholars such as Gayraud Wilmore, DeOtis Roberts, Major Jones, William Jones, Charles Long, Pauli Murray, Jacqueline Grant, and Cornel West have elaborated their own views of what a program of black theology should include.[16] The most important result of this theological movement is that it not only legitimated the study of black churches and black religious phenomena in academic institutions, but it gained recognition for the intellectual perspectives and writings of black people in a way and to an extent that had never existed before in the United States. The movement has also been valuable both for the external critique it provided of American society and for the internal dialogue it stimulated within the black community—a dialogue involving both affirmation and criticisms of black churches and leaders—thus helping to forge a progressive path to the future. These important achievements notwithstanding, the question presents itself: How influential has this new movement of black liberation theology been among the black clergy and the black churches over the past twenty years?

This study is the first to give a systematic sociological examination of the influence of black liberation theology on the urban black clergy nationwide. In our urban questionnaire we asked the pastors of 1,531 urban churches, "Have you been influenced by any of the authors and thinkers of black liberation theology (e.g., James Cone, Gayraud Wilmore, DeOtis Roberts, Major Jones, William Jones, etc.)?" and to elaborate on their answers. In our rural questionnaire, we asked a somewhat different question to the pastors of 619 rural churches in an attempt to explore the influence of the older liberation tradition, "Does your ministry relate in any way to the freedom and liberation of black people?—If yes, explain how it relates (e.g., preaching about buying land, voting, getting an education, community activism and social concerns, etc.)."[17]

The responses of the black urban clergy show a dramatic shift on this question. Where previous responses on the black consciousness profile have been running about two-thirds affirmative and one-third negative, this question shows the reverse: yes (34.9 percent) and no (65.1 percent). Both the survey data and the qualitative responses show that thus far the movement of black liberation theology has had a relatively limited influence upon the urban clergy and their congregations. A little more than one-third of the black pastors interviewed claimed any influence from this movement.

Further analysis of the urban data indicates that age, education, and denomination were the most significant variables in determining the responses. The eta scores on age (.24320) and education (.23976) showed strong substantive relationships. Clergy who are forty and under claimed to be more strongly influenced by black liberation theology than those who are older. Education was also very strongly associated with knowledge of black liberation theology. Pastors with a high school and less educational background said that they were minimally influenced by liberation theology, while those with a college 5 plus education have the most positive views of the movement. The majority of the less educated pastors have neither heard of the movement nor of the names of theologians associated with it. Among educated clergy familiar with the movement, James Cone has the highest name recognition.

These differences are not surprising, since black liberation theology is a relatively recent intellectual movement occurring largely among the educated elite of the black clergy. Thus, although the movement has had some influence among the most recently trained clergy and those who sustain a self-directed continuing education program, the great majority of black urban ministers in the United States—at least two-thirds of them—have not been affected by the movement at all.

The liberation motif as the dependent variable also showed wide variation among the denominations, especially between the A.M.E.

(66.2 percent positive) and COGIC (17.9 percent positive). The eta score on the denomination variable (.29419) indicated a strong substantive relationship. As mentioned, black liberation theology is still a pioneer area not yet subscribed to by many black urban clergy. In short, the denominations with higher educational levels among their clergy such as the A.M.E., along with the intellectual elite of the Black Church (theologians, scholars, and divinity school students), are the major proponents of this view. The fact that the Pentecostal ministers of the Church of God in Christ, which has the largest sector of lower-class members among the seven denominations, have been scarcely influenced by this theological perspective suggests some of the class limitations of this movement. The major formulators of black theology have been unable to move beyond their middle-class origins, even though a major tenet of black liberation theology is to do theology from the "bottom up," from the perspective of the oppressed in American society. Accordingly, the names and works of the major black theologians remain unfamiliar to the majority of black pastors in most of the historic denominations. The findings suggest one of two possibilities: either a much more intense educational effort on the part of the intellectual elite is required before black liberation theology is fully acceptable, or the theological formulation itself must undergo major revision.

Our field experiences with black clergy nationwide revealed that the majority of them are still educated and socialized in the ministry in an apprenticeship mode, learning on the job from senior clergy. Whatever academic education occurs for many of them takes place in small local Bible schools or classes sponsored by local clergy associations.[18] Much of their reading matter comes from their own denomination, and the books they purchase and read usually consist of devotional and prayer books or collections of sermons. It is this local level of clergy education that the new black liberation theology has thus far failed to penetrate.

In contrast to the extensive networks and thousands of local base communities developed in the Latin American liberation theology movement, many of which are led by lay members, our field experience has shown that the new black liberation theology movement in the United States has yet to fully develop its organizational and institutional potential among African American Christians. Black churches represent an enormous potential network for the development of base groups committed to liberation. But this potential has remained largely unrealized over the past two decades. Another instructive comparison with the Latin American situation is the attention paid to the development of teachers and teaching materials, to the hermeneutical task of helping lay people interpret and analyze their own situations of oppression. Paulo Freire's classic work, *Pedagogy of the Oppressed,* is but one illustration of this process. More recently, biblical scholars in Latin America have applied their skills to the task of popularizing the liberation message.[19] But the point of the comparative lesson is clear. Unless the movement of black liberation theology reaches beyond its present location in an intellectual elite and gives more attention to the development of hermeneutical traditions within the African American community and to a mass education of clergy and laity in the churches, the movement will continue to have minimal influence among its key constituencies.

As noted above, information regarding the influence of black theology on clergy pastoring rural churches is not available. Information regarding the continuing influence of the older stream of liberation motifs among the 363 black rural clergy of 619 rural churches showed a dramatically different outcome from the urban clergy's responses to the black liberation theology movement cited above. Of the rural pastors, 286 (78.6 percent) replied affirmatively that their ministries had related to the freedom and self-sufficiency of African Americans. Only 36 (10 percent) responded negatively, with 41 (11.4 percent) giving no response. Illustrative of such orientations are these comments by rural clergy:

No. 0368: "Try to give hope to a cast down people, to get an education, to become leaders in every respect, to develop thinking, to gain power over their own lives."
No. 0043: "We encourage them to stand on their own feet, venture out and try to come up with new ideas. Be self-employed."
No. 0044: "I tell them that they ought to buy a home, get their children an education, open a savings account."
No. 0046: "Talk about how people suffered in slavery—[Frederick] Douglass, etc. Tell them the importance of owning land. Be a man."
No. 0067: "I teach them that real freedom comes when you vote and elect good leaders."

Such remarks attest to the continuing influence of the older liberation tradition among the rural clergy. The motifs of this tradition are far more pragmatic, relating to the everyday survival needs of church members and stressing the virtues of uplift and self-help. This older tradition is also more reformist in its strategy of social change than some of the more radical visions of the intellectuals in the black liberation theology movement.

The two liberation traditions are not necessarily contradictory, however, but are potentially complementary. In some respects, the split in the liberation traditions parallels the historic debate between Booker T. Washington and W. E. B. Du Bois.[20] Washington's emphasis upon self-help and economic uplift via industrial education for the masses reflects the older tradition of liberation motifs, whereas Du Bois's advocacy of a liberal arts education for the "Talented Tenth," and his later, more radical, social vision for American society, find a resonance in the social location and work of the present intellectuals of the black liberation theology movement. Some merging of the two traditions would seem to be in the best interests of the black estate, and in fact as will be seen, such a merger is being attempted in the ecumenical program of the Congress of National Black Churches.

Summary of the Black Consciousness Profile

The influence upon black clergy by the social movements of the 1960s and 1970s is apparent. Black pastors are conscious of the need to provide black role models for their members, particularly the children. Most of them perceive the role of the Black Church as the gatekeeper of the black historical heritage. The vast majority of black churches (86 percent) contribute to church-related black colleges. Slightly over half of the clergy feel that ministry in a black denomination is essentially different because of the racial and economic conditions of African American people. The most significant indicator of the influence of black consciousness is the claim by two-thirds of the clergy of a change in sermon content. However, when it comes to personal theology, tension and ambivalence are evident. The black liberation theology movement has attempted to mold a social gospel of reform and revolution by drawing upon recent and past sources of black nationalism, liberation stories and motifs from the biblical tradition, and a critical sociology of race relations. Recently Cornel West and James Cone have begun to incorporate major aspects of the Marxist tradition as another theological resource.[21]

However, our survey indicates the limited impact that this intellectual movement has had among the urban clergy and, it may therefore be presumed, among rural church clergy as well, since two-thirds of the rural pastors reside in urban areas. On the other hand, the older tradition of liberation motifs is still strong among rural church clergy and, it is reasonable to presume, enjoys a substantial audience among urban clergy as well. Indeed, the tradition of community outreach and service, to which the discussion will turn shortly, is highly compatible with this older tradition.

The Black Consciousness Scale

As part of this study of the effects of black consciousness upon the clergy and their churches, we devised a black consciousness scale for the first six items in our black consciousness profile (since the questions regarding liberation traditions differed in our urban and rural surveys, we excluded that item from the scale in order to apply it to the total sample). The six items were recoded and tested for reliability so that a black consciousness scale score was used to divide clergy responses into "low," "moderate," and "high" expressions of black consciousness.[22] Low represented 0 to 2 positive responses, moderate equaled 3 to 4 positive responses, and high meant 5 to 6 positive responses.[23] The resulting percentage distribution of the scale for the entire sample was as follows: low=10 percent; moderate=51 percent; and high=39 percent. These percentages from the scale again confirm the fact that black clergy in our study have certainly been influenced by the black consciousness movement of the late 1960s and early 1970s.

The black consciousness scale was also used to examine the effects and relationship of variables like age, denomination, and education upon the clergy's expressions of black consciousness. Table 23 represents the results of a multiple classification analysis of the black consciousness scale in terms of these three variables.[24] All of the three main effects were significant at the .01 level and no confounding interaction effects were significant at the .01 level.

As table 23 indicates the variable of denomination and education have strong relationships with the black consciousness scale. Methodists, in particular, tend to respond most favorably to the black consciousness items (0.07). The Baptists tended to be evenly divided between positive and negative responses to black consciousness (0.00), while the Pentecostals as a denomination were the most

Table 23: Multiple Classification Analysis of the Effect of Age, Denomination, and Education on the Clergy's Black Consciousness (as Measured by the Black Consciousness Scale)

		VARIABLE AND CATEGORY	
		Unadjusted Deviation	Adjusted Deviation
	Number	Eta	Beta
Denomination			
Baptist	787	−0.01	0.00
Methodist	603	0.09	0.07
Pentecostal	290	−0.17	−0.14
Other	59	0.09	0.00
		0.32	0.26
Age			
1 to 34	247	0.09	0.04
35 to 49	486	0.03	0.04
50 to 64	646	−0.02	−0.00
65 plus	360	−0.08	−0.05
		0.20	0.12
Education			
Less than high school	283	−0.13	−0.09
High school graduate	242	−0.09	−0.06
Some college	320	−0.04	−0.04
College graduate	238	0.02	0.01
College plus	656	0.10	0.08
		0.33	0.24

Multiple R^2=0.184
Multiple R=0.429
Missing=156 (8.2 percent)
Total N=1,739

strongly negative (−0.14). The overall beta score of 0.26 indicates a strong substantive relationship between black consciousness and denomination.

In earlier sections of this chapter we discussed some of the possible reasons why Methodist clergy have tended to show a stronger positive response to black consciousness. Methodists organized into denominations earlier than their Baptist and Pentecostal counterparts, and they became the bearers of a proud historical heritage. The fact that the African Methodist Episcopal Church and the African Methodist Episcopal Zion Church, in particular, consciously took the appellation "African" as part of the names of their denominations during the late eighteenth and early nineteenth centuries was probably reinforced by the pronounced tendency during the more recent period of the black consciousness movement to identify positively with Africa. Although a few individual Baptist churches such as the First African Baptist Church of Savannah acknowledged their African heritage, neither the major black Baptist denominations nor the Church of God in Christ used African within their names. The Methodist clergy, on the whole, tend to be slightly more highly educated as a group than their Baptist or Pentecostal counterparts. However, as indicated in table 23, there were no significant confounding effects between denomination and education (or age).

Education is also strongly related to the direction of responses on the black consciousness scale as indicated by the beta score of 0.24. Table 23 shows a sharp division between those who are college graduates and above and those who have less than a college education. The adjusted deviation scores show a negative trend for the categories "less than high school" (−0.09) to "some college" (−0.04). The positive responses begin with "college graduate" (0.01) and increases sharply with "college graduate plus" (0.08). The data on education indicate that the more education a pastor has, the greater the tendency to identify with elements of black consciousness in the religious sphere.

Age is also related to the direction of responses on the black consciousness scale but not as strongly as the other two variables. The unadjusted eta score is 0.20 and the adjusted beta score is 0.12. It appears from an analysis of the responses that those who are younger (ages 1–49) tend to respond more favorably to the black consciousness items (0.04), while those who are older, especially 65 plus, tend to respond more negatively (−0.05).

The Black Consciousness Scale and Black Church Community Outreach Programs

A multiple classification analysis was done on the data in the study in an attempt to assess whether the degree of black consciousness

Table 24: Percentage of Congregations within Categories of Black Consciousness, Denomination, Size of Congregation, and Location Having Various Community Outreach Programs (Adjusted for the Effects of Other Entered Variable Using Multiple Classification Analysis)

PROGRAM	TOTAL	BLACK CONSCIOUSNESS SCALE		
		Low	Medium	High
Ecumenical Programs				
Community service	23		Not significant	
Social problem oriented	7	2	6	9
Interracial cooperation	24		Not significant	
Governmental Programs				
(Any type)	8	8	6	11
Housing construction	1		Not significant	
Cooperation with Social Agencies in Dealing with Community Problems				
Cooperation (Any)	72	52	71	78
Civil rights organizations	43	22	33	40
Employment problems	5		Not significant	
Welfare rights and housing	7	2	6	9
Community crisis events	12		Not significant	
Other	17	10	16	20
Nonchurch Groups Which Use the Church Building				
(Any)	43	28	39	52
Civil rights organizations	15	6	14	19
Civic associations	21	14	18	26
Political organizations	6	3	5	8
Fraternal organizations	6	2	5	8

Not significant: controlled relationship is not significant at .01.
Not entered: relationship was not significant in screening ANOVA which included the variables of black consciousness scale, denomination, size of congregation, and location.

expressed by the clergy had any significant impact or influence in the involvement of their churches within the community and the kinds of outreach and social action programs that these churches sponsored. Table 24 shows the relationship between the community outreach programs sponsored by black churches in our sample and the variables of the black consciousness scale, denomination, size of congregation, and location (urban/rural). The table gives the percent-

aptist	Methodist	Pentecostal	Other	1–99	100–199	200–599	600+	Rural	Urban
	DENOMINATION				SIZE OF CONGREGATION			LOCATION	
	Not entered			16	18	28	28	15	25
	Not entered			3	7	8	11	2	8
	Not entered			14	20	29	31	10	27
	Not entered			3	5	9	19	Not entered	
	Not entered			0	0	0	0	Not entered	
	Not entered			54	74	77	90	Not entered	
	Not entered			23	36	39	47	53	40
	Not entered			3	4	3	12	Not entered	
	Not entered			Not entered				1	8
	Not entered			8	10	15	16	6	13
	Not entered			Not entered				8	9
	Not entered			27	37	70	67	Not entered	
	17	11	28	9	13	13	22	Not entered	
	Not entered			13	15	23	25	Not entered	
	Not entered			2	4	9	10	Not entered	
	Not entered			3	5	6	12	Not entered	

In none of the cases included in table 24 were the interaction effects significant at .01.

ages of congregations within each category. The phrase "not significant" means that the controlled relationship was not significant at the 0.01 level. "Not entered" indicates that the relationship was not significant at the 0.01 level in a screening analysis of variance which included these variables. None of the cases included in the table showed significant interaction effects at the 0.01 level.

Although there is no comparable data yet, we suspect that black churches, on the whole, are more socially active in their communities than white churches and that they also tend to participate in a greater range of community programs. The reasons for this statement are twofold: first, white churches do not have the kind of institutional centrality in their communities that black churches have; second, there are far more competing secular institutions among whites. Probably the only time when white churches and pastors in the United States experienced a similar kind of centrality in their communities occurred in the colonial period when churches were at the center of social life and pastors were considered the major community leaders. Second, black churches have a greater range of social problems to contend with. Since close to 35 percent of the black population is mired in an economic underclass, many of the elite black churches that we encountered in the field tended to be involved in community programs for social betterment. Some examples of these churches and their projects will be discussed later. In our study the variables of size of congregation and the degree of black consciousness as measured by the black consciousness scale were most strongly related to community outreach programs. On the whole, denomination and location (urban/rural) were not significantly related, except in a few cases.

It is reasonable to expect that the size of the congregation is an important factor in determining the availability of community programs. Larger black churches tend to have more financial resources and facilities, a more highly educated leadership, and more people available to staff their programs. Our results tend to support this observation. There also appears to be an ascending symmetrical relationship between community outreach programs and the size of the church. Fewer of the smaller churches (below 100 members) have programs and facilities in comparison to the large churches (600-plus members). Larger churches are also much more active in the community and in relating to community problems and ecumenical groups. For example, table 24 shows that 90 percent of the largest churches (600-plus) indicated that they cooperated with social agencies in dealing with community problems, and only 54 percent of the smallest (below 100) did so. This pattern of more community involvement by larger black churches runs throughout the study.

A second pattern that emerges from the data is that a larger percentage of the pastors in the high category of the black consciousness scale were more involved in community outreach programs than those in the low category of the scale. For example, although 72 percent of the total sample said they cooperated with social agencies regarding community problems, only 52 percent of the pastors in the low category did so, compared to 78 percent of those in the high. A similar example is found in the results of the use of church buildings by nonchurch groups for meetings and events: 43 percent of the total sample allowed the use of their buildings, but only 28 percent in the low category and 52 percent of the high.

While 43 percent of all the churches cooperated with civil rights organizations, only 22 percent of those in the low category did so compared with 40 percent of the high category. One interesting anomaly: 53 percent of black rural churches reported cooperation with civil rights groups, while only 40 percent of urban churches did so. This anomaly, which is probably due to the major impact and more dramatic success of the civil rights movement in southern rural areas than in the urban North, runs counter to the slightly greater involvement of urban churches in most programs. For example, 25 percent of urban churches were involved in ecumenical programs, compared to 15 percent of rural churches. However, the southern states were the main arena for the movement and much of the organizing by civil rights workers occurred in rural areas. These areas also lack the variety of competing institutions and social agencies which urban churches must deal with. The results of the survey do not mean that all of these rural churches participated in the civil rights movement in the 1960s, but they do indicate that twenty years later many of the pastors of black rural churches feel the need for cooperation with civil rights organizations.

About 8 percent of the churches in the study participated in government programs of all types. The most common ones were Headstart, day-care centers, and senior citizen programs. Only 1 percent of the churches were involved in government-sponsored housing construction. Again, we do not know what the comparable data is for white churches, but we suspect that there is far less participation by them in government-sponsored programs.

Black Churches and Community Outreach: A Few Examples

The range of these community outreach programs is best conveyed by examining some concrete examples. The Concord Baptist Church of Brooklyn, with about 15,000 members on the roll, illustrates the relationship between the size of the church, a socially aware clerical leadership, and church sponsorship of social service programs in the community. Situated in the economically depressed Bedford-Stuyvesant area, Concord Baptist has a staff of three full-time professional social workers. The church contributes toward their salaries and office expenses, and the social workers also use grants and private consulting services to make ends meet. A federal credit union, which the church helped to start, is housed in the spacious gymnasium and serves both church members and the larger community. Pastored and led by Rev. Dr. Gardner C. Taylor, Concord has built a complex of buildings to serve as a nursing home for senior citizens and the elderly. It also has an active program of church members who visit shut-ins in the Bedford-Stuyvesant area. Under the directorship of the pastor's wife, the church runs a private elementary and junior high school to offer a quality education and to deal with a deteriorating public educational system. Besides an active youth recreation program, Concord also sponsors a clothing bank and a child-care center. The pastor and a staff of five associate ministers provide psychological and spiritual counseling and are active in politics, often responding to crisis events. Nonchurch groups use the large gymnasium, which seats more than a thousand, for meetings and community events.

Bethel A.M.E. Church in Baltimore, one of the oldest churches in the denomination, claims a membership of 6,000 and, like Concord, is located in a deteriorating neighborhood. Pastored by a former civil rights activist, Rev. Dr. John Bryant, Bethel has built and runs its own private academy through the elementary grades. The church also sponsors a daily soup kitchen to feed the hungry. It provides meeting space for a variety of civil rights and community action groups. The active members are divided into task force groups to deal with a range of social problems from teenage pregnancy to drug addiction. They also try to combine a deep spirituality as evidenced by the "gifts of the Spirit" with their social and community concerns. More will be said about Bethel A.M.E. of Baltimore in chapter 13.

As the son of a famous bishop within his denomination and a bishop himself, Rev. Dr. Ozro T. Jones, Jr., pastor of the 3,000-member Jones Temple Church of God in Christ in Philadelphia, has also tried to combine the deep piety of Pentecostalism's emphasis upon speaking in tongues, or glossolalia, with expressions of social concern. Bishop Jones attempted to express his concern by being available on a daily basis to deal with people's problems. The church has participated in the food distribution program of the federal government and it has its own clothing bank. Much of the church's outreach to the community is through the private counseling of the pastor and his active members.

These are a few examples of the attempts by some black churches from the three major traditions of Baptists, Methodists, and Pentecostals to get involved in the problems facing black communities. As we mentioned earlier, in the field we have seen many different kinds of creative examples in the involvement of black churches in their local communities' problems: construction of apartment buildings for lower-income and middle-income families, the establishment of nursing homes, senior citizen centers and private schools, programs like Headstart and day-care centers, tutoring and reading programs, employment and job referral programs, clothing banks, soup kitchens, food distribution points, drug and alcohol rehabilitation programs, and classes for pregnant teenagers and young mothers. Black church congregations also constitute informal social service networks where information and some help is available through the efforts of members. One example of the formal cooperation of black churches with social service agencies is the "One-Church One-Child" program of the Illinois Department of Family Services which enlisted the help of black churches in Chicago to find families for more than 700 African American children who were awaiting adoption in 1981 in the city. By 1986 more than 600 of the children had been adopted by families within those churches and fewer than 60 of them were left.[25]

Black Ecumenism: Expression of Black Consciousness

Just as black consciousness is related to community outreach, so does it correspond to participation in interdenominational, social change-oriented movements of the Black Church. Indeed, the ecumenical movements constitute in many respects the vanguard of the Black Church, providing a home for the progressive-minded, radical-acting clergy and laypersons who find themselves out-of-step, if not out-of-favor, with their more conservative brethren.

That a liberation motif was extant in the Black Church prior to the civil rights movement and the new black revolution is attested by the fact of an organization such as the Fraternal Council of Negro Churches. Founded in 1934 by A.M.E. bishop Reverdy C. Ransom, the Fraternal Council remained active in varying degrees for three decades. Under the forceful leadership of Rev. William H. Jernigan, a prominent Baptist of the 1940s and 1950s, the Fraternal Council's Washington bureau functioned as a significant lobby for the social, economic, and political interests of the Black Church constituency—which is to say, the whole of the African American community.

The Fraternal Council declined with the establishment of the National Council of Churches in 1950, and gradually ceased operation with the ascendancy of the civil rights movement. A key organization rendering the Fraternal Council obsolete was the Southern Christian Leadership Conference, organized in 1957, which served as the vehicle for coordinating local direct action movements across the South under the leadership of Martin Luther King, Jr. Though not deliberately organized as such, this midwife of black consciousness clearly was ecumenical in its character and in its consequences. Not only was the national body church-oriented—as evidenced by its very name and by the ministerial composition of its board of directors—but local affiliates and chapters also very often were led by ministers who conducted their local campaigns through the structures and resources of local church bodies.

The ecumenical organization that came into being self-consciously responding to the new revolution was the National Conference of Black Churchmen (NCBC). Organized in 1967, NCBC was the religious counterpart of the secular black power movement. Born out of confrontation with the white church, which seemed offended and threatened by the challenge it recognized in black militancy, NCBC became the primary agency for interpreting that militancy to the white religious establishment. NCBC's task was twofold, however, as it also sought to develop the consciousness of black clergy which had grown moribund in the mode of "Negroness" that had dominated the church for the better part of the century. In contrast to SCLC's emphasis on desegregation and political enfranchisement in the South, NCBC stressed economic development in the North. Few of the organization's announced intentions in that arena were actualized, however, before the conservative backlash of the 1970s caused it and other militant organizations to reduce operations. NCBC was only marginally functional from 1973 until the early 1980s, when it became totally inactive. In consequence, NCBC's principal legacy is the extent to which it served, under the leadership of Gayraud Wilmore, as the forum for incubating and nurturing the emergent black theology of that era.

As NCBC declined, many of the early participants in its theological commission found an avenue for pursuing the theological expressions of black liberation and empowerment in the Black Theology Project (BTP), one of the several ethnic-based liberation theology projects organized in 1976 under the auspices of Theology in the Americas (TIA), a movement originally initiated to establish a dialogue between Latin American and North American theologians. After several years of erratic activity, the Black Theology Project began meeting on a regular basis in 1984; it has since achieved substantial autonomy from TIA.

Predating both NCBC and BTP are two other ecumenical organizations, both of which are still functioning. The Interdenominational Theological Center (ITC), a consortium of six black seminaries chartered in Atlanta in 1958, is concerned with providing theological training for African American clergy. The National Black Evangelical Association (NBEA), organized in 1963, is made up largely of members of the evangelical wing of American Protestantism who, through the influence of the black consciousness movement, have reclaimed the historic liberation motif of the Black Church. NBEA, with its dual emphasis on spirituality and social change, may provide the most clear-cut demonstration of black ministers being influenced by the new revolution.

Two more recent ecumenical movements share a common founding date of 1978: Partners in Ecumenism (PIE) and the Congress of National Black Churches (CNBC). First proposed by members of the National Association of Ecumenical Staff (NAES) and organized as an entity within the National Council of Churches, PIE's fundamental purpose, as the name indicates, is the fostering of partnerships between black and white churches at the local as well as the national level, specifically for the reason of pursuing social, political, and economic changes in the life circumstances of residents of the nation's central cities. Under the guiding hand of its director, Don Jacobs (now retired), PIE continued NCBC's precedents for challenging the white church to be more responsive to black concerns. It also has provided a forum in which progressive black churchmen and churchwomen from both black and white denominations can carry on a dialogue with one another free of the restrictions attending their respective denominations.

In contrast to most of the black ecumenical movements in which membership is on an individual basis and is extended to white denominations, CNBC is an organization of black denominations having a national constituency (that is, the seven denominations which are the focus of this study). CNBC, founded and chaired in its first several years by A.M.E. bishop John Hurst Adams, most nearly resembles the Fraternal Council of Negro Churches in its adoption of a conciliar model. Its progress agenda, however, is less that of political lobbying and systematic theologizing, than it is of social and economic institution-building within the black community. Utilizing the resources of the Black Church, the goal of the congress is to build cooperative institutions—for example, insurance, banking, purchasing, and publishing—which will serve to empower African Americans in pragmatic and structural ways. CNBC, more than any of the other movements, is the institutional embodiment of the black consciousness movement, representing, as it does, a creative effort to merge the radical social vision of black theology and the older liberation tradition of reform, self-help, and economic uplift.[26]

Conclusion

Throughout this chapter we have attempted to document the empirical evidence for a major change among the black clergy and churches in the United States since the last national study of black urban and rural churches by Mays and Nicholson in 1934.[27] The civil rights movement and the black consciousness phase which followed it mark an entirely new stage in the annals of African American history and empirical studies of the Black Church which do not take this factor into account have missed an important dimension of what is new and different about black churches and clergy over the past 50 or more years. For example, methodological approaches such as Mukenge's "political economy" study, The Black Church in Urban America, tend to have a reductionistic view of the role of ideas and cultural values in the study of religion. The political economy approach, which is influenced by Marxist assumptions, ultimately views ideas and the cultural sphere and religion itself as distorted ideological reflections of the material or economic base.[28] Furthermore, this methodology also repeats the error of viewing African Americans and their institutions like churches as being merely reactive to changes in the larger political economy of the society. The revisionist historians of American slavery have correctly pointed out that the slaves were not automatons only responding to the conditions of the plantation system but they also created their own worldviews, and social and cultural institutions infused with the African heritage.[29] Just as the slaves were molders and shapers of their environment, using their own heritage and creative impulses, so, too, have the black clergy and their congregations transformed themselves. If the transformation is incomplete, it is nevertheless substantial. Sociological studies of the Black Church need to be sensitive to the cultural world and worldview created by African Americans. The black consciousness movement and its diverse manifestations in plays, novels, scholarly studies, songs, sermons, oral histories, and genealogies have been the most recent products of this phase of the new black revolution.

As our study has shown, the influence of black consciousness upon the black clergy and their churches has had mixed results. While the majority of black clergy have tended to put more emphasis upon their denomination's historical heritage, black pride, the need for black role models in Sunday School literature, and a more unique sense of how black churches differ from others, most of them have not been influenced by the new movement of black liberation theology.

Max Weber has argued that religious ideas can have an impact upon people's lives, however unintentional that impact might be, and thereby affect their living conditions.[30] The results of our black consciousness scale show that having a high degree of black consciousness is strongly related to the kinds of community outreach programs which the black clergy and their churches support. As we have argued in chapter 1, a dialectical model of the Black Church, which stresses the constant dialectical interaction between the sphere of ideas, values, and culture, and the material or economic conditions of a society, allows for a much more realistic and holistic view. It also acknowledges the creative contributions which the black clergy and churches have made in charting their own paths to liberation. The advent of desegregation through the civil rights movement and the influence of the black consciousness movement have probably led to a greater political awareness among Black Church constituencies, a controversial topic that we will examine in the next chapter.

8 "Now Is the Time!" The Black Church, Politics, and Civil Rights Militancy

We have also come to this hallowed spot to remind America of the fierce urgency of now. This is not the time to engage in the luxury of cooling off or to take the tranquilizing drug of gradualism. Now is the time to make real the promises of democracy; now is the time to rise from the dark and desolate valley of segregation to the sunlit path of racial justice; now is the time to lift our nation from the quicksands of racial injustice to the solid rock of brotherhood; now is the time to make justice a reality for all God's children. It would be fatal for the nation to overlook the urgency of the moment. This sweltering summer of the Negro's legitimate discontent will not pass until there is an invigorating autumn of freedom and equality.*

"Run, Jesse, Run!" "If not now, when? If not Jesse, who?" "Now is the time!"

In political revival meetings and voter registration drives in black communities across the country during the summer and fall of 1983, thousands of ordinary black folk chanted for their favorite preacher-politician to enter the presidential contest. Rev. Jesse Jackson's controversial candidacy in the 1984 and 1988 presidential primaries for the Democratic party is to be understood in the context of black religious history in the United States. Too often scholars and journalists have sharply demarcated religion and politics into separate spheres, thereby misunderstanding much that has happened in black history and the continuing role of the Black Church. As Manning Marable has pointed out:

*Martin Luther King, Jr., excerpt from the "I Have a Dream" speech at the March on Washington, August 28, 1963, reprinted in James M. Washington, editor, *A Testament of Hope: The Essential Writings of Martin Luther King, Jr.*, pp. 217–18.

196

The majority of Black theologians and sociologists of religion tend to make a radical separation between Black faith and the specific political praxis of Black clergy. Most political science research on the Civil Rights Movement concentrates on King's role as a centrist within the broad and often fractious united front that constituted the desegregationist campaign, and ignores the historical relationship between Black politics and faith. Few historians have seriously explored the Movement's impact on the evolution of the Black Church.[1]

In the previous chapter we pointed out some of the profound effects that the new black revolution in consciousness has had among black churches and clergy since the civil rights period. Jesse Jackson's candidacy and the election of more than 7,000 black officeholders nationwide are only some of the visible signs of this cultural revolution. Others include a large increase in the numbers of black students in colleges and graduate schools since 1960, a viable and growing black middle class, and a period of creative ferment of black literary and intellectual talent that is reminiscent of the achievements of the Harlem Renaissance. Although in the 1980s under the Reagan administration there has been some erosion in the gains made by black people, particularly in the areas of affirmative action, social welfare programs, and the enforcement of civil rights legislation, which have contributed to the growth of the black underclass, there has also been a strong and concerted resistance to these efforts at retrenchment within the black community. One of the major sources of this resistance includes some national black church leaders, clergy, and churches, and Jesse Jackson's presidential candidacy must be understood as a symbol of this continued resistance.[2]

A Critique of the Myth of the Black Church and Politics

In spite of the evidence of the recent activism by black clergy and churches in Jackson's campaign, there remains a widespread tendency among some black intellectuals and among many academics to completely separate religion from politics, and even to denigrate religion as an illusory ideology or as a childhood fantasy that will pass away with maturity.[3] In the revised version of his 1964 empirical study of the relationship between black religiosity and political activism during the civil rights movement, Gary Marx found an inverse relationship between intensity of religious belief and practice and

intensity of political activism. Using the words of his famous name-
sake, he concluded that black religion was an "opiate" of the masses
and tended to depress civil rights militancy.[4] A black scholar and
professor of political science at Yale University, Adolph L. Reed, Jr.,
has written a biting and controversial critique of Jesse Jackson's 1984
presidential campaign, charging that Jesse's candidacy usurped the
rational democratic political processes within the national black
community and ultimately will hurt the development of an effective
black political movement. In his chapter, "Mythology of the Church
in Afro-American Politics," Reed lambasts the historical view of a
politically active black church and argues that the process of differentiation in the black community has reached the point in the
1980s so that "DuBois's 1903 prediction of the supersession of a
clerically grounded leadership appeared to have reached fruition."[5] In
other words, there appears to be a complete differentiation of spheres
between the Black Church and politics, and the black clergy are no
longer needed as political leaders. Moreover, he argues that the "institutional logics and functions" of the Black Church are incompat-
ible with politics. Reed concludes: "The problem at the core of the
political mythology of the black church is not simply its historical
inaccuracy or even its disturbing implications for the development
and maintenance of rational, democratic discourse in the black community. A matter for equal concern is that the projection of the
church as the source of leadership authenticity assigns responsibility
for political legitimation to an intrinsically antipolitical agency."[6]

Reed's assertion that the Black Church is an intrinsically antipolitical agency represents a serious misunderstanding of the relationship between religion and politics and a gross distortion of the
political functions which black churches have performed historically. This chapter will provide a critique of Reed's and Gary Marx's
views of the myth of the Black Church and politics by examining the
following: first, a historical overview and summary of the political
role and functions of black churches; second, a consideration of the
Black Church and electoral politics, including some information on
religion and the Congressional Black Caucus; third, contemporary
empirical data on the civil rights militancy debate on the political
involvement of black churches and clergy; and finally, a summary of
the lessons that can be drawn from historical and empirical studies
for a theoretical view of the relationship between religion and politics.

Before proceeding to the historical overview of black churches and politics, our definition of politics as used in this chapter will be clarified because it extends beyond the usual views of politics as "electoral politics" and "protest politics." Politics in black churches involves more than the exercise of power on behalf of a constituency; it also includes the community building and empowering activities in which many black churches, clergy, and lay members participate in daily. As Peter Paris has pointed out, a broad definition of politics is required in order to obtain an adequate view of the involvement of black churches in the political sphere. He further defines politics as "building structures for human associations."[7] We adopt this broader view of politics because both forms of protest and electoral politics are only made possible by the prior foundation of community building activity and black churches are examples of structures for human association par excellence. The broader definition of politics is also needed because black churches have been and continue to be a central part of black communities; there is no radical disjunction between them.[8]

The one constant factor in any survey of the relationship between black churches and politics is the history of white domination and racial oppression. In all of the varieties of black political strategies and tactics that have unfolded over several hundred years, the target has always been the white system of domination and oppression that has often attempted to define the limits and choices of the African American subculture.[9] It is in relationship to this history of domination that the political activities of black churches and black communities must be seen.

A Historical Overview of Black Churches and Politics

Slavery and Abolitionism: The Development of the Survival
and Liberation Traditions

In chapter 1 we argued for a theoretical view which stressed the institutional centrality of black churches in black communities. This centrality of religion was achieved through a gradual historical process which involved several factors. First, prior to and during the rise of the Atlantic slave trade, the traditional worldviews, cosmologies, and societies of the Africans themselves were permeated by religion, with no division between sacred and secular, especially between religion and politics. Under the sacred canopy of traditional African religions, kings and queens and chiefs were not only political leaders but religious ones as well.[10] It is important to stress this cultural starting point since the Africans who were brought as slaves to the new world did not come as "blank slates," or "tabula rasae," but they came as human beings who were already socialized in their own traditions and values. The debate about how much of African culture survived in the new world, especially in the United States, has been covered elsewhere and will not be addressed here.[11] What is important about that debate is the growing recognition that a home-grown, indigenous African American culture, a fusion of elements from Africa, Europe, and the United States, was created during the several centuries of slavery and the period of Jim Crow segregation that followed it.[12]

A second important factor in the development of the institutional centrality of black churches involved the great ambivalence among white people toward religion and toward the conversion of slaves. Most of the early colonies were founded by religious groups like the Puritans, who were seeking the freedom to practice their religion without persecution. Although Indians and Africans were viewed as subhuman, efforts toward their conversion were pressed. As early as 1667 the Virginia colony passed laws, which other colonies followed, that permitted the baptism and conversion of slaves without setting them free.[13] In 1701 the Anglican Society for the Propagation of the Gospel in Foreign Parts began their missionary efforts among the slaves and Indians, but it was not until the early decades of the nineteenth century during the Second Great Awakening that many of the slaves became converted. But for most whites, Christianity was largely viewed as an instrument of social control, to produce "obedient and docile" slaves.[14]

While the social control aspects of Christianity were quite effective when intermeshed with other constraints such as laws, illiteracy, and an omnipresent threat of extermination, religion became the only institutional area where the slaves also exercised a measure of freedom, despite the many efforts to hinder or control their religious life. Sometimes stealing off to the backwoods and bayous of southern plantations, or meeting clandestinely in the slave quarters, and at times even openly in services with whites present, they performed their own rituals, songs, and other cultural forms of religious worship. They also developed their own leaders so that the "invisible institution"—the underground slave religion—could effectively merge with the rise of institutional black churches in the latter half of the eighteenth and early nineteenth centuries.[15] As a consequence of these historical factors, religion among black people became the only institutional area which was permitted to develop to any significant degree. During several centuries of slavery, political, economic, educational, and other cultural and social institutions were deemed illegal and remained relatively undeveloped. Finally, as the only significant social institution other than the black family, the Black Church took on multiple roles and burdens that differed from its white counterpart. This historical fact of institutional centrality is an important starting point for any analysis or discussion of the Black Church and politics.

Gayraud Wilmore's classic study, *Black Religion and Black Radicalism*, remains the best historical overview of the involvement of black religious groups and individuals in black-oriented efforts in political and social change in the United States.[16] As Wilmore, Lincoln, and others have pointed out, the mere fact of black survival in a total system of dehumanization and exclusion is by itself a significant political act.[17] Even a Marxist historian such as Eugene Genovese concluded in his studies of slavery that slave religion played a major role in the survival of the slaves by preventing their complete dehumanization when it presented alternative views of their human worth in God's eyes.[18] Social scientists and other observers have tended to use typologies like "otherworldly" and "pie in the sky" to describe the ecstatic emotionalism often found in black religious groups and therefore judge them to be apolitical.[19] But they have often missed the fact that even the most otherworldly religious group has contributed to black survival, both personal and collective. Survival in the midst of extreme dehumanization like slavery requires political cunning and sometimes that is the most that can be managed. Survival also has the political potential of contributing future leaders and activists in later generations who are in a better position to produce significant political and social changes.[20] As Mary Berry and John Blassingame have commented about the "survival tradition" among the slaves: "In spite of all the cruelty and deprivation inherent in slavery, the blacks survived and preserved their sense of manhood and womanhood. . . . It was only in the 1960s that masses of blacks discovered that many of the values and customs of whites were less functional for the survival of an oppressed minority than those of their slave ancestors."[21] After the period of slavery when more political options were possible, the survival tradition among blacks became largely a pre-political condition, but one with political potential. Survival was the requisite first step toward actualizing the political potential among black people in either protest or electoral politics. This important dimension of survival and black religion's contribution to it has often been ignored in discussions of religion and politics.

Beyond mere survival, black churches and clergy have also been continually involved in a broad range of political activities, both reformist and radical. These reformist and radical activities stemmed from the liberation tradition of the heritage of black churches, which were based on their own interpretations of Old Testament stories, prophetic pronouncements, and New Testament apocalypse. For example, the social teachings of the black churches, as Paris has indicated, have maintained a constant critical posture against racism in American society from the beginning and their politics were largely reformist in nature.[22] The origins of most of the major black denominations were rooted in the fact of racial discrimination and the desire for independence.[23] During the period of slavery these social teachings were put into practice as numerous black clergy, lay leaders, and churches became involved in the underground railroad, working with white abolitionists such as the Quakers to help facilitate the escape of slaves to the North. While there is a certain truth to Benjamin Quarles's assertion that every black person by virtue of being black was an abolitionist, most of the active black leaders of abolitionism were related to churches.[24] For example, the basement of the Mother Bethel A.M.E. Church in Philadelphia was used by Bishop Richard Allen to hide escaped slaves and numerous other black church leaders and their congregants risked their freedom and sometimes their lives to further the cause of freedom. However, the A.M.E. Zion Church became known as the freedom church because it was the spiritual home for some of the most famous of the legendary figures of the abolitionist movement: Frederick Douglass, Harriet Tubman, Sojourner Truth, Rev. Jermain Louguen, Catherine Harris, Eliza Ann Gardner, and Rev. Thomas James.[25] Others like Rev. Henry Highland Garnet, David Walker, Bishop Richard Allen, and Rev. Absalom Jones were also motivated by the liberation tradition.

The liberation tradition of the Black Church also included radical revolutionary activity that in certain instances even supported the use of violence to achieve freedom and justice. American historians of slavery often tend to overlook the fact that the three largest slave revolts in American history were led by slave preachers, who used their status as religious leaders to mobilize thousands of African slaves. The Old Testament narratives of Exodus and the prophets and the New Testament apocalypse were for them compelling signals of God's concern for their freedom.[26] The sense that slavery was inconsistent with the will and the character of God was subliminal to all slave religion, thus the three largest slave revolts in American history were planned and led by slave preachers: Gabriel Prosser in 1800 near Richmond; Denmark Vesey in 1822 in Charleston, South Carolina; and Nat Turner in 1831 in Southampton County, Virginia. Both Gabriel Prosser's attempt in 1800 in Richmond and Denmark Vesey's aborted revolt in 1822 in Charleston failed because of betrayals. Nat Turner's bloody insurrection in 1831 in Southampton only partially succeeded. Yet all of the actual and failed attempts at revolt served to unmask the prevailing myth that the slaves were content and happy with their condition. Since church meetings were the only types of gathering permitted, worship services, prayer meetings, and Bible study sessions were often the context in which these insurrections were planned. Few scholars have recognized that the otherworldly orientation of mysticism, accompanied by apocalyptic visions and eschatological beliefs, can have profound revolutionary this-worldly effects. The mystical prophets such as Nat Turner and John Brown foresaw in their apocalyptic visions that the system of slavery could only be overturned by violent means.[27] It took the Civil War to bring about the destruction of the slave system, the bloodiest war in the history of the United States in terms of the number of American lives lost in proportion to the total population.

In elaborating on the survival and liberation traditions that is rooted in slave religion but finds its expression in all forms of black religion, politics, and culture, Wilmore writes:

> What may be called the liberation tradition in black religion also begins with the determination to survive, but because it is exterior rather than primarily interior (and for that reason its carriers find more space in which to maneuver) it goes beyond strategies of sheer survival to strategies of elevation—from "make do" to "must do more." Both strategies are basic to Afro-American life and culture. They are intertwined in complex ways throughout

the history of the diaspora. Both are responses to reality in a dominating white world. Both arise from the same religious sensibility and inheritance that took institutional form in Afro-Christian and Afro-Islamic cults and sects from the mid-eighteenth century onward.[28]

As the above historical examples illustrate, the movement from the pre-political survival mode to involvement in the liberation stage can occur in a variety of ways. It can occur as a result of the deep moral convictions held by most abolitionists that slavery was wrong both in the eyes of God and fellow human beings. It could also occur by means of a religious vision, a deeply felt experience that one is called by God to carry out a special task of liberation as exemplified by the black preachers who led slave revolts. Sometimes the move from survival to liberation occurs as a result of a specific triggering incident or event which forces people into action like Rosa Parks's refusal to move to the back of the bus in Montgomery in 1955, and in the lynching incident to be described later in this chapter. In whatever way the move from survival to liberation occurred, black people were inspired and motivated to participate in political action.

From Reconstruction to the Twentieth Century: Accommodation and Resistance

The Civil Rights Act of 1867 brought the franchise to the former slaves in the South and to other black people in the North. African Americans were able to participate in electoral politics for a brief time during the Reconstruction period beginning in 1867. But this participation was severely curtailed after Rutherford B. Hayes's infamous southern compromise of 1877, which removed federal troops from the South in exchange for southern electoral votes in a deadlocked presidential contest. However, during their brief time of effective franchise thousands of former slaves registered to vote and they succeeded in electing twenty black congressmen and two black senators. In 1870 an A.M.E. clergyman, Rev. Hiram Revels of Mississippi, became the first black citizen and the first black senator elected to Congress. Also Rev. Richard H. Cain served four years in the state senate and two years in the House of Representatives; he became a bishop in the A.M.E. Church in 1880. These two clergy-politicians at the national level represented only the tip of the iceberg of black clerical involvement in politics. A large number of black clergy were involved in local and state politics; many were either appointed or elected to leadership posts. In his chapter on "The Call of Politics," Carter G. Woodson gives brief sketches of about twenty black clergy who were active in local and state politics during the Reconstruction period. For example, Dr. William Simmons was a county clerk, county commissioner, and chairman of the county campaign committee in Florida; and Rev. G. W. Gayles served in the Mississippi legislature and as a state senator.[29] Woodson also astutely points out that even clergy who were not directly involved in politics nevertheless wielded political influence through their reputations as great preachers and church leaders.[30]

The influence of the Black Church was such that various factions sought to influence the black vote through its leadership on the theory that the church functioned substantially as a political organization. As John Van Dusen has observed: "The most effective method (of controlling the black vote) was to bribe the preachers, since the Negro church was a kind of political organization and those who voted contrary to the direction of their spiritual guides were ostracized and sometimes expelled from the church."[31]

The most radical political voice in the late nineteenth century was Bishop Henry McNeil Turner of the A.M.E. Church. As an organizer for the Republican party, Turner helped to build a black political base in Georgia. As a theologian he raised a considerable controversy through his black nationalist liberation theology which began with the premise that "God Is a Negro." Turner was the singular voice among black clergy that called for reparations for slave labor. He also supported the emigration movement back to Africa.[32]

The removal of the protection provided by federal troops, unrestrained Ku Klux Klan violence, economic discrimination, an ever-increasing number of restrictive black codes, and electoral obstacles such as poll taxes and frivolous registration procedures finally led to a virtually complete disenfranchisement of black voters in the South by the end of the nineteenth century. Jim Crow segregation was ratified and legitimated by the highest court in the land through the doctrine of "separate but equal" laid down in the *Plessy v. Ferguson* decision of 1896. Thereafter, for close to a hundred years, from the failure of Reconstruction until the passage of the Voting Rights Act of 1965, the Black Church became the main area for black political activity. Excluded from the mainstream electoral process, black people voted and chose their leaders in their churches, selecting pastors, bishops, trustees, deacons and deaconesses, the presidents of the conventions, women's auxiliaries, and the like. This surrogate politics carried on in the Black Church became an intensive training ground of political experience with all of the triumphs and disappointments of which the political process is capable. It was the one area of social life where leadership skills and talents could be honed and tested, and it was the only area for most African Americans where the struggle for power and leadership could be satisfied.

Prior to the Reconstruction period and particularly after its failure, black churches in the South performed a variety of roles and functions that could easily provide the transition to the arena of protest and electoral politics. Due to their social cohesion and independence, black churches often formed a potent political base, especially the larger churches. Ultimately, basic political and sociological questions needed to be asked: Where are the people socially organized? How can they be politically mobilized? In almost all black communities, the most persistent answer was the churches. It has been a continuous tradition for black churches to let both black and white politicians speak from the pulpit during political campaigns. Politicians sought access to natural constituencies, and the churches and clergy gained some leverage and influence. Sometimes the clergy ran for political office themselves, a phenomenon rooted in the American tradition of voluntary associations and developed more extensively in the black community.

In a society dominated by patriarchal values, the Black Church became especially important for black men who were denied the normative masculine role in every area of social life. From the period of slavery until the civil rights era, adult black males were usually called "boy" by white southerners and only the black minister was given a title such as "preacher" or "Rev." Black women were also denigrated by always being called by their first names without customary titles. Men and women of talent were called to be preachers and only the most politically astute could reach the levers of power as bishops and presidents of the black denominations and as the pastors of large congregations.

Black Church leadership at its highest levels has always presumed a political astuteness unique to the calling. Management and leadership of a large black congregation presupposed, first of all, the exclusion of a segregated society and the concomitant authority and responsibility derived from the people who were affected by that segregation. Hence, the black church leader of consequence must have extraordinary bureaucratic and leadership skills as well as political ability. The opportunity to develop these skills was necessarily to be learned on the job in the church, but they were skills which could be easily transferred outside the church should opportunity ever present itself. Fund-raising, public speaking, organization and mobilization, campaign strategy, and administration were skills which retained their viability in almost any sphere of human enterprise.

Black clergy, particularly those who were employed full-time by the larger churches in the community, were expected to speak out about the pressing issues of the day, especially about the problems of racial discrimination. Such "race men" and "race women" were usually shielded from adverse economic retaliation by the independence provided by their clerical leadership. As one woman said regarding this role in an oral history interview in Poughkeepsie, New York: "What are you [ministers] scared of? The city is not paying you a salary, we poor black people is taking care of you."[33] The expectation is for black clergy to speak out on the difficult issues and their economic independence has profound political implications for the future. At a time when more black people are entering the professional fields in growing numbers, many of them are discovering the difficulty of raising a critical voice because of the fear of jeopardizing career advances or suffering from other economic repercussions.

The Black Church also has political meaning for the masses as Frazier correctly observed.[34] Because their voices and votes counted in this universe of black activity, the black churches were able to enlist the deepest loyalties of their constituents. If church politics became the surrogate politics of the black community, the lessons of democratic polity, of political evaluation, and the exercise of the right and the responsibility to vote took on meaning and provided an easier transition to mainstream political participation after the most obstructive barriers to civil rights had been removed.

From the Great Urban Migrations to the Civil Rights Period:
A Deradicalized Black Church?

The long-term decline of sharecropping and individual farm ownership, and the growing need for cheap labor in northern industry overcame whatever lingering resistances there may have remained in the rural black communities scattered throughout the southern black belt. However, the ruptures and dislocations incident to America's participation in the World Wars completed the impetus for a change of place and pace for a people wed to the plantation. Millions of black people left the black belt in search of jobs and a better life.

The effects of the great migrations upon black churches were twofold. First, rural churches in the South sustained a considerable loss in membership and clergy. The reduced congregations and the decline in available leadership required a majority of these churches to abandon weekly services in favor of services that were held once or twice a month, or even less frequently than that since most pastors now had several churches.[35] Second, the established urban churches in the North and West were the prime beneficiaries of the new hordes of migrants, but not exclusively by any means. Many migrants felt uncomfortable in the large black churches, and when they did, they and their pastor from "down home" established smaller churches, many of which were located in rented storefronts in poorer sections of cities. Some of these smaller churches were to be considered mission churches of their original rural church at home. Others were the spiritual enclaves of various elders and pastors whose call to spiritual leadership arrived with them in this new land of promise.

If urban life was confusing and complex for both the rural migrants and their pastors, the political situation was even more complicated. The translocated pastors soon learned that certain adjustments had to be made in the traditions of leadership between pastor and congregation, and that the autocratic style that many clergy had become accustomed to in the rural South would need to be modified. Some of the leading black clergy in urban areas also realized the need for secular, broad-based civil rights organizations like the National Association for the Advancement of Colored People and the National Urban League. Clergymen such as Rev. Reverdy Ransom and J. Milton Waldron were influential members of W. E. B. Du Bois's Niagara Movement that presaged the founding of the interracial NAACP in 1909 as the guardian and advocate for black rights in the political arena. In 1911 another interracial organization, the National Urban League, was created largely through the influence of Booker T. Washington to assist urban African Americans in improving employment and economic opportunities. From the beginning both the NAACP and National Urban League found their primary black support in the Black Church and through the active participation of the black clergy. Gayraud Wilmore has captured the spirit of the relationship with the observation that "the NAACP met in many churches immediately after the benediction was pronounced. It used to be a truism in many communities that 'the black church was the NAACP on its knees.' "[36]

The Great Depression of 1929 had a devastating impact in black communities and its repercussions were felt throughout the decade of the 1930s in the dwindling social outreach activities sponsored by black churches. Nevertheless, many black churches continued to be involved in local urban politics during the interwar years, primarily as mobilizers of the black vote in cities like Chicago, where African Americans became an important part of Big Bill Thompson's Republican political machine.[37] Black clergy like Archibald Carey and some secular black leaders became part of what Martin Kilson has called the "client-patron" politics of black communities during this era; African Americans were clients of white political patrons such as Thompson and later Mayor Richard J. Daley.[38] But the large numbers of unlettered rural migrants, and the devastating economic conditions which gripped the black communities pushed many black churches into a conservative political stance, and many of the new storefront churches withdrew into a revivalistic sectarianism. Wilmore has characterized this interwar period as the "deradicalization of the Black Church."[39] The deradicalization thesis is based on sociological studies of black churches by Mays and Nicholson, Frazier, Drake and Cayton, and Myrdal, which detected a strong conservative strain among black clergy and churches, a withdrawal from political and social involvement in their communities, and a pronounced tendency toward assimilation into mainstream white culture, accompanied by a denial of black heritage and black nationalism. Finally, it was a time when the black sects and cults like Father Divine's Peace Mission, Daddy Grace's United House of Prayer for All People, W. D. Fard's and Elijah Muhammad's Nation of Islam made their colorful impact. Many of the negative views of black churches in relation to black radicalism are rooted in the studies of this period.[40] But while few black churches exhibited the characteristics of a militant black nationalism like Marcus Garvey's United Negro Improvement Association or Elijah Muhammad's Nation of Islam, they were not necessarily depoliticized.[41] Many northern black churches continued to play a role in mobilizing black voters and providing a forum where political candidates could address the members of the black community. Even in the South where black disenfranchisement was the order of the day, black pastors like Martin Luther King, Sr., led the members of the Ebenezer Baptist Church in an attempt to register to vote in 1935 in Atlanta.[42] Other issues of interest to black people were similarly put forward through the agency of the churches. Philip Randolph's fledgling black labor union, the Brotherhood of Sleeping Car Porters, for example, used the black local churches as a primary organizational base for recruitment and financial support. Brotherhood meetings in black churches drew "surprisingly large attendance, ranging as high as 1,500 at the Metropolitan Community Church in Chicago and 2,000 at the Abyssinian Baptist Church in New York."[43]

Black laywomen also learned about running for office, campaigning, voting, and leading in the women's conventions of their denominations, in the Sunday School and missionary conventions, and in the national network of Negro women's clubs. The women's conventions of each of the seven historic black denominations formed a power bloc in their denominational structures around which even the most authoritarian bishops and church leaders learned to tread lightly. These conventions have been among the most independent national organizations of black women and their political role and influence have not been adequately examined. During the interwar period several of these women like Dr. Mary McCleod Bethune and Mrs. Nannie Helen Burroughs, who were staunch Baptists, and Dr. Arenia C. Mallory of the Church of God in Christ were active on the national political scene as well as in the women's conventions of their denominations.[44] With her close friendship with Eleanor Roosevelt, Dr. Bethune reached national political prominence in FDR's administration.

Prior to the civil rights movement, many black church leaders sometimes courted low visibility, preferring a behind the scenes approach toward civil rights and economic issues. They attempted nonconfrontational negotiations with the local white employers for access to jobs in hospitals, schools, factories, and department stores for black workers. A few clergy like Adam Clayton Powell, Jr., of the Abyssinian Baptist Church in Harlem adopted more radical strategies such as civil rights protests in the streets on economic issues. In the late 1930s Powell, from his base in the 8,000 member Abyssinian Baptist Church, organized the Greater New York Coordinating Committee to focus attention on job discrimination. Later broadened to include other voluntary religious and secular groups, the coordinating committee initiated boycotts and picketing for jobs, and it ultimately became the political instrument which broke the power of New York's Tammany Hall political organization in Harlem. In 1944 Powell was elected to the House of Representatives, the first black politician from the East to serve in Congress.[45] He eventually became the chairman of the House Committee on Education and Labor, making him the most powerful black politician since Reconstruction. An effective if controversial preacher-politician, Adam Clayton Powell, Jr., made major legislative contributions that paved the way for the rise of the civil rights movement.

If the interwar years were a relatively quietistic time for black church leadership, with such notable exceptions as Powell, the civil rights period ushered in by *Brown v. Board of Education* in 1954 was a period of considerable turmoil and violence. It was also a time of intense black politicization. Ironically, the first area of American society to be desegregated was the U.S. Army under orders from President Harry Truman in compliance with the Civil Rights Act of 1947. The next target was public schools and education. The case which came to symbolize a decisive break with the past began when Rev. Oliver Leon Brown of the St. Mark's A.M.E. Church in Topeka, Kansas—supported by the NAACP Legal Defense Fund—sued the Board of Education on behalf of his nine-year-old daughter Linda Brown and all other black children similarly injured by segregation in the public schools. The resultant Supreme Court decision granting the relief requested set in motion the civil rights movement which reached its zenith under the leadership of Martin Luther King, Jr., with reverberations around the world. It was Dr. King who led the year-long Montgomery bus boycott, begun in December 1955, and which culminated in a decisive defeat of segregation in the public transportation system of that one-time capital of the Confederacy. While King provided the public leadership, it was the black church women of the Women's Political Council in Montgomery who provided the network of organization and support. Two years later King organized the Southern Christian Leadership Conference as the political arm of the Black Church. SCLC gave decisive focus and direction to local church involvement in the civil rights movement, and hundreds of black clergymen and their congregations made extraordinary sacrifices to move the cause forward.

Black churches were the major points of mobilization for mass meetings and demonstrations, and black church members fed and housed the civil rights workers from SNCC, CORE, and other religious and secular groups. Most of the local black people, who provided the bodies for the demonstrations, were members of black churches acting out of convictions that were religiously inspired. Black church culture also permeated the movement from oratory to music, from the rituals and symbols of protest to the ethic of nonviolence.[46] It is estimated that several hundred churches in the South were bombed, burned, or attacked during the civil rights years, with ninety-three of those occurring between 1962 and 1965, with more than fifty in Mississippi alone; the white opposition understood the importance of the black churches.[47]

The civil rights movement is a major watershed in the annals of Black Church history and the history of the nation, and the role of the Black Church in whatever success that movement has accomplished is self-documented. Martin Luther King, Jr., emerged from the civil rights tumult as the symbolic and mythical figure of that era. The movement has not been completed; and the crusaders have not yet "overcome." Before his death, King and other civil rights leaders were involved in organizing the Poor People's Campaign in Washington, D.C., because they realized that true freedom presupposes freedom from want. The next phase of the movement was the need to focus on economic issues and economic inequality. Having the civil right to sit in a restaurant if one could not afford to eat there was a hollow victory indeed, so the new black political strategy was to use political power via protest and electoral politics as a leverage for economic access and opportunity.

The Black Church and Electoral Politics

The Phenomenon of Political Alienation

The phenomenon of political alienation among the black masses has rarely been studied but it is usually raised in every election campaign in the form of the question: "Why don't African Americans, the largest minority group in the population, vote?" For example, among the 17 million black people of voting age in 1983, only 10 million were registered to vote.[48] The usual answer proffered by scholars like Gary Marx and Adolph Reed is that this alienation from politics is

caused by a deep involvement in religion, a religious otherworldli-
ness that directs the believers' attention toward the pie-in-the-sky
rather than toward the troubles of this world. Furthermore, they
argue that the institutional logic of black churches is intrinsically
apolitical since the solutions sought are divine miracles rather than
the hard-nosed, daily, pragmatic give and take of politics.

These answers greatly underestimate both the depth of alienation
among the black masses, particularly the lower classes, and the role
of black churches. The alienation of many lower-class African Americans does not stem from an otherworldly outlook but from the
constant disappointments and daily betrayals they have come to
expect from mainstream pragmatic politics in the United States.
They have seen different faces but have long since despaired of the
same broken promises of "40 acres and a mule," whatever its latest
cosmetics and persuasion. The objective conditions of their everyday
lives in poverty and discrimination confirm for them the nature of
the American political reality. Their alienation is rooted in a deep
distrust of a system that has constantly failed and excluded them.[49]
In other words, the alienation of the masses from the system of
electoral politics is more likely to be based on a realistic, this-worldly
assessment derived from past and present experiences than on their
expectation of supernatural deliverance. As Linda Jones, one of the
politically alienated among the black poor said, "I don't vote for the
simple reason that I don't believe most of the things the candidates
are telling people, and my vote might count but then yet I think: I'm
just one person you know. That's the attitude of a lot of people and I
guess that's why they can't really change or get the President who
they want."[50]

While there is a sector of black churches and clergy who stress an
otherworldly, pie-in-the-sky attitude toward everyday social and political problems, our research data on the seven mainline black denominations, which represent more than 80 percent of all black
Christians, indicate that only 8.4 percent of the clergy supported the
view of noninvolvement in such problems. In other words, the vast
majority (91.6 percent) of black clergy nationwide advocated church
involvement in social and political issues, and they advocated expressing their views in support of those interests with which they
identified. These findings will be elaborated in more detail in the
section below on the civil rights militancy debate. However, these
results are important in debunking the myth that religious aliena-

tion is the cause for the political alienation of large numbers of black people from the electoral process. The causes for that alienation are to be found in the political system itself, and in the continuing dilemma of racism in a society which wants to be perceived as democratic and under God.

The historical role of black churches in providing a training ground for the development of leadership skills and a practice of democratically selecting leaders, combined with our research findings, point to a different scenario of churches actually helping to overcome this alienation from electoral politics. As the dominant institutions, black churches have played the dual role of preserving the black heritage and at the same time of acting as a cultural broker of the values of the larger society, part of the dialectical tension that is inherent in the Black Church tradition. This role as cultural broker has emphasized participation in the political process, "to fulfill your duty as a responsible American citizen." As we indicated earlier, the politics of black churches have largely been reformist in nature; there have been very few examples of support for revolution. Paris's study of *The Social Teaching of the Black Churches* has confirmed this reformist political perspective.[51]

The findings of a study by Cavanaugh and Foster of Jesse Jackson's 1984 campaign in the presidential primaries provide further confirmation of the mobilizing potential of black churches in the electoral process. In seeking "black political empowerment" Jackson received more than 80 percent of the black vote in most states and he encouraged the registration of more than 1 million black voters since the 1980 primaries. In the massive mobilization and fund-raising, Jackson's network of black ministers and churches was important. Cavanaugh and Foster wrote:

> The black church was an important element in the Jackson campaign. Black ministers frequently emerged as the chairmen of local Jackson organizations. Virtually everywhere, black ministers solicited both financial and organizational support from their congregations, often through the simple expedient of "passing the plate" during a service. The national Jackson for President Campaign Committee even sent a memorandum to thousands of black ministers in March detailing how they could raise funds for the candidate without violating federal election law. The first Sunday in April was set aside as "A Jackson for Jackson Day," a plea for individual $20 contributions in black churches across the nation.[52]

Besides Jackson, there are other examples of the political role of black churches and clergy. Prior to the historic turnout of black voters for Jesse, the 1976 presidential election of Jimmy Carter was both "the largest black vote in history" and "the most decisive and influential exercise of minority political power in this century," according to John Lewis of the Voter Education Project.[53] Hidden behind those startling headlines was the fact that when the peanut farmer from southwest Georgia was running in the presidential primaries, Representative Andrew Young and Martin Luther King, Sr., took Jimmy Carter directly to the black churches and clergy, bypassing the Congressional Black Caucus which was deeply divided about whom to support. In a *New York Times* article, Shirley Chisholm made the following comment about Young's role: "He caught a lot of black politicians sleeping in the black community. . . . He used his network of black ministers to get to voters in the black community. Andy shrewdly outwitted and outmaneuvered black politicians."[54] In another *New York Times* article about politics in Harlem, the reporter indicated that the Baptist Ministers Conference of Greater New York and Vicinity, which met at the Convent Avenue Baptist Church on Monday afternoons, was one of the most powerful black political caucuses in New York City. If mass support was needed for an issue or a project, then, this was the group to address. For example, during the meeting when the authors of this study approached the Baptist Ministers Conference for their support of our survey efforts of black churches in New York City, representatives from Caesar Chavez's United Farm Workers' were also present soliciting their support for a nationwide lettuce boycott. Entitled "Preaching and Politics on Weekly Agenda for Baptist Ministers," the writer said that at times during the meeting it seemed that the priorities were in reverse order.[55]

As we have shown, black churches have a long tradition of involvement in electoral politics but the specific dynamics and influence of churches on black elected officials has not been explored. We turn next to the results of a study of religion and the Congressional Black Caucus.

Religion and the Congressional Black Caucus

In her 1982 unpublished M.A. thesis, "Black Politics, Black Faith," Mary Sawyer, a former aide to Representative Mervyn Dymally, examined both the religious background and the influence of religion on the political stance of fourteen members and former members of the Congressional Black Caucus. At the time of the interviews twelve were present members of the caucus (out of a total of eighteen) and two were former members. These fourteen respondents represented half of the total of twenty-eight African Americans who had served in Congress from 1954 to 1982.[56]

Three of the fourteen were ordained clergy (Walter Fauntroy, Andrew Young, and William Gray); two others were deeply religious and active lay leaders in their churches (Parren Mitchell and Shirley Chisholm); several were sons or daughters of ministers (Barbara Jordan, Harold Washington, and William Gray); one was connected to religion by profession as a mortician (Charles Diggs); two advocated a socialist posture but they also supported a stance of "civil religion" (Ron Dellums and John Conyers). All fourteen described themselves as being religious or spiritual persons but liberal in their religious outlook as opposed to fundamentalist.[57] Eleven grew up in all black churches, two in predominantly black congregations, and one in a mixed church. Ten have memberships in all black churches and three in mixed congregations. Ten also felt that their church was supportive of their political involvement, while two saw their church as only tolerant and one as not supportive. However, thirteen of the fourteen said that their activities as public officials were guided by their own religious convictions.[58]

Sawyer also examined the extent to which these fourteen individual congressional members related to the church institution in their professional capacity as politicians. The results are summarized as follow:[59]

    10 speak in black churches in the district during campaigns;
    13 receive pastoral endorsements;
    11 utilize church members as volunteers in their campaigns;
     9 report church involvement in voter registration and get-out-
        the-vote drives;
     5 receive financial contributions from the churches;
     5 have ministerial committees in their campaigns;
    10 receive endorsements of ministerial bodies (one noted he has
        also been opposed by some).

Among the list of broad conclusions drawn by Sawyer from her study, several are relevant to our discussion of black churches and politics. First, the congressional members "accept, welcome, initiate—indeed, often rely upon—participation in and support of politi-

cal activities by black churches and ministers in their districts."
However, she noted that these representatives are generally not influenced or guided by the policy positions of religious bodies. Second,
they are guided by their own personal religious orientation and theology in political stances, especially in their commitment toward policies that eliminate injustices and oppression. Third, they are reformist in political orientation, seeking to modify the existing system so
that it actualizes the American creed, rather than attempting any
radical transformation.[60]

Before leaving the topic of religion and the Congressional Black
Caucus, a brief case study of one of its newest members, Rev. Floyd
Flake, Representative of the Sixth Congressional District of Queens,
New York, will be insightful.

The Election of Congressional Representative Floyd Flake, from Community Organizing to Political Mobilization

The doctrine of the separation of church and state has had an inhibiting effect on the phenomenon of clergy running for political office.
Yet throughout American history there have been isolated examples
of this phenomenon in both black and white communities. Among
whites recent examples include Father Drinan's election to the
House of Representatives and Pat Robertson's presidential campaign
in 1988. For African Americans preachers were always considered
among the prime community leaders and during Reconstruction the
first black person elected to Congress was the clergyman-politician
Senator Hiram Revels of Mississippi in 1870, and Rev. Richard Cain
also became a congressman during Reconstruction. Among the numerous preacher-politicians in the black community the most notable included: Adam Clayton Powell, Jr., who chaired the House Committee on Education and Labor; Andrew Young, mayor of Atlanta;
Walter Fauntroy, who is the delegate of the District of Columbia to
Congress; William Gray III, former chairman of the powerful Budget
and Finance Committee of the House and recently elected majority
whip in Congress, the third highest post;[61] and John Lewis, member
of the House from Georgia. In the fall of 1986 one of the newest
additions to Congress was Floyd H. Flake, pastor of the Allen A.M.E.
Church, who was elected from the sixth congressional district of
New York City. Flake's election is an illustration of the mobilizing
potential inherent in a black church base.

After leaving his position as university chaplain and dean of students at Boston University, Flake was appointed in 1976 by his bishop to the pastorate of the Allen A.M.E. Church in Jamaica, Queens, a respectable working-class church of 1,400 members with a $250,000 annual budget. In his community near Kennedy international airport, Flake decided to test his ideas about community development and education. Over the next decade he promoted a neighborhood revitalization program, establishing church-based corporations that worked with city agencies to rehabilitate local stores and homes.[62] Under his leadership the church built an $11 million senior citizen housing complex, including a senior citizen center that serves hot meals to over 200 elderly persons on a daily basis. He also completed the $3.8 million Allen Christian School and Multi-Purpose Center, which has an enrollment of 480 students from kindergarten to eighth grade. The church also sponsored a home care agency in cooperation with the city of New York to provide home attendants for people who require such help. It also has a health center to provide clinical, pregnancy, postnatal, and other services.[63] By 1987 Allen A.M.E. Church had five thousand members, eight subsidiary corporations with one thousand employees, and a yearly budget of $12 million.

Flake had his first personal experience of electoral politics when he was elected as a Jesse Jackson delegate to the 1984 Democratic Convention; after he helped to lead the local effort to mobilize black voter registration. Following the suicide of Queens borough president Donald Manes in 1986 and the unexpected death of Representative Joseph F. Addabbo a month later, Flake was encouraged to run for Addabbo's vacated post by a group of local black ministers, using the religious community as a base of support. The white-dominated Queens Democratic organization supported black assemblyman Alton R. Waldron, Jr., and attempted to have Flake's petitions disqualified on a technicality so he could not run as an independent.[64] Flake took the case to court and won a place on the ballot but it was too late to have his name added to the absentee ballots, which gave Waldron the slim margin needed for victory. Waldron served the remaining time on Addabbo's term and had to face Flake again in the 1986 Democratic primary. Flake won the primary with 21,831 votes to Waldron's 18,295, and he easily won the general election.[65]

On the mixing of religion and politics, Flake said, "Politics is a reality of our structure and our lives; to suggest that religion and politics have no plane on which they can reside together would be a bit foolish. Those decisions that are made by politicians affect the lives of the people who are the 'saved or the unsaved.' "[66] In describing his style of prophetic ministry, he believes that there are ethical limits in being involved in the political structure. "The prophet must have a clear perspective and a clear vision of [his or her] roles. There must be some coalescing, [church and politics], in order to garner for our people the things which are rightfully theirs, . . . as taxpayers, as a people."[67]

Floyd Flake's election as a congressional representative is important as a case study because it offers a number of lessons on the relationship of religion and politics. First, it illustrates the potent role of black churches as the bases for political mobilization and defeating the candidate of the regular political party. American electoral politics depend upon the role of voluntary associations and in black communities churches are the dominant voluntary associations par excellence. Second, Flake's story points out the limitations of academic discussions of religion and politics because politics is often too narrowly defined as "electoral politics" and it often does not include the kind of community organizing and empowering activities which constitute the usual form of politics in black churches. Feeding hungry people, housing them, tending to their physical, psychological, and spiritual needs, providing dignity and status are ultimately ways of being political because political power grows out of organized and mobilized people. As the *Amsterdam News* reported about Flake's victory, people saw how he made a difference in transforming both the church and the community with the limited resources available to him, and "they felt that as Congressman he could use the same model to change Southeast Queens."[68] Third, clergy cannot run successfully for political office without doing the prior work of community organizing and caring for people. Historical examples like Powell and recent ones like Gray and Flake underscore the lesson. As Flake commented, "The church is not just a building, it is a community. The people are the church."[69]

In our profile of 2,150 rural and urban black churches, we presented our findings on both the internal church maintenance activities and their attempts to reach out to the community. As we argued above, community organizing, community building, and empowering activities should be considered part of the overall topic of the Black Church and politics. We reiterate some of our earlier findings in order to emphasize our broader view of this subject. In re-

Table 25: Black Churches and Community Outreach
Programs

Programs and Agencies	Number	Percent
Civil rights organizations (NAACP, SCLC, voter registration, etc.)	627	(31.5)
Employment agencies and problems	45	(2.3)
Day-care centers and nurseries	20	(1.0)
Drug and alcohol abuse agencies and problems	45	(2.3)
Senior citizen or elderly groups	64	(3.2)
Welfare rights and housing	78	(3.9)
Police community relations (crime, recruitment of minorities, etc.)	75	(3.8)
Food programs and clothing banks (breakfast programs, clothing for poor, etc.)	54	(2.7)
Tutoring and educational programs (reading, unwed mothers, legal rights, etc.)	41	(2.1)
Health related agencies and problems (hospitals, Red Cross, health clinics, etc.)	66	(3.3)
Local community crisis events (school desegregation, local protests, etc.)	111	(5.6)
Emergency land fund (help farmers keep land)	2	(0.1)
Youth agencies (YM/YWCA, Scouts, 4-H, etc.)	14	(0.7)
Other	159	(8.0)
No cooperation with any agencies or programs	588	(29.5)
No response	161	(7.5)

Total $N=2,150$

sponse to the question of whether their church has "cooperated with social agencies or other nonchurch programs in dealing with community problems," the black pastors of 1,459 (67.9 percent) churches responded affirmatively, while 596 (27.7 percent) said no and the "no response" was 95 (4.4 percent). Those who answered yes were asked to list the nonchurch programs and social agencies that their church cooperated with. Table 25 presents the total number and percentage of churches, as well as a list of the types of programs and agencies.

The fact that civil rights organizations and programs were actively supported by 627 (31.5 percent) churches illustrates how the civil rights movement has become a major watershed period in the history of the Black Church. Churches that participated in local community crisis events like school desegregation and demonstrations numbered 111 (5.6 percent). Welfare rights and housing ranked third with 78 (3.9 percent) churches, while police community relations programs were a close fourth with 75 (3.8 percent) churches. Churches that cooperated with health related agencies and problems numbered 66 (3.3 percent), and 64 (3.2 percent) churches were involved with senior citizen programs. These results show that black churches are much more active in a wide variety of community support and outreach programs than the stereotype of a withdrawn, noninvolved Black Church.

Another example of the cooperation of black churches with social agencies is the "One-Church One-Child" program of the Illinois Department of Family Services, in which black families adopt black children through their churches. Before the program began in 1981 a backlog of more than 700 black children in Chicago were awaiting adoption, and since that time fewer than 60 remain.[70] The black Catholic priest, Father Clemens, who has adopted two teenage sons, was the original inspiration of this program.

In spite of the fact that civil rights organizations rank at the top of the list of secular groups with which churches work, an academic debate about the relationship between the Black Church and civil rights militancy has been brewing over the past twenty years.

The Civil Rights Militancy Debate

With the publication of his book, *Protest and Prejudice,* in 1967, Gary Marx started the formal academic debate among scholars about the effects of religion on civil rights protests and militancy.[71] His statistical study of religiosity and militancy was based on a metropolitan sample of 1,119 interviews with African Americans collected in 1964 as part of the University of California's *Five Year Study of Anti-Semitism in the United States.* He combined information on subjective importance, attendance, and orthodoxy into a measure of religiosity and showed an inverse relationship between religiosity and militancy, a relationship which remained even after applying controls for education, age, region, sex, and denomination. Marx's general conclusion was that religious involvement tends to act as an opiate rather than as an inspiration for civil rights militancy. Further, he leaves the general impression that black religion in particular acts as an opiate to militancy since only the African Americans who were members of white denominations tended to be militant.[72]

In 1986 Adolph Reed, Jr., rekindled the debate by referring approvingly to the conclusions of Marx's study of the dampening effect of religiosity upon civil rights militancy in his own scathing attack on the "mythology of a church-based politics" in the black community. In his wide-ranging critique of Jesse Jackson's 1984 presidential campaign, *The Jesse Jackson Phenomenon*, Reed lambasts the view that black clergy and churches were in the forefront of civil rights protests.[73] It is a curious omission that Reed has not examined one of the most important studies in the civil rights militancy debate by Hart Nelsen and Anne Nelsen, *Black Church in the Sixties*. In this section we will summarize the Nelsens' reanalysis and critique of Marx's data and conclusions. We will also present our own research results derived from interviews with 1,894 black clergy representing 2,150 churches on their attitudes toward civil rights militancy and political involvement.

In their secondary analysis of Marx's data, the Nelsens point out that he failed to control the effects of sectarianism and leaves the reader with the general impression that religiosity in general is inversely related to militancy.[74] Besides an undifferentiated view of religiosity, they also criticize Marx's "orthodoxy index" because it is "more sectlike than churchlike."[75] Finally, the Nelsens show that there are two components of the religiosity style, orthodoxy and sectarianism, which are separately related to militancy, with the former having a positive association and the latter a negative one. They conclude:[76]

> In sum, a churchlike orientation inspires militancy, while a sectlike orientation acts as an opiate for militancy. Rising educational levels are coupled with a decrease in sectarianism but not in orthodoxy, signifying that Marx's comment about the necessity for a loss of the hold of religion over black people reflects both a viewpoint in the tradition of Frazier (i.e., that religion bars the assimilation of black people) and a belief that sectarianism is not rapidly disappearing among these Americans. In both cases Marx appears to be wrong: not all religion is inversely

related to militancy, and sectarianism would appear to be waning as black educational levels rise.

The Nelsens' critique is very important because they show that only a certain kind of religiosity, namely a strong "otherworldly sectarianism," fits into the mold of the opiate thesis of both Karl Marx and Gary Marx. That kind of sectarianism tends to depress civil rights militancy and activism. However, there is also the form of a churchlike this-worldly religiosity, which can be just as committed to religious institutions, beliefs, and practices, but which is also supportive of civil rights militancy, too. The distinction between types of religiosity is important because the ethical dimension of religion or the prophetic type of religious faith, which we have called the liberation tradition of the Black Church, is too often ignored or omitted in discussions of religion and politics.

The Nelsens' insight regarding the decline of black religious sectarianism and a rise in black educational levels has been borne out by our field observations of COGIC (chapter 3). Once rejected as a cult, COGIC is now a full-fledged member of the National Council of Churches and is probably that body's fastest growing constituency. Ironically, while Pentecostals retain with pride the most distinctive hallmarks of their religious heritage, they have become increasingly identified with the black working and middle classes. The fuzzy line distinguishing COGIC from other mainline black denominations is blurred further by its avid embrace of the contemporary charismatic movement which seems to transcend the conventional shibboleths of Protestant and Catholic communions. Hence the sectarian label which evoked visions of fragmentary religious aggregations distinguished by unacceptable estatic, demonstrable behavior may no longer be reliable a a typological index. Expressive behavior is not likely to disappear from black churches anytime soon; indeed, its adoption could help white mainstream churches cope with recent membership declines. As one Pentecostal preacher observed: "When black folks yield to the spirit, they call it 'emotionalism.' When white folks do the same thing, they call it 'therapy.' Call it what you want, it helps the helpless and it packs the pews. There can't be a whole lot wrong with that!"[77]

In our study of the relationship between black churches and politics, we replicated questions which were asked in earlier Gallup poll surveys on the civil rights militancy of the clergy and on the political involvement of black churches. Our study tends to support the earlier findings of the Gallup surveys and Nelsen and Nelsen's contention that black people in general are much more supportive of civil rights militancy among their clergy.

In response to the question of whether the respondents would approve or disapprove of clergy in their own church taking part in protest marches on civil rights issues, 91 percent of the black clergy surveyed supported participation in civil rights protests while only 9 percent disapproved. The results of statistical tests of significance showed that there were no significant variations regarding age, sex, region, or location. However, education showed a somewhat stronger relationship with the civil rights item but only the denominational variation reached a level of both statistical and substantive significance.

Table 26 shows that there is some relationship between the educational level of the clergy and the approval of civil rights militancy although the eta score of .16682 does not indicate a level of substantive significance. However, the data indicate that the less educated pastors are less positive of civil rights militancy and the more educated clergy tend to have a higher degree of approval. The approval rate for college 5 plus was 96.2 percent and 83.5 percent for the less than high school graduate category.

In table 26 civil rights militancy as a dependent variable has a very strong relationship with denominational affiliation (eta=.28828). Although there is not much variation between the other denominations, COGIC still remains the exception. All the other six black mainline denominations show a rate of approval within the 90 percentile range, while COGIC has a 78 percent positive response. Again, this may be an indication of COGIC's focus on religious experience, and it also reflects a somewhat lower educational background for most of its clergy. However, this somewhat lower rate of approval for civil rights militancy by COGIC clergy does not imply a negative view since the majority do approve. It is important to remember that Martin Luther King, Jr., and the sanitation workers' strike in Memphis in 1968 used the Charles H. Mason Temple Church of God in Christ as their headquarters. Also during the fierce struggle to desegregate Mississippi, many COGIC churches participated and a number of them were bombed.

At the peak of civil rights demonstrations in March 1965, using the same question on civil rights militancy that we asked above, the Gallup Poll surveyed 273 black respondents, of whom 88 percent

Table 26: Civil Rights Militancy and Political Involvement of Black Clergy and Churches

Civil Rights Militancy

Q. How would you feel about clergy in your own church taking part in protest marches on civil rights issues? Would you approve or disapprove of this?

	Number (Percent)	Eta Coefficient	
Approve	1,567 (91.0)	Age	0.11705
Disapprove	158 (9.0)	Education	0.16682
Missing=169 (8.9 percent)		Denomination	0.28828*
N=1,894			

Political Involvement

Q. Should the churches keep out of political matters, or should they express their views on day-to-day social and political questions?

	Number (Percent)	Eta Coefficient	
Express views	1,657 (91.6)	Age	0.04858
Keep out	149 (8.4)	Education	0.11418
Missing=88 (4.6 percent)		Denomination	0.12078
N=1,894			

*Significant Eta result

responded affirmatively, compared to 30.5 percent of 2,205 white respondents.[78] Our survey of 1,894 urban and rural black clergy shows that 91 percent would approve of civil rights militancy, a rate which is comparable to the earlier black lay respondents in the Gallup survey. In an unpublished in-house study of leadership training institutes of the Second Episcopal District of the A.M.E. Church completed in 1986 by Mamiya, 71 percent of 127 A.M.E. lay leaders approved of civil rights militancy by their clergy, 6 percent disapproved, and the rest did not respond or had no opinion on the question.[79] Although the majority of lay leaders approve, they also appear to be more ambivalent toward civil rights militancy than the clergy of their churches.

We also replicated the Gallup poll question, asking the clergy whether churches should keep out of political matters or should they express their views on day-to-day social and political questions. As mentioned earlier, the results in table 26 indicate that an over-whelming majority of black clergy (91.6 percent) support the position of churches expressing their views on day-to-day social and political questions. Only 8.4 percent of the sample said that churches should keep out of social and political involvement.

Due to the unanimity of the response, there were no significant variations in the data regarding age, education, denomination, re-gion, or location as shown in table 26. Part of the reason for this high rate of positive response is due to the fact that the Black Church has been the dominant social and cultural institution in the black com-munity so that the separation between religion and politics has not been made so readily. Because of its dominant role many churches and preachers had to be involved in the political arena.

According to comparative data in the Gallup surveys of March 1957 and February 1968, 68.4 percent of 231 nonwhites, compared to 46.4 percent of whites favored the social prophecy role for the church. In contrast, the 91.6 percent approval rate for political in-volvement of churches by our sample of black clergy nationwide is a much higher rate of approval than among lay nonwhites and whites. In the unpublished 1986 study mentioned above, 87.4 percent of the A.M.E. lay leaders supported a social prophecy role for churches of the Second District, while 3.2 percent said to keep out of such matters, and 9.4 percent had no response or no opinion.[80] A general conclu-sion that can be drawn from the results of several surveys over a twenty-year period is that there is a broad support and consensus in the black community, both within and without the churches, among clergy and laity, for a social prophecy role for black churches. The attitude is pervasive that the churches should be involved in and express their views on everyday social and political issues. It is also clear that black people generally support a much more activist role for their churches than do whites. As far as it is known, black churches have not suffered the kinds of loss in membership and financial support that some more liberal white denominations have experienced because of their involvement in social and political is-sues. James Harris's study of the attitudes of black clergy and laity toward political involvement by their churches has also confirmed our findings.[81]

In sum, a very high percentage of African Americans, clergy and laity, were in favor of a civil rights protest role on the part of their ministers and a social prophecy role on the part of their churches. The results of the studies support a refutation of the stereotype of apolitical and docile black clergy and churches. Of course, the passage of time and the successes of the civil rights movement may have helped to legitimate a more active role in the secular arena on the part of churches and clergy. It is also important to emphasize that our major field survey of black clergy and churches was completed in 1983 before Jesse Jackson's 1984 campaign. The widespread support that Jesse won from black churches and clergy, even an endorsement from the previously conservative National Baptist Convention, U.S.A., Inc., has probably led to a greater politicization of the religious sector of the black community and one could expect even higher levels of support for political involvement and civil rights militancy.[82] However, in spite of these high levels of support for civil rights militancy and political involvement by black clergy and laity in the 1980s, it is important to remember that there is also a political ambiguity in the Black Church tradition and a developing pluralism in political attitudes in the black community, which we will examine next.

The Political Ambiguity of the Black Church

In his provocative and insightful essay, "The Ambiguous Politics of the Black Church," Manning Marable raises questions which reflect the ambiguity toward politics among black religious leaders. He asks,

> Why has the Black Church as an institution failed repeatedly to evolve into a coherent agency promoting the liberation of Afro-American people, and why has it succeeded to reveal itself as an essential factor in Black struggles at certain difficult historical periods? Why is the stereotypical Black preacher the frequent object of embarrassment, ridicule and scorn for the Black petty bourgeoisie and to much of the Black working class, yet simultaneously he continues to be a critically important contributor to the total sum of Black social, cultural, economic and political life? How can such a church create Martin Luther King and Daddy Grace, Ben Chavis and Reverend Ike? Why, in short, does the Black Church continue to perform its fundamentally ambiguous role in the Black experience?[83]

The ambiguity of the Black Church toward politics, which Marable correctly perceives, is mainly derived from the fact that black churches are institutional expressions of the phenomenon of double-consciousness which Du Bois has located at the heart of black spirituality and existence in the United States, the constant dialectical tension of being African and American at the same time.[84] In chapter 1, which gave an outline of theoretical assumptions of this study, we elaborated on the dialectical model of the Black Church, which asserted that the empirical existence of black churches are also involved in a constant series of dialectical tensions: between the survival and liberation traditions; between the process of cultural assimilation and the assertion and preservation of a unique African American cultural heritage; between accommodation to the American mainstream and being independent of it. Numerous studies over the years have attested to the fact that the vast majority of black people deeply desire to be a part of the American mainstream in politics and economics, "without having the doors of Opportunity" closed roughly in their faces because of race.[85] Countless ways and strategies have been devised by African Americans and their institutions such as churches to become part of this mainstream—from fighting and dying in all of America's wars, accumulating educational credentials, joining political parties, and even to passing as white for those that could. In criticism and defiance of the racial barriers, they have also asserted their independence by separating from white institutions and upholding a proud black tradition. Yet racial factors have continued to be an important conscious and unconscious dynamic in the American political scene as Jesse Jackson's 1984 and 1988 campaigns have demonstrated.[86]

Another reason for the ambiguous politics among black clergy and churches is partly due to the strong evangelical tradition that is part of the heritage of the Black Church. Many black slaves became Christians as a result of the Second Great Awakening, which started in the frontier states of Kentucky and Tennessee and spread to the plantations of the South through the efforts of circuit riders and other clerical itinerants. There is some evidence that this born-again, evangelical tradition has continued to have a strong influence among black Christians. According to a national survey of evangelicals by the Princeton Religion Research Center, 44 percent of the black respondents identified themselves as a born-again or evangelical Christian.[87] On the whole, the evangelical tradition, especially in the

South, tends to be highly correlated with political and behavioral conservatism among whites. However, many black evangelicals tend to be conservative in their religious views but liberal in their political positions. The fundamental critique of racism in American society, which is found in the black religious heritage, is partly responsible for this more liberal view.[88] While the majority of black evangelicals tended to register as Democrats, there was still a segment of them that advocated noninvolvement in politics or rejected any influences of the recent black consciousness movement. For example, the results of our study and other surveys showed that about 8 percent of the clergy and 31 percent of the laity supported noninvolvement of clergy and churches in politics.[89] The results of the black consciousness scale in chapter 7 showed that about one-third of the pastors tended to reject racial identifications of their churches and activities. These data underscored the ambiguity of the Black Church toward politics and were also indicative of the growing pluralism in perspectives among churches and clergy. In spite of this ambiguity, questions must be raised about the future role of black churches in the political arena and what kind of institutional strategy would be the best for the interests of the black community.

The Black Church and Politics in the Future: Competition or Cooperation?

In his 1903 essay, "On the Wings of Atlanta," Du Bois predicted that the old leaders of Negro opinion, the black preacher and the black teacher, would be replaced by other professionals in an urban setting: "The leaders of Negro opinion, in the little groups where there is a Negro social consciousness, are being replaced by new; neither the black preacher nor the black teacher leads as he did two decades ago. Into their places are pushing the farmers and gardeners, the well-paid porters and artisans, the businessmen,—all those with property and money."[90]

Du Bois was only partially correct in pointing to the impact of an urban, secular environment upon a mostly rural, church-oriented people residing in the southern black belt. While some degree of differentiation has occurred, particularly in regard to the class structure of the black community, it is less clear that the clergy and churches have completely lost their leadership role and influence among African Americans. Although their historical role may have diminished somewhat—especially with the emergence of a growing number of grass roots community leaders who were trained in the poverty programs of the 1960s and the rise of professional black politicians who will use their offices to dispense jobs and patronage—it is not certain that this political involvement by black churches and clergy is over or will ever be over. Indeed, the economic independence of these churches and clergy has encouraged this political involvement for the reasons mentioned earlier. Where black business owners, corporate executives, and other black professionals must be much more careful and diplomatic in raising their critical, prophetic voices about racial or political issues for fear of offending their white colleagues or employers, the independent base of black churches still permits this freedom. In many black communities, the people still expect their clergy to exhibit an unmistakable racial consciousness and to speak out on racial issues.

Economic independence appears to be a prerequisite for a continuous critical political stance in American society. For example, in the 1986 Howard Beach racial incident which took the life of Michael Griffith, a young black worker, four of the most active protest leaders were black clergy (Herbert Daughtery, Calvin Butts, Benjamin Chavis, and Al Sharpton), two were black lawyers (Vernon Mason and Alton Maddox, Jr.), and one was a local community activist (Sonny Carson). Except for Chavis, whose position as executive director of the Commission of Racial Justice for the United Church of Christ allowed him to take radical positions, all of the protest leaders were economically based in the black community. Furthermore, a fact which Du Bois and others have overlooked in pondering the leadership role of the black clergy is that some astute black pastors in the early twentieth century saw the need for creating secular vehicles to deal with the more complex political and social environment of northern and southern cities. For example, as we pointed out earlier, politically progressive clergy like Reverdy Ransom were members of Du Bois's 1905 Niagara Movement, and in 1909 they supported the founding of the NAACP as an interracial vehicle to protest for black rights in the political arena. In 1911 under the impetus of Booker T. Washington's influence and philosophy, the National Urban League was created as an interracial organization focusing upon the improvement of economic opportunities for urban Negroes.[91] Although Washington was known as an educator and considered as the national leader of Negro people in his time, he often functioned as an unordained preacher and had an enormous influence among black Baptists.[92] Throughout their histories both the NAACP and the National Urban League were supported by black clergy and churches. In fact, in many local chapters clergy and church members formed the backbone of these secular organizations.

Examples of politically active black churches in the 1980s included the Shiloh Baptist Church of Washington, D.C.; the Abyssinian Baptist Church in Harlem; Allen A.M.E. Church in Jamaica, Queens; and Ward A.M.E. Church in Los Angeles. Shiloh Baptist has allowed many controversial and nonconformist politicians like Mayor Marion Barry to speak from its pulpit and it also held a "Marion Barry Appreciation Day." Shiloh also became the showcase when President and Mrs. Reagan served as hosts for a night of spiritual and gospel music for the television series, "In Performance at the White House." Rev. Henry C. Gregory, pastor of Shiloh, said, "The church itself does not support any political candidate. It will open the doors to anybody."[93] In 1982 his church also erected a $5.5 million Family Life Center in an attempt to deal with the urban problems of the depressed Shaw ghetto. Rev. Calvin Butts, pastor of the Abyssinian Baptist Church who has also served as its executive minister, has been considered one of the more politically astute black leaders in New York City. He has mediated in a number of racial crisis incidents in New York City, including the police brutality hearings of Congressman John Conyers, the Howard Beach case, and the problems of the Health and Hospital Corporation of New York. Although Butts has been highly critical of the mayor of New York City, Abyssinian has allowed Koch and other politicians to speak in the church. The case of the preacher-politician Congressman Floyd Flake of the Allen A.M.E. Church has already been covered above. Flake's colleague, Rev. Frank Reid, III, of the Ward A.M.E. Church in Los Angeles has been considered one of the more politically radical and outspoken clergy in southern California. He has opened his church to a prison ministry, a soup kitchen, and has provided general support for grassroots community leaders. Finally, the son of the presiding bishop of the Church of God in Christ, J. O. Patterson, Jr., has served as a state senator in the Tennessee legislature, the first black person elected from Shelby County since Reconstruction.

The relationship between black churches and black secular organizations is often a symbiotic, cooperative one rather than a competitive situation. As mentioned above, many black clergy saw urban society in the twentieth century as far more complicated than their former small southern towns and rural settings, which required the creation of alternative organizations. Stricter interpretation and enforcement of the separation of church and state provisions of the Constitution by the Supreme Court also reinforced this direction. However, in spite of the proliferation of many of these groups in urban society, no black secular organization has been able to match the membership and resource commitment by black people to their churches.[94] The story of Beulah Mae Donald's struggle with the Klan, which we turn to next, is an illustration of that kind of commitment on a personal level.

Private Faith and Politics: The Lawsuit Against the Ku Klux Klan

Discussions about the Black Church and politics often miss the role of a believer's individual faith in nurturing and sustaining political activity over a long period of time. Much of the academic discussion revolves around the relevance or irrelevance of churches to politics, pointing to examples or counterexamples as we have done. However, there are instances when the importance of an individual's faith in providing courage and hope overwhelms intellectual abstractions and makes concrete the relationship between faith and politics. The story of Mrs. Beulah Mae Donald's $7 million victory in a lawsuit against the Ku Klux Klan is such an instance.[95]

On March 21, 1981, Michael Donald, age 19, the youngest of Mrs. Donald's six children, was found hanging from a camphor tree with a thirteen-loop noose around his neck in Mobile, Alabama. Although the two klansmen responsible for the brutal lynching were eventually brought to trial after several years of investigation, Mrs. Donald, supported by the Southern Poverty Law Center, persisted in her quest for justice by bringing a civil suit in 1984 against the members of Unit 900 and the United Klans of America. In February 1986 an all-white jury delivered a historic $7 million verdict against the United Klans, the largest of the Klan organizations in the United States. It was the first time that a Klan group had been held financially liable for acts committed by its members.[96]

Hidden behind the headlines of Mrs. Donald's courageous stand was her deep religious piety. Her life was bounded by work, church,

and children. Divorced, she raised her six children alone, taking all of
them to church on Sunday and spending all day there. "I'm a strong
believer. I don't know about man, but I know what God can do."[97]

During the course of the trial one of the klansmen on the stand
turned to her and begged for her forgiveness. Mrs. Donald replied, "I
do forgive you. From the day I found out who you all was, I asked God
to take care of y'all, and he has."[98] She has also opposed the death
penalty for the klansmen. "You can't give life, so why take it?" asks
Beulah Mae Donald. "You kill an innocent person, that person stays
with you day and night."[99]

In her long and painful six-year struggle with the Klan, "A lot of
good people," said Mrs. Donald, "black and white, have called me and
said 'Have strength in the Lord.' " That is where she found it.[100]

Mrs. Donald's story of private faith and politics illustrates the relationship between the survival and liberation traditions of the Black
Church. As a single mother of six children, her major concern was
just to survive every day and to raise the kids as best as she could. Her
black church provided the context for that survival with spiritual
guidance, comfort, and emotional support for her and her children.
Yet there were crisis events like her son's lynching that triggered her
movement from mere survival to courageous acts of liberation. Few
Americans fully appreciate the gravity and danger of challenging the
Klan in a southern city like Mobile, Alabama. But in her journey of
liberation, Mrs. Donald continued to rely upon religious faith and
church community for support. With the money from the lawsuit,
she planned to buy a house closer to her church.[101]

Concluding Summary: Theoretical Propositions on the Black Church and Politics

Throughout this chapter our main purpose has been to elaborate the
roles and functions of black churches in politics through a historical
overview and some contemporary survey data. We have also tried to
provide a corrective to some misconceptions about the Black Church
and politics. Except for the elaboration of the survival and liberation
strands in the Black Church heritage, we have not attempted to
propose a general theory of the relationship between religion and
politics. However, the historical studies and the empirical data do
provide some insights or lessons that may be helpful in developing a

series of theoretical propositions, which may lead to a more general theory. The following propositions also act as a summary of the major themes and findings of our study:

1. As the primary social and cultural institution, the Black Church tradition is deeply embedded in black culture in general so that the sphere of politics in the African American community cannot be easily separated from it. Much of the black political tradition derives from a broader religious background. For example, the speaking style of black politicians has been influenced by the cadence, repetition, and rhythmic delivery of the black preacher. Audience participation, too, in black political rallies is directly influenced by the style of response found among black church congregations. The constant visits by both black and white politicians to speak in black churches during political campaigns also make black churches a prime vehicle for the political socialization of church members.

2. The Black Church heritage has contributed to both the survival and liberation traditions that have shaped black attitudes toward politics. Many of the famous historical figures in slave revolts, abolitionism, electoral politics, and civil rights protests have either been clergy or closely identified with black churches.

3. The major function of black churches in electoral and protest politics is to act as mobilizing and communicative networks in local and national settings. No other black institutional area has this mobilizing potential or as extensive a constituency. There are thousands of black churches and clergy nationwide and millions of members; this kind of national institutional network cannot be easily replaced or supplanted.

4. Politics must be broadly defined beyond electoral politics and protest politics to include the community organizing and community building activities that are part of the ministry of many black clergy and churches.

5. Economic independence of persons and institutions is a major prerequisite for effective political activity, especially in protest politics. The "race men" and "race women" of the past still have a role to play in speaking out about racial problems.

6. A deep religious faith can be the bedrock for sustaining a person in courageous political acts of liberation. Religious piety does not have to be an opiate; it can be an inspiration to civil rights militancy.[102] Other-worldly religious transcendence can be related dialectically to the motivation, discipline, and courage needed for this-worldly political action.

7. While the process of differentiation in professions and institutions has continued over the past eighty years so that the Black Church no longer enjoys the near-monopoly in black leadership that it once did, the black clergy and the Black Church will continue to be a significant force in leadership and sustenance in electoral and protest politics, Du Bois's vision of a supersession of clerical leadership in the black community notwithstanding. Black churches still provide a natural training ground for the development of leadership skills that can be transferred to almost any arena, especially politics. Full-time black clergy, especially of the larger black churches, have a degree of economic and political independence that most black professionals do not possess. Hence, they lack the inhibiting restraints that are common among other potential leaders.

8. Part of the misunderstanding of the role of black churches in politics is due to different assumptions in disciplinary boundaries and theoretical views. The social sciences tend to emphasize a view of increasing secularization of religion in modern society and a complete separation of spheres and functions like those of politics, economics, and education.[103] As faith communities, black churches are social embodiments of theological views and convictions which emphasize involvement and concern in all spheres of life, not just the institutionally religious. The movement of the social sciences, like that of science in general, is toward continuously discrete analysis and differentiation, while theological and moral views move toward unifying all aspects of life and society.

Far from being an antipolitical agency, as has been suggested, the history and the sociology of black churches indicate that they have played a very significant role in politics in the past and in the present and will most likely do so in the future. Yet, the politics of the Black Church has been an ambiguous one as Marable has observed.[104] It has existed in a dialectical tension between the survival and liberation traditions, between a conservative and radical politics, between the doubleness of an African and American heritage. Like most black people, the Black Church has desired to become part of the American political mainstream, but at the same time, it has also jealously guarded its independence. As we pointed out in chapter 1, the dialectical model of the Black Church is the best way of understanding the political pluralism that exists among black churches. This ambiguity and dialectical view will also be found in the concerns of the next chapter.

9   The American Dream and the American Dilemma: The Black Church and Economics

The American Negro problem is a problem in the heart of the American. It is there that the interracial tension has its focus. It is there that the decisive struggle goes on. This is the central viewpoint of this treatise. Though our study includes economic, social, and political race relations, at bottom our problem is the moral dilemma of the American—the conflict between his moral valuations on various levels of consciousness and generality.*

The Puritan wanted to work in a calling; we are forced to do so. . . . In the field of its highest development, in the United States, the pursuit of wealth, stripped of its religious and ethical meaning, tends to become associated with purely mundane passions, which often actually give it the character of sport. . . . The modern man is in general, even with the best will, unable to give religious ideas a significance for culture and national character which they deserve.**

For more than a century foreign observers like Max Weber and Alexis de Tocqueville, and American social scientists like Robert Bellah have recognized the predominance of economic values in the United States.[1] Americans have given the highest priority to economic acquisition and consumption so that the American dream of upward mobility is permeated by those values. However, as Weber has pointed out in the quote above, the religious background which contributed to the rise of the spirit or ethos of modern industrial capitalism in the West is often ignored. Many American economists

---

*Gunnar Myrdal, *An American Dilemma: The Negro Problem and Modern Democracy*, 1:xliii.

**Max Weber, *The Protestant Ethic and the Spirit of Capitalism*, pp. 181–83.

also continue to ignore the relationships between religion and economic behavior. Yet an estimated 40 to 55 percent of all annual retail sales occur during the religious holiday period which begins with the holy day of American civil religion, Thanksgiving, and includes both Hanukkah and Christmas. As Max Stackhouse has also pointed out, both the form and the ethos of the modern limited liability corporation owe their origins to religious roots.[2] A similar attitude prevails with respect to African Americans. Most economic studies of the black community tend to ignore the contributions of their religious background to black economic mobility and development.[3] This chapter will examine several dimensions of the contributions of the Black Church to black economic development in the past and present, and it will also point out some of the contradictions which exist between economics, race, and religion in the United States.

Economics and Race: The Origins of the American Dilemma

The Atlantic slave trade and the institution of slavery in the United States were rooted in the pursuit of economic gain. The Africans were pursued, purchased, and enslaved solely for the cheap labor they could provide on farms and plantations. They were the economic tools for the system of chattel slavery that reduced human beings to forms of property. Although their exact numbers will never be known, the estimates range between 3.5 million to over 50 million Africans who were forcibly taken from Africa, and for every African who survived the rigors of transport to the New World about five others died.[4] The numbers of lives lost during the five centuries of the Atlantic slave trade reached Holocaust proportions. All of the later rationalizations developed about the slave trade as "civilizing the Africans" or "bringing heathens into the fold of Christianity" were subordinated to their fundamental economic purpose. Although the arrival of the first twenty Africans is usually dated as 1619 in the Jamestown colony of Virginia, there were earlier arrivals of African slaves in North America: Lucan Vasquez de Ayllon brought one hundred slaves near to the Jamestown site in 1526 and slaves were present in St. Augustine, Florida, from 1565.[5] Several historians have pointed out that in the beginnings of economic development in the colonies, race was not the primary consideration since even white indentured servants and American Indians were tried out as slaves.[6]

However, the economic calculus of the European colonial mind finally settled upon the Africans as the most cost efficient prospects for enslavement because they were strong and durable, able to withstand the hot summers of the South, distant from the effective security systems of their own people, and above all, their distinctly visible physiologies, their black skin and African features, which contrasted sharply with the Euro-American norm. Moreover, the supply of Africans seemed inexhaustible.[7] Inevitably, physical phenomenology—the fact that Africans looked different from the white men claiming to be their masters—became the basis for the intertwining of race and economics and the development of a racial caste system in the United States.

Since economic values are both primary and predominant in American society, and are commonly used to determine social relations and social status, the most severe forms of racial discrimination against black people have been economic in character. A brief survey of the labor history of African Americans over several centuries provides the evidence for this proposition. During the period of slavery, from the seventeenth century until the Civil War, the majority of black people in the United States were slaves, providing a large segment of the American economy with free labor. These slaves were, of course, in turn dependent upon their masters and the plantation system for food, shelter, and clothing, a dependence orchestrated to ensure contingent survival, and no more. The small number of free black people, or "freedmen" as they were called, also lived marginally in northern and southern cities. From 1840 until the twentieth century, the free African Americans, who were later joined by their newly emancipated brethren in 1865, faced increased competition for jobs, especially in northern cities, from the newly arrived European immigrants which included Germans, Irish, Italians, Poles, and Jews. A comparative study of the labor history of a number of ethnic groups in a small northern city during the late nineteenth century shows that while the Irish initially suffered economically from anti-Catholic bias, the second and third generations were able to achieve economic mobility. However, even with the passing of several generations, black workers in that city did not experience intergenerational mobility and were usually trapped in the lowest occupational strata. Most black women remained in domestic and laundry work and most black men were common laborers or in service occupations like waiters and valets.[8] The conclusions of a study of black labor in Poughkeepsie, New York, can be generalized to other American cities

in the nineteenth century. For large numbers of African Americans
the myth of Horatio Alger remained a myth rooted in pigmentation,
which even the strongest educational attainments and hard work
could not overcome.

During the first four decades of the twentieth century some black
people found access to economic mobility by migrating to northern
industrial centers and replacing white workers in periods of war. But
Gunnar Myrdal, the Swedish sociologist who was invited by the
Carnegie Commission to do a major study of American society, was
puzzled by the deep contradiction that he saw between the high
democratic ideals, the American creed that Americans professed to
believe in, and their actual behavior and practices. Above all, he was
so struck by the discrimination against and the general suppression
of African Americans that he entitled his study *An American Dilemma*. High rates of poverty, unemployment, and underemploy-
ment were found among black people in both urban and rural areas.
Economic discrimination based on race was also accompanied by the
subtle institutional violence of residential segregation, poor housing,
deficient schools, hunger, malnutrition, and higher rates of infant
mortality. The statistical evidence for this coincidence of race and
economics is found in Census Bureau data from 1947 to 1987: the
unemployment rate of black adults has on the average been twice
that of whites and the median black family income has ranged between 51 to 62 percent of white family income.[9] Throughout the
decade of the 1980s the unemployment rate of black teenagers has
hovered between 38 to 50 percent. Black-owned businesses have long
been an area of stunted growth; in 1972 black-owned businesses were
2.7 percent of all business firms. In 1986 the National Urban League
reported that black businesses represented "only 2 percent of all
businesses."[10]

In spite of the harsh realities of the American racial dilemma, the
majority of African Americans have desired to be part of the American dream and to share more equally the fruits of their singular
contributions to this land of opportunity. No one else has expressed
more eloquently this deep abiding faith of African Americans in the
tradition of American upward mobility than Martin Luther King, Jr.,
in his "I Have a Dream" speech delivered in Washington, D.C., in
1963:

> It is obvious today that America has defaulted on this prom-
> issory note insofar as her citizens of color are concerned. Instead

of honoring this sacred obligation, America has given the Negro people a bad check; a check which has come back marked "insufficient funds." We refuse to believe that there are insufficient funds in the great vaults of opportunity of this nation. And so we've come to cash this check, a check that will give us upon demand the riches of freedom and the security of justice.[11]

In the face of the stark economic discrimination faced by black people, what have been the responses of their churches toward the American dilemma in the past and in the present? And what is the relationship between black churches and the economic sphere? In the following sections, we will examine the economic ethic of the mainline black churches and also present some data about black churches as financial institutions and the kinds of economic projects they are supporting.

The Economic Ethic of the Black Church: The Black Self-Help Tradition and the Survival and Liberation Strategies

In the previous chapter on the Black Church and politics we elaborated on the survival and liberation strategies found in the responses of black churches toward politics. Briefly, the survival strategy stressed surviving the brutalities and dehumanization of slavery and racial abuse by any means possible. At times, mere survival was a major accomplishment. But survival always carried with it the potential for change in the future. For most of the black masses survival was the immediate goal, although they had deeper yearnings for freedom and equality. In time the goal of liberation was to move beyond mere survival and to press aggressively for full freedom and common parity, using both reformist and radical political strategies and activities. Both the survival and liberation traditions can be found in the economic realm because the economic ethic of the Black Church also involves a dialectical tension between these two poles.

The survival strategy in the everyday economic life of black people was to just get by or "survivin' one day at a time." Survival meant to eke out a living by whatever means possible. It meant to stay alive "until my chance comes." Studies of extremely poor black people have shown that many of them relied upon an economy of bartering, exchanging, and trading goods and possessions.[12] They also tended to rely upon an extended kinship network, of real and fictive kin. Kin relations frequently provided the only real safety net that they knew, from borrowing and lending money, moving in with kinfolk during times of crises, and relying upon kin for surrogate child-care while parents worked, or during extended periods of nuclear family reversal. Nevertheless, as important as the stage of survival economics was for poor people, it was inevitably marked by extreme dependency, uncertainty, and insecurity.

The liberation strategy in the black community, on the other hand, focused on gaining both upward mobility from poverty and eventual economic independence. There was an understanding that real freedom only comes with the attainment of a measure of economic independence and the creation of an independent economic base. However, upward mobility or becoming middle class was not an end in itself, but it was important because it allowed for the possibility of devising strategies for a greater economic independence in the future. The liberation view also emphasized self-determination, dignity, and a pride in the African and African American heritage and institutions. This liberation perspective tended to be critical of those economic aspects of the capitalist system that tend to dehumanize and oppress people.

The Black Church is a reflexive institution that moves constantly between the poles of survival and liberation in the political and economic arenas. On one hand, for its own economic survival it is an institution that has taken part in the financial and economic transactions of the larger society and it has largely accepted capitalism as an economic system. On the other hand, the Black Church is the most economically independent institutional sector in the black community. It does not depend upon white trustees to raise funds, for example, as do most of the black colleges. Nor does it depend upon white patronage to pay its pastors or erect its buildings.[13] At the same time the seven historically black denominations are justifiably proud of their own histories and contributions to black culture. To collapse the dialectical tension to either the survival pole or the liberation one is to distort the history of the Black Church and to misunderstand the complexity of its dynamic functions.

The economic ethic of the Black Church was forged in the crucible of the slave quarters from whence an ethos or spirit of survival and self-help emerged. The origins of the black self-help tradition were found in the attempts of slaves to help each other survive the traumas and terrors of the plantation system in any way they could. Mothers relied on older relatives or neighbors in the slave quarters to watch the children while they spent the day in the fields. During illness, injury, and death the slaves learned to take care of each other and depend on one another because there was no one else. When death or sale took the parents of young children, the children were raised and cared for by other slaves, irrespective of kinship or lack of it. Since there were no legal slave marriages (although the slaves created their own legitimating rituals like "jumping the broom") there were also no illegitimate children. By law, the father of a slave child was unknown. Children were not stigmatized as bastards as in the English tradition but all children were accepted and loved, whatever the circumstances of their birth.[14] The tradition of mutual aid lay deep in the African heritage, which stressed a greater communalism and social solidarity than either European or American customs allowed. These incipient traditions of mutual aid and self-help in the slave quarters were formalized and legitimated with the Christianizing of the slaves in the eighteenth and nineteenth centuries.

Mutual aid or beneficial societies and churches were among the first social institutions created by black people. They often existed in a symbiotic relationship. Sometimes mutual aid societies led to the formation of black churches, and at other times these societies were organized under the rubric of the churches.[15] Freedmen often played a leading role in establishing both institutions. For example, in April 1787 Richard Allen and Absalom Jones founded one of the earliest mutual aid-benefit societies called the Free African Society. Out of that society in 1794 Allen organized the Mother Bethel A.M.E. Church of Philadelphia. A few weeks earlier Jones had become the pastor of the St. Thomas African Episcopal Church, the first church to be spawned by the Society.[16] These societies themselves were often quasi-churches, attempting to meet both religious and social needs. As Wilmore points out: "Wherever the Societies were organized they began as protests against white prejudice and neglect and with the objective of providing not only for religious needs, but for social service, mutual aid and solidarity among 'people of African descent.'"[17] Mutual aid-benefit societies spread rapidly in northern urban areas where there were a large number of free blacks. By 1830 in Philadelphia, for example, there were more than a hundred of these societies with an average membership of seventy-five.[18] In terms of functions and purpose, these societies were the forerunners of both the NAACP and the National Urban League.

Another early set of institutions that were important in the formation of the black self-help tradition were the quasi-religious fraternal lodges, the Masons and the Odd Fellows. Each fraternal lodge also developed an auxiliary group for women like the Daughters of the Eastern Star for the Masons. Prince Hall, a Methodist minister, established the African Masonic Lodge of Boston in 1775 and the Negro Odd Fellows were founded by Peter Ogden in 1843. The lodges' secret rituals and ceremonies and distinctive regalia lent identity and prestige to the membership, but the organizations also performed significant functions of mutual aid and security.

Black churches, mutual aid societies, and the fraternal lodges contributed to the formation of the black self-help tradition and to the establishment of an economic ethos of uplift for the race that emphasized the following virtues and moral values: industry, thrift, discipline, sobriety, and long-term sublimation rather than immediate gratification. Of these three institutions, black churches led in spreading this ethic of economic rationality among the newly freed masses during the Reconstruction period, partly because they were the most inclusive community institutions and their membership often included members from both the mutual aid societies and lodges. For example, the A.M.E. Church *Review*, the leading African American magazine in the post-Civil War era, published many articles which stressed "the importance of economic and moral development, self-help, and racial solidarity."[19] Before he became a bishop, Benjamin Tucker Tanner, editor of the A.M.E. *Christian Recorder* from 1868 to 1884, urged black people to imitate the economic advancement of Jews in Europe. He also called for collective support for an African American press on a racial basis.[20]

From their pulpits many black preachers preached the moral messages of saving for a rainy day, learning to read and write, getting an education, finding a job and working hard, supporting the family, and raising the children respectably and industriously. They also emphasized the principal moral maxims of evangelical Christianity which did not countenance such activities as smoking, drinking, or dancing. The sermons were reinforced by smaller groups in Sunday School, prayer meetings, and Bible study sessions. Above all, in numerous small, rural southern towns and tightly knit black urban communities, the power of moral sanctions and disciplinary measures were wielded by the deacons and deaconesses. Being cut off from the fellowship of the church in those communities often meant an uncomfortable social isolation.

Thus far, no studies have been done on the role of the Black Church in the economic mobility of black people and the creation of a viable and stable black middle class. Yet, it is clearly evident that black churches had a major role in establishing the black self-help tradition during a time when there were no social welfare agencies and private philanthropy was reserved for other groups. The Black Church assumed the task of helping black people internalize the ethic of economic rationality that would lead to economic mobility. Black church leaders were well aware of the role of racism in retarding this mobility, and they knew from experience that they and their children would have to put forth maximum efforts for minimal achievements. To reduce the trauma of these realities as much as possible, the black churches took on economic roles and functions and created institutional vehicles they might otherwise have left to other entities.

The Economic Roles and Functions of the Black Church in the Past: A Historical Overview

In his examination of the economic situation in African American communities, Du Bois concluded that any study of "economic cooperation among Negroes must begin with the Church group."[21] He was referring to the founding and establishment of black churches during the period of slavery and in the aftermath of the Civil War. Black church members literally pooled their pennies and meager resources to buy land to erect church buildings in both the North and the South. During Reconstruction when many African Americans left the plantations or were driven off, they often settled in nearby black communities, working as sharecroppers on their former master's land or as tenant farmers. These communities were often led by their pastors, and their churches became the first communally built institutions. As the central and dominant institutions in their various communities, black churches performed other critical roles and functions in the economic sphere to ease somewhat the onerousness of abject deprivation.

Du Bois's statement about the Black Church in economic cooperation can be expanded beyond its description of the church's roles as the first communal enterprise and as a cultural broker for the ethic of economic rationality. Black churches and their allied institutions like the mutual aid societies, the quasi-religious fraternal lodges, and the benevolent and burial associations, which often met in the churches, helped to create the first major black financial institutions: the black-owned banks and the black life insurance companies.

The role of churches, lodges, and mutual aid-benevolent associations in creating financial institutions did not begin en masse until after the collapse of the Freedman's Savings and Trust Company in 1874, which had "the most far-reaching economic influence" on the black community.[22] Chartered by Congress in 1865, the Freedman's Savings and Trust Company was the major bank which held most of the savings of many newly emancipated African Americans, the bounties which black soldiers received upon joining the Union army, and the deposits of numerous philanthropic organizations, benevolent associations, and churches. Its collapse resulted from both the national recession of 1873 and the incompetency of bank officials. Yet the collapse of the Freedman's bank and the loss of hard earned savings created a major distrust among many African Americans toward banks, which for some took more than a decade to overcome and then only at banks organized by institutions they trusted. That distrust has not been fully dissipated in some sectors even to this day, and its effect lingers on in conventions which remain suspicious of black enterprise. According to Blassingame, for many other African Americans this distrust toward banks and other financial institutions never completely disappeared, but it helped to intensify a focus upon spending one's earnings for immediate pleasures.[23] In 1887 there was not a single black-owned bank but by 1908 fifty-five banks had been started and forty-seven were in operation.[24]

Toward the end of the nineteenth and at the beginning of the twentieth century the first black insurance companies began to appear, developing from the financial resources of both the mutual aid and burial societies and the fraternal orders. In examining the origins of one of the largest black life insurance companies, North Carolina Mutual, Meier and Rudwick see the following pattern: "In the life of John Merrick, the man chiefly responsible for North Carolina Mutual, one of the two largest black life insurance companies, one observes the evolution of Negro insurance from the quasi-religious fraternity society through the chartered mutual-aid organization to the legal reserve company."[25] Merrick founded North Carolina Mutual in 1898, while Alonzo Herndon established the rival Atlanta Life

Insurance Company in 1905. The Afro-American Industrial Insurance Society of Jacksonville, founded in 1901, began as a mutual benefit society in the Baptist church pastored by Rev. J. Milton Waldron.[26]

The fraternal lodges and churches helped to capitalize black banks like the True Reformers' Bank in Richmond, and the Capital Savings Bank of Washington, D.C., both founded in 1888. The fraternal orders were the primary mobilizers of black finance but the churches ranked second.[27] Clergymen often played a prominent role in organizing insurance societies and banks. As Meier and Rudwick pointed out, "The True Reformer's Bank, the Galilean Fishermen's Bank, and the St. Luke's Bank were all either founded by ministers or closely connected with the churches."[28] The historical museum in the basement of the Sixteenth Street Baptist Church in Birmingham, Alabama, has records of the Penny Saver Bank which was established by that church for its members in the late nineteenth century. The bank's first president was the pastor.[29] Many of these black banks did not survive the Great Depression, but they serve as a historical reminder of the multifaceted economic role of black churches and clergy.

The benevolent and burial associations were also an important economic base since many black funeral parlors and mortuaries grew out of them. By the nature of their function, all of the funeral parlors and mortuaries were also quasi-religious institutions with strong ties to churches. In every black community there was at least one black funeral home and the mortician and his family were usually part of the economic elite. Many poor people bought into burial plans, paying 5 to 10 cents a week for burial insurance, which would assure them of a decent burial. In spite of the trials and travails of a life of poverty, to be properly buried was for most of the black poor a final testimonial of their own decency and human worth. The traditional African American custom of the open funeral casket prompted many people to buy burial insurance, to make certain that their last impressions were favorable and acceptable.

The practice of segregated cemeteries in the North and the South and the difficulties of obtaining loans from white lending agencies also led to the establishment of black cemetery associations and building and loan associations. The first building and loan association in Philadelphia was founded in 1886 and in twenty years there were ten such associations. Pastors also provided the leadership in many of these associations.[30]

The economic role of black churches gained impetus in the twentieth century, under the leadership of Booker T. Washington, who was widely regarded as the national Negro leader of his time, a role which Frederick Douglass had assumed during the latter years of abolitionism and the Civil War years. Both men were deeply religious, closely tied to churches and they often functioned as unofficial preachers. Douglass had been an ordained deacon in the A.M.E. Zion Church, while Washington developed a strong following among black Baptists, and Tuskegee Institute was considered an unofficial black Baptist institution. Although Booker T. Washington was a complex and shrewd man with conservative political views, he also espoused racial solidarity and saw group economic unity—or "Negro support of Negro business"—as the only path toward economic progress and uplift for a largely rural and destitute people.[31] The gospel of wealth that Washington preached espoused the major values of the Protestant ethic: thrift, industry, and self-help. He felt that "economic accumulation" and the "cultivation of morality" were the major means of black acceptance in American society. By demonstrating their worth through frugality, hard work, and achievement, the African American's economic progress would lead to social equality and political rights; Washington eschewed political protests and did not press for the franchise. His views on economics represented a microcosm of the opinions of many black church leaders.[32] Within their views, there is an ambiguous tension between the racial pride, unity, and independence of the Black Church tradition and the deep desire to be part of the American mainstream. Du Bois's description of the dilemma of "double consciousness," of preserving the goodness of being African and American at the same time, is exemplified on the institutional level.[33] Rather than challenging the basis of American capitalism, most black people and their churches wanted to be a part of it.

Washington's mainstream economic views attracted the loyal support of business leaders like Andrew Carnegie, who bankrolled many of Washington's activities and helped him start the National Negro Business League, the first national organization focused upon advancing the economic concerns of the black businessman. The league was a splendid platform for Washington's ideas of economic uplift and it brought him into contact with many African American entrepreneurs starting small businesses in urban areas. The league also facilitated the dialogue between business and clergy leaders.

Another institutional vehicle which Washington indirectly influenced was the founding of the National Urban League in 1911. Conservative black disciples of Washington, white philanthropists, and social workers established the Urban League specifically to improve the employment opportunities of urban African Americans. In the first few decades of the organization the philosophy and strategy of the Urban League was one of a "moral gradualism," attempting to convince white employers of the "moral righteousness and economic value of hiring Negroes."[34] Following Washington's lead, growing numbers of black clergy leaders also saw the need for establishing secular organizational vehicles like the NAACP and the National Urban League in dealing with the more complex urban environments of the Northeast and Midwest. While the NAACP took the more political and legal path in dealing with civil rights cases, the Urban League focused on jobs and the general economic conditions of black people.

Throughout the massive migrations from the rural South, individual churches and clergy in northern cities helped the migrants gain employment by announcing jobs from the pulpit or by posting them on the church bulletin board. That tradition of helping people find employment continues to this day in many leading black churches. It was not unusual for city bureaucrats or heads of companies who were seeking qualified black candidates for jobs to turn to the pastors of large black urban churches for suggestions and names. Just as experienced white politicians have learned of the communicative network and value of speaking in leading black churches during an election campaign, the same phenomenon has applied to the area of employment and economics. During the Depression years some black churches held classes in the fundamentals of job seeking and household economics for the newly arrived rural migrants. For example, in 1936 Dr. Robert Wesley Morgan, a black dentist and leading A.M.E. Zion layman, taught classes in economics and household finances at both the Catharine Street A.M.E. Zion Church and the Ebenezer Baptist Church in Poughkeepsie.[35] Besides these classes, Dr. Morgan with the black pastors and local lay leaders of Poughkeepsie's black community negotiated behind the scenes for access by black people to jobs in hospitals, schools, and stores which had been closed to them. Prior to the civil rights movement, many pastors and leading lay members of the fledgling black middle class took a less visible, behind-the-scenes approach toward civil rights and economic issues, especially negotiating for access to jobs.[36]

As we mentioned previously, only a few clergy like Adam Clayton Powell, Jr., of the Abyssinian Baptist Church in Harlem took more radical and publicly visible measures by leading civil rights protests in the streets on economic issues. A. Phillip Randolph was one of the leading vocal activists prior to the 1950s.[37] Through the journal *The Messenger*, which he coedited with Chandler Owen, Randolph attempted to spread his Marxist analysis of racial prejudice and discrimination, which he felt was used by capitalists as a means of keeping black and white workers from effectively uniting. Although his message was never completely understood except by a few intellectuals, Randolph's most effective contribution to the economic situation of African Americans was his organizing of the Brotherhood of Sleeping Car Porters in the mid-1920s. The brotherhood became one of the most effective black labor unions, and to keep it going, Randolph spent a good deal of time speaking at organizing meetings held in black churches.[38] In spite of his criticism of the clergy and churches, and of the black middle class for neglecting the needs of the deprived masses, Randolph understood well the need for keeping in touch with the church, a people-based institutional sector. He knew too that power lay in organizing the masses, and he could scarcely afford to alienate the organizations with the largest memberships in the black community. Even though his own planned march on Washington for jobs during the Second World War did not materialize, he planted the idea which culminated in the highly successful civil rights March on Washington during the summer of 1963.

Black churches, mutual aid-benefit societies, and fraternal lodges were attempts at creating moral communities that would spread the ethos of economic uplift and self-help. They were partially successful in doing this in both rural and urban settings. However, as voluntary associations that were open to membership by anyone who wanted membership subject to certain minimal criteria, these organizations could not effectively enforce an internal discipline to regulate strictly day-to-day personal behavior. Ivan Light has argued that in certain black groups like Father Divine's Peace Mission a level of strict internal discipline was achieved critical to the order and function of the society as an economic entity. While recent studies like Robert Weisbrot's have confirmed the formidable economic abilities of Divine's Peace Mission, the kind of internal discipline it entailed could not be effectively realized within the more democratic traditions of black churches as compared to the strict authoritarianism of such closed, tightly knit, cult type organizations.[39]

On the other hand, while some black sectarian groups like Father

Divine's Peace Mission and Elijah Muhammad's Nation of Islam were successful in instilling a stern economic and behavioral discipline, there is good evidence that the mainline black churches were also successful in creating an ethos of upward mobility among its members. In one of the few studies to examine the interaction between religion and economic behavior, Gerhard Lenski observed the following about black Protestants in Detroit in the late 1950s:

> One of the more surprising findings in this area concerned the Negro Protestant churches and their relationship to the spirit of capitalism. We had expected that involvement in the Negro Protestant churches would be negatively linked with commitment to the spirit of capitalism, since the group as a whole lacked a strong commitment. However, such was not the case. Those who were active in the Negro Protestant churches were more likely to express views consonant with this spirit than were marginal members. . . . Active Negro Protestant churchgoers actually show a higher frequency of responses compatible with a capitalist orientation than active Catholics.[40]

In one of the first community studies published by an American sociologist, *The Philadelphia Negro*, Du Bois in 1899 summarized the multi-leveled economic functions that black churches have performed historically:

> The Negro churches were the birthplaces of Negro schools and of all agencies which seek to promote the intelligence of the masses; and even to-day no agency serves to disseminate news or information so quickly and effectively among Negroes as the church. . . . Consequently all movements for social betterment are apt to center in the churches. Beneficial societies in endless number are formed here; secret societies keep in touch; cooperative and building associations have lately sprung up; the minister often acts as an employment agent; considerable charitable and relief work is done and special meetings held to aid special projects. The race problem in all its phases is continually being discussed, and, indeed from this forum many a youth goes forth inspired to work.[41]

Before presenting our data on black churches and economics in the 1980s, a brief excursus on the Black Church and education is necessary. Although the topic of education could warrant a separate chapter, we decided to include it in this chapter on the Black Church and economics because in American society at large and in the black community in particular, education is traditionally considered the primary means of achieving economic mobility, and personal and social fulfillment.

The Black Church and Education

No other area of black life received a higher priority from black churches than education. Despite the fact that teaching a slave to read and write was illegal during slavery, one of the most persistent desires of the slaves was to be educated. First of all, literacy was the key to the scriptures, the Word of God, but education was also a rebuttal of the prevailing allegation that black people were a different order of human being, incapable of learning and manipulating the master's language. For many slaves education was tied to their religion, a coveted doorway to the faith and its promises. In *Deep Like the Rivers*, Thomas Webber showed the close link between the rudimentary education of the slaves and the Christianity they adopted.[42] The slaves who learned to read and write often began with the Bible. After emancipation, the newly freed people of all ages swamped the schools. For example, in 1867 there is evidence that all of the classes in Savannah that were opened to educate the former slaves were filled to capacity, despite the absence of a correlation between literacy and employment—given the devastated conditions of the southern economy after the Civil War.[43] Sunday schools were often the first places where black people made contact with the educational process, first hearing, then memorizing, and finally, learning to read Bible stories.

With the aid of the Freedman's Bureau, some white philanthropists, and missionaries from the American Mission Society, individual black churches began to establish schools. A few of these schools, which were often housed in the basements of black churches, later became famous black colleges. Morehouse College in Atlanta, for example, traced its history to a school founded after 1866 in the basement of the Springfield Baptist Church in Augusta.[44] Started as a school in the basement of the Friendship Baptist Church in Atlanta, Spelman College is also a vivid contemporary example of the role of the Black Church in education. Although it became a predominantly Baptist institution under Booker T. Washington's influence, Tuskegee Institute began as a school which met in the basement of Butler Chapel A.M.E. Zion Church in Tuskegee, Alabama.[45]

Besides individual churches, all of the primary black denominational bodies among the Baptists, Methodists, and Pentecostals
established their own colleges and seminaries. In our historical chapters on each of these denominations, a list of their educational institutions is given. The importance of these denominational schools
showed the primacy which the Black Church gave to the area of
education, often establishing black schools whether or not they also
had white philanthropy. Since many of the famous black colleges and
universities such as Howard, Fisk, Talladega, and Hampton Institute
were founded with the aid of white philanthropy and white missionaries, some scholars have undervalued the independent contribution
of the Black Church in this area.[46] However, regardless of their primary sources of origin, all these black schools stressed the importance of religion and moral education for the uplift of the race as it
was obvious to all parties that socialization was closely tied to the
educational process. The molding of young minds in the crucible of
education would become determinative of the future options and
economic opportunities for African Americans. Throughout the
twentieth century many black churches continue to contribute
scholarship funds for promising young members in their congregation who are willing to struggle for college degrees; and they are often
given special recognition and encouragement during the worship
services.

In our study it was found that 86 percent of the black pastors of
2,150 churches responded affirmatively when asked whether their
church supported church-related black colleges. Only 14 percent said
no. Although the exact amount of each church's contribution is not
known, one can assume that there is a very high level of support for
these colleges within the major black denominations. For example,
the General Baptist Convention of the Commonwealth of Virginia,
the largest black Baptist organization in the state, donated $400,000
to the Virginia Union University and Seminary in 1988.[47] Yet, even
this level of support by black churches cannot entirely overcome the
precarious financial situation experienced by many black colleges
since the desegregation of the schools, especially in the South. The
black colleges and universities accounted for about 37 percent, or a
little more than one-third, of the black college student population in
1985. Desegregation and the recruitment of black students by elite
white colleges and universities have also reduced the pool of students
from black middle-class families who have traditionally attended the
historic black colleges. In a study of the future of black colleges and

universities, Garibaldi and his associates estimated that only about half of the more than one hundred institutions of higher education will survive into the twenty-first century.[48] A number of church-related black colleges are already threatened by an unstable financial situation, and each black denomination will have to make major decisions about the schools they support. One attractive option is the consolidation of colleges and seminaries on the model of the Inter-denominational Theological Center in Atlanta, which serves as an umbrella and cooperative enterprise for seven black theological seminaries.

The support and involvement of black churches in education ultimately leads to the question of what kind of viability the churches themselves have as economic institutions.

The Black Church as an Economic Institution

Black churches have not only been the spawning ground for a variety of economic enterprises such as funeral homes, benevolent associations, banks, and insurance companies, but they are themselves significant economic and financial institutions. As a community-based institution, the finances of the local black church often reflect the economic conditions of its members. Much of the class character of the churches, from elite ones to storefronts, is determined by this important index. Nevertheless, as important as black churches are in the profiles of their respective communities, not much hard information is known about their financial activity. Any research on the economic character of black churches is severely limited by the inadequate records kept by many of these churches, or by the extreme difficulty in gaining access to these records if they exist.[49] At the present time most of the financial data on black churches must be interpreted with extreme caution; a statement which applies to our own study which recorded an inordinate number of "no responses" to questions about church finances. In spite of these limitations we present the findings we have since they can act as relative benchmarks about black churches as economic institutions. The data also shed some light on the kinds of economic activity that some churches have undertaken in the contemporary period. The dollar amounts in the survey reflect the value of the dollar during the five-year period from 1979–1984.

The data in table 27 indicate that the average yearly church in-

Table 27: Church Income

Q. What is the average yearly income of this church?

Income Estimate	Total	Urban	Rural
$1 to $4,999	232 (10.8%)	110 (7.2%)	122 (19.7%)
$5,000 to $9,999	224 (10.4%)	116 (7.6%)	108 (17.4%)
$10,000 to $14,999	212 (9.9%)	136 (8.9%)	76 (12.3%)
$15,000 to $24,999	242 (11.3%)	162 (10.6%)	80 (12.9%)
$25,000 to $49,999	342 (15.8%)	270 (17.6%)	72 (11.7%)
$50,000 and over	543 (25.3%)	513 (33.5%)	30 (4.8%)
No response	355 (16.5%)	224 (14.6%)	131 (21.2%)

Estimated total average income of all churches $15,000 to $24,999
Estimated total average income of urban churches $15,000 to $24,999
Estimated total average income of rural churches $9,000 to $15,000

Total N=2,150
Urban N=1,531
Rural N=619

come for 2,150 churches is in the category of $15,000 to $24,999; the
mean income for 1,531 urban churches also fell in the same range.
For 619 rural churches the average income ranged from $9,000 to
$15,000.[50]
   In response to the question, "What is the main way of raising
income for this church?" the pastors could choose among several
ways their church raises income. The results in table 28 indicate that
the vast majority, 1,836 (85.4 percent) churches relied on offertory
collections, while 1,176 (54.9 percent) also used the pledge system.
Churches that sponsored special fund-raising drives numbered 995
(46.3 percent), and only 47 (2.2 percent) had any endowment income.
Churches that also used other means of raising funds like church
dinners, church sales, musical events, and fashion shows numbered
1,608 (74.8 percent). The finding on endowment income is significant because it points to the fact that very few black churches have
any endowment income to sponsor programs. In our field experience
it appeared that the knowledge about financial vehicles like endowment income for churches was not pervasive among black pastors. In
comparison, many white churches use endowment income to maintain their physical plant and to run programs.

Table 28: Methods of Raising Income for the Church

Q. What is the main way of raising income for this church? (Allowed to choose more than one)

Methods	Total	Urban	Rural
Pledge system	1,176 (54.9%)	884 (57.7%)	328 (53.0%)
Offertory collections	1,836 (85.4%)	1,319 (86.2%)	513 (82.9%)
Special fund-raising drives	995 (46.3%)	667 (43.6%)	328 (53.0%)
Endowment income	47 (2.2%)	31 (2.0%)	13 (2.1%)
Other means (church dinners, etc.)	1,608 (74.8%)	1,093 (71.4%)	515 (83.2%)

In terms of budget allocation the high levels of "no response" (45 to 47 percent) from the clergy indicate a need for great caution in interpreting the results. For the Baptists with an independent or congregational polity, the results were: missions and benevolence 6.39 percent; program of the local church 53.07 percent; national programs or causes 3.55 percent; and secular institutions 2.39 percent. Given the high levels of no responses to this question, a revised estimate of budget allocation among Baptist churches would be about 85 percent for the program of the local church (most of which goes for the salary of the pastor and building maintenance); 6 to 10 percent for missions and benevolence; and a total of about 5 percent for national programs or causes and secular institutions. For the Methodists (A.M.E., A.M.E. Zion, and C.M.E.) and the Pentecostals (COGIC) who subscribe to a connectional polity, the question asked how much the church paid in general claims (apportionments) to the general church in the last fiscal year. The average amount of general claims contributed by 781 Methodist and COGIC churches was $4,259.58.

The survey also examined other financial holdings of black churches like investments (financial); businesses (commercial businesses, for example, book stores, parking lots, or service enterprises such as housing projects and child-care centers); and income producing property (rental housing and land). Table 29 shows that 336 (15.6 percent) churches responded affirmatively to the question of any financial investments, while 1,688 (78.5 percent) replied no. Most of the investments held by black churches consisted of money market

Table 29: Church Investments, Businesses, and Income
Producing Property

Investments: Q. Does your church have any investments?

	Total	Urban	Rural
Yes	336 (15.6%)	270 (17.6%)	66 (10.7%)
No	1,688 (78.5%)	1,168 (76.3%)	520 (84.0%)
No response	126 (5.8%)	93 (6.1%)	33 (5.3%)

Businesses: Q. Does this church operate any businesses (e.g., commercial businesses like a bookstore, religious articles store, parking lot, or service enterprises like housing projects, child-care centers, etc.)?

	Total	Urban	Rural
Yes	149 (6.9%)	134 (8.8%)	15 (2.4%)
No	1,946 (90.5%)	1,349 (88.1%)	597 (96.4%)
No response	55 (2.5%)	48 (3.1%)	7 (1.1%)

Income-producing property: Q. Does this church own any income-producing property?

	Total	Urban	Rural
Yes	291 (13.5%)	262 (17.1%)	29 (4.7%)
No	1,796 (83.5%)	1,217 (79.5%)	579 (93.5%)
No response	63 (2.9%)	52 (3.4%)	11 (1.8%)

Total N=2,150
Urban N=1,531
Rural N=619

---

certificates or high interest bank accounts. Some churches have invested in city and state bonds, but only a handful of them have developed a stock portfolio.

In response to the question of operating commercial businesses or service enterprises, 149 (6.9 percent) said yes, while 1,946 (90.5 percent) said no. The most common type of businesses operated by black churches included parking lots and child-care centers. In regard to income producing property, 291 (13.5 percent) said yes and 1,796 (86.1 percent) replied negatively. The most common types of income producing property were rental houses and leased land. One rural church outside Jackson, Mississippi, received royalties from a natural gas well on its property.

A number of large black churches have revived the tradition of church involvement in businesses and the economic development of their communities. America's largest black church with an estimated 15,000 members, the Concord Baptist Church in Brooklyn, pastored by Gardner Taylor, operated a nursing home, a private school from elementary to the eighth grade, a clothing bank, a credit union, and had two full-time social workers on its staff. Under the leadership of Rev. William A. Jones, the 4,000 member Bethany Baptist Church in Brooklyn raised $1 million to open the Harvest Manor Restaurant that employs forty-four people and serves lunch and dinner every day.[51] Rev. Floyd Flake's Allen A.M.E. Church in Jamaica, Queens, has set up a church-sponsored housing corporation that rehabilitated 10 stores in the neighborhood, a housing development fund, a home care agency, a 300-unit, $11 million complex for senior citizens, and a 480-pupil elementary school. In Miami, Florida, under the leadership of Rev. Henry Nevin, the St. John's Baptist Church organized the St. John's Community Development Corporation, a nonprofit agency designed to rehabilitate the neighborhood surrounding the church.[52] Other examples of large black churches involved in economic development projects include[53] (1) Allen Temple Baptist Church in Oakland, California, under the guidance of Rev. Dr. J. Alfred Smith, pastor and president of the Progressive National Baptist Convention, operated a 75-unit housing development for low-income and elderly citizens and another 51-unit project. It also had a job information center, a blood bank, and a credit union with $1 million in assets. (2) The Hartford Avenue Baptist Church in Detroit established a multipurpose social service agency that handled everything from medical needs to counseling. It also runs a print shop, a book bindery, an auto shop, a 460-pupil school, and a $2 million credit union. (3) New Zion Baptist Church in Louisville ran a 117-bed nursing home. (4) Rev. W. N. Daniel of the Antioch Baptist Church in Chicago's Southside led his congregation in several housing development projects: first, a $7 million, 810-unit development; second, a $4 million, 195-unit development in Fort Wayne, Indiana; and third, a 230-unit, $12 million complex in Englewood called Haven Homes. (5) In the largest housing cooperative project of its kind in the nation, fifty-five East Brooklyn churches are building 5,000 owner-occupied row houses within ten years, the Nehemiah Houses (in honor of the fifth-century prophet who rebuilt Jerusalem). About 40 percent of the owners of these houses will come from public housing projects.[54]

Probably the wealthiest black church we encountered in the field was the Wheat Street Baptist Church in Atlanta. Led by a famous preacher and financier, William Holmes Borders, Wheat Street had the largest property holdings of any black church in the United States, infusing the surrounding community with more than $15 million worth of development. The church had built a middle-class apartment building, Wheat Street Towers, rented out a number of storefronts along Auburn Avenue, and owned fifteen acres of property in downtown Atlanta. Borders had also set up the first federal credit union sponsored by any church and is considered one of the pioneers in church-sponsored public housing. The examples of Borders and Wheat Street and the other examples given above, however, appear to be more the exception than the rule since the vast majority of black pastors and churches do not seem to have much knowledge about financial investments and economic development. Much of the economic development is being undertaken by large, elite black churches which usually have well-educated, activist, and economically astute pastors. But the examples do point to the potential in economic development by black churches.

The survey also examined the ownership of church buildings, whether the property was mortgaged, the estimated value of church-held property, and the level of church debt. Table 30 shows the responses in regard to the ownership of church buildings and any mortgages on the property. 1,944 (90.4 percent) churches claimed that they owned their church building, while 117 (5.4 percent) rented and 47 (2.2 percent) had "other arrangements," usually meeting in someone's home. If the building was owned, the survey inquired whether the property was mortgaged. About one-third, 679 (31.6 percent) churches, replied yes that the property had a mortgage on it. But close to two-thirds, 1,282 (59.6 percent) churches said no, implying that they had outright ownership of their buildings. These two findings that 90 percent of black churches owned their buildings, and close to 60 percent of the churches had no mortgages confirm the economic independence of this institutional sector. There are probably very few other institutions in the black community that can match this level of ownership and independence.

In response to the question of giving an estimate of the value of

Table 30: Ownership and Mortgage Data of Church
Buildings

Ownership: Q. Is the church building owned or rented?

	Total	Urban	Rural
Owned	1,944 (90.4%)	1,378 (90.0%)	566 (91.4%)
Rented	117 (5.4%)	101 (6.6%)	16 (2.6%)
Other	47 (2.2%)	16 (1.0%)	31 (5.0%)
No response	42 (2.0%)	36 (2.4%)	6 (1.0%)

Mortgage: Q. If owned, is the property mortgaged?

	Total	Urban	Rural
Yes	679 (31.6%)	543 (35.5%)	136 (22.0%)
No	1,282 (59.6%)	830 (54.2%)	452 (73.0%)
No response	189 (8.8%)	158 (10.3%)	31 (5.0%)

Total N=2,150
Urban N=1,531
Rural N=619

overall church-held property, the average for 1,944 churches was
$349,411.12. For 1,369 urban churches the average estimated value
was $453,963.17, while for 575 rural churches the average was
$100,436.33. While these estimates appeared to be high, during the
five-year period of the survey property values in both urban and rural
areas constituted a highly inflated sector of the economy. A fact to
keep in mind regarding church financing is that although the average
value of church property holdings may seem high, the actual real
property estimate may be much lower. Most banks are reluctant to
foreclose their financial dealings on church properties because of the
negative public image this may produce. Also when church buildings
are closed, they are difficult to convert to other business uses without extensive renovations and capital investment.

The estimated overall level of church debt averaged $53,853.99 for
968 churches (45.02 percent). The urban-rural breakdown was an
average of $62,734.00 for 771 urban churches, and $19,099.89 for
197 rural churches. However, the majority of black churches, 1,182
(54.98 percent), did not have any debt. This finding contrasts signifi-

cantly from Mays and Nicholson's concern that 71.3 percent of the churches in their study were indebted.[55] Almost all of the church debt for both urban and rural churches is due to the construction of new buildings or renovations of older ones. The rapid escalation in heating costs has also increased church debt.

While the findings of our nationwide field survey of 1,863 pastors of 2,150 black churches was based on personal interviews, we did not project any national economic figures because of the problems associated with church record keeping and access. However, a study by Martin Larson and Stanley Lowell does offer some estimates which underscore the idea that black churches are important economic institutions. In a 1981 article on the "Economics of the Church," using the statistics provided by Larson and Lowell's *The Religious Empire*, David Smallwood estimated that at least 20 million black Americans are religious and these 20 million constitute about 15 percent of an estimated total of 135 million religious Americans. "As such," he wrote, "blacks contribute about 15 percent of the total plate offerings, some $1.7 billion."[56]

Other studies confirm the continuing importance of the area of religion to African Americans. In a 1987 preliminary report of a two-year study on philanthropy in black America for the Joint Center for Political Studies, Emmett Carson cited the finding that, "Over two-thirds (68 percent) of all dollars that are contributed by blacks to charity go to the church."[57] While no total dollar figures are given by the Joint Center study, the 68 percent given by black people to the church is a much higher rate than the 46.9 percent of all charitable giving that went to the religious category nationwide, as reported by the AAFRC Trust for Philanthropy in *Giving USA*.[58] Although it is a well established fact that religion receives the highest percentage of all charitable giving in the United States, not much was known about the black rate of charitable contributions. When the 7.4 percent which is given to "religious organizations" in the Joint Center report is added to the 68 percent given to "own church," the black rate reaches an amazing 75.4 percent of all charitable giving that properly belongs in the category of "giving to religion."[59] Updating Smallwood's estimates, the total amount given by African Americans to religion can easily surpass $2 billion annually, a figure which does not include volunteer time. In the Joint Center report Carson estimated that "About the same percentage of blacks and whites (35.3 percent and 34.6 percent, respectively) volunteered for church activities—by far the largest recipient of volunteer services."[60] According to the AAFRC Trust for Philanthropy report, about 39.5 million Americans in 1986 contributed time to religious organizations and the estimated value of this time was $35 billion.[61] While no specific estimated value has been given to the volunteer time that African Americans give to religion, the total amount would certainly run into billions of dollars each year, giving significant economic clout to the area of religion in the black community.

If volunteer behavior in terms of time and money can be taken as an indicator of a people's loyalty and commitment, then according to the Joint Center study results, the 75.4 percent total in charitable giving and the 35.3 percent in volunteer time accorded to the area of religion by black people far outstrips any other sector of institutional concern. For example, the next highest categories to religion include 6.6 percent given to hospitals and medical centers, 6.2 percent to social welfare organizations, and 3.8 percent to educational organizations; in terms of volunteer time, the next highest category, education groups, received 11.6 percent from black volunteers.[62]

Data from the Princeton Religion Research Center of May 1987 on levels of religious involvement also confirm the continuing importance of religion to the majority of black people. According to *Emerging Trends*, 78 percent of African Americans are "churched," compared to 72 percent nationwide; 37 percent of African Americans are "superchurched," compared to 31 percent nationwide; the "unchurched" rate among black people is 22 percent, compared to 28 percent nationwide; and 3 percent of black people claim to be "totally nonreligious," compared to 4 percent nationwide.[63] All of the church affiliation rates of African Americans tend to be slightly higher than the national rate. The weekly church attendance rates of black people at 43 percent in 1986 is also slightly above the national average of 40 percent.[64]

In sum, all of the data point to a highly significant role for black churches as economic institutions. Although some erosion has taken place in the loyalty of African Americans to their churches during the great migrations and the process of urbanization, religion still emerges as one of the strongest, most stable, and most independent institutional areas in the black community nationwide. Taking into account the value of their property and holdings, the amount of charitable donations given, and the value of volunteer labor, the total institutional area of religion in the black community represents untold billions of dollars. Yet the irony remains that most black churches are not wealthy institutions, and that close to half of the black clergy nationwide (45.1 percent) must work at another full-time occupation in order to support themselves. However, valid questions are being raised both within and without the Black Church about the use and stewardship of these actual and potential economic resources. We turn to two final topics which are directly related to these concerns: the Black Church and black economic development, and economic challenges for the Black Church.

The Black Church and Black Economic Development: The Opportunities Industrialization Centers and New Directions

> It was generally agreed among the black churches that the economic standing of the race was directly proportional to the level of educational and moral development. Hence they believed that improvement in the latter would result in a corresponding improvement in the former. Although many black economic enterprises had their beginnings in the black churches, and although the churches themselves constituted major economic institutions, they never gave high institutional priority to black economic development. Hence the churches expended much less energy in that sphere of their life than in education, moral training, and civil rights. The reasons for this are multiple, but a major one is that blacks viewed education and civil rights as necessary conditions for economic development.[65]

Peter Paris's astute observation that black churches never gave black economic development a high institutional priority, in spite of their own significant economic roles in past history, is supported by the results of our survey and field observations. While a few elite black churches and pastors have been engaged in important projects that could help the economic development of their local areas, the majority of pastors and churches lacked adequate knowledge about financial investments and about the economic development of their own institutions and that of the surrounding community. One of the major weaknesses of the historic black denominations is in the area of training and teaching their denominational leaders, pastors, and laity about all aspects of economic stewardship, from careful record keeping, financial accountability, and investments to the economic development of their communities. However, since the civil rights period of the late 1960s there has been a very important development among black churches regarding economic issues in the black community, namely, the Opportunities Industrialization Centers under the leadership of Rev. Leon Sullivan of Philadelphia.

The Opportunities Industrialization Centers grew out of the experience of the civil rights struggles in Philadelphia and developed under the leadership of Leon Sullivan, pastor of the Zion Baptist Church. Educated at the Union Theological Seminary in New York and having served under the tutelage of Adam Clayton Powell, Jr., at the Abyssinian Baptist Church, Sullivan organized the Selective Patronage Campaign in the late 1950s, which was supported by four hundred black ministers in Philadelphia. The campaign successfully boycotted the Tasty Baking Company, Sun Oil, Gulf Oil, Atlantic-Richfield, and Pepsi Cola. This success led to requests from potential white employers for black employees with skills in technical fields which many African Americans did not possess at that time. Sullivan then recognized the need for a community-based employment training facility, which was founded in 1964 as the Opportunities Industrialization Centers of America.[66] Another economic development project which helped to prepare the way for OIC was Sullivan's "10–36" plan initiated in 1962 in his church. The plan called for church members to contribute $10 for 36 months to support the Philadelphia Community Investment Cooperative. The group of 227 original subscribers grew to over 5,000 with about 400 black churches participating, and $200 of every $360 subscription was invested in the for-profit Progress Investments Associates, while the remaining $160 was donated to Zion Non-Profit Charitable Trust. The Progress Investments Associates built Progress Plaza Shopping Center, the first and largest black-owned and operated shopping complex in the United States. It also constructed an apartment building, a garment manufacturing plant and a chain of convenience stores. Zion Non-Profit Charitable Trust used foundation and government grants to sponsor programs like housing for the disadvantaged, remedial education, and other human services activities.[67] Through these projects Sullivan was resurrecting the historical role of black clergy and churches being involved in the stimulation of economic development.[68]

Following its organization in 1964, the Opportunities Industrialization Centers of America quickly became a nationwide phenomenon, operating in seventy cities within five years and handling federal government contracts worth $18 million. President Johnson's War on

Poverty programs and Sullivan's old mentor, Rep. Adam Clayton Powell, Jr., aided in the development of an oic-federal connection.[69] A distinctive feature of the oic approach was the development of a close working relationship with the private sector, which facilitates job placement activities and generates corporate contributions that have permitted oic's to keep their training cost per participant quite low.[70] Another distinctive feature of oic job training programs involved the attempt to stimulate a moral commitment from the trainees and to inspire them by providing classes on black history and self-esteem. This spiritual and moral dimension of oic distinguished it from federal government manpower and other job training programs. The expansion of oic programs has depended upon the support of local ministers and churches in various communities, a pattern that is consistent with its origins.[71] Although oic does not have any formal ties with churches, four of the top five officers of oic's national board of directors were ministers.

By emphasizing a community based vocational training and job placement operation, the oic experience has been a relatively successful one. At its height in 1980 oic was operating in more than 160 cities and close to 700,000 people had been trained and placed in jobs. However, a total evaluation and history of the oic experiment nationwide has not yet been done. There have been stories of successes as well as failures since each center operates relatively autonomously. The severe budget cutbacks on social programs during the Reagan years have also hampered oic programs and some $77 million in federal funding has been lost.[72] Yet many centers have survived and an oic International with branches in Africa has been established.

As a charismatic and diplomatic figure, Leon Sullivan's career deserves scholarly evaluation. He is perhaps the most prominent example of the modern black minister involved in the complexities of economic development issues. Sullivan was the first black person to sit on the board of directors of General Motors. In his concern for the improvement of conditions for black workers in South Africa, he devised the famous "Sullivan Principles" between 1975 and 1977, which were adopted by some American companies. However, when the Reagan administration began to use his principles to rationalize its policy of "constructive engagement" in its benign posture toward apartheid in South Africa, Sullivan rejected Reagan's strategy and called for a deadline of May 31, 1987, for the abolition of apartheid by the South African government. Thereafter, Sullivan pressed a campaign for $100 billion in divestment pledges by American interests in South Africa, and by July 1986, he had gathered some $40 billion in pledge divestments.[73] Sullivan's involvement in the South Africa issue has helped to broaden the international economic and political perspectives of many black church leaders, who were often accused of having only parochial concerns.

Besides Sullivan and the Opportunities Industrialization Centers, a more recent example of the Black Church's involvement in economic development concerns the projects of the Congress of National Black Churches. In 1978 the congress held its first organizational meeting at the Indianapolis-based Lilly Endowment, and elected Bishop John Hurst Adams of the A.M.E. Church as its first president. Made up primarily of representatives from each of the seven historic black denominations, the congress decided to undertake the task of social and economic institution-building in the black community. Under Bishop Adams's leadership the congress addressed itself to overcoming the economic vulnerabilities of the black community by using the resources of the Black Church in cooperative economic ventures. Relying partly on the results of the early phases of this study, which pointed to the lack of basic life and health insurance benefits among the majority of black clergy, the congress began the process of establishing a joint insurance program in which all black clergy and even laity can participate in. Further, as mentioned in chapter 7, the congress plans to establish a large, cooperative publishing company. Almost all of the historic black denominations have extensive, individual publishing operations for church literature, but except for Johnson Publications, which has a very limited book division, there is no independent African American publisher of serious nonreligious literature. Because very few aspiring black writers addressing black interests are able to penetrate the white publishing circles, the African American subculture is seriously underexpressed, and the vast black economic potential that lies in the Americas, Africa, and the Caribbean remains unrealized.

Another new direction in economic development by churches is the project to sponsor a national bank credit card by the Christian Methodist Episcopal Church, the first attempt of its kind by any religious denomination. The C.M.E. Church hopes to raise revenue from the credit cards for its educational, economic, social-welfare, and health programs since the denomination would earn one-half of

1 percent in royalty fees each time the card is used. Floyd R. Chapman, executive director of the c.m.e. Economic Development Commission, has estimated that the church could earn $1 million a year if only 50,000 of its 750,000 members signed up for the card.[74] The card is issued by the First National Bank of Louisville, Kentucky, as part of its "affinity bank card program," which has become a popular fundraising tool for some large universities, trade associations, and charitable organizations.

The political efforts by black civil rights groups in the economic arena such as Jesse Jackson's People United to Save Humanity or Operation PUSH, the Southern Christian Leadership Conference, the NAACP, and the National Urban League should also be considered in any discussion of the Black Church and economics since the membership of those groups tend to overlap with black church membership. Moreover, PUSH, SCLC, and the NAACP have had ministerial leadership. Under Jackson's leadership, Operation PUSH has negotiated with a number of American corporations and firms to open up franchise possibilities and employment for blacks. PUSH has held its general meetings on Saturday in order not to conflict with the worship services of black churches on Sunday morning. However, the format and atmosphere of its meetings is that of a quasi-church. In 1988 SCLC conducted a campaign among the black churches of Atlanta to withdraw their money from white banks and to deposit it in black banks, after it was discovered that these white banks were discriminatory in making loans to black people and businesses. Although the political efforts of groups like PUSH and SCLC have not been adequately evaluated, they do illustrate the current black strategy of using political leverage to gain economic access and opportunity. The constant interaction between politics, economics, and religion has been evident in most of the civil rights activities since 1954. For example, the Montgomery bus boycott was an economic weapon designed to achieve the desegregation of buses, and the black churches, clergy, and church members constituted the mobilizing network. Since the passage of the Civil Rights Act of 1964 and the Voting Rights Act of 1965, the focus has been to use black political power to open up economic opportunities for the masses of black people.

By devising new institutions and by focusing upon structural ways of attacking the economic conditions of African Americans, the Congress of National Black Churches and the economic projects by the c.m.e. Church and civil rights organizations represent some of the more hopeful signs to emerge in the decade of the 1980s. All of these groups are attempting to deal with the difficult complexities of a technological society and at the same time revive the tradition of the involvement of black clergy and churches in the economic arena. If they succeed, the Black Church will be in a favorable position to deal with some of the economic challenges in the twenty-first century.

Toward the Twenty-First Century: Economic Challenges for the Black Church

In their 1945 classic, *Black Metropolis*, Drake and Cayton described a rapidly developing class structure among Negroes in "Bronzeville," the inner-city of Chicago. Just after a few decades of rural to urban migration, they estimated that 5 percent were in the upper class, 30 percent in the middle class, and 65 percent in the lower class.[75] Since the Drake and Cayton study, there has been an ongoing dispute among social scientists about how to define class and socio-economic status among African Americans. Yet, in spite of this debate, all of the data point to the important fact that there are currently more black people in the working and middle classes or above, in contrast to the 1945 data.[76] Robert Hill has held to the following class divisions: one-third middle class, one-third working class, and one-third lower class or poor. Andrew Billingsley has shown that about two-thirds of the black community are in the category of "middle income."[77] Reynolds Farley has argued that black economic progress since 1960 has been a mixed phenomenon, showing gains in areas like educational attainment and income but also a lack of progress in the unemployment of black men, rise in poverty rates, and high degrees of residential and school segregation.[78] The growth of middle-income families among blacks should not obscure the fact that black median family income is still about 60 percent of whites and whites have an intergenerational wealth base of ten times as much family wealth as African Americans. One-third of black families have no family wealth, while much of the economic advantage of the past that whites have accumulated is perpetuated through family wealth and inheritance.[79] The category of lower class has been divided between a lower-class group of the "working poor" and the "dependent poor" or "underclass," namely, those who persist in poverty for several generations.

While the black poor constituted about one-third (30 to 36 percent) of the black population in the 1980s, much of the scholarly and political debate has focused on the black underclass, which is estimated to be about half of impoverished African Americans or 18 percent.[80] According to William Julius Wilson's recent study, *The Truly Disadvantaged*, the black poor, especially the underclass, live in extremely deprived sectors of ghetto communities. Using data from Chicago, Wilson argues that the problems of the underclass are compounded because most of the upwardly mobile black people and their corresponding institutions have left the most deprived sectors of the ghetto, leaving the underclass more isolated and alienated. Prior to the civil rights period, there were black middle-class and working-class role models and institutions like black churches available to help the truly disadvantaged. The industrial base of large cities such as factories and manufacturing industries has moved to the sun belt or to Third World countries so that the jobs which provided the typical entry level positions for the very poor are no longer available. Wilson feels that even the elimination of racism, which is often the goal of race-specific social policies, would not significantly affect the black poor unless something was done to change both the larger economy and the communities they live in.[81]

As we have shown in our historical overviews of the seven major black denominations, most of black church members are middle class and working class or in the coping middle income category. The three Methodist denominations (A.M.E., A.M.E. Zion, and C.M.E.) were composed largely of middle-income members. Although the type of edifice that people worship in can be deceiving, they do give an indication about the economic level of the majority of the members of that church. For example, storefront churches are usually found in the most depressed areas of a ghetto because landlords who own commercial space cannot find anyone to rent to, except church people who may also use part of that space as living quarters for the pastor and family members. In our survey of 2,150 churches we came across only one Methodist storefront church. About 7 percent of our sample were storefront churches and these were usually Baptist or Pentecostal (COGIC). However, the majority of Baptists and Pentecostals were also from the working and middle classes. One of the most significant class shifts over the past fifty years has been among the Pentecostals. As Drake and Cayton noted in their study, if anyone said that they were "sanctified," it was immediately assumed that they were lower class.[82] Although the Pentecostals are still classified by some scholars as lower class, the class situation with the Church of God in Christ is changing rapidly.[83] It is estimated that more than half of COGIC members are now within the coping middle-income strata (largely working-class and some middle-class members). Many of their churches are also reflecting this economic change from storefront to regular church edifices. Pentecostals are also developing their own scholars, a number of whom are enrolled in doctoral programs in major divinity schools. As we pointed out in chapter 4, the Church of God in Christ has moved quite rapidly in establishing a national headquarters in Memphis and in developing a cohesive administrative bureaucracy. In this regard, they have already surpassed some of their Methodist and Baptist counterparts.

The major challenge facing a predominantly middle- and working-class Black Church is whether it can effectively reach out to the extremely deprived members of the truly disadvantaged. While many middle-income black church congregations have a few poor members in their midst, recent studies like Wilson's point to a major and growing class division in the black community with the extremely poor being more and more isolated and alienated from even black institutions. More than any other institution, some black churches have shown in their past history the ability to span class divisions and to unify people in the spirit of enthusiastic worship.[84] Yet as class differentiation has continued, the question is whether black middle- and working-class churches will continue to devise programs, provide leadership, and reach out effectively to the truly poor. Many poor people do not feel comfortable in middle-income churches. Thus far, at least politically, the black middle and working classes have not abandoned the poor since the majority of black voters have tended to be among the most liberal and reform-minded voters on the American political scene. One advantage that many black churches have is the fact that the majority of them are still located in the ghetto, although new churches are now being formed in black suburban areas. Black churches can take advantage of their location and begin the difficult task of organizing these deprived inner-city communities and providing a political voice and community infrastructure; whether they will do so remains to be seen. Before his death, Martin Luther King, Jr., issued this economic challenge to the black middle class: "It is time for the Negro middle class to rise up from its stool of indifference, to retreat from its flight into unreality and to bring its full resources—its heart, its mind and its checkbook to the aid of the less fortunate brother."[85]

On the other side of the class divide is the challenge presented by the concerns of the young, black, urban professionals (often called "Buppies"), who have been enamored of their newly found education, wealth, and status, and like their white counterparts revel in the pursuit of "conspicuous consumption" and an intensified focus upon self.[86] Some of the Buppies have left the church and the black community, since they do not want to be constrained by traditions which they feel are irrelevant to their present needs. There is some evidence, however, that other black professionals, especially those who have worked in the white corporate world for at least a decade, tend to feel socially isolated among their white colleagues. In their book on *Black Life in Corporate America,* George Davis and Gregg Watson discussed the problems of isolation and alienation that many black middle managers have felt in large corporations.[87] The lack of any social or communal support system is felt most acutely for African Americans who both live and work in white suburban areas. However, where there are enough black professionals, there has been a tendency not only to form social clubs but also to establish churches. For example, in the IBM-dominated mid-Hudson region, the Bethel Missionary Baptist Church of Wappingers Falls, known colloquially as the "IBM church," was established in 1966 by a congregation made up of predominantly black IBM'ers, a scant fourteen years after the corporation hired its first black engineer.[88]

A political and ideological issue with economic repercussions, which has been sharpened by the cutbacks experienced during the years of the Reagan administration, concerns the degree to which black communities and their churches have become dependent upon large-scale federal government programs and how this has affected the economic initiatives of the churches and their self-help tradition. Black neoconservatives have argued that the black self-help tradition has been eroded with Roosevelt's New Deal in 1935 which set up a welfare system, and that the problem was exacerbated with Johnson's War on Poverty. While black liberals have pointed out that even with all of the resources which black communities and churches could muster through self-help efforts, the social and economic problems faced by poor black people are so deeply systemic and institutionalized that only the federal government has the economic resources to make the major breakthroughs.[89] This issue has been falsely polarized by the either/or options presented by the debate since both federal resources and the black self-help tradition are required for any real progress in racial and economic justice. As we pointed out earlier, some large black churches and progressive pastors have mobilized both their congregations' economic resources and federal programs and grants in order to attack the problems of housing, unemployment, health care, and education in their communities.

The final and most crucial challenge facing the Black Church is to decide what kind of economic system would best serve the needs of everyone, with justice, equity, and fairness in the twenty-first century. Thus far, black churches have accepted the American political economy of capitalism "as is." Even Jesse Jackson's economic platform in the 1988 presidential primary campaign was not sharply critical of capitalism as an economic system, except for a few minor modifications. However, some black intellectuals, like social scientists Walter Rodney and Manning Marable and theologians like Cornel West and James Cone, have been calling for a more radical restructuring of the capitalist economic system.[90] They see the roots of racism deeply embedded in and intertwined with an economic worldview that is premised upon inequality. Whether African Americans and their churches will accept the more radical critique of capitalism will depend upon the conditions of their economic progress. If the American racial dilemma does not render intolerable black attempts at achievement, mobility, and economic equality and their pursuit of the promises of the American dream, then most African Americans will continue to accept and support the present economic system, and rely on reformist strategies of change. However, if the dilemma of racism continues to pose obstacles toward that progress then the radical critique of capitalism will inevitably gain a growing constituency, even among the black churches and clergy. Since the 1960s the record of economic progress among African Americans has been a mixed one, with some gains due to the pressure of civil rights groups and a growing number of losses during the Reagan years.[91] For a revolutionary ethos to succeed in the black community, there must be considerable economic regression across all strata of African Americans, not only among the poor.

Summary and Conclusion

The American dream of upward mobility and achievement unfettered by skin color still remains a major goal and hope for the majority of African Americans. But even after several centuries that dream is still complicated by the American dilemma of racial and economic inequality. In this chapter we have pointed out that economic values have been predominant in American society so that much of the discrimination suffered by black people has been economic in character, beginning with chattel slavery or human beings treated as objects of property. As one of the earliest and certainly the most dominant institution, the Black Church has had and will continue to have a very important role in the economic situation of black communities. The following statements summarize the varied economic roles of the Black Church:

1. The Black Church helped to create the black self-help tradition and an ethos of economic rationality for free and enslaved blacks. The economic ethic of the Black Church played a crucial role in the transition from slavery to freedom, teaching the values of long-term sublimation instead of instant gratification, saving for a rainy day, getting an education, and keeping the family together.

2. Through its priestly functions, the Black Church provided comfort, nurture, and care among an outcast people, "a refuge in a hostile white world," as Frazier described it, where they could sing, shout, laugh, and cry among those who understood and shared the pain.[92] The weekly worship service gave them the strength to go back to their jobs to survive another day, another week. But black churches also took part in the liberation tradition by becoming economically independent institutions.

3. Black churches, along with the quasi-religious mutual aid societies and fraternal orders, created important economic institutions during the late nineteenth and early twentieth centuries such as black banks, black life insurance companies, mortuaries and funeral parlors, building and loan associations, and cemetery associations. However, in spite of its role in creating these institutions, the Black Church has placed more emphasis and resources in education, civil rights, and developing moral character than in the economic arena. The large migrations from the South, the effects of the Great Depression, and the institution of federal government social welfare programs also took their toll on the economic initiatives of the Black Church.

4. Black churches are themselves significant economic institutions in black communities. Recent studies indicate that the churches and the area of religion receive the highest percentage of charitable donations (75.4 percent) and volunteer time (35.3 percent).

The cumulative property value of churches and some of their enterprises run into billions of dollars. The irony, however, is that the churches often reflect the economic circumstances of their congregations so that close to half of the black clergy nationwide must work at another full-time occupation in order to support themselves and their families.

5. Spurred by their participation in the activism of the civil rights period, and in war on poverty programs, a growing number of pastors of large black churches are becoming involved again in economic initiatives and projects in their own communities. Cutbacks by the Reagan administration in social programs have also forced many churches to take on the concerns of housing, health care, senior citizens, tutoring, and soup kitchens. One of the largest job training and employment programs, the Opportunities Industrialization Council was started by a Baptist minister, Leon Sullivan of Philadelphia. The largest black-owned shopping mall was also initiated by Sullivan's efforts.

6. If the Black Church has a major weakness, it is in the area of economics and finances. Black denominations need to be more concerned about the poor financial and membership record keeping in black churches. Poor record keeping has been one of the major sources for conflict in church disputes and schisms. The lack of adequate records also hinders a denomination's knowledge about itself and hampers any long-range planning. Most black clergy require more training in the area of church finances and the wise economic uses of church resources.

Even before Dr. King's death in 1968 there was a growing realization that the frontier area for the civil rights movement concerned economic justice and equal opportunity. Having the civil right to sit in a restaurant was not enough if a person could not afford to eat there. King's support of the striking sanitation workers in Memphis and his plans for a Poor People's Campaign underscore his vision of the need for economic justice. The progress toward that goal has been mixed thus far. Upwardly mobile and middle-class African Americans have benefited most from Affirmative Action programs and policies, while the sector of the truly disadvantaged has increased dramatically. Middle-class black churches and church members are being challenged to reach out more effectively to the poor. The majority of the truly disadvantaged are made up of women and children, topics which are the focus of the following chapters.

10 The Pulpit and the Pew:
The Black Church and Women

If the man may preach, because the Saviour died for him, why not the woman? seeing he died for her also. Is he not a whole Saviour, instead of a half one? as those who hold it wrong for a woman to preach, would seem to make it appear.*

Then that little man in black there, he says women can't have as much rights as men, because Christ wasn't a woman! Where did your Christ come from? Where did your Christ come from? From God and a woman! Man had nothing to do with Him.**

In the sanctuary of a black Baptist church in Chicago in 1971 at a meeting of the National Committee of Black Churchmen, the following incident took place. Two black women approached the pulpit at different times during the meeting: one was a theology student, so that she could place a recording device; and the other was a Presbyterian church executive, who wished to address the committee. The pastor approached each woman and asked her to remove herself from the pulpit area, explaining that the women church officers had passed a ruling that no woman could stand behind the pulpit for any reason. They wanted to ensure that no woman would be elevated over another in the church, and they insisted that the image of the clergy should remain exclusively male. This incident is one illustration of the fact that traditionally in the Black Church, the pulpit has been viewed as "men's space" and the pew as "women's place."[1]

*Excerpt from Jarena Lee's account of her religious experience and call to preach in Bert J. Loewenberg and Ruth Bogin, editors, *Black Women in Nineteenth-Century America*, p. 139.
**Excerpt from Sojourner Truth's "Ain't I a Woman" speech at the 1851 woman's rights convention in Akron, Ohio, ibid., p. 236.

274

All of the seven mainline black denominations are characterized by a predominantly female membership and a largely male leadership, despite the fact that the major programs of the Black Church in politics, economics, or music depend heavily upon women for their promotion and success. However, although the public figures have usually been men, black women in each of the seven denominations have carved out their own space for leadership and power in the women's conventions of their denomination. These women's conventions are among the largest organized groups of black women in the United States.[2] Women serve in myriad roles in black churches as evangelists, missionaries, stewardesses, deaconesses, lay readers, writers on religious subjects, Sunday School teachers, musicians, choir members and directors, ushers, nurses, custodians, caterers and hostesses for church dinners, secretaries and clerks, counselors, recreation leaders, and directors of vacation Bible schools. Women are also the designated "mothers of the church," an honorific title usually reserved for the wife of the founder or for the oldest and most respected members. In some black churches pastors usually consult with the church mother before making an important decision because she can exercise countervailing power among some key church members. The phenomenon of the "church mother" has no parallel in white churches; it is derived from the kinship network found within black churches and black communities.

Both historical and contemporary evidence underscore the fact that black churches could scarcely have survived without the active support of black women, but in spite of their importance in the life of the church, the offices of preacher and pastor of churches in the historic black churches remain a male preserve and are not generally available to women. There are exceptions and the focus of this chapter will be on black women as preachers and pastors, past and present, because this issue continues to be a controversial one for the Black Church. We will present an overview of some examples of black preaching women and their struggles to achieve recognition and official status within black churches, and we will also present the data on the attitudes of the black clergy of 2,150 urban and rural churches toward women as preachers and pastors. Finally, in the section on trends in black churches we will briefly examine the movement of black womanist theology, patterns among black women clergy and offer a possible explanation for the sexual imbalance within black church congregations.

Daughters of Thunder:
A Historical Overview of Black Preaching Women

A proper examination of the role of active religious leadership among black women must begin with African religious traditions, because the Christianity that was brought to the slaves on the plantations or to free blacks in urban areas did not encourage leadership roles for women, especially in regard to preaching. The main gospel message preached by whites often stressed the role of submissiveness taught by the apostle Paul: "wives obey your husbands; slaves obey your masters." It also included the added injunction that "women should be silent in the church." The fact that the African slaves were previously socialized into their own religious traditions before enslavement provides another reason for beginning with Africa.

According to John Mbiti, women played major roles in African traditional religion. They were priestesses, queens, midwives, diviners, and herbalists; they were among the major practitioners of both good and evil witchcraft. There were also female deities in the complex cosmology of different ethnic groups. Since childbearing was considered a blessing and childlessness a curse, the skills of midwifery were important and sacred.[3] Among the Lovedu people the queen was not primarily a ruler but a rainmaker who had the power to make rain for her people and withhold it from the enemy.[4] According to Geoffrey Parrinder, "Women may be priestesses, and frequently they are as prominent as men in the conduct of religious affairs. The psychic abilities of women have received recognition and scope to a much greater degree in African religion than they have in Islam or Christianity where women are still barred from the priesthood."[5]

In the transition from Africa to the New World, the importance of the religious role of women was seen most clearly in the Afro-Caribbean and Afro-Latin religious traditions like the Voudou of Haiti, the Santeria of Cuba, the Shango of Grenada and Trinidad, the Obeah of Jamaica, and the Candomble and Umbanda of Brazil, where the survival of African religious influences were strongest.[6] In all of these African-influenced New World religions, women continued their roles as priestesses. In the United States where Protestant Christianity dominated, the African religious influences survived in more indirect and sublimated forms. However, the strongest African influences were found in the Voudou traditions of New Orleans.

Raboteau and Sobel indicate that the cult of the Marie Laveaus, grandmother, mother, and daughter, had a persistent influence in the religious milieu among blacks and whites in New Orleans.[7] In the black folk religious tradition women continued their religious roles in the healing arts by prescribing herbs and roots as medicines and folk remedies, in childbirth by acting as midwives, and in fortune-telling via ecstatic trances. Sometimes they also acted as conjurers and mediums on plantations.[8] Raboteau cites the examples of Sinda, an elderly slave woman on Frances Kemble's plantation, who "exerted considerable religious influence among the slaves as a prophetess" and of Maum Katie of the Sea Islands, over a century old, who was a " 'spiritual mother,' a fortune teller or, rather, prophetess, and a woman of tremendous influence over her spiritual children."[9]

In both African and African American cultures, the influence of the oral tradition was an important background factor in the desire of black women to preach. In West African cultures, history and genealogy were recorded through oral transmission and memory, constantly repeated on ritual occasions and passed on from generation to generation. The skills of storytelling and oration were highly valued and prized.[10] The development of the African American heritage of oral tradition received its impetus from two influences: Africa and slavery. The slave system feared the literate slave and placed a ban on teaching slaves to read and write. While some slaves learned to read and write clandestinely, this banning, which lasted for several centuries, resulted in a greater emphasis on the oral tradition in black culture. From songs and sermons to an ever-expanding array of speeches, jokes, folk tales, musical forms, raps, and street talk, the African American oral tradition has been a creative reservoir for black culture.[11]

The origins of the religious role models for black preaching women is uncertain since Christianity was spread among most of the slave population largely by male preachers, black and white. The historical records reflect very little influence, if any, from white women preachers who were active in the South. But it appears that a combination of several factors legitimated this preaching role for black women: first, the African strain in their African American heritage which made possible prominent roles in religion for women both in Africa and on American plantations; second, the influence of the black oral tradition elevated preaching and the ability to speak in public to one of the highest levels of art forms; third, the independence and internal strength that black slave women had to develop in a plantation system that often took their men or their children away. All of these factors were combined in an institution that placed a premium upon charismatic personality and ability to preach. The final ingredient was the Protestant notion of a "call," a vocation endorsed by the Almighty, to preach and to minister to the needs of an abused and outcast people. The call was a deep personal experience, a long lasting, unshakable conviction that they were somehow chosen to do this difficult task in the face of seemingly insurmountable barriers.

American society considered the slave woman primarily as a source of cheap labor and as a breeder, the instrument by which the slave status would be passed on "durante vita," from generation to generation and the supply of slaves could be ensured indefinitely. The patriarchal values of the larger society and of Christianity itself also added the burden of sexism, including sexual exclusion from the vocation of ministry. As the invisible, underground religion of the slave churches merged into visible, institutional black churches of Baptist and Methodist persuasion, the freedmen and former slaves who founded these churches often accepted in toto the rules, beliefs, hierarchy, structure, and patriarchal conventions of their white counterparts from whose churches they were now separated. The role of preacher and pastor in the Black Church was also complicated by the long history of the exclusion and denigration of black males from the normal prerogatives of masculine identity and power in American society, unable to fulfill their expected economic and political roles. As we mentioned in chapter 8, only the black preacher achieved a modicum of recognizable status in a society where all African Americans and whatever their attainment were presumed to be incurably defective. In the limbo of a caste society, as Albert Raboteau has pointed out, the slave "preacherman" was "relatively mobile and privileged."[12] In the common, black folk idiom the best preachers, those who were able to stir a crowd with fiery, silver-tongued oratory, bringing them to an enthusiastic, spirit-filled catharsis, was often known as a "son of thunder."[13] Hence, the roadblocks to preaching for black women were further compounded by the complex problem of black male identity in a racist society. If the ministry was the only route to even a shadow of masculinity, the inclusion of women seemed very much like a gratuitous defeat for everybody. But there were some "daughters of thunder" who would not be denied by such a rationale; they too felt the divine call to preach.

That there were slave women who preached in clandestine services on the plantations is undoubted, but the recorded evidence for them is scanty. None of the black women prior to the late nineteenth and mid-twentieth centuries were ever officially recognized or ordained as preachers and pastors by any black denomination.[14] Instead, they were required to take sublimated paths to the ministry as exhorters, teachers, missionaries, evangelists, religious writers, and wives of clergymen. For example, the earliest published book by any black American was the religious poetry of Phyllis Wheatley in 1773.[15] While Wheatley (1754?–1784) confined her expressions of deep religious piety to her writing, other black women were more vocal. In 1889 the Philadelphia Quakers posthumously published the story of a former slave woman from Maryland who was only called Elizabeth in a tract entitled, *Elizabeth, A Colored Minister of the Gospel Born in Slavery.*[16] Elizabeth (1766–1867) began to preach at the age of 30 and once was threatened with arrest by officials in the Virginia Commonwealth for preaching without a license. Asked if she was ordained, she answered, "Not by the commission of men's hands; if the Lord has ordained me, I need nothing better." They let her go.[17]

The first official challenge to the restrictions on women preachers in a black denomination came from one of the most famous daughters of thunder, Jarena Lee (1783–185?). Probably born free in Cape May, New Jersey, in 1783, Jarena worked as a house servant in homes close to the Philadelphia border. Almost mystical, she had a number of ecstatic religious experiences and visions, and subsequently felt the call to preach at the age of twenty-four. In 1809 she approached the pastor of the newly established Bethel African Methodist Episcopal Church in Philadelphia, Richard Allen, and sought a license from him to preach. Although Allen could see women leading prayer meetings, he drew the theological line against female preaching and refused to issue the license requested.[18] However, impelled by her call Jarena Lee preached without it. In 1811 she married an A.M.E. clergyman, Rev. Joseph Lee, pastor of a society at Snow Hill. A year after the A.M.E. Church was officially established as a connectional denomination in 1816, Mrs. Lee again sought the newly elected Bishop Allen's permission and legitimation for her activities. Methodist Church polity did not include female preachers and Allen could not ordain her. However, he did permit her to hold prayer meetings and to "exhort." He further encouraged her by admitting Jarena to meetings with recognized ministers and gave her speaking engagements in the churches under his jurisdiction.[19] Although she described herself as "the first female preacher of the African Methodist Episcopal Church," Jarena's claim was not officially sanctioned by the denomination with full ordination.[20]

While Jarena Lee remained patient but persistent in her desire to preach, other women became extremely frustrated at the roadblocks in black churches and joined white denominations or other religious groups. Such was the case of Rebecca Cox Jackson (1795–1871), a younger contemporary of Jarena Lee, who at the age of thirty-five experienced a profound spiritual awakening and also felt called to preach. Her brother, who was a prominent clergyman in the Bethel A.M.E. Church, her husband, and the A.M.E. clergy opposed her vocation because she was "a woman aleading men," and her radical Holiness beliefs, which included celibacy, were considered heretical and threatening.[21] Jackson eventually severed ties with her family and church and joined the religious sect called the Shakers, whose emphasis upon spirituality, celibacy, and feminist theology (doctrine of the Four-in-One Godhead of Father, Son, Mother, and Daughter) were attractive to her. The Shaker's recognition of her as an authentic prophet became the decisive factor in Mrs. Jackson's willingness to forsake former friends and family and affiliate with the communalistic society. She moved to the Shaker community in Watervliet, New York, and later accompanied by another black disciple, Rebecca Perot, Jackson moved back to Philadelphia to establish a predominantly black Shaker sisterhood.[22]

Amanda Berry Smith (1837–1915) was another A.M.E. preaching woman who also finally chose an alternative path in dealing with her denomination's half-hearted attempts to include women in its ordained ministry.[23] Smith joined the Holiness movement during the second half of the nineteenth century and became known as one of the great itinerant Holiness preachers. Between 1871 and 1878 she preached frequently at camp meetings and maintained only loose nominal ties with Methodism. The Holiness movement grew out of John Wesley's attempts to seek spiritual perfection and to lead a more holy life, which was achieved in the personal experience of "sanctification," a second gift of grace. Although it was Methodist in origin, the Holiness movement soon became interdenominational and independent. In later years it was linked to Pentecostalism. As a gifted singer, preacher, evangelist, and missionary, Amanda Smith helped to pave the way for hundreds of black women who also felt the call to preach and founded their own independent, "sanctified" storefront churches during the great urban migrations of the twentieth century. Smith's unusual missionary experience led her to preach in England, serve for two years in India, and eight years in Liberia. However, her views of Africa were marked by the ambivalence which also characterized the perspectives of many black and white American missionaries in the nineteenth century, who perceived African culture as pagan and considered Western Christianity as superior.[24] But Amanda Berry Smith's story is essentially that of a humble black washerwoman who became an internationally famous preacher and missionary. Toward the end of her life she worked with black orphans and established the Amanda Smith Industrial Orphan Home for colored children in Harvey, Illinois, in 1899.[25]

While many other black preaching women in the nineteenth century could be cited, the examples given above serve to illustrate the different paths and orientations that these women took in fulfilling their call to preach. It would be remiss in a historical overview to ignore the other religious women who chose far more sublimated paths to ministering to the needs of their people by participating in more secular activities such as abolitionism, women's rights, the antilynching campaign, and teaching and education. Many of these community service and political activities stemmed from a moral concern to uplift the race that was deeply rooted in religious motivation.

Sublimated Paths to Ministry in the Black Church

While Christianity originally provided the major legitimation for the system of slavery in the United States, eventually it also stimulated the moral impulses for its abolition. Throughout much of the nineteenth century the abolitionist movement became the mechanism by which religious people, black and white, could put their faith into practice. Among the many black women participants, Maria W. Stewart (1803–79), Harriet Tubman (1823–1913), and Sojourner Truth (1797–1883) were examples par excellence of religious abolitionism. In a speech before the newly formed "Afric-American Female Intelligence Society" in Boston in 1832, Maria W. Stewart became one of the first women of any color to deliver public political speeches and she was also the first black woman political writer. Influenced by David Walker, the militant author of "Walker's Appeal," and by the Old Testament view of an avenging God, Stewart called for the abolition of slavery by violence if necessary. Besides abolitionism, Maria Stewart also became a champion for women's rights, especially for "the fair daughters of Africa." Although she was a member of Boston's African Baptist Church, her combination of faith and politics in the abolitionist struggle transcended denominational lines.[26]

Called the "Moses" of her people, Harriet Tubman made nineteen trips to the South between 1850 to 1857 and led more than three hundred slaves to freedom as the prime "conductor" of the Underground Railroad. A staunch member of the A.M.E. Zion Church, she used familiar spirituals such as "Steal Away to Jesus" as codes for escape-oriented communication. During the Civil War Tubman served the Union army as a spy, scout, and nurse and she became famous as the only woman to successfully plan and execute a military campaign behind enemy lines.[27] Where Tubman was short and wiry, her compatriot and sister in the struggle, Sojourner Truth, was six feet tall and a striking presence.

Born Isabella Baumfree, a slave in Ulster County, New York, she took the name Sojourner Truth on June 1, 1843, after one of her many religious visions. Although she, like Harriet Tubman, was a member of the Zion Church in New York, her mystical personality could not be confined by a church structure, nor by the religious cult called the Mathias group that she briefly experimented with, before she finally set forth on her own antislavery crusade. For Sojourner Truth the freedom movement was "the secular counterpart of spiritual salvation."[28] Among the many fine orators for abolitionism, she was one of the few who could match the wit, eloquence, and power of Frederick Douglass to change the mood and direction of a meeting. Once when Douglass, a licensed deacon in the Zion Church, had concluded a despairing speech, Sojourner stood up and stunned both the meeting and the deacon by asking, "Frederick, is God dead?"[29] Sojourner Truth and Douglass, who was one of the most prominent male feminists of his day, also provided the link between abolitionism and the women's suffrage movement. In popular demand as a suffrage speaker, Sojourner's brief but classic speech, "Ain't I a Woman?"

criticized the views of men and of white women for neglecting the plight of black women.

If they could not become preachers, large numbers of religiously motivated black women felt that they were called to teach. The vocation of education attracted numerous black women because the educational needs of the black community were great, especially after the Civil War when thousands of former slaves crammed the churches which often doubled as schoolhouses. Teaching was also attractive because it was considered a proper female occupation by the larger society, and in the black community teachers were highly respected. Frances Jackson Coppin and Dr. Anna Julia Cooper serve as examples of educators in the nineteenth century, while Dr. Mary McCleod Bethune and Nannie Helen Burroughs are twentieth-century examples of noted black women educators of legendary acclaim. All of them were active members of black churches. Frances Coppin (1836–1913) and Anna Cooper (1858–1964) were among the most brilliant educators to emerge from the nineteenth century. Coppin was an ex-slave whose greatest desire was "to get an education and to teach my people." She graduated from the Rhode Island Normal School and was the second black woman to receive a degree from Oberlin College, where she later taught. At a time when there was considerable skepticism about the intellectual capacity of African Americans, she taught black students to master Greek and mathematics. Coppin served as principal for the Institute for Colored Youth in Philadelphia, and later in life she became president of the Home Mission Society of the A.M.E. Church. She also spent several years in Africa when her husband was elected as an A.M.E. bishop and served his term overseas.[30]

Born a slave in Raleigh, North Carolina, in 1858, Anna Julia Cooper lived for 106 years and spanned both the nineteenth and twentieth centuries. She attended St. Augustine Normal School, married a minister from the West Indies, and after his death she went north to study, receiving her college degree from Oberlin in 1884. For decades she served as a teacher and then as principal of the M Street High School in Washington, D.C., which became the famous Dunbar High School, known for black high achievers. Close to retirement age, she went to Paris and completed a Ph.D. in Latin in 1925. In that same year she also published a book on Charlemagne and a study of French attitudes toward slavery. From 1929 to 1941 Dr. Cooper served as president of the Frelinghuysen University in Washington, a school for working black adults. Cooper's great concern was for the equal education of black women because the conventional wisdom often held that education for women was a useless frill.[31]

Both Dr. Mary McCleod Bethune (1875–1955) and Mrs. Nannie Helen Burroughs (1883–1961) probably would have become preachers if their respective denominations, the NBC and A.M.E., had allowed it. But the barriers for black Baptist women to achieve full ordination and acceptance were even more difficult than for Methodist women in the past and in the present. In consequence, both Dr. Bethune and Mrs. Burroughs chose to carry out their ministry in education and politics. They also symbolized the different political orientations which would emerge among black people in the twentieth century. From 1865 until the Great Depression, the majority of black voters were loyal Republicans, "the party of Lincoln the Emancipator." Nannie Helen Burroughs was active in Republican politics and remained so even though many blacks were switching allegiance during the era of the New Deal. In 1900 in Richmond, Virginia, Burroughs launched her famous career in religious leadership with her address to the National Baptist Convention, "How the Sisters Are Hindered from Helping."[32] For many years she served as corresponding secretary for the Woman's Convention, Auxiliary to the National Baptist Convention, U.S.A., Inc., and helped to influence women to provide political support for issues like suffrage for blacks and women, the antilynching campaign, temperance, decent housing, greater employment opportunities for black women, and labor laws to protect women and children.[33] As a well-known educator, Burroughs founded the National School for Girls in Washington, D.C., whose curriculum combined both aspects of the Du Bois versus Washington debate, liberal arts and training in the skills of household and domestic services. Burroughs also served as the editor of the *Christian Banner* and was a prolific writer and lecturer on religious topics.

Mary McCleod's frail health as a child of slave parents in South Carolina eventually thwarted her attempts to become a missionary to Africa. Instead, she became a teacher and founded the Daytona Normal School, which evolved into the Bethune-Cookman College. As president of the college, she often preached in the required chapel services. Dr. Bethune was active in the women's club movement and served as president of the National Council of Negro Women. Through her friendship with Eleanor Roosevelt she was able to influence the social policies of FDR's New Deal, and she became the highest ranking Negro administrator in the federal government, serving in the National Youth Administration and as director of the Division of Negro Affairs.[34]

Probably all of these women and many unnamed others would have become ordained as clergy if that were an option available to them, because the Black Church and their Christian beliefs were the central values of their lives. Instead they had to channel their energies and service into other areas of life. While the world is richer for their activities, unfortunately they could not have their ministries officially legitimated by the institution they were devoted to.

The Black Denominations and the Ordination of Women

The first black denomination to officially ordain women to the ministry was the African Methodist Episcopal Zion Church. In 1891 at the Second Ecumenical Conference Bishop James Walker Hood defended the right of women to be elected delegates to the general conference of the denomination. He said that, "there is one Methodist-Episcopal Church that guarantees to women all rights in common with men."[35] Several years later, he acted on his words. At the Seventy-Third Session of the New York Annual Conference held at the Catharine Street A.M.E. Zion Church in Poughkeepsie on May 20, 1894, Bishop Hood ordained Mrs. Julia A. Foote (who was a conference missionary) "deacon." On May 19, 1895, Mrs. Mary J. Small, wife of Bishop John B. Small, was ordained deacon by Bishop Alexander Walters at the Sixty-Seventh Session of the Philadelphia and Baltimore Conference. In 1898 Mrs. Small became the first woman of Methodism to be ordained "elder" by Bishop Calvin Pettey at the Philadelphia and Baltimore conference. After transferring to the New Jersey conference, Mrs. Foote was also ordained an elder by Bishop Alexander Walters in 1900.[36] Thus, Mrs. Small and Mrs. Foote became the first women to achieve the rights of full ordination to the ministry by any Methodist denomination, black or white. The A.M.E. Zion Church's ordination of women preceded similar action by the other black Methodist denominations and by the United Methodist Church by half a century.

The struggle for full ordination by black women in the other two black Methodist bodies, the African Methodist Episcopal Church and the Colored Methodist Episcopal Church, was considerably more protracted. Black women in the A.M.E. Church were not allowed full ordination until 1948. Prior to that time there were many attempts by A.M.E. women and their male supporters to obtain the rights of ordination for preaching women. At the 1868 General Conference the denomination created the post of stewardess, the first official position for women whose main task was to look after other women and to assist the male stewards, class leaders, and pastors. The 1884 General Conference approved of the licensing of women to preach but without ordination. In response to the growing pressure from women, in 1900 the A.M.E. Church created the position of deaconess, again without ordination, despite the fact that men were always ordained when they became deacons.[37] In creating the post of deaconess without ordination, the A.M.E. Church responded to women in the same manner as the northern and southern white Methodist bodies had done.[38]

The C.M.E. Church did not allow full ordination for women until 1954. On the issue of women, this southern black Methodist denomination was much more traditionalist and conservative than their northern counterparts. Partly due to its late organization as a separate denomination in 1870, it was not until 1902 that the women of the C.M.E. Church were able to organize the Women's Home Missionary Society and only in 1918 did the Women's Connectional Missionary Council receive approval as an organization. As Bishop Othal H. Lakey described it in his history of the C.M.E. Church, "it is quite evident that neither the bishops nor the General Conference viewed an organization for women in the same manner in which they viewed other needs of the church." Further, the bishops and the general conference would allow the women of the church to have their own connectional organization to run "as long as they did not conflict or interfere with the church itself."[39] With the concerns of women in the church given a low priority, the ordination of women as pastors and preachers in the C.M.E. Church would not occur until the beginning of the modern civil rights era in the 1950s.

For women in the three black Baptist denominations (National Baptist Convention, U.S.A., Inc., National Baptist Convention of America, Uninc., and Progressive National Baptist Convention), the struggle and quest for full ordination into the ministry has been even more difficult. The complete history of black preaching women among the Baptists is undocumented and difficult to trace because the independent church polity of the Baptists ensures the autonomy of each congregation in matters of faith and practice. However, in the earliest Separate Baptist churches of the South, women were ordained as deaconesses, and some unordained women were allowed to preach. As the Baptist faith spread during the First Awakening in the mid-eighteenth century, there was a "remarkable freedom of participation by women."[40] As Sobel has observed, "Black women found much room for involvement, expression, and leadership in the Baptist churches, which was in keeping with both the Southern Separatist tradition and earlier African traditions. . . . Women were given formal roles as deaconesses and served on committees to work with women who had violated Baptist ethics. . . . Southern black women even attended the meetings of the American Baptist Missionary Convention in the North.[41] However, in 1800 when the Separate and Regular Baptists merged that freedom became far more restricted, and eventually, in both black and white churches leadership became almost exclusively male. While women never lost the post of deaconess, their role as preachers was practically eclipsed. After the Civil War many of the black Baptist clergy became members of the Southern Baptist Convention, but due to unequal treatment and racism they began their movement toward independence in 1880, a process which was completed in 1895 with the formation of the National Baptist Convention (NBC).[42] Schisms among the black Baptists led to the formation of the National Baptist Convention of America (NBCA) in 1915 and the Progressive National Baptist Convention (PNBC) in 1961. While there is no specific policy against the ordination of women in any of the black Baptist denominations, the general climate has not been supportive of women preaching and pastoring churches. However, in recent years there has been a small minority of black clergymen who have sponsored women candidates for ordination in their associations. The Baptist principle of congregational autonomy has been helpful in these cases since the independence of each church and pastor cannot be challenged by any denominational authority.

Among the large variety of Pentecostal groups the Church of God in Christ, the largest black Pentecostal denomination, has taken a firm policy stand against the full ordination of women as clergy. Although COGIC has recognized the numerous contributions that women have made in the affairs of the church, COGIC's *Official Manual* argues on scriptural grounds against ordaining women as elder, bishop, or pastor.[43] Although it has recognized that women were important in the ministry of the New Testament era, the denomination has found no mandate for ordaining women to the previously mentioned positions. COGIC has allowed women to preach in their churches but only as evangelists or missionaries, performing a teaching function that does not carry a mandate for ordination. There are, however, a few exceptions on record where widows have temporarily carried on the work of their deceased husbands. Many Pentecostal churches are kin-type churches, which are passed on in a hereditary manner from fathers to sons or, if sons are lacking, to wives. While proprietary churches are common among the Baptists where the congregation owns the church property, the mixed polity of COGIC has permitted the development of kin churches, which are often not only named after the founder but also passed on in the extended family. While COGIC is a connectional church with a hierarchical structure of bishops and strict denominational ties, the denomination also encourages its clergy to found and develop their own churches in the manner of the churches having an independent polity like the Baptists. There is no itinerancy requirement such as the Methodists have which requires pastors to be reassigned after a term of years. Hence, in COGIC the pastor's tenure in a particular church is usually for the long term, and may well be for life. In some cases a few congregations have preferred to have the wife of the founder continue as their minister instead of an outsider. In spite of its official policy of prohibiting women pastors, there seems to be a tacit understanding in the denomination which quietly tolerates such situations by allowing the woman to complete the ministry of her late husband as *shepherd sans portfolio.*

The official restrictions against ordaining women clergy in some of the major black denominations combined with sexist attitudes have often prompted many black women to start their own independent Holiness or Pentecostal churches. Such churches usually begin in private homes or apartments, eventually moving to storefronts. Some of the more charismatic women preachers have been able to attract substantial followings and build large churches. Elder Lucy Smith who established the All Nations Pentecostal Church in Chicago in the 1930s and Bishop Ida Robinson who founded the Mount Sinai Holy Church of Philadelphia in 1924 come to mind. More recent examples include Rev. Dr. Barbara King of the Hillside International Truth Center in Atlanta, and Rev. Johnnie Colemon of the

Christ Universal Temple in Chicago. Both King and Colemon, who have reputations as charismatic preachers, have several thousand members in each of their own congregations. In proportion to their respective numbers in the population, there have probably been more black women as preachers and pastors than there have been white women counterparts. White ethnic experience has not proved as fertile for the emergence of a strong preaching tradition among women, nor has there been the apparent reception that some black women preachers have found outside the structures of the major black churches.

Inevitably, this brief historical survey of the policies of the major black denominations toward women clergy raises questions about the contemporary attitudes of black clergy toward the issue of women as pastors and preachers and whether there has been any improvement in attitudes of clergy in the last quarter of the twentieth century with the growing pressures of the feminist movement. We turn now to an examination of the results of our survey on clergy attitudes toward women clerics.

Contemporary Black Clergy Attitudes Toward Women as Preachers and Pastors

In our nationwide survey of the black clergy of 2,150 churches, only sixty-six, or 3.7 percent, were female in spite of special efforts to interview black female clergy.[44] Our best estimate is that fewer than 5 percent of the clergy in the historic black denominations are female. Although there are probably more black women proportionately who were clergy than white women, the vast majority of them are found in storefront churches or in independent churches.

On the question of whether the clergy approved or disapproved of a woman as the pastor of a church, a Likert scale was used to measure the strength of the response. The results indicated that the following variables showed some relationship to the strength of the response: sex, age, education, and denomination. In regard to the sex of the clergy respondent, the eta coefficient of 0.16774 in table 31 indicated a moderate degree of relationship with approval of women as pastors. For the women interviewed, fifty-two (81.5 percent) out of a total of sixty-four approved of women pastors, while twelve (18.5 percent) disapproved. For the men, the approval and disapproval rates were

Table 31: Women as Pastors by Sex, Age, and Education

VARIABLE		
SEX	Male	Female
Strongly approve	249 (15.0%)	37 (58.0%)
Approve	593 (35.8%)	15 (23.5%)
Disapprove	406 (24.5%)	7 (11.4%)
Strongly disapprove	409 (24.7%)	5 (7.1%)
Eta coefficient=.16774		
AGE	Under 30	Over 65
Strongly approve	18 (16.2%)	40 (13.1%)
Approve	60 (53.0%)	84 (27.5%)
Disapprove	18 (15.4%)	76 (25.0%)
Strongly disapprove	18 (15.4%)	105 (34.4%)
Eta coefficient=.17047		
EDUCATION	Less Than High School Graduate	College 5 Plus
Strongly approve	28 (10.5%)	147 (23.2%)
Approve	87 (32.7%)	276 (43.6%)
Disapprove	68 (25.5%)	114 (18.0%)
Strongly disapprove	84 (31.3%)	97 (15.2%)
Eta coefficient=.23188		

almost even, with only a slight majority 842 (50.8 percent) approved of women pastors, while 815 (49.2 percent) disapproved. Among the men there were some very strong feelings in the negative direction. For example, on the Likert scale 409 (24.7 percent) of the men strongly disapproved and only 249 (15.0 percent) strongly approved, while thirty-seven (58.0 percent) of the women strongly approved and five (7.1 percent) strongly disapproved. While it seemed a curious phenomenon to have women clergy who strongly disapproved of women as pastors, these women probably became ministers after their husbands' deaths, often reluctantly taking over their ministries. Further, despite their own roles as clergy, they may also be reflecting the official policies of their denominations against ordaining women as pastors, particularly in the Church of God in Christ and among some Baptist associations.

The results of table 31 showed some symmetry with respect to age and the approval of women as pastors. Seventy-eight (69.2 percent) of those who were under thirty approved—and they were more liberal in their attitudes toward women pastors—while 124 (40.6 percent) of those over 65 approved and 181 (59.4 percent) disapproved. The eta coefficient of 0.17047 also indicated a moderate relationship between the variable of age and approval of women pastors.

However, a strong statistical and substantive relationship existed between the educational level of the clergy and their attitudes toward women as pastors. The eta coefficient was 0.23188. It is important to note in table 31 that the majority of black clergy were negative in their attitudes until the category of those who have graduate training, college 5 plus, is considered. The data indicated that for those clergy who were less than a high school graduate, 152 (56.8 percent) disapproved of women as pastors and only 115 (43.2 percent) approved. But 423 (66.8 percent) of clergy in the college 5 plus category indicated their approval of women as pastors, while only 211 (33.2 percent) disapproved. The results were somewhat symmetrical with those in the lowest educational categories having the highest disapproval rates and those with the most education having the highest positive attitudes toward women pastors. The data also indicated that clergy with some college education have more positive views than those with only a high school education or less.

A very strong relationship existed between the variable of denomination and attitudes toward women as pastors (WP). Table 32 presents the results of chi-square cells, giving the breakdown of the seven black denominations and their rates of approval or disapproval of women pastors. The eta coefficient is 0.57607 with WP dependent and 0.26827 with denomination dependent. As the cells indicated, the three Baptist denominations and the Pentecostals (COGIC) tended to be highly negative in their attitudes toward women as pastors. The three Methodist denominations, on the other hand, were much more strongly positive. The A.M.E. Zion Church led with a 94.2 percent approval rate, the C.M.E. Church with 92 percent, and the A.M.E. Church with 88 percent.

Among the Baptists, the Progressive National Baptist Convention tended to be only slightly more progressive on this issue of women pastors than the other conventions. PNBC had a total approval rate of

Table 32: Women as Pastors by Denomination

Denomination:	NBC, Inc.*	NBC, Uninc.*	PNBC
WP			
Strongly approve	31 (6.6%)	10 (5.6%)	12 (9.2%)
Approve	94 (19.9%)	34 (19.8%)	43 (33.5%)
Disapprove	140 (29.7%)	76 (44.7%)	44 (33.6%)
Strongly disapprove	207 (43.9%)	51 (29.9%)	31 (23.7%)
Totals	472 (28.2%)	171 (10.2%)	130 (7.8%)

Eta coefficient=.57607
Missing=225 (11.9%)
N=1,894

* These Baptist denominations are known more popularly by their "Inc." and

42.7 percent and a total disapproval rate of 57.3 percent. The largest black Baptist body, NBC, U.S.A., Inc., was very strongly negative toward women pastors with 43.9 percent of their clergy strongly disapproving and a total disapproval rate of 73.6 percent. The total approval rate of the NBC, U.S.A., Inc., was 26.5 percent. The NBC, America, Uninc., had a total approval rate of 25.4 percent and a total disapproval rate of 74.6 percent.

The Church of God in Christ also had a high disapproval rate of 73.4 percent, with the second highest rate of 36 percent who strongly disapproved of women as pastors. The total approval rate was 26.6 percent. As it was noted in the previous historical section, COGIC has an explicit denominational policy against the ordination of women as pastors. In COGIC women can become evangelists, an official church position, but not pastors. The few women who were pastors of churches in the denomination were widows who succeeded their husbands because their congregations felt more comfortable with the former pastor's kin leading the church, or because there are usually no survivor's benefits in the black churches, and succession may be an instrument of economic survival.

Among the major black denominations, a distinction is usually made between pastors and preachers, with pastor being the official ordained leader of a church, while a preacher may be anyone who preaches with or without benefit of ordination or denominational

A.M.E.	A.M.E. Zion	C.M.E.	COGIC	Totals
74 (29.7%)	65 (33.6%)	50 (30.9%)	20 (6.9%)	262 (15.7%)
146 (58.3%)	118 (60.6%)	99 (61.0%)	57 (19.7%)	591 (35.4%)
24 (9.6%)	8 (3.8%)	4 (2.5%)	108 (37.4%)	404 (24.2%)
6 (2.4%)	4 (2.0%)	9 (2.0%)	104 (36.0%)	412 (24.7%)
250 (15.1%)	195 (11.7%)	162 (9.7%)	289 (16.3%)	1,669 (100%)

"Uninc." designations. Their abbreviated titles are the NBC, USA Inc. and NBC, America Uninc.

recognition as a pastor. There are instances of officially ordained preachers who may or may not be the pastor at any given time. They may teach in seminaries, or function as executives and administrators. Some Baptist churches permit women to be preachers or exhorters (that is, they can preach from the pulpit) but they are not allowed to carry out certain other pastoral functions, especially the rituals of baptism and communion. However, the distinctions are seldom rigid in conventional understanding, and the terms are often used interchangeably. A "jackleg preacher" is the pejorative idiom for a "self-called" preacher without credentials of any kind.

The Methodist-Baptist difference in our data is partly due to the fact that some of the black Methodists, like the A.M.E. Zion Church, have a longer historical and denominational tradition of allowing women to be ordained as pastors. The Zion Church began the official ordination of women as deacons and elders between 1894 and 1900. Furthermore, it did not develop euphemistic categories like "deaconess," which became an officially recognized but unordained subordinate office for women in the other Methodist bodies, both black and white. The leadership provided by a small group of liberal feminist A.M.E. Zion bishops (Hood, Walters, Small, and Pettey) in the late nineteenth century was crucial to this process of legitimating women as pastors. Our survey results of contemporary black clergy nationwide reflected the continuing vitality of this liberal tradition.

Zion clergy were the strongest supporters of women as pastors. Women in the A.M.E. and C.M.E. churches had a longer and much more difficult struggle, but the majority of clergy in these denominations also voiced support for women as pastors.

Black Clergy Views on Women as Pastors: Pro and Con

The qualitative section of the survey allowed the clergy who wished to do so to amplify their feelings and thoughts on one of the more controversial issues addressed by black churches. The following were some examples of verbatim pro and con statements made by the clergy who are identified only by interview number:

Negative Reactions

The clergy who disapproved of women as pastors of churches generally cited biblical support. Most frequent examples referred to the absence of women among the 12 disciples; Adam and Eve stories; and St. Paul's injunctions on the conduct of women in the church, that is, to keep silent. Others cited their denomination's restrictions, and still others the physical limitations of women.

> No. 0358: "They do not have any business preaching. She has no voice. If she has any questions, let her ask her husband at home."
> No. 1865: "Okay to preach but not as pastor. The doctrine of COGIC doesn't approve of the term preachers [for women]. [Call them] Evangelists."
> No. 1935: "Women have been preaching for years but not identified as preachers. That role pastor has not been distinguished for her. As one within, I could not accept a woman pastor—a masculine role."
> No. 1419: "She can be a 'pastor's helper'—but God didn't make her job to be a pastor; they may have the educational ability, but they're not God-approved."
> No. 1420: "Theoretically [they have] co-equal positions but no women are pastors. 'Spiritual leaders' or 'church mothers' are female counterparts to ministers; other positions [are] held—deaconesses, missionaries."
> No. 1422: "[The] responsibility of the pastor is too strenuous for women. The pastor is on call 24 hours but there are certainly

times when women are incapacitated, i.e., during pregnancy, during times of menstrual cycle. However, I feel a woman can be an 'evangelist.' Deacons must do 'dirty work'—How can you expect a woman to do such? She loses her femininity and it diminishes her womanhood."

No. 1725: "In order to pastor, one must be blameless and the husband of one wife, that's what the Bible says, and there is no way a woman can be the husband of one wife. I don't care what kind of operation she has."

No. 1836: "When a woman brings a message she is preaching. But when it comes to pastoring it's not her place, according to the Bible."

No. 1901: "In her discourse [she] can go whatever route she chooses to go to make plain the Gospel, but [do] not call it preaching, call it teaching."

Positive Reactions

The clergy who approved of women as pastors either cited biblical support, or relied on the theological argument that God is all powerful and can do anything. Many of those who were favorable also had direct experiences with women who were preachers and pastors. Some pastors referred to the analogy between racial discrimination and sexual discrimination. In terms of biblical examples, Mary and Martha are called the first bearers of the good news of the resurrection.

No. 0125: "A woman minister shows more concern to her flock."

No. 1189: "If the Lord can cause rocks to cry out, surely he can call women."

No. 1403: "Adam and Eve—If [Eve] woman can lead men to hell, why can't she lead them to heaven."

No. 1507: "Value is not determined by sex."

No. 0101: "I don't think God is a sexist. Men must not do to women what whites have done to us on the basis of a false anthropological view of human nature in a backward sociology."

No. 1913: "I cannot restrict God to [the] male population of the church. The Holy Spirit on the day of Pentecost was not discriminatory. There are varied ministries and room in those also."

No. 1748: "I am a woman. I understand women to be more thorough and genuine in caring and nurturing."

No. 1506: "They are my fellow yokemen. I strongly approve. I would be happy to serve under a woman pastor."

No. 1249: "I think women have a place in the Christian ministry, although presently I am still mentally studying this situation in my own mind. I am convinced, however, God cannot be limited to who he might call into his service."

No. 1942: "The few [women] I have known were excellent speakers, good administrators and well educated."

No. 0324: "In Christ there is neither male nor female. The call is not a sex affair but a divine call of God. Women are doing a better job. In the last days all children shall prophesy. Women keeping silent in the church was a discipline and [has] nothing to do with preaching. God sees where he can use one."

The negative and positive reactions of the black clergy given above represented the range of feelings elicited in our open-ended interview section. Both the interview materials and data demonstrated that the struggle for black women to become preachers and pastors in the mainline black denominations is fraught with difficulty. Although there has been a long historical heritage of some black preaching women, the black religious tradition usually had a male as the authority figure, as preacher and pastor, with female as followers. This tradition, however, has been subjected to increasing criticism in recent years and it is slowly changing. In a field interview, Rev. Dr. Gardner C. Taylor, former president of the Progressive National Baptist Convention and pastor of Brooklyn's Concord Baptist Church, the largest black church in the United States, admitted that he had great difficulties with this question of the role of women as pastors. "I came to appreciate women," Taylor said, "as I taught women in school. I began to see an inkling of spiritual and religious leadership in them. I am open to this if a woman has been properly trained in the ministry."

In an interview with *The Cornerstone*, Rev. Dr. T. J. Jemison, president of the National Baptist Convention, U.S.A., Inc., said,

It's not widely known that the National Baptist Convention, USA, Inc., has had three women pastors within the past twenty-five years. One of those pastors was Rev. Trudy Trim of Chicago, who assumed that role following the death of her husband. She too recently passed. Also when Rev. Plummer of Cleveland, Ohio became ill, his wife carried on in his absence. Many of our churches today have women assistants. The secretary of our convention, Dr. Richardson, is pastor of the Grace Church in Mount Vernon, New York. His assistant pastor is a woman, Rev. Flora Bridges. The editor of our convention's newspaper is Rev. Roscoe Cooper of Richmond, Virginia. The assistant in his church is also female. . . . I welcome women and have nothing against them. Of course, most Baptists will come to accept this very slowly. My father was adamantly against this trend and so are most of my colleagues.[45]

Earlier generations of black preaching women during the urban migrations either founded independent churches, or they submitted to the secondary religious leadership positions created for them in the black denominations. The present generation of black preaching women, however, is insistent in their pursuit of leadership roles on parity with men, and they have won the support of some of their black clergy colleagues. About 51.1 percent of the black clergy interviewed in our study approved of women as pastors. However, our study also detected stronger, more intense feelings among the ministers who disapproved of women pastors. In spite of this intense opposition, which finds its primary focus among the Baptists and Pentecostals, the challenge of black women to open the doors of the Black Church to equal opportunities to serve shows no sign of abatement. In the next section we will examine some of the emerging trends among black women clergy.

Trends Among Contemporary Black Preaching Women

In contrast to earlier generations of their sisters who were often unlicensed or forced to found their own independent churches, black women preachers are far more likely to pursue the path of professionalization through full ordination. Two historical factors have influenced their search for official legitimation from black and white church denominations. One is that sudden postwar proliferation of Christian churches in the 1950s in the United States which led to an expanded need for professional clergy. Responding to this need, about one-third of the Protestant denominations in the World Council of Churches changed their disciplines to allow for the full ordination of women.[46] Second, the black consciousness movement of the late 1960s pushed the view of black leadership, and the feminist movement of the early 1970s fostered a quest for equality in all leadership positions and occupational arenas, including the church, as Delores Carpenter has pointed out in her study of black women clergy graduates of seminaries.[47] Because American women have a long tradition of church involvement in designated roles, the search for new involvements in positions of church leadership seemed consistent with the emerging ethos of sexual parity which was beginning to alter counterpart stereotypes in the secular world. For many women, the church was a comfortable and familiar environment to work in.

The first major trend was a move toward professionalization among black clergywomen. From 1930 to 1980 the movement of black and white women into the professional ministry has increased 240 percent.[48] But, according to Carpenter, the number of black women graduates from accredited theological seminaries increased 676 percent from 1972 to 1984.[49] The greater proportion of black women seeking theological credentials and ordination reflected both the paucity of their numbers in seminaries prior to the civil rights movement, and a tripling of the number of black college graduates who were twenty-five years and older, from 7 percent in 1960 to 20 percent in 1980.[50]

Another recent trend among black preaching women is their tendency to seek ordination and employment in the mainline, predominantly white denominations. More than half of the 380 ordained black women in Carpenter's study turned to the white denominations, partly because of the increased opportunity for ordination and employment, and the more rigid resistance and obstacles they experienced with the mainline black churches. Major white denominations like the United Church of Christ, the United Methodist Church, the Presbyterians, Episcopalians, Lutherans, and others have moved rapidly in the past two decades to include women among the ranks of ministers at almost all levels. Some of these white denominations have been more liberal and progressive on the issue of women clergy than most of the black denominations. Both white and black women have been attracted by these increased opportunities to move from the pew to the pulpit, and to other leadership positions in their denominations. Carpenter has raised doubts, however, about how long this trend of black women preachers moving into white denominations will or can be sustained. The vast majority of these women are being assigned to the predominantly black parishes within these white denominations and it may only be a matter of time before these limited options will be filled and "the doors will shut."[51]

Furthermore, this projection is exacerbated by the suspicion of white paternalism and the resentment some black women feel at being showcased as evidence of white Christian liberalism. As one black United Methodist clergywoman pointed out in an interview, the cost of being a token person in a white denomination can be very high. She claimed that she was used as a "public relations piece," photographed and invited to dinners with the board of trustees of her seminary. Even as an ordained minister, she said, "I am viewed as a freak. Always singled out and critiqued, always asked to represent my race and/or my gender. I am always a minority—always without colleague support of the same gender/race."[52] Dr. Katie Cannon, an African American theologian, underscored the personal problems of tokenism in a white, male-dominated environment:

> I was quite successful in seminary because I knew how to behave in men's space so as not to threaten them. My stance was primarily that of the fly on the wall—a fly with many privileges granted to me as long as I remembered my place/space. Sometimes I was permitted to soar like a mighty eagle and other times I sat quietly like a bump on a log. Knowing the difference made me constantly feel as if I was driving with one foot on the accelerator and the other one simultaneously on the brakes. This meant that even though I was producing at top quality on one side of my brain, my soul sagged and ached with the heavy load of the precariousness of my tokenism.[53]

According to Cynthia Epstein, being black and female is one of the most cumulatively limiting of all the negatively evaluated statuses, and the majority of black women professionals in most occupations are often seen as inappropriate, or they are undervalued.[54] This view is common among professional black clergywomen in white denominations who must struggle not only with sexism but must do so against a backdrop of pervasive racial chauvinism.

A final trend found among both white and black clergywomen is their struggle to advance beyond entry level or auxiliary-style appointments or elections. While the reception of women as professional clergy has increased sharply over the last two decades, their advancement into positions of real power and prestige has been slow and dilatory. For example, while most newly ordained clergy can expect to begin pastoring in rural or small marginal urban churches, women are far more likely than men to move to second or third lateral appointments rather than truly promotive stations. Few women are chosen for the large established churches of the central city, or for posh, prestigious suburban churches. Interviews with men and women clergy and presiding elders in the Second District of the African Methodist Episcopal Church have confirmed the fact that the greatest challenge in the future is to have women move into the prestige churches in the district. The Second District, which encompasses the Washington-Baltimore region, is considered to be one of the most progressive in the A.M.E. Church and the clergy and laity have been receptive to women as pastors of churches. Yet one presiding elder confessed his skepticism regarding the future of women clergy:

> Acceptance has been terrific. We have not experienced any opposition to women as ministers. In fact, the women have turned the situation around in a number of problem churches. However, in this District all of the appointments have been beginning appointments. Some of the women are in their third and fourth years, the time of advancement. It remains to be seen whether they will experience the same kind of acceptance in larger churches as they did in smaller ones. It is a question in my mind.[55]

The apprehensions of the presiding elder are shared both by the women clergy in the Second District who want to move up, and by some of the male A.M.E. clergy who expressed concern about perceived competition for favorable posts in one of the few districts in the A.M.E. Church with a surplus of available ministers.[56]

Thus far, the only black women clerics to be elected as bishops are Leontyne C. Kelly of the United Methodist Church and Barbara C. Harris, who in 1988 was chosen a suffragan or assistant bishop for the diocese of Massachusetts of the Episcopal Church in an emotionally charged and highly controversial departure from tradition. None of the black Methodist denominations have yet elected a woman bishop and it will be some time before they do so. Bishop John Adams of the Second District of the A.M.E. Church probably speaks for most of his denomination when he predicts that "women will achieve the post of bishop in due time when they have accumulated enough experience as pastors and presiding elders and developed a reputation for leadership in the A.M.E. Church." But many women clergy in his church feel that his formula is a catch-22, and that the road ahead for women aspiring for the episcopacy is long and fraught with obstacles.[57]

In spite of the great difficulties and obstacles they have encountered in their attempts to become professional ministers, black women have forged ahead to answer their own spiritual calling to serve and to provide their own contributions to the church as a liberating force in American society. In Mozella Mitchell's study of black female religious professionals, 98 percent reported that they would not leave their vocation despite their feeling that they were heavily exploited and that coworkers often treated them with indifference or suspicion. The women are confident that they are qualified to minister to people's multidimensional needs and that God will support them in their ministry even if no one else does.[58]

The quest for professionalization among black preaching women has not only affected the practices of churches and church bureaucracies but it has also involved all of the intellectual fields concerned with the academic training of clergy in seminaries and divinity schools. Black liberation theology, which was described earlier in chapter 7, has also given rise to a new movement of black women who were concerned about critical theological reflections from their own perspective and context. We turn to a brief description of some of the major features of an emerging womanist theology.

Womanist Theology and Ethics: Theological Reflections from the Experiences of Black Women

Much of the debate concerning black women and the rise of the feminist movement over the past twenty years has focused on two issues: a stress upon the continued need for racial unity in a white society and a puzzlement over why more black women have not joined the feminist movement. Historians such as Paula Giddings have summarized the internal debate over racial unity in the black community by pointing out that black women were often relegated to supporting roles in the civil rights movement while black men were looked upon as leaders. Although black women formed the backbone of both the civil rights movement and the Black Church, they were kept in the background to take orders and not to give them.[59] White racism, it is argued, produced a stereotyped emasculation of the black male, therefore black men should be supported in leadership positions. Other versions of the argument stressed the need for priority on racial issues since white feminism was not necessarily seen by black women as a disavowal of white racism.

The priority of racial unity is related to the question of why more

African American women have not joined the feminist movement. The Combahee River Collective, a group of black feminists, have written, "Accusations that Black feminism divides the Black struggle are powerful deterrents to the growth of an autonomous Black women's movement."[60] Another reason is that the contemporary feminist movement in the United States is largely dominated by the concerns and organizations of white, middle-class women. The needs and struggles of African American women and women of color, many of whom are poor, are scarcely addressed by white feminists, and black women were never given a significant voice or leadership role in feminist organizations. Most black women felt that white women are often too trapped by their socialization in the racism of American society to reach effectively beyond their own concerns. For example, while white women protested the sexist treatment of women in beauty contests and Miss America pageants, they have never questioned or challenged the underlying conventional standards of beauty. Caucasian features are still preferred: white skin, long blonde or brunette hair, a narrow nose, thin lips, and blue eyes. Verbal and nonverbal statements about what is considered beautiful or ugly, and the acceptability of physical appearance have far-reaching consequences in the development of self-confidence and personal identity. But since the feminist movement has had difficulty in coming to terms with the pluralism of women of different races and classes in their midst, the arguments for gender solidarity are viewed with suspicion by most black women.

As a consequence of their perceived rejection by their white sisters, African American feminists have felt more comfortable organizing their own units of advocacy and protest. Womanist theology is a product of the black nationalism inherent in black liberation theology focused on black feminist concerns. The term "womanist" is derived from Alice Walker's view that the experiences of black women are significantly different from those of white women so that a term other than feminist is needed. Also the word womanist is considered more reflective of both the language and the ethos of the black community:

> Womanist, from womanish, (Opp. of "girlish," i.e., frivolous, irresponsible, not serious). A Black feminist or feminist of color. From the Black folk expression of mothers to female children, "You acting womanish," i.e., like a woman. Usually referring to outrageous, audacious, courageous, or willful behavior. Wanting

to know more or in greater depth than is considered "good" for one. Interest in grown-up doings. Acting grown up. Being grown up. Interchangeable with another black folk expression: "You trying to be grown." Responsible. In charge. Serious.[61]

According to theologian Jacqueline Grant, womanist theology not only proceeds from the particular context of the suffering and experiences of African American women but that context, which brings together the issues of race, sex, and class, provides the broadest and most comprehensive base for liberation theology. Womanist theology agrees with the critique of white racism and the need for black unity expressed in black liberation theology, and it agrees with the criticism of sexism and the need for the unity of women in feminist theology. However, womanist theology moves beyond both by providing its own critique of racism in feminist theology and of sexism in black theology. It also adds the dimension of class since most black women have been poor. As Grant has argued, "Black feminism grows out of Black women's tri-dimensional reality of race/sex/class. It holds that full human liberation cannot be achieved simply by the elimination of any one form of oppression. Consequently real liberation must be 'broad in the concrete'; it must be based upon a multi-dimensional analysis."[62]

Since all liberation theologies have focused on the situation of the poor and oppressed and upon the divine identification with the "least of the people," womanist theology has asserted that the poor black woman is an appropriate Christ figure for contemporary American society. The context and reality of black women's experiences contain a dynamic universalism that connects them intrinsically with the suffering and oppression of others: "They share race suffering with Black men; with White women and other Third World women, they are victims of sexism; and with poor Blacks and Whites and Other Third World peoples, especially women, they are disproportionately poor."[63]

Katie Cannon has extended the womanist tradition into ethics by reflecting on the moral situation of black women in the past and the present. She has also opened the area of black literature as a creative resource for ethical reflection by examining the life and works of Zora Neale Hurston.[64]

Womanist theology is only one form of the theological debate addressed by African American feminist theologians and preaching women. However, it is an important intellectual trend that is likely to continue to grow along with the dramatic increase of black women students now entering seminaries and divinity schools. How these trends will affect the membership of black churches in the future is still unknown since the movement is still in its infancy. And whether and to what extent black women preachers and theologians will be able to find significant response among the black women laity must also await the evaluation that only time can provide. In the meantime, we turn to an examination of another important question that involves gender identity in the black churches, or why the membership ratio of women to men is so distinctly disproportionate.

Black Women, Black Men, and the Black Church: Where Have All the Black Men Gone?

Any casual observer of a Sunday worship service in the typical black church is immediately struck by the predominance of female members. Depending on the congregation, between 66 to 80 percent of its membership is usually composed of women. In our survey of 2,150 churches male membership averaged 30 percent. There are about 2.5–3 females to every male member. The usual anguished lament and questions heard from pastors and laity are: "Where have all the black men gone?" "Why don't more black men attend church?"

The answer to the relative absence of males in black churches is found in a complex of cultural and demographic factors. American culture has always tended to identify lay religion with women, and women have, in fact, always been more strongly represented in both church and synagogue attendance and membership. According to a national sample, 45 percent of all women attended church or synagogue every week compared to 34 percent of all men; 75 percent of all women were members of a church or synagogue versus 63 percent for men.[65] The patriarchal values of American society have identified church attendance and membership with the enterprise of cultural maintenance and value transmission rather than one that is instrumental or economic. The traditional view of women's roles is aptly summarized by the familiar German aphorism: kinder, kueche, kirche (children, kitchen, church). Convention expects women to be the moral exemplars of the society, and to provide the major socialization for children. Even in the black community where women have usually performed significant instrumental tasks by working full time, they are still expected to fulfill the cultural maintenance and value transmitting roles reserved for them. The cultural explanation for men is quite different. It includes Sunday distractions such as sports or other recreation, and extended rest as a reward for a full week of labor. Among the lower classes, teenage black males are often socialized by their male role models to view too much church involvement as a sign of weakness or an absence of machismo: "Time to be a man and learn the ways of the world. Leave the church to the women."[66]

Besides the cultural explanations, there are also demographic factors which affect the greater disproportion of female members in black churches than in white ones. First, in the United States women outlive men by a ratio of seventy-nine years to seventy-two years. Similarly, the average life expectancy of black women is about ten years longer than that of black men, seventy-four years to sixty-five years.[67] Age is also a key factor in comparing the religiosity of men and women, with the highest intensity of religious behavior coming after age fifty for both sexes.[68] Thus, many of the older members of black churches tend to be widows. Second, there are fewer black males than females nationally. Depending on the region of the country, there are 18 to 25 percent fewer black men than women in the age group between seventeen and forty-five years old, which is traditionally considered the prime marriageable years. For example, in central Harlem there are seventy-five men to every hundred women.[69] Although the birthrate of black male and female babies is about even, by the advent of the young adult years there are fewer black men available in the overall pool. According to the 1970 and 1980 censuses, there were more than 1 million black women in this age group compared to men. In his study of the structural constraints and ideological preferences involved in black marriage rates and the growth of singlehood among African Americans, Robert Staples estimated that in all age groups there may be "an excess of three million black women without the opportunity to find an available or desirable mate."[70] Finally, the factors which reduce the black male population are many and diverse: early death due to the factors of poverty, malnutrition, and racism; high rates of homicide and school dropouts; a prison population that is disproportionately black (49 percent nationwide, higher in individual states); the military, which has a large number of minority recruits (25 percent); the toll of hard drugs and life on the streets; and high rates of unemployment among black teenagers and young adults, especially males (50 percent).

This shortage of black males is not only felt in black churches but it has repercussions in all areas of life in black communities including dating and marriage, the phenomenon of female headed households, and the numbers of black male members in any black organization, excluding the fraternities and lodges. The shortage has reached the level of crisis proportions, particularly among teenage and young adult black males, which we will describe in more detail in the next chapter.

A question that is often raised in discussions about the entry of more women into positions of pastors and preachers in the Black Church is whether the presence of women in leadership posts will drive away black men. While there have been no studies of this question, the analysis of the shortage of black men presented above indicates that their absence is less a question of the sex of the pastor and more a question that is rooted in cultural and demographic factors. The current shortage of black men exists while the pastors of 95 percent of the mainline black churches are male. The current male members, who make up one-third of the membership of black churches, are there for religious reasons and the sex of the leader will probably not make a substantial difference. In fact, one popular folk explanation of the predominance of female members in black churches is related to the power of sexual attraction between the male pastor and his largely female followers. While the power of the patriarchal heritage cannot be summarily dismissed, it would seem just as reasonable to expect that a female pastor would attract a largely male following. But that has not happened because the shortage of male participation is rooted in structural factors that also include the high rates of unemployment among black men. Until these societal problems are resolved it is unlikely that black churches or other black organizations will experience a resurgence of black male membership.

Summary and Conclusion

In examining the topic of black women and the black church we have focused largely on the efforts of black women to become officially recognized preachers and pastors in the mainline, historic black denominations, an issue that continues to be of implicit concern in all black churches. Even in those black denominations (mainly Methodist) where women have been officially accepted as pastors and preachers, their upward mobility to larger black churches, historically famous preaching posts, and positions like bishop remains troubled with varying degrees of hindrances and resistances. Our survey results indicate that although close to half of the black clergy nationwide approved of women as pastors and preachers, there are still strongly entrenched negative attitudes among some clergy and laity. As a result of the opposition they have encountered in the historic black denominations, a growing number of theologically trained black women have opted for posts in white denominations that have shown more progressive attitudes on the issue of sexuality. Whether and when this trend will change depends upon the changes in attitude and practice among the historic black churches toward greater tolerance and equal treatment of women clergy.

In our historical overview we have attempted to show that the quest for parity by black preaching women derives largely from the African heritage of African American culture. Traditional African religions have usually given women a greater role in the religious sphere, from feminine depictions of certain deities, to roles as priestesses, diviners, herbalists, and midwives. It was, therefore, much more natural for black women to seek leading religious roles as preachers and pastors when the transition to Christianity was made As a consequence, there probably have been more black women preachers historically in proportion to their numbers in the total population than white women preachers. Many of these black women have had to serve their churches in unofficial and unrecognized positions as preachers, or under titles as exhorters, evangelists and missionaries, and more often in sublimated career paths such as teaching. During the mass migrations of African Americans to the urban centers of the North beginning with World War I, many black women preachers avoided the strictures of the traditional black denominations by founding independent storefront churches. Today a few black women pastor independent, proprietary churches with substantial memberships.

The issues of sexism and feminism in the black community are often overshadowed by the problem of race. Racism in American society is so pervasive and controlling in the lives of African Americans that the problems of sexual discrimination often get considerably less attention. However, during the decade of the 1980s more and more college educated black women addressed the issues of differential gender expectations in a growing black feminist movement. Women in the Black Church have responded with creative attempts at theological analysis and reflection in the womanist theological movement. The prevailing message of black feminism or womanism is that the analysis issues of race and class in the black community can no longer ignore the oppression of sexism. Furthermore, they assert that black clergy and church leaders should recognize that the existence and survival of black churches is overwhelmingly indebted to the efforts and contributions of the women in the pews. If and when these laywomen take up the issue of sexual discrimination in the Black Church, far-reaching changes will occur.

Another vexing problem concerns the relationship between black churches and young people, the children, teenagers, and young adults who represent the future of the Black Church. Since a church without youth is by definition committed to mortality, how the Black Church will fare in the twenty-first century must necessarily be determined to a substantial degree by its ability to attract, hold, and service a constituency of young people. In the next chapter we examine a set of issues and problems that also demand the attention of black church leaders and members.

11 "In My Mother's House": The Black Church and Young People

Beneatha: "Mama, you don't understand. It's all a matter of ideas and God is just one idea I don't accept. . . . There is simply no blasted God—there is only man and it is he who makes miracles!"
(Mama slaps Beneatha powerfully across her face.)
Mama: "Now—you say after me, in my mother's house there is still God. (Pause) In my mother's house there is still God."
Beneatha: "In my mother's house there is still God."*

The powerful emotional scene and confrontation between mother and daughter regarding God's existence and influence in Lorraine Hansberry's classic work summarizes the concerns of this chapter, the relationship between the Black Church and young people. Black parents, like Mama and her husband in *A Raisin in the Sun*, have usually tried to raise their children properly by taking them to church every Sunday. But like Beneatha, many young African Americans, teenagers and young adults, have increasingly questioned the need for God and the relevancy of the Black Church to their own lives in the world as they have come to see it. Black artists and writers such as Hansberry and James Baldwin have constantly pointed to the city, the urban milieu with its different values and pluralistic lifestyles, as the locale where the future changes and challenges for black churches and black families lie.[1] During the period of the massive black migrations to urban areas from World War I until the late 1960s, the majority of black migrants continued to use their churches as the major communal institutions, and many of them still do so in the 1980s, as we have indicated in previous chapters. However, among certain sectors of the black community,

*Lorraine Hansberry, *A Raisin in the Sun*, p. 39.

fissures in the previous dominance of the Black Church have developed and important challenges and problems are emerging, especially among young people. As one concerned c.m.e. pastor said in his survey interview in Harlem, "For the first time in Black history, we are seeing an unchurched generation of young Black people growing up in urban areas. In previous generations, you could always assume some knowledge of Black Church culture, like favorite hymns or prayers or some rituals. Today, there are teenagers out there [in the streets] who have no knowledge of and no respect for the Black Church and its traditions."[2]

The new generation of black young people, who were born in northern and western urban areas after the civil rights era in the 1970s and 1980s, represents this potentially large unchurched group to which the pastor referred.[3] Not all of this generation is unchurched but, as we shall point out, certain growing segments of them are. In this chapter we will examine two major challenges that confront black churches: the problem of identity among young black children and the issue of the growing sectors of unchurched black teenagers and young adults. We will relate the findings of our field interviews with black clergy to these issues. How seriously do the clergy and the Black Church take the challenges posed by recalcitrant young people? What kinds of programs and solutions do they propose? Will the clergy, like Mama in *Raisin*, attempt to reinforce the traditional solutions or will they attempt to seek new ways to cope with the dilemmas posed by the erosion of the religious tradition? Before addressing these questions, we offer a brief historical overview of the relationships between black churches, black families, and their children because it is easy to forget the real strengths that exist in the black community and to get lost in the thicket of pathological statistics of contemporary urban society.

The Enduring Institutions: Black Families and Black Churches

In their fine history of the African American experience in America, Mary Berry and John Blassingame recognized that black families and black churches have constituted the "enduring institutions" in black communities.[4] In the interaction between these two major institutional sectors of family and church, there has always existed a historical tradition of special caring for young children. The precariousness of existence during the centuries of slavery and the continued state of racial oppression thereafter have contributed to a view of children that was not widespread in American society. Since young children were often taken away from their mothers and sold as slaves, an informal system of adoption for children and a system of "fictive kinship" were developed among black extended families. As it was mentioned earlier, children, who were born out of wedlock, were not shunned nor stigmatized as bastards or labeled as illegitimate as they were in the English and American traditions, but they were accepted as members of the extended family. If there were no parents, or if the mother had a difficult time, the children were often informally adopted by grandparents or by fictive uncles and aunts, black adults who were not blood relatives.[5] Children were children, no matter the circumstances of birth, and they were treated with a care and indulgence peculiar to the precarious conditions of oppressed people. Sacrifices of material goods, food, money, labor, and even lives were made on behalf of the children by parents, whose only hope was that their children would live to see a better day.

As the only communal institutions in most urban and rural black communities, black churches were intimately involved in the complex network of black extended families. Some churches were totally dominated by one or a few kin groups so that the phenomenon of the "family church" or "kin church" was widespread, especially in rural areas where departed relatives of the extended family were buried in the church cemetery. Such cemeteries were the common features of a society which from birth through death required and legitimated the segregation of the races in both the North and the South. Even today, it is not unusual to find a family church and its supporting kin group in the rural South holding a memorial service for a former member who had migrated to a northern city and had died and was buried there. As it was mentioned in chapter 5, the profound loyalty and commitment of the family members toward the family church is a major reason why many black rural churches are still in existence.

Black families and churches are involved in a dynamic interactive relationship. Families constituted the building blocks for black churches and the churches through their preaching and teaching, symbols, belief system, morality, and rituals provided a unity—a glue that welded families and the community to each other. After the Civil War, for example, black churches legitimated the informal marital relationships of many former slaves and sought to restore the

role of black males as husbands and providers.[6] Parents often brought
their children to church, sometimes even forcing them to go, because
they deeply believed that the church would provide a dose of moral
education for the children and open up the spiritual dimensions of
their lives. Churches also provided Sunday school for children and
adults, and for many black people for a long period of time the church
was the place where they first began to learn rudimentary reading
skills. Although worship services were oriented toward the adult
members, special Sunday services were set aside for the participation
of children and children's choirs on "Children's Day," or "junior
church" occasions.[7] The birth of a new child was first publicly announced in church, and there the infant was consecrated by the
pastor. Black clergy not only provided marriage counseling to pro-
spective couples, but if that family remained with the church, the
pastor was often sought out for advice on important decisions and at
points of family crisis. A stable family life was an important goal for
the churches in their quest to build community.[8]

Black churches not only provided spiritual uplift, they also provided important social occasions where people could meet and interact with each other. Going to church in many black communities
was, and in some instances still is, an all day affair. Sunday church
dinners are an important tradition and some church kitchens have
gained a local or regional reputation for their culinary art, as is the
case at the Mother Zion Church in New York City, for example.[9] All
of these social affairs from dinners to church picnics and bus tours to
visit other churches, or to vacation spots included families and children. For many youngsters the first trip out of their local community
was usually to a church sponsored event. At least one black denomination, the African Methodist Episcopal Church, has developed
its own bus company, Allen Transportation, and a supporting travel
agency. A few churches also provide recreational events and sponsor
athletic teams. Finally, black churches have served as concert halls,
art galleries, and public forums of African Americans, and the first
public performance seen or given by many black children often occurred in the church.

Perhaps one of the most important functions that black churches
performed for young people was to provide a place where they could
meet older adults, men and women, who could serve as role models
for them. Much of the socialization for children and youth occur
through the process of role modeling—observing, evaluating, emu-
lating, and filing away for later use the behavior, examples, and

values of others. Studies have shown that black pastors and laity have been important role models for black youth. Both Carter G. Woodson and Charles S. Johnson have pointed to the molding influences of churches on rural youth, who were not only aware of the positive aspects of going to church but were also critical of the double standards in adult behavior.[10] In John Scanzoni's 1971 study of black families, the minister ranked second behind the school teacher among the adult role figures who showed an interest in black youth. Not surprisingly the Sunday school teacher ranked third, so that two out of the top three adult role models for Scanzoni's sample of black youth were related to the Black Church.[11] We will return to this important topic of role models in the section on teenagers and young adults after examining the challenge which the problem of identity among young black children presents to black churches.

Black Children, White Dreams:

Description of the Problem of Racial Identity Among Black Children[12]

From 1939 until the early 1950s the husband and wife team of black psychologists Drs. Kenneth and Mamie Clark published a series of studies on the racial self-identification of black children. These studies played an important role in the 1954 Supreme Court decision in the celebrated *Brown v. Board of Education* case which desegregated public schools.[13] The case, which was brought by Leon Oliver Brown, pastor of the St. Mark's A.M.E. Church in Topeka, Kansas, and the NAACP Legal Defense Fund on behalf of nine-year-old Linda Brown and other black children, used the results of the doll-choice tests developed by the Clarks to show the detrimental effects of a segregated and inferior school system on black children. According to the Clarks, 67 percent of the black children preferred to play with a white doll but 66 percent of them also identified with the black doll. However, they concluded that the 34 percent of black youngsters who did not identify with the black doll suffered from low self-esteem.[14]

Since the pioneering studies by the Clarks, other social scientists have performed similar tests with different variations, but their results have also shown that more than half of the black children involved have indicated a preference for white dolls and about one-third of the children tended to misidentify themselves.[15] In their

survey of the social history of these doll-choice tests and studies of
racial identity among young black children from the 1940s until the
1980s, Fine and Bowers have pointed out that during the period of
black consciousness in the late 1960s and 1970s the percentages of
black children choosing the black doll rose to 70 percent and 64
percent, signifying almost a reversal of the earlier studies.[16] They
argued that the social attitudes of black pride and the broader public
support of Great Society programs fostered a greater sense of opti-
mism and hope which may have influenced the results of the studies
conducted during this period. Likewise, they hypothesized that the
setbacks in economic conditions and a diminishing of black pride
symbols that blacks have experienced in the 1980s would also be
reflected by studies of racial identity in that decade. Fine and Bowers
reported that their results in 1984 indicated a break with the trend
toward increasing preference for a black doll that was found in the
late 1960s and 1970s; black children expressed less preference for a
black doll and their levels of racial self-identification reverted back to
those reported in the 1940s. Black boys in their study also preferred
and identified more with the white doll than black girls.[17]

At the 1987 meeting of the American Psychological Association
(APA), psychologist Darlene Powell-Hopson reported on her study of
155 black and white youngsters between ages three to six in Headstart programs and preschools in New York City, Long Island, and in
Connecticut.[18] According to Powell-Hopson, 64 percent of the black
children selected white dolls, a finding that seems to support Fine
and Bowers's view of a decline in racial self-identification in the
1980s.[19]

Research results have shown that doll-choice studies are affected
by the age, social class, and gender of the children.[20] But the psychological dynamics of doll selection remain unclear and scholars have
debated its meaning: for example, whether the fact that some black
children select or identify with a white doll is indicative of low self-
esteem or whether it is just a reflection of broader societal attitudes
(via media and schooling) or the attitudes of the testers. However, the
most important point is that all of the studies indicate a level of
ambivalence among many black children toward their own racial
identity.[21] Even middle-class black children were found to experience
high rates of racial rejection because many of them grew up in white
suburbs. These middle-class children also exhibited more positive
self-esteem as individuals but less positive racial self-esteem as
members of a minority group.[22] Furthermore, the vast majority of

white children (90 percent or more) in these studies have not shown any ambivalence toward their own identities since they more accurately identified themselves via the color of the dolls. Even more disturbing were the tendencies of both black and white children to express in open-ended interviews and free association play that the black doll was "dirty" or "bad."[23] As Powell-Hopson said in an interview, her study does not show that black youngsters "are full of self-hatred or that they want to be white. It does mean that the message they're getting is that it's preferable to be another race."[24]

The ambivalence in identity that black children showed in the doll-choice tests was also confirmed by the fieldwork and participant observation that Robert Coles did in his classic work, *Children of Crisis*. In 1964 Coles noted that Negro children tended to draw themselves and their friends as smaller than white children or as being in subservient positions to whites.[25] In reflecting upon the meaning of race, he said:

> In a very real sense being Negro serves to organize and render coherent many of the experiences, warnings, punishments and prohibitions that Negro children face. The feelings of inferiority or worthlessness they acquire, the longing to be white they harbor and conceal, the anger at what they find to be their relatively confined and moneyless condition, these do not fully account for the range of emotions in many Negro children as they come to terms with the "meaning" of their skin color.[26]

Much of the meaning of skin color for black children, according to Coles, comes in the period of "preparation," the lessons devised by black parents to teach their children how to cope in a white dominated society. To learn to put on the defensive armor against the subtle and not so subtle attacks and insults.

While the raw violence and physically closed doors of segregated institutions during the period of Coles's study have been declared illegal, black parents and major black institutions like the Black Church must still struggle with the meaning of race, particularly where children are concerned.

The Black Church and the Problem of Racial Identity Among Black Children

The continuing ambivalence of racial identity among black children in the 1980s as revealed by the studies mentioned above, strikes at the core of the doctrinal position of the Black Church and poses a major challenge to it. During slavery, African American Christians embraced the biblical view of human personality, that each person, slave or free, was a child of God. This doctrine of the infinite worth of human personality and the equality of all human beings in the eyes of God prevented the complete dehumanization of the slaves. Since black churches were one of the few institutions to emerge intact from the period of slavery, they always viewed their task as a holistic one, dealing not only with spiritual concerns but also with the spheres of politics, economics, education, and the various dimensions of culture.

Black churches have always provided a community and an atmosphere where people could be affirmed and accepted as they are. One of their major strengths was to provide a place where the status and dignity of even the lowliest person could be affirmed. A janitor could become a deacon of the church and a domestic could be the head usher. Hence, the invisible people, who were not recognized and who were often rejected by the larger society, received status and recognition in this institution. Nevertheless, a major problem for many contemporary black churches is the disproportionate focus of their programs and efforts on adults. Black youth, especially young children, became a kind of afterthought in the church's schedule of significant ministry. While Sunday Schools continue as a traditional part of the typical black church, many perform functions more akin to babysitting than education and socialization. Too many black pastors do not concern themselves with this aspect of ministry, but tend to delegate the religious education of their youth to someone else.

For the vast majority of black pastors, preaching was still seen as their major task. In our survey of pastoral responsibilities, 919 (60.0 percent) of 1,531 clergy ranked preaching as their top priority, while 358 (23.4 percent) ranked teaching as their primary responsibility. No other pastoral responsibility (administration; visitation; community leadership; leadership of groups within the church; leading worship; fund raising) received more than 5 percent support. One pastor put these results in perspective when he replied in his interview, "Black folks have a different religious orientation from white folks. There is little emphasis put upon Home and Foreign Mission and Christian Education. White folks work from the building of their Educational department, but black folks operate from the pulpit as great preaching stations. Great emphasis is put upon preaching in the Black Church."[27]

While black congregations and clergy will continue to place priority upon preaching, especially charismatic preaching, as their primary task, the results of our survey and the studies of the problem of racial identity among young black children suggest that more attention needs to be paid to the education and socialization of black youth. Black churches can begin with the religious education that is within their control, especially with Sunday School education and literature. In the black consciousness profile of our survey, we asked the clergy, "Is it important to have black figures in your Sunday School literature?" Out of a total of 1,765 respondents, 1,215 (68 percent) replied affirmatively, while 550 (32.0 percent) said no. The majority of those who responded negatively to the question felt, "skin color is of no great significance in relating the message of Jesus."[28] One pastor said, "Yes. Because it gives them a self-awareness and self-esteem so they don't feel inferior. If they see white images, they think you have to be white to succeed."[29] Another pastor elaborated on his affirmative response by saying, "Well, there is the particular literature where Jesus was carrying a cross and Simon the black man helped him carry it. I think it is important to have blacks portrayed and Moses' wife was an Ethiopian. These characters need to be portrayed so blacks will not feel like they are a minority in religion."[30]

Although the majority of black clergy felt that it was important to have black figures portrayed in Sunday School literature, an informal survey of that literature used by the major black denominations revealed that only the black Methodist denominations (A.M.E., A.M.E. Zion, and C.M.E.) were consistent in having black figures in their Sunday day school literature.[31] Many black Baptist and Pentecostal churches continued to use educational materials put out by white denominations, especially the Southern Baptists. In fact there is an increasing trend among black Baptists, especially in the South, of maintaining secondary affiliations with the Southern Baptists, entitling them to receive Sunday school materials and educational support from the white denomination.[32]

While some black churches undoubtedly use educational materials from white denominations primarily out of financial considerations, our research suggests that the major black denominations and churches need to pay closer attention to the programs of religious education and to the materials used in their Sunday schools. Each of the seven major black denominations own their individual publishing house and printing facilities. Some of these publishing houses are multi-million dollar operations, having the capability of printing their own instructional literature, magazines, brochures, and books. Where black churches and clergy are serious about helping young black children in resolving the problem of an ambivalent racial identity, they are already substantially equipped to address this problem. One pastor underscored this view in the plaintive question he raised in his interview. "The Church has an obligation to teach about the contributions of our race. . . . If we don't do this, where are our kids going to get it?"[33] The process of identity formation is a very subtle one, and the selection and presentation of Sunday school materials, as innocuous as they seem, send messages to young children about what is important and unimportant about themselves and their society, no less than what should have religious significance in their lives.

Besides the question of religious education and Sunday schools, black churches and families may need to consider changes in the larger social systems that affect the socialization of black youth, particularly the media and the public schools. Studies show that many black children spend from two to five hours per day watching television.[34] Although there has been an increase in the number of positive roles and family programs like the "Bill Cosby Show," most major programs and characters are still dominated by whites, including the news media. The numbers of African Americans working in all types of media still remain quite low. For example, only 2 percent of journalists for daily newspapers are black. Only a handful of 1,710 daily newspapers are black owned.[35] There is a paucity in black television programming, and in the decade of the 1980s African Americans owned only 8 television stations out of 1,138 commercial stations across the country. As Jesse Jackson pointed out to the National Association of Broadcasters, "This is a lily white industry."[36]

In 1967 Jonathan Kozol's *Death at an Early Age* stunned many educators and parents because he showed via his own teaching experience in a public school in Roxbury (Boston) how the pride, self-esteem, and motivation of many young black children get destroyed by the not-so-subtle attitudes and messages of their teachers and school administrators. From culture-bound tests and tracking systems to judgments about art, civilization, and history, the message is sent that people of color are second class, not good enough.[37] Both Albert Memmi and Eugene Perkins have demonstrated that the educational system forms a critical part of the socialization of oppressed people, particularly the young.[38] As Woodson has long recognized, by controlling a Negro's mind, you also control his actions: "You do not need to send him to the back door. He will go without being told. In fact, if there is no back door, he will cut one for his special benefit. His education makes it necessary."[39]

The recognized biases of American public education when coupled with negative economic realities lead inevitably to "death at an early age," or to very high levels of drop out among young African Americans. Although the number of black youth attending high schools has increased from a total of 6 percent of all high school students in 1960 to 10 percent in 1980, there has also been a high rate of black students dropping out of school. During the 1980s the black drop-out rate has averaged about 25 percent nationally, but in some urban school systems that rate exceeded 50 percent.[40]

The historic antiracist stance of black churches has supported the goal of cultural pluralism and ethnic diversity in the media and in public school systems. Cultural pluralism and an informed citizenry require the recognition and inclusion of black history and culture in the content of school curricula and television programming. Pluralism also suggests the need to increase the numbers of black people working in the schools, the media, and other sectors of society. When this happens, black workers can become significant role models for all black youth. As the doll-choice studies showed, the levels of racial preference and self-identity among black children can be influenced by a positive environment, positive reinforcement by culturally sensitive teachers, and an emphasis upon black pride; but they can also be reversed by negativity. In an article, "An Advocacy Agenda for Black Families and Children," Marian Wright Edelman of the Children's Defense Fund has outlined the premises and steps that are needed to change the negative situation for black children. Edelman acknowledges that it will require a long and persistent struggle to change the conditions of racial inequality in American society, and she underscores the fact that the effort will require not only the resources of the government but also the strengths and fortitude of black families and institutions like the Black Church.[41] Significantly, Edelman quotes with approval Nannie Burroughs, a black Baptist churchwoman who spoke of the need for black people to

organize "inside," to reemphasize the moral and spiritual dimensions of life, and to teach black children, "the internals and the
eternals rather than the externals. Be more concerned with putting in
than getting on. We have been too bothered about the externals—
clothes or money. What we need are mental and spiritual giants who
are aflame with a purpose."[42]

The issue of racial identity among black children also involves the
larger task of providing a critique of Eurocentric values that are
embedded in the English language. In our Western culture where the
term "black" is often equated with evil and uncleanness, and "dark"
is a pejorative word signifying diminished value or obscurity, African
American clergy, theologians, educators, and others in position to
interpret reality to black youth have a unique responsibility to work
at changing the valence of insidious language.[43] Until a reconstruc-
tive approach to language takes place, it seems doubtful that the confused interpretations of the color-based identity can be completely
overcome. The ambivalence of black identity illustrated in the studies we mentioned previously may have significant implications in
later life. While the majority of black children eventually come to
terms with their racial identity as they grow older, there are some
children whose self-confidence, self-worth, and adequacy may be
permanently affected.[44] In *Manchild in the Promised Land*, Claude
Brown gives the following example: "The secretary told me that Mr.
Stillman wasn't going to be in all day but that Mr. Upshur would see
me as soon as he was free. I sat down and waited for a few minutes and
Mr. Upshur came in. When he said he was Mr. Upshur, I knew he
couldn't help me. He was colored. What could he do for anybody?"[45]

The issue of an ambivalent racial identity among black children
presents a major challenge to the claims of the Christian message of
the Black Church that salvation brings wholeness to human personalities and a healing of broken lives. The command to love your
neighbor as yourself is rendered problematic without self-acceptance.
Claude Brown's observations lead us to consider some of the issues
and challenges involving the Black Church, teenagers, and young
adults.

The Black Church and the Challenges of Black Youth in Poverty

Most of the pressing issues for black churches, black families, and
the black community stem from that sector of the black population

that is still mired in poverty, which social scientists have labeled the underclass. Poor black families make up about one-third of all black families but only about half of these poor families (16 to 18 percent of the total) are caught in a cycle of several generations of welfare dependency, which has been widely publicized by the media.[46] The other half of poor families are the working poor, whose marginal incomes are supplemented by food stamps. However, as Douglas Glasgow has pointed out, the numerical size of the black underclass involves a "staggering magnitude," if one also includes the unemployed; the close to 1 million black men who have given up looking for jobs and are no longer counted by the census; blacks in prisons; about 3 million blacks in rural hamlets in small southern towns; and the new "homeless" black poor. The total estimate may be close to 10 million people.[47] Although there has been a considerable debate about the causes of the underclass phenomenon, the following three factors have played an important role: first, the structural transformation of the American economy from an industrial to a post-industrial, technological society which has removed manufacturing and low skilled jobs from the central cities; second, high rates of unemployment among black males due to this transformation and continuing racial discrimination; and third, public policies of the federal government.[48]

An important characteristic of the underclass is the large number of black females who are poor. Of the 4.6 million black families with children, 2.6 million are headed by single women. Among the 8.9 million poor black Americans, 6.2 million were females and/or persons in female-headed households.[49] In 1960 22.4 percent of black families were headed by females but that number has increased to 42 percent in 1983.[50] Glasgow's critique of the feminization of poverty thesis has correctly pointed to two major causes of the large number of poor black females and the rise in female-headed households: first, the racial discrimination which places the income of black women in the lowest ranks; and second, the high rates of black male unemployment.[51] Studies have shown that there usually is a rise in female-headed households among blacks and whites whenever there is a rise in long-term male unemployment because the men usually leave their families to look for jobs, or are forced to leave by welfare policies. Indeed, male unemployment may be the single most important factor in explaining female-headed households.[52] For our purposes it is important to recognize that close to half (49 percent) of all black youth grow up in female-headed households, which means that increasingly many of them are growing up in poverty and their life chances and opportunities are considerably diminished.

As mentioned earlier in this chapter, a major challenge to the Black Church concerns a growing sector of unchurched black youth, largely teenage and young adult black males from the underclass, who are located in northern and western urban centers.[53] This phenomenon is also beginning to appear in southern cities like Atlanta, but the South as a region has always had a stronger religious culture than other parts of the country. In a study of black male youths and church attendance in Tennessee, Dr. Ruth Dennis of the Meharry Medical School said, "Even though we see daily evidence of the return of individuals to church, from our study, we also see evidence of the church . . . losing ground as it relates to black male youth, adolescent, young adult and adult."[54] The socialization process for many black males growing up in urban ghettos involves "the street institution," as Eugene Perkins calls it, learning the survival tactics of street life and eventually becoming involved with a formal or informal street gang for protection.[55] Gang membership often leads to illegal activities such as robbery and stealing, prostitution, and the sale and/or use of drugs. An inordinate proportion of homicides and other victims of crime are young black males. According to Claude Brown, it is the type of drug used, like PCP, or angel dust, and cocaine in the form of crack, and the viciousness of the crimes committed that distinguishes the black gangs of the 1980s from those of the 1950s.[56] The turf wars of the 1950s were far more ritualized, involving demonstrations of individual bravado and combat over territory, than the drug wars of the 1980s where whole families are often massacred. However, socialization into gang activity often involves countervailing pressures against involvement in any mainstream activities or institutions, especially black churches which are usually identified in street culture as the province of older black women or "straight" types.

During the 1980s black teenagers and young adults, ages seventeen to thirty-five, have experienced extremely high unemployment rates ranging from 40 percent to over 50 percent; in some black communities like New York's Bedford-Stuyvesant and the Bronx, the unemployment rate for teenagers soared to 80 percent.[57] In terms of gender, black male teenagers and young adults had an average unemployment rate of more than 50 percent in 1984, compared to the 46 percent for black females.[58] The great concern of these high rates of teenage and young adult unemployment during the Reagan years is that a large segment of black youth will not acquire the work experience, the discipline and motivation, much less the skills necessary for long-term participation in the labor force. A lost generation of black young people is being created in many central cities and some rural areas.

Besides unemployment, a common experience for many black teens and young adults, especially males, is imprisonment. Nationally, the incarceration rate of black men has averaged between 46 percent to 48 percent in the 1980s, with higher rates in states like New York (50 to 53 percent between 1979 to 1986) and throughout the South (54 percent).[59] While women as a whole made up about 4 percent of the total prison population in 1981, black women constituted about 51 percent of all women prisoners.[60] The rates of recidivism, of returning to prison, varies with age; younger inmates, between ages seventeen to twenty-four, have the highest rates, 60–70 percent, and older inmates, over age forty-five, have rates below 5 percent.

The United States ranks third among industrial nations, behind South Africa and the Soviet Union, in having the largest prison populations. In 1985 there were more than 500,000 prisoners in U.S. state and federal prisons, which corresponds to a rate of imprisonment of 201 per 100,000 population. However, if the imprisonment rates for black Americans alone are examined, a different picture arises. According to the New York State Coalition for Justice and the Center for Justice Education, there is a severe factor of racial discrimination in the criminal justice system that pervades the extremely high imprisonment rates of black people in America. For example, they point out that in 1984 South Africa had a black incarceration rate of 504 per 100,000.[61] But New York State's 1985 rate of "776 blacks imprisoned per 100,000 is one and one-half times greater than South Africa's and more than ten times the rate for whites."[62] Furthermore, blacks in New York were more likely to receive jail and prison sentences than probation, while there were three times more whites on felony probation as there were in prison. About 70 percent of the total state prison population in New York were in the age category of sixteen to thirty-five years old.[63] In Albany County, New York, it is estimated that if one adds the number of blacks incarcerated in city and county jails to the state prison population, more than 10 percent of the young black male population will be in jails or prisons.[64] The imprisonment rates of blacks in southern states were also higher than that of South Africa.[65] High rates of unemployment and high rates of incarceration among the black, urban poor are tied together. Increasingly, it appears that prisons are being used as part of a social policy, to deal with these high rates of unemployment and poverty among minority groups in the United States.

While some form of incarceration is a major experience for the majority of young black men in the underclass, teenage pregnancy among many young black women has reached crisis proportions. Teenage pregnancy is not a specifically black problem, since it is a consequence of the sexual revolution of the 1960s and all sectors of American society have been affected, especially the traditional socializing institutions of church and family. However, as Joyce Ladner points out, a hesitancy and a defensiveness to recognize or deal with developing social problems in the black community by academics, intellectuals, leaders, and experts on the black family have contributed to the present crisis.[66] Most of the births to black and white adolescents are out of wedlock. According to the Children's Defense Fund, in 1982 teenagers accounted for 24.6 percent of all black births and 12.3 percent of all white births.[67] In a "Fact Sheet" on teenage pregnancy, K. A. Moore pointed out that by age twenty, 41 percent of black females and 19 percent of white females have given birth.[68] Teenage births are problematic because they involve higher rates of infant mortality, emotional immaturity of the mother who is often still a child herself, lack of support and responsibility by the father, little education of both parents, and a constant series of health, medical, and economic problems.[69] The majority of black teenage mothers live in conditions of poverty and are often part of a generational phenomenon of teen mothers in their families.[70]

Perhaps the most serious aspect of this problem of teen pregnancy is the fact that most of these young people are alienated, disadvantaged, and disconnected from the mainstream of the society and the black community. Widespread alienation from the traditional norms and institutions that once socialized black youth constitutes a major problem for many black churches, as Ladner has indicated. She also points to the failure of many churches in confronting the problem: "The black church, which serves as a focal point for the community, has not assumed a leadership role on teen pregnancy prevention. Most black churches tend to be conservative on the issues of premarital sex, contraceptives, and abortion, especially for teens. Therefore, only the most secular-oriented progressive churches can be expected to take a leadership position on this problem."[71] Ladner is correct in her insight that teen pregnancy is a major challenge to the traditions of black churches. The fact is that the whole Christian tradition has had great difficulty in dealing with the issues of sexuality, involving not only premarital sex, abortion, and homosexuality, but also including the acceptance of women clergy as we indicated in the previous chapter. Ladner's criticism also leads to questions of what the black churches are doing for black young people? What kinds of programs do they sponsor and what has been effective in attracting teenagers and young adults? What can black churches do in regard to the challenges of black males in prison and teenage pregnancy? We turn next to the results of our survey on the relationship between black churches and clergy and teenagers and young adults.

The Black Church and Young People:
The Views of the Clergy and the Programs of the Churches

In our field survey of black churches we were concerned with black teenagers, ages thirteen to sixteen, and young adults between the ages of seventeen to thirty-five. The terms "youth" and "young people" are used interchangeably for both groups, unless questions are specified for one age category. In responding to the question of whether their church had any difficulty in recruiting and maintaining teenagers and young adults in their churches, close to half of the clergy, 996 (48.4 percent), said yes they had difficulty, while slightly more than half, 1,061 (51.6 percent), said that they had no difficulty. The fact that the responses were almost evenly divided indicated that many black churches have been experiencing difficulties with both teenagers and young adults. From our field experiences with black churches, we have noted that they do better with teenagers than with young adults. If any age group tends to be missing in many black churches, it is likely to be the young adult group (ages seventeen to thirty-five).

Table 33 presents the results of responses to the question, "What is the church doing in terms of outreach programs for young people?" The top three youth programs sponsored by churches included: youth group activities (such as youth choir, Baptist Training Union or other youth group) 433 (20.1 percent); evangelism (rallies, revivals,

Table 33: Outreach Programs for Youth

Q. What is the church doing in terms of developing outreach programs for youths?

Type of Program	Number	Percent
Evangelism (rallies, revivals, special services)	431	20.0
Educational programs (Bible study, discussion groups, vacation Bible school)	245	11.4
Recreational programs (sports, athletic teams, summer fun)	145	6.7
Social programs (fashion/talent shows, picnics, dinners, skating parties)	39	1.8
Youth group activities (youth choir, youth group, Scouts, clubs)	433	20.1
Counseling by minister	35	1.6
Community service oriented programs (tutoring, visit hospitals/elderly)	76	3.5
Scholarship aid	10	0.5
Hiring of special youth minister	43	2.0
Other	218	10.1
Church does nothing for youth	317	14.7
No response	158	7.6

N=2,150

and special services) was a close second with 431 (20.0 percent); educational programs (such as Bible study, discussion groups, lectures, and films) 245 (11.4 percent). However, 317 (14.7 percent) said that their churches did nothing for youth. In examining the results, it is interesting to note that the programs which require the attention of the clergy to youth activities and problems ranked quite low. For example, thirty-five (1.6 percent) said they had counseling by the minister and only forty-three (2.0 percent) churches hired a special youth minister.

In responding to the question, "Why do you think young people leave the church?" the results in table 34 show that 538 (25.0 percent) of the clergy feel that the primary reason is because "young people are either bored, and/or the church does not have a relevant program for

Table 34: Reasons Young People Leave the Church

Q. Why do you think young people leave the church?

Reasons	Number	Percent
1. Youth not given chance by adults to participate in a meaningful way in church programs	463	21.5
2. Youth bored and/or does not have a relevant program for them	538	25.0
3. Youth lack knowledge and understanding of the church's importance	144	6.7
4. Stage of life—time to become independent, search and test things out for themselves	316	14.7
5. Lack of intellectual challenge from clergy and church adults (lack of education on part of clergy, ignorance, etc.)	45	2.1
6. Outgrew their childhood faith and beliefs	18	0.8
7. Critical of the hypocrisy of the church or minister—double standards	49	2.3
8. Other	416	19.3
No response	138	6.4

$N=2,150$

them"; 463 (21.5 percent) of the respondents felt that the "youth are not given a chance by adults to participate in a meaningful way in church programs"; adults tended to dominate in most church programs. However, 316 (14.7 percent) of the pastors felt that young people in late adolescence and young adulthood were in a stage of life, a time to become independent, to search and test things out for themselves. In other words, it was natural for them to rebel against adult authority, express doubt, and not attend church. A smaller number, 144 (6.7 percent), of the pastors felt that young people left churches because they "lacked the knowledge and understanding of the church's importance." Interestingly, reasons like the "lack of intellectual challenge," or "hypocrisy in the church," or "outgrowing one's childhood faith and beliefs" ranked below 3 percent. The clergy did not perceive that secularization in this age group was an important rationale for leaving the church.

Our study also examined the views of clergy regarding whether

Table 35: Young People Return to Church

Q. Of the young people who left your church, do they return later in life?

	Number	Percent
Yes	1,783	82.9
No	99	4.6
No response	268	12.5

$N=2,150$

Q. If so, when did they return to church?

	Number	Percent
Never return or very seldom return when they leave	35	1.6
After marriage and first child is born (raising a family)	370	17.2
Middle age years (30s or 40s)	537	25.0
Old age years (after age 65)	50	2.3
Encounter a personal crisis or in deep trouble	240	11.2
After a religious conversion	96	4.5
Other	451	21.0
No response	371	17.2

$N=2,150$

these young people who left their churches ever returned later on in their life, and if so, when did this return to church occur for them? Table 35 presents the results of the clergy responses. A large majority of the pastors, 1,783 (82.9 percent), felt that many of these young people do return to church later in their lives and only 99 (4.6 percent) said that they do not return. The clergy who answered affirmatively were also asked to reflect from their own experiences and delineate when these young people returned to church. The data showed that 537 (25.0 percent) of the pastors felt most young people returned to church during their middle age years (mid-thirties to mid-fifties), while 370 (17.2 percent) said, "after marriage and the first child is born" (that is, raising a family). These top two categories of middle age and raising a family were very similar and tended to reflect views of about half of the clergy (42.2 percent) that a period of settling down after the testing and experimentation of adolescence and young adulthood was the crucial period for a return to church. However, 240 (11.2 percent) of the clergy said that when young people encounter a personal crisis or are in deep trouble, they tend to return. Curiously, only ninety-six (4.5 percent) said that the return occurred after religious conversion, and fifty (2.3 percent) claimed the time for the return was in the old age years (after age 65). Only thirty-five (1.6 percent) said that in their experience these young people "never return or very seldom return when they leave."

The results of table 35 also point to the importance of life stages in a discussion of religious maturity and growth. The psychoanalyst Erik Erikson stressed the importance of stages in a life cycle of human development and maturation.[72] In his work on the lives of Martin Luther and Mahatma Gandhi, Erikson emphasized the role of the identity crisis during adolescence as a critical part of the religious formation of these great men.[73] However, embedded in Erikson's dynamic scheme is the view that an identity crisis is also possible during the stages of middle age and old age. Apparently, in the experience of the black clergy we interviewed, the crises of middle age, which also coincide with raising a family, were a pivotal time for a return to religion and church. There is also some evidence that age is a very important factor in determining the degree of religiousness and that religiousness increases steadily with age. Both men and women, fifty years and older, showed the highest levels of religiousness, with older women (32 percent) having higher levels than older men (17 percent).[74] The period of old age is a far more reflective time of life when a person has retired from active pursuit of a career or job and when one's own death approaches. Erikson has called this period a time of attaining wisdom.[75]

Table 36 shows the distribution of responses to the question, "What special techniques and programs have you found to be successful in attracting young people?" According to the clergy, the top attraction for teenagers and young adults by far was music and choir, which was chosen by 413 (19.2 percent) of the sample. The type of music preferred by most teenagers and young adults was modern gospel. Furthermore, 283 (13.2 percent) of the respondents said that

Table 36: Successful Techniques and Programs for Young People

Q. What special techniques and programs have you found to be successful in attracting young people?

Program or Technique	Number	Percent
Allow greater participation and involvement in the leadership and decisionmaking of church	283	13.2
More understanding and tolerance for young people's lifestyles (openness)	134	6.2
Athletic and recreational programs (sports, picnics, camping)	260	12.1
Music and choir	413	19.2
Community service programs	20	0.9
Bible study and educational programs	149	6.9
More emphasis on evangelism and outreach programs	163	7.6
Relevant preaching	79	3.7
Young people's club (youth groups, etc.)	125	5.8
Other	247	11.5
No response	277	12.9
N=2,150		

there was a need to "allow the young people greater participation and involvement in the leadership and decisionmaking of the church"; and 260 (12.1 percent) chose athletic and recreational programs (such as social events or picnics) to encourage young people to become involved in the church. The usual traditional church programs for young people tended to rank lower: 163 (8.7 percent) said there was a need for more emphasis upon evangelism and outreach programs; 149 (6.9 percent) advocated Bible study and educational programs; 134 (6.2 percent) of the pastors saw the need for more understanding and tolerance for young people's life-styles (openness and encouragement); but curiously, only seventy-nine (3.7 percent) of the clergy saw "relevant preaching" as the best way to attract young people, and community service programs received the least support, twenty (0.9 percent).

Table 37: Recruitment to the Ministry by
Local Church

Q. In the past five years, how many young people from
your church have decided to enter the ministry?

Number of Candidates	Frequency	Percent
None	989	46.0
One	373	17.3
Two	278	12.9
Three	198	9.2
Four	86	4.0
Five	67	3.1
Six	37	1.7
Seven	26	1.2
Eight	19	0.9
Nine or more	77	3.6

$N=2,150$

Finally, our survey asked the pastors, "In the past five years, how many young people from your church have decided to enter the ministry?" The rationale for asking this question was to obtain a benchmark for future studies on the recruitment of young people to the ministry. While the call by God to the ministry in the mainline black churches involved an intense personal experience and decision by the candidate, role models or influential persons were also important in the process. Choosing the ministry as a career and profession means that a young person has usually had very effective role model(s). As the results in table 37 indicate close to half of the churches in our sample, 989 (46 percent), had no candidates for the ministry in their church over the past five years. But slightly more than half of the churches, 1,161 (54 percent), had at least one candidate for the ministry during that period. Whether these percentages are average, below average, or above average is not known since this question of recruitment into the ministry has not been studied in black churches on a national scale before. About one-third of those with an affirmative answer, 373 (17.3 percent), sent one person to the ministry, and 278 (12.9 percent) had two candidates. A much smaller number,

seventy-seven (3.6 percent), of the churches were successful in having nine or more ministerial candidates. A very important finding
about recruiting candidates to the ministry is the fact that a few of
the churches were highly productive, while 46 percent did not produce one candidate. This finding points out the importance of keeping track of the more successful churches and pastors by theological
seminaries and divinity schools that are interested in recruiting
black candidates. Rather than approaching colleges and universities
as the recruiting ground, selected individual black churches and
pastors may be more fruitful. Usually the pastors of these churches
have been highly successful role models in inspiring young people to
enter the ministry. For example, Rev. John Bryant of the Bethel A.M.E.
Church in Baltimore has sent more than seventy-five candidates to
divinity schools in less than ten years, with about twenty-five of
them studying for the ministry at the Divinity School of Howard
University. Martin Luther King, Jr.'s life and ministry have similarly
inspired countless others to follow in this profession.

In our survey of programs held by black churches for young people,
most of the activities were traditional programs such as youth choirs,
youth groups, evangelistic programs, Bible study, recreational and
social events. None of the traditional church programs for black
children, teenagers, and young adults specifically addressed the major issues covered in the first half of this chapter: the ambivalence in
racial identity found to be widespread among many black children;
the high levels of unemployment among black teenagers; the large
numbers of young black men in prisons; and the high rates of teenage
pregnancy and female-headed households.

All of these crisis issues are both symptoms and consequences of a
continuing racial oppression in the United States. As Wilson has
pointed out, the social isolation experienced by the members of the
black underclass and their cultural traits and behavior are adjustments and adaptations made to the social structural constraints and
opportunities in the larger society.[76] In other words, there is a continuous dialectical interplay, an interaction, between the behavior of
black young people and their parents in the ghetto and the resistances and unequal opportunity they encounter in the institutions of
society. Neoconservative analysts have stressed the need to change
personal behavior and cultural characteristics that impede upward
mobility, and liberal reformers have advocated changes in the institutional sector.[77] As we have argued previously, it is obvious that both

aspects are needed, changes inside the black community to stimulate motivation and changes outside in the discriminatory way institutions operate in society, in order to achieve a transformation of the ghettos and the life chances of black youth. While the majority of black churches are not addressing these crisis issues through their traditional programs, it would be a mistake to imply that therefore nothing is being done by black churches. Some progressive pastors and churches have devised creative programs to begin dealing with these issues. We turn first to the critical issue of high rates of unemployment among black young people.

The Black Church and Young People:
The Self-Help Tradition and the Problem of Unemployment

In chapter 9 we presented a brief historical sketch of the development of the self-help (mutual aid) tradition in black churches and also gave an outline of how these churches helped to develop an ethos of mobility and achievement among their members. While much more historical work is needed to fill in the details of the role of black churches in the economic transformation of the black community, there has developed a corpus of studies on the role of American religion and mobility, beginning with Max Weber's *The Protestant Ethic and the Spirit of Capitalism*, to establish a similar plausible hypothesis in regard to black churches.[78] Black churches do have a role in the contemporary unemployment crisis among black teenagers and young adults by returning to an emphasis of its self-help tradition.

In the research project on *The Black Youth Employment Crisis*, sponsored by the National Bureau of Economic Research, Richard Freeman has examined the relationship of churchgoing to the socioeconomic performance of black male youths from inner-city tracts. In examining who escapes and who is left behind in the ghetto, Freeman has found that the background factors of inner-city youths like churchgoing behavior and the welfare status of their families are good predictors of success or failure. By focusing on the allocation of time in the daily activities of the youth in relationship to these background factors, Freeman concluded: "More specifically, the empirical analysis shows, first, that the principal variable on which the paper focuses, churchgoing, is associated with substantial differences in the behavior of youths, and thus in their chances to "escape" from inner-city poverty. Churchgoing affects allocation of time, school attendance, work activity, and the frequency of socially deviant activity."[79] Freeman cautions against making direct causal links regarding churchgoing behavior, since his study could not adequately differentiate whether churchgoing was merely an indication of "good kids" or whether it really changed their behavior. However, he does feel that his results suggest that some part of the churchgoing effect is "the result of an actual causal impact" because churchgoing black youths do not have "better market opportunities than others."[80] The influence of role models in the family, whether the parents work or are on welfare, was also a critical factor in who escapes and who stays among the youth.[81]

Although Freeman does not postulate it, one can extend his insights by arguing that black teenagers and young adults from the underclass who continue their churchgoing behavior probably have a better chance of escaping from the ghetto. The reason is that within black churches these young people will encounter both the self-help tradition, which is constantly reinforced by preaching from the pulpit, and role models of working adults. Although the adults may be from the working poor or marginally employed, they are still role models that can positively influence youth who may not experience people who work in their own families. It also takes a level of disciplined behavior and a rational allocation of time to attend church and participate in its activities. Furthermore, Wilson's concept of the social isolation of the underclass is important in this context. Part of the reason for the continued deprivation of the black underclass, according to Wilson, is the gradual withdrawal not only of employment opportunities in central cities but also the quiet disappearance of members of the black working and middle classes. This does not mean that all upwardly mobile blacks have moved to the suburbs as demographic studies on the high rates of residential segregation in the United States have shown.[82] But it does mean that the social contact between members of different economic groups that was once available in cohesive black communities has gradually disappeared with upward mobility and movement to the better parts of urban environments. What churchgoing behavior can do for black young people is to reduce the social isolation of their backgrounds and put them in contact with important role models. The successful internalization of the values of the black self-help tradition is depen-

dent upon a socializing environment that will continually reinforce
and reaffirm those values in a caring way. While there may be a few
alternative institutions that can perform some of these functions,
like a highly motivated, disciplined athletic team with an astute
coach or a black fraternity/sorority group, none of them have the
extensive network of black churches in thousands of large and small
black communities across the country.

Although there have been no longitudinal studies of black storefront churches and the mobility of their members, the Church of God
in Christ, the largest black Pentecostal denomination, serves as a
historical example of the possibility of economic transformation
inherent in a black religious tradition. Established as a Pentecostal
denomination in the early twentieth century by Bishop Charles H.
Mason, the vast majority of COGIC's members were illiterate, poor,
rural migrants in urban centers. Throughout the migration period
from the 1930s through the 1950s, they appeared in sociological
studies as the "sanctified people" in storefront churches whose ecstatic worship, speaking in tongues, and lower-class background were
either scorned or ridiculed.[83] In the mid-1950s with eight hundred
churches, Bishop Mason and COGIC applied for membership in the
National Council of Churches and they were immediately rejected
because they were regarded as a cult. Fifteen years later they returned
with 8,000 churches and the National Council was willing to accept
COGIC as a full-fledged black denomination.[84] As the fastest growing
black denomination, in 1979 COGIC listed 10,000 churches and
10,000 clergy in their first published *International Directory*.[85] Furthermore, its members have been gradually moving into middle-
income status as members of the black middle and working classes.
Although COGIC probably still has the larger sector of poor members
among the seven major black denominations, the numerous storefront churches which once characterized the extreme poverty of its
past are quickly disappearing.[86] Now COGIC members shout and
carry on their ecstatic traditions in more and more middle-class
church buildings. The Church of God in Christ, the largest black
Pentecostal body, is only one example among other black religious
groups that have undergone class changes in the past thirty years.[87]

While COGIC illustrates the power and potential of the black self-
help tradition in black churches, that tradition becomes less effective
in the face of the legal and structural constraints of a de jure segregated society. Only when those barriers were removed by the civil

rights movement through more than a decade of struggle, thousands of upwardly mobile black people, who had been prepared for years by their churches, were able to take advantage of these opportunities and begin their move out of poverty. In other words, significant economic transformation required both a widespread internalization of the self-help tradition and the removal of external barriers along with the provision of reasonably equal opportunities in employment. The high rates of unemployment among black teenagers and young adults will not be significantly reduced without a double-pronged strategy of change, working both inside the black community to affect the motivational values of black youth and outside to change the way institutions operate. Some black churches have begun to work on the unemployment problem by providing job training and education through the Opportunities Industrialization Centers that Leon Sullivan developed. However, as Wilson has argued, a comprehensive set of public policies and programs will be required for long-term change.[88] The self-help tradition and job training are futile without the creation of new and meaningful employment possibilities for black youth.

We have elaborated on the issue of the high rates of unemployment among black teenagers and young adults because it is the key issue that has ramifications for a whole range of cyclical social problems that affect poor black families, from inadequate housing and educational opportunities to female-headed households. Studies have shown that high rates of unemployment among black males, in particular, have affected the structure of many poor families. Unemployment is tied to other problems like crime, drugs, homicide, and prisons. We turn next to a brief overview of the programs that black churches have undertaken in order to address problems that affect poor black families.

The Black Church and Young People: Progressive Programs for Black Families

In the city of Detroit where some 10,000 abandoned houses are being used as crack houses by drug dealers, the 12th Street Missionary Baptist Church has launched a campaign to begin dealing with the problem. Through a church-sponsored community group called Reach, the pastor, Rev. Lee Earl, church members, and neighbors started efforts to buy these abandoned houses. After tracking the absentee landlords and negotiating with the city on delinquent taxes, the group began buying the houses for $8,000 each. Then they repaired the houses through the labor of church volunteers and hired unemployed persons and sold them to low-income residents in the neighborhood for $18,000 to cover the purchase and renovation. Most of these residents perform church work or work on the renovation in lieu of down payments; no closing or application fees are charged.[89] For example, Melanie Ruffin, a legal secretary, church member, and single parent of two sons, moved into one of the houses and is doing part-time typing for the church as her down payment. She did not fit the desired profile of banks and realtors for a home owner.[90] Although the program was initially started as a way of getting rid of drug dealers, it also began to meet the housing needs of low income neighbors. After renovating a dozen houses, Reach received a $150,000 grant from the city to rehabilitate twelve more. Their eventual goal is to stabilize two square miles of Detroit's West Side in their continuous battle with mobile drug dealers.

The example of the 12th Street Missionary Baptist Church is only one of the ways in which black communities are mobilizing to combat the drug problem. Other examples include the efforts of both orthodox Muslims and members of the Nation of Islam in providing community patrols in Brooklyn and in Washington, D.C., to prevent drug dealing.[91] The strong-arm tactics of the Muslims were matched by the Baptist antidrug crusader of Harlem, the late Rev. Obadiah T. Dempsey of Harlem, who gained notoriety as the "pistol packing preacher" because of the death threats he received in his antidrug efforts. Dempsey's colleague Rev. Wyatt T. Walker of the Canaan Baptist Church has developed a more sedate drug rehabilitation and counseling program in his Harlem church.[92]

Rev. Henry Gregory of the Shiloh Baptist Church in Washington, D.C., led his church to develop the Family Life Center, which has become the institutional vehicle for a variety of creative programs for black youth and families. With grants from the Ford and Meyers foundations, the Family Life Center is sponsoring the "Male Youth Enhancement Program." The major aim of the program is to help boys from the poverty-stricken Shaw neighborhood become adults without being entrapped by drugs, premature parenthood, and street gang activities. The goal of the program is centered on academic achievement, but sports are used as the "hook" to attract and keep the youngsters involved.[93] After the University of Maryland star basketball player Len Bias died of a drug overdose at a dorm party celebrating his being named as the Boston Celtics' first draft choice, Shiloh's Family Life Center also began sponsoring a series of ad hoc conferences on sports and drugs at local junior high schools in the District of Columbia. They recruited volunteer pro basketball players from the Washington Bullets to give talks at the programs. They found that sports was a good way to reach many young black males because it appeals to their macho self-image and still provides a constructive way of challenging their energy. However, they also found that sports programs achieve their maximum potential when they are tied to educational programs. Other black churches in our study also used sports and recreation as an incentive to attract male teenagers, like karate and boxing programs. The Abyssinian Baptist Church in Harlem sponsored and paid all costs for a fully outfitted football team.

The Family Life Center of the Shiloh Baptist Church also sponsors a math and science tutorial program, which is family-oriented. This tutorial program, funded by a grant from the Carnegie Foundation, differs from others in that the instructor tutors not only the child but also the parent(s). The whole family is involved in the tutorial process and reinforcement of the lessons occurs all around; the parent reinforces the child and vice versa. Besides developing skills in math and science, a long-term goal is to encourage black students to consider careers in these areas where black representation has been historically low. After their first year the results show that the children in the program have done very well in school. The National Urban Coalition is interested in using this math and science tutorial program as a pilot project that can be replicated in other localities.[94]

The Shiloh Baptist Church was also one of the few black churches that has taken the prison problem seriously—the incarceration of large numbers of teenage and young adult black males and some females. In our field survey of black church programs in the community, the vast majority of churches (99 percent) did not mention involvement in this issue at all. While there were some black clergy who served as prison chaplains, very few black congregations and church members have become involved in prison ministries. Yet, more than half of the inmates in many prisons do not receive any visits from family or friends. Muslim groups have been more active and seemingly more effective in carrying out a ministry to incarcerated men and women than most black Christians.[95] According to Gregory, Shiloh's prison program had three parts: first, they attempted to recruit church members and others to tutor reading in the prison's literacy program; second, some church members and the pastor became religiously involved by holding occasional worship services, leading Bible study groups, and by providing counsel and advice; third, an ex-offender group, which was organized by the ex-offenders themselves, was allowed to meet weekly in the church building. Gregory pointed out that Shiloh was able to develop a lot of creative programs because they allow small groups to form and pursue a particular interest; the church has about ninety of these organizations.[96] The Bethel A.M.E. Church in Baltimore has also developed a prison ministry program that not only involves church members visiting inmates but also helping their families; former inmates are encouraged to join the church.

A consortium of ten churches in Chicago has developed a comprehensive, ecumenical program, Project IMAGE, to strengthen the image, role, and presence of black males in families, churches, schools and communities. A similar program called Black Manhood Training: Body, Mind, and Soul was developed by Courtland Lee of the University of Virginia and it is being used in several southern black churches to train deacons in youth counseling.[97] The Concord Baptist Church of Brooklyn has raised a $1 million Christfund to help finance activities for black youth and children. Christfund has supported the Billie Holiday Theater for young performing artists and sent a choir on a singing tour of Rome.[98]

With grants from the Ford and Lilly Endowment foundations, the Congress of National Black Churches has developed an ambitious program called Project Spirit, which is designed to meet the needs of black youth and families in poverty. Operating in fifteen inner-city churches in Oakland, California, Atlanta, and Indianapolis, each program has three major objectives: after-school tutorials and counseling for children in elementary grades; an education program for the parents so that they can be better advocates for their children; and a pastoral counseling program to make the clergy of inner-city churches more effective in dealing with problems like parent-child communication, sexuality, and pregnancy.[99] A comprehensive program of education like Project Spirit also has the possibility of developing the kinds of support and affirmation needed to combat the problem of ambivalence in racial identity found among so many black children.

In Durham, North Carolina, the Church Connection Project involves six churches in health care, including birth control for teen-age women. The churches cooperate with the Lincoln Community Health Center.[100] Conceived by a laywoman, Michele Bowen-Spencer, the Church Connection Project trains volunteer church members to work with the youth of their church. Seminars on con-troversial topics like the AIDS crisis or sexually transmitted diseases are held.[101] The Bethel A.M.E. Church in Baltimore has also devised Teen PEP (Pregnancy Education Program), which not only attempts to help teenage mothers, but also attempts to involve and educate the young fathers about their responsibilities.[102]

Although all of the projects covered above are sponsored by black churches within the seven historic black denominations, there were also creative projects for families and youth in some predominantly black churches in major white denominations. For example, the Lincoln Congregational Temple of the United Church of Christ in Washington, D.C., has developed the Adopt-A-Family program. Fam-ilies in distress are matched with others who agree to provide any kind of support except financial. The relationship is solemnized in a church service. For example, a women's social club adopted an un-employed, single mother of two and trained her to be a receptionist; she now has a full-time job.[103] An interdenominational coalition of black churches and pastors in Illinois encourages adoption by black families in the One Church, One Child program, co-sponsored with the Illinois Department of Social Services. Each pastor encourages the families in his congregation to adopt at least one child. The number of black children awaiting adoption has been cut from seven hundred to about sixty, even though many of the children are older and thus are considered difficult to adopt. The inspiration for this project was provided by a black Catholic priest, Father George Clem-ents of the Holy Angels Church in Chicago, who adopted two teenage boys himself.[104]

The Memorial A.M.E. Zion Church of Rochester, New York, has sponsored a Summer Fun Project since 1985. It is a program which combines educational, recreational, spiritual, and creative activities in a unique way for youth between ages five to twelve years. Besides the usual summer fun activities like arts and crafts, nature hikes, swimming and camping, the uniqueness of its program lies in its reinforcement of Afro-American culture. The program is supported completely by the church and the parents of the youth. Rev. William Gipson, the assistant minister, said: "We play games to develop verbal skills and to build social skills. We spend a lot of time talking about self and what it means to be an African American. The concept of "self"—who we are—is interwoven into all of our activities. It is very important for us as a summer camp in an African American church to do something in the way of affirming who these young people are."[105] Programs like Memorial A.M.E. Zion Church's Summer Fun Project appear to be one way for black churches to begin dealing with the problem of racial ambivalence among young black children described earlier. The psychological studies, however, indicate that such efforts of reinforcing positive racial identity need to come earlier, before the age of five.

These programs for black families and youth represented some of the more creative and progressive programs that black churches have undertaken in the decade of the 1980s. Although these programs were initiated by the more enlightened pastors and congregations, supported by foundation and government grants, they illustrate the potential role in social change that black churches can play in their communities. However, most of these churches by themselves lack the adequate financial resources and staff to attack the enormous cyclical problems of poverty and powerlessness that confront many black families and youth. Foundation personnel, social workers, staff members of government agencies, and other professionals have only recently begun to rediscover what civil rights workers in the South during the 1960s learned, that is that black churches are natural grass roots community organizations which can be mobilized for change. The mounting problems of poor black families and youth have reached such a crisis level in black communities that a partnership between black churches and the agencies concerned about these social problems is urgently indicated in the attempts to resolve them.

The coming decade of the 1990s will probably see more and greater efforts in community organizing among the poor by black clergy and churches. The strategies for dealing with black children, teenagers, and young adults and their families will include a mix of traditional programs like youth choirs, evangelism, and revivals with progressive programs like the Family Life Center and others mentioned above. A pluralistic approach is needed to reach black young people with diverse interests. Historically, among black churches there has seldom been a discrete bifurcation of the social and religious dimensions of life, to the end that black churches have usually been more willing to participate in a greater range of social, political, and economic projects than their white counterparts. The participation of some black churches in progressive programs to ameliorate the problems of black youth and families is a continuation of this long tradition.

Before we conclude this chapter, we turn briefly to the topic we began with, Lorraine Hansberry's inquisitive, iconoclastic, yet searching character of Beneatha, the college student who wants to become a doctor. Daughter Beneatha symbolically represents not only the black intellectual class but also the growing numbers of college educated young adults who have professional aspirations. What is the relationship of the Black Church to young people of the black middle class?

In My Mother's House: The Black Church and Young People of the Black Middle Class

We have focused much of our attention on the relationship between black churches and black youth in poverty because it is with that segment of the black population that most of the problems have reached crisis levels. There is also some evidence that a large and growing sector of underclass black youth, males in particular, are also unchurched or have minimal contact with black churches and clergy.[106] But what about the youth of the black middle class or those upwardly mobile young people who have made it to college in spite of their background in poverty? How do black churches relate to their concerns and problems?

At the present time there is no evidence of a large-scale abandonment of black churches by the black middle class. The practice, too, of upwardly mobile black people joining white churches or denominations, which Frazier once saw as their assimilative destiny, has been stemmed by the resurgence of black consciousness and an affirmation of black institutions.[107] If members of the black middle class join churches, they tend to join the elite black churches. Only the Roman Catholic Church has experienced a rise in black membership among the major white denominations; much of this is due to a surge in West Indian immigrants, especially Haitians, and to the preference of some black parents for the discipline provided by urban parochial schools. There is evidence that most of the black middle-class members and pastors of elite black churches in urban and rural areas have used their churches as institutional bases for innovative programs in their communities. We have provided examples of these programs and activities in this chapter and in chapters 8 and 9. But what about their children, especially college educated young adults? There is no evidence that large numbers of middle-class, black young adults have left their churches. But the possibility is there since higher education, especially the scientific and liberal arts education of most American colleges, tends to encourage skepticism and doubt particularly where religion is concerned. As James Hunter pointed out in his study of the future leaders of evangelicalism in the United States, even the higher education at strict evangelical colleges tends to have a secularizing effect.[108]

Besides the secularizing impact in the future of growing numbers of college educated black young people, what kinds of challenges do they present to black churches and clergy? The first and most obvious concern is that the educational levels of many of these professionally educated young adults have already surpassed that of the majority of black clergy in the United States. In our study about 39 percent of the clergy said that they had received one or more years of graduate education beyond four years of college. Although we did not ask about their completion of graduate seminary education, Dr. James Costen, president of the Interdenominational Theological Center in Atlanta, a consortium of six black seminaries, has estimated that only about 10 to 20 percent of the black clergy nationwide had completed their professional education (Master of Divinity level).[109]

A related concern is that this growing educational gap between the clergy and educated black young adults may lead to a situation of alienation from black churches. Some of the traditional black preaching styles and the traditional formulas designed to elicit an emotional response from the audience may no longer have an impact upon these young adults. They expect more probing sermons and intellectual challenge, as well as spiritual nurture. Like Beneatha they also expect intelligent answers to their questions rather than a slap on the face or a reassertion of traditional authority. If these young adults remain members of black churches, they will probably place greater demands upon the clergy for pastoral counseling. There is already some evidence that pastoral counseling is a growing need within the Black Church.[110] According to the results of our study, since women clergy are perceived as better and more skillful counselors because they tend to be better listeners, this demand for more pastoral counseling could lead to more opportunities for women pastors. Family issues will also take a prominent place on the agenda of these churches. Finally, some of these college-educated young adults will also demand that their church and pastor be more relevant to the political and social issues in the larger community.

In the future as more and more young black professionals become part of the American mainstream and work for predominantly white corporations and institutions, black churches may be recognized as the premier carriers and preservers of the black ethnic heritage. Whether these young professionals will join and support the historic black churches, as their parents did, may depend upon how the clergy and the churches respond to their challenges. It will also depend upon whether the clergy can accommodate and find use for their professional skills in the ministry of the church without feeling threatened by them. If creative responses are lacking and these young adults continue to feel alienated then they will leave their mother's houses and black churches behind.

Summary and Conclusion

In this chapter, we pointed to the important roles that black churches and families, the enduring institutions, have had in providing the major socialization for many black young people, children, teenagers, and young adults in the past. Black pastors, Sunday school teachers and other lay members were significant role models for the young. We also summarized some of the research and literature on two major issues of black youth which should be of concern to leaders, pastors, and members of the Black Church. First, the problem of the ambivalence of racial identity, as expressed in the doll-choice tests, is found to be widespread among many black children, regardless of class. The gains in racial pride and identity in the children's test scores that were made in the 1960s have reverted to the pre-civil rights levels. But more important than test scores were the continued verbal interpretations of both black and white children in the 1980s that the color black was "dirty." This research is important to black churches because it suggests the need to review their use of Sunday school literature and Bible lessons. The ambivalence of racial identity among many black children also challenges one of the central tenets of the Christian tradition of the wholeness of human personality and self-acceptance, to "love thy neighbor as thyself."

The second set of challenges concerns the crisis conditions found among the majority of poor black youth and their families. Since the 1960s almost all of the problems of the black underclass have worsened, from high rates of unemployment—especially among teenagers and young adults—to high levels of incarceration in prisons, teen pregnancy, and female-headed households. About half of all black children are presently growing up in female-headed households, and the majority of these in conditions of extreme poverty. Increasingly, recent studies have been showing the growth of an unchurched segment of underclass black teenagers and young adults, which is a new phenomenon with implications for black churches in the future. One can no longer assume that the black poor in the future will always be the loyal churchgoers they have been in the past. However, the self-help tradition of black churches can be an important aid in attempts to resolve these problems. Churchgoing behavior was found to be an important background factor among black youth who escaped from the ghetto. Some enlightened black clergy and churches have begun to undertake programs to attack the problems of underclass youth and their families. The needs and interests of young people from the black middle class will also demand attention from black churches and clergy.

In our research of the programs and techniques that pastors have found successful in reaching young people, the highest rated answer was music, from youth choirs and concert events to the training of young people in vocal and instrumental forms. The musical heritage of the Black Church has been one of the enduring gems of black culture that has enriched the cultures of the world. We turn next to a historical overview of this important form of ministry provided by the Black Church.

12 The Performed Word: Music and the Black Church

Make a joyful noise unto the Lord, all ye lands
Come before his presence with singing
—Psalm 100

I got a song, you got a song
All God's children got a song
When I get to heaven gwine to sing-a-my song
I'm gwine to sing all over God's heaven!
—Traditional African American Spiritual

The sermon, or more accurately, the *preaching* is the focal point of worship in the Black Church, and all other activities find their place in some subsidiary relationship. In most black churches music, or more precisely, *singing* is second only to preaching as the magnet of attraction and the primary vehicle of spiritual transport for the worshiping congregation. In some of the more traditional churches even the sermon (and often the prayers of the ministers or deacons) are still "sung" in a kind of ritualistic cadence peculiar to the Black Church.[1] The preacher who is particularly skilled at this kind of musical eloquence is usually highly regarded as adept in his profession, and his church is almost certain to be blessed with a large and faithful membership.

In the Black Church good preaching and good singing are almost invariably the minimum conditions of a successful ministry. Both activities trace their roots back to Africa where music and religion and life itself were all one holistic enterprise. There was no disjunction between the sacred and the secular, and music, whether vocal or instrumental, was an integral aspect of the celebration of life, as indeed was the dance which the music inspired in consequence of its evocation of the human spirit. So it was that music initially assumed a major role in the black experience in religion as the West African

346

diaspora sought to adapt to the new forms of spiritual intercourse to which they were eventually introduced in the United States. First of all, music served the important function of convoking the cultus, that is, assembling the faithful to a common place and a common experience of worship. Once this was accomplished it functioned to transcend or to reduce to insignificance those social, cultural, or economic barriers which separate individuals in their secular interests in order that genuine corporate worship might take place.

Congregational singing is a well-known device for the temporary reduction of social alienation and for the accomplishment of an ad interim sense of community. In the Black Church singing together is not so much an effort to find, or to establish, a transitory community as it is the reaffirmation of a common bond that, while inviolate, has suffered the pain of separation since the last occasion of physical togetherness. In the words of James Cone: "Black music is unity music. It unites the joy and the sorrow, the love and the hate, the hope and the despair of black people; . . . It shapes and defines black being and creates cultural structures for black expression. Black music is unifying because it . . . affirms that black being is possible only in a communal context."[2] Undoubtedly this was a significant factor in the failure of blacks to find meaningful participation in the white churches of the slave era where they could not express themselves or celebrate their sense of community through the communal songs born of a common experience.

Since there was no substantial involvement of the transplanted Africans in American Christianity until the early eighteenth century, there was an interspace of almost one hundred years during which there was no significant, identifiable cult of African spirituality capable of sustaining the body of religious traditions they are presumed to have brought with them. This problem was exacerbated by the deliberate dispersion of Africans speaking the same language and sharing common tribal affiliations as a hedge against conspiracy or insurrection. For the same reasons, the practice of heathen rites, that is, African religion, was generally forbidden in any case, as was the use or possession of the drums upon which the celebration of traditional African rituals depended. In spite of such obvious obstacles to the retention and the transmission of the African's cultural heritage in the new context of the American experience, the evidence that critical elements of that heritage managed to survive and their adaptation in the New World is substantial, especially in religion.[3]

Black singing and the performance practices associated with it is perhaps the most characteristic logo of the African heritage retentive in the Black Church, whether it is the singing of songs or the "singing" of sermons and prayers. A study of black singing, then, is in essence a study of how black people "Africanized" Christianity in America as they sought to find meaning in the turn of events that made them involuntary residents in a strange and hostile land.

The first black church of record was established at Silver Bluff, South Carolina, sometime between 1750 and 1777. However, because of the universal proscription against black churches and the inconvenience associated with permitting African Americans to attend white churches, the Christian experience was hardly available to black interest before the revival movement known as the Second Great Awakening, which swept the American frontier between 1780 and 1830. While African Americans gained some introduction to Christian life through the efforts of the Anglican sponsored Society for the Propagation in Foreign Parts after 1701, the plantation based services of the s.p.g. missionaries and their successors made only a modest impact upon the captive slave population, which if it heard them at all, heard them without zeal. But it was the spiritual romance of the camp meetings of the Awakening that first stirred the religious imagination of the black diaspora, and brought thousands of displaced African Americans and their descendants into meaningful Christian communion for the first time.

The Black Spirituals: Spontaneous Creation in Preaching and Prayer

In the early days of the Black Church the spontaneous creation of spirituals during the preaching event was a common feature of black worship. These spirituals undoubtedly grew out of the preacher's chanted declamation and the intervening congregational responses. Little by little this musical call and response became a song. Having witnessed such an event at a religious meeting of slaves on a Georgia plantation, Ella Clark shared this reminiscence:

> So many wonder about the origin of spirituals. . . . A large number had their origin in the camp meetings and other religious services where emotions were stirred and excitement was at a high pitch. The words and music were spontaneous and extemporaneous, and were in a large measure their own, suggested by

some strong sentences in the sermon, or some scripture emphasized and repeated. More often than not the preacher was interrupted in his sermon by a song leader who was moved to answer
him in song.[4]

Some spirituals generated from the extemporaneous preaching
event may have lasted only for the heightened moment, while others were perpetuated through the oral tradition. Oral transmission
meant that spirituals were constantly recomposed and rearranged, so
that a single spiritual might eventually have numerous musical and
textual variations. This process was complicated by the fact that true
to their African counterparts the spirituals were a principal means of
transmission of oral history. Hence, they were subject to constant
embellishment as the black experience unfolded against a backdrop
of divine succor and leadership.

Like the sermon, prayer was also delivered in a kind of sing-song
declamation which evoked musical response from the worshipers.
Natalie Curtis Burlin describes in detail a spiritual emanating from
an extemporaneous prayer event:

> Minutes passed, long minutes of strange intensity. The mut-
> terings, the ejaculations, grew louder, more dramatic, till sud-
> denly I felt the creative thrill dart through the people like an
> electric vibration, that same half-audible hum arose,—emotion
> was gathering . . . then, up from the depths of some "sinner's"
> remorse and imploring came a pitiful plea . . . sobbed in musical
> cadence. From somewhere in the bowed gathering another voice
> improvised a response . . . then other voices joined the answer,
> shaping it into a musical phrase; and so, before our ears, as one
> might say, from this molten metal of music a new song was
> smithed out, composed then and there by no one in particular
> and by everyone in general.[5]

Calculated Composition

There is little documentation regarding the notion that spirituals
were the formal compositions of individuals, but the most likely candidate for this recognition is once again the creative black preacher.
Scarcely literate, he did not notate his compositions of course, but
probably kept tempering a catchy tune and text until a spiritual song
was fashioned. Many ex-slaves confirmed this procedure when re-
calling that the songs they sang during slavery were taught to them

by their preachers. Such evidence has led contemporary researchers to conclude that a substantial number of spirituals were composed by black preachers specifically for liturgical use.

Eileen Southern locates the first general recognition of the spiritual as a distinctive form of black worship in the camp meetings of the revival movement called the Second Awakening:

> They were singing songs of their own composing, which was even worse in the eyes of the officials. The texts of the composed songs were not lyric poems in the hallowed tradition of Watts, but a stringing together of isolated lines from prayers, the Scriptures, and orthodox hymns [with] the addition of choruses and . . . refrains between verses. . . . Nevertheless from such practices emerged a new kind of religious song that became the distinctive badge of the camp meeting movement. . . .
> Song leaders added choruses and refrains to the official hymns. . . . They introduced new songs with repetitive and catchy tunes. Spontaneous songs were composed on the spot. . . . The new songs were called "spiritual songs" as distinguished from the hymns and psalms.[6]

Whatever its origin, it seems clear that it was the "Negro Spiritual" which first developed as the signature of serious black involvement in American Christianity. William B. McClain describes the spirituals as "songs which speak of life and death, suffering and sorrow, love and judgment, grace and love, justice and mercy, redemption and conciliation."[7] The spiritual was the expression of the full range of life experiences garnered by the slave. At Fisk University where the Negro spiritual first gained international acclaim through the performances of the famous Fisk Jubilee Singers in the late nineteenth century, they were described by Professor John Wesley Work as the slave's "sweet consolation and his messages to Heaven, bearing sorrow, pain, joy, prayer and adoration." Comments Work, "The man though a slave, produced the song, and the song in turn produced a better man. . . . How could a man be base who looked ever to the hills? . . . The creator of those songs had now become his own creation."[8]

Textual Sources of the Spiritual

Howard Thurman explains that "It was dangerous to let the slave understand that the life and teachings of Jesus meant freedom for the captive and release for those held in economic, social, and political bondage."[9] In consequence the slaves fashioned most of their spirituals from the Old Testament narratives, which were appealing because of their simplicity, and because of God's direct intervention in human affairs in the interest of the oppressed. But in spite of the strongest restrictions against black literacy, some slave preachers learned to read and introduced themselves and their congregations to the New Testament. A spiritual recorded at a mid-nineteenth-century North Carolina revival is evidence:

> A local preacher among them started some well known hymn of which they would sing a line, and then Joe [the preacher] would improvise a chorus to which they all kept admirable tune and time. A favorite chorus was
>
> > I want to die in the field of battle
> > Good Lord when I die;
> > I want to die in the field of de battle
> > Fighting for the Lord.
>
> This would [be followed by] a line of "I want to die like Moses died," and [then] with Elijah, Daniel, David, and all the Old Testament saints, and then Peter and John, Martha and Mary would be taken [up], until they were exhausted.[10]

Among the few spirituals which mention Jesus specifically are "Ride on King Jesus," "A Little Talk with Jesus Makes it Right," and "Steal Away to Jesus." These depict Jesus as protector, comforter, friend, redeemer, and refuge, rather than as liberator.

Not all spirituals were biblically derived. Several evolved from private moments of "instant religion." This is particularly evident in the sorrow songs, such as "I've Been 'Buked and I've Been Scorned," "Sometimes I Feel like a Motherless Child," and "Nobody Knows the Trouble I've Seen."

Eschatology in the Spiritual

It is understandable that spirituals were typically other-worldly in theology, for there was nothing in the present world which offered much consolation to the slaves. "When all hope for release in this world seems unrealistic and groundless," explains Howard Thurman, "the heart turns to a way of escape beyond the present order."[11] Paradoxically, though many of the spirituals spoke of "heaven," this eschatological realm was actually anchored firmly in this world, first in their coded meaning, and second in their therapeutic value as survival tools. Regarding the former, James Cone offers this insight:

> Although the black spirituals had been interpreted as being exclusively otherworldly and compensatory, our research into the testimonies of black slave narratives and other black sayings revealed that the theme of heaven in the spirituals and in black religion generally contained double meanings. "Steal away" referred not only to an eschatological realm, but it was also used by Harriet Tubman as a signal of freedom for slaves who intended to run away with her to the north, or to Canada.[12]

It is likely, then, that to the slave heaven meant both that eschatological realm, *and the North*—whichever happened to have come first; or the latter first and the former later.

On the other hand, through the singing of spirituals the enslaved were able to release their repressed emotions and anxieties and simultaneously experience the exhilaration of being creative under circumstances of unbelievable stress. They sang, hummed, clapped, moaned, stomped, and swayed themselves into a remarkable transcendence over their oppressive condition, and so dredged up the spiritual inspiration needed to endure until God would move to change their circumstances for the better.

The Shout

A stubborn retention of African religious ritual firmly fixed in the transition to Christian forms in America is the "ring shout" or simply "shout." After the regular religious services were over, or on special "praise nights," the benches in the early black churches or "praise houses" would be pushed back against the wall so that the dancing could begin. The dancers or "shouters," as they were called, would form a circle, and to the cadence of a favorite shout song or "running spiritual" would begin a slow, syncopated shuffling, jerking movement "bumped" by the handclapping or body slapping of those waiting on the sidelines. The tempo gradually quickened, and during the course of the dance (which might last for seven or eight hours), shouters who became possessed, or who dropped from sheer exhaustion, were immediately replaced by others waiting to take their places. An 1862 account of a shout observed on St. Helena Island, South Carolina, gives a detailed description of this very popular ritual:

> [W]e went to the "shout," a savage, heathenish dance out in Rina's house. Three men stood and sang, clapping and gesticulating. The others shuffled along on their heels following one another in a circle and occasionally bending the knees in a kind of curtsey. They began slowly, a few going around a[nd] more gradually joining in, the song getting faster and faster til at last only the most marked part of the refrain is sung and the shuffling, stamping, and clapping gets furious.[13]

While some first-hand observers went so far as to describe the shouters as "getting the power," or being "filled with the Spirit," others considered the shout to be a remnant of savage idol worship or to be mere "frolic."

Eileen Southern writes with insight about the true meaning of the shout and about the cultural perspectives that obscure its significance:

> While white observers admitted the strange attraction of the shout, they generally disapproved of it, regarding the holy dance as barbaric and even lascivious. Knowing nothing of African traditions, the observers failed to appreciate the two most important elements of the shout:
> (1) Shouters used dance as a means of communication with God in the same way that song and prayer are used, and (2) Shouters reached the highest level of worship when the Holy Spirit entered their bodies and took possession of their souls. *Nowhere in the history of the black experience in the United States was the clash of cultures—the African versus the European more obvious than in the differing attitudes taken towards ritual dancing and spirit possession.* [Italics supplied.][14]

In traditional African religions, music included dancing; no distinction is made. All forms of music involved bodily movement. For the Africans who converted to evangelical Christianity, the prohibition against dancing had to be respected. Black Christians justified their ring shout by saying that dancing involved crossing one's feet; in shouting the feet did not cross but it involved a slow shuffle step and a swaying bodily movement.[15]

Such cultural differences die hard and they transcend racial boundaries. In the early days of the developing Black Church, A.M.E. Bishop Daniel Alexander Payne, founder of Wilberforce University, was unrelenting in his denunciation of spirituals, which he called "cornfield ditties," and the ring dance, which he described as "ridiculous and heathenish." Even James Weldon Johnson concluded that shouts were "neither true spirituals nor truly religious." Instead, he considered them "semi-barbaric remnants of primitive African dances" which were at best "quasi-religious."[16] But if these black critics seemed overly sensitive in their denunciations, perhaps John Work's review of the reasons will be helpful in at least giving perspective to their annoyance. Professor Work writes (whose life's work with the Fisk Jubilee Singers was devoted to the performance of the spirituals): "Naturally enough when the Negro found himself free, he literally put his past behind him. It was his determination that as far as within him lay, not one single reminder of that black past should mar his future. So away went all those reminders into the abyss of oblivion."[17] Consigned to the "abyss" with the spiritual, the ring dance or the shout has been largely abandoned, except in black Holiness and Pentecostal sects where forms of the "holy dance" are still continued.[18] The spirituals live on in other forms.

Hymn-Lining Tradition

The tradition of lined hymn singing in the Black Church commenced in the early nineteenth century. Its precursor was the psalm-lining of the Calvinists, which was perpetuated in the American colonies by the Puritans. *The Bay Psalm Book* (1640), the first church music published in America, was their source of texts. In the singing of the psalms, a deacon or preacher intoned a line or couplet which was then sung by the congregation. This responsorial delivery was the answer to the dilemma of pervasive illiteracy among the Puritans, no less than to the lack of hymn books.

The publication of Dr. Isaac Watts's *Hymns and Spiritual Songs*, in 1707, initiated the interest in hymnody. Watts's hymns, with their vivid imagery, gradually displaced the pallid, metricized psalmody. Eventually, those slaves permitted to attend church with their masters would acquire the lining technique and that style of singing gradually became commonplace in their own Baptist and Methodist churches. But as the late Wendell Whalum observed, "The Black

Methodists and Baptists endorsed Watts's hymns, but the Baptists 'blackened' them."[19] What Whalum meant was that since Watts's hymns were texts only, the borrowed tunes from Euro-American hymns and folk songs were Africanized by the distinctive mode of black singing. Some of the tunes may also have been of African origin; or, like some spirituals, may have been spontaneous creations of an individual or a congregation of black worshipers. But regardless of origin, because of the tradition of improvisation during performance, every melody executed in the black idiom was a new creation each time it was sung.

Although it was most frequently Watts's hymns which were sung in the lined style, an 1862 account of a religious meeting of slaves proves that some original textual creations did evolve extemporaneously: "The prayer over, they all rise and sing, the leader 'deacon' [gives] out one line at a time in his sing-song and at the top of his voice, and the whole congregation sings in the most intensified hardshell twang they can possibly attain. Frequently the leader makes up his hymn as he goes along."[20] Since the hymn-liner composed as he proceeded, the lined style was probably responsible for the creation of certain of the hymns we now identify as spirituals.

Meter Music

The lined style of unaccompanied singing is called "meter music" because the hymn texts are constructed in poetic meter. The most frequently used meters in hymnody are *short, common,* and *long.* In the Watts style of singing the particular meter determines how a hymn is to be lined, and what tunes can be used.

Short meter (SM) is a four-line stanza with six syllables in lines one, two, and four, and eight syllables in line three (6.6.8.6.). The deacon or preacher, in this instance, intones a couplet which the congregation echoes in a slow, drawn-out intonation (for example, "Come, Ye That Love the Lord").

Common meter (CM) is literally the most common. It is a four-line stanza with eight syllables in lines one and three, and six syllables in lines two and four (8.6.8.6.). Here, also, the leader intones couplets (for example, "Amazing Grace, How Sweet the Sound").

Long meter (LM) should not be confused with the term "long-metered singing," which blacks use to describe the elongated lined singing style. Long meter is a four-line stanza with eight syllables per line (8.8.8.8.). Here, the leader intones only one line before the congregation takes it up (for example, "Go Preach My Gospel, Saith the Lord").

Post-Bellum Period to the Present

In the post-Emancipation era the lined singing style of Dr. Watts's hymns became even more prominent in the Black Church. First of all, the educated or progressive class of blacks disdained the spirituals because they were reminiscent of slavery. And secondly, the spirituals of the "invisible" slave church were antistructural, while worship in the institutional church was very structured. Wyatt T. Walker provides further explanation regarding the appeal of Watts's hymnody:

> Since the lyrics were from the dominant white culture and slaves were now free, the impulse for imitation was natural and understandable, religiously and otherwise. Given the association that the spirituals had with the slave experience and the quest for expanding the Black people's religious life and expression, the meter music found fertile ground for development and use immediately following the freeing of the slaves.[21]

But this style was also appealing because the metrical quatrains with rhymed line endings made the texts lyrical and easy to remember. And of course, the responsorial pattern of singing was traditional.

Hymn-lining, long discontinued in the white church and in most black churches as well, is still to be found occasionally in a few black congregations in the South, particularly in rural areas, and sometimes in storefronts of the lower economic strata in the cities of the North. In some churches of predominately middle-income Baptists, it is practiced in prayer meetings and informal devotional services carried on by the senior adults. In Baptist churches with a preponderance of lower income members, it is even more prominent, and may be the principal mode of congregational singing.

Social Salvation Hymns in the Black Church

Social gospel hymnody reflects the emphasis on the social concerns of the church which evolved during the historic "social gospel movement" which challenged American Christianity from about 1880 to 1930. In contrast to evangelical hymnody, which addresses the redemption and salvation of the individual, this social hymnody stressed the collective life, rebuked the sins of society, and predicated the establishment of the kingdom of God on earth as the fulfillment of God's plan for perfect brotherhood: "The new hymns have been increasingly songs of human brotherhood; of the redemptive social order rather than the salvation of the individual soul; and of the higher patriotism which looks beyond the nation to mankind."[22] These hymns, therefore, were particularly important to black Christians who were the principal victims of adverse social conditions.

Much of this hymnody, first published in journals of social science, was eventually compiled in special editions. Among them were Mabel Mussey's *Social Hymns of Brotherhood and Aspiration* (1914), and Henry Sloane Coffin and Ambrose W. Vernon's *Hymns of the Kingdom of God* (1926). The poems in these and similar collections gradually penetrated the hymnals of virtually every Protestant denomination, including the mainline black denominations. The four most recent A.M.E. Church hymnals (1892, 1941, 1954, 1984), for example, symbolize its acceptance in the Black Church in that they show increased emphasis on social themes from one edition to the next. The 1892 volume, *The African Methodist Episcopal Church Hymn and Tune Book* contains (out of 760 pieces) seven social gospel hymns.

The 1941 *A.M.E. Hymnal*, also known as the *Richard Allen A.M.E. Hymnal*, contains (out of 461 pieces) eighteen social gospel hymns. The 1954 *A.M.E.C. Hymnal* contains (out of 673 pieces) twenty-six social gospel hymns. And the 1984 *A.M.E.C. Bicentennial Hymnal* contains (out of 670 pieces) twenty-five social gospel hymns.[23] While these figures represent only one of the major black churches, (and one which from its inception has held a strong emphasis on social issues), other black churches have similar histories of social gospel involvement. The choice of such hymns for congregational singing was vocal and spiritual affirmation of the nascent social theology struggling for expression in the Black Church.

Because there was no social gospel hymnody written by blacks to accost their specific social circumstances (and there would not be any until the civil rights movement), the social hymns of white writers had to suffice. But only some of their hymns were directly relevant to African American social concerns, while most were not.

One social gospel hymn by John Oxenham that became popular

among black Christians was "In Christ There Is No East or West." Set
to the melody of a black spiritual, this hymn opens with a celebration
of human fraternity:

> In Christ there is no east or west
>> In Him no south or north,
> But one great fellowship of love
>> Throughout the whole wide earth.
>
> In Him shall true hearts everywhere
>> Their high communion find;
> His service is the golden cord
>> Close binding all mankind.

These two stanzas anticipate the third which offers a dictum the
oppressed needs to have reaffirmed as often as possible: There is not
only no east or west and no south or north, but of critical importance,
there is also no black or white in the family of God:

> Join hands, then, brothers of the faith,
>> Whate'er your race may be;
> Who serves my Father as a son
>> Is surely kin to me.

In addressing the idea of human oneness in the body of Christ, the
hymnist also suggests that there is an equality in Him which ignores
the accidents of race:

> In Christ now meet both east and west,
>> In Him meet south and north:
> All Christly souls are on in Him
>> Throughout the whole wide earth.

"America the Beautiful," "My Country 'Tis of Thee," and "The
Star Spangled Banner" are nationalistic social gospel hymns frequently sung in black churches on ceremonial occasions. Heard less
often is "God Save America," by William G. Ballantine, even though
it speaks of "higher patriotism" which transcends national affinity in
a more universal interest.[24]

> God save America! Here may all races
>> Mingle together as children of God,
> Founding an empire on brotherly kindness,
>> Equality in liberty, made of one blood!

This hymnody looks beyond denominationalism to ecumenism,
beyond nationalism to universality, and focuses the attention of the

worshipers, not only on the salvation of their individual souls, but also on the salvation of their larger collectivity beyond the bounds of race. Hence, it is a development of significance often overlooked in the assessment of the moral maturity of the Black Church.

Gospel Music

According to Eileen Southern, just as the spiritual was a development of the camp meeting phenomenon of the Second Awakening, so did the Protestant City Revival Movement create gospel hymnody, a new song genre "more relevant to the needs of the common people in the rapidly growing cities. . . . The gospel song evolved in urban settings, in huge temporary tents erected for revival meetings by touring evangelists in football stadiums and mammoth tabernacles."[25] Black gospel quickly distinguished itself from its white counterpart by the body rhythms, the call and response patterns and the improvisations characteristic of African music. Perhaps for these same reasons, gospel music became anathema for more traditionally oriented churches and their leaders and spokesmen. Sociologist Joseph R. Washington, whose strong misgivings about black folk religion in general were voiced in his well-known book, *Black Religion*, is caustic in his assessment of black gospel:

> The joy expressed in meetings [ghetto religious services] was sealed within, giving birth to the most degenerate form of Negro religion—gospel music.
>   Gospel music is the creation of a disengaged people. Shorn from the roots of the folk religion, gospel music has turned the freedom theme in Negro spirituals into licentiousness. Ministers who urge their people to seek their amusement in gospel music and the hoards of singers who profit from it lead the masses down the road of religious frenzy and escapism.[26]

In a later work, *Black Sects and Cults*, Washington comments that gospel music is basically blues and jazz disguised in "spiritual garb," and that "jackleg preachers" go from "rags to riches" by bringing these masqueraded secularisms into sacred worship.[27] Sociologist E. Franklin Frazier is considerably more benign in his assessment. "Gospel songs," Frazier avers, "express the deep religious feelings of the Negro masses who are increasingly exposed to life in the American community."[28] These negative assessments aside, black gospel music has undergone several developmental phases and it has a pervasive appeal in most black worship settings.

The Transitional Period of Gospel Music

There is common agreement among students of the phenomenon that distinctive black gospel music is rooted in the ghetto experiences of African Americans in the large cities of America, and that its development transcends at least three identifiable stages. The first stage has been called the transitional period, or the pre-gospel era. This epoch commenced around 1900 with the gospel hymns of Rev. Charles Albert Tindley, a black Methodist minister born in Maryland around the beginning of the Civil War. In the Methodist tradition of itinerancy, Tindley preached throughout the area and gained some prominence as a camp meeting preacher and singer. By the turn of the century he had settled in Philadelphia where he founded the church which now bears the name Tindley Temple United Methodist Church. Tindley's church became famous for its concerts and new music, much of which was written by himself. In 1916 he published *New Songs of Paradise*, a collection intended for informal worship. This early collection included the song that would fifty years later be known around the world as the signature of the civil rights movement, "I'll Overcome Someday." These were the first black gospel songs ever to be published, and they eventually found a place in the music of the Black Church, regardless of denomination. By the beginning of World War II the collection had gone through seven editions.

Tindley wrote songs incorporating the black folk imagery which attempted to interpret the oppression African Americans faced as they settled in the cities of the North, an experience not essentially different from that which produced the spirituals. Unlike the spirituals, however, the Tindley gospel songs have few references to the Old Testament characters and events. The Tindley hymns (which are congregational songs), admonish those who suffer the storms of life to stand fast in Christ. They are songs of dependency ("I Will Go if My Father Holds My Hand"), songs of ascendancy ("A Better Home"), songs of hope ("Some Day"), and songs of faith ("I'll Overcome Someday"). But the Tindley songs are not simply other-worldly. They are also addressed to helping the oppressed to survive *this* world.

Nevertheless, Tindley's hymns still tend to have a heavenward polarity. Like the spirituals, they depict heaven as the ultimate triumph over earthly oppression, a utopian realm of relaxation and family reunion. It is not the descendance of the Kingdom of God to earth preached by such social gospelers as A.M.E. Bishop Reverdy Ransom but the ultimate harvest to be reaped once the storms of this life have been successfully weathered.

The Traditional Period: The Golden Age of Gospel

The traditional period, also called the "golden age of gospel," commenced around 1930 with the compositions of Thomas A. Dorsey. Admittedly influenced by Tindley's songs, Dorsey earned the title "The Father of Gospel" due to his tireless promotion of the idiom. An ex-blues musician who first learned his music in the church and later played piano for Ma Rainey, "Georgia Tom" (as he was then known) brought elements of the blues into gospel. His blues-like gospel songs reflect the same eschatology as the Tindley hymns in their quest for the glorious hereafter that lies just beyond our present travail:

> Precious Lord, take my hand,
> Lead me on, Let me stand,
> I am tired, I am weak, I am worn;
> Through the storm, through the night
> Lead me on to the light,
> Take my hand, precious Lord,
> Lead me home.

Other gospel composers and arrangers who helped spread the gospel of "gospel" are Kenneth Morris, Sallie Martin, Roberta Martin, Theodore Frye, Lucie Campbell, and J. H. Brewster. These writers, along with Dorsey, transformed the congregational gospel hymns of Tindley into songs for church choirs, soloists (for example, Mahalia Jackson), and ensembles—sextets (for example, the Dixie Hummingbirds), quintets (for example, the Five Blind Boys of Mississippi), and quartets (for example, the Sensational Nightingales). But it was Dorsey who first called the church songs "gospel songs."

The transition from congregational hymns to songs for specialized soloists and ensembles had important sociological consequences. While the former united worshipers through the collective activity of singing and declaring theological and doctrinal commonalities, the new style required the congregation to assume the role of audience. In essence, worshipers became bystanders who witnessed the preaching and personal testimonies of singers. At best the congregation was to share in those attestations by affirmative "amens," nodding, humming, clapping, swaying, or occasionally by singing along on choruses and vamps. One unexpected consequence was that black worshipers and concertgoers often became the audience to a new homiletical gospel experience.

The emergence of a gospel circuit of specialized ensembles and talented soloists performing what seemed to some to be blues disguised in spiritual dress inevitably drew fire from some elements of the Black Church. The comments of E. Franklin Frazier are illustrative: "Some of the so-called advanced Negro churches resented these gospel singers and refused to permit them to sing within their churches. They have gradually become more tolerant and let down the bars as the Gospel Singers have acquired status and acceptance within the white world."[29] Although this new music was not readily accepted when it first appeared, in retrospect it sounds almost traditional in comparison with contemporary gospel.

Contemporary Gospel Music

The contemporary period in gospel music dates from the late 1960s and early 1970s when the transition from the typical gospel chorus accompanied by a piano and handclapping performing in a church had been superseded by ensembles featuring strings, brasses, synthesizers, and electronic instruments performing in a concert hall. The other thrust of the contemporary gospel expression is provided by a new generation of performers or presenters who use the gospel medium as a new homiletical instrument. Some representatives of this new genre are Edwin Hawkins, Andre Crouch, Tremaine Hawkins, and such clergypersons as Rev. James Cleveland, Rev. Al Green, and evangelist Shirley Caesar, who literally preach their compositions to their concert hall congregations. This calling to the "gospel ministry" broadens considerably the penetration and the acceptability of gospel as a legitimate and powerful expression of black religion. Contemporary gospel has also made greater use of communications media like radio, television, records, and film.

Just as the spirituals were taken outside the formal worship context by the Jubilee Singers of Fisk University to be performed throughout the nation and the world, so it was with gospel brought by performers into the concert halls and recording studios of America. The first instance necessitated the concerted arrangements of spirituals which made them more aesthetic than cathartic. The second inevitably required some musical and textual secularization of gospel. In consequence, the musical development of gospel began to sound more like pop music and jazz, and it seemed to be the catchy rhetorical metaphors and phrases, in what was otherwise a sincere, sacred song, which caught the imagination of the audience. This, in essence, was the secularism which Joseph Washington so adamantly denounced, and it is the principal dilemma which continues to disturb conservative clergy and laity in the contemporary Black Church.

In spite of the controversy surrounding it, during this period gospel has not only found a place beside concerted spirituals in the otherwise classical repertoire of black college choirs, but separate gospel choirs also developed and eventually found wide acceptance, although official administrative approval (and funding) were usually delayed and always apprehensive. Today the black college that does not have a black mass choir or some other form of gospel enterprise is the exception rather than the rule. Even black college students who attend white colleges and universities have often established gospel choirs as an affirmation and continuation of their heritage.

Because gospel has been popularized by college ensembles, students are attracted to those churches in the surrounding community which have contemporary gospel choirs, and usually attend services on the Sundays when those choirs perform. As a result, gospel music groupies of part-time college-age churchgoers have evolved. In lieu of a full commitment to the churches they attend is a fervent subscription to the contemporary gospel they have come to identify as belonging to them and to their generation. In our field research we found that the black churches that were most successful in attracting young adults also sponsored gospel music programs.

Gospel in Pentecostalism

Gospel music has played a critical role in the development of Pentecostalism, and reciprocally, Pentecostalism has performed an indispensable service in the development and acceptance of contemporary gospel. It is hardly incidental that the Pentecostal bodies are by far the fastest growing denominations in the Black Church.

> The gospel tradition was influenced by the older styles of the Negro religious music, and here the split of Holiness groups from the orthodox Negro church was an important event, for it was among the Holiness groups that the free expression of religious and musical behavior common to the rural Southern Negro began to assert itself and undergo further development in an urban setting.
>
> While the use of instruments was forbidden in the orthodox Negro church, their introduction by Holiness groups gave the music a "different sound than just handclapping."[30]

The Church of God in Christ, more than any other single denomination, has pioneered in the creation of contemporary gospel. It produced such performers as the Hawkins Singers, Andre Crouch, and the Clark Sisters, and their influence has been such that every contemporary gospel choir of whatever church is almost inevitably brushed with elements of Pentecostalism through its music and its performance practices. Only in the Holiness-Pentecostal churches is gospel the customary denominational music.

The style of gospel which prevails at any given Pentecostal church depends partly on the age of the singers. The senior adults tend to prefer the transitional and traditional gospel songs of the Tindley and Dorsey eras, and they sing these when they gather for prayer meetings and pre-worship devotional services which are not usually attractive to youth. On the other hand, the young adults prefer contemporary gospel, and it may predominate the main worship service itself. But whatever the period, the singing is almost sure to be rendered in the form of gospel. "The standard hymns that are used are done much differently than they are written in the hymnals, especially in matters of accent, rhythm, and key. Hymnals are used primarily for the words and melodic line. For the most part, hymns are trans-literated into a Gospel mode."[31] The development of gospel music illustrates the dynamic and dialectical interaction between religious and secular forms of black music. Many black musicians and artists received their initial musical training in black churches, developed their talent further in concert halls, nightclubs, and juke joints, and their musical style was combined with the words from hymns or newly created sacred songs in the churches.

Shout

The rhythmically accentuated gospel songs performed by the young adult choirs in the Holiness-Pentecostal churches frequently prompt a "shout" (or holy dance), which E. Franklin Frazier identifies as the "chief religious activity of the members of the Holiness cults."[32] The shout is to gospel and its cult what the ring-shout was to the spiritual and the slaves, and what spirit possession was to African sacred song. In all of its forms, the basic religious phenomenon is a spiritual possession experience in which the worshiper "gets happy" or is "anointed by the spirit" and praises God in paroxysmal dance. Frazier believed it to be the "maximum of free religious expression on the part of the participants."[33] In shouting, as in the ring-shout and the African trancelike dance, there is a kind of culturally restricted choreography which distinguishes it from secular dance. There is also a method of determining whether the shouter is "dancing in the spirit" or "dancing in the flesh." By suddenly halting the gospel shout music, one is able to check for authenticity. If the dancing continues without the music, it is assumed that it is genuine and induced by the Holy Spirit. But if it ceases, apparently it was not so holy after all and was merely rhythmically induced.[34]

Whether shouting is intense religious expression or simply the opiate of an oppressed people, or both, is not to be determined here, for there are logical arguments supporting both the spiritual and scientific premises. What is indisputable, however, is that the shout serves as a testimony to the shouter's felt sense of Spirit Baptism or sanctification. The shouter is, therefore, someone special in the congregation, a "somebody" who possesses that much-approved "good old-time religion." The result, whether intentional or not, is status, respect, and attention in the church, an achievement which may be difficult to attain in society at large.

Concerted Spirituals

Following emancipation some members of the African American elite refused to sing spirituals in their churches because they reminded people of the degradation of slavery and they were considered too crude for the formal worship exemplified by the white churches that blacks often sought to emulate. This attitude is best summarized by A.M.E. Bishop Daniel Payne's famous putdown of the spirituals as "cornfield ditties."[35] Acceptance of these songs came only after they were embellished and rendered in the sophisticated idiom of the European anthem. These anthemized spirituals were a novel development in the Black Church, for they constituted the first substantial body of composed Black sacred music not categorized as folk song. They were neither perpetuated through the oral tradition like spirituals, nor were they simply musical sketches of what was to be filled in with improvisation like the early gospel songs. What the arranger notated in the musical language of the European school was that which was to be sung by trained voices.

The creators of spirituals were untrained, of course, and the writers of gospel were generally self-taught. But the composers of the concerted spirituals were generally among black America's best-trained musicians, educated at the nation's, even the world's, most prestigious universities and conservatories of music. Among this elite coterie was R. Nathaniel Dett (1882–1943). Dett studied at the Oliver Willis Halstead Conservatory of Music in Lockport, New York (1901–3). He received his bachelor of music degree from the Eastman School of Music in 1930. He continued his education intermittently at the American Conservatory of Music, Columbia University, the University of Pennsylvania, Harvard University, the Fontainebleau School in Paris, and in Munich. Like most of his contemporaries, Dett earned a living as a music educator, having taught and directed choirs at Lane College, Lincoln University (Missouri), Bennett College, and Hampton Institute. And like the Fisk Jubilee Singers, Dett's Hampton Choir performed throughout the United States and Europe, bringing worldwide acclaim not only to Hampton and to himself, but to the spiritual. A portion of each concert program was devoted to his musical arrangements, of which "Don't Be Weary, Traveler," "Listen to the Lambs," "Let Us Cheer the Weary Traveler," and "Don't You Weep No More, Mary," were the most familiar.

Dett's credentials and career are representative of numerous black composers who arranged spirituals for concert performance. Among them are H. T. Burleigh, John Wesley Work, Hall Johnson, Clarence Cameron White, Samuel Coleridge-Taylor, J. Rosamond Johnson, William Dawson, and William Grant Still. Their works were sung by concert soloists like Roland Hayes and Paul Robeson, and by black college choirs like the Fisk Jubilee Singers and the Hampton Singers. Today, choir directors, perhaps at every black college and university in the nation, maintain this tradition of arranging and performing spirituals. Among them are Roland Carter at Hampton Institute, Wendell Whalum at Morehouse College, Nathan Carter at Morgan State University, Charles Gilchrist at North Carolina Central University, and Robert Leigh Morris at Jackson State University.

The traditional method of arrangement in the anthem style has been to cast the familiar text and tune of a spiritual into a homophonic (occasionally contrapuntal) setting for choir, with or without a featured soloist and piano accompaniment. For Dett this modernization process did not necessarily improve the spiritual,[36] but it did solve the problem of assimilating it into the sophisticated worship services of the elite black churches:

> It occurred to this writer that if a form of song were evolved which contained all the acceptable characteristics of Negro folk music and yet would compare favorably in poetic sentiment and musical expression with the best class of church music, it would be a means of solving this peculiar problem, for being created out of native material, it would save to the Negro and his music all the peculiar and precious idioms, and as a work of art would summon to its interpretation the best of his intellectual and emotional efforts.[37]

On the one hand, the African American religious tradition is maintained through the modernization of spirituals; while, on the other, the arranged spiritual ceases to be authentic and actually becomes an anthem. It ceases to be the congregational folk song that the worshipers sing, or to which they can clap, sway, and respond verbally. It becomes a concert piece to be appreciated artistically. Anthemization, then, has replaced one of the remaining African remnants of religious antistructure with even more structure. It has taken much of the spirit out of the spiritual and has replaced the cathartic with the aesthetic. Critics complain that it has made the Black Church more like the white church and less like itself.

Spirituals Arranged as Hymns

The more recent hymnals of mainline black denominations include a selection of spirituals arranged in four-part harmony as standard hymns. Some hymnologists choose to distinguish these from traditional Euro-American hymns by terming them folk hymns. The 1984

A.M.E.C. *Bicentennial Hymnal*, for instance, contains twenty-five folk hymns arranged by such historic black composers as H. T. Burleigh and John Wesley Work, and such contemporary arrangers as the late Wendell Whalum. Included are old favorites like "Go Tell It on the Mountain," "We Are Climbing Jacob's Ladder," "There Is a Balm in Gilead," and "Swing Low, Sweet Chariot."

While concerted spirituals are performed by skilled senior choirs, hymnic versions are sung congregationally as were the original spirituals. There is a significant variance, however. The original spirituals were executed improvisatorily and had sufficient space for emotional antistructure. Conversely, hymnic arrangements are generally sung in unison and are highly structured. The more restricted structure allows very little spiritual freedom for church members spontaneously getting happy or crying out in a passion of sorrow. Yet, since hymnody is so important in Methodist and Baptist churches of the higher socioeconomic strata, hymnic arrangements are a means of preserving the spiritual in a musical form to complement their more sophisticated taste, while also perpetuating the important element of congregational singing. Furthermore, hymnized spirituals sung congregationally are more cathartic and less aesthetic than the anthemized spirituals performed chorally. Although the formal structure of the hymn tends to preclude emotional antistructure, congregational singing can nevertheless be cathartically therapeutic. In fact, in the elite black churches where impassioned expression is considered eccentric, singing is the principal mode of emotional release.

Civil Rights Hymnody: Protest Songs of the Civil Rights Era

During the abolitionist movement in America, protest songs evolved at the hands of such white abolitionists as John Greenleaf Whittier, Elizabeth Margaret Chandler, and William Lloyd Garrison. At the request of the American Anti-Slavery Society, Edwin F. Hatfield, a Presbyterian minister, compiled this hymnody into a volume titled *Freedom's Lyre: Or, Psalms, Hymns, and Sacred Songs, for the Slave and His Friends* (1840). In this collection were both authentic abolitionist hymns and adaptations of extant evangelical hymns. Of the latter, key words and phrases were altered in order to superimpose meaning relative to abolition.

It was this liberative theme of abolitionist hymnody synthesized with the language of social gospel hymnody and the dialectical imagery of the black spirituals which can be summed up as the major constituents of the songs of the new abolitionist or civil rights movement. Although all of these were requisite ingredients, it was the abolitionist element of unconditional liberation that supplied the radical edge which rounded out the character of the freedom songs.

Adaptations of Spirituals and Gospels in the Civil Rights Movement

Like the abolitionist hymnody, some freedom songs were composed specifically for the civil rights movement, while most were adaptations of extant songs—in this instance, spirituals and gospels. These genre, which typified a heavenward polarity much like Watts's hymns, also required textual modifications in order to assimilate them into the freedom movement. The gospel song, "If You Miss Me from Praying Down Here," for example, was changed to "If You Miss Me from the Back of the Bus." The spiritual "This Little Light of Mine" became "This Little Light of Freedom." And the spiritual "Woke Up This Morning with My Mind on Jesus" became "Woke Up This Morning with My Mind Stayed on Freedom."

The singing of a particular song during a sit-in, protest march, freedom ride, mass meeting, or other protest activities, typically lasted twenty to twenty-five minutes. This necessitated the composition of new verses for the sake of textual variety during these lengthy involvements. Sometimes verses were prepared for a specific protest occasion; other times they evolved extemporaneously from the emotion generated by the occasion.

The anthem of the civil rights movement, "We Shall Overcome," is a synthesis of the spiritual "I'll Be Alright" and the C. A. Tindley hymn "I'll Overcome Someday." The melody is that of the spiritual, and the lyric a variation on Tindley's text. A side-by-side comparison of the two stanzas is instructive:

I'll overcome some day.	We shall overcome
I'll overcome some day,	We shall overcome
I'll overcome some day;	We shall overcome someday.
If in my heart I do not yield	If in our hearts we do believe
I'll overcome some day.	We shall overcome someday.

Even though the first person singular personal pronoun "I" was traditionally considered "communal" in black culture, the creators of civil rights songs always used the first person plural pronouns—"we" and "our." This was a feature of abolitionist hymnody and social gospel hymnody as well, and in each case the collective language of these protest songs was intended to foster a sense of community as the protesters sought to act as one consolidated body.

Not all extant church songs required textual alteration to meet the needs of the protesters. The spiritual "Wade in Water," for instance, was sometimes sung in wade-in demonstrations which aimed to integrate public swimming pools.[38] Spirituals like "Over My Head I See Freedom in the Air" and "Free at Last" could also be interpreted with relevant intent without textual modification. Although freedom from life and freedom from slavery often had synonymous meaning to the enslaved,[39] their original intent became tangential in the new context in which these songs were sung. What is important is that for the freedom fighters the messages had functional meaning related to their quest for civil rights. The songs of the movement also functioned to sustain the emotional intensity of involvement and commitment among its members. So it is that during this era of protest African Americans "returned to the spirituals, not as songs of faith but as sources of spirited support."[40] Without the enormous contributions of civil rights hymnody, the movement would have been rendered drab and lifeless.

Original Freedom Songs

Like abolitionist hymns, not all freedom songs were adapted from extant material. Some were composed by individuals specifically for events at hand. Each community typically had its own talented songwriters and thus its own freedom songs, the verses of which varied according to the mode of protest in that particular community. Atlanta lauded Bayard Rustin, "an old Lion of the Movement," who was closely associated with Martin Luther King, Jr.[41] Stated Rustin, "I was a singer and I wrote songs and they were topical about what was happening, and Abernathy would usually introduce them."[42] Greenwood, Mississippi, had Sam Block whose song, "Freedom Is a Constant Dying," is a personal reflection of the suffering endured during the struggle:

They say freedom is a constant dying (repeat 3 times)
O Lord, we died so long
We must be free.
We must be free.

In Sam Block's reminder: "O Lord, we died so long / We must be free" is evidence that these militant protest songs veiled in lamentation have much in common with the "sorrow songs." In a sense they are the neospirituals of the new abolitionists who sought a second emancipation for their people.

Professional Freedom Singers

Given the African American penchant for making and for being entertained by music, it was inevitable that the freedom songs, or some of them, would find professional expression. One very distinctive retention of African Americans from the African experience is the celebration of every phase of life with music, and the thin, wavy line that separates the religious enterprise from any other. For the African all life was religious, and religion was all of life. And life without music was no life to speak of. In consequence, the disjunctions between the sacred and the secular in music are not always apparent, especially to those who perform it. In the course of the freedom movement many new songs were composed to address specifically the goals and the interests of the struggle. Other familiar songs were adapted. These original and adapted freedom songs were not only sung congregationally at mass meetings and demonstrations, they were also performed professionally by ensembles like the Nashville Quartet, Guy Carawan and the Freedom Singers, Carlton Reese's Gospel Freedom Choir of the Alabama Christian Movement for Civil Rights, and the Freedom Singers.

Of these groups, the Freedom Singers, an affiliate of the Student Non-violent Coordinating Committee, gained a national reputation:

> The Freedom Singers were the major group responsible for spreading freedom songs over the nation. Their main body of songs came from the Nashville sit-ins, the Albany movement and the songs of the jailed CORE and SNCC freedom riders at Parchman penitentiary, Mississippi. . . .
> The group was formed with the aim of raising money and spreading the ideas of SNCC. All the singers were SNCC field secretaries.

They did not sing with instruments. They used the same basic equipment—hands, feet and strong voices—that they used while leading mass meetings in the South.[43]

And

... there has never been a singing movement like this one. Perhaps it is because most of them were brought up on the gospel songs and hymns of the Negro church in the South; perhaps also because they are young; probably most of all because what they are doing inspires song. They have created a new gospel music out of the old, made up of songs adapted or written in jail or on the picket line. Every battle station in the Deep South now has its Freedom Chorus, and the mass meetings there end with everyone standing, led by the youngsters of SNCC, linking arms, and singing.[44]

The Music of the Freedom Movement

The lyric religion of the freedom songs was a principal stimulus in the sustained efforts of the civil rights movement to achieve social change through nonviolent protest. As one student of the movement observed: "When police clubs, snarling dogs and hoses start to attack the line of march, praying to one's self gives some courage, but when hundreds sing their hopes together the songs provide the shield and identification necessary to withstand even the fury of the hostile mob."[45] Having been at the forefront of countless freedom marches and mass meetings, Martin Luther King, Jr., confirmed the power and the indispensability of music in the struggle:

An important part of the mass meetings was the freedom songs. In a sense the freedom songs are the soul of the movement. They are more than just incantations of clever phrases designed to invigorate a campaign; they are as old as the history of the Negro in America. They are adaptations of the songs the slaves sang—the sorrow songs, the shouts for joy, the battle hymns, and the anthems of our movement. I have heard people talk of the beat and rhythm. "Woke Up This Morning with My Mind Stayed on Freedom" is a sentence that needs no music to make its points. We sing these freedom songs today for the same reason the slaves sang them, because we too are in bondage and the songs add hope to our determination that "we shall overcome."[46]

While King's statement emphasizes the importance of the texts of the freedom songs, psychologist Carl Seashore offers an instructive comment on the critical part that rhythm played in the protest songs: "Rhythm gives us a feeling of power; it carries. . . . The pattern once grasped, there is an assurance of ability to cope with the future. This results in . . . a motor attitude, or a projection of the self in action; for rhythm is never rhythm unless one feels that he himself is acting it, or, what may seem contradictory, that he is even carried by his own action."[47] Hence, when King says, "These songs bind us together, give us courage together, help us to march together," he is perhaps unconsciously including in his assessment a tribute to Seashore's dictum that rhythm "carries."

The songs of the civil rights era were the first openly armigerous or militant music to come out of the Black Church. The spirituals, while based upon freedom themes, were not extrinsically militant; they were "songs of protest, in acceptable and thinly veiled form against the conditions of life."[48] Abolitionist hymnody, though composed under the aegis of religion on behalf of the slaves, was basically the work of white abolitionists; and social gospel hymnody, a white Protestant entity, decried the sins of society but remained only tangential to the critical issues of African American social concern. The blues lamented the social, political, and economic oppression common to the black experience, but they were outside the legitimate periphery of the Black Church. And of all these genre, it is paradoxical that gospel is the most Christocentric and yet the least radical.

The freedom songs did not passively lament the black condition; they made God active in human history day by day with social agitation. African Americans were not just singing about freedom, they were systematically seeking it, and their songs were deliberate instruments tactically utilized in the effort. Freedom songs chronicle the historic events of the various forms of protest, personal reflections, testimonials, and religious responses to the oppressive forces opposing the struggle for freedom. As the spirituals provide an authentic window for religion in the life of the slave, so do the freedom songs offer a documentary on what the lives of black people were like in America one hundred years after slavery had ended.

Types of Music in the Contemporary Black Church

Charles Wesley wrote more than seven thousand hymns, setting the musical tone for the Protestant Church in America for generations.

Today, fewer than one hundred are used in the Black Church. James Cone explains that a major reason for the decline of Wesleyan hymnody is that in European hymnody in general the textual focus is seldom on liberation. Freedom has always been an intimate concern of the Black Church, and in its pilgrimage toward that goal, the much used songs of Charles Wesley seemed increasingly inexpressive of the urgencies felt by black people. "White Christianity may refer to liberation in limited times and places, as shown by the abolitionists, the social gospel preachers, and the recent appearance of liberation theologians in Europe and North America, but liberation is not and never has been the dominant theme in white church songs, prayers, and sermons."[49] In the chronology of A.M.E. church hymnals of 1892, 1941, 1954, and 1984, there is a steady decrease in the number of Wesley hymns, from 210 (out of 760 hymns) in the 1892 volume to forty-six (out of 670) in the 1984 volume. Of the forty-six Wesley hymns in the 1984 A.M.E. Church Bicentennial Hymnal, only two, "Come, Thou Long-Expected Jesus" and "Try Us, O God," could be considered thematically significant to black worshipers. And in Songs of Zion, a 1981 "songbook from the black religious tradition" sponsored by the United Methodist Church, of 285 offerings only two were from Charles Wesley, and one of those, "Father I Stretch My Hands to Thee," was in the special category of "response." By contrast, Songs of Zion lists ninety-eight songs as "Negro Spirituals and Afro-American liberation Songs."[50]

It has been said of Wesley that "one of the most characteristic features of his hymns is the way in which, no matter with what earthly subject they begin, they end in heaven."[51] And even those based on social themes are "never in danger of becoming earthbound."[52] However, despite the elements of lethargy that linger from the early days of its development when the open appreciation for freedom was tantamount to insurrection, on the whole the Black Church has both revered Charles Wesley and transcended him. Certainly the theology implicit in his hymns does not express the full range of Black Church interests for today, nor do they address with sufficient candor and specificity the critical issues of African American existence in a world where God is expected to identify himself with the oppressors of the earth *in this world.* "Singing," says W. B. McClain in Songs of Zion, "is as close to worship as breathing is to life" and life in the contemporary Black Church is earth-oriented though heaven-bound.

Wattsian Hymnody

On the whole, Isaac Watts's hymns have been more successful in the Black Church than Charles Wesley's. Again using the chronology of A.M.E. hymnals of 1892, 1941, 1954, and 1984 as a barometer, while the 1892 hymnal has (out of 461 hymns) forty-six by Watts, the 1984 hymnal retains thirty-six (out of 670).

The imagery in Watts's hymns has always found favor with the African American worshiper. They were the principal hymns sung in the lined tradition during the antebellum and post-bellum eras, such that lined singing was commonly known as the "Dr. Watts style." During the "golden age of gospel," ensembles like the Clara Ward Singers performed the Watts hymns in a gospel idiom along side the gospel songs of Thomas Dorsey and J. H. Brewster. Currently many of the Watts hymns are traditional in the Black Church:

> O God, our help in ages past,
> Our hope for years to come,
> Our shelter from the stormy blast,
> And our eternal home.

Compared to the hymns of Wesley and other evangelicals, Watts's hymns more often seem to have particular signification for contemporary African American worshipers, but like the former, they also tend to have a heavenward bent which is generally pronounced in the closing stanza. Often commencing with a social theme, Watts's hymns almost predictably take a Calvinistic excursus toward heaven (much like the sermon climaxes of the black folk preacher). Consequently, the Old Testament theology of God as liberator of the oppressed is severely dampened by the centrality of praise for the Sovereign Lord.

Social Gospel Hymnody

Although social gospel hymnody is a white Protestant entity, social hymns like "Onward Christian Soldiers" and "In Christ There Is No East or West" are more relevant to African American liberation than evangelical hymnody. In spite of their empiricism, however, social gospel hymns have failed to displace, not only the Watts and Wesley hymns, but also the old favorites of James Montgomery ("Angels from the Realms of Glory"), John Newton ("Amazing Grace"), William Cowper ("There Is a Fountain Filled with Blood"), and Fanny J. Crosby ("Jesus Is Tenderly Calling You Home").

This preference for the evangelical is not necessarily a reaffirmation of the other-worldly focus that has been considered traditional to the Black Church. It is in part attributable to the deep cisterns of spirituality with which the black diaspora have been endowed by African traditional religions. Second, it is a result of attachment to the favorite old tunes and texts whose familiarity gives consolation to those who must constantly endure disconsolation. Again, change does not come readily to religion in any case, for religion is the prime custodian of what tradition has sanctified. The newer hymns of the social gospel have not prevailed against these odds, however unseemingly the paradox, for they come closer to the liberation theology of the freedom songs than any other music in the Black Church.

The Hymn-Lining Tradition

The lined tradition has been partially maintained in the contemporary Black Methodist churches. In the A.M.E. Church, for example, the congregational chanting of the Lord's Prayer (immediately following the sermon) is lined-out by the minister, but usually in a spoken rather than sing-song declamation. Further, when introducing the morning hymn, the A.M.E. minister reads a stanza or two, and then advises the congregation that they are to stand and sing with the choir. By the initial lining, deference is paid to tradition when that feature was a necessary modus vivendi because of the generalized illiteracy among church members and the lack of hymnals.

In the early Black Baptist and Methodist "word hymnals," the meter indications (SM, CM, LM) enabled the song leader to select short, common, and long meter tunes (maintained by the oral tradition) to match the meter of the poetry. Although modern hymnals have texts and tunes already suited, the meters are provided to allow their interchanging. Some of the more sophisticated hymnals go so far as to include a metric index which facilitates commutation. This would enable a pastor to introduce to a congregation a new or more theologically suitable common meter hymn paired with a well-known common meter tune. While this technique is rarely used in the Black Church, by maintaining the familiar the minister is likely to be more successful in introducing the unfamiliar. The black Methodists have transformed the lined tradition into something creative and functional in the methodic mode of worship, but, history is indebted to the Baptist churches for keeping alive this authentic tradition which is nearly two centuries old in the Black Church.

Gospel Music

While gospel music has been generally accepted by most black churches, there are still some prominent segments within elite black Baptist and Methodist churches and among some traditionalists who customarily express annoyance with, or outright rejection of gospel music, both in terms of its often problematic theology and because of its alleged secularity. The problem begins with the fact that gospel choirs often select their repertoires based on what is popular on the radio or television, despite the fact that not all gospel packaged commercially is ideal for worship. Because commercialization presupposes secularization, it is inevitable that many metaphors and musical embellishments acceptable for secular performance are considered unacceptable in a worship setting. Another problem is that gospel songwriters compose their songs based on their personal theology, or without consideration of theological implications rather than with any official theological canon in mind. Generally speaking, the theology of contemporary gospel may be loosely classified as continuing in the evangelical tradition of Tindley and Dorsey, hence, there can be a musical retreat from what is happening in the black community rather than a response to it. Finally, there is probably a denominational bias against gospel in some churches because of its strong Pentecostal identification. This is a problem of increasing significance for both the Black Church and American Christianity in general, Catholic as well as Protestant, as the contemporary charismatic movement presses hard against conventional concepts in the characterization of religion in America. We turn next to some sociological data on the Black Church and music.

Sociological Data on the Black Church and Music

In our survey of 2,150 black churches nationwide, we found that the vast majority of churches had at least two or more choirs. Table 38 indicates that only 436 (20.3 percent) churches had only one choir.

Table 38: Church Music: Number of Choirs in
Black Churches

Number	Total	Urban	Rural
One	436 (20.3%)	265 (17.4%)	171 (27.7%)
Two	514 (23.9%)	319 (20.8%)	195 (31.5%)
Three	428 (19.9%)	312 (20.4%)	116 (18.7%)
Four	291 (13.5%)	245 (16.0%)	46 (7.4%)
Five	209 (9.7%)	167 (10.9%)	42 (6.8%)
More than 5	132 (6.2%)	111 (7.2%)	21 (3.4%)
No response	140 (6.5%)	112 (7.3%)	28 (4.5%)

Total N=2,150
Urban N=1,531
Rural N=619

Average number of choirs per church=2.89 or 3 choirs

The average number of choirs for the total sample was 2.89 (or three) choirs per church. This average number gives an indication of how important music and singing are in black churches. Even poor black churches with very few material resources invested what little they had in their musical program. In our previous findings regarding paid church staff members in black churches, musicians (choir directors, pianists, and organists) ranked first, ahead of church secretaries and custodians. The results in table 38 also point to a slight urban-rural difference in the number of choirs supported by the churches. The majority of the rural churches, 366 (59.2 percent), had only one or two choirs, while the majority of the urban churches, 835 (54.5 percent), had three or more choirs. Obviously, black urban churches have a larger population base to draw on.

In attempting to assess the changing scene of music in the Black Church, the survey also asked pastors what types of music are approved for use in the church. Table 39 shows that the vast majority of black churches 2,084 (96.9 percent) approved of the use of some form of gospel music (the survey did not distinguish between the types of gospel music given in the historical overview above), and only 33 (1.5 percent) did not approve. Spirituals were also approved by the majority of respondents, 2,002 (93.1 percent), with a slight urban-rural difference: 1,486 (97.1 percent) urban churches approved of spirituals, while only 516 (83.4 percent) of rural churches did so.

Table 39: Church Music: Type of Music Approved for Use in Worship Services

	Total	Urban	Rural
I. Gospel music?			
Yes	2,084 (96.9%)	1,489 (97.3%)	595 (96.2%)
No	33 (1.5%)	21 (1.4%)	12 (1.9%)
No response	33 (1.5%)	21 (1.4%)	12 (1.9%)
II. Spirituals?			
Yes	2,002 (93.1%)	1,486 (97.1%)	516 (83.4%)
No	114 (5.3%)	24 (1.6%)	90 (14.5%)
No response	34 (1.6%)	21 (1.4%)	13 (2.1%)
III. Other black music (e.g., jazz, blues, etc.)?			
Yes	448 (20.8%)	408 (26.6%)	40 (6.5%)
No	1,595 (74.2%)	1,030 (67.3%)	565 (91.2%)
No response	107 (5.0%)	93 (6.1%)	14 (2.3%)

Total *N*=2,150
Urban *N*=1,531
Rural *N*=619

The greatest ambivalence was shown toward other types of black music like jazz and blues, for use in black churches. Only 448 (20.8 percent) said they approved of the use of jazz and blues in church settings, while 1,595 (74.2 percent) said no, they disapproved. There is a significant urban-rural difference in the attitudes of pastors toward the use of other black music in church: 408 (26.6 percent) of the urban pastors said that they approved of using other black music and only forty (6.5 percent) of the rural pastors approved. The black clergy of urban churches were far more willing to experiment with other types of black music for use in worship than the rural clergy. In some of the non-Pentecostal urban churches we visited the pastors were willing to allow the use of musical instruments other than the piano and organ, like drums, trumpets, saxophones, and clarinets. For example, a Baptist pastor in Newport News, Virginia, who was a trained professional musician, taught youngsters in his church how to use different musical instruments during the week; a full set of drums was placed next to the piano in his church's sanctuary.

The whole musical scene in the Black Church is a fluid, dynamic, and constantly changing one. Before he died, Duke Ellington composed many pieces of jazz-based sacred music that could be played in worship settings. Just as the introduction of a blues' rhythm and style in the synthetic product called gospel music caused enormous controversy among black church members, the introduction of more jazz into worship settings will also stir the pot. For example, W. C. Handy's father, an A.M.E. pastor, once viewed his son's work as the "devil's music." However, with the passage of time gospel music has received near universal acceptance in most quarters of the Black Church, as our data above has indicated. Among those who are on the cutting edge of musical experimentation in the Black Church is Rev. Wyatt Tee Walker of the Canaan Baptist Church in Harlem. With his keen sense for dramatic presentation, Walker's congregation meets in a converted theater. The gospel choirs at Canaan are accompanied by instrumental groups and sometimes appropriate modern dance segments are incorporated into the worship setting. Walker has also written a book that relates Black Church music to social change.[53] The Word is performed not only in his sermons, but in the musical program of the church.

Conclusion

As some commentators have observed, the contributions of African Americans to the musical heritage of the United States have been enormous, often constituting the original and primary innovations in music from spirituals and gospel to blues, ragtime, jazz, rock and roll, soul, and rap; the core of American music has derived from black culture.[54] Walker has extended that insight by arguing that black religious music has been "the primary root of all music born in the United States."[55] However, in spite of the importance of the topic of music in the life of the Black Church, very little attention has been paid to it by the scholars of religion and there have been even fewer empirical studies.[56] We have attempted to fill the gap by providing a broad survey of the development of music in the Black Church and by examining some of the new trends in musical experimentation. As we pointed out at the beginning of this chapter, the music performed in black churches is a major way of attracting members and sustaining their spiritual growth. Just as we can speak about the charisma of the preacher, that ineffable quality or gift that draws and attracts people, there can also be the charisma of music in the form of a choir, choir director, soloist, or musical program. Our field research has shown that among black young people, teenagers and young adults, gospel music programs constitute the major drawing card.

Music in the Black Church is a dynamic phenomenon, always subject to the tension between religious traditions and customs and the musical styles of the day. However, the boundary line between sacred and secular black music is often a thin one. We have pointed out that one of the trends of music in black churches is to find appropriate ways of incorporating musical styles like jazz and blues and even modern dance into worship settings. In our last chapter we turn to other trends that will probably affect black churches in the twenty-first century.

13 The Black Church and the Twenty-First Century: Challenges to the Black Church

At the beginning of the last decade of the twentieth century the black churches are, on the whole, still healthy and vibrant institutions. While there has been some chipping away at the edges, particularly among unchurched underclass black youth and some college educated, middle-class young adults, black churches still remain the central institutional sector in most black communities. Based on the indices of church membership, church attendance, and charitable giving in 1987, different studies have pointed out the following: about 78 percent of the black population claimed church membership and attended once in the last six months; blacks (44 percent) tend to have slightly higher rates of weekly church attendance than white Protestants (40 percent); and they have the highest rates of being superchurched (attending church more than on Sundays) among all Americans (37 versus 31 percent). Furthermore, if time and money are an indication of loyalty, black churches received a far higher percentage of the charitable dollar and more volunteer time than that given to any other organization by black people.[1] The seven major black denominations have not suffered the kind of severe decline in membership experienced by some mainstream white denominations like the Disciples of Christ (40 percent), the United Presbyterian Church (33 percent), or the Episcopal Church (33 percent).[2]

We have covered a broad range of topics, providing overviews of the seven major historic black denominations, presenting the demographic profiles of rural and urban black churches and clergy, examining the impact of the black consciousness movement upon the black clergy, and analyzing the relationships between black churches and the spheres of politics, economics, and music. We also focused on some specific problems regarding the relationship between black churches and black women clergy, and their tenuous hold on segments of the black urban youth and young adult population. We conclude this study by attempting to provide some clues toward answering the following questions: what does the future hold for black churches and clergy? What kinds of challenges lie ahead for this institutional sector that has played such a heroic role in the past? What are the assessments of black clergy regarding some problematic areas facing their own institutions?

The Challenge of Two Black Americas and Two Black Churches?

The process of secularization in black communities has always meant a diminishing of the influence of religion and an erosion in the central importance of black churches. Secularization is accompanied by the twin processes of increasing differentiation and increasing pluralism that tend to diminish the cultural unity provided by the black sacred cosmos.[3] There is some evidence that the present and past central importance of the Black Church may be threatened by the virtual explosion of opportunities, which are now becoming available to recent black college graduates. An officially segregated society contributed to the dominant role black churches were able to maintain as one of the few cohesive black institutions to emerge from slavery. Talented black men and women developed their leadership skills in black churches and used them as launching pads for professional careers in the church or elsewhere in black society like education, music, and entertainment. With the breakdown of official segregation, some opportunities in previously closed professions in law, medicine, politics, and business have opened up as never before. Also many white colleges, universities, and graduate schools have been seeking black students to bolster their black enrollment. As Freeman has pointed out in his study of black elites, recent black college graduates have been able to achieve income parity with their white counterparts for the first time in history, an occurrence beyond reach of the vast majority of black workers.[4] Even with some decline in black college enrollment during the Reagan years, the total numbers of black college graduates since the 1960s will still represent an unprecedented phenomenon in black history. How black churches and their leadership grapple with this challenge will determine whether they will be faced with the same problems of attrition and decline now affecting several white mainstream denominations.

Whether black churches will have the clergy with educational training equal to that of their lay members is also in question. At one time black clergy were among the most highly educated members of the community, and a number of black colleges and universities were founded for the training of the clergy. However, as we pointed out in the profile of urban clergy in chapter 6, that is no longer the case. With the proliferation in available professions for young people, the question of whether the ministry of the Black Church will continue to attract the best and the brightest is still unresolved.

As we mentioned, some studies have pointed out the increasing bifurcation of the black community into two main class divisions: a coping sector of middle-income working-class and middle-class black communities, and a crisis sector of poor black communities, involving the working poor and the dependent poor.[5] The demographic movement of middle-income blacks out of inner city areas and into residential parts of the cities, older suburbs, or into newly created black suburbs, has meant a growing physical and social isolation of the black poor. For example, since the 1960s, 48 percent of the black population of Atlanta has moved out of the central city into surrounding counties.[6] The gradual emergence of two fairly distinct black Americas along class lines—of two nations within a nation— has raised a serious challenge to the Black Church. The membership of the seven historic black denominations is composed largely of middle-income working-class and middle-class members, with a scattering of support from poorer members, especially those in southern rural areas who tend to be among the most loyal members.[7] But black pastors and churches have had a difficult time in attempting to reach the hard-core urban poor, the black underclass, which is continuing to grow.[8] In past generations some of the large urban black churches were one of the few institutions that could reach beyond class boundaries and provide a semblance of unity in black communities.[9] The challenge for the future is whether black clergy and their churches will attempt to transcend class boundaries and reach out to the poor, as these class lines continue to solidify with demographic changes in black communities. If the traditional Black Church fails in its attempt to include the urban poor, the possibility of a Black Church of the poor may emerge, consisting largely of independent, fundamentalist, and Pentecostal storefront churches. There also may emerge cults and sectarian forms of new religious movements among the black poor, similar to those exotic groups that emerged in the 1930s like those of Father Divine, Daddy Grace, Mother Horne, Elder Solomon Lightfoot Michaux, Rabbi Cherry, and Elijah Muhammad.[10] One of the few hopeful signs that the historic black churches will be able to provide a measure of unity beyond class boundaries involves the rise of a neo-Pentecostal movement in some black denominations.

The Challenge of Church Growth: A Case Study of the Rise of a Neo-Pentecostal Movement in the A.M.E. Church

While some recent studies have pointed to the phenomenon of a growing sector of unchurched black people, especially among black males in northern urban areas, scant attention has been paid to the rise of a neo-Pentecostal or charismatic movement that has contributed to the opposite phenomenon of church growth among some black church denominations.[11] Just as some of the white mainstream church denominations, including the Roman Catholics, have experienced a charismatic or neo-Pentecostal movement among some of their churches, a similar phenomenon has also occurred among some of the middle-class black denominations like the African Methodist Episcopal Church.[12] Rev. Dr. John Bryant, Jr., who was the former pastor of the Bethel A.M.E. Church in Baltimore until he was elected a bishop of the denomination in 1988, has been one of the central figures in leading and influencing A.M.E. pastors and laity in the direction of neo-Pentecostalism. The most significant fact about this movement in the A.M.E. Church has been the enormous church growth it has produced in almost all of the churches associated with it. For example, when Bryant took over the Bethel A.M.E. Church of Baltimore in the mid-1970s the church had about five hundred members; within ten years its membership had grown to over six thousand members, making it the largest A.M.E. congregation in the nation. Besides Bethel, several of the largest A.M.E. churches in the country associated with the movement were pastored by Bryant protégés. Rev. Frank M. Reid III of Ward A.M.E. in Los Angeles, Rev. Floyd Flake of Allen A.M.E. in Queens, Rev. Fred Lucas of Bridgestreet A.M.E. in Brooklyn, Rev. Grainger Browning of Fort Washington A.M.E., just outside Washington, D.C., and Rev. Dr. Kenneth Robinson of Payne Chapel A.M.E. in Nashville are representative. While some of the church growth took place in older, urban

A.M.E. churches like Bethel, Bridgestreet, and Ward, others occurred in churches in residential working-class neighborhoods such as Allen A.M.E. in Jamaica, Queens, and in churches in newly created black suburbs such as Fort Washington A.M.E. The Allen A.M.E. Church grew from 1,400 members to over five thousand, and Fort Washington A.M.E. from twenty-five members to over a thousand members in two years.[13]

The membership of most of these neo-Pentecostal churches consists of a mix of a middle-income working-class and middle-class blacks, who make up the majority of traditional A.M.E. membership and some of the black urban poor, the latter tending to be attracted by the informal, less structured, and highly spirited worship services. Neo-Pentecostalism in black churches tends to draw upon the reservoir of the black folk religious tradition which stressed enthusiastic worship and Spirit filled experiences. One of the appeals of the current movement is its emphasis upon a deeper spirituality, the need for a second blessing of the Holy Spirit. The older Holiness-Pentecostal movement of the late nineteenth century emerged out of Methodism and John Wesley's search for spiritual perfection, which was carried one step further by the Pentecostalists with their stress on another blessing of the Spirit (with its evidence of glossolalia, interpretation and prophesying, or other "gifts of the Spirit").

Another characteristic of the neo-Pentecostal movement in the A.M.E. Church concerns its curious combination of a deep Pentecostal spiritual piety and the A.M.E. tradition of involvement in progressive politics and political activism. The pastors as well as the laity associated with movement churches are caught up in the most intense, enthusiastic worship featuring the traditional Pentecostal phenomena referred to above. The lay members of these churches tend to be intensely involved with church activity on a daily basis, from prayer meetings and Bible study to adult education classes. Drums, tambourines, cymbals, and such instruments as electric guitars have also been introduced into worship services. The charismatic style of worship is much more emotionally oriented than the traditional A.M.E. emphasis upon "order and decorum." However, the A.M.E. tradition of political involvement seems unaffected. In contrast to most white churches in which the Pentecostal spirit and political conservatism seem to appear in tandem, the majority of the black pastors and their churches in the neo-Pentecostal movement tend to be politically progressive. Like Bishop Bryant, many of them were veterans of the civil rights struggle of the 1960s and this background has influenced their political views. Some of these activists felt burned out by the continuous struggle and sought a deeper, spiritual side. Under Bryant's leadership, Bethel established a private Christian school for elementary grades with future plans for a high school. It also ran a soup kitchen for the poor and it has been active in city politics by providing a forum for officials and candidates. Rev. Floyd Flake used his church base at Allen A.M.E. to conduct a successful election campaign to become congressman of his district, after the church had organized more than $20 million worth of community projects in the neighborhood. Rev. Grainger Browning of the Fort Washington A.M.E. Church calls on each family of his mostly middle-class congregation to contribute a new pair of shoes on the Sunday before Labor Day. On Labor Day the church dispenses to anyone a pair of shoes without cost. Rev. Frank Reid III of Ward A.M.E. in Los Angeles has been one of the more vocal black clergy in political affairs in Southern California, supporting black nationalists and being involved in police-community relations issues. Ward A.M.E. sponsors a prison ministry program that involves church members in Bible study and prayer sessions with inmates in prisons and halfway houses, and supplies food and clothing to their families. A program to help church members adopt black children, called "Room for One More," was devised by a laywoman at Ward.[14] Rev. Dr. Kenneth Robinson, who is also a practicing physician, has persuaded his congregation at Payne Chapel A.M.E. to hold neighborhood health fairs in Nashville, where health professionals from the church provide free medical screening and advice.

For the A.M.E. charismatics, today's neo-Pentecostalism also differs from the traditional Pentecostalism in that it combines both the "letter and the spirit," transcending the sheer emotionalism of the past. Many of the pastors and some of the laity of the new charismatic movement have had a college education and formal theological education in seminaries. Supporters argue that the merger of the letter and the spirit, the intellect and the emotions, is a corrective to traditional African Methodism, which allegedly tended to kill off the emotional side of worship and rituals prompting many to opt for other denominations like the Baptists or Pentecostals. Spirited, enthusiastic worship, they say, can attract people, and is not contrary to genuine A.M.E. tradition. In support of this argument it is said that the place where worship has the most vitality among A.M.E.s is in

South Carolina where enthusiastic and spirited worship is normative, and where "there are more A.M.E.s than anywhere in the
world."[15]

The neo-Pentecostal movement has been a source of spiritual
revitalization among the A.M.E.s and a rich source of ministerial
candidates. For example, the Bethel A.M.E. Church in Baltimore has
sent more than twenty-five students to divinity schools like Howard
Divinity and the Interdenominational Theological Center. Bethel
has also had more than fifty assistant ministers in training, serving at
the church.

While the neo-Pentecostals in the A.M.E. Church have produced
enormous church growth and a revitalized energy and enthusiasm in
some congregations, there are severe critics of the movement who
resent the threat to traditional worship in an atmosphere of order and
decorum. They also criticize the spiritual chauvinism of many charismatics who tend to view their way as the only way. The charismatic
movement represents a powerful potential for the revitalization of
the A.M.E. Church, but it could also produce a serious schism with
the whole church ending up as the loser.

There is some evidence that this neo-Pentecostal movement has
also involved black church denominations other than the A.M.E.
Church, including a few churches in the A.M.E. Zion Church and
some middle-class Baptist churches.[16] These churches have also exhibited similar characteristics such as rapid and enormous church
growth in membership. However, the extent of this neo-Pentecostal
phenomenon among black churches is unknown because it has not
been examined thoroughly. Nevertheless, the challenge which neo-
Pentecostalism poses for the Black Church is real, and the issue of
how to benefit from this potential of church growth and spiritual
revitalization without alienating the pillars of normative tradition,
both lay and clergy, and without producing a crisis of schism is a
challenge most black churches must inevitably address.

The Islamic Challenge to the Black Church

The resurgence of Islamic fundamentalism has been a worldwide
phenomenon in recent years and it has implications for the general
religious situation in the United States and for black Christian
churches. Black communities have been particularly vulnerable to
the Islamic challenge since the largest indigenous sector of Ameri-

cans who have become Muslims are from the black population. The influence of varieties of Islam among blacks in the United States has had a long history, stemming from the African Muslims who were brought to North America as slaves and who constituted as much as 20 percent of the slave population on some large southern plantations.[17] However, much of the African Islamic influence did not survive the period of slavery, and the main bearers of that tradition came through the writings of intellectuals like Edward Wilmot Blyden, a late nineteenth-century advocate of African Islam.[18] But it was the leaders of "proto-Islamic" movements during the black urban migrations of the twentieth century who prepared the way for a much wider acceptance of Islam. Muslim advocates such as Noble Drew Ali of the Moorish Science Temple in 1913 and Master Wali Fard and the Honorable Elijah Muhammad of the Nation of Islam during the years of the Great Depression opened the door of Islam to black America with a dramatic appeal to heritage and history.[19] The Nation of Islam survived to become the nucleus of a rapidly proliferating Islamic growth in America transcending racial and ethnic boundaries.

The Nation of Islam, which was founded by Master Farad Muhammad in 1930 and led by Elijah Muhammad from 1934 until 1975, has a challenging and controversial history.[20] Under the influence of Minister Malcolm X, Elijah's national representative, the Nation made its greatest impact on the black community and American society during the 1960s and early 1970s when America was searching for change but adamantly resisting changing. Malcolm X and the Nation are credited with the primary ideological foundations that led to the development of the concepts of "black power," "black pride," and "black consciousness" which stirred black youth and reverberated all through the civil rights movement of the period. Malcolm X was more deeply aware than many less controversial leaders that the struggle for civil rights and integration were meaningless if the integrity and independence of black selfhood were drowned in a sea of whiteness. Malcolm's biting critique of the "so-called Negro" and his emphasis upon the recovery of an independent black selfhood helped to change the language and vocabulary of an entire society from "Negro" to "black."[21]

Under Wali Fard and Elijah Muhammad the Nation of Islam was essentially a proto-Islamic religious black nationalism that was often at odds with the traditional doctrines of orthodox Islam.

Since the death of Elijah Muhammad in 1975, many members of

the Nation of Islam, or the Black Muslims, have followed their new leader Imam Warith Deen Muhammad in making the transition to orthodox Sunni Islam. Warith began dismantling the exclusive black "nation" by accepting whites into the movement and then proceeded to gradually discard all the precepts and practices taught by Elijah, which he considered in violation of the spirit and the letter of orthodox Islam. "There is no black Muslim or white Muslim," he declared, "all are Muslims, all children of God."[22] Under Warith Muhammad the movement changed its name, first to the World Community of al-Islam in the West, then to the American Muslim Mission, finally finding its long-sought "true" identity in the world brotherhood of traditional Islam. Imam Warith Muhammad was recognized and accepted by world Muslim leaders, who honored him with the office of certification for Muslims from the United States who go on the annual pilgrimage, or Hajj, to Mecca. Muslim imams or leaders of the "Jummah," or Friday prayer services, are now commonly accepted as members of black ministerial alliances across the country.

An estimated 100,000 former members of Elijah Muhammad's old Nation of Islam followed Warith Deen Muhammad into Islamic orthodoxy as Sunni Muslims. Imam Muhammad's newspaper, *The Muslim Journal*, has also been one of the pioneers in using the term African American in reference to black Americans. Perhaps another 20,000 or so are led by Minister Louis Farrakhan, who continues the provincial black nationalist teachings of Master Fard and Elijah Muhammad. Farrakhan's followers retained the original designation of the Nation of Islam along with its ideology. While there have been smaller splinter groups led by rival leaders, the fluidity of membership in these groups has made it very difficult to obtain an accurate assessment of membership figures. However, over the fifty-eight-year history of the Nation and its evolution to orthodox Islam, it is estimated that several million black people, mostly black men, have passed through these various Islamic and proto-Islamic movements.[23] In 1989 the *New York Times* has estimated that about 1 million of the 6 million Muslims in the United States are African Americans, and close to 90 percent of new converts are black.[24]

Islam has proven itself to be a viable religious alternative to black Christian churches, especially for many black males, who have experienced difficulty with normative social and economic adjustments. In fact, the membership of Islamic masjids or mosques has always tended to be heavily made up of black men, a segment of the black population which black churches have had great difficulty in recruiting. The attraction of Islamic movements to black males may be due to several reasons, among them the legacy of the militant and radical black nationalist Malcolm X has been a profound influence on these young men. As a culture hero, Malcolm X was seen as the uncompromising critic of American society. Another reason is that the Muslims project a more macho image among black men. The Qur'an advocates self-defense while the Christian Bible counsels turning the other cheek. The *lex talionis,* "an eye for an eye, a life for a life," has a persuasive appeal to the oppressed whose cheeks are weary of inordinate abuse. Black sports heroes such as Muhammad Ali and Kareem Abdul-Jabbar have further legitimated the Islamic option by converting to Islam and taking on Muslim names. Black parents who are not Muslims frequently give their children Muslim names as a statement of solidarity with some features of Islam and as a way of announcing their independence from Western social conventions, or as a means of identifying with an African cultural heritage. Finally, many black men have been attracted to Islamic alternatives because the Muslims have been very active in working in prisons and on the streets where they are, a ministry which is not pronounced in most black Christian churches.

A full decade before the turn of the twenty-first century, if the estimate of 6 million Muslims in the United States is reasonably accurate, Islam has become the second largest religion in America, after Protestant and Catholic Christianity. American Judaism with a steadily declining membership is now third. While much of this Islamic growth is independent of the black community, the possibility of a serious impact on the Black Church cannot be peremptorily dismissed. The phenomenon of more black males preferring Islam while more black females adhere to traditional black Christianity is not as bizarre as it sounds. It is already clear that in Islam the historic black church denominations will be faced with a far more serious and more powerful competitor for the souls of black folk than the white churches ever were. When is the question, not whether.

"E Pluribus Unum," Out of Many, One?: The Challenge of Black Ecumenism

The potential power of the Black Church as a social institution has never been fully realized and it probably never will be so long as sectarianism is the norm. However, there have been men and women throughout black history who have dared to dream that out of the denominational pluralism that has characterized the situation of black churches, there might one day arise a unity, and perhaps an organic union and merger, so that the several black churches could speak with one effective voice and move with one unified spirit and singleness of purpose. They have dreamed that these churches could pool their financial, material, and human resources to better serve their people, eliminating the duplication and replication of services such as individual multi-million dollar publishing houses for each denomination. From the very beginnings of the historic black denominations there were serious discussions between black Methodist leaders of Philadelphia-Baltimore and New York City about merging into one denomination. In fact, the New York leaders of the A.M.E. Zion Church did adopt as their official name "the African Methodist Episcopal Church in America" before relationships between the communions degenerated and the word "Zion" was added to differentiate themselves from the Philadelphia-Baltimore Methodist movement that became known as the A.M.E. Church.[25] Throughout the nineteenth and twentieth centuries there have been sporadic efforts at ecumenical merger between various members of the historic black denominations. For example, the National Baptist Convention, U.S.A., Inc., was formed in 1895 through the merger of three Baptist groups, but two schisms in 1915 and in 1961 also produced two new and independent denominations, the National Baptist Convention of America, and the Progressive National Baptist Convention. Another cooperative attempt, the Fraternal Council of Churches which was founded in 1934 by A.M.E. Bishop Reverdy C. Ransom, was active in the 1940s and 1950s.[26] The period of civil rights ferment and black consciousness has also spawned a wide variety of black ecumenical movements such as the Southern Christian Leadership Conference, the National Black Evangelical Association, and the National Conference of Black Churchmen.[27] One of the more successful ventures in black ecumenism was the Interdenominational Theological Center, founded in 1957. ITC represents the cooperative efforts of six denominational bodies, including black Episcopalians and black United Methodists, to provide a common center for theological training by pooling their separate resources and services.

During the decade of the 1980s several other major efforts in black ecumenism have emerged: Partners in Ecumenism (PIE); and the Congress of National Black Churches (CNBC). A merger of three black denominations is planned, consisting of the African Methodist Episcopal Zion Church, the Christian Methodist Episcopal Church and the Union American Methodist Episcopal Church. Both PIE and CNBC were established as ecumenical groups in 1978, although with different purposes and constituencies. Founded under the auspices of the National Council of Churches to promote social change programs through the common efforts of black and white churches, Partners in Ecumenism challenged the NCC and white denominations to be more responsive to black concerns, and provided a platform for progressive black and white clergy. In contrast, the Congress of National Black Churches, which began with a membership restricted to black denominations with a national constituency, is concerned with social and economic programs that promote institution building in black communities through such programs as collective purchasing, banking, insurance, and communications.[28] Plans call for a cooperative publishing house adequate to meet the printing and publishing needs of member denominations and secular black writers. The congress also sponsors a large-scale social program called Project Spirit which attempts to relate black churches, families, and children in after-school programs focused on developing self-esteem among the children in an enriched cultural ethos in Atlanta, Indianapolis, and Oakland.

The planned merger of the C.M.E. Church, the A.M.E. Zion Church, and the U.A.M.E. Church may be completed by the early 1990s, thereby strengthening historic black Methodism at a time when membership in some of the churches involved is beginning to decline. Merger may help to resolve some problems common to black churches such as an aging clergy, dwindling financial resources, inefficient use of duplicated church properties and personnel. However, church mergers are among the most complicated of human endeavors, and the restructuring of ecclesiastical entities seem to founder more often than they succeed. Human interests vested in positions of power and leadership must be resolved once the doctrinal and ritual preferences have been resolved. Traditions are not readily relinquished, even in the face of the obvious, and emotions sometimes speak with more authority than either reason or practicality.[29] Nevertheless, the planned merger of these three black Methodist denominations has heightened speculations about the possibility of their merger with the A.M.E. Church at some time in the future, and of the possibility that the black Baptist denominations may also consider reunion with each other. The split between the National Baptist Convention, U.S.A., Inc., and the Progressive National Baptist Convention is fairly recent and probably not irreparable, though the divisions of separation between the two older Baptist conventions have had more time to harden. But the hopes among some black and white Christians that the Black Church will eventually merge itself into mainline white Christianity seem increasingly unrealistic as these racial communions seem more and more resigned to the realities of religious separation in a society where secular separation remains the ideological norm.

As the United States moves into the technological space age of the twenty-first century, the collective efforts of black ecumenical groups will become increasingly important both to preserve their religious and cultural integrity and to oppose the subtle manipulations of an information society.

The Problems Facing the Black Church: The Black Clergy Perspective

We turn now to the views of the black clergy who were asked what they considered to be the most important problem facing black churches. Table 40 presents the results of clergy's responses. However, since only 57 percent (1,218) of the clergy responded, out of a total 2,150, the results need to be interpreted with caution. As table 40 shows, 472 (22.0 percent) of the clergy interviewed felt that the leading problem facing the Black Church was the "lack of evangelism in fulfilling its religious role" (failure to proclaim the gospel, or not being a true Christian); 251 (11.7 percent) claimed that "secularization—loss of respect for the church, and dwindling membership" was a major problem; while 123 (5.7 percent) said "Sin." 108 (5.0 percent) of the clergy felt that the lack of adequate finances was a major problem of their churches; 103 (4.8 percent) said that their church's leadership or denominational hierarchy was at the core of the Black Church's problems; only sixty-two (2.9 percent) saw the Black Church's major problem stemming from an "uneducated or untrained clergy"; and fifty-one (2.4 percent) claimed that the major problem concerned "problems with young people—loss of young

Table 40:   Clergy Views of the Church's Major Problem

Q. What do you consider to be the church's major problem today?

Major Problem	Number	Percent
Sin	123	5.7
Lack of evangelism in fulfilling its religious role (failure to proclaim the gospel, not being a true Christian, etc.)	472	22.0
Secularization (loss of respect for church, dwindling membership, etc.)	251	11.7
Problems with young people (loss of young people due to dominating elders, loss of interest, etc.)	51	2.4
Criticisms of church's leadership	103	4.8
An uneducated or untrained clergy	62	2.9
Lack of adequate finances	108	5.0
Racism in the larger society	9	0.4
Social conditions and the problems of black people	39	1.8
No response	932	43.3

$N=2,150$

people due to domination by elders, loss of interest, etc." Much of the clergy's perceptions tended to focus on problems internal to their churches rather than on the larger society. For example, only thirty-nine (1.8 percent) considered that the major problem of the Black Church was the "social conditions and problems of black people," and even fewer, nine (0.4 percent), said "racism in the larger society" was what they felt as the church's major problem.

A few clergy elaborated in open-ended interviews on what they saw as some of the major problems facing the Black Church. Rev. Dr. Thomas Kilgore, former president of the Progressive National Baptist Convention, pastor, theologian, and a college chaplain at the University of Southern California, commented at length:

> I see rough days ahead for the Black Church because of the following: (1) Selfish expectations of black preachers [what he called "the anniversary syndrome," of preachers wanting to receive money for whatever they did for people]. (2) Failure of the

Black Church [as a whole] to work for the renewal of the Black family. (3) Church leaders and pastors who are always seeking ways of raising money instead of just being good stewards. (4) Failure to understand the importance of supporting the educational institutions. Another would include poor planning in evangelism.[30]

While Kilgore did not see these problems as fatal ones to the life of the Black Church, he did feel that they were some of the major issues which black churches and clergy had to deal with if they were going to move in a more progressive direction in the future.

A Baptist pastor of a rural church in Mississippi said, "The need in the rural areas is to have only one pastor be shepherd and steward to one local congregation. So that instead of having one man pastor 3 or 4 churches, [let him] pastor only one church, to give specialized attention to that one congregation."[31]

An A.M.E. pastor in North Carolina argued for the need for a more comprehensive perspective: "I believe the primary problem facing the church today is the struggle to hammer out a course of action. A theological and philosophical outlook that will reflect a guidance toward the future liberation it projects."[32]

Finally, one pastor spoke about the constant need to be reminded about the rich, historic legacy of the Black Church in the black experience: "The church has many critics but no rivals in what it has meant in the life of the people—in saving and developing them. Without the Black Church, black leadership and black organization would hardly have developed. Especially as a positive influence in the black experience, black consciousness would have been devoid of real hope and black life would have been completely dehumanized. The Black Church is the biggest happening in the black experience in the United States of America."[33]

These brief quotes and the survey results from the clergy interviewed give an indication of what black clergy perceived to be some of the major problems and issues that confront them and their churches.

As we mentioned at the beginning of this chapter, black churches remain strong and viable institutions and they still constitute the central institutional sector of most black communities. Nevertheless, this does not obscure the fact that there are major challenges and problems confronting these churches. The most serious one concerns the growing class divide between the coping sector of middle income blacks and the working poor, and the crisis sector of the dependent poor. Moreover, the resources and ingenuity of the Black Church and its leadership will be taxed increasingly to reach the growing segments of the unchurched among the recently educated black middle class as well as the urban poor. The Black Church, on the whole, is thriving, but it cannot rest on its laurels because of these concerns, nor must it underestimate the Islamic challenge on the horizon. Islam is a proven universal religion that is undergoing a worldwide fundamentalist resurgence and the Muslims in black communities have proven themselves to be highly motivated evangelists.

On the other hand, some black churches have also demonstrated a capacity to sustain extraordinary growth. The neo-Pentecostal movement that is influencing some black denominations like the A.M.E. Church has combined the deep spirituality of traditional black Pentecostalism with a highly educated clergy and sophisticated social ministries. In the twentieth century the Church of God in Christ has shown the most rapid growth among all of the historic black denominations, clearly attesting to the power of the Pentecostal thrust. If the neo-Pentecostal movement continues to surge through the black denominations, close to half of all black Christians in the twenty-first century may reflect its impact.

In the latter half of the twentieth century the historical black denominations have found that black ecumenical efforts, either in the form of cooperative social, political, and economic projects between denominations, or in the merger of several black denominations, are one of the best means to deal with a complex and modern technological society. The complicated and highly institutionalized nature of racism in American society requires collective resources and efforts.

The Black Church has always been a spiritual refuge with a social consciousness which has at some times and places been more pronounced than at others. While this unevenness exasperates those who have a one dimensional perspective of the Black Church, its genius is that it recognizes human beings as both spirit and body with a duality of needs which must be addressed, because both are constantly at risk in American society. Effective mission is the ability to determine where the emphasis should be placed in the light of existing realities. Contemporary needs are both deeply spiritual and agonizingly physical, and the resultant burden of the Black Church has never been more critical or more challenging.

The church is moving to address these needs, not with perfect symmetry, but with persistence. The Black Church is, after all, no more and no less than the black people who comprise it, and it mirrors the imagination, the interest, and the sense of urgency of the black community it serves and symbolizes.

Today's Black Church is struggling for relevance in the resolution of today's black problems: racism; drug abuse; child care; health and welfare; housing; counseling; unemployment; teenage pregnancy; the false securities of conspicuous consumption; and the whole tragic malaise with which society in general is burdened. It must address all these social challenges without abandoning its distinctive mandate to assist human beings in their efforts to find conciliation and comfort with their Creator. There is no moratorium on the human need for spiritual and moral nurture.

A Concluding Unscientific Postscript: Policy Recommendations for the Black Church

While it would be presumptive to try to determine for the churches involved the implications of the findings of this study, certain realities do suggest themselves to the authors as having significance for the future of the Black Church in America.

After delving into the scholarly literature on the history, sociology, and demographics of black churches and black communities, and after traveling thousands of miles, crisscrossing the United States in pursuit of interviews with black clergy in rural and urban churches, large and small, the sense of the spiritual and cultural munificence with which the Black Church has endowed the lives and experiences of black people, past and present, is inescapable. Black churches are not perfect institutions but with all their limitations they represent the institutionalized staying power of a human community that has been under siege for close to four hundred years. Black personalities, movements, and ideologies have waxed and waned over the years, and will continue to do so, but black churches have remained a firm anchor stabilizing the black experience and giving it meaning through the uncertain eras of change and counter-change. Nevertheless, there are areas of proper concern for the Black Church, just as there are for any prudent institution that cares about a future of service and relevance. Some conclusions we reached have already been suggested by other researchers, and their consideration is already on the agenda of some churches. Others are not as obvious and probably require a kind of self-study or inventory by the churches themselves before the full impact of existing or portending problems can be assessed. Here are some suggestions:

The Need for a Better-Trained and Better-Educated Clergy

If we were asked to make a single policy recommendation that we consider critical for the future of black churches, it would be the need for more, better-trained, and better-educated black clergy. Although this need has been raised before by Woodson, Mays and Nicholson, and countless other denominational leaders, seminary presidents, and professors, there is but meager evidence that it has been taken seriously by the Black Church as a whole. The short-run prognosis of the needs of the Black Church from the perspectives of the powers in control was geared consciously or unconsciously to a cultural and educational ceiling in the black community that has since been shattered. Our survey and field experiences indicate quite clearly that the most creative and innovative forms of ministry in black communities today are being carried out by the better-educated clergy at the large urban black churches.[34] However, even if size were held constant, the better-educated clergy tend to be more resourceful in serving smaller urban churches or even rural ones. They are also more aware of both the internal needs of their congregations, as well as the external needs in their surrounding communities. While we recognize that formal seminary education is not a panacea for all the ills of black churches, or for society, the time when the unlettered preacher could build a large congregation by sheer dint of energy and determination is rapidly passing. Increasing levels of education among black people will need to be met by their intellectual peers in the ministry. As we mentioned in chapter 1, the ideal black preachers are able to combine the best formal education with the best of the black religious tradition.

The ministry of the Black Church is the *only* profession where only one out of every four or five practitioners has graduated from professional school. Professional education could help enhance the skills and effectiveness of black clergy not only in the areas of spiritual nurture, theological understanding, biblical interpretation, preaching, and counseling, but also in financial accountability and economic development, record keeping, and political awareness and moral responsibility. In an age of increasing specialization and the development of technical expertise, the ministry remains one of the few professions for generalists, those much needed people who attempt to relate to the whole spectrum of human needs in the interests of a broader and deeper humanity. Once again, the inherent genius of the Black Church is its holistic ministry that seeks to encompass all of life because human beings are not only spiritual, but also physical and social creatures.

The evangelical traditions of the past which set the norm for the emergent black denominations only required evidence of a sincere call from God to the ministry. A prudent policy for the future would add professional education and a full-time clergy to that norm. The inherent fractures of life in the black community will increasingly require full-time attention from professionals fully prepared to give counsel, leadership, and succor in an era in which the traditional reservoir of humanitarian concern are increasingly depleted.

Improved Benefits for Black Clergy

As we have indicated in our profiles of urban and rural black clergy, the benefits offered to the majority of them are either minimal or nonexistent. Their counterparts in the white mainstream denominations can usually expect a parsonage or housing allowance, some form of travel allowance, and almost always health and pension benefits. While the black Methodists (A.M.E., A.M.E. Zion, C.M.E.) do much better on the whole than the norm for the Black Church, a common or unified health and pension system sponsored by all the black denominations would be beneficial both for individual clergy and black ecumenical efforts. At the very minimum, every black clergy ought to have the security of some health and pension benefits. It would help to relieve some of the anxiety and economic pressures that some aging black clerics feel that keeps many of them in their pulpits in declining effectiveness and long past reasonable retirement age to make ends meet. Further, it should be easier to unite the black denominations around some basic needs such as health and pension benefits, posing no threat to creedal differences and beliefs. Some of the younger black clergy we met in the field have joined white denominations because they felt that the security and benefits were essential to an effective ministry. As the black denominations confront the coming problem of finding leadership for their churches, the issue of benefits will take on compelling significance.

The Problem of Understaffing of Black Churches

In their 1934 study of *The Negro's Church*, Mays and Nicholson were concerned about the problem of overchurching because in their view, there were too many churches in urban and rural black communities.[35] However, since the 1930s we have come to appreciate the myriad functions that these churches and clergy perform, providing for spiritual and counseling needs, as well as dealing with some of the social problems that exist. Nevertheless, a major problem for the future will almost certainly have to do with the insufficiency of clerical supply to meet the needs of the existing churches. There is an aging clergy in both urban and rural churches with a median age of fifty-two years, which means that about half of the clergy nationwide are at or above that age. In the early years of the twenty-first century when most of these clergy have either retired or reached retirement age, many churches in the mainline black denominations will begin to experience chronic problems in supplying their pulpits. Our interviews in the field indicated that the ministry as a choice of profession among younger and more talented black people is diminishing as career options in law, medicine, and business proliferate. If this trend continues, probably as it will, some urban black churches will have to resort to the itinerant and absentee ministry of their rural counterparts.

Fortunately, there has been an increased interest in the ministry among black women, and the decade of the 1980s has shown the largest and most dramatic increases in black women seminarians in major divinity schools. Black women are stepping forward to offer their participation in the leadership of the most historic and most independent institution in the black community, an institution in which their membership is traditionally double that of their male counterparts. The black churches may do well to be instructed by the experience of certain mainline white denominations which have already been traumatized by the failure to prepare adequately for the acceptance of women in the clergy. If the present denominations are unwilling or unable to make room for a future that includes women in positions of clerical leadership, then they should prepare for the development of counterpart schismatic organizations which will. The black Methodists have shown considerably more flexibility than the Black Church at large in its reception of women clergy at entry level. But even more flexibility will be needed if women are to be routinely appointed to pulpits in keeping with their credentials, experience, and ability, and if they are not to be locked out of the higher ecclesiastical and administrative positions like bishop or convention president. For most of the black Baptist denominations, and for the Church of God in Christ, the issue of women clergy is particularly worrisome, and its potential for church schism should not be underestimated. But there are no islands that lie safely beyond the shoals of controversy. Black women clergy are a potential resource for helping to alleviate some of the future problems of efficient full-time clerical leadership, a resource the Black Church can ignore only at its peril.

Black Families

The black family is the primary unit of the Black Church. The historic Black Church was a gathering of families and extended families worshiping in a sanctuary they themselves erected, and buried in due course in the churchyard that was already hallowed by the memories of past generations it enshrined. There is a symbiosis between the black family and the church which makes for mutual reinforcement and creates for most black families their initial or primary identity. Probably the most crucial of all concerns is the need to bolster the personal and cultural identity and the self-esteem of black youngsters at all socioeconomic levels. The findings reported in chapter 11 indicate that most of the identity scores on the doll tests involving black children in the 1980s have returned to the low levels observed by Kenneth and Mamie Clark prior to the Supreme Court desegregation decision of 1954. Project Spirit, sponsored by the Congress of National Black Churches, is an attempt to develop self-esteem and cultural identity in afterschool programs in three cities. The project could well be expanded to the mutual benefit of churches, the community, and the children whose identity needs are generally undernourished. Many churches could also influence a positive sense of black identity by the simple stratagem of a more judicious selection of Sunday school literature and other publications. Despite the overabundance of black church publishing houses, very many black churches continue to use materials originating in white denominations which are not necessarily sensitive to the needs of black children.

Above all, cultural identity and self-esteem are affected most significantly by the adult role models provided by black churches, both clerical and lay. In the past when black churches had even fewer economic resources than now, Du Bois found that they were still able to provide significant role models and inspiration for black youth.[36] A related concern is the escalating problems of black teenagers and young adults in the crisis sector of the black community, the dependent poor or underclass. Black teenage females have among the highest pregnancy rates in the world, and black males have the highest homicide and incarceration rates in the United States.[37] There is a continuing debate among social analysts as to whether these social problems are merely symptoms of the need for a structural reform in the American economy, or are indicators of the need for a deeper social revolution to change the pattern of race and class oppression embedded in our capitalistic system.[38] While the long-term strategies for change are still unclear, there are short-term strategies and steps that black churches and denominations can take to help poor black teenagers and young adults toward meaningful survival. The physical and social isolation of poor black communities suggest a need for black churches and other concerned groups to return to the community organizing attempts of the 1960s. High-profile role models, community organizers, street workers, teachers, coaches, recreation leaders, and clergy who are sent specifically to work with black youth and their families could play a significant part in the revitalization of poor communities. Black churches could also establish mission churches, beginning with "house churches" in the apartments of large housing projects or other areas where the poor reside. There is some evidence that poor black young people, when connected to mainstream organizations like churches, youth groups, or athletic teams sponsored by churches, have a better chance of moving out of poverty conditions than those condemned to the anonymity of poverty, or the dubious identity of the street.[39] There are examples of churches that have begun to act on these problems like the Church Connection in Durham, North Carolina, that provides support services for black female teenagers, and the Male Youth Enhancement

Program of the Family Life Center at the Shiloh Baptist Church in Washington, D.C. While a few black churches have undertaken meaningful prison ministries, the vast majority have not. Islamic groups have a far stronger presence in the prisons than black Christian churches in the struggle for the souls and allegiance of poor black men and women. If the Black Church should ask itself why it needs to be reconnected with the hard-core urban black poor, the answer is as simple as it is obvious: one-third of the black population will be responsible for more than half of all black children growing up in the decade of the 1990s. The future of the Black Church in the twenty-first century will depend as much on how it responds to the poor in its midst as to the externals of racism, the abstractions of ecumenism, or the competitive threat of a resurgent Islam. Past tradition has cast the Black Church as the proverbial "rock in a weary land"—the first and the last sure refuge of those who call it home, and all those who live in the shadow of its promises.

Appendix: National Sample for the Black Church in the African American Experience

This appendix will describe the sampling technique used in the nationwide survey of black clergy and black churches of the seven major historical black denominations. As it was reiterated earlier in the profiles of black rural and urban churches, the major obstacle for survey research is that national lists of clergy and churches for these denominations were not available for a representative random sample to be drawn. The representativeness of any sample of black churches, especially for the black Baptist groups, is currently questionable and will remain so, until membership and clergy records are kept. Since black churches are predominantly pastor-centered institutions, with the black clergy having a greater degree of authority than their white counterparts, the survey focused on the pastor as the major bearer of information about black churches.

A regional research strategy was followed, dividing the country into Northeast, South, Midwest, Southwest, and West. After experimenting with mailed questionnaires and telephone survey techniques, we found that the black clergy responded the best and were more cooperative with face-to-face personal interviews, the most costly method. Regional surveys were conducted using personal interviews with clergy who were randomly selected from lists provided by local clergy associations in cities and towns in each region. Our national sample was drawn from regional subsets and constitutes a selected sample of black churches from the historic black denominations. In view of the problems of an unknown universe and a lack of national lists, our basic research strategy was to aim at a large sample size of interviews from different regions of the country. At this point in time we cannot claim a completely representative random national sample; however, we believe that our selected sample is reasonably representative. The only regional bias in the study is due to the fact that our entire sample of 619 churches for the rural phase of the study was done in southern black belt counties.

With the exception of a white A.M.E. female clergy person, all of our interviewers were black and displayed some knowledge of and sensitivity toward black churches. The majority of interviewers were students in

Table A.1: Profile of Black Church Sample

1. Total Church Marginals
Total sample=2,150 churches; 1,894 clergy.
Urban sample=1,531 urban churches (80.8%); 1,531 urban clergy.
Rural sample=619 rural churches (19.2%); 363 rural clergy.

2. Primary Denominational
Affiliation

	Number	Percent
A. Baptists total 1,028 (47.8%)		
NBC, U.S.A., Inc.	630	29.3
NBC, Am., Uninc.	209	9.7
PNBC	189	8.8
B. Methodists total 724 (33.7%)		
A.M.E.	309	14.4
A.M.E. Zion	232	10.8
C.M.E.	183	8.5
C. Pentecostals total 316 (14.7%)		
COGIC	316	14.7
D. Other black churches	68	3.2
No response	14	0.7

divinity schools and colleges. All of them were trained in administering the interview schedule by the field director of the survey. Regional coordinators for major metropolitan areas provided oversight for the interviews, checking to see that the interviews were actually done, and made the necessary contacts with local black clergy associations and bishops in the area. Regional coordinators were either seminary faculty members or senior pastors with graduate training. As mentioned previously, the rural study used the Interdenominational Theological Center in Atlanta as a base.

Interviewers were instructed to make random selections from the lists of clergy provided by the local clergy associations; for example, interview every fifth pastor and to select another name if there was a refusal. Rates of cooperation varied in different regions, with a high of 80 percent in Alabama and a low of 20 percent in the New York metropolitan area. The overall rate of cooperation was about 33 percent. Interviewers were asked to inspect the church records when they were available. The field director also made random callbacks and site visits to check on the accuracy of the interview data. The project also hired two full-time black

Table A.2: Estimated Distribution of Black Church Membership in 1989

Church Denomination	Number in Millions	Percent
African Methodist Episcopal	2.2	9.3
African Methodist Episcopal Zion	1.2	5.1
Christian Methodist Episcopal	0.9	3.8
Church of God in Christ	3.7	15.6
National Baptist Convention, U.S.A., Inc.	7.5	31.6
National Baptist Convention of America	2.4	10.1
Progressive National Baptist Convention	1.2	5.1
Smaller black communions	1.4	5.9
Predominantly white Protestant groups	1.2	5.1
Roman Catholic*	2	8.4
Total	23.7	100

Sources: Figures for the seven largest denominations were obtained from executives and published reports of the respective denominations. These figures are estimates for 1989. Updated sources for other categories are James S. Tinney, "Selected Directory of Afro-American Religious Organizations, Schools, and Periodicals," 1977; "The Black Church in America," *Dollars and Sense*, June/July 1981.

*The Roman Catholic figure is from the *New York Times*, July 15, 1989, and the Gallup survey. Since 1985 black Roman Catholics have been among the fastest growing religious groups, largely due to the influx of Haitians and other black people from the Caribbean region. Upwardly mobile African Americans have been attracted to parochial school education as a result of the problems of urban public school systems.

researchers who did interviews nationally and helped to fill the gaps in denominational quotas in each region.

Pre-testing for the field questionnaires began in 1978 and the field study took five years to complete. Aspects of the study were updated by two in-house field studies done for the black Methodist denominations in 1985 and 1986. In table A.1 a profile of our Black Church sample is presented. A breakdown of the primary denominational affiliation of our sample can be compared with the estimates of total Black Church membership in table A.2. This comparison indicates that in our national selected sample, we oversampled the black Methodist denominations by about 15 percent. The oversampling was partly due to the fact that each denomination is very strong in a particular state. For example, the A.M.E. Church has its largest following in South Carolina, the A.M.E. Zion Church in North Carolina, and the C.M.E. Church in Tennessee. Methodist clergy also tended to be more cooperative in their willingness to be interviewed. The oversampling, however, did not add significant bias to the sample.

The following is a listing by states and counties of the metropolitan and nonmetropolitan areas covered by our national sample. The Southern Regional Council's definition of "rural" as consisting of a standard metropolitan statistical area of under fifty thousand population was used, as well as demographic maps of the southern black belt counties produced by the council. Cities with the largest black populations were given priority in each regional area, then smaller cities with a sizable proportion of black people were added to cover different types of metropolitan areas.

Metropolitan Areas Covered in Urban Sample

Northeast

New York State: New York, New York (Manhattan); Kings County (Brooklyn); Bronx County (Bronx); Queens County (Queens); Richmond (Staten Island); Eastchester (Mount Vernon, Yonkers); Nassau; Suffolk; Westchester.

New Jersey: Essex County (Newark, Orange, and East Orange); Hudson County (Jersey City and Hoboken).

Pennsylvania: Philadelphia County (city of Philadelphia); Delaware County; Chester County; Montgomery County; Bucks County.

South

Georgia: DeKalb and Fulton counties (Atlanta); Macon County (city of Macon); Muscogee County (city of Columbus).

Tennessee: Hamilton County (city of Chattanooga); Shelby County (city of Memphis).

Virginia: Norfolk County (city of Norfolk); Portsmouth County (city of Portsmouth).

North Carolina: Durham County (city of Durham); Wake County (city of Raleigh).

South Carolina: Charleston County (city of Charleston); Richland County (city of Columbia).

Alabama: Etowah County (city of Gadsden); Jefferson County (city of Birmingham); Montgomery County (city of Montgomery).

Mississippi: Hinds County (city of Jackson); Washington County (city of Greenville).

Southwest

Texas: Dallas County (city of Dallas); Houston County (city of Houston).

Midwest

Illinois: Cook County (city of Chicago, also Evanston); DuPage County; Will County.

Michigan: Wayne County (city of Detroit); Oakland County; Macomb County.

Missouri: Cass County; Clay County (Kansas City); Jackson County (Kansas City; Johnson County; Lafayette County; Platte County; St. Louis and St. Charles counties (city of St. Louis).

Kansas: Wyandotte County (Kansas City, Kansas); Johnson County; Leavenworth County.

West

California: Los Angeles County (city of Los Angeles); Ventura County; San Francisco County (city of San Francisco); Alameda County (cities of Oakland and Hayward); Contra Costa County (cities of Richmond and Berkeley).

Nonmetropolitan Areas Covered by the Rural Sample

Georgia counties: Baker; Bibb; Calhoun; Clay; Dooly; Early; Peach; Pulaski; Randolph; Stewart; Sumpter; Terrell; Twiggs; and Wilkes.

North Carolina counties: Bladen; Burke; Chatham; Columbus; Hoke; Robeson; Sampson; and Warren.

South Carolina counties: Abbeville; Allendale; Berkeley; Calhoun; Clarendon; Fairfield; Lee; Orangeburg; Sumter; and Williamsburg.

Virginia counties: Southampton and Sussex.

Florida counties: Gadsden; Jefferson; and Leon.

Alabama counties: Autauga; Bullock; Chambers; Coosa; Dallas; Greene; Lowendes; Russell; and Wilcox.

Mississippi counties: Bolivar; Claiborne; Coahoma; Copiah; Holmes; Jefferson; Madison; Sharkey; Sunflower; and Yazoo.

Notes

1 The Religious Dimension

1. See the following as examples: W. E. B. Du Bois, editor, *The Negro Church*; Carter G. Woodson, *The History of the Negro Church*; Benjamin Mays and Joseph Nicholson, *The Negro's Church*; and E. Franklin Frazier and C. Eric Lincoln, *The Negro Church in America: The Black Church Since Frazier*. Lincoln was one of the first scholars to note that the change in terminology was not merely nominal but it reflected a deeper change in attitudes among the black population.

2. The term "Greater Black Church" can be used to encompass both the historic black denominations and the predominantly black congregations in white denominations.

3. Roof and McKinney estimate that "roughly 85 percent of all black Protestant memberships are in the black denominations," which includes only six of the seven we have listed. Like most analysts of black churches, they have excluded the Church of God in Christ. They also estimate that most of the white denominations have a small proportion of black members, about 2 to 3 percent black membership is the typical pattern. See Wade Clark Roof and William McKinney, *American Mainline Religion: Its Changing Shape and Future*, pp. 140–41. For the derivation of our estimate of more than 80 percent of black Christians in the seven historic black denominations, see the appendix. The 80 percent figure is also given in the estimates of black membership in the seven historic black denominations in the special issue on "The Black Church in America," "Church Denominations," in *Dollars and Sense* 7 (1981), no. 2, edited by Donald C. Walker. Their estimates were made by U.S. Census Bureau statistician John Raye.

4. Charles H. Long has made a number of forays in an attempt to construct a general phenomenology of black religion based on the history of religions approach. He is correct in his perception that most U.S. scholars of black religion tend to delimit their analyses within Christian boundaries. For the general theoretical outlines of his religious hermeneutic, see Long's *Significations: Signs, Symbols, and Images in the Interpretation of Religion*. For a general typology of black religious institutions, see Hans Baer and Merrill Singer, "Toward a Typology of Black Sectarian Response to Racial Stratification," *Anthropological Quarterly* 54 (1981): 1–14.

5. For the classic definition of the sacred or the holy in the study of religion see Rudolf Otto, *The Idea of the Holy.*

6. In *The Sacred Canopy*, Peter L. Berger provided the theoretical basis for a social analysis of sacred cosmologies. Mechal Sobel was one of the first scholars to successfully examine the process of creating sacred cosmologies in the West African tradition, in slave religion, and in the creation of an Afro-Baptist faith. See Sobel's *Trabelin' On: The Slave Journey to an Afro-Baptist Faith.*

7. See Emile Durkheim, *The Elementary Forms of the Religious Life.* For Durkheim's elaboration on the influence of social processes upon hermeneutics and cultural interpretation, see Emile Durkheim and Marcel Mauss, *Primitive Classification.*

8. A good sociological analysis of the process of creating worldviews is found in Peter L. Berger and Thomas Luckmann, *The Social Construction of Reality: A Treatise in the Sociology of Knowledge.* The historical work of Melville Herskovits, John Blassingame, Eugene Genovese, Herbert Gutman, and Albert Raboteau are a few examples of the recent trend in scholarship which recognized that black slaves were not merely robots responding to the demands of the slave system, but they were also active creators of their own forms of culture and worldview.

9. Examples of this view are found in the works of E. Franklin Frazier and Gunnar Myrdal. See the "Assimilation" and "Compensatory" models of the Black Church in section 3 of this chapter.

10. Nathan Glazer and Daniel Patrick Moynihan, *Beyond the Melting Pot,* p. 51.

11. For the tenacity of residential and educational segregation, see the studies by Gary Orfield, *Public School Desegregation in the United States 1968–1980;* and Gary Orfield and William Taylor, *Racial Segregation: Two Policy Views.*

12. As scholars like Melville Herskovits have pointed out, more of African culture survived in the Caribbean and Latin American countries like Brazil than in the United States. See Melville J. Herskovits, *The Myth of the Negro Past.* For an overview of the influences of African religious traditions in the New World, see George Eaton Simpson, *Black Religions in the New World.*

13. See the following: Henry H. Mitchell, *Black Belief: Folk Beliefs of Blacks in America and West Africa;* James Cone, *A Black Theology of Liberation;* and Gayraud Wilmore, *Black Religion and Black Radicalism: An Interpretation of the Religious History of Afro-American People.* Also see Theo Witvliet, *The Way of the Black Messiah.*

14. See Wilmore, *Black Religion and Black Radicalism,* pp. 75–78.

15. See the ending of Dr. King's "I Have a Dream" speech in James M. Washington, editor, *A Testament of Hope: The Essential Writings of Martin Luther King, Jr.,* p. 220. For an attempt to construct a black theology of freedom, see Long, *Significations,* chapters 9–12. For Long, freedom is a fundamental construct of both the human condition and religion.

16. See W. E. B. Du Bois, *The Souls of Black Folk*, p. 211.

17. Sobel, *Trabelin' On*, p. 107.

18. Ibid., p. 108.

19. Ibid., p. 109.

20. One example of this is the formation of caucuses of black priests, nuns, and bishops who are attempting to include more of their Afro-Christian heritage in their services. See the issue on "The Black Catholic Experience," in *U.S. Catholic Historian* 6 (1986), no. 1.

21. Tillich's theology of culture involved a dialectical relationship between religion and culture. His broad definition of religion as "ultimate concern" or "ultimate value" makes it possible to see how religion sacralizes the central values of a culture or a group of people. In Tillich's view of Christianity, however, he also provided for the possibility of religion transcending culture and providing a critique of it in his notion of the "protestant principle." For a general summary of Tillich's view of religion and culture, see James Luther Adams, *Paul Tillich's Philosophy of Culture, Science, and Religion*. For the self-transcendence of the Spirit, see Paul Tillich, *Systematic Theology*, 3:50–98.

22. Much of the discussion and debate about American civil religion and the religious quality of political nationalism have tended to miss this point.

23. For examples, see Lawrence H. Mamiya and C. Eric Lincoln, "Black Militant and Separatist Movements," in the *Encyclopedia of the American Religious Experience*, 2:755–71.

24. In the sphere of black music, one example of the attempt to impose rigid sacred/secular distinctions is found in work of LeRoi Jones (Amiri Baraka), *Blues People: Negro Music in White America.* For example, Jones traces the origins of the blues to the "secular" work songs and field hollers of the slaves, instead of what he calls their "sacred" Afro-Christian music. Clearly the distinctions represent Jones's own modern divisions rather than those of the slaves. Charles Keil in *Urban Blues*, pp. 32–41, has criticized Jones for failing to see the interactive and dialectical nature of black music, the constant interchanges between spirituals, gospel, blues, and jazz. Keil has argued that Jones seems to feel that gospel and blues are worlds apart; consequently, he (Jones) has missed the important role of storefront churches in the development of the blues tradition since so many blues musicians received their musical training in these churches. The musicians often move back and forth between church and nightclub. Scholars of black music have often missed the "mutual malleability" of that music and the "flexibility of African cultural systems."

25. See the following: Du Bois, editor, *The Negro Church*; Woodson, *The History of the Negro Church*; Frazier and Lincoln, *The Negro Church in America*; Albert Raboteau, *Slave Religion: The "Invisible Institution" in the Antebellum South*; and John Blassingame, *The Slave Community: Plantation Life in the Antebellum South.*

26. Frazier, *The Negro Church in America*, p. 23ff. Also see Raboteau, *Slave Religion*.

27. W. E. B. Du Bois, *Economic Cooperation Among Negro Americans*, p. 54.

28. For a more extensive list of these early black churches, see Edward D. Smith, *Climbing Jacob's Ladder: The Rise of Black Churches in Eastern American Cities, 1740–1877*, chapters 2, 3.

29. Talcott Parson's structural-functionalist analysis of modern society into separate spheres underlies the view of complete differentiation. For the effects of this process on religion, see Robert Bellah, *Beyond Belief: Essays on Religion in a Post-traditional World*; Thomas Luckmann, *The Invisible Religion*; and Berger, *The Sacred Canopy*.

30. For the dynamic interplay between black musical styles and their historical development, see Eileen Southern, *The Music of Black Americans: A History*. See Southern's brief description of Dorsey, pp. 402–4.

31. Hart M. Nelsen and Anne Kusener Nelsen, *Black Church in the Sixties*, pp. 8–13.

32. Although the Nelsens have combined their first model as the "assimilation-isolation model," we have separated them into two models to clarify their different sources. Frazier and Lincoln, *The Negro Church in America*, pp. 78–81, 85–86.

33. Anthony M. Orum, "A Reappraisal of the Social and Political Participation of Negroes," *American Journal of Sociology* 72 (July 1966): 33. Charles E. Silberman, *Crisis in Black and White*, p. 144.

34. St. Clair Drake and Horace Cayton, *Black Metropolis: A Study of Negro Life in the North*, 2:424. Gunnar Myrdal, *An American Dilemma: The Negro Problem and Modern Democracy*, p. 928.

35. Nelsen and Nelsen, *Black Church in the Sixties*, pp. 11–13.

36. These six main pairs of polar opposites are derived from some of the usual typologies used in the sociology of religion and from past studies of black churches which tend to overemphasize one pole of a dialectic, e.g., other-worldly.

37. John Brown was one of the few whites to advocate the overthrow of the slave system via violent means; he also was a mystic like Nat Turner. See Wilmore's account in his chapter, "Three Generals in the Lord's Army," in *Black Religion and Black Radicalism*. Also see Wilmore's fine analysis of the tradition of eschatology in black religion in his *Last Things First*.

38. See John Mbiti, *African Religions and Philosophy*; and Ali Mazrui, *The Africans: A Triple Heritage*. For the development of oral tradition among Afro-Americans, see Lawrence Levine, *Black Culture and Black Consciousness*.

39. See Manning Marable, *How Capitalism Underdeveloped Black America*, p. 26.

40. For a sociological elaboration of the idea of "mediating structures" in

society, see Peter L. Berger and John Richard Neuhaus, *To Empower People: The Role of Mediating Structures in Public Policy.*

41. Alex Haley's story of his grandfather several generations removed, Kunta Kinte, is a poignant example of the themes of accommodation and resistance on an individual level. Although he always attempted to escape bondage but never succeeded, Kunta Kinte's masters attempted to force him to take the name Toby. Even though he finally acquiesced to the name while he was being brutally whipped, Kunta Kinte never gave in spiritually; he resisted being "Toby-ized." See Alex Haley, *Roots: The Saga of an American Family.* We are also indebted to Rev. Calvin Butts of the Abyssinian Baptist Church for coining the term "Toby-ize."

42. The "church-sect" typology, which is usually used in the study of black churches, has been omitted from this list because of its conservative tendency of emphasizing the inhibition of social change. The prophetic dimension tends to be left out. For a more elaborate critique, see Nelsen and Nelsen, *Black Church in the Sixties*, pp. 2–5.

43. Wilmore, *Black Religion and Black Radicalism.*

44. Marable, *How Capitalism Underdeveloped Black America*, chapter 7.

45. See Du Bois's famous elaboration of his phenomenology of Afro-American consciousness in *The Souls of Black Folk*, pp. 45–46. It is significant that this description of "double-consciousness" is found in his essay, "Of Our Spiritual Strivings," indicating what he thought were the ultimate concerns of black people.

46. This view of a "collective double-consciousness" is similar to Durkheim's use of the concept "collective representation."

2   The Black Baptists

1. Miles Mark Fisher, "What is a Negro Baptist?" *The Home Mission College Review* 1 (May 1927), no. 1.

2. James M. Washington, *Frustrated Fellowship: The Black Baptist Quest for Social Power*, chapters 5, 6.

3. James S. Tinney, "Selected Directory of Afro-American Religious Organizations, Schools, and Periodicals," in *The Black Church: A Community Resource*, Dionne J. Jones and William H. Matthews, editors, pp. 168–73. Accurate statistics on black Baptists are particularly difficult to obtain due to the simultaneous affiliations of churches, associations, and state conventions with more than one national convention, resulting in double counting. More recent estimates for the Southern Baptist Convention and American Baptist Churches Convention place black membership at 250,000 and 400,000 respectively, much of which would reflect dual affiliations. See Leroy Fitts, *A History of Black Baptists*, pp. 302, 308. Conversely, many small churches are not affiliated with any convention at all, and so are not included in any reported membership figures.

4. Jacobus Arminius, a Dutch Protestant theologian, modified the harshness of the Calvinistic doctrine of predestination by asserting that human beings have a certain amount of free will in regard to their actions.

5. For the best dating records on early black Baptist churches, see Sobel, *Trabelin' On*, p. 250ff.

6. Scholars like Carter G. Woodson and Mechal Sobel tend to accept the latter dates between 1773 and 1775. However, a field trip to the Silver Bluff Baptist Church by Lincoln and Mamiya found that the cornerstone of the church claims a founding date of 1750. The cornerstone reads "Silver Bluff Baptist Church, Organized 1750, Rev. J. A. Goflin Pastor, Remodeled 1920, Rev. A. W. Vincent Pastor." The discrepancy has not yet been cleared up.

7. Emmett T. Martin and Nellie C. Waring, *History Book of the Springfield Baptist Church, Augusta, Georgia, 1781–1979*.

8. Fisher, "What Is A Negro Baptist?"

9. Ibid.

10. Accounts differ as to when the convention first proposed incorporating and whether the proposal was made in response to the withdrawal of the Publishing Board, or whether it was in response to the threatened withdrawal, or if it helped precipitate the conflict leading to the withdrawal. Leroy Fitts suggests that the convention merely revised its constitution in 1916, and did not technically incorporate until the 1930s. See Fitts, *A History of Black Baptists*, p. 94.

11. The 1989 estimates cited above were obtained from interviews with officials of NBC, U.S.A., Inc.

12. Washington, *Frustrated Fellowship*, pp. 195–96.

13. The names and dates were obtained from officials of NBCA.

14. The 1989 estimates were derived from interviews with officials from NBCA. Figures for the number of churches were arrived at by prorating statistics provided by state conventions and associations reporting in 1982 and cited in the convention's *Official Journal* of 1983. The number of clergy was provided by NBCA officials.

15. See the account given by Charles Hamilton, *The Black Preacher in America*, pp. 159–63. Also see Fitts, *A History of Black Baptists*, pp. 98–105.

16. Fitts, *A History of Black Baptists*, pp. 98–105.

17. Hamilton, *The Black Preacher in America*, p. 125.

18. Charles Butler, "PNBC: A Fellowship of Partners," *The Crisis* 89 (November 1982), no. 9, pp. 44–45. Also see James S. Tinney, "Progressive Baptists," *Christianity Today* (October 9, 1970), pp. 42–43.

19. The 1989 figures cited were estimates derived from interviews with PNBC officials and raise certain questions. For example, such large churches normally would have staffs of several ministers. Apparently only senior pastors are included in this census.

20. The data cited above were obtained from PNBC officials.

21. Distinctions may be made between "Regular" or "District" associa-

tions, which belong to state conventions, and through them to the National Convention, and "General" associations, which belong to the National Convention only, having status comparable to a state convention, but more than a regular district association. A further point of confusion is that a given state may have as many as three or four separate state conventions.

22. "Yearbook of the East Cedar Grove Missionary Baptist Association," held at the Siloam Baptist Church Eighty-Ninth Annual Session, Rougemont, North Carolina, July 4, 5, 1984, p. 22.

23. John Snyder, "The Baptists," *The Crisis* (May 1920), p. 12. The reference to the role of trustees more aptly describes deacons. Particularly in rural areas, where three or four churches were served by one pastor, the power and authority of the head deacon was unquestioned.

24. For the names of the women see Dr. T. J. Jemison's quote in chapter 10, pp. 296–97.

25. Sandy Dwayne Martin, "Black Baptists, Foreign Missions, and African Colonization, 1814–1882," in *Black Americans and the Missionary Movement in Africa*, edited by Sylvia M. Jacobs, p. 64. Also see Leroy Fitts, *Lott Carey, First Black Missionary To Africa.*

26. Quoted in St. Clair Drake, *The Redemption of Africa and Black Religion*, p. 51.

27. Joseph H. Jackson, *A Story of Christian Activism: The History of the National Baptist Convention, U.S.A., Inc.*, p. 41.

28. Ibid., pp. 5–10.

3 The Black Methodists

1. Application for admission into the African Methodist Episcopal Church, in Daniel A. Payne, *History of the African Methodist Episcopal Church*, p. 471.

2. Othal Hawthorne Lakey, *The History of the C.M.E. Church*, pp. 105–8.

3. Harry V. Richardson, *Dark Salvation: The Story of Methodism as It Developed Among Blacks in America*, pp. 79, 84.

4. James S. Tinney, "Selected Directory of Afro-American Religious Organizations, Schools, and Periodicals," pp. 182–87.

5. Richardson, *Dark Salvation*, pp. 294–95, n. 3.

6. Ibid., pp. 284, 295.

7. William J. Walls, *The African Methodist Episcopal Zion Church: Reality of the Black Church*, p. 41.

8. Richardson, *Dark Salvation*, pp. 50–75.

9. Richard Allen, *The Life, Experience and Gospel Labors of the Rt. Rev. Richard Allen*, George A. Singleton, editor, p. 25.

10. Ibid.

11. The term "Society" originally referred to a group of Anglicans in a given geographical area who had adopted John Wesley's "methods." Each

society was divided into two or more "classes," the term for a cadre or cell of
people who met together regularly for prayer and Bible study, each having a
lay "class leader" who monitored the spiritual welfare of the class members.
Eventually, the societies evolved into "congregations" of churches, also referred to as "charges." Today, ministers are still appointed to charges, which
may be either a station (one church) or a circuit (two or more churches,
usually in rural areas). The class structure is retained at least nominally by
all the Methodist denominations, and is enjoying resurgence among some
local churches. The African societies that emerged in this era were not,
however, necessarily Methodist, or even explicitly religious.

12. Allen, *The Life, Experience and Gospel Labors of the Rt. Rev. Richard
Allen*, pp. 24–25.

13. Richardson, *Dark Salvation*, p. 72.

14. Wilmore, *Black Religion and Black Radicalism*, p. 60.

15. Richardson, *Dark Salvation*, pp. 94–95.

16. Charles Spencer Smith, *A History of the African Methodist Episcopal
Church*, p. 501.

17. Howard D. Gregg, *History of the African Methodist Episcopal
Church*. See the sections on Department of Missions and Overseas Work,
pp. 193–205.

18. The 1989 estimates cited above were obtained from A.M.E. Church
officials and it was compared with 1984 data from the report, "A Summary of
the Results of the Committee on Restructure," 1984, A.M.E. Church.

19. The itinerant ministry (more commonly called "traveling" ministry
in the A.M.E. Zion Church) denotes full acceptance in an annual conference
of the church, including eligibility for appointment by a bishop to pastor a
local church. Its origins are in the system devised by Wesley in which
traveling preachers went from town to town to preach to societies before
there were established churches and a separate Methodist Episcopal denomination. To be excluded from the itinerancy meant that blacks were not
in "full connection" with the church and could only preach in a local church
under the supervision of a white pastor. Additionally, not being ordained,
they could not perform important ministerial functions.

20. After Methodist churches per se were established, they retained the
structure of the predecessor societies to the extent of dividing members into
small groups called classes for purposes of spiritual disciplines and fiscal
accountability. Blacks commonly were assigned to separate classes.

21. Walls, *The African Methodist Episcopal Zion Church*, p. 58.

22. "Charge" refers to a local pastoral appointment, which may be either a
station (one church, which holds services every Sunday) or a circuit (two or
more churches, usually in rural areas, holding services every other Sunday or
less). At the time Zion Church and Asbury Church constituted a circuit
charge.

23. Walls, *The African Methodist Episcopal Zion Church*, pp. 49–50.

24. The 1989 data cited above were obtained from A.M.E. Zion Church officials.

25. Hunter D. Farish, *The Circuit Dismounts: A Social History of Southern Methodism*, p. 170.

26. Isaac Lane, *Autobiography of Bishop Isaac Lane, LL.D. With a Short History of the C.M.E. Church in America and of Methodism*. Quoted in Othal Hawthorne Lakey, *The Rise of Colored Methodism*, pp. 68–69.

27. For all quoted materials on the organizing General Conference of the C.M.E. Church, see Richardson, *Dark Salvation*, p. 226ff.

28. Edward W. Wheeler, "Uplifting the Race: The Black Minister in the New South, 1865–1902," p. 49.

29. The 1989 estimates cited above were derived from interviews with C.M.E. officials.

30. Daniel Coker, *Journal of Daniel Coker* (Baltimore: Edward J. Coale and the Maryland Auxiliary Colonization Society, 1820; John D. Toy, Printer), p. 17ff.

31. Ibid., pp. 23, 28, 42, 44. For a summary of A.M.E. Church's conflict with the American Colonization Society, see Lawrence H. Mamiya, "A Social History of the Bethel A.M.E. Church in Baltimore: The House of God and the Struggle for Freedom," to be published in a book on the history of American congregations, edited by James Lewis and James Wind, to be published by the University of Chicago Press in 1991. For an assessment of the impact of black missionary activity in Africa, see Sylvia M. Jacobs, editor, *Black Americans and the Missionary Movement in Africa*.

32. Gregg, *History of the African Methodist Episcopal Church*, pp. 193–205.

33. Lakey, *The History of the C.M.E. Church*, pp. 573–77.

4   The Black Pentecostals

1. Bishop James Oglethorpe Patterson (presiding bishop), and Bishop German R. Ross (general secretary), eds., *Church of God in Christ International Directory*.

2. Tinney, "Selected Directory of Afro-American Religious Organizations, Schools, and Periodicals," pp. 188–215.

3. Catherine L. Albanese, *America: Religion and Religions*, pp. 105–6; 126–27; 232–33.

4. James S. Tinney, "Black Origins of the Pentecostal Movement," *Christianity Today* (October 8, 1971).

5. James S. Tinney, "Black Pentecostals: The Difference Is More Than Color," *Logos* 2 (May/June 1980), pp. 16–19.

6. The outline of this biographical sketch is derived from the account given by Bishop Mason's second child, Mary Mason, which is found in *History and Formative Years of the Church of God in Christ with Excerpts from*

the *Life and Works of Its Founder—Bishop C. H. Mason*, reproduced by James Oglethorpe Patterson, German R. Ross, and Julia Mason Atkins, editors.

7. The summary of Bishop Mason and the building of the first church were derived from oral history interviews by Lawrence Mamiya and Larry Murphy with Mrs. Marguerite Walton and Mrs. Olivia L. Martin and other older members of the St. Paul Church of God in Christ, August 12, 1982 in Lexington, Mississippi. Mrs. Martin also wrote a sketch of the early history. Dr. Larry Murphy of the Garrett-Evangelical Theological Seminary provided technical assistance with video and tape recordings.

8. Patterson, Ross, and Atkins, editors, *History and Formative Years*, p. 63.

9. Ibid., p. 19. Also see Anqunett Fusilier, editor, "The Divine Origins of the Church of God in Christ," *The Cornerstone* (1985), pp. 32–33.

10. Ibid.

11. Ibid.

12. Nelsen and Nelsen, *Black Church in the Sixties*, pp. 22–23.

13. See the account given by Vincent Synan, *The Holiness-Pentecostal Movement in the United States*, chapters 5, 8.

14. Mary Mangum Johnson assisted by Inez Cole Barber, *The Life and Works of Mother Mary Mangum Johnson: Founder of the Church of God in Christ in the State of Michigan*, p. 14. (Mother Johnson died in 1935 at the age of 90.) The authors acknowledge and thank COGIC Bishop Ithiel Clemmons of Brooklyn, N.Y., for making this rare booklet available to them. Bishop Clemmons and Bishop German Ross, general secretary of COGIC, were consultants to the research project on the Church of God in Christ.

15. Fusilier, "The Divine Origins of the Church of God in Christ," p. 33.

16. Patterson, Ross, and Atkins, *History and Formative Years*, pp. 77–81. In Weberian terms, the Church of God in Christ had passed from its initial charismatic phase to the routinization of charisma and the beginnings of its bureaucratic phase.

17. The background information on Bishop Patterson is summarized from Frances Burnett Kelly and German R. Ross, *Here Am I, Send Me*.

18. Reported 1989 estimates were derived from interviews with COGIC officials.

19. Elder C. F. Range, Jr., Elder Clyde Young, Bishop German R. Ross, and Dr. Roy L. H. Winbush, editorial commission, *Official Manual with the Doctrines and Disciplines of the Church of God in Christ*, pp. 130–31.

20. Ibid., p. 130.

21. Ibid., pp. 4–19.

22. Ibid., pp. 17–20.

23. Ibid., pp. 20–27.

24. The bookstore at the Church of God in Christ headquarters in Memphis sold the following guide on church nursing that was produced by the NBCA: Ruby G. Lockridge, *A Guide for Church Nursing*.

25. Dovie Marie Simmons and Olivia L. Martin, *Down Behind the Sun: The Story of Arenia Conelia Mallory.*

26. For some of the recent studies on independent African churches, see the following: Sheila S. Walker, *The Religious Revolution in the Ivory Coast: The Prophet Harris and the Harrist Church;* J. Akinyele Omoyajowo, *Cherubim and Seraphim: The History of an Independent African Church;* and Wyatt MacGaffey, *Religion and Society in Central Africa: The Bakongo of Lower Zaire.*

5 Profile of Rural Clergy and Churches

1. See Du Bois, *The Negro Church;* Frazier, *The Negro Church in America;* and Woodson, *The History of the Negro Church.*

2. C. Eric Lincoln, foreword to the first edition of Wilmore, *Black Religion and Black Radicalism,* p. vii.

3. Mays and Nicholson, *The Negro's Church.*

4. The seven historic black denominations included in the study are the African Methodist Episcopal Church, the African Methodist Episcopal Zion Church, the Christian Methodist Episcopal Church, the National Baptist Convention, U.S.A., Inc., the National Baptist Convention of America, Uninc., the Progressive National Baptist Convention, and the Church of God in Christ.

5. The following weighting system was devised to account for rural pastors having more than one church:

If rural church = 1 or 0, clergy weight = 1
"   "   "   = 2,   "   "   = 0.5
"   "   "   = 3,   "   "   = 0.33
"   "   "   = 4,   "   "   = 0.25
"   "   "   = 5,   "   "   = 0.20
"   "   "   = 9,   "   "   = 0.11

Dr. David Roozen of the Institute of Social and Religious Research at the Hartford Theological Seminary did the project's statistical and computer work. However, the authors are completely responsible for any interpretations given to the data.

6. For example, see Ida Rousseau Mukenge, *The Black Church in Urban America: A Case Study in Political Economy;* Arthur Paris, *Black Pentecostalism: Southern Religion in an Urban World;* and Hamilton, *The Black Preacher in America.*

7. Cf. Mays and Nicholson, *The Negro's Church;* Charles Spurgeon Johnson, *Growing Up in the Black Belt: Negro Youth in the Rural South;* Charles Spurgeon Johnson, *Shadow of the Plantation;* Richardson, *Dark Glory;* and Ralph Felton, *Go Down Moses: A Study of 21 Successful Negro Rural Pastors.*

8. We are grateful for the careful monitoring done by Dr. James Shopshire now of Wesley Theological Seminary, a sociologist of religion and one of our regional coordinators, who was based at ITC at the beginning of the study. We also acknowledge the help of Rev. Owen Brooks and the offices of the Delta Ministry in Greenville, Mississippi, during the pretesting phase of the rural study.

9. U.S. Department of Commerce, *The Social and Economic Status of the Black Population in the United States: An Historical View, 1790–1978.* Current Population Reports, Special Studies Series P. 23, No. 80.

10. Daniel M. Johnson and Rex Campbell, *Black Migration in America: A Social Demographic History.*

11. For some literature on the black migrations, see the following: ibid.; Jacqueline Jones, *"To Get Out of This Land of Sufring": Black Migrant Women, Work and Family in Northern Cities, 1900–1930.* Working Paper No. 91; and Marcus E. Jones, *Black Migration in the United States with Emphasis on Selected Central Cities.*

12. Richardson, *Dark Glory,* p. 65.

13. For example, see Ralph Felton's study of positive examples of rural black clergy, *Go Down Moses.*

14. Richardson, *Dark Glory,* pp. 65–66.

15. In their 1933 study, *The Negro's Church,* Mays and Nicholson raise the problem of "overchurching" as the central dilemma for black churches, both urban and rural. While there is the problem of depleting valuable resources in having too many churches, there are some deep cultural and economic reasons for this development. First, America's rigid system of racial exclusion made the job of "preacher" one of the few dignified roles with a large degree of independence and authority. The greater emphasis upon a charismatic personal style in the black community is one of the primary reasons for the origin of new churches. Second, for a long period of time black churches were the only institutions completely controlled by the people. The high degree of personal investment in these churches makes it difficult to give up easily. Third, the variety of churches meet a pluralism of religious and social needs. Fourth, it is doubtful that the Roman Catholic strategy of one large parish church with twenty-five clergy would work in the black community. Decentralized centers seem to work best among the rural proletariat, although some degree of consolidation is desirable and perhaps inevitable.

16. Although the civil rights movement proper began with the organization of the Montgomery bus boycott in December 1955, the 1954 Supreme Court decision in Brown vs. Board of Education provided the legal legitimation for the movement.

17. For the opiate thesis concerning black churches, see Gary Marx, *Protest and Prejudice.* In chapter 8 we deal more extensively with Marx's thesis.

18. Hilton, *The Delta Ministry,* p. 182.

19. For a theoretical typology of the relationship between black religious groups, stratification, and social action, see the article by Baer and Singer, "Toward a Typology of Black Sectarian Response to Racial Stratification."

20. Ralph Felton, *These My Brethren: A Study of 570 Negro Churches and 542 Negro Homes in the Rural South*, pp. 61–62.

21. Richardson, *Dark Glory*, p. 123.

22. Felton, *These My Brethren*, pp. 58–59.

23. It is estimated that between 60–66 percent of the black clergy work at secular jobs to support themselves. The underreporting of income figures is widely known in church circles and any income data should be taken with a grain of salt. In a number of interviews the clergy said that they would only give their church support figures.

24. Richardson, *Dark Glory*, p. 71.

25. U.S. Department of Commerce, *The Social and Economic Status of the Black Population*.

26. Felton, *Go Down Moses*, p. 41.

27. Ibid., pp. 78–79.

28. "Regular church attendance" patterns are different in black and white churches. Although the majority go every Sunday, some black church members attend only on the "first" and "third" Sundays, while others go on the "second" and "fourth." Still others attend once a month. Yet, all of them consider themselves to be "regular churchgoers." Thus far, most surveys of black church attendance have failed to deal adequately with the cultural nuances and assumptions regarding attendance. A careful national study of black church attendance, which needs to be done, can be complex and costly.

29. The revised figures are based on a check of the figures reported by the rural clergy and the financial records kept by the church secretary in 10 percent of the rural churches where such records were available. In 70 percent of the cases the pastor tended to underestimate the income figures he had given. Estimated revisions were based upon our field experience.

30. Mays and Nicholson, *The Negro's Church*, p. 254.

31. These insights are based on field observances and the literature on power relations and schisms in black churches; cf. Mays and Nicholson, *The Negro's Church*, pp. 11–13, 278–98; Hamilton, *The Black Preacher in America*, pp. 19–23; Mukenge, *The Black Church in Urban America*, pp. 125–26; and Melvin D. Williams, *Community in a Black Pentecostal Church: An Anthropological Study*, pp. 58–61.

32. Hamilton, *The Black Preacher in America*, pp. 19–28.

33. Cushing Strout, *The New Heavens and New Earth: Political Religion in America*, p. 106.

34. Mays and Nicholson, *The Negro's Church*, p. 254.

35. Felton, *Go Down Moses*, p. 97.

36. Ibid., p. 96.

37. Frazier and Lincoln, *The Negro Church in America: The Black Church Since Frazier.*

38. Williams, *Community in a Black Pentecostal Church: An Anthropological Study;* Paris, *Black Pentecostalism.*

39. Nelsen and Nelsen, *Black Church in the Sixties.* Also see Mukenge, *The Black Church in Urban America.*

40. Eugene Genovese, *Roll, Jordan, Roll: The World the Slaves Made.* Also see Raboteau, *Slave Religion.*

41. Frazier, *The Negro Church in America.*

42. Wilmore, *Black Religion and Black Radicalism.*

43. U.S. Department of Commerce, *The Social and Economic Status of the Black Population in the United States,* p. 63.

44. The prediction is given in the Glenmary Research Center study, David Dybiec, editor, *Slippin' Away: The Loss of Black Owned Farms.* Also see "Nation's Farms Decrease: Black Farms Nearly Gone," *Jet* 70 (April 7, 1986): 14.

45. In their 1981 study Johnson and Campbell point out that between 1970 and 1975, 238,000 blacks moved outside the South while 302,000 moved to the South with a net gain of 64,000 black population for the South. "The most significant change was the Northeast where for every one migrant to the Northeast, two were moving to the South" (Johnson and Campbell, *Black Migration in America,* p. 170). Data from the National Urban League study of reverse migration indicate that between 1975 and 1980 some 415,000 blacks moved to the South, while only 220,000 left the South for a net gain of 195,000. James D. Williams, editor, *The State of Black America 1984,* p. 172.

46. The title of William Julius Wilson's book, *The Declining Significance of Race,* unfortunately tends to obscure his important thesis of growing class divisions in the black community due primarily to the structural changes in the movement of American society from an industrial to a postindustrial, technological economy. The escalator opportunities in heavy industries are no longer available to the urban black underclass, and technological society demands more educational skills. National Urban League data indicate that 28 percent of 4.9 million black families in 1970 were headed by women; by 1982 almost 41 percent of 6.4 million black families were female-headed households (Williams, *The State of Black America 1984,* p. 173).

47. Hart M. Nelsen, "Unchurched Black Americans: Patterns of Religiosity and Affiliation," *Review of Religious Research* 29, no. 4 (June 1988): 402.

6   Profile of Urban Clergy and Churches

1. One example of a freedman who was enslaved was Solomon Northrup. See John Hope Franklin, *From Slavery to Freedom,* p. 213.

2. August Meier and Elliot Rudwick, *From Plantation to Ghetto,* pp. 173–74.

3. Ibid., p. 83.

4. According to Edward Smith's study of the rise of black churches in eastern American cities, there was also an African Union Society in Providence, Rhode Island, which merged into a nonsectarian church, the African Union Meeting House, in 1820. Both churches in Providence and Newport later lost their nonsectarian character. See Edward D. Smith, *Climbing Jacob's Ladder: The Rise of Black Churches in Eastern American Cities, 1740–1877,* published for the Anacostia Museum by the Smithsonian Institution, pp. 56–57. Meier and Rudwick gave the founding date of the African Union Society of Newport as 1780; cf. *From Plantation to Ghetto,* pp. 83–86. If they are right about the founding date, then the historical view that the Free African Society of Philadelphia was the first mutual aid society needs to be corrected. It is also unclear where the term "society" comes from in many of these mutual aid groups. It could be from general usage, but the Puritan minister, Cotton Mather, drew up *Rules for the Society of Negroes* in 1693, which is the earliest recorded account of blacks organizing for religious meetings. Cf. Smith, *Climbing Jacob's Ladder,* p. 26.

5. Meier and Rudwick, *From Plantation to Ghetto,* pp. 83–86.

6. Carter G. Woodson, *A Century of Negro Migration.*

7. Jones, *Black Migration in the United States,* p. 31.

8. The phrase is taken from the letter of a Biloxi, Mississippi, mother, dated April 27, 1917. The full text can be found in Emmett J. Scott, collector, "Letters of Negro Migrants, 1916–1918," *Journal of Negro History* 4, no. 3 (July 1919): 318. See also Jones, *"To Get Out of This Land of Sufring": Black Migrant Women, Work and the Family in Northern Cities, 1900–1930,* Working Paper No. 91, p. 6.

9. For a fine account of the Kansas Exodus and the major reasons for black migration, see Johnson and Campbell, *Black Migration in America.*

10. Du Bois is quoted in Meier and Rudwick, *From Plantation to Ghetto,* p. 215. For a concrete example of his observation, see his classic study, *The Philadelphia Negro: A Social Study.*

11. U.S. Department of Commerce, *The Social and Economic Status of the Black Population of the United States: An Historical View, 1790–1978,* table 8, p. 15.

12. See Allan H. Spear, *Black Chicago: The Making of a Negro Ghetto 1890–1920.* Johnson and Campbell, *Black Migration in America,* p. 81.

13. Scott, collector, "Letters of Negro Migrants, 1916–1918," p. 420.

14. Meier and Rudwick, *From Plantation to Ghetto,* p. 215.

15. Jones, *"To Get Out of This Land of Sufring,"* p. 43.

16. Mays and Nicholson, *The Negro's Church,* p. 96. Although they used these figures to show the increase in urban church membership, Mays and Nicholson also had some doubt about the accuracy of the *Federal Census of Religious Bodies.*

17. For example, see Drake and Cayton's comments on this price inflation of older church and synagogue properties in *Black Metropolis*, 2:415.

18. Mays and Nicholson, *The Negro's Church*, pp. 175, 215–23.

19. Drake and Cayton, *Black Metropolis*, 2:415.

20. Emmett J. Scott, collector, "More Letters From Negro Migrants, 1916–1918," *Journal of Negro History* 4, no. 4 (October 1919): 465. The parenthesis represents the authors' emendation.

21. Ibid., pp. 459–65.

22. Ibid. For example, Professor Larry Murphy of the Garrett-Evangelical Theological Seminary in Evanston, Illinois, has been collecting oral history and videotaped materials of church members in Chicago who migrated from rural counties in Mississippi. Since the church was the major communal institution in rural areas, it was not unusual for people from the same church to plan to move together.

23. Myrdal, *An American Dilemma: The Negro Problem and American Democracy*, 2:863.

24. For the deradicalization thesis, see chapter 6 of Gayraud Wilmore's excellent study, *Black Religion and Black Radicalism*. Much more historical work needs to be done on the period of the migrations, particularly the Depression years and its effects on the churches. Although this period has been covered by a number of studies, including Mays and Nicholson, Drake and Cayton, Myrdal, and Frazier, most of these studies were done in the city of Chicago by social scientists trained at the University of Chicago. Whether the Chicago School of Sociology had any value or ideological biases needs to be examined. Historical studies of other cities (Detroit, Cleveland, Cincinnati, and Indianapolis) in the North and especially those in the South like Atlanta and New Orleans would be helpful in resolving this debate.

25. See Gilbert Osofsky, *Harlem: The Making of a Ghetto*, chapters 2, 3. For Chicago, see Spear, *Black Chicago*, and Drake and Cayton, *Black Metropolis*, vol. 2.

26. For race relations in northern cities and a description of the riots, see Osofsky, *Harlem*, chapter 8; and Spear, *Black Chicago*, chapter 11.

27. For example, see Gary Orfield's study, *Public School Desegregation in the United States, 1968–1980*.

28. Although Ida Mukenge has a fine descriptive analysis of the class differentiation occurring among the black population and their churches during the interwar period, she tends to overemphasize the sacred-secular tensions in the urban environment. Mukenge fails to see that the creation of secular political organizations like the NAACP was also encouraged by some black clergy who saw the need for such vehicles in dealing with a more complex situation. Much more will be said about the problems of a political economy approach in chapter 7. Cf. Mukenge, *The Black Church in Urban America*.

29. Meier and Rudwick, *From Plantation to Ghetto*, p. 199.

30. For one of the best explanations and overview of the relationship between class structure, stratification, and social status in the traditional black community, see Andrew Billingsley, *Black Families in White America*, chapter 5.

31. Vattel Elbert Daniel, "Ritual and Stratification in Chicago Negro Churches," *American Sociological Review* 7 (June 1942): 354; also see Nelsen and Nelsen, *Black Church in the Sixties*, p. 121. For an updated attempt to develop a typology of black religious groups and stratification, see the article by Baer and Singer, "Toward a Typology of Black Sectarian Response to Racial Stratification," *Anthropological Quarterly* 54 (1981): 1–14.

32. Drake and Cayton, *Black Metropolis*, 2:670. For an updated study of the black Spiritualist movement, see Hans Baer, *The Black Spiritualist Movement: A Religious Response to Racism*.

33. See Arthur Fauset's study, *Black Gods of the Metropolis*. For an overview and update of some of these religious groups and militant movements, see Mamiya and Lincoln, "Black Militant and Separatist Movements," in the *Encyclopedia of the American Religious Experience*, 2:756–71.

34. For his pessimism and negative judgments, see Frazier's "Conclusion," in Frazier, *The Negro Church in America*, p. 90.

35. Trained in the Chicago School of Sociology, Frazier reflected the views of his teachers that American slavery had destroyed all remnants of African culture and tradition. This view is elaborated in his studies of both the Negro family and Negro religion.

36. See Herbert Gutman's criticism of Frazier's monocultural model and Gutman's formulation of a bicultural model in his classic study, *The Black Family in Slavery and Freedom, 1750–1925*, pp. 259–62.

37. Nelsen and Nelsen, *Black Church in the Sixties*.

38. The fifteen major cities in the sample included New York, Newark, Philadelphia, Atlanta, Birmingham (Alabama), Jackson, Dallas, Houston, Chicago, Detroit, Kansas City, St. Louis, Oakland, San Francisco, and Los Angeles. The black churches in the Washington, D.C., area were surveyed in another study conducted by researchers from Howard University and our results will be compared with theirs. See Diane R. Brown and Ronald W. Walters, *Exploring the Role of the Black Church in the Community*.

39. Ibid., pp. 12–14.

40. Mays and Nicholson, *The Negro's Church*, pp. 54–55.

41. This estimate was given by Dr. James Costen, president of the Interdenominational Theological Seminary in Atlanta. His estimate also corresponds to the views of several denominational leaders who were interviewed as part of this project.

42. Brown and Walters, *Exploring the Role of the Black Church in the Community*, table 2.1, p. 13.

43. For a foundational view of tent-making ministries, see Johannes C. Hoekendijk, *The Church Inside Out*.

44. Besides the interviews of our field study, evidence for the problems of having two full-time jobs comes from interviews with A.M.E. clergy from the Second Episcopal District of the A.M.E. Church. See Lawrence H. Mamiya, "The Second Episcopal District of the African Methodist Episcopal Church Under the Leadership of Bishop John Hurst Adams: Evaluations of the Leadership Training Institutes and the Phenomenon of Church Growth in the District," unpublished study funded by the Lilly Endowment, January 1986.

45. For a historical overview of the importance of oral tradition in the formation of black culture, see Levine, *Black Culture and Black Consciousness*.

46. According to Bishop William J. Walls of the A.M.E. Zion Church, he started out to research the history of the church and he ended up with a history of the race. See Walls, *The African Methodist Episcopal Zion Church: Reality of the Black Church*. Using the metaphor of "river," Vincent Harding's historical reflections on the black journey toward freedom also follows a similar path of emphasizing the role of black churches and black religion. See Vincent Harding, *There Is a River: The Black Struggle for Freedom in America*.

47. Most scholars follow Carter G. Woodson's dating of the Silver Bluff Baptist Church between 1773–75. However, during a field visit to Silver Bluff, we discovered that the cornerstone of the church had a founding date of 1750 inscribed on it. There has been an ongoing dispute among the early black churches as to which one was first. Mechal Sobel in her classic work on early black Baptists, *Trabelin' On*, gave a founding date of 1758 for the African Baptist or "Bluestone Church" in Lunenberg, Virginia (now Mecklenberg). Cf. Sobel, *Trabelin' On*, pp. 250, 256. The Springfield Baptist Church in Augusta, Georgia, has claimed that it is an offshoot of the Silver Bluff congregation and therefore deserves to be considered the first continuous black church in existence, although its founding date was 1788. The First African Baptist Church of Savannah, established in 1787, has also made its claims to be the first black church.

48. There have been very few studies of urban storefront churches, which have usually been local in scope; there are no national studies. From field observations in a number of cities we have learned that storefront churches tend to appear in greatest frequency in some of the most depressed areas. For example, in 1982 in a two-block area on Fulton Avenue in one of the poorest sections of Bedford-Stuyvesant in Brooklyn, we counted twenty-two storefront churches.

49. In our national study we found only one Methodist storefront, which was an A.M.E. mission church.

50. Brown and Walters, *Exploring the Role of the Black Church*, pp. 19, 43.

51. Mays and Nicholson, *The Negro's Church*, pp. 123–26.

52. Drake and Cayton, *Black Metropolis*, 2:670.

53. Brown and Walters, *Exploring the Role of the Black Church*, pp. 31–

33. Brown and Walters do make the important observation that the missionary societies within black churches often provided unspecified neighborhood services.

54. Ida Wells-Barnett was the prime mover behind the antilynching campaign in the late nineteenth and early twentieth centuries. See Ida Bell Wells, *U.S. Atrocities* (London: 1892). On the civil rights period, see the following: Aldon D. Morris, *The Origins of the Civil Rights Movement: Black Communities Organizing for Change.* Thus far, the best film documentary on the civil rights movement is Henry Hampton's "Eyes On the Prize."

55. See the following: Williams, *Community in a Black Pentecostal Church;* Paris, *Black Pentecostalism;* Mukenge, *The Black Church in Urban America;* Nelsen and Nelsen, *Black Church in the Sixties.*

56. Brown and Walters, *Exploring the Role of the Black Church.*

57. The percentages are derived from the continuing studies of the work group on mainline Protestant denominations, sponsored by the Lilly Endowment. According to one of the publications, the United Methodist Church has lost about 1 million members and the United Presbyterian and Episcopal churches about half a million members. Other denominations like the United Church of Christ and Lutherans have also been affected by a substantial decline in membership. See Carl Dudley, *Where Have All Our People Gone?: New Choices for Old Churches,* p. 4. For the most comprehensive study of the phenomena of church decline and growth, see the collection of essays in *Understanding Church Growth and Decline: 1950–1978,* edited by Dean R. Hoge and David A. Roozen.

58. The figure of 10,000 COGIC churches is derived from the national directory of churches and clergy, which the denomination published and released in 1980. There is ample evidence that many scholars did not view the Church of God in Christ, the largest black Pentecostal body, as one of the historic black denominations but as an extreme sectarian group. Our study has differed from these scholars by considering the Church of God in Christ as a major black denomination. For example, Hans Baer and Merrill Singer have placed the Church of God in Christ outside the stream of the mainline black church denominations and in the category of sectarianism. Baer and Singer, "Toward a Typology of Black Sectarian Response to Racial Stratification." In his fine book, *The Social Teaching of the Black Churches,* Peter Paris has only used black Methodist and black Baptist sources for reconstructing the social ethics of the mainline black churches. The usual tendency of most scholars has been to ignore the rise of the Holiness-Pentecostal stream of the Black Church tradition, which has proven to be the fastest growing area of black religion in the twentieth century. Wilmore in *Black Religion and Black Radicalism,* p. 154, indicated that the Church of God in Christ grew from 30,263 members in 1926 to over a reported 3 million members in 1983.

59. The observations presented here came from interviews the coauthors

had with leaders of the seven black denominations. Our denominational and black church consultants for the study were Bishop John H. Adams of the African Methodist Episcopal Church; Bishop James L. Cummings of the Christian Methodist Episcopal Church; Bishop J. Clinton Hoggard of the African Methodist Episcopal Zion Church; Bishop German Ross of the Church of God in Christ; Rev. F. Benjamin Davis of the National Baptist Convention of America; Rev. Manuel L. Scott of the National Baptist Convention, U.S.A.; Rev. Thomas Kilgore, Jr., of the Progressive National Baptist Convention; Bishop S. S. Morris, Jr., of the African Methodist Episcopal Church; Dean Lawrence Jones of the Howard University Divinity School; and Rev. Leon Watts, professor of religion at Yale Divinity School. As mentioned earlier, none of the denominations keep accurate membership figures, so that the estimates of church growth and decline are only educated guesses, based on interviews with denominational leaders and field visits to rural and urban churches. Lincoln and Mamiya also served as consultants for an in-house study of the c.m.e. Church, which was commissioned by the College of Bishops. The results of the telephone survey of eighty-eight c.m.e. clergy and 415 laity by Don Regusters of Associate Control, Research and Analysis, of Washington, D.C., were analyzed by the coauthors, resulting in some policy and planning recommendations. The study was completed by May 1985.

60. For a good overview of past and present attempts at merger by black denominations, see Mary R. Sawyer, *Black Ecumenism: Cooperative Social Change Movements in the Black Church*.

61. Since the retirement of Rev. Dr. Joseph Harrison Jackson from the presidency of the National Baptist Convention, U.S.A., in 1984, his successor, Rev. T. J. Jemison of Louisiana, has attempted to woo the Progressive National Baptist Convention back into the fold. The 1961 split resulted from the dissatisfaction of the progressive civil rights clergy like Gardner Taylor and the opposition that Joseph Jackson asserted against the policies and tactics of Martin Luther King, Jr., and the civil rights movement.

62. See Wade Clark Roof, *Race and Residence in American Cities*, vol. 441. For a historical example of how residential segregation has affected the location of black churches over a period of one hundred years, see Lawrence H. Mamiya and Lorraine Roberts, "Invisible People, Untold Stories: A Historical Overview of the Black Community in Poughkeepsie," in *New Perspectives on Poughkeepsie's Past: Essays to Honor Edmund Platt*, edited by Clyde Griffen.

63. For example, see Thomas A. Clark, *Blacks in Suburbs: A National Perspective*.

64. Ronald Smothers, "Atlanta Still on a Roll, but New Doubts Arise," *New York Times*, July 14, 1988, p. A-21.

65. For example, the Fort Washington a.m.e. Church grew from twenty-six members to more than a thousand in two years. See Mamiya, "The Second Episcopal District of the African Methodist Episcopal Church."

66. Isabel Wilkerson, "Study Finds Segregation in Cities Worse Than Scientists Imagined," *New York Times*, August 5, 1989, p. A-6. According to University of Chicago researchers Douglas S. Massey and Nancy A. Denton, African Americans suffer from "hypersegregation," a deeper and more profound degree of racial segregation.

67. Frazier, *The Negro Church in America*, p. 83. It is unclear what data Frazier was relying upon for his assertions. See also Robert L. Wilson, *The Northern Negro Looks at the Church*, pp. 24–31. For both Frazier and Wilson, class mobility among African Americans has usually meant switching to a higher status denomination, i.e., a white denomination.

68. According to Dean Hoge's study of Roman Catholicism, the number of black converts to Catholicism has declined since the 1960s, largely because of a decline in Catholic schools and the rise in black consciousness. Data from the National Office of Black Catholics indicate that only 8 percent of recent adult converts were black. Dean Hoge, *Converts, Dropouts, Returnees: A Study of Religious Change Among Catholics*, p. 30.

69. B. Drummond Ayres, Jr., "Black Priest Is Termed Threat to Catholic Unity," *New York Times*, July 15, 1989, p. A-6. The figures are from Archbishop John May of St. Louis, president of the National Conference of Catholic Bishops, in response to the problem of Father George A. Stallings's attempt to start an independent black Catholic movement with Imani Temple.

70. Like black Protestants, black Catholics have also formed black caucuses and pressure groups. The National Office of Black Catholics is one result of their efforts. For a historical overview of black Catholicism, see "The Black Catholic Experience," in the *U.S. Catholic Historian*, vol. 5, no. 1, 1986.

71. See *Emerging Trends*, published by the Princeton Religion Research Center, vol. 9, no. 5 (May 1987): 5. The only data that tend to contravene these findings are found in the Princeton Religion Research Center's study, *The Unchurched American . . . 10 Years Later*, p. 37. The church membership rate for black people was recorded as 64 percent, which is a 13 percent drop from the rate reported in 1987. Since this recent finding is so anomalous from other studies of black church membership over the past 20 years, including Gallup's own findings, we reserve judgment until other studies confirm or discount this result. Thus far, our church sources have not supported a large loss in church membership.

72. Roof and McKinney, *American Mainline Religion*, p. 91.

73. Du Bois, *The Philadelphia Negro;* see his analysis of "The Seventh Ward," pp. 58–72. Drake and Cayton, *Black Metropolis*, 2:524–25. The "Shadies" for Drake and Cayton were those who participated in illegal enterprises, a group which cut across class lines. Elliot Liebow, *Talley's Corner: A Study of Negro Streetcorner Men*. Prior to the civil rights movement, the characterization of the unchurched in these community studies really meant those who were marginally socialized into the Black Church tradition

or those who were rebelling against it. It did not mean that they had virtually no contact with Black Church culture, as we will point out in chapter 11.

74. For a profile of this group, see Michael R. Welch, "The Unchurched, Black Religious Non-Affiliates," *Journal for the Scientific Study of Religion* 17 (September 1978): 289–93.

75. Nelsen, "Unchurched Black Americans: Patterns of Religiosity and Affiliation," *Review of Religious Research* 29, no. 4 (June 1988): 398–412. Nelsen's fine reanalysis of the Gallup study and of other data is a significant contribution to the field. However, we do have some questions about the adequacy of using a telephone survey in regard to lower-income or poor black Americans, who may be left out by such a method. It is estimated that only about 80 percent of Americans have telephones in their homes; most of the truly disadvantaged cannot afford the service.

76. Cf. Frazier, *The Negro Church in America*, p. 82. Mukenge tends to psychologize the functions of urban black churches because she sees their future role only in the area of mental health and psychological stability. Mukenge, *The Black Church in Urban America*, p. 204. Also see Nelsen, "Unchurched Black Americans," pp. 408–9.

77. Nelsen, "Unchurched Black Americans," p. 408.

78. See Paris, *The Social Teaching of the Black Churches* for the continuous antiracial, ethical stance among the Black Baptists and Methodists. For the historical tradition of black religious radicalism or the prophetic stance, see Wilmore, *Black Religion and Black Radicalism*. As mentioned earlier, Vincent Harding has also written about the black journey toward freedom in *There Is a River*.

79. Roof and McKinney, *American Mainline Religion*, p. 91.

80. Billingsley, *Black Families in White America*, chapter 5.

7 The Black Consciousness Movement

1. Morris, *The Origins of the Civil Rights Movement: Black Communities Organizing for Change*, pp. 79–81.

2. Ibid., p. 77.

3. See Clarence Crane Brinton's important study of the factors involved in the process of revolutions, *The Anatomy of a Revolution*, and Chalmers Johnson's focus on the role of new principles and values in his *Revolutionary Change*. For the importance of consciousness-raising in the process of social change, see the following: G. W. F. Hegel's classic description of the dialectical change in consciousness in the master-slave relationship in his essay "Lordship and Bondage" in *The Phenomenology of Mind*; and Paulo Freire, *Pedagogy of the Oppressed*.

4. C. Van Woodward, "After Watts—Where Is the Negro Revolution Headed?" *New York Times Magazine*, August 29, 1965, p. 82.

5. See Randall Burkett, *Garveyism as a Religious Movement*; and Robert

A. Hill, editor, *The Marcus Garvey and the Universal Negro Improvement Association Papers*. Although Marcus Garvey's Universal Negro Improvement Association is still the largest recorded black social movement, its political impact on the structures of American society was limited. Garvey's arrest for mail fraud and deportation from the United States, and his subsequent split with the New York chapter of UNIA, the movement's largest chapter, prevented a greater impact.

6. Isabel Wilkerson, "Many Who Are Black Favor New Term for Who They Are," *New York Times*, January 31, 1989, pp. A-1, A-14.

7. Frazier, *The Negro Church in America* and Lincoln, *The Black Church Since Frazier*.

8. Among the many efforts at constructing a systematic theology from a black perspective, James Cone's pioneering work, *Black Theology and Black Power*, still stands out. For a summary overview of individual theological efforts in the United States and Africa, see Josiah Young's *Black and African Theologies: Siblings or Distant Cousins?* Also see Gayraud Wilmore and James Cone, editors, *Black Theology: A Documentary History, 1966–1979*. The sociological study by Nelsen and Nelsen, *Black Church in the Sixties*, hints at this change in their proposed "ethnic community-liberation" model of black churches but its main thrust is a reanalysis of the civil rights militancy debate. Mukenge's *The Black Church in Urban America: A Case Study in Political Economy*, tends to dismiss the significance of this change in consciousness as merely ideological without any impact upon social structure. We argue the contrary case in this chapter.

9. In his zealous crusade for education among African Methodists, Bishop Daniel Payne developed a strong disdain for aspects of the African cultural heritage which he noticed in worship services. To him "ring shouts" and "cornfield ditties" were manifestations of ignorance. Cf. Clarence E. Walker, *A Rock in a Weary Land: The African Methodist Episcopal Church During the Civil War and Reconstruction*, p. 24.

10. This observation on the class status of the membership of the Church of God in Christ comes from personal field experience and from personal interviews with COGIC Bishop Ithiel Clemmons, who helped our project as a historical consultant. Our other survey data indicate that almost all of the storefronts in our study were either COGIC or Baptist (7 percent or 107 storefronts), reflecting the class diversity in those two denominations. In our nationwide survey, we found only one A.M.E. storefront which was serving as a mission church.

11. For the role of the preacher and the sermon in black churches, see the following: Henry H. Mitchell, *Black Preaching*; and Hamilton, *The Black Preacher in America*.

12. See Charles M. Wiltse, editor, *David Walker's Appeal*. For Bishop Turner's quote, see Wilmore, *Black Religion and Black Radicalism*, p. 125.

13. For an overview of these movements and their significance, see the

article "Black Militant and Separatist Movements" by Mamiya and Lincoln in *Encyclopedia of American Religious Experience*.

14. See Wyatt MacGaffey's fascinating account of this small, early movement in his *Religion and Society in Central Africa: The Bakongo of Lower Zaire*, pp. 208–11. For an excellent analysis of later independent church movements in Central Africa, especially that of Simon Kimbangu, see MacGaffey's *Modern Kongo Prophets*.

15. Cone, *Black Theology and Black Power*.

16. For the best overview, see Wilmore and Cone, editors, *Black Theology: A Documentary History, 1966–1979*. Also see the following: J. DeOtis Roberts, *Liberation and Reconciliation*; William R. Jones, *Is God a White Racist?* Major J. Jones, *Black Awareness*; and Cornel West, *Prophesy Deliverance!*

17. The reason for asking a different question to the rural clergy was the desire to get some empirical data on the influence of the older liberation tradition. In doing the field survey we felt that the black urban clergy would probably be more knowledgeable about the new black liberation theology movement than those serving in rural areas. We also reasoned that if the urban clergy were not greatly influenced by this new movement, then the same results would probably apply to the rural clergy, two-thirds of whom live in urban areas.

18. This kind of education in local Bible schools or classes applies particularly to the black clergy who serve in rural areas, small towns and cities, and sometimes in large metropolitan areas that have not been influenced by the major divinity schools or seminaries.

19. Freire, *Pedagogy of the Oppressed*. Elsa Tamez, *Bible of the Oppressed*.

20. For an overview of the significance of the Washington-Du Bois debate, see Mary Berry and John Blassingame's assessment, *Long Memory: The Black Experience in America*, pp. 272–79.

21. West, *Prophesy Deliverance!* West's book contains the most extensive use of Marxism by any of the currently known black liberation theologians. In his more recent writings James Cone has shifted from his earlier Barthian theological structure to a greater incorporation of Marxism. See Cone's essay, "The Black Church and Marxism: What Do They Have to Say to Each Other?" published as an Occasional Paper from the Institute for Democratic Socialism, New York: April 1980.

22. The six items in the black consciousness scale were recoded so that 2= "positive" black consciousness response and 1= "negative" response, with "no answer" =0. Responses were then summed over the six items and divided by the number of items answered. Persons not answering 5 or 6 (all) of the items were coded as "no answer." Cronbach's alpha for the scale was .58 (standardized item alpha) using the weighted sample for the rural clergy who pastor more than one church (which is used throughout the analysis). The removal of any one item from the scale did not increase alpha.

Raw scale scores (BCS6) could range from 1 to 2 (6/6 to 12/6). "No answers" were excluded from further analysis. The mean of the black consciousness scale is 1.6 and the standard deviation is .27.

23. The actual scale score indicated that "low" =1 through 1.33; "moderate" =1.34 through 1.67; and "high" =1.68 through 2.

24. Denomination was recoded into four categories (from the seven denominations examined to Methodists, Baptists, Pentecostals, and others); age was divided into four categories and education into five categories.

25. A New York Times article by John Herbers, "10 Agencies Win Grants for Innovative Projects," reported on this Ford Foundation funded project, September 26, 1986, p. A-18.

26. This discussion of ecumenical movements is based largely on Mary Sawyer, "Black Ecumenism: Cooperative Social Change Movements in the Black Church."

27. Mays and Nicholson, The Negro's Church.

28. See Mukenge's The Black Church in Urban America. While Mukenge has some good historical data on the class changes occurring among black people, her critique of ideas like black religion and theological views of blackness as merely uninfluential ideologies tend to reflect the one-sided reductionistic Marxist assumptions inherent in the political economy approach. The dialectical tension between ideas and social structure is ultimately dissolved. See pp. 193–202 in Mukenge for statements on the noncausal role of religious ideas in explaining structural and functional changes. See Max Weber's critique of the Marxian approach on this issue of the role of religious ideas and change in Hans Gerth and C. Wright Mills, editors, From Max Weber: Essays in Sociology.

29. For examples of the revisionist view of slavery, see the following: Genovese, Roll, Jordan, Roll: The World the Slaves Made; Blassingame, The Slave Community; Gutman, The Black Family in Slavery and Freedom, 1750–1925; and Raboteau, Slave Religion.

30. Max Weber, The Protestant Ethic and the Spirit of Capitalism; and Gerth and Mills, From Max Weber.

8   Church, Politics, and Civil Rights

1. Marable, How Capitalism Underdeveloped Black America, p. 196.

2. Some of the national black church leaders include Bishop John Hurst Adams of the A.M.E. Church who was the first president of the Congress of National Black Churches; Rev. Benjamin Hooks, president of the NAACP; and Rev. William Gray III, who is chairman of the Budget Committee of the House of Representatives. Besides this resistance to Reagan, there has also been a small coterie of black neoconservative leaders such as Thomas Sowell, Walter Williams, Clarence Pendelton, and Glenn Loury.

3. The references are to the Marxist view of religion as "false consciousness" and to the Freudian analysis of religion as a phase of childhood projec-

tion, which continue to have widespread currency among intellectuals in academia.

4. Marx, *Protest and Prejudice*.

5. Adolph L. Reed, Jr., *The Jesse Jackson Phenomenon*, p. 44.

6. Ibid., p. 60.

7. Peter Paris, *Black Leaders in Conflict*.

8. See Peter Paris's arguments about the Black Church and the black community in *The Social Teaching of the Black Churches*, pp. 22–23, n. 14.

9. Genovese has also argued in *Roll, Jordan, Roll* that black political choices during slavery were limited by the white system of domination. Such a view corresponds to our emphasis upon a dialectical analysis of the Black Church in relationship to other institutional spheres of society. Also see George Friedrich Hegel's dialectical analysis of the tensions and contradictions involved in "Lordship and Bondage" in *The Phenomenology of Mind*, pp. 233–40.

10. See Mbiti, *African Religions and Philosophy*; and Raboteau, *Slave Religion*, chapter 1.

11. The debate on African survivals in Afro-American culture involved the two main protagonists, E. Franklin Frazier, who argued that African culture had been stripped away by slavery, and Melville Herskovits, who gave examples of African survivals in Caribbean and Afro-American culture. Albert Raboteau has given the best summary of the debate involving black religion, while Herbert Gutman has given one of the best resolutions of the debate regarding the black family. See the following: Frazier and Lincoln, *The Negro Church in America: The Black Church Since Frazier*; E. Franklin Frazier, *The Negro Family in the United States*; Herskovits, *The Myth of the Negro Past*; Raboteau, *Slave Religion*, chapter 1; and Gutman, *The Black Family in Slavery and Freedom*, *1750–1925*.

12. Herbert Gutman has argued the anthropological idea of the spread of a uniform Afro-American culture among southern plantation slaves by the early nineteenth century. He criticized the mimetic theories of Frazier and Gunnar Myrdal, who asserted that American Negro culture was a distorted and pathological version of general American culture, and argues for a "bicultural model," the creation of a unique Afro-American culture as shown in slave rituals, naming practices, and kinship network. Cf. Gutman, *The Black Family in Slavery and Freedom*, pp. 259–62. C. Eric Lincoln has proposed a similar view, suggesting that a unique black American culture was created during the slave period and after, with black religion playing an important formative role. See his introductory essays in *The Black Experience in Religion*, edited by Lincoln. Also see chapter 2 in Lincoln, *Race, Religion, and the Continuing American Dilemma*.

13. See Lester B. Scherer, *Slavery and the Churches in Early America, 1619–1819*, p. 30.

14. Raboteau, *Slave Religion*.

15. E. Franklin Frazier coined the term "the invisible institution" to designate slave religion. Frazier, *The Negro Church in America.* See also Raboteau, *Slave Religion;* and Lincoln, *Race, Religion, and the Continuing American Dilemma,* pp. 41–59.

16. Wilmore, *Black Religion and Black Radicalism.* It is a curious fact that scholars like Adolph Reed, Jr., tend to ignore Wilmore's valuable historical study on the subject of the Black Church and radical black politics, which has been available for more than a decade, and continue to rely on simplistic views of black religion. Reed's faulty and one-sided historical treatment of the history of black churches tends to skew his discussion of both the past and present roles of black churches in politics.

17. Ibid., pp. 15–39. Lincoln, *Race, Religion, and the Continuing American Dilemma,* chapter 2.

18. Genovese, *Roll, Jordan, Roll: The World the Slaves Made.*

19. Reed, *The Jesse Jackson Phenomenon,* chapter 4. Reed follows in the tradition of E. Franklin Frazier in viewing black churches as ultimately dysfunctional in integrating black people into the American democratic system. For a sophisticated "two-by-two" typological table, using "church" versus "sect" and "other worldly" versus "this worldly," see Baer and Singer, "Toward a Typology of Black Sectarian Response to Racial Stratification," *Anthropological Quarterly,* 54 (1981): 1–14.

20. Wilmore, *Black Religion and Black Radicalism,* pp. 227–34.

21. Berry and Blassingame, *Long Memory: The Black Experience in America,* pp. 12, 16.

22. Paris, *The Social Teaching of the Black Church.*

23. For historical overviews on the founding of black denominations, see Richardson, *Dark Salvation: The Story of Methodism as It Developed Among Blacks in America;* and Washington, *Frustrated Fellowship: The Black Baptist Quest for Social Power.* As noted earlier, the only exception to this pattern of withdrawing from a white denomination was the Church of God in Christ, the largest black Pentecostal denomination. Although it was founded in 1897 in Lexington, Mississippi, the Church of God in Christ did not spread rapidly until after the Azusa Street Revival in 1907 when Bishop Charles H. Mason officially took over the denomination. From 1907 to 1914 Bishop Mason ordained large numbers of white Pentecostal clergy as ministers of the Church of God in Christ. However, by 1914 the racial factor reared its ugly head when many white Pentecostal clergy withdrew to form their own denomination, the Assemblies of God. The brief interracial period among Pentecostals ended by 1924. See the account given by Vincent Synan in *The Holiness-Pentecostal Movement in the United States,* chapters 5, 8.

24. Benjamin Quarles, *Black Abolitionists.*

25. Wilmore, *Black Religion and Black Radicalism,* p. 121.

26. Ibid., pp. 53–63.

27. For the best summary of Prosser, Vesey, Turner, and Brown, see

"Three Generals in the Lord's Army," in Wilmore, *Black Religion and Black Radicalism*.

28. Ibid., p. 227.

29. Woodson, *The History of the Negro Church*, pp. 198–223. Woodson's list is not a complete one by any means. As far as it is known, a complete listing of all black clergy participating in any level of politics during the Reconstruction period has not been done.

30. Ibid.

31. John G. Van Dusen, "The Negro in Politics," *Journal of Negro History* 21 (July 1936): 257. Also see Mary Sawyer's M.A. thesis, *Black Politics, Black Faith*, pp. 48–49. For a published summary of her findings, see Sawyer, "A Moral Minority: Religion and Congressional Black Politics," *Journal of Religious Thought* 40 (Fall–Winter, 1983–84), no. 2:55–66.

32. Henry McNeil Turner, "God Is a Negro," *The Voice of Missions*, African Methodist Episcopal Church, February 1, 1898. Also quoted in Wilmore, *Black Religion and Black Radicalism*, p. 125.

33. Oral history interview with Mrs. Earline Patrice in *For Their Courage and for Their Struggles: The Black Oral History Project in Poughkeepsie, New York*, edited by Lawrence H. Mamiya and Patricia A. Kaurouma, pp. 71–72.

34. Frazier, *The Negro Church in America*, p. 49.

35. Richardson, *Dark Glory*.

36. Wilmore, *Black Religion and Black Radicalism*, p. 142.

37. Harold Gosnell, *Negro Politicians: The Rise of Negro Politics in Chicago*. The A.M.E. clergyman Archibald Carey was one of the most active political figures in the black community.

38. Martin Kilson, "Political Change in the Negro Ghetto, 1900–1940s," in *Key Issues in the Afro-American Experience*, edited by Nathan I. Huggins, Martin Kilson, and Daniel Fox, 2:171.

39. Wilmore, *Black Religion and Black Radicalism*, chapter 6.

40. For an overview of these studies, see chapter 1 above.

41. Before the deradicalization thesis can be firmly accepted, careful historical studies need to be made of the activities of black churches during this period. A number of questions need to be explored: what did black churches do for the masses of migrants? Did they sponsor any social or welfare programs in their communities? Were the clergy involved with politics or did they surrender that sphere to the cults and sects? Did these colorful cults and sects dominate the news coverage during this period so that the political activities of black churches were not covered? What exceptions were there—e.g., Reverdy Ransom, Adam Clayton Powell, Sr., and Jr.? What was happening in Atlanta with Daddy King and William Holmes Borders? And most significant of all, how did the members of the black bourgeoisie who opted for white churches compare with those who remained in black churches?

42. Taylor Branch, *Parting the Waters: America in the King Years, 1954–*

1963. Branch has provided some examples that some of the leading black clergy in Atlanta continued to be politically active during the 1930s and 1940s.

43. Edward Peeks, *The Long Struggle for Black Power*, p. 285.

44. Both Dr. Bethune and Mrs. Burroughs were active members of the National Baptist Convention. As the founder and president of Bethune Cookman College, Dr. Bethune also served as president of the National Council of Negro Women for fourteen years and, through her friendship with Eleanor Roosevelt, she was influential in some of the social programs of the New Deal. See Rackham Holt, *Mary McLeod Bethune: A Biography.* Nannie Burroughs served as the corresponding secretary and a key leader of the Baptist Women's Convention, influencing their political stands on women's suffrage and involvement in Republican electoral politics. Most blacks prior to the New Deal were loyal members of the party of Lincoln. See Evelyn Brooks, "Religion, Politics, and Gender: The Leadership of Nannie Helen Burroughs," *Journal of Religious Thought* 44 (Winter–Spring 1988), no. 2. Dr. Mallory was an active member of the Church of God in Christ (Pentecostals) and president of the Saints Academy and Junior College in Lexington, Mississippi. See Simmons and Martin, *Down Behind the Sun: The Story of Arenia Conelia Mallory.*

45. Adam Clayton Powell, Jr., *Marching Blacks: An Interpretive History of the Rise of the Black Common Man*, pp. 95–103. Also see Kilson, "Political Change," pp. 179–80.

46. Morris, *The Origins of the Civil Rights Movement.*

47. Hilton, *The Delta Ministry*, p. 182.

48. John E. Jacob, "An Overview of Black America in 1983," *The State of Black America 1984.*

49. For examples of this deep alienation particularly among the underclass, see William Julius Wilson, *The Truly Disadvantaged: The Inner City, the Underclass, and Public Policy*; and Douglas Glasgow, *The Black Underclass: Poverty, Unemployment, and Entrapment of Ghetto Youth.*

50. Linda Jones (pseudonym), "I Don't Vote," *New York Times*, July 14, 1976, p. A-35.

51. Paris, *The Social Teaching of the Black Churches.*

52. Thomas E. Cavanaugh and Lorn S. Foster, *Jesse Jackson's Campaign: The Primaries and Caucuses, Election '84 Report #2*, p. 13.

53. "Role of Black Voters in 1976 Election of Carter," *New York Times*, January 15, 1977.

54. Paul Delaney, "Many Black Democratic Leaders Voice Doubt, Fear, and Distrust About Carter," *New York Times*, July 6, 1976.

55. George Vecsey, "Preaching and Politics on Weekly Agenda for Baptist Ministers," *New York Times*, November 6, 1976.

56. Sawyer, *Black Politics, Black Faith*, M.A. thesis, pp. 105–6. See also chapter 5.

57. Ibid., pp. 105–6.

58. Ibid., p. 106.

59. Ibid., p. 107.

60. Ibid., pp. 119–21.

61. Representative Gray is also the senior pastor of the Bright Hope Baptist Church in Philadelphia. Robin Toner, "William H. Gray, 3d," *New York Times,* June 15, 1989, p. B-8.

62. Clifford D. May, "Queens Congressman Balances Duties in Church and the Capitol, " *New York Times,* March 30, 1987, pp. B-1, B-5.

63. Ibid. Also see "Gospel Balance. . . . It's Happening in Jamaica, New York," by Rev. Brenda Huger Hazel, assistant minister at Allen A.M.E. Church, *The Cornerstone,* edited by Anqunett Fusilier (1985), pp. 10–12.

64. May, "Queens Congressman Balances Duties," p. B-5.

65. "Results of Balloting in New York and Connecticut," *New York Times,* September 11, 1986, B-12.

66. Hazel, "Gospel Balance," p. 11.

67. Ibid.

68. Simon Anewkwe, "Flake, Vann, and Green Win Over Challengers," *Amsterdam News,* November 8, 1986, vol. 77, no. 45:1.

69. Ibid. Flake's success as a politician also illustrates some of the dilemmas of black church involvement in electoral politics. By 1988 Flake's church had been the recipient of some $5.3 million in New York City grants from Mayor Edward Koch's administration, whom Flake has politically supported. After Koch's attacks on Jesse Jackson in the 1988 primary campaign, some black leaders and newspapers have begun to question Flake's silence on Koch.

70. The "One-Church One-Child" program is funded by a grant from the Ford Foundation. See John Herbers, "10 Agencies Win Grants for Innovative Projects," *New York Times,* September 26, 1986, p. A-18.

71. Marx, *Protest and Prejudice.*

72. See Hart Nelsen's comments about this insight on Marx's work in Nelsen and Nelsen, *Black Church in the Sixties.*

73. Reed, *The Jesse Jackson Phenomenon,* chapter 4. While Reed is correct in pointing out that the black clergy did not lead all of the civil rights protests, he tends to overstate his case by ultimately denying the Black Church and clergy any role in political legitimacy. Reed also fails to take into account the fact that a number of leaders of secular civil rights groups like SNCC and CORE were clergy or seminarians, like John Lewis and Charles Sherrod of SNCC and James Farmer of CORE, and others, like Bernice Reagon Johnson and the SNCC Freedom Singers, were closely associated with black churches. An issue more important than whether a demonstration or protest was led by black clergy is the fact that the civil rights movement participated in an overall Black Church culture that permeated the movement in its nonviolent beliefs and practices, rituals, symbols, speaking styles, audience response, civil rights hymnody, and above all, meeting places in urban and

rural areas in the South. As civil rights workers throughout the South knew from experience, there were no legitimate mass meeting places other than black churches, especially in the rural areas. This is the main reason why an estimated 300 or more black churches were bombed or attacked from 1954 to 1968 throughout the South with close to half of that number occurring in Mississippi itself. Furthermore, the majority of local civil rights participants were ultimately affiliated with black churches. Reed needs to consider whether the civil rights movement could have occurred without black churches and clergy.

74. Nelsen and Nelsen, *Black Church in the Sixties*, p. 122.

75. Ibid., p. 109.

76. Ibid., pp. 122–23.

77. Interview no. 2005, "The Black Church in the Black Experience," National Black Church Research Project, Duke University.

78. Summaries of the Gallup surveys are found in Nelsen and Nelsen, *Black Church in the Sixties*, especially in chapter 5.

79. Mamiya, "The Second Episcopal District of the African Methodist Episcopal Church Under the Leadership of Bishop John Hurst Adams," January 1986, p. 27. This unpublished in-house study was funded by the Black Church Research Advisory Committee of the Lilly Endowment.

80. Ibid.

81. See James H. Harris, *Black Ministers and Laity in the Urban Church: An Analysis of Political and Social Expectations*. The majority of Harris's sample of 338 respondents felt that aggressive political leadership by black ministers was very important; see p. 29.

82. Rev. Joseph H. Jackson, former president of the National Baptist Convention, U.S.A., Inc., had been identified with political conservatism when he refused to support Dr. King and the civil rights movement. His successor, Rev. Jemison, has supported Jesse Jackson's candidacy.

83. Marable, *How Capitalism Underdeveloped Black America*, p. 211. The essay on the Black Church is chapter 7 of the book.

84. Du Bois, *The Souls of Black Folk*, pp. 45–46.

85. Besides Du Bois's expression of this desire among black people, see Myrdal, *An American Dilemma*, vols. 1, 2; and Lincoln, *Race, Religion, and the Continuing American Dilemma*.

86. Even with Jackson's more accommodative and toned down approach in the 1988 campaign, all of the political pundits have failed to take his candidacy seriously even though he has been one of the consistent front-runners.

87. *Emerging Trends*, vol. 9, no. 2 (February 1987): 4.

88. See Paris, *The Social Teaching of Black Churches*. For the view of conservative religion and liberal politics among African Americans, see Kelly Miller Smith, "Religion as a Force in Black America," James D. Williams, editor, *The State of Black America 1982*, pp. 210–17. Past political

experiences with the civil rights movement have taught many blacks of the need for federal government action to counter the racial practices of institutions and individuals.

89. The findings are from two unpublished in-house surveys: Lawrence H. Mamiya and C. Eric Lincoln, "Analysis of the Results of the Christian Methodist Episcopal Church Membership Survey," in 1985; and Mamiya, "The Second Episcopal District of the African Methodist Episcopal Church Under the Leadership of Bishop John Hurst Adams," in 1986. Both studies were funded by the Lilly Endowment.

90. Du Bois, *The Souls of Black Folk*, p. 113. Also see Reed's reference to the "supersession" of the black clergy as political leaders: Reed, *The Jesse Jackson Phenomenon*, p. 44.

91. August Meier and Elliot Rudwick, *From Plantation to Ghetto* (New York: Hill and Wang, revised edition, 1970). See pp. 214–23 on the history of the founding of both the NAACP and the National Urban League.

92. See Louis R. Harlan, *Booker T. Washington: The Wizard of Tuskegee, 1901–1915*.

93. Kenneth M. Noble, "A Church Where Things Happen," *New York Times*, August 23, 1984.

94. The contemporary evidence for this commitment in terms of membership, time, and commitment is presented in chapter 9.

95. See the following articles on Mrs. Donald's lawsuit against the Klan: Robin Toner, "Victim's Mother Tells of Klan Fight," *New York Times*, March 6, 1986; and Jessica Kornbluth, "The Woman Who Beat the Klan," *New York Times Magazine*, November 1, 1987, pp. 26–39.

96. Toner, "Victim's Mother Tells of Klan Fight."

97. Kornbluth, "Woman Who Beat the Klan," p. 31.

98. Ibid., p. 38.

99. Ibid., p. 34.

100. Toner, "Victim's Mother Tells of Klan Fight."

101. After moving into her new home, Mrs. Donald passed away in September 1988. See the newsletter of the Southern Poverty Law Center.

102. See the thesis of Nelsen and Nelsen, *Black Church in the Sixties*.

103. For the classic view of this phenomenon of secularization, see Max Weber's essay, "Asceticism and the Spirit of Capitalism," where he argues that the modern capitalistic economy, stripped of its religious and ethical moorings, has turned into the "iron cage" (das stahlhartes Gehaüse). Weber, *The Protestant Ethic and the Spirit of Capitalism*, p. 181.

104. Marable, *How Capitalism Underdeveloped Black America*, chapter 7.

9   The Church and Economics

1. Weber, *The Protestant Ethic and the Spirit of Capitalism*. In his astute observations of American life Tocqueville noted the strong strain of individ-

ualism among Americans, especially in their economic activity. Alexis de Tocqueville, *Democracy in America*, trans. George Lawrence, edited by J. P. Mayer. In his study of Japan's modernization, Robert Bellah asserts that Japan is a society characterized by political values, while in the United States economic values are dominant. Robert N. Bellah, *Tokugawa Religion*, p. 5. Also see Robert N. Bellah, Richard Madsen, William M. Sullivan, Ann Swidler, and Steven M. Tipton, *Habits of the Heart*.

2. Max L. Stackhouse, *Public Theology and Political Economy: Christian Stewardship in Modern Society*, chapter 7.

3. Frank G. Davis, *The Economics of Black Community Development*. In Davis's study the role of churches in potential and actual black economic development is not even considered.

4. For a summary of the controversy involving the numbers of slaves taken from Africa, see Johnson and Campbell, *Black Migration in America*, p. 9ff. Also see Phillip Curtin, *The Atlantic Slave Trade*. Using Basil Davidson's estimates of the 50 million figure, Walter Rodney has developed a chart and argument that the Atlantic slave trade was a major factor which led to the underdevelopment of Africa as a continent, and consequently to the modernization of Europe and the United States. Walter Rodney, *How Europe Underdeveloped Africa*. See p. 106 for the chart comparing the population figures for Europe, Asia, and Africa over a 400-year period. The stagnation of the African population figures is startling. For the 5-to-1 ratio of lives lost to survivors in the New World, see Julius Lester, *To Be a Slave*.

5. Johnson and Campbell, *Black Migration in America*, pp. 7–8.

6. See Daniel P. Mannix, *Black Cargoes*, pp. 54–55; Daniel Lacy, *The White Use of Blacks in America*, pp. 9–22; and Lerone Bennett, *Before the Mayflower: A History of the Negro in America 1619–1964*, pp. 36–37. There is some historical debate about the status of the first twenty Africans in the Jamestown colony. Although they were viewed as indentured servants like many whites under British laws, the Dutch man-of-war that brought them to Jamestown was engaged in the African slave trade. The Dutch also brought slaves to New Amsterdam as early as 1625.

7. Bennett, *Before the Mayflower*.

8. Clyde Griffen and Sally Griffen, *Natives and Newcomers: The Ordering of Opportunity in Mid-Nineteenth Century Poughkeepsie*. Also see Mamiya and Roberts, "Invisible People, Untold Stories," pp. 76–104.

9. For one of the best compilations of socioeconomic data on the black population, see the special publication by the U.S. Department of Commerce, Bureau of the Census, *The Social and Economic Status of the Black Population in the United States*, Special Studies Series P. 23 No. 80. Although the Census Bureau data officially compare black unemployment and median family income for the period 1947 to 1974, updates of the data from 1974 to 1987 can be found in the economic studies of the National Urban League in their publications, edited by James D. Williams, *The State of Black*

America. Also see Reynolds Farley and Walter Allen, *The Color Line and the Quality of Life in America.*

10. Williams, editor, *The State of Black America 1986*, p. 181.

11. Martin Luther King, Jr., "I Have a Dream," speech at the March on Washington, August 29, 1963, in Washington, *A Testament of Hope*, p. 217.

12. See Carole Stack's study, *All My Kin: Strategies for Survival in a Black Community*. Stack's fine study is marred by the fact that she focuses entirely upon kin relationships and does not examine relationships to black churches.

13. Although there have been instances where whites paid for some large black church structures as a trade-off for political support, for every such case there have been many more independently built black churches.

14. Blassingame, *The Slave Community*, chapter 3. For an account of the development of slaves rituals, practices, and a kinship system see Herbert Gutman, *The Black Family in Slavery and Freedom, 1750–1925.*

15. Meier and Rudwick, *From Plantation to Ghetto*, p. 83.

16. Ibid., pp. 85–92. An even earlier mutual aid-benefit society was the African Union Society founded in 1780 in Newport, Rhode Island.

17. Wilmore, *Black Religion and Black Radicalism*, p. 113.

18. Meier and Rudwick, *From Plantation to Ghetto*, p. 90.

19. August Meier, *Negro Thought in America 1880–1915*, pp. 44–45.

20. Ibid., p. 45.

21. Du Bois, *Economic Cooperation Among Negro Americans*, p. 54.

22. John Blassingame, *Black New Orleans, 1860–1880*, p. 67.

23. Ibid., pp. 67–68.

24. Locations of the banks were as follows: eleven in Mississippi, ten in Virginia, five in Oklahoma, four in Georgia, four in Tennessee, four in North Carolina, four in Texas, two in Alabama, and one each in Arkansas, Pennsylvania, and Illinois. See Flournoy A. Coles, Jr., *Black Economic Development*, pp. 105–6.

25. Meier and Rudwick, *From Plantation to Ghetto*, p. 197ff.

26. Meier, *Negro Thought in America 1880–1915*, p. 142. In 1989 North Carolina Mutual is the largest black-owned business in Durham, N.C., and the Afro-American Life Insurance Company is the largest black-owned business in Florida.

27. Coles, *Black Economic Development*, p. 106. Fraternal orders were quasi-religious institutions in their beliefs and rituals, and many of them received their start in Negro churches. However, according to Light, there also was some hostile competition between some clergy and fraternal leaders for the allegiance of the masses. See Ivan H. Light, *Ethnic Enterprise in America: Business and Welfare Among Chinese, Japanese, and Blacks*, pp. 138–39. See also Drake and Cayton, *Black Metropolis*, 2:210.

28. Ibid., 2:198.

29. Notes of field visit, May 1979. The Sixteenth Street Baptist Church in Birmingham was bombed in 1963 during the civil rights movement and four young girls attending Sunday school were killed.

30. Meier and Rudwick, *From Plantation to Ghetto*, p. 196. They also point to the example of the pastor of the Berean Presbyterian church in Philadelphia, who organized the largest building and loan association in the state of Pennsylvania because he wanted his church to offer this service, p. 198.

31. Ibid., p. 211. Much has been made of the Washington versus Du Bois debate about educational strategy since Washington called for practical, vocational training in the industrial arts and agricultural techniques, while Du Bois supported a liberal arts college education for the "Talented Tenth." Both strategies reflected the background and socialization of each man: Du Bois was the urbane New England intellectual, trained at Fisk, Berlin, and Harvard; Washington was the former slave, educated at Hampton Institute and founder of Tuskegee Institute in the black belt of Alabama.

32. Ibid., 203–4. Washington's philosophy was influential among some black Baptist leaders.

33. Du Bois, *The Souls of Black Folk*, p. 5.

34. Meier and Rudwick, *From Plantation to Ghetto*, p. 223.

35. Mamiya and Roberts, "Invisible People, Untold Stories," p. 89.

36. This less visible, quieter, behind-the-scenes approach by most church leaders toward community problems and issues during the migrations and Depression years (1920–1950) probably led many researchers to assume that black churches had lost their previous activist stance and commitment. In fact, after reviewing the studies by Mays and Nicholson, Frazier, and Drake and Cayton, Gayraud Wilmore has labeled this period "the deradicalization of the Black Church." However, the authors of this study feel that black churches and clergy had not lost their activism but many of them took this more indirect, behind-the-scenes approach toward problems. It is more difficult to find evidence for this approach since newspapers tend to cover only the more visible, controversial cases of protest or more colorful events like those of Father Divine and Daddy Grace. But there is some evidence in the oral history reports by black people, who were leaders during this era, which showed their continued concern and efforts. It is also true that the resources of many black churches and clergy in northern urban areas were also burdened by the needs and massive waves of migrants, especially during the Depression years. As the data in Mays and Nicholson's study showed, many black urban churches were heavily indebted as they built new buildings or bought older church edifices from whites in order to accommodate the growing numbers of migrants. See Mays and Nicholson, *The Negro's Church*, pp. 171–97.

37. Other black activists in the early twentieth century included Ida B. Wells, Monroe Trotter, Anna Julia Cooper, Mary McCleod Bethune, James Ford, Cyril Briggs, W. E. B. Du Bois, Marcus Garvey, Reverdy Ransom, and Nannie Burroughs.

38. Meier and Rudwick, *From Plantation to Ghetto*, p. 226.

39. Light, *Ethnic Enterprise in America*, pp. 131–51. Also see Robert

Weisbrot's fine reassessment of Father Divine's movement, *Father Divine and the Struggle for Racial Equality*. Although the Black Church has been stereotyped as an authoritarian institution and black clergy viewed as autocratic leaders (cf. Frazier), it should not be forgotten that ultimately it is the lay members who elect their pastors, bishops, and other church leaders. Compared to cult type groups, there are far more democratic traditions within the mainline black churches.

40. Gerhard Lenski, *The Religious Factor: A Sociological Study of Religion's Impact on Politics, Economics, and Family Life*, p. 122.

41. Du Bois, *The Philadelphia Negro: A Social Study*, p. 207.

42. Thomas Webber, *Deep Like the Rivers: Education in the Slave Quarter Community, 1831–1865*.

43. Cf. Gutman, *The Black Family in Slavery and Freedom, 1750–1925*. The slaves craved education for two reasons: first, it would help prove that they were not the brute animals that whites took them to be; second, reading the Bible themselves was an important motivation, regardless of whether that education led to a job.

44. *History Book of the Springfield Baptist Church, Augusta, Georgia: 1787–1979*, edited by Martin and Waring. A copy of this in-house publication was obtained during a field visit to Springfield Baptist and the nearby Silver Bluff Baptist Church by the authors in June 1983.

45. In his address at Livingstone College at its twenty-fifth anniversary celebration, Dr. Washington referred to this connection: "There is, however, another connection between Tuskegee Institute and Livingstone College, and the great church which stands behind Livingstone, which makes Tuskegee feel very near to the African M.E. Zion Church, for Tuskegee Institute had its birth in a church of your denomination in 1881. Mr. Adam Lewis, one of the most prominent members of your church, had begun to lay the foundation of the Tuskegee Institute before I went to Alabama, and it was in the church of which he was a member that Tuskegee Institute was born." This excerpt of Washington's address is found in Walls, *The African Methodist Episcopal Zion Church: Reality of the Black Church*, p. 331.

46. Nelsen and Nelsen, *Black Church in the Sixties*. The Nelsens argue, "The church's relationship to education is considerably more difficult to pin down," p. 30. They argue that the white missionaries and teachers sent to educate the freedmen and the efforts of white northern denominations to found schools made it hard to differentiate black church efforts in this area.

47. Interview by Lawrence Mamiya with Rev. Cessar Scott, executive minister of the General Baptist Convention of Virginia, January 15, 1989.

48. Antoine Garibaldi, editor, *Black Colleges and Universities: Challenges for the Future*.

49. For many black churches the keeping of financial records tends to be fairly informal with the pastor or one or two laypersons counting the offertory contributions and making payments as needed. The lack of adequate fi-

nancial records and the finances of black churches have often been a point of contention and controversy resulting in church conflicts and schisms. Until this situation is rectified, the financial situation of many black churches will remain clouded not only for researchers but also for interested church members. Poorly kept financial records by black churches still remain a vulnerable point as Mays and Nicholson pointed out over fifty years ago. Mays and Nicholson, *The Negro's Church*, pp. 190–91.

50. The financial data represent information reported by the clergy interviewed. Where they were available, the financial records of the churches were checked against the reported data and adjustments made. Financial records were available in about 20 percent of the urban churches and 10 percent of the rural churches.

51. Dorothy J. Gaithers, "Church Opens a Restaurant in Brooklyn," *New York Times*, April 23, 1983.

52. "Church Businesses Spread the Gospel of Self-Help," *Ebony*, February 1987, p. 61.

53. Ibid., pp. 62–64.

54. This coalition of East Brooklyn Churches also includes predominantly black congregations from white denominations like the Roman Catholics and Lutherans.

55. Mays and Nicholson, *The Negro's Church*, p. 175.

56. David Smallwood, "Economics of the Church," in *Dollars and Sense* special issue, "The Black Church in America," edited by Donald C. Walker, vol. 7, no. 2 (June/July 1981): 81. Smallwood bases his estimates on *The Religious Empire: The Growth and Danger of Tax Exempt Property in the United States*, by Martin A. Larson and C. Stanley Lowell. Using Larson and Lowell's estimate of an $11 billion total in plate offerings ($7 billion from Protestants and $4 billion from Catholics), Smallwood takes 24 percent of $7 billion (for black Protestants) and 3 percent of $4 billion (for black Catholics). The estimate is that black Protestants contribute about $1.6 billion and black Catholics about $100 million.

57. Emmett D. Carson, "Survey Dispels Myth That Blacks Receive but Do Not Give to Charity," *Focus* 15, no. 3 (March 1987): 5.

58. American Association of Fund-Raising Council, *Giving USA:* "Estimates of Philanthropic Giving in 1986 and the Trends They Show," pp. 61–68.

59. Carson, "Survey Dispels Myth," p. 5. It is not clear why Carson separates the amount given by blacks to their "own church" from the amount they give to "religious organizations." The amounts given to both categories need to be added together to give an accurate picture of what black people give in general to religion.

60. Ibid.

61. AAFRC, "Estimates of Philanthropic Giving in 1986," p. 63.

62. Carson, "Survey Dispels Myth," p. 5.

448   Notes

63. *Emerging Trends*, vol. 9, no. 5 (May 1987): 5. The definitions of the scale are as follows: "Superchurched" persons must state a religious preference, are members of a church, attend church regularly, and say religion is "very" important in their lives. "Churched" persons are church members and attend church regularly, regardless of the importance they attribute to religion in their lives. "Unchurched" are those who are not church members and do not attend church regularly, regardless of their other responses.

64. *Emerging Trends*, vol. 9, no. 1 (January 1987): 2.

65. Paris, *The Social Teaching of the Black Churches*, pp. 69–70.

66. Sonja H. Stone, "The Opportunities Industrialization Centers as a Religio-Economic Institution," August 1986, p. 8. Unpublished paper which was prepared as a background paper for the Black Church in the African American Experience Research Project.

67. Ibid., p. 13.

68. Indeed one of Sullivan's economic development tutors was the famous Father Divine who had his headquarters in Philadelphia as Sullivan was beginning his ministry at Zion Baptist Church. Father Divine was the black economic genius of the Great Depression, feeding and housing thousands of people when the federal government could not. Divine's method of economic cooperation among poor people as a means of uplift fascinated Sullivan.

69. Stone, "The Opportunities Industrialization Centers," p. 9.

70. James B. Stewart, "The Black Church as a Religio-Economic Institution," August 1986. Unpublished paper prepared as a background paper for the Black Church in the African American Experience Research Project, p. 23.

71. Ibid.

72. Stone, "The Opportunities Industrialization Centers," p. 5.

73. Ibid., p. 11.

74. "Church Issues Credit Card," Louisville, Gannett News Service, *Poughkeepsie Journal*, July 16, 1988, p. 12.

75. Drake and Cayton, *Black Metropolis*, 2:522.

76. The main dispute is whether class should be defined by income or by occupation. Economist Andrew Brimmer and sociologist Robert Hill define middle class by individual and/or family income ($20,000 to $50,000), while sociologist Bart Landry follows the Weberian tradition of defining middle class by an individual's occupation. Hill contends that much of the rise in the black middle class is due to having two wage earners in a black family rather than one among whites. Landry argues that income alone is an insufficient criterion since it doesn't indicate future potential and stability as do occupational criteria. See the following: Andrew Brimmer and Robert Hill, "The New Black Middle Class,"*Ebony*, August 1987; Robert Hill, "The Black Middle Class: Past, Present, and Future," *The State of Black America 1986*; Bart Landry, "The New Black Middle Class (Part 1)," *Focus*, vol. 15, no. 9 (September 1987); and Bart Landry, "The New Black Middle Class (Part 2),"

Focus, vol. 15, no. 10 (October 1987). Using individual income, Hill estimates that 27 percent of black families had incomes of $25,000 and over in 1983. Based on income and occupation, Landry estimates the black middle class as 37 percent.

77. Robert Hill, "The Black Middle Class Family: Past, Present, and Future," pp. 43–64. Also see Andrew Billingsley, "Black Families in a Changing Society," in *The State of Black America 1987*, pp. 97–111.

78. Reynolds Farley, *Blacks and Whites: Narrowing the Gap?* For more recent data, see Farley and Allen, *The Color Line.*

79. For the study on family wealth, see "Census Bureau Study of Personal and Family Wealth Disparity Between Blacks and Whites," *New York Times,* July 19, 1986, p. A-1.

80. For an overview of the controversy over the term "underclass," see Wilson's *The Truly Disadvantaged*, chapter 1. Wilson argues that this debate between conservatives and liberals about the use of the term tends to obscure some fundamental shifts in the American political economy of large industrial cities, namely, the loss of manufacturing and factory jobs that were essential for access to work experience and job mobility. Also see Isabel Wilkerson, "Growth of the Very Poor Is Focus of New Studies," *New York Times,* December 20, 1987, p. A-26.

81. Wilson, *The Truly Disadvantaged;* see his arguments in chapters 5, 6, and 7. While Wilson has good insights about the limitations and lack of universal appeal of race-specific social policies like affirmative action, a major problem with his analysis of American society is his failure to deal adequately with "institutional racism." In his previous work, *The Declining Significance of Race,* Wilson argued that the legal or de jure desegregation of society had occurred as a result of the civil rights movement, thereby leaving much of what is called racism only in the personal dimension, as individual incidents of racism, for example, name calling, or insults. He does not deal with the fact that there can be institutional barriers and mechanisms, or institutional ways of acting in a racial manner, for example, using zoning laws to promote segregation or culturally biased testing. Affirmative action programs were designed to deal with this factor of institutional racism. Furthermore, although Wilson is correct in perceiving that race-specific social policies like affirmative action have helped the black middle and working classes more than the underclass, the fact that they have been successful in most instances points to their continued need. Our position is that both race-specific and universal social policies are needed at this stage in American society. If Wilson's universal policies succeed in providing the uplift needed by the most deprived members of the underclass, they will still need something like affirmative action to ensure equal opportunity and treatment in businesses, jobs, schools, and the disbursement of government tax revenues.

82. Drake and Cayton, *Black Metropolis*, 2:670.

83. See Baer and Singer, "Toward a Typology of Black Sectarian Response to Racial Stratification," *Anthropological Quarterly* 54 (1981): 1–14. Although Baer and Singer tend to classify the Church of God in Christ with the sectarian characteristics of lower socioeconomic groups, the present and future estimates are that the denomination is becoming largely middle income. The estimates are based on field observations of COGIC churches and conversations with COGIC bishops and administrative personnel at COGIC headquarters in Memphis. "Middle income" should not be confused with "middle-class" status, which usually indicates a college education besides income. Being middle income among African Americans is also a precarious state, vulnerable to sudden economic shifts. Usually it requires at least two working members of a black family to reach that level.

84. While class divisions do afflict black churches, Drake and Cayton have pointed out that the large institutional urban churches or what they have called "mixed type churches" have demonstrated the ability to bring together people from different class strata. Their success involved allowing different adult subgroups to form within the church. These subgroups made poor people feel comfortable among those like themselves, yet other programs brought them into contact with middle-class members. See Drake and Cayton, *The Black Metropolis*, 2:670ff.

85. Martin Luther King, Jr., *Where Do We Go from Here?* p. 132. Also see Hill, "The Black Middle Class Family: Past, Present, and Future," p. 57.

86. See the descriptions in Charles H. Nichols, "Recreative and Creative Involvement in Culture," in Joseph R. Washington, Jr., editor, *Dilemmas of the New Black Middle Class*, p. 70. Nichols also refers to Christopher Lasch's *The Culture of Narcissism: American Life in an Age of Diminishing Expectations*. For more recent popular descriptions of the ambivalence found among the black middle class, see the following: C. King, "We're Black Yuppies. Which World Would We Belong in?" *Glamour* 85 (May 1987): 78. R. Lacayo, "Between Two Worlds: The Black Middle Class," *Time* 133 (March 19, 1989): 58–62.

87. George Davis and Gregg Watson, *Black Life in Corporate America: Swimming in the Mainstream.*

88. Mamiya and Roberts, "Invisible People, Untold Stories," pp. 26–30.

89. For one example of this debate between black neoconservatives and liberals, see Williams, editor, *The State of Black America 1986*, for the debate on "U.S. Social Policy: Obstacle or Opportunity for Disadvantaged Americans." Essays by Bernard Anderson, "The Case for Social Policy," and by Glenn C. Loury, "Beyond Civil Rights."

90. Rodney, *How Europe Underdeveloped Africa*, p. 106. Rodney presents a chart showing comparative population growth estimates over four centuries and the effect of the slave trade in stripping African countries of millions of potential workers. See Manning Marable's application of Rodney's analysis to the United States in his *How Capitalism Underdeveloped*

Black America. Among the black theologians, Cornel West has developed the most extensive and sophisticated critique of American capitalism and related it to the traditions of the Black Church in his *Prophecy Deliverance!* Partly due to West's influence and to his dialogues with Latin American liberation theologians, James Cone has begun to incorporate a Marxist analysis into his theological reflections. See Cone's essay, "The Black Church and Marxism: What Do They Have to Say to Each Other?"

91. For a summary of economic gains and losses, see Farley, *Blacks and Whites.* Also see Farley and Allen, *The Color Line.*

92. Frazier, *The Negro Church in America,* p. 50.

10 The Church and Women

1. For a recounting and interpretation of the incident, see Jacquelyn Grant, "Black Women and the Church," in Gloria T. Hull, Patricia Bell Scott, and Barbara Smith, editors, *All the Women Are White, All the Blacks Are Men, BUT SOME OF US ARE BRAVE: Black Women's Studies,* pp. 141–52; and Cornish Rogers, "Feminists: Soul and Sense," in *The Christian Century* (February 1974), pp. 172–74. Rogers interprets this incident as a "painful reminder of the reality of black male powerlessness and efforts of black church women to bolster males egos." The church women have decided that the "women rule and the men preside."

The division of the pulpit as men's space and the pew as women's place is not only found in black churches but also in most white churches. This division follows the patriarchal view that the public sphere is male space and the private sphere is female space. Besides Christianity, Judaism and Islam have also been deeply affected by this sexual division of public and private.

2. In spite of their historical importance, very little research has been done on the history of any of the women's conventions of the seven denominations. See the work of Evelyn Brooks on Nannie Burroughs and the Woman's Convention of the National Baptist Convention, U.S.A., Inc. Brooks, "Religion, Politics, and Gender: The Leadership of Nannie Helen Burroughs." Also see Evelyn Brooks, "In Politics to Stay: Black Women Leaders and Party Politics in the 1920s," in Louise Tilly and Patricia Gurin, editors, *Women in Twentieth-Century American Politics.*

3. Mbiti, *African Religions and Philosophy.* See chapter 11.

4. Geoffrey Parrinder, *African Traditional Religion.*

5. Ibid., p. 101.

6. For an overview of these traditions, see Simpson, *Black Religions in the New World.*

7. Raboteau, *Slave Religion,* pp. 75–87. Sobel indicates that the first Marie Laveau was a "small black Congo woman," whose African practices were handed down to her daughter, who became a Haitian Voudou practitioner. Her granddaughter became the most important Voudou practitioner

in America, the "Voudou Queen" of New Orleans. See Sobel, *Trabelin' On*, pp. 49–50.

8. See Sobel, *Trabelin' On*, pp.42–45, 66–71, for an excellent description of conjure in black folk religion, which lasted into the twentieth century.

9. Raboteau, *Slave Religion*, p. 238.

10. Mbiti, *African Religions and Philosophy*. See the section on history and time in African cosmologies, pp. 27–31.

11. For examples and an elaboration of the powerful role of oral tradition in black culture, see Levine, *Black Culture and Black Consciousness*.

12. Raboteau, *Slave Religion*, p. 253.

13. Ibid., p. 81ff. While the folk idiom "son of thunder" was used to designate the booming voiced, fiery preacher, the origin of the term may also be related to "Shango," the West African god of thunder and lightning, whose symbol was the axe. Many African American folk customs are related to thunder.

14. For example, Carter Woodson's famous work, *The History of the Negro Church*, does not list one woman preacher from the period of slavery into the twentieth century.

15. Phillis Wheatley, *Poems on Various Subjects, Religious and Moral*.

16. Elizabeth, *Elizabeth, A Colored Minister of the Gospel Born in Slavery*.

17. See the section on Elizabeth, in Loewenberg and Bogin, *Black Women in Nineteenth-Century America*, p. 127.

18. Jarena Lee, *Religious Experience and Journal of Mrs. Jarena Lee*. For background information on Mrs. Jarena Lee, see the following: Loewenberg and Bogin, *Black Women in Nineteenth-Century America*, pp. 135–41; and Jualynne Dodson, "Nineteenth-Century A.M.E. Preaching Women," in Hilah F. Thomas and Rosemary Skinner Keller, editors, *Woman in New Worlds*, pp. 276–89. Also see the account given of Mrs. Lee in the introductory essay, "Three Women and the Black Church," by Marilyn Richardson, editor, in *Black Women and Religion: A Bibliography*.

19. Dodson, "Nineteenth-Century A.M.E. Preaching Women," p. 278.

20. Loewenberg and Bogin, *Black Women in Nineteenth-Century America*, p. 136.

21. See the introductory essay by Jean McMahon Humez, editor, *Gifts of Power: The Writings of Rebecca Jackson, Black Visionary, Shaker Eldress*.

22. Ibid.

23. According to Dodson, the A.M.E. Church created the post of "stewardess," to recognize women who would merely be assistants to male stewards, class leaders, and the pastor. See Dodson, "Nineteenth-Century A.M.E. Preaching Women," p. 282.

24. Amanda Berry Smith, *An Autobiography: The Story of the Lord's Dealings with Mrs. Amanda Smith, the Colored Evangelist, Containing an Account of Her Life Work of Faith, Her Travels in America, England, Scot-*

land, India, and Africa as an Independent Missionary. See Loewenberg and Bogin for Amanda Smith's view, *Black Women in Nineteenth-Century America*, p. 143. Also see Sylvia M. Jacobs, editor, *Black Americans and the Missionary Movement in Africa*.

25. See the introduction by Jualynne Dodson to Smith, *An Autobiography: The Story of the Lord's Dealings with Mrs. Amanda Smith, the Colored Evangelist.*

26. Marilyn Richardson, editor, *Maria W. Stewart: America's First Black Woman Political Writer*. Also see Loewenberg and Bogin, *Black Women in Nineteenth-Century American Life*, pp. 183–200.

27. See Bettye Collier-Thomas, *Black Women in America: Contributors to Our Heritage*, for a profile of Harriet Tubman.

28. Loewenberg and Bogin, *Black Women in Nineteenth-Century America*, p. 234.

29. Sojourner Truth, *The Narrative of Sojourner Truth, A Bondswoman of Olden Times Emancipated by the New York Legislature in the Early Part of the Present Century, with a History of Her Labors and Correspondence.* See also Bettye Collier-Thomas, *Black Women in America*, for a profile of Sojourner Truth.

30. Frances Jackson Coppin, *Reminiscences of School Life and Hints on Teaching*. For background see Loewenberg and Bogin, *Black Women in Nineteenth-Century America*, pp. 302–16.

31. Anna Julia Cooper, *A Voice from the South: By a Black Woman of the South*. Also see Loewenberg and Bogin, *Black Women in Nineteenth-Century America*, pp. 317–18.

32. Brooks, "Religion, Politics, and Gender: The Leadership of Nannie Helen Burroughs," p. 5. Nannie Helen Burroughs, *Grow: A Handy Guide for Progressive Churchwomen*.

33. Ibid.

34. For a profile of Dr. Mary McLeod Bethune, see Collier-Thomas, *Black Women in America*.

35. Walls, *The African Methodist Episcopal Zion Church*, p. 479.

36. According to Methodist-Episcopal polity, the ordained ministers are of two orders, deacons and elders. A deacon can preach, *assist* at the administration of Holy Communion, baptize and administer matrimony, and try disorderly members. Eldership is the highest of holy orders. Only an elder can consecrate the elements of Holy Communion. Besides the duties of preaching, baptism, and marriage, an elder is usually the pastor of a church. Cf. Walls, *The African Methodist Episcopal Zion Church*, pp. 103–4.

37. For a summary of this history, see Dodson, "Nineteenth-Century A.M.E. Preaching Women."

38. The Methodist Episcopal Church, North, recognized deaconesses in 1888 and the Methodist Episcopal Church, South, accepted them in 1902. For both deaconess is not an ordained position but the special status of a full-

time church worker. See Jackson W. Carroll, Barbara Hargrove, and Adair T. Lummis, *Women of the Cloth: A New Opportunity for the Churches*, p. 28.

39. See Lakey, *The History of the C.M.E. Church*, pp. 406, 408.

40. See the summary given by Carroll et al., *Women of the Cloth*, p. 22.

41. Sobel, *Trabelin' On*, p. 233.

42. Washington, *Frustrated Fellowship: The Black Baptist Quest for Social Power*, part 3.

43. See the *Church of God in Christ Official Manual*, by the Editorial Commission, pp. 144–46.

44. Our interviewers in the field were instructed to make special efforts to interview black female clergy of the seven historic black denominations even if they were not in the random sample.

45. Anqunett Fusilier, editor, "National Baptist Convention U.S.A., Inc. Socio-Economic Programs Sweep the Nation Under the Leadership of Dr. T. J. Jemison," *The Cornerstone*, p. 22.

46. See John Lynch, "The Ordination of Women: Protestant Experience in Ecumenical Perspective," *Journal of Ecumenical Studies* 12 (1975), no. 2:195. According to Lynch, most predominantly white denominations did not have to change their doctrines but only adjusted their disciplines to allow full ordination of women.

47. Delores Carpenter, "The Effects of Sect-Typeness Upon the Professionalization of Black Female Masters of Divinity Graduates, 1972–1984," Ph.D. dissertation, p. 136. The authors wish to acknowledge and thank Rev. Dr. Dolores Carpenter for sharing a copy of her dissertation with them.

48. Carroll et al., *Women of the Cloth*, p. 4.

49. Carpenter, *The Effects of Sect-Typeness*, pp. 136ff. Also see Marjorie Hyer, "Black Women, White Pulpits," *Washington Post*, October 12, 1985.

50. Hyer, "Black Women, White Pulpits."

51. Interview with Carpenter in Hyer, "Black Women, White Pulpits."

52. Respondent no. 7 in a study by Deborah May, "The Impact of Racism and Sexism upon Black Clergywomen," unpublished study for a senior thesis in Women's Studies at Vassar College, April 30, 1985, p. 44. The authors wish to thank Ms. May for permission to cite her excellent study.

53. Katie G. Cannon, in *God's Fierce Whimsy: Christian Feminism and Theological Education*, edited by Katie G. Cannon, Beverly W. Harrison, Carter Heyward, Ada Maria Isasi-Diaz, Bess B. Johnson, Mary D. Pellauer, Nancy D. Richardson, p. 46. Also cited in May, "The Impact of Racism," p. 44.

54. Cynthia Epstein, "Positive Effects of the Multiple Negative: Explaining the Success of Black Professional Women," *American Journal of Sociology* 78 (January 1973), no. 4:917. Also see May, "The Impact of Racism."

55. Mamiya, "The Second Episcopal District of the African Methodist Episcopal Church," p. 6.

56. Ibid.

57. Ibid.

58. See Mozella G. Mitchell, "The Black Women's View of Human Libera-

tion," in *Theology Today* 39 (January 1983): 421–25. Also see May, "The Impact of Racism," p. 45.

59. See Paula Giddings's excellent historical overview of the internal and external debates regarding the role of black women in both the civil rights and feminist movements. Paula Giddings, *When and Where I Enter: The Impact of Black Women on Race and Sex in America*, chapters 17, 18.

60. The Combahee River Collective, "A Black Feminist Statement," in *All the Women Are White, All the Blacks Are Men*, edited by Hull, Scott, and Smith, p. 19.

61. Alice Walker, *In Search of Our Mother's Garden*, p. xi. Also quoted in Jacqueline Grant, "Womanist Theology: Black Women's Experience as a Source for Doing Theology, with Special Reference to Christology," in *The Journal of the Interdenominational Theological Center*, 13 (Spring 1986), no. 2:200. Grant leaves out Alice Walker's other definitions of womanist.

62. Grant, "Womanist Theology," p. 199.

63. Ibid., p. 208.

64. Katie G. Cannon, *Black Womanist Ethics*.

65. *Emerging Trends* 10 (January 1988), no. 1:1, 4.

66. Lawrence Mamiya, interviews with inmates at the Green Haven Correctional Facility, New York, May 6, 1988; quote from Elijah. Also see the literature on lower-class black male socialization: Malcolm X and Alex Haley, *The Autobiography of Malcolm X*; Claude Brown, *Manchild in the Promised Land*; and Eugene Perkins, *Home Is a Dirty Street: The Social Oppression of Black Children*. More contemporary data for unchurched black males over the age of eighteen is presented in chapter 11.

67. See the data between 1981 to 1983 covered by Jacquelyne Johnson Jackson's study, "Aged Black Americans: Double Jeopardy Re-examined," in *The State of Black America 1985*, edited by James D. Williams, pp. 143–83.

68. *Emerging Trends* 9 (November 1987), no. 9:1.

69. See Robert Staples's essay, "The Myth of Black Matriarchy," in *The Black Male in America*, edited by Doris Y. Wilkerson and Ronald L. Taylor, p. 183, n. 23.

70. Robert Staples, "Race and Marital Status: an Overview," in Harriet Pipes McAdoo, editor, *Black Families*, p. 174. Also see Robert Staples, *The World of Black Singles*. Staples points out the structural constraints affecting the black middle class, especially in regard to the large numbers of black female college graduates compared to black male graduates. The overall ratio is 2–1 and in some categories like the elite colleges and universities as high as thirty-eight women to every male. In 1988 there were about 100,000 more black women in colleges than black men.

11   The Church and Young People

1. See James Baldwin's somewhat autobiographical account in *Go Tell It on the Mountain*, a play that reflects the rural-urban migration.

2. Interview no. 1099.

3. Studies have shown that religion in the South as a region is still more highly influential among both blacks and whites. For a historical perspective, see Albanese, *America: Religion and Religions.* For demographic studies, see Bernard Quinn et al., *Churches and Church Membership in the United States, 1980,* and Roof and McKinney, *American Mainline Religion.*

4. Berry and Blassingame, *Long Memory: The Black Experience in America,* pp. 70–113.

5. For the historical evidence for informal adoption and fictive kinship, see Gutman's *The Black Family in Slavery and Freedom, 1750–1925.*

6. Frazier and Lincoln, *The Negro Church in America: The Black Church Since Frazier,* pp. 37–40.

7. Carter G. Woodson uses the phrase "junior church," and Charles S. Johnson refers to "Children's Day," to describe the special activities of rural churches for youth. Carter G. Woodson, *The Rural Negro,* p. 171. Charles Spurgeon Johnson, *Growing Up in the Black Belt: Negro Youth in the Rural South,* p. 141.

8. For a theological interpretation of the relationship between black families and black churches, see DeOtis Roberts, *Roots of a Black Future: Family and Church.*

9. See the *New York Times* article on the church kitchen at Mother Zion, "Typical Sunday Dinner for Worshipers at Harlem's Mother African Methodist Episcopal Zion Church," August 26, 1981.

10. Woodson, *The Rural Negro,* chapters 8, 9. Johnson, *Growing Up in the Black Belt,* chapter 5. Although Allison Davis and John Dollard's *Children of Bondage: The Personality Development of Negro Youth in the Urban South* was written as part of the American Youth Commission's project on Negro youth, as was Johnson's *Growing Up in the Black Belt,* their work was not very helpful in delineating the influence of urban black churches. Davis and Dollard's focus on the development of personality types and on deviance tends to skew the portrait of urban Negro youth.

11. John H. Scanzoni, *The Black Family in Modern Society,* p. 117.

12. The title of this section and the next, "Black Children, White Dreams," is taken from Thomas Cottle's study of urban black children, *Black Children, White Dreams.*

13. Most scholars tend to cite the famous 1947 study by Kenneth B. Clark and Mamie B. Clark, "Racial Identification and Racist Preference in Negro Children," in T. M. Newcomb and E. L. Hartley, editors, *Readings in Social Psychology,* pp. 169–78. The 1947 study was preceded by two others: Kenneth B. Clark and Mamie P. Clark (1939), "The Development of Consciousness of Self and the Emergence of Racial Identity in Negro Preschool Children," *Journal of Social Psychology* 10: 591–99; and Kenneth B. Clark and Mamie P. Clark (1940), "Skin Color as a Factor in Racial Identification of Negro Preschool Children," *Journal of Social Psychology,* SPSS Bulletin 11:

156–69. In the doll-choice tests the child, who is presented with a black and a white doll, is given the following instructions: 1. Show me the doll you would like to play with (preference). 2. Show me the doll that looks nice. 3. Show me the doll that looks bad. 4. Show me the doll that looks like a Negro child. 5. Show me the doll that looks like you (expressed self-identification).

14. Clark and Clark, "Skin Color as a Factor in Racial Identification." Also see Michelle Fine and Cheryl Bowers, "Racial Self-Identification: The Effects of Social History and Gender," *Journal of Applied Social Psychology* 14 (1984): 2:136–43.

15. For overview summaries of these studies, see the following: J. Porter and R. Washington, "Black Identity and Self-Esteem: A Review of Studies of Black Self-Concept," *Annual Review of Sociology* 5 (1979): 53–54. Also see Judith Porter's fine book, *Black Child, White Child: The Development of Racial Attitudes.* For studies into the decade of the 1980s, see Fine and Bowers, "Racial Self-Identification."

16. In their 1970 study Hraba and Grant found that 70 percent of black children preferred the black doll. J. Hraba and C. Grant, "A Reexamination of Racial Preferences and Identification," *Journal of Personality and Social Psychology* 16 (1970): 398–402. In 1977 Winnick and Taylor reported that 64 percent of black children chose the black doll; cf. Porter and Washington, "Black Identity and Self-Esteem."

17. Fine and Bowers, "Racial Self-Identification," pp. 138–43. On the predicted gender difference the authors reported that 57 percent of the boys versus 35 percent of the girls preferred to play with the white doll, and 83 percent of the girls versus 60 percent of the boys identified themselves with the black doll.

18. A summary of the 1987 APA meeting was reported in the following: Daniel L. Goleman, "Black Child's Self-Views Still Low," *New York Times,* August 13, 1987, p. A-13; and "A Question of Black Pride," by Anastasia Toufexis and D. Blake Hallanan, *Time* (September 14, 1987), p. 74. Sharon McNichol did a study of black children in Trinidad and found even stronger preferences among the children there for the white dolls than in the U.S. study by Powell-Hopson.

19. Darlene L. Powell-Hopson, "The Effects of Modeling, Reinforcement, and Color Meaning Word Associations on Doll Color Preferences of Black Preschool Children and White Preschool Children," Ph.D. dissertation, Hofstra University, 1985. The study also showed that white preference of both black and white children could be modified with intervention by experimenters who modeled black preference responses, read a story depicting black children positively, and reinforced children who chose black dolls. The post-test showed that 67 percent of the children preferred the black doll. The study has implications for teachers' attitudes.

20. For the effects by age and social class, see Porter, *Black Child, White Child,* pp. 74–86, 87ff. Porter shows that for black children between ages 3–

6, there is a majority preference for white skin color, which diminishes gradually between ages 7–10. By ages 11–12 there is a preference for brown skin color. In terms of class, awareness of racial differences is more prevalent among lower-class children, both black and white. Black middle-class children tend to be more individualistically inclined with regard to identity. For the effects by gender, Fine and Bowers (1984) show that black males, ages 4–6, were more likely to prefer and identify with white dolls.

21. Fine and Bowers, "Racial Self-Identification," p. 137.

22. Porter, Black Child, White Child, pp. 138–39.

23. Ibid., pp. 66–69.

24. Interview with Darlene Powell-Hopson in Toufexis and Hallanan, "A Question of Black Pride."

25. Robert Coles, Children of Crisis, pp. 64–65.

26. Ibid., pp. 336–37.

27. Interview no. 1453.

28. Interview no. 1623.

29. Interview no. 1423.

30. Interview no. 1425.

31. The informal survey of Sunday school literature was conducted as part of the "Black Church in the African American Experience" project by Lawrence Mamiya in field visits to black churches and interviews with denominational leaders. Some pastors were asked for a sample of their educational materials.

32. Observation of Dr. David Shannon, vice president of academic affairs, Interdenominational Theological Center, Atlanta, May 13, 1988. Shannon's view is based on contact with Baptist clergy in the South.

33. Interview no. 1188.

34. Porter, Black Child, White Child, pp. 18–19. Porter cites Suzanne Keller's study, "The Social World of the Urban Slum Child," American Journal of Orthopsychiatry 33 (1963): 823–31. Although Keller's study applies specifically to lower-class black children, one can also generalize about the influence of television on middle-class children, black and white.

35. For specific data on blacks in the media, see Samuel L. Adams, "Blackening in Media: The State of Blacks in the Press," The State of Black America 1985, edited by James D. Williams, pp. 65–103.

36. Pat Patterson, "Blacks and the Media in the 1980s," The State of Black America 1982, edited by James D. Williams, pp. 239–63.

37. See Kozol's comments about the judgments of the art teacher and its effects on the children. Jonathan Kozol, Death at an Early Age: The Destruction of the Hearts and Minds of Negro Children in the Boston Public Schools, pp. 148–50.

38. Albert Memmi, The Colonizer and the Colonized; and Perkins, Home Is a Dirty Street: The Social Oppression of Black Children.

39. Carter G. Woodson, The Mis-Education of the Negro, p. xiii.

40. Billingsley, "Black Families in a Changing Society," p. 102.

41. Marian Wright Edelman, "An Advocacy Agenda for Black Families and Children," in Harriet McAdoo, editor, *Black Families*, pp. 291–300.

42. Ibid., p. 295. Also see Nannie Burroughs, "Unload Your Uncle Toms," in Gerda Lerner, editor, *Black Women in White America: A Documentary History*.

43. For example, see Joseph R. Washington, Jr., *Anti-Blackness in English Religion, 1500–1800*. Also see the work of black theologians like James Cone, Gayraud Wilmore, and Cornel West.

44. Porter, *Black Child, White Child*, pp. 28–30.

45. Claude Brown, *Manchild in the Promised Land*, p. 75. Also see Porter, *Black Child, White Child*, p. 141.

46. The most prominent example of media focus on the dependency phenomenon is found in Bill Moyers's television documentary on "The Vanishing Black Family," produced for PBS in 1987. Moyers unfairly tends to take the problems of underclass black families as being representative of the whole.

47. Douglas G. Glasgow, "The Black Underclass in Perspective," in *The State of Black America 1987*, p. 131.

48. Ibid., pp. 129–44. Also see Wilson, *The Truly Disadvantaged*. Both Glasgow and Wilson summarize the impact of the public policy debate. Liberals see the rise in poverty and the underclass due to the severe reduction in programs to aid the poor and in the restrictions placed upon having males in the home by welfare departments. Neoconservatives have argued the need to change lower-class behavior and the dependency syndrome generated by the welfare system.

49. Ibid., p. 136.

50. James D. McGhee, "The Black Family Today and Tomorrow," *The State of Black America 1985*, p. 2.

51. Ibid., pp. 135–38.

52. See Glasgow, "The Black Underclass in Perspective," pp. 137–38. Glasgow also refers to a study in progress by Betty J. Collier Watson, "Income, Employment, and Family Formation: A Pilot Study." Also see Wilson, *The Truly Disadvantaged*, pp. 72–73, 82–83. Wilson also points out that due to the relative absence of black males, black female heads of households are less likely to remarry if divorced and white female headed households tend to be of shorter duration, p. 172.

53. For some empirical data on this phenomenon, see Richard B. Freeman's study, "Who Escapes? The Relation of Churchgoing and Other Background Factors to the Socioeconomic Performance of Black Male Youths from Inner-City Tracts," in *The Black Youth Employment Crisis*, edited by Richard B. Freeman and Harry J. Holzer. Freeman found "more inner-city youths never attending church and fewer attending once a week or more than other youths," p. 362.

54. Ruth Dennis, "The Young Black Male and the Church," a paper read at the Vanderbilt Divinity School, November 21, 1980, for a conference on the Black Male in Religious Context. Excerpts of the study were quoted in Kelly Miller Smith, "Religion as a Force in Black America," in *The State of Black America 1982*, edited by James D. Williams, p. 230.

55. Perkins, *Home Is a Dirty Street: The Social Oppression of Black Children*, chapters 3, 4. Although Perkins has a fine analysis and understanding of underclass black youth, much of his work is limited to black male socialization.

56. Claude Brown, "Manchild in Harlem," *New York Times Magazine*, September 16, 1984, p. 38ff. Also see Brown's article, "Crack and the American Dream: Lost Opportunities in the Ghetto," special to the *Los Angeles Times*, reprinted in the *Poughkeepsie Journal*, May 26, 1988.

57. David Swinton, "The Economic Status of Blacks 1986," in *The State of Black America 1987*, Janet Dewart, editor, pp. 58–59.

58. Billy J. Tidwell, "A Profile of the Black Unemployed: A Disaggregation Analysis," *The State of Black America 1987*, Janet Dewart, editor, p. 227. See the data in table 1.

59. Joan Petersilia, *Racial Disparities in the Criminal Justice System*, p. 1. Also see Roi D. Townsey, "The Incarceration of Black Men," in *Black Men*, edited by Lawrence E. Gary, p. 229–31.

60. Vernetta Nix Williams, writer, and Travis L. Francis, editor, "Women in Prisons," *Criminal Justice Issues*, January 1983, vol. 7, no. 2:1–2.

61. Jim Murphy, "A Question of Race: Minority/White Incarceration in New York State" (Albany, New York: New York State Coalition for Criminal Justice and Center for Justice Education, 1987), p. 2. Data on South African prisons are taken from *Report of the Department of Justice, Republic of South Africa* for the period July 1, 1983, to June 30, 1984. South African population data is from *Statesman's Year Book 1985/1986*.

62. Murphy, "A Question of Race."

63. Ibid., pp. 3–4.

64. Ibid.

65. According to the *Southern Coalition Report*, seven out of the top ten states having the largest prison populations in the United States were in the South, where blacks constitute 54 percent of the total. See the *Southern Coalition Report on Jails and Prisons* 7 (Spring 1980), no. 2.

66. Ladner rightly points out that negative reactions to the Moynihan Report's heavy emphasis upon social pathologies led to this defensiveness and hesitancy; the reactions led to emphasizing the strengths of black families. The crises of the 1980s, however, have led to a more balanced approach of recognizing strengths but also of dealing with problematic areas. See Joyce Ladner, "Teenage Pregnancy: The Implication for Black Americans," in *The State of Black America 1986*, edited by James D. Williams, pp. 68–70.

67. Children's Defense Fund, "Black and White Children in America:

Key Facts." Washington, D.C., 1985. Also see Ladner, "Teenage Pregnancy," p. 70.

68. K. A. Moore, "Fact Sheet" (on teenage pregnancy). Also see Ladner, "Teenage Pregnancy," p. 70.

69. Ladner, "Teenage Pregnancy," pp. 71–73.

70. Ibid., p. 74.

71. Ibid., p. 75.

72. The view of life cycle was first elaborated in Erik Erikson's *Childhood and Society*.

73. See Erik Erikson's *Young Man Luther: A Study in Psychoanalysis and History*, and *Gandhi's Truth: On the Origins of Militant Nonviolence*. Also see *Encounter with Erikson: Historical Interpretation and Religious Biography*, edited by Donald Capps, Walter H. Capps, and M. Gerald Bradford.

74. See "Age a Key Factor in Comparing Religiousness of Men and Women," in *Emerging Trends* 9, no. 9 (November 1987): 1. Respondents were asked to rate themselves on a scale from 1 to 10 regarding how well the term, "religious person," fits them. A score of 10 represented a perfect description and 1 a totally wrong description.

75. Erik Erikson, *The Life Cycle Completed*. Also see Daniel Goleman, "Erikson, in His Own Old Age, Expands His View of Life," *New York Times*, June 14, 1988, pp. C-1, C-14.

76. See Wilson, *The Truly Disadvantaged*, pp. 61–62.

77. Charles Murray has been one of the leading neoconservative analysts. See his critique of the welfare system and poverty program policies in *Losing Ground: American Social Policy, 1950–1980*. Robert Hill, Joyce Ladner, Andrew Billingsley, Douglas Glasgow, and others have constituted the liberal wing of the social policy and poverty debate. Hill's *The Strengths of Black Families* is one example of the policy position in the debate on black families stirred by Daniel Patrick Moynihan in 1965.

78. Max Weber, *The Protestant Ethic and the Spirit of Capitalism*. Gerhard Lenski's study, *The Religious Factor*, is one of the few examinations of black religious belief and economic behavior. Lenski said the following: "We had expected that involvement in the Negro Protestant churches would be negatively linked with commitment to the spirit of capitalism, since the group as a whole lacked a strong commitment. However, such was not the case. Those who were active in the Negro Protestant churches were more likely to express views consonant with this spirit than were marginal members." Lenski, *The Religious Factor*, p. 122.

79. Freeman, "Who Escapes? The Relation of Churchgoing and Other Background Factors to the Socioeconomic Performance of Black Male Youths from Inner-City Tracts," p. 372.

80. Ibid., p. 373.

81. Ibid., p. 374.

82. According to a 1987 study of residential segregation, Douglas S. Massey and Nancy A. Denton found that blacks remain the "most residentially segregated minority group in America," about 1.6 times higher than Hispanics and twice that of Asians. Even when blacks move to suburbs, they are often subjected to high levels of segregation, they reported. Results of the study were presented at meetings of the Northeast-Midwest Institute. See "Persisting Segregation Reported," Gannett News Service, Poughkeepsie Journal, June 23, 1988, p. 1.

83. For example, see Drake and Cayton, Black Metropolis, 2:636ff. Also see Zora Neale Hurston's previously unpublished study, The Sanctified Church.

84. However, COGIC has not joined the National Council of Churches probably because its stance on homosexuality may have prevented its membership. The Community Metropolitan Churches, made up of mostly gay congregants, were members.

85. Church of God in Christ International Directory 1978–1979. Bishop J. O. Patterson, presiding Bishop; Bishop German R. Ross, general secretary.

86. As we pointed out in chapter 9, only 7 percent of the churches in our study were storefront churches, mainly of Baptist and COGIC persuasion.

87. One could point to the black Methodists (A.M.E.; A.M.E. Zion; and C.M.E.), who are predominantly middle income, and a number of black Baptists. Groups like the Muslims have also been affected. See Lawrence H. Mamiya, "From Black Muslim to Bilalian: The Evolution of a Movement," Journal for the Scientific Study of Religion 21, no. 2 (June 1982): 138–52.

88. For examples of comprehensive policies, see Wilson, The Truly Disadvantaged, chapter 7.

89. Isabel Wilkerson, "Detroit Citizens Join with Church to Rid Community of Drugs," New York Times, June 29, 1988, p. A-14.

90. Ibid.

91. Thomas Morgan, "Muslim Patrol Reduces Crime in Brooklyn Area," New York Times, February 25, 1988.

92. Both Dempsey and Walker were interviewed as part of our field survey.

93. "Black Churches, Endangered Children," editorial page, New York Times, May 23, 1988, p. A-18.

94. Telephone interview by Lawrence Mamiya with Henry Gregory of the Shiloh Baptist Church, July 6, 1988.

95. Imam Warith Deen Muhammad, the leader of the former American Muslim Mission, has a strong, devout following in many prisons. This group of Sunni Muslims has developed programs for men and women in prison and when they are released.

96. Ibid.

97. Alex Poinsett, "Suffer the Little Children," Ebony (August 1988), p. 148. Poinsett indicates that black churches have more youth-oriented programs than any other institutions.

98. Ibid. Dr. Taylor of Concord has also suggested that ten thousand black churches could raise $250,000 each, creating a permanent funding base for community activities.

99. "Black Churches, Endangered Children." Project Spirit grew out of attempts by Bishop John Hurst Adams to found a school for ethnic education for the children of Watts when he was the pastor of the Grant A.M.E. Church in Los Angeles. See the work developed by Adams and Trevlyn Reed, *Ethnic Educational Materials for Young Children*.

100. Ibid.

101. Emily Smith, "The Church Connection," *Durham Morning Herald*, November 20, 1988. The six participating churches are Fisher Memorial United Holy Church of America, Covenant United Presbyterian Church, Community Baptist Church, Mt. Gilead Baptist Church, Mt. Vernon Baptist Church, and Russell Memorial A.M.E. Church.

102. Lawrence Mamiya, field interview conducted at the Bethel A.M.E. Church in Baltimore, May 21, 1989.

103. Ibid.

104. Ibid.

105. Marsha Jones, "Memorial A.M.E. Zion Church: 161st Anniversary Celebration," in *About . . . Time Magazine*, Rochester, N.Y. (May 1988), p. 25.

106. See Dennis, "The Young Black Male and the Church," pp. 230–33. Dennis feels that the majority of young black males in her study had quit attending church before age seventeen. Also see Freeman, "Who Escapes? The Relation of Churchgoing and Other Background Factors to the Socioeconomic Performance of Black Male Youths from Inner-City Tracts."

107. Frazier, *The Negro Church in America*, chapter 5. During the 1950s when Frazier did his study there was a pattern of upwardly mobile blacks joining white churches. However, the civil rights movement and the period of black consciousness that followed largely stemmed that movement. There has been no evidence of a surge of black membership in white denominations. For example, a study of the black clergy in the Episcopal Church reports on the problems of recruiting and deploying these clergy. If black people were joining the Episcopal Church in large numbers, the problem of placing their black priests would not be an issue. See Franklin D. Turner and Adair T. Lummis, *Black Clergy in the Episcopal Church: Recruitment, Training, and Deployment*. The study of Episcopal clergy was conducted in 1979 and published thereafter.

108. James Davidson Hunter, *Evangelicalism: The Coming Generation*, pp. 165–78.

109. Interview by Mamiya with Dr. James Costen, May 23, 1988, in Durham, N.C. Costen felt that only about 15 percent of the black clergy nationwide had completed their professional training. The evangelical Christian tradition of the black Baptists, Methodists, and Pentecostals does not require

a seminary education for ordination. After their initial call, most black clergy go through a period of apprenticeship with a more experienced pastor.

110. For the growing focus on the importance of pastoral counseling in black churches, see the following: Henry H. Mitchell and Nicholas Cooper Lewter, *Soul Theology: The Heart of American Black Culture;* David Hurst, "Shepherding Black Christians," Ph.D. dissertation; Edward P. Wimberley, *Pastoral Care in the Black Church;* and Carroll M. Felton, Jr., *The Care of Souls in the Black Church: A Liberation Perspective.*

12 Music and the Church

1. For an analysis and examples of the sung sermon, see the fine study by Gerald L. Davis, *I Got the Word in me and I can sing it, you know: A Study of the Performed African-American Sermon.* The title of our chapter, "The Performed Word" borrows from Davis's view of performance in the sermon and extends it to the musical ministry of the Black Church. The Word is performed and made alive not only in the preaching but also in the music.

2. James H. Cone, *The Spirituals and the Blues,* p. 5.

3. Cf. Miles Mark Fisher, *Negro Slave Songs in the United States;* Mitchell, *Black Preaching;* and Southern, *The Music of Black Americans.*

4. Ella Anderson Clark, "The Reminiscences of Ella Anderson Clark," MS, pp. 41–42, James Osgood Andrew Clark Papers.

5. Natalie Curtis Burlin, "Negro Music at Birth," *The Musical Quarterly* 5 (October 1919): 88.

6. Southern, *The Music of Black Americans* (second edition), p. 85.

7. William B. McClain, "The Liturgy of Zion." (Unpublished manuscript.)

8. John Wesley Work, *Folk Songs of the American Negro,* pp. 110–20.

9. Howard Thurman, *Deep River and the Negro Spiritual Speaks of Life and Death,* p. 21.

10. William Grove Matton, "Memoirs 1859–1887," MS, chapter 6, p. 2.

11. Thurman, *Deep River,* p. 29.

12. James H. Cone, *For My People: Black Theology and the Black Church,* p. 63.

13. Laura M. Townes, Diary, MS, April 28, 1862 entry, Penn School Papers.

14. Southern, *The Music of Black Americans,* pp. 170–71.

15. See LeRoi Jones's explanation of this shout phenomenon among converted slaves in *Blues People.*

16. James Weldon Johnson and J. Rosamond Johnson, editors; *The Book of American Negro Spirituals,* p. cc.

17. Work, *Folk Songs.*

18. One example of a modified "ring-shout" is found in the offertory ritual of Daddy Grace's United House of Prayer for All Peoples. With Bishop Daddy Grace William McCullough sitting on his elevated throne, the congregation formed a large circle and to the accompaniment of a brass band, members

shuffled forward swaying from side to side and dropped their offering in collection plates at the front. As a form of offertory musical chairs, people who ran out of money sat down, while others continued. Unpublished field study of Daddy Grace's United House of Prayer for All People by Lawrence H. Mamiya, Union Theological Seminary, 1967.

19. Wendell P. Whalum, "Black Hymnody," *Review and Expositor* 70, no. 3 (Summer 1973): 347.

20. Simeon A. Evans to Mother, MS, August 21, 1862.

21. Wyatt Tee Walker, *"Somebody's Calling My Name": Black Sacred Music and Social Change*, p. 84.

22. Henry Wilder Foote, *Three Centuries of American Hymnody*, p. 307.

23. Compiled by Jon Spencer, editor, *Journal of Black Sacred Music*, 1988.

24. Foote, *Three Centuries*, p. 307.

25. Southern, *The Music of Black Americans*, p. 402.

26. Joseph R. Washington, Jr., *Black Religion*, pp. 51–52.

27. Joseph R. Washington, Jr., *Black Sects and Cults*, p. 78.

28. Frazier, *The Negro Church in America*, p. 89.

29. Ibid., p. 78.

30. George Robinson Ricks, *Some Aspects of the Religious Music of the United States Negro*, pp. 131, 132.

31. Paris, *Black Pentecostalism*, p. 57.

32. Frazier, *The Negro Church in America*, p. 61.

33. Ibid., p. 59.

34. William T. Dargan, "Congregational Gospel Songs in a Black Holiness Church: A Musical and Textual Analysis," p. 63.

35. Walker, *A Rock in a Weary Land*, pp. 22–24.

36. R. Nathaniel Dett, "Negro Idioms in Motets and Anthems," Program Notes.

37. R. Nathaniel Dett, "Development of Negro Religious Music," in *Negro Music*, p. 5.

38. Mancel Warrick et al., *The Progress of Gospel Music: From Spirituals to Contemporary Gospel*, p. 56.

39. Thurman, *Deep River*, p. 32.

40. Washington, *Black Religion*, p. 207.

41. Howell Raines, *My Soul is Rested: Movement Days in the Deep South Remembered*, p. 52.

42. John Dunson, *Freedom in the Air: Movement Songs of the Sixties*, pp. 66–67.

43. Ibid., p. 64.

44. Howard Zinn, SNCC: *The New Abolitionists*, p. 4.

45. Dunson, *Freedom in the Air*, pp. 66–67.

46. Martin Luther King, Jr., *Why We Can't Wait*, p. 61.

47. Carl E. Seashore, *Psychology of Music*, p. 162.

48. Washington, *Black Religion*, p. 207.

49. James H. Cone, "Black History: The Black Church's Role, Theology, and Worship seen in an Historical and Theological Interpretation," visiting lecture, Duke University, January 11, 1981.
50. J. Jefferson Cleveland and Verolza Nix, editors, *Songs of Zion.*
51. Frank Baker, *Charles Wesley's Verse,* pp. 15–16.
52. J. Ellsworth Kalas, *Our First Song: Evangelism in the Hymns of Charles Wesley,* p. 33.
53. Walker, *"Somebody's Calling My Name": Black Sacred Music and Social Change.*
54. Ibid., p. 15. Also see the following: Levine, *Black Culture and Black Consciousness;* and Southern, *The Music of Black Americans.*
55. Walker, *"Somebody's Calling My Name": Black Sacred Music and Social Change.*
56. To his credit, James Cone saw the importance of black music as a major resource for black liberation theology in his book, *The Spirituals and the Blues.* However, many of the classic historical and sociological studies of black churches by G. Carter Woodson, Benjamin Mays and Joseph Nicholson, St. Clair Drake and Horace Cayton, E. Franklin Frazier, and Gayraud Wilmore have neglected this vital area.

13 Challenges for the Twenty-First Century

1. For data on church membership and rates of being churched, see *Emerging Trends* 9, no. 5 (May 1987): 5.
2. The estimates of decline among white mainstream churches were derived from the research group on Congregational Studies, sponsored by the Lilly Endowment. Also see Roof and McKinney, *American Mainline Religion.*
3. For general theoretical descriptions of the effects of the process of secularization on religion, see Peter Berger, *The Sacred Canopy,* chapters 2, 3.
4. Richard B. Freeman, *Black Elite: The New Market for Highly Educated Black Americans,* pp. 27–40.
5. For example, see Wilson, *The Truly Disadvantaged.* Also see the socioeconomic data of the National Urban League in the annual publication, *The State of Black America,* 1986, 1987, 1988. The descriptive terms "coping" and "crisis" sectors of the black community are derived from Professor Martin Kilson in his presentation on black clientage politics in the working group on Afro-American Religion and Politics at the W. E. B. Du Bois Institute, Harvard University, October 29, 1988.
6. Smothers, "Atlanta Still on a Roll, but New Doubts Arise," *New York Times,* July 14, 1988, p. A-21.
7. Nelsen, "Unchurched Black Americans."
8. Laura Sessions Stepp, "Black Church Losing Historic Role: Drug Use, Teen Pregnancies Seen as Consequences," *Washington Post,* August 20, 1988, p. A-6.

9. Drake and Cayton, *Black Metropolis*, vol. 2.

10. See Joseph Washington, *Black Sects and Cults*. For an overview of five major groups, see Mamiya and Lincoln, "Black Militant and Separatist Movements."

11. See Nelsen, "Unchurched Black Americans." Also see Welch, "The Unchurched, Black Religious Non-Affiliates." The most recent study of the unchurched was done by George Gallup, Jr.'s organization. See Princeton Religious Research Center, *The Unchurched American . . . 10 Years Later*. For a profile of the black unchurched, see Robert J. Taylor, "Correlates of Religious Non-Involvement Among Black Americans," *Review of Religious Research* 30, no. 2 (December 1988): 126–39.

12. Meredith McGuire, *Pentecostal Catholics: Power, Charisma and Order In a Religious Movement*.

13. See the unpublished in-house study by Lawrence H. Mamiya, "The Second Episcopal District," pp. 4–5.

14. *1984–1985 Annual Report*, Ward African Methodist Episcopal Church, Rev. Frank Reid III pastor, pp. 25–28.

15. Ibid.

16. For example, there is a Four Square Gospel A.M.E. Zion Church with several thousand members in Fort Washington.

17. Allan D. Austin, *African Muslims in Antebellum America: A Sourcebook*.

18. Edward W. Blyden, *Islam and the Negro Race*. Also see Hollis Lynch, *Edward Wilmot Blyden: Pan Negro Patriot*.

19. For overviews of the Moorish Science Temple and the Nation of Islam, see Mamiya and Lincoln, "Black Militant and Separatist Movements." The term "proto-Islam" was coined by C. Eric Lincoln, "The American Muslim Mission in the Context of American Social History," in *The Muslim Community in North America*, edited by Earle H. Waugh, Baha Abu-Laban, and Regula B. Qureshi.

20. For the best historical overview of the origins of the movement, see C. Eric Lincoln, *The Black Muslims in America*.

21. See Mamiya and Lincoln, "Black Militant and Separatist Movements," p. 767.

22. "Rule Switch Allows Whites as Muslims," *Nashville Tennessean*, June 19, 1975. For an examination of the reasons for the change to orthodox Islam, see Lawrence H. Mamiya, "From Black Muslim to Bilalian: The Evolution of a Movement," *Journal for the Scientific Study of Religion* 21, no. 2 (June 1982): 138–52.

23. Bruce M. Gans, and Walter L. Lowe, "The Islam Connection," in *Playboy*, May 1980.

24. Ari L. Goldman, "Mainstream Islam Rapidly Embraced by Black Americans," *New York Times*, February 21, 1989, pp. 1, B-4.

25. Walls, *The African Methodist Episcopal Zion Church*, pp. 73–84.

26. See Mary Sawyer, "Black Ecumenical Movements: Proponents of So-

cial Change," *Review of Religious Research* 30 (December 1988), no. 2:152–53.

27. Ibid., see figure 1.

28. This section on black ecumenism is indebted to Sawyer's work, "Black Ecumenical Movements," pp. 154–55.

29. Mamiya and Lincoln, "Policy and Planning Implications of the Christian Methodist Episcopal Church Survey."

30. Interview with Rev. Dr. Thomas Kilgore in Los Angeles.

31. Interview no. 505.

32. Interview no. 0101.

33. Interview no. 1094.

34. Woodson, *The History of the Negro Church*. Benjamin Mays and Joseph Nicholson, *The Negro's Church*.

35. Mays and Nicholson, *The Negro's Church*, chapter 11.

36. Du Bois, *The Philadelphia Negro*, p. 207.

37. See the data in chapter 11. Ladner, "Teenage Pregnancy," and Petersilia, *Racial Disparities in the Criminal Justice System*.

38. Neoliberal analysts like William Julius Wilson see the problems of the black underclass rooted in structural changes in the economy, and he believes that structural economic reforms will remove both the conditions of poverty and the behavior associated with it. Wilson argues for universal, nonracial social policies. See Wilson's *The Truly Disadvantaged*. Radical Marxist analysts like Manning Marable argue for the need of a social revolution since racism is deeply embedded in the system of capitalism itself. However, Marable's vision of a social democracy and how to get there still remain vague. See *How Capitalism Underdeveloped Black America*.

39. Freeman, "Who Escapes? The Relation of Churchgoing and Other Background Factors to the Socioeconomic Performance of Black Male Youths from Inner-City Tracts."

Selected Bibliography: Sources Consulted

Books

Adams, James Luther.
Paul Tillich's Philosophy of Culture, Science, and Religion. New York: Harper and Row, 1965.

Albanese, Catherine L.
America: Religion and Religions. Belmont, Calif.: Wadsworth Publishing, 1981.

Allen, Richard.
The Life, Experience and Gospel Labors of the Rt. Rev. Richard Allen. George A. Singleton, editor. New York: Abingdon, 1960.

Austin, Allan D.
African Muslims in Antebellum America: A Sourcebook. New York: Garland, 1984.

Baer, Hans.
The Black Spiritualist Movement: A Religious Response to Racism. Knoxville: University of Tennessee Press, 1984.

Baker, Frank.
Charles Wesley's Verse. London: Epworth, 1984.

Baldwin, James.
Go Tell It on the Mountain. New York: Dell, 1952.

Barrett, Leonard.
Soul-Force: African Heritage in Afro-American Religion. Garden City, N.Y.: Anchor, 1974.

Bellah, Robert N.
Tokugawa Religion. Boston: Beacon, 1970.
Beyond Belief: Essays on Religion in a Post-traditional World. New York: Harper and Row, 1970.

Bellah, Robert N., et al., editors.
Habits of the Heart. Berkeley: University of California Press, 1985.

Bennett, Lerone.
Before the Mayflower: A History of the Negro in America 1619–1964. New York: Penguin, 1976 revised.

Berger, Peter L.
The Sacred Canopy. Garden City, N.Y.: Doubleday, 1967.

Berger, Peter L., and John Richard Neuhaus.
To Empower People: The Role of Mediating Structures in Public Policy.

469

Washington, D.C.: American Enterprise Institute for Public Policy Research, 1977.

Berger, Peter L., and Thomas Luckmann.
The Social Construction of Reality: A Treatise in the Sociology of Knowledge. Garden City, N.Y.: Doubleday, 1966.

Berry, Mary, and John Blassingame.
Long Memory: The Black Experience in America. New York: Oxford University Press, 1982.

Billingsley, Andrew.
Black Families in White America. Englewood Cliffs, N.J.: Prentice-Hall, 1968.

Blassingame, John.
The Slave Community: Plantation Life in the Antebellum South. New York: Oxford University Press, 1972.
Black New Orleans, 1860–1880. Chicago: University of Chicago Press, 1973.

Blyden, Edward W.
Islam and the Negro Race. London: Edinburgh University, 1967 reprint.

Branch, Taylor.
Parting the Waters: America in the King Years, 1954–1963. New York: Simon and Schuster, 1988.

Brawley, Benjamin.
A Social History of the American Negro. New York: Macmillan, 1921.

Breitman, George, editor.
Malcolm X Speaks. New York: Merit, 1965.
Malcolm X on Afro-American History. New York: Pathfinder, 1985 reprint.

Brinton, Clarence Crane.
The Anatomy of a Revolution. New York: W. W. Norton, 1938.

Brown, Claude.
Manchild in the Promised Land. New York: Macmillan, 1965.

Brown, Diane R., and Ronald W. Walters.
Exploring the Role of the Black Church in the Community. Washington, D.C.: Mental Health Research and Development Center and Institute for Urban Affairs and Research, Howard University, no publication date given, c. 1982.

Burkett, Randall.
Garveyism as a Religious Movement. Metuchen, N.J.: Scarecrow and ATLA, 1978.

Burkett, Randall, and Richard Newman, editors.
Black Apostles: Afro-American Clergy Confront the Twentieth Century. Boston: G. K. Hall, 1978.

Burroughs, Nannie Helen.
Grow: A Handy Guide for Progressive Churchwomen. Washington, D.C.: National Baptist Convention, n.d.

Butler, Alfloyd.
The Africanization of American Christianity. New York: Carlton, 1980.

Byers, David M., and Quinn, Bernard.
New Directions for the Rural Church. New York: Paulist, 1978.

Cannon, Katie G.
Black Womanist Ethics. Atlanta: Scholars Press, 1988.

Cannon, Katie G., Beverly W. Harrison, Carter Heyward, Ada Maria Isasi-Diaz, Bess B. Johnson, Mary D. Pellauer, Nancy D. Richardson, editors.
God's Fierce Whimsy: Christian Feminism and Theological Education. New York: Pilgrim, 1985.

Capps, Donald, Walter H. Capps, and M. Gerald Bradford, editors.
Encounter with Erickson: Historical Interpretation and Religious Biography. Missoula, Mont.: Scholars Press for the American Academy of Religion and the Institute of Religious Studies, University of California, Santa Barbara, 1977.

Carpenter, Delores.
"The Effects of Sect-Typeness Upon the Professionalization of Black Female Masters of Divinity Graduates, 1972–1984." Ph.D. dissertation, Department of Sociology, Rutgers University, 1986, mimeo.

Carroll, Jackson W., Barbara Hargrove, and Adair T. Lummis.
Women of the Cloth: A New Opportunity for the Churches. Harper and Row, 1981.

Cavanaugh, Thomas E., and Lorn S. Foster.
Jesse Jackson's Campaign: The Primaries and Caucuses, Election '84 Report #2. Washington, D.C.: Joint Center for Political Studies, 1984.

Childs, John Brown.
The Political Black Minister: A Study in Afro-American Politics and Religion. Boston: G. K. Hall, 1980.

Clark, Thomas A.
Blacks in Suburbs: A National Perspective. New Brunswick, N.J.: Rutgers University, Center for Urban Policy Research, 1979.

Cleveland, J. Jefferson, and Verzola Nix, editors.
Songs of Zion. Nashville: Abingdon, 1981.

Coles, Flournoy A., Jr.
Black Economic Development. Chicago: Nelson Hall, 1975.

Coles, Robert.
Children of Crisis. Boston: Little, Brown, 1954.

Collier-Thomas, Bettye.
   Black Women in America: Contributors to Our Heritage. Washington,
   D.C.: Bethune Museum-Archives, 1983.
Collins, Sheila.
   The Rainbow Challenge: The Jackson Campaign and the *Future of U.S.
   Politics.* New York: Monthly Review Press, 1985.
Cone, James.
   Black Theology and Black Power. New York: Seabury, 1969.
   A Black Theology of Liberation. Philadelphia: Lippincott, 1970.
   The Spirituals and the Blues. New York: Seabury, 1972.
   For My People: *Black Theology and the Black Church.* Maryknoll, N.Y.:
   Orbis, 1984.
Cooper, Anna Julia.
   A Voice from the South: By a Black Woman of the South. Kenia, Ohio:
   Aldine Publishing, 1892.
Coppin, Frances Jackson.
   Reminiscences of School Life and Hints on Teaching. Philadelphia: A.M.E.
   Book Concern, 1913.
Cottle, Thomas.
   Black Children, White Dreams. Boston: Houghton Mifflin, 1974.
Curtin, Phillip.
   The Atlantic Slave Trade. Madison: University of Wisconsin Press, 1969.
Dargan, William T.
   "Congregational Gospel Songs in a Black Holiness Church: A Musical
   and Textual Analysis." Ph.D. dissertation. Wesleyan University, 1982.
Davis, Allison, and John Dollard.
   *Children of Bondage: The Personality Development of Negro Youth in the
   Urban South.* Washington, D.C.: American Council on Education,
   1940.
Davis, Frank G.
   The Economics of Black Community Development. Washington, D.C.:
   University Press of America, 1978.
Davis, George, and Gregg Watson.
   Black Life in Corporate America: Swimming in the Mainstream. New
   York: Doubleday, 1985.
Davis, Gerald L.
   *I Got the Word in me and I can sing it, you know: A Study of the
   Performed African-American Sermon.* Philadelphia: University of
   Pennsylvania Press, 1985.
de Tocqueville, Alexis.
   Democracy in America, trans. George Lawrence, edited by J. P. Mayer.
   New York: Doubleday/Anchor, 1969.

Drake, St. Clair.
The Redemption of Africa and Black Religion. Chicago: Third World, 1970.
Drake, St. Clair, and Horace Cayton.
Black Metropolis: A Study of Negro Life in the North. New York: Harper and Row, 1962, revised and enlarged, 2 volumes.
Du Bois, W. E. B.
Economic Cooperation Among Negro Americans. Atlanta: Atlanta University Press, 1907.
The Souls of Black Folk. New York: New American Library, 1969 edition.
The Philadelphia Negro: A Social Study. New York: Schocken Books, 1970 edition.
Du Bois, W. E. B., editor.
The Negro Church. Atlanta: Atlanta University Press, 1903.
Dudley, Carl.
Where Have All Our People Gone?: New Choices for Old Churches. New York: Pilgrim, 1979.
Dunson, John.
Freedom in the Air: Movement Songs of the Sixties. New York: International, 1965.
Durkheim, Emile.
The Elementary Forms of the Religious Life. New York: Free Press, 1965 edition.
Durkheim, Emile, and Marcel Mauss.
Primitive Classification. Chicago: University of Chicago Press, 1963.
Dybiec, David, editor.
Slippin' Away: The Loss of Black Owned Farms. Atlanta: Glenmary Research Center, 1988.
Elizabeth.
Elizabeth, a Colored Minister of the Gospel Born in Slavery. Philadelphia: Tract Association of Friends, 1889.
Erikson, Erik.
Childhood and Society. New York: W. W. Norton, 1950.
Young Man Luther: A Study in Psychoanalysis and History. New York: W. W. Norton, 1958.
Gandhi's Truth: On the Origins of Militant Nonviolence. New York: W. W. Norton, 1969.
The Life Cycle Completed. New York: W. W. Norton, 1982.
Farish, Hunter D.
The Circuit Dismounts: A Social History of Southern Methodism. Richmond: Dietz, 1938.

Farley, Reynolds.
Blacks and Whites: Narrowing the Gap? Cambridge, Mass.: Harvard University Press, 1984.

Farley, Reynolds, and Walter Allen.
The Color Line and the Quality of Life in America. New York: Russell Sage Foundation, 1987.

Fauset, Arthur.
Black Gods of the Metropolis. Philadelphia: University of Pennsylvania Press, 1944; revised, 1970.

Felton, Carroll M., Jr.
The Care of Souls in the Black Church: A Liberation Perspective. New York: Martin Luther King Fellows Press, 1980.

Felton, Ralph.
These My Brethren: A Study of 570 Negro Churches and 542 Negro Homes in the Rural South. New York: Committee for the Training of the Negro Rural Pastors of the Phelps-Stokes Fund and the Home Missions Council of North America, 1950.
Go Down Moses: A Study of 21 Successful Negro Rural Pastors. Madison, N.J.: Department of Rural Church, Drew Theological Seminary, 1952.

Fisher, Miles Mark.
Negro Slave Songs in the United States. New York: Citadel, 1953.

Fitts, Leroy.
A History of Black Baptists. Nashville: Broadman, 1985.
Lott Carey, First Black Missionary to Africa. Valley Forge, Penn.: Judson, 1978.

Foote, Henry Wilder.
Three Centuries of American Hymnody. Hamden, Conn.: Shoe String, 1940.

Fordham, Monroe.
Major Themes in Northern Black Religious Thought 1800–1860. Hicksville, N.Y.: Exposition, 1975.

Franklin, John Hope.
From Slavery to Freedom. New York: Alfred A. Knopf, 1956; revised, 1970.

Frazier, E. Franklin.
The Negro Church in America. New York: Schocken Books, 1964.
The Negro Family in the United States. Chicago: University of Chicago Press, 1969, revised edition.

Frazier, E. Franklin, and C. Eric Lincoln.
The Negro Church in America: The Black Church Since Frazier. New York: Schocken Books, 1974.

Freeman, Richard B.
Black Elite: The New Market for Highly Educated Black Americans.
New York: McGraw-Hill, 1976.

Freeman, Richard B., and Harry J. Holzer, editors.
The Black Youth Employment Crisis. Chicago: University of Chicago
Press, 1986.

Freire, Paulo.
Pedagogy of the Oppressed. New York: Orion, 1968.

Garibaldi, Antoine, editor.
Black Colleges and Universities: Challenges for the Future. New York:
Praeger, 1984.

Gary, Lawrence E., editor.
Black Men. Beverly Hills, Calif.: Sage, 1981.

Genovese, Eugene.
Roll, Jordan, Roll: The World the Slaves Made. New York: Pantheon,
1974.

Gerth, Hans, and C. Wright Mills, editors.
From Max Weber: Essays in Sociology. New York: Oxford University
Press, 1958.

Giddings, Paula.
*When and Where I Enter: The Impact of Black Women on Race and Sex in
America.* New York: William Morrow, 1984.

Glasgow, Douglas.
*The Black Underclass: Poverty, Unemployment, and Entrapment of
Ghetto Youth.* New York: Vintage, 1981.

Glazer, Nathan, and Daniel Patrick Moynihan.
Beyond the Melting Pot. Cambridge, Mass.: MIT Press and Harvard University Press, 1963.

Gosnell, Harold.
Negro Politicians: The Rise of Negro Politics in Chicago. Chicago: University of Chicago Press, 1935.

Gregg, Howard D.
History of the African Methodist Episcopal Church. Nashville: A.M.E.C.
Publishing House, 1980.

Griffen, Clyde, and Sally Griffen.
Natives and Newcomers: The Ordering of Opportunity in Mid-Nineteenth Century Poughkeepsie. Cambridge, Mass.: Harvard University Press, 1978.

Griffen, Clyde, editor.
*New Perspectives on Poughkeepsie's Past: Essays to Honor Edmund
Platt.* Poughkeepsie, N.Y.: Dutchess County Historical Society, 1988.

Gutman, Herbert.
   The Black Family in Slavery and Freedom, 1750–1925. New York: Pantheon, 1976.
Haley, Alex.
   Roots: The Saga of an American Family. Garden City, N.Y.: Doubleday, 1976.
Hamilton, Charles.
   The Black Preacher in America. New York: William Morrow, 1972.
Hansberry, Lorraine.
   A Raisin in the Sun. New York: New American Library, 1958.
Harding, Vincent.
   There Is a River: The Black Struggle for Freedom in America. New York: Harcourt Brace Jovanovich, 1981.
Harlan, Louis R.
   Booker T. Washington: The Wizard of Tuskegee, 1901–1915. New York: Oxford University Press, 1983.
Harris, James H.
   Black Ministers and Laity in the Urban Church: An Analysis of Political and Social Expectations. New York City: University Press of America, 1987.
Hegel, Georg Wilhelm Friedrich.
   The Phenomenology of Mind. New York: Harper and Row, 1967 edition.
Herskovits, Melville J.
   The Myth of the Negro Past. Boston: Beacon, 1969 edition.
Hilton, Bruce.
   The Delta Ministry. New York: Macmillan, 1969.
Hill, Robert.
   The Strengths of Black Families. New York: National Urban League, 1971.
Hill, Robert A., editor.
   The Marcus Garvey and the Universal Negro Improvement Association Papers. University of California Press, volume 1 (1983); 2 (1983); 3 (1984).
Hoekendijk, Johannes C.
   The Church Inside Out. Philadelphia: Westminster, 1964; English edition, 1966.
Hoge, Dean R.
   Converts, Dropouts, Returnees: A Study of Religious Change Among Catholics. New York: Pilgrim, 1981.
Hoge, Dean R., and David A. Roozen, editors.
   Understanding Church Growth and Decline: 1950–1978. New York: Pilgrim, 1979.

Holt, Rackham.
  Mary McLeod Bethune: A Biography. New York: Doubleday, 1964.
Huggins, Nathan I., Martin Kilson, and Daniel Fox, editors.
  Key Issues in the Afro-American Experience. New York: Harcourt Brace
  Jovanovich, 1971, volumes 1, 2.
Hull, Gloria T., Patricia Bell Scott, and Barbara Smith, editors.
  *All the Women Are White, All the Blacks Are Men, BUT SOME OF US
  ARE BRAVE: Black Women's Studies.* Old Westbury, N.Y.: Feminist
  Press, 1982.
Humez, Jean McMahon.
  *Gifts of Power: The Writings of Rebecca Jackson, Black Visionary, Shaker
  Eldress.* Amherst: University of Massachusetts Press, 1981.
Hunter, James Davidson.
  Evangelicalism: The Coming Generation. Chicago: University of Chi-
  cago Press, 1987.
Hurst, David.
  Shepherding Black Christians. Ph.D. dissertation. Claremont, Calif.:
  Claremont School of Theology, 1980.
Hurston, Zora Neale.
  The Sanctified Church. Berkeley, Calif.: Turtle Island, 1983.
Jackson, Joseph H.
  *A Story of Christian Activism: The History of the National Baptist
  Convention, U.S.A., Inc.* Nashville: Townsend, 1980.
Jacobs, Sylvia M., editor.
  Black Americans and the Missionary Movement in Africa. Westport,
  Conn.: Greenwood, 1982.
Johnson, Chalmers.
  Revolutionary Change. Boston: Little, Brown, 1966.
Johnson, Charles Spurgeon.
  Growing Up in the Black Belt: Negro Youth in the Rural South. New
  York: American Council on Education, 1941; reprint Schocken, 1967.
  Shadow of the Plantation. New York: Phoenix, 1966 reprint.
Johnson, Clifton H., editor.
  *God Struck Me Dead: Religious Conversion Experiences and Autobiogra-
  phies of Ex-Slaves.* Philadelphia: Pilgrim, 1960.
Johnson, Daniel M., and Rex Campbell.
  Black Migration in America: A Social Demographic History. Durham,
  N.C.: Duke University Press, 1981.
Johnson, James Weldon, and J. Rosamond Johnson, editors.
  The Book of American Negro Spirituals. New York: Viking, 1925.
Johnson, Mary Mangum, assisted by Inez Cole Barber.
  *The Life and Works of Mother Mary Mangum Johnson: Founder of the
  Church of God in Christ in the State of Michigan.* No publisher or date
  given.

Johnston, Ruby F.
  The Development of Negro Religion. New York: Philosophical Library,
  1954.
  The Religion of Negro Protestants. New York: Philosophical Library,
  1956.
Jones, Dionne J., and William H. Matthews, editors.
  The Black Church: A Community Resource. Washington, D.C.: Howard
  University Institute for Urban Affairs and Research, 1977.
Jones, Jacqueline.
  "To Get Out of This Land of Sufring": Black Migrant Women, Work and
  Family in Northern Cities 1900–1930. Working Paper No. 91. Wellesley
  College Center for Research for Women. Wellesley, Mass., 1982.
Jones, LeRoi (Amiri Baraka).
  Blues People: Negro Music in White America. New York: William Mor-
  row, 1963.
Jones, Major J.
  Black Awareness. Nashville: Abingdon, 1971.
Jones, Marcus E.
  Black Migration in the United States with Emphasis on Selected Central
  Cities. Saratoga, Calif.: Century Twenty-One Publishing, 1980.
Jones, William R.
  Is God a White Racist? Garden City, N.Y.: Doubleday/Anchor, 1973.
Joyner, Charles.
  Down by the Riverside: A South Carolina Slave Community. Urbana:
  University of Illinois Press, 1984.
Kalas, J. Ellsworth.
  Our First Song: Evangelism in the Hymns of Charles Wesley. Nashville:
  Discipleship Resources, 1984.
Keil, Charles.
  Urban Blues. Chicago: University of Chicago Press, 1966.
Kelly, Frances Burnett, and German R. Ross.
  Here Am I, Send Me. Memphis: Church of God in Christ Publishing
  House, 1970.
King, Martin Luther, Jr.
  Why We Can't Wait. New York: Mentor, 1964.
  Where Do We Go from Here? New York: Harper and Row, 1967.
Kozol, Jonathan.
  Death at an Early Age: The Destruction of the Hearts and Minds of Negro
  Children in the Boston Public Schools. Boston: Houghton Mifflin,
  1967.
Lacy, Daniel.
  The White Use of Blacks in America. New York: McGraw-Hill, 1972.

Lakey, Othal Hawthorne.
The Rise of Colored Methodism. Dallas: Crescendo, 1972.
The History of the C.M.E. *Church.* Memphis: C.M.E. Publishing House, 1985.

Lane, Isaac.
Autobiography of Bishop Isaac Lane, LL.D. With a Short History of the C.M.E. *Church in America and of Methodism.* Nashville: C.M.E. Church, 1912.

Larson, Martin A., and C. Stanley Lowell.
The Religious Empire: The Growth and Danger of Tax Exempt Property in the United States. Washington, D.C.: R. B. Luce, 1976.

Lasch, Christopher.
The Culture of Narcissism: American Life in an Age of Diminishing Expectations. New York: W. W. Norton, 1979.

Lee, Jarena.
Religious Experience and Journal of Mrs. Jarena Lee. Philadelphia: The author, 1849.

Lenski, Gerhard.
The Religious Factor: A Sociological Study of Religion's Impact on Politics, Economics, and Family Life. Garden City, N.Y.: Doubleday, 1963 revised.

Lerner, Gerda, editor.
Black Women in White America: A Documentary History. New York: Vintage, 1972.

Lester, Julius.
To Be a Slave. New York: Dell, 1968.

Levine, Lawrence.
Black Culture and Black Consciousness. New York: Oxford University Press, 1978.

Liebow, Elliot.
Talley's Corner: A Study of Negro Streetcorner Men. Boston: Little, Brown, 1967.

Light, Ivan H.
Ethnic Enterprise in America: Business and Welfare Among Chinese, Japanese, and Blacks. Berkeley: University of California Press, 1972.

Lincoln, C. Eric.
The Black Muslims in America. Boston: Beacon, 1961.
Sounds of the Struggle: Persons and Perspectives in Civil Rights. New York: William Morrow, 1967.
Race, Religion, and the Continuing American Dilemma. New York: Hill and Wang, 1984.

Lincoln, C. Eric, editor.
The Black Experience in Religion. Garden City, N.Y.: Doubleday, 1974.
Martin Luther King, Jr.: A Profile. New York: Hill and Wang, 1970.

Lockridge, Ruby G.
A Guide for Church Nursing. Nashville: The National Baptist Publishing Board of the National Baptist Convention of America, 1974.

Loewenberg, Bert J., and Ruth Bogin, editors.
Black Women in Nineteenth-Century America. University Park: Pennsylvania State University Press, 1978.

Long, Charles H.
Significations: Signs, Symbols, and Images in the Interpretation of Religion. Philadelphia: Fortress, 1986.

Lovell, James, Jr.
Black Song: The Forge and the Flame. New York: Macmillan, 1972.

Lovett, Leonard.
"Black Holiness-Pentecostalism: Implications for Ethics and Social Transformation." Ph.D. dissertation. Emory University, 1979.

Luckmann, Thomas.
The Invisible Religion. New York: Macmillan, 1967.

Lynch, Hollis.
Edward Wilmot Blyden: Pan Negro Patriot. New York: Oxford University Press, 1970.

McAdoo, Harriet Pipes, editor.
Black Families. Beverly Hills: Sage, 1981.

MacGaffey, Wyatt.
Modern Kongo Prophets. Bloomington: University of Indiana Press, 1983.
Religion and Society in Central Africa: The Bakongo of Lower Zaire. Chicago: University of Chicago Press, 1986.

McGuire, Meredith.
Pentecostal Catholics: Power, Charisma and Order in a Religious Movement. Philadelphia: Temple University Press, 1982.

Malcolm X and Alex Haley.
The Autobiography of Malcolm X. New York: Grove, 1965.

Mannix, Daniel P.
Black Cargoes. New York: Viking, 1962.

Mapson, J. Wendell, Jr.
The Ministry of Music in the Black Church. Valley Forge, Penn.: Judson, 1984.

Marable, Manning.
How Capitalism Underdeveloped Black America. Boston: South End, 1983.

Marx, Gary.
Protest and Prejudice. New York: Harper and Row, revised edition, 1969.
Mays, Benjamin, and Joseph Nicholson.
The Negro's Church. New York: Russell and Russell, 1969, reissue.
Mazrui, Ali.
The Africans: A Triple Heritage. Boston: Little, Brown, 1986.
Mbiti, John.
African Religions and Philosophy. New York: Praeger, 1969.
Meier, August.
Negro Thought in America 1880–1915. Ann Arbor: University of Michigan Press, 1969.
Meier, August, and Elliot Rudwick.
The Making of Black America. New York: Atheneum, 1969.
From Plantation to Ghetto. New York: Hill and Wang, 1970, revised.
Memmi, Albert.
The Colonizer and the Colonized. Trans. Howard Greenfield. New York: Orion, 1965.
Mitchell, Henry H.
Black Preaching. Philadelphia: Lippincott, 1970.
Black Belief: Folk Beliefs of Blacks in America and West Africa. New York: Harper and Row, 1975.
Mitchell, Henry H., and Nicholas Cooper Lewter.
Soul Theology: The Heart of American Black Culture. San Francisco: Harper and Row, 1986.
Morris, Aldon.
The Origins of the Civil Rights Movement: Black Communities Organizing for Change. New York: Free Press, 1984.
Moses, Wilson Jeremiah.
Black Messiahs and Uncle Toms: Social and Literary Manipulations of a Religious Myth. University Park: Pennsylvania State University Press, 1982.
Mukenge, Ida Rousseau.
The Black Church in Urban America: A Case Study in Political Economy. New York: University Press of America, 1983.
Murray, Charles.
Losing Ground: American Social Policy, 1950–1980. New York: Basic Books, 1984.
Myrdal, Gunnar.
An American Dilemma: The Negro Problem and Modern Democracy. New York: Harper and Row, 1944, volumes 1, 2.

Nelsen, Hart M., and Anne Kusener Nelsen.
  Black Church in the Sixties. Lexington: University of Kentucky Press,
  1975.

Nelsen, Hart M., Raytha L. Yokley, and Anne K. Nelsen, editors.
  The Black Church in America. New York: Basic Books, 1971.

Newcomb, T. M., and E. L. Hartley, editors.
  Readings in Social Psychology. New York: Holt, 1947.

Omoyajowo, J. Akinyele.
  *Cherubim and Seraphim: The History of an Independent African
  Church.* New York: NOK Publishers International, 1982.

Orfield, Gary.
  Public School Desegregation in the United States, 1968–1980. Washington, D.C.: Joint Center for Policy Studies, 1983.

Orfield, Gary, and William Taylor.
  Racial Segregation: Two Policy Views. New York: Ford Foundation, 1979.

Osofsky, Gilbert.
  Harlem: The Making of a Ghetto. New York: Harper and Row, 1971,
  second edition.

Otto, Rudolf.
  The Idea of the Holy. New York: Oxford University Press, 1967, reprint.

Paris, Arthur.
  Black Pentecostalism: Southern Religion in an Urban World. Amherst:
  University of Massachusetts Press, 1982.

Paris, Peter.
  Black Leaders in Conflict. New York: Pilgrim, 1978.
  The Social Teaching of the Black Churches. Philadelphia: Fortress, 1985.

Parrinder, Geoffrey.
  African Traditional Religion. New York: Harper and Row, 1976.

Patterson, James Oglethorpe, and German Ross, editors.
  Church of God in Christ International Directory. Memphis: Church of
  God in Christ Publishing House, 1980.

Patterson, James Oglethorpe, German R. Ross, and Julia Mason Atkins,
  editors.
  *History and Formative Years of the Church of God in Christ with Ex-
  cerpts from the Life and Works of Its Founder—Bishop C. H. Mason.*
  Memphis: Church of God in Christ Publishing House, 1969.

Payne, Daniel A.
  History of the African Methodist Episcopal Church. Nashville: A.M.E.
  Church, 1891. Reprint: New York, 1968.

Peeks, Edward.
  The Long Struggle for Black Power. New York: Charles Scribner's Sons,
  1971.

Perkins, Eugene.
Home Is a Dirty Street: The Social Oppression of Black Children. Chicago: Third World, 1975.

Petersilia, Joan.
Racial Disparities in the Criminal Justice System. Santa Monica, Calif.: Rand, June 1983.

Porter, Judith.
Black Child, White Child: The Development of Racial Attitudes. Cambridge, Mass.: Harvard University Press, 1971.

Powell, Adam Clayton, Jr.
Marching Blacks: An Interpretive History of the Rise of the Black Common Man. New York: Dial, 1945.

Powell-Hopson, Darlene L.
"The Effects of Modeling, Reinforcement, and Color Meaning Word Associations on Doll Color Preferences of Black Preschool Children and White Preschool Children." Ph.D. dissertation, Hofstra University, 1985.

Princeton Religion Research Center. George Gallup, executive director.
The Unchurched American . . . 10 Years Later. Princeton: Princeton Religion Research Center, 1989.

Quarles, Benjamin.
Black Abolitionists. New York: Oxford University Press, 1969.

Quinn, Bernard, et al.
Churches and Church Membership in the United States, 1980. Atlanta: Glenmary Research Center, 1982.

Raboteau, Albert.
Slave Religion: The "Invisible Institution" in the Antebellum South. New York: Oxford University Press, 1978.

Raines, Howell.
My Soul Is Rested: Movement Days in the Deep South Remembered. Baltimore: Penguin, 1983.

Range, C. F., Jr., Clyde Young, German R. Ross, and Roy L. H. Winbush, editors.
Official Manual with the Doctrines and Disciplines of the Church of God in Christ. Memphis: Church of God in Christ Publishing Board, 1973.

Reed, Adolph L., Jr.
The Jesse Jackson Phenomenon. New Haven, Conn.: Yale University Press, 1986.

Richardson, Harry V.
Dark Glory: A Picture of the Church Among Negroes in the Rural South. New York: Friendship, 1947.

Dark Salvation: The Story of Methodism as It Developed Among Blacks in America. Garden City, N.Y.: Doubleday, 1976.

Richardson, Marilyn, editor.
Black Women and Religion: A Bibliography. Boston: G. K. Hall, 1980.
Maria W. Stewart: America's First Black Woman Political Writer. Bloomington: Indiana University Press, 1987.

Ricks, George Robinson.
Some Aspects of the Religious Music of the United States Negro. New York: Arno, 1977.

Roberts, J. DeOtis.
Liberation and Reconciliation. Philadelphia: Westminster, 1971.
Roots of a Black Future: Family and Church. Philadelphia: Westminster, 1980.

Rodney, Walter.
How Europe Underdeveloped Africa. London: Bogle-L'Ouverture, 1972.

Roof, Wade Clark.
Race and Residence in American Cities. Philadelphia: American Academy of Political and Social Science, 1979.

Roof, Wade Clark, and William McKinney.
American Mainline Religion: Its Changing Shape and Future. New Brunswick, N.J.: Rutgers University Press, 1987.

Sawyer, Mary R.
"Black Politics, Black Faith." M.A. thesis, Divinity School of Howard University, 1982.
"Black Ecumenism: Cooperative Social Change Movements in the Black Church." Ph.D. dissertation, Duke University, 1986.

Scanzoni, John H.
The Black Family in Modern Society. Boston: Allyn and Bacon, 1971.

Scherer, Lester B.
Slavery and the Churches in Early America, 1619–1819. Grand Rapids, Mich.: Eerdmans, 1975.

Seashore, Carl E.
Psychology of Music. New York: McGraw-Hill, 1938.

Sernett, Milton.
Black Religion and American Evangelicalism: White Protestants, Plantation Missions and the Flowering of Negro Christianity, 1787–1865. Metuchen, N.J.: Scarecrow and American Theological Library Association, 1975.
Afro-American Religious History: A Documentary Witness. Durham, N.C.: Duke University Press, 1985.

Shopshire, James Maynard.
"A Socio-Historical Characterization of the Black Pentecostal Movement in America." Ph.D. dissertation. Northwestern University, 1975.

Silberman, Charles E.
Crisis in Black and White. New York: Random House, 1964.

Simmons, Dovie Marie, and Olivia L. Martin.
Down Behind the Sun: The Story of Arenia Conelia Mallory. Memphis: Riverside Press, 1983.

Simpson, George Eaton.
Black Religions in the New World. New York: Columbia University Press, 1979.

Smith, Amanda Berry.
An Autobiography: The Story of the Lord's Dealing with Mrs. Amanda Smith, the Colored Evangelist, Containing an Account of Her Life Work of Faith, Her Travels in America, England, Scotland, India, and Africa as an Independent Missionary. Chicago: Meyer, 1891. Reprint, New York: Oxford University Press, 1988.

Smith, Archie, Jr.
The Relational Self: Ethics and Therapy from a Black Church Perspective. Nashville: Abingdon, 1982.

Smith, Charles Spencer.
A History of the African Methodist Episcopal Church. Philadelphia: A.M.E. Church, 1922.

Smith, Edward D.
Climbing Jacob's Ladder: The Rise of Black Churches in Eastern American Cities, 1740–1877. Washington, D.C.: Smithsonian Institution, 1988.

Smith, Timothy L.
Revivalism and Social Reform in Mid-Nineteenth Century America. Nashville: Abingdon.

Sobel, Mechal.
Trabelin' On: The Slave Journey to an Afro-Baptist Faith. Westport, Conn.: Greenwood, 1979.

Southern, Eileen.
The Music of Black Americans: A History. New York: W. W. Norton, 1971, second edition, 1983.

Spear, Allan H.
Black Chicago: The Making of a Negro Ghetto, 1890–1920. Chicago: University of Chicago Press, 1967.

Stack, Carol B.
All My Kin: Strategies for Survival in a Black Community. New York: Harper and Row, 1974.

Stackhouse, Max L.
Public Theology and Political Economy: Christian Stewardship in Modern Society. Grand Rapids, Mich.: Eerdmans, 1987.

Staples, Robert.
The World of Black Singles. Westport, Conn.: Greenwood, 1981.

Strout, Cushing.
The New Heavens and New Earth: Political Religion in America. New York: Harper and Row, 1974.

Synan, Vincent.
The Holiness-Pentecostal Movement in the United States. Grand Rapids, Mich.: Eerdmans, 1971.

Tamez, Elsa.
Bible of the Oppressed. Maryknoll, N.Y.: Orbis, 1982.

Thomas, Hilah F., and Rosemary Skinner Keller, editors.
Woman in New Worlds. Nashville: Abingdon, 1981.

Thompson, Robert Farris.
Flash of the Spirit. New York: Random House, 1983.

Thurman, Howard.
Deep River and the Negro Spiritual Speaks of Life and Death. Richmond, Ind.: Friends United, 1975.

Tillich, Paul.
Systematic Theology. Chicago: University of Chicago Press, 1963, volume 3.

Tilly, Louise, and Patricia Gurin, editors.
Women in Twentieth-Century American Politics. New York: Russell Sage Foundation, 1988.

Truth, Sojourner.
The Narrative of Sojourner Truth, a Bondswoman of Olden Times Emancipated by the New York Legislature in the Early Part of the Present Century, with a History of Her Labors and Correspondence. The author, 1875. Reprinted by Arno Press and *New York Times,* 1968, and Johnson Publishing, 1970.

Turner, Franklin D., and Adair T. Lummis.
Black Clergy in the Episcopal Church: Recruitment, Training, and Deployment. Office of Black Ministries, Seabury Professional Services, n.d.

U.S. Department of Commerce, Bureau of the Census.
The Social and Economic Status of the Black Population in the United States: An Historical View, 1790–1978. Current Population Reports. Special Studies Series, P. 23, No. 80. Washington, D.C.: U.S. Government Printing Office, 1980.

Walker, Alice.
In Search of Our Mother's Garden. San Diego: Harcourt Brace Jovanovich, 1983.

Walker, Clarence E.
A Rock in a Weary Land: The African Methodist Episcopal Church Dur-

ing the Civil War and Reconstruction. Baton Rouge: Louisiana State University Press, 1982.

Walker, Sheila S.
The Religious Revolution in the Ivory Coast: The Prophet Harris and the Harrist Church. Chapel Hill: University of North Carolina Press, 1983.

Walker, Wyatt Tee.
"Somebody's Calling My Name": Black Sacred Music and Social Change. Valley Forge, Penn.: Judson, 1979.

Walls, William J.
The African Methodist Episcopal Zion Church: Reality of the Black Church. Charlotte, N.C.: A.M.E. Zion Publishing House, 1974.

Warrick, Mancel, et al.
The Progress of Gospel Music: From Spirituals to Contemporary Gospel. Washington, D.C.: Vantage, 1977.

Washington, James M.
Frustrated Fellowship: The Black Baptist Quest for Social Power. Macon, Ga.: Mercer University Press, 1986.

Washington, James M., editor.
A Testament of Hope: The Essential Writings of Martin Luther King, Jr. San Francisco: Harper and Row, 1986.

Washington, Joseph R., Jr.
Black Religion. Boston: Beacon, 1964.
Black Sects and Cults. Garden City, N.Y.: Anchor/Doubleday, 1973.
Anti-Blackness in English Religion 1500–1800. New York: Edwin Mellin, 1984.

Washington, Joseph R., Jr., editor.
Dilemmas of the New Black Middle Class. Philadelphia: University of Pennsylvania's Afro-American Studies Program, 1981.

Webber, Thomas.
Deep Like the Rivers: Education in the Slave Quarter Community, 1831–1865. New York: W. W. Norton, 1978.

Weber, Max.
The Protestant Ethic and the Spirit of Capitalism. New York: Charles Scribner's Sons, 1958.

Weisbrot, Robert.
Father Divine and the Struggle for Racial Equality. Champaign: University of Illinois Press, 1983.

Wells, Ida B.
On Lynchings: Southern Horrors; A Red Record; Mob Rule in New Orleans. New York: Arno, 1969.
U.S. Atrocities. London, 1892.

West, Cornel.
Prophesy Deliverance! Philadelphia: Westminster, 1982.

Prophetic Fragments. Grand Rapids, Mich.: Eerdmans and Africa World Press, 1988.

Wheatley, Phillis.
Poems on Various Subjects, Religious and Moral. London: A. Bell, 1773.

Wheeler, Edward L.
Uplifting the Race: The Black Minister in the New South, 1865–1902. Lanham, Md.: University Press of America, 1982.

Wilkerson, Doris Y., and Ronald L. Taylor, editors.
The Black Male in America. Chicago: Nelson Hall, 1970.

Williams, Ethel L., and Clifton F. Brown.
Afro-American Religious Studies: A Comprehensive Bibliography with Locations in American Libraries. Second edition. Metuchen, N.J.: Scarecrow, 1979.

Williams, James D., editor.
The State of Black America 1982. New York: National Urban League, 1982.
The State of Black America 1984. New York: National Urban League, 1984.
The State of Black America 1985. New York: National Urban League, 1985.
The State of Black America 1986. New York: National Urban League, 1986.

Williams, Melvin D.
Community in a Black Pentecostal Church: An Anthropological Study. Pittsburgh: University of Pittsburgh Press, 1974.

Williams, Walter L.
Black Americans and the Evangelization of Africa, 1877–1900. Madison: University of Wisconsin Press, 1982.

Wilmore, Gayraud.
Black Religion and Black Radicalism: An Interpretation of the Religious History of Afro-American People. Maryknoll, N.Y.: Orbis, 1983, second edition.
Black and Presbyterian: The Heritage and the Hope. Philadelphia: Geneva, 1983.
Last Things First. Philadelphia: Westminster, 1982.

Wilmore, Gayraud, and James Cone, editors.
Black Theology: A Documentary History, 1966–1979. Maryknoll, N.Y.: Orbis, 1979.

Wilson, Robert L.
The Northern Negro Looks at the Church. New York: Department of Research and Survey of the National Division, Board of Missions of the United Methodist Church, 1968.

Wilson, William Julius.
The Declining Significance of Race: Blacks and Changing American Institutions. Chicago: University of Chicago Press, 1980.
The Truly Disadvantaged: The Inner City, the Underclass, and Public Policy. Chicago: University of Chicago Press, 1987.
Wiltse, Charles M., editor.
David Walker's Appeal. New York: Hill and Wang, 1965.
Wimberley, Edward P.
Pastoral Care in the Black Church. Nashville: Abingdon, 1979.
Witvliet, Theo.
The Way of the Black Messiah. Oak Park, Ill.: Meyer Stone, 1987.
Woodson, Carter G.
The History of the Negro Church. Washington, D.C.: Associated Publishers, 1972, third edition.
A Century of Negro Migration. Washington, D.C.: Association for the Study of Negro Life and History, 1919.
The Rural Negro. New York: Russell and Russell, 1930; reprint 1969.
The Mis-Education of the Negro. Washington, D.C.: Associated Publishers, 1933; reprint 1977 by AMS.
Work, John Wesley.
Folk Songs of the American Negro. Nashville: Press of Fisk University, 1915.
Young, Josiah.
Black and African Theologies: Siblings or Distant Cousins? Maryknoll, N.Y.: Orbis, 1986.
Zinn, Howard.
SNCC: The New Abolitionists. Boston: Beacon, 1965.

Articles, Journals, and Monographs

Adams, John Hurst, and Trevlyn Reed.
Ethnic Educational Materials for Young Children. Los Angeles: Educational Growth Organization, 1970.
Adams, Samuel L.
"Blackening in Media: The State of Blacks in the Press." James D. Williams, editor. *The State of Black America 1985.* New York: National Urban League, 1985.
American Association of Fund-Raising Council (AAFRC).
"Estimates of Philanthropic Giving in 1986 and the Trends They Show." *Giving USA.* New York: AAFRC Trust for Philanthropy, 1987.
Baer, Hans, and Merrill Singer.
"Toward a Typology of Black Sectarian Response to Racial Stratification." *Anthropological Quarterly* 54 (1981): 1–14.

Berenson, William M., Kirk W. Elifson, and Tandy Tollerson, III.
"Preachers in Politics: A Study of Political Activism Among the Black Ministry." *Journal of Black Studies* 24 (June 1976): 373–92.

Billingsley, Andrew.
"Black Families in a Changing Society." Janet Dewart, editor. *The State of Black America 1987*. New York: National Urban League, 1987.

Brooks, Evelyn.
"Religion, Politics, and Gender: The Leadership of Nannie Helen Burroughs," *Journal of Religious Thought* 44 (Winter–Spring 1988), no. 2.
"In Politics to Stay: Black Women Leaders and Party Politics in the 1920s." Louise Tilly and Patricia Gurin, editors, *Women in Twentieth-Century American Politics*. New York: Russell Sage Foundation, 1988.

Brown, Claude.
"Manchild in Harlem." *New York Times Magazine* (September 16, 1984): 38ff.

Burlin, Natalie Curtis.
"Negro Music at Birth." *The Music Quarterly* 5 (October 1919).

Burroughs, Nannie.
"Unload Your Uncle Toms." Gerda Lerner, editor. *Black Women in White America: A Documentary History*. New York: Vintage, 1972.

Butler, Charles.
"PNBC: A Fellowship of Partners," *The Crisis* 89 (November 1982).

Carson, Emmett D.
"Survey Dispels Myth That Blacks Receive but Do Not Give to Charity." *Focus*. Washington, D.C.: Joint Center for Political Studies (March 1987), vol. 15, no. 3.

Clark, Ella Anderson.
"The Reminiscences of Ella Anderson Clark," MS. James Osgood Andrew Clark Papers. Special Collections Department. Atlanta: Emory University.

Clark, Kenneth B. and Mamie P. Clark.
"The Development of Consciousness of Self and the Emergence of Racial Identity in Negro Preschool Children." *Journal of Social Psychology* 10 (1939): 591–99.
"Skin Color as a Factor in Racial Identification of Negro Preschool Children." *Journal of Social Psychology, SPSS Bulletin* 11 (1940): 156–69.
"Racial Identification and Racial Preference in Negro Children." T. M. Newcomb and E. L. Hartley, editors. *Readings in Social Psychology*. New York: Holt, 1947: 169–78.

Cone, James.
"The Black Church and Marxism: What Do They Have to Say to Each Other?" An Occasional Paper from the Institute for Democratic Socialism. New York (April 1980).

Daniel, Vattel Elbert.
"Ritual and Stratification in Chicago Negro Churches." *American Sociological Review* 7 (June 1942): 352–61.

Dargan, William T.
"Congregational Gospel Songs in a Black Holiness Church: A Musical and Textual Analysis." Ph.D. dissertation, Wesleyan University, Middletown, Conn., 1982.

Dett, R. Nathaniel.
"Negro Idioms in Motets and Anthems." Program Notes, Concert by the Hampton Institute Choir. Symphony Hall, Boston. March 20, 1929.

Dodson, Jualynne.
"Nineteenth-Century A.M.E. Preaching Women." Hilah F. Thomas and Rosemary Skinner Keller, editors. *Woman in New Worlds*. Nashville: Abingdon, 1981: 276–89.

Ebony Magazine.
Thad Martin, "The Black Church: Precinct of the Black Soul." *Ebony* (August 1984).
Marilyn Marshall, "Leontine T. C. Kelly: First Black Woman Bishop." *Ebony* (November 1984).
"Church Businesses Spread the Gospel of Self-Help." *Ebony* (February 1987).
Andrew Brimmer and Robert Hill, "The New Black Middle Class." *Ebony* (August 1987).
Alex Poinsett, "Suffer the Little Children." *Ebony* (August 1988).

Edelman, Marian Wright.
"An Advocacy Agenda for Black Families and Children." Harriet McAdoo, editor, *Black Families*. Beverly Hills: Sage, 1981.

Emerging Trends.
Princeton Religion Research Center (January 1987), vol. 9 no. 1.
Princeton Religion Research Center (February 1987), vol. 9, no. 2.
Princeton Religion Research Center (May 1987), vol. 9, no. 5.
Princeton Religion Research Center (November 1987), vol. 9, no. 9.
Princeton Religion Research Center (January 1988), vol. 10, no. 1.

Epstein, Cynthia.
"Positive Effects of the Multiple Negative: Explaining the Success of Black Professional Women." *American Journal of Sociology* 78 (January 1973), no. 4.

Evans, Simeon A.
Simeon A. Evans to Mother, MS, August 21, 1862. Department of Archives and Manuscripts. Louisiana State University, Baton Rouge.

Fine, Michelle, and Cheryl Bowers.
"Racial Self-Identification: The Effects of Social History and Gender." *Journal of Applied Social Psychology* 14 (1984), no. 2:136–43.

Fisher, Miles Mark.
"What Is a Negro Baptist?" *The Home Mission College Review* 1 (May 1927), no. 1.
Francis, Travis L., editor, and Veretta Nix Williams, writer.
"Women in Prisons." *Criminal Justice Issues*. New York: Commission for Racial Justice of the United Church of Christ (January 1983), vol. 7, no. 2.
Freeman, Richard B.
"Who Escapes? The Relation of Churchgoing and Other Background Factors to the Socioeconomic Performance of Black Male Youths from Inner-City Tracts." Richard B. Freeman and Harry J. Holzer, editors. *The Black Youth Employment Crisis*. Chicago: University of Chicago Press, 1986.
Fusilier, Anqunett, editor.
"The Divine Origins of the Church of God in Christ." *The Cornerstone*. San Antonio, Tex.: Cornerstone Publishing, 1985.
"National Baptist Convention U.S.A., Inc., Socio-Economic Programs Sweep the Nation Under the Leadership of Dr. T. J. Jemison." *The Cornerstone*. San Antonio, Tex.: Cornerstone Publishing, 1985.
Gans, Bruce M., and Walter L. Lowe.
"The Islam Connection." *Playboy* (May 1980).
Glasgow, Douglas G.
"The Black Underclass in Perspective." Janet Dewart, editor. *The State of Black America 1987*. New York: National Urban League, 1987.
Glenn, Norval D., and Erin Gotard.
"The Religion of Blacks in the United States: Some Recent Trends and Current Characteristics." *American Journal of Sociology* 83 (September 1977): 443–51.
Goatley, Wilbert H.
"The Black Church in Rural America." *Review and Expositor* 70, (Summer 1973), no. 3.
Grant, Jacqueline.
"Womanist Theology: Black Women's Experience as a Source for Doing Theology, with Special Reference to Christology." *The Journal of the Interdenominational Theological Center* 13 (Spring 1986), no. 2.
Harding, Vincent.
"Religion and Resistance Among Antebellum Negroes, 1800–1860." *The Making of Black America*. August Meier and Elliott Rudwick, editors. New York: Atheneum, 1969.
Hazel, Brenda Huger.
"Gospel Balance. . . . It's Happening in Jamaica, New York." *The Cornerstone*. Anqunett Fusilier, editor. San Antonio, Tex.: Cornerstone Publishing, 1985.

"The Black Catholic Experience," *U.S. Catholic Historian* 6 (1986), no. 1.
Hill, Robert.
"The Black Middle Class: Past, Present, and Future." *The State of Black America 1986*. New York: National Urban League, 1986.
Hraba, J., and C. Grant.
"A Reexamination of Racial Preferences and Identification." *Journal of Personality and Social Psychology* 16 (1970): 398–402.
Hunt, Larry L., and Janet G. Hunt.
"Black Religion as Both Opiate and Inspiration of Civil Rights Militancy: Putting Marx's Data to the Test." *Social Focus* 56 (January 1977): 1–14.
Jackson, Jacqueline Johnson.
"Aged Black Americans: Doubled Jeopardy Re-examined." *The State of Black America 1985*. James D. Williams, editor. New York: National Urban League, 1985.
Jacob, John E.
"An Overview of Black America in 1983." *The State of Black America 1984*. New York: National Urban League, 1984.
Johnston, Ronald.
"Negro Preachers Take Sides." *The Black Church in America*. Hart M. Nelsen et al., editors. New York: Basic Books, 1971.
Jones, Marsha.
"Memorial A.M.E. Zion Church: 161st Anniversary Celebration." *About . . . Time Magazine*. Christopher J. Kauffman, editor. Rochester, N.Y.: May 1988.
Keller, Suzanne.
"The Social World of the Urban Slum Child." *American Journal of Orthopsychiatry* 33 (1963): 823–31.
King, C.
"We're Black Yuppies. Which World Would We Belong In?" *Glamour* 85 (May 1987): 78.
King, Martin Luther, Jr.
"The Case Against Tokenism." *New York Times Magazine* (August 5, 1962).
Kornbluth, Jessica.
"The Woman Who Beat the Klan." *New York Times Magazine* (November 1, 1987), pp. 26–39.
Lacayo, R.
"Between Two Worlds: The Black Middle Class." *Time* 133 (March 19, 1989): 58–62.
Ladner, Joyce.
"Teenage Pregnancy: The Implication for Black Americans." James D. Williams, editor. *The State of Black America 1986*. New York: National Urban League, 1986.

Landry, Bart.
"The New Black Middle Class (Part I)." *Focus.* Washington, D.C.: Joint
Center for Political Studies, September 1987, vol. 15, no. 9.
"The New Black Middle Class (Part 2)." *Focus.* Washington, D.C.: Joint
Center for Political Studies, October 1987, vol. 15, no. 10.

Lee, Carlton L.
"Religious Roots of the Negro Protest." *Assuring Freedom to the Free.*
Arnold Rose, editor. Detroit: Wayne State University Press, 1964.

Lincoln, C. Eric.
"The Development of Black Religion in America." *Review and Expositor*
70 (Summer 1973), no. 3: 295–308.
"200 Years of Black Religion." *Ebony* (August 1975): 84–89.
"Contemporary Black Religion: In Search of a Sociology." *Journal of the
Interdenominational Theological Center* 5 (Spring 1978): 91–104.
"White Christianity and Black Commitment: A Comment on the Power
of Faith and Socialization." *Journal of the Interdenominational Theo-
logical Center* 6 (Fall 1978): 21–31.
"Black Family, the Black Church, and the Transformation of Values."
Religious Life 47 (Winter 1978): 486–96.
"Black Religion in North Carolina from Colonial Times to 1900." *The
Black Presence in North Carolina.* Jeffrey J. Crow and Robert Winters,
Jr., editors. Raleigh: North Carolina Museum of History, 1978.
"The Black Church in the American Society: A New Responsibility?"
Journal of the Interdenominational Theological Center 6 (Spring 1979):
83–93.
"The American Muslim Mission in the Context of American Social His-
tory." *The Muslim Community in North America.* Earle H. Waugh,
Baha Abu-Laban, and Regula B. Qureshi, editors. Edmonton: University
of Alberta Press, 1983: 215–33.

Lincoln, C. Eric, and Lawrence H. Mamiya.
"Daddy Jones and Father Divine: The Cult as Political Religion." *Religion
in Life* 49 (Spring 1980), no. 1: 6–23.
"In the Receding Shadow of the Plantation: A Profile of Rural Clergy and
Churches in the Black Belt." *Review of Religious Research* 29 (June
1988), no. 4: 349–68.

Lynch, John.
"The Ordination of Women: Protestant Experience in Ecumenical Perspective." *Journal of Ecumenical Studies* 12 (1975), no. 2.

McGhee, James D.
"The Black Family Today and Tomorrow." James D. Williams, editor. *The
State of Black America 1985.* New York: National Urban League, 1985.

Madron, Thomas W., Hart M. Nelsen, and Raytha L. Yokley.
"Religion as a Determinant of Militancy and Political Participation

Among Black Americans." *American Behavioral Scientist* 17 (July–
August 1974): 783–97.

Mamiya, Lawrence H.
"Minister Louis Farrakhan and the Final Call: Schism in the Muslim
Movement." *The Muslim Community in North America.* Earle H.
Waugh, Baha Abu-Laban, and Regula B. Qureshi, editors. Edmonton,
Alberta: University of Alberta Press, 1983.
"From Black Muslim to Bilalian: The Evolution of a Movement." *Journal
for the Scientific Study of Religion* 21 (June 1982), no. 2: 138–52.
"The Black Muslims as a New Religious Movement: Their Evolution and
Implications for the Study of Religion in a Pluralistic Society." *Conflict
and Cooperation Between Contemporary Religious Groups.* Chuo Aca-
demic Research Institute. Tokyo: Nakamura, 1988.

Mamiya, Lawrence H., and Patricia A. Kaurouma.
*For Their Courage and for Their Struggles: The Black Oral History Proj-
ect of Poughkeepsie, New York.* Poughkeepsie, N.Y.: Urban Center for
Africana Studies, 1978.

Mamiya, Lawrence H., and C. Eric Lincoln.
"Black Militant and Separatist Movements." *Encyclopedia of the American Religious Experience.* Charles H. Lippy and Peter W. Williams,
editors. New York: Charles Scribner's Sons, 1988, 2: 755–71.

Mamiya, Lawrence H., and Lorraine Roberts.
"Invisible People, Untold Stories: A Historical Overview of the Black
Community in Poughkeepsie." *New Perspectives on Poughkeepsie's
Past: Essays to Honor Edmund Platt.* Clyde Griffen, editor. Poughkeep-
sie, N.Y.: Dutchess County Historical Society, 1988.

Martin, Emmett T., and Nellie C. Waring.
*History Book of the Springfield Baptist Church, Augusta, Georgia: 1787–
1979.* Augusta, Ga.: Springfield Baptist Church, 1979.

Matton, William Grove.
"Memoirs 1859–1887," MS. Manuscript Department. Durham, N.C.:
Duke University.

Mitchell, Mozella G.
"The Black Women's View of Human Liberation." *Theology Today* 39
(January 1983): 421–25.

Moore, K. A.
"Fact Sheet" (On teenage pregnancy). Washington, D.C.: Child Trends,
1985.

Murphy, Jim.
"A Question of Race: Minority/White Incarceration in New York State."
Albany: New York State Coalition for Criminal Justice and Center for
Justice Education, 1987.

Murphy, Larry George.
"The Church and Black Californians: "A Mid-Nineteenth Century Struggle for Civil Justice." *Foundations* 18 (April–June 1975): 165–81.

Nelsen, Hart M.
"Unchurched Black Americans: Patterns of Religiosity and Affiliation,"
Review of Religious Research 29 (June 1988), no. 4: 398–412.

Newspaper Articles (listed chronologically):
"Rule Switch Allows Whites as Muslims," *Nashville Tennessean*, June
19, 1975.

Paul Delaney, "Many Black Democratic Leaders Voice Doubt, Fear, and
Distrust About Carter." *New York Times*, July 6, 1976.

"I Don't Vote." *New York Times*, July 14, 1976, A-35.

George Vecsey, "Preaching and Politics on Weekly Agenda for Baptist
Ministers." *New York Times*, November 6, 1976.

"Role of Black Voters in 1976 Election of Carter." *New York Times*,
January 15, 1977.

"Typical Sunday Dinner for Worshippers at Harlem's Mother African
Methodist Episcopal Zion Church." *New York Times*, August 26, 1981.

Dorothy J. Gaithers, "Church Opens a Restaurant in Brooklyn," *New York
Times*, April 23, 1983.

Kenneth M. Noble, "A Church Where Things Happen," *New York Times*,
August 23, 1984.

Marjorie Hyer, "Black Women, White Pulpits." *Washington Post*, October 12, 1985.

Robin Toner, "Victim's Mother Tells of Klan Fight," *New York Times*,
March 6, 1986.

"Census Bureau Study of Personal and Family Wealth Disparity Between
Blacks and Whites." *New York Times*, July 19, 1986, A-1.

"Results of Balloting in New York and Connecticut." *New York Times*,
September 11, 1986, B-12.

John Herbers, "10 Agencies Win Grants for Innovative Projects." *New
York Times*, September 26, 1986, A-18.

Simon Anewkwe, "Flake, Vann, and Green Win Over Challengers." *Amsterdam News*, November 8, 1986, vol. 77, no. 45:1.

Clifford D. May, "Queens Congressman Balances Duties in Church and
the Capitol," *New York Times*, March 30, 1987, B-1, B-5.

Daniel Goleman, "Black Child's Self-Views Still Low," *New York Times*,
August 13, 1987, A-13.

Isabel Wilkerson, "Growth of the Very Poor Is Focus of New Studies,"
New York Times, December 20, 1987, A-26.

Thomas Morgan, "Muslim Patrol Reduces Crime in Brooklyn Area," *New
York Times*, February 25, 1988.

"Black Churches, Endangered Children," *New York Times*, May 23, 1988, A-18.

Claude Brown, "Crack and the American Dream: Lost Opportunities in the Ghetto," special to the *Los Angeles Times*, reprinted in the *Poughkeepsie Journal*, May 26, 1988.

Daniel Goleman, "Erikson, in His Own Old Age, Expands His View of Life," *New York Times*, June 14, 1988, C-1, C-14.

Isabel Wilkerson, "Detroit Citizens Join with Church to Rid Community of Drugs," *New York Times*, June 29, 1988, A-14.

"Persisting Segregation Reported," Gannett News Service, *Poughkeepsie Journal*, June 23, 1988, 1.

Ronald Smothers, "Atlanta Still on a Roll, but New Doubts Arise," *New York Times*, July 14, 1988, A-21.

"Church Issues Credit Card." Louisville, Gannett News Service, *Poughkeepsie Journal*, July 16, 1988.

Laura Sessions Stepp, "Black Church Losing Historic Role: Drug Use, Teen Pregnancies Seen as Consequences," *Washington Post*, August 20, 1988, A-6.

Emily Smith, "The Church Connection," *Durham Morning Herald*, November 20, 1988.

Isabel Wilkerson, "Many Who Are Black Favor New Term for Who They Are," *New York Times*, January 31, 1989, A-1, A-14.

Ari L. Goldman, "Mainstream Islam Rapidly Embraced by Black Americans," *New York Times*, February 21, 1989, 1, B-4.

Robin Toner, "William H. Gray, 3d," *New York Times*, June 15, 1989, B-8.

B. Drummond Ayres, Jr., "Black Priest Is Termed Threat to Catholic Unity," *New York Times*, July 15, 1989, A-6.

Isabel Wilkerson, "Study Finds Segregation in Cities Worse Than Scientists Imagined," *New York Times*, August 5, 1989, A-6.

Orum, Anthony M.
"A Reappraisal of the Social and Political Participation of Negroes." *American Journal of Sociology* 72 (July 1966): 33.

Patterson, Patrick.
"Blacks and the Media in the 1980s." James D. Williams, editor. *The State of Black America 1982.* New York: National Urban League, 1982.

Porter, J., and R. Washington.
"Black Identity and Self-esteem: A Review of Studies of Black Self-Concept." *Annual Review of Sociology* 5 (1979): 53–54.

Reid, Frank, III.
1984–1985 Annual Report. Los Angeles: Ward African Memorial Episcopal Church.

Roberts, Harry W.
"The Rural Negro Minister: His Personal and Social Characteristics." *Social Forces* 27 (March 1949): 291–300.

Rogers, Cornish.
"Feminists: Soul and Sense." *The Christian Century* (February 1974):
172–74.

Sawyer, Mary R.
"A Moral Minority: Religion and Congressional Black Politics." *Journal of Religious Thought* 40 (Fall–Winter 1983–1984), no. 2: 55–66.
"Black Ecumenical Movements: Proponents of Social Change." *Review of Religious Research* 30 (December 1988), no. 2.

Scott, Emmett J., collector.
"Letters of Negro Migrants, 1916–1918." *Journal of Negro History.* G. Carter Woodson, editor, vol. 4, no. 3, July 1919.
"More Letters from Negro Migrants, 1916–1918." *Journal of Negro History.* G. Carter Woodson, editor, vol. 4, no. 4, October 1919.

Simpson, George Eaton.
"Black Pentecostalism in the United States." *Phylon* 34 (February 1974):
203–11.

Smallwood, David.
"Economics of the Church." *Dollars and Sense,* special issue on "The Black Church in America," edited by Donald C. Walker (June/July 1981), vol. 7, no. 2.

Smith, Kelly Miller.
"Religion as a Force in Black America." *The State of Black America 1982.* James D. Williams, editor. New York: National Urban League, 1982: 210–17.

Southern Coalition Report on Jails and Prisons 7 (Spring 1980), no. 2.

Snyder, John.
"The Baptists." *The Crisis* (May 1920).

Stone, Sonja H.
"Oral Tradition and Spiritual Drama: The Cultural Mosaic for Black Preaching." *Journal of the Interdenominational Theological Center* 8 (Fall 1980): 17–27.

Swinton, David.
"The Economic Status of Blacks 1986." Janet Dewart, editor. *The State of Black America 1987.* New York: National Urban League, 1987.

Taylor, Robert J.
"Correlates of Religious Non-Involvement Among Black Americans." *Review of Religious Research* 30 (December 1988), no. 2:126–39.

Tidwell, Billy J.
"A Profile of the Black Unemployed: A Disaggregation Analysis." Janet Dewart, editor. *The State of Black America 1987.* New York: National Urban League, 1987.

Tinney, James S.
"Progressive Baptists." *Christianity Today* 15 (October 9, 1970): 42–43.
"Black Origins of the Pentecostal Movement." *Christianity Today* 16 (October 8, 1971): 4–6.
"Black Pentecostals: The Difference Is More Than Color." *Logos* 2, no. 1 (May/June 1980): 16–19.

Toufexis, Anastasia, and D. Blake Hallanan.
"A Question of Black Pride." *Time* 130 (September 14, 1987): 74.

Townes, Laura M.
Diary of Laura M. Townes. MS. Penn School Papers, Southern Historical Collection. University of North Carolina, Chapel Hill.

Townsey, Roi D.
"The Incarceration of Black Men." Lawrence E. Gary, editor. *Black Men.* Beverly Hills: Sage, 1981.

Turner, Henry McNeil.
"God Is a Negro." *The Voice of Missions,* African Methodist Episcopal Church, February 1, 1898.

Turner, Ronny E.
"The Black Minister: Uncle Tom or Abolitionist?" *Phylon* 34 (March 1974): 86–95.

Van Dusen, John G.
"The Negro in Politics." *Journal of Negro History* 21 (July 1936): 257.

Walker, Donald C., editor.
"The Black Church in America," in *Dollars and Sense* 7 (June/July 1981), no. 2.

Welch, Michael R.
"The Unchurched, Black Religious Non-Affiliates," *Journal for the Scientific Study of Religion* 17 (September 1978): 289–93.

Williams, Vernetta Nix, and Travis L. Francis.
"Women in Prisons." *Criminal Justice Issues* 7, no. 2 (January 1983): 1–2.

Whalum, Wendell H.
"Black Hymnody." *Review and Expositor* 70 (Summer 1973), no. 3.

Wilson, Bobby M.
"Church Participation: A Social Space Analysis in a Community of Black In-Migrants." *Journal of Black Studies* 10 (December 1979): 198–217.

Wimberly, Anne S.
"Spirituals as Symbolic Expression." *Journal of the Interdenominational Theological Center* 5 (Fall 1977): 23–32.

Woodward, C. Vann.
"After Watts—Where Is the Negro Revolution Headed?" *New York Times Magazine,* August 29, 1965.

Unpublished Papers

The following unpublished background papers were prepared for the "Black Church in the African American Experience" Research Project, Department of Religion, Duke University. References in this text are to these background papers and not to any subsequent publication by the authors.

McClain, William B.
  "Blacks in the United Methodist Church." August 1986.

Nelson, Douglas J.
  "A Brief History of the Church of God in Christ, Inc." August 1986.

Satterwhite, John H.
  "The Black Methodist Churches." August 1986.

Stewart, James B.
  "The Black Church as a Religio-Economic Institution." August 1986.

Stone, Sonja H.
  "The Opportunities Industrialization Centers as a Religio-Economic Institution." August 1986.

The following unpublished studies were also referred to:

McClain, William B.
  "The Liturgy of Zion." Unpublished manuscript.

Mamiya, Lawrence H.
  "The Second Episcopal District of the African Methodist Episcopal Church Under the Leadership of Bishop John Hurst Adams: Evaluations of the Leadership Training Institutes and the Phenomenon of Church Growth in the District." January 1986. Study funded by the Lilly Endowment.

Mamiya, Lawrence H., and C. Eric Lincoln.
  "Analysis of the Results of the Christian Methodist Episcopal Church Membership Survey." April 1985. Study funded by the Lilly Endowment.

May, Deborah.
  "The Impact of Racism and Sexism Upon Black Clergywomen," unpublished study for a senior's thesis in Women's Studies at Vassar College, April 30, 1985.

Index

Abdul-Jabbar, Kareem, 391
Abernathy, Ralph David, 36, 142, 370
Abolitionists: women as, 281–83
Absentee pastor, 96
Abyssinian Baptist Church (New
York), 8, 25, 27, 121, 139, 142–43,
210, 231, 248, 263, 338
Adams, C. C., 37
Adams, Charles, 14
Adams, John Hurst, 194, 265, 300
Addabbo, Joseph F., 218
Adopt-A-Family, 340
Affirmative Action, 273
Africa: A.M.E. in, 54, 69, 74; A.M.E.Z.
in, 38; Baptists in, 45–46; C.M.E. in,
38; COGIC in, 84, 90; economic po-
tential of, 265; musical heritage of,
346–48, 352–53, 359, 365, 380; OIC
in, 264; Pentecostals in, 79; re-
ligious tradition of women in, 276,
277, 307. *See also* Black sacred
cosmos
Afric-American Female Intelligence
Society, 281–82
African Baptist (Bluestone) Church
(Mecklenburg, Va.), 23
African Baptist Church (Boston), 25,
282
African Baptist Missionary Society
(ABMS), 26, 29, 45
African Conference (Methodist), 57
African Masonic Lodge (Boston), 243
African Methodist Episcopal Church
(A.M.E.), 48, 49–56; and abolitionism, 202; and black consciousness
in sermons, 176; and civil rights,
225–26; and clergy education, 130,
133 (table 8); and distinctiveness of
the Black Church, 173; and economics, 55, 56; and education, 52–
53, 56; foreign missions of, 53–54,
74–75; growth of, 158; and liberation theology, 179–80; and neo-
Pentecostalism, 158, 385–88; organization of, 55–56; origins of,

49–52; and politics, 204–5; polity
of, 54–55, 69, 70, 71, 73; schisms in,
48 (1885), 49 (1907); size of, 54; and
social services, 52, 55; and social
prophecy, 226; and urban growth,
119; and women, 279–80, 285–86,
291, 293–94 (table 32). *See also*
Methodists
African Methodist Episcopal Zion
Church (A.M.E.Z.), 56–60; and abolitionism, 58; and clergy education,
133 (table 8); and education, 60; foreign missions of, 74–75; and neo-
Pentecostalism, 388; organization
of, 58–59; origins of, 56–58; polity
of, 59–60, 69, 70–71, 72–73; and
schism (1881), 48; and segregation,
56; size of, 58; and the Underground
Railroad, 58; and union, 158, 363;
and whites, 58; and women, 58, 285,
291, 293–94 (table 32). *See also*
Methodists
The African Missions, 45
African Union Church, 49
African Union First Colored Method-
ist Church (A.U.M.P.), 49
African Union Society, 116
Afro-American Industrial Insurance
Society of Jacksonville, 246
AIDS, 340
Alabama Christian Movement for
Civil Rights, 371
Albany movement, 371
Alger, Horatio, 239
Ali, Muhammad, 391
Ali, Noble Drew, 125, 389
Allen, Richard, 50; and the A.M.E.Z.,
57; as businessman, 132; as founder
of FAS, 8, 51, 116, 242; and freedom,
5; and Underground Railroad, 202;
withdrawal from Methodists, 50–
52, 65; and women preachers, 279–
80
Allen A.M.E. Church (Jamaica, N.Y.),
217, 218, 231, 257, 385, 386, 387

501

Baumfree, Isabella. *See* Truth, Sojourner
Bay Psalm Book, 354
Beatrice the Madonna, 177
Bedford-Stuyvesant, 190, 322
Bellah, Robert, 236
Beneatha (*Raisin in the Sun*), 309, 342, 343
Benedict College (Columbia, S.C.), 29
Benefits, clerical, 101, 133–35 (table 10), 400–401
Benevolent societies, 245, 246, 249. *See also* Mutual aid societies; Free African Society
Bennett College (Greensboro, N.C.), 66
Berry, Mary, 201, 310
Bethany Baptist Church (Brooklyn), 257
Bethel A.M.E. Church (Baltimore), 74, 137, 140, 142, 190, 332, 339, 340, 385, 386, 387, 388
Bethel Missionary Baptist Church (Wappinger Falls, N.Y.), 270
Bethune, Mary McLeod, 89, 210, 283, 284–85
Bethune-Cookman College (Daytona Beach, Fla.), 66, 284
Betty (slave), 50
Bias, Len, 338
Bible Way Churches of Our Lord Jesus Christ, World Wide, 78
Billie Holiday Theater, 339
Billingsley, Andrew, 123, 162, 267
Bishop, Josiah, 24
Black Church. *See* Clergy; Rural churches; Rural clergy; Urban churches; Urban clergy
Black Church in the Sixties, 10–11, 126, 222
The Black Church in Urban America, 126, 194
Black consciousness, 389; and black ecumenism, 191–94; conclusions about, 194–95; origins of, 165–68; profile of clerical, 168–89; scale of, 183–91
Black consciousness profile, 168–89; and black figures in educational literature, 169 (chart 1), 173–74; and black liberation theology, 169 (chart 1), 176–83; distinctiveness of the Black Church, 169 (chart 1), 173, 174; methodology of, 168; ministry

of the Black Church, 168–70 (chart 1); mission of the Black Church, 169 (chart 1), 170–71; in sermons, 169 (chart 1), 175–76; support for education, 169 (chart 1), 171–72
Black consciousness scale, 183–90; and church size, 187 (table 24), 188, 190; and civil rights, 189, 190; and community outreach examples, 185–91 (table 24)
Black Hebrews, 125
Black Life in Corporate America, 270
Black Manhood Training: Body, Mind, and Soul, 339
Black Methodists for Church Renewal, 67
Black Metropolis, 11, 121, 146, 160, 267
Black Power, 175, 195, 389
Black Pride, 175, 192, 389
Black Religion and Black Radicalism, 201
Black sacred cosmos, 2–7, 17
Black Theology and Black Power, 278
Black Theology Project (BTP), 193
Blassingame, John, 201, 245, 310
Block, Sam, 370–71
Blues music, 361, 362, 379 (table 39), 381
Blyden, Edward Wilmot, 389
The Book of Discipline: in A.M.E., 54, 57, 59, 60, 70, 71–72; in A.M.E.Z., 57, 59, 60, 70, 71–72; in C.M.E., 62, 64, 72; in M.E. Church, 68
Borders, William Holmes, 176, 258
Booth, L. Venhael, 37
Bowen-Spencer, Michele, 340
Bowers, Cheryl, 314
Boyd, Henry Allen, 34
Boyd, R. H., 33, 34
Boyd, T. B., Jr., 34
Boyd, T. B. III, 34
Brewster, J. H., 361, 375
Bridges, Flora, 297
Bridgestreet A.M.E. Church (Brooklyn), 385, 386
Bronx, 322
Bronzeville, 267
Brotherhood of Sleeping Car Porters, 210, 249
Brown, Diane R., 127, 130, 152, 157
Brown, Claude, 320, 322
Brown, John, 203

The Authors

C. Eric Lincoln is Professor of Religion and Culture at Duke University. He is the author of many books on black religion, including *The Black Church Since Frazier*, and has edited the C. Eric Lincoln Series in Black Religion.

Lawrence H. Mamiya is Associate Professor of Religion and African Studies at Vassar College. He is the author of sociological studies on black churches, the Nation of Islam, the Muslim movement, and history projects.

2847